Frommer's®

Cambodia & Laos

1st Edition

by Daniel White

WILEY

Wiley Publishing, Inc.

ABOUT THE AUTHOR

Daniel White is a British writer who has been published in major magazines and newspapers in Europe and Asia. He has written for publications such as the UK's *Guardian, Observer, Maxim,* and *Marie Claire.* He has also worked on guidebooks and political commentaries as both a writer and editor, and was editor-in-chief of the now defunct *Absolute Phuket* magazine in Thailand. He has traveled the corners of Southeast Asia by motorcycle, and is currently working on a website project chronicling his trips on two wheels. Previously based in London and Paris, he has been based in Bangkok since 2002.

Published by:

WILEY PUBLISHING, INC.

111 River St.
Hoboken, NJ 07030-5774

ISBN 978-0-470-49778-4

Editor: Jamie Ehrlich
Production Editor: Jana M. Stefanciosa
Cartographer: Roberta Stockwell
Photo Editor: Richard Fox
Production by Wiley Indianapolis Composition Services

Front cover photo: Young monk dresses below Bousra waterfall in Sen Monorom, Mondulkiri province, Cambodia. ©Dan Morris / Alamy Images
Back cover photo: Patuxai Monument in Vientiane, Laos. ©SuperStock / AGE Fotostock, Inc.

For information on our other products and services or to obtain technical support, please contact our Customer Care Department within the U.S. at 877/762-2974, outside the U.S. at 317/572-3993 or fax 317/572-4002.

CONTENTS

13 LUANG PRABANG & NORTHERN LAOS 252

14 CENTRAL LAOS 297

15 SOUTHERN LAOS 307

16 FAST FACTS 321

17 KHMER & LAO GLOSSARY 325

INDEX 331

LIST OF MAPS

ACKNOWLEDGMENTS

Concerning Cambodia, thanks to journalist Luke Hunt for his feedback on history and politics, his unwavering disdain for pointless violence, his understanding of elevated artillery positions, and his good humor on the rare occasions when England beat Australia at cricket. Thanks to Derek and Wendy for their wonderful welcomes to the weary and their friendship and peace. Thanks to Hurley Scroggins for his huge commitment to Cambodia over many years and the generous way he shares his knowledge with his peers. Thanks to Dr. Trudy Jacobsen for sharing her hugely useful academic knowledge on colonial history and her skill at pool. Thanks to Hem Sopheap and Cat Sien for the incredible insights they have given me into Cambodian family life.

Concerning Laos, thanks to all those motorcyclists who have spent years traveling those rough, rough roads on two wheels and were so helpful in pointing me in interesting directions: Rhodie, David Unkovich, Jim Barbush, Mrs Quynh, and Richard Gunston.

Back at the mothership, thanks to colleagues and friends Greg Lowe and Chris Mitchell for the feedback. Thanks to Jamie Ehrlich in New York, editor of this guide, for being so concise in her feedback.

—Daniel White

HOW TO CONTACT US

In researching this book, we discovered many wonderful places—hotels, restaurants, shops, and more. We're sure you'll find others. Please tell us about them, so we can share the information with your fellow travelers in upcoming editions. If you were disappointed with a recommendation, we'd love to know that, too. Please write to:

Frommer's Cambodia & Laos, 1st Edition
Wiley Publishing, Inc. • 111 River St. • Hoboken, NJ 07030-5774

AN ADDITIONAL NOTE

Please be advised that travel information is subject to change at any time—and this is especially true of prices. We therefore suggest that you write or call ahead for confirmation when making your travel plans. The authors, editors, and publisher cannot be held responsible for the experiences of readers while traveling. Your safety is important to us, however, so we encourage you to stay alert and be aware of your surroundings. Keep a close eye on cameras, purses, and wallets, all favorite targets of thieves and pickpockets.

FROMMER'S STAR RATINGS, ICONS & ABBREVIATIONS

Every hotel, restaurant, and attraction listing in this guide has been ranked for quality, value, service, amenities, and special features using a **star-rating system.** In country, state, and regional guides, we also rate towns and regions to help you narrow down your choices and budget your time accordingly. Hotels and restaurants are rated on a scale of zero (recommended) to three stars (exceptional). Attractions, shopping, nightlife, towns, and regions are rated according to the following scale: zero stars (recommended), one star (highly recommended), two stars (very highly recommended), and three stars (must-see).

In addition to the star-rating system, we also use eight feature icons that point you to the great deals, in-the-know advice, and unique experiences that separate travelers from tourists. Throughout the book, look for:

(Finds)	Special finds—those places only insiders know about
(Fun Facts)	Fun facts—details that make travelers more informed and their trips more fun
(Kids)	Best bets for kids, and advice for the whole family
(Moments)	Special moments—those experiences that memories are made of
(Overrated)	Places or experiences not worth your time or money
(Tips)	Insider tips—great ways to save time and money
(Value)	Great values—where to get the best deals
(Warning!)	Warning—traveler's advisories are usually in effect

The following **abbreviations** are used for credit cards:

AE	American Express	**DISC**	Discover	**V**	Visa
DC	Diners Club	**MC**	MasterCard		

TRAVEL RESOURCES AT FROMMERS.COM

Frommer's travel resources don't end with this guide. Frommer's website, **www.frommers. com**, has travel information on more than 4,000 destinations. We update features regularly, giving you access to the most current trip-planning information and the best airfare, lodging, and car-rental bargains. You can also listen to podcasts, connect with other Frommers.com members through our active-reader forums, share your travel photos, read blogs from guidebook editors and fellow travelers, and much more.

The Best of
Cambodia & Laos

The countries of Cambodia and Laos immediately conjure up many images: ancient temples in the mist; colorfully dressed ethnic hill tribes working terraced rice paddies up steep hillsides; weathered colonial charm; remote river journeys with breathtaking sunsets; religious ceremonies reflecting centuries of cultural complexity; and busy markets, fantastic food, and natural riches. Robustly emerging from an era of conflict, these two countries once again offer those who visit all these things and more.

1 FAVORITE CAMBODIA EXPERIENCES

- **Contemplating the Bayon:** The Bayon in Angkor Thom is simply one of the most enigmatic and remarkable buildings in the world. Huge faces of a god-king stare out lazily from the rocky walls. You contemplate them and they contemplate you as they have millions before you. This is a truly mystical place. See p. 116.
- **Dancing the Ramvong:** The Khmers' traditional dance involves walking around slowly in a circle while making delicate shapes with their hands. If you pass by a wedding or a celebration of any sort, or indeed go to a local disco or dance hall, you will see this dance. You will almost certainly be dragged over to join them. If you find yourself in a rural village, you may see old women doing the dance with no accompaniment at all, as the other villagers hoot with laughter. Join in—it's great fun. See p. 24.
- **Enjoying Fresh Coffee and Baguettes by the Tonle Sap:** Although imperialism may not be a good thing, the French occupation of Indochina left the region with a legacy of great breakfasts. In Phnom Penh, the riverfront of Sisowath Quay is the busy place to be seen.

It is a wonderful venue to enjoy this Gallic legacy while watching the world go by. Head to any other waterfront throughout Laos or Cambodia and the experience will be equally fulfilling.
- **Haggling in the Market:** Psar Toul Tom Poung (p. 87) and many other markets in Cambodia are busy, congested, and packed with everything you can imagine. Actually purchasing something requires the negotiating skills of a UN diplomat. Not too forceful, not too reticent, one has to strike exactly the right balance between bonhomie and confidence in order to secure the right price. If your vendor is grinning from ear to ear as you leave, then you have definitely lost the contest. No matter. If you got it right, you will have enjoyed the experience and be smiling too.
- **Dolphin Spotting on the Mekong:** Up the Mekong in Kratie resides the very rare freshwater Irrawaddy dolphins. They are incredibly shy creatures (this might be partly due to the locals' past method of catching fish with live grenades). Traumatized as they justifiably may be, they do break the surface of the water every now and then, often in pairs, and there is something very

rewarding about sitting in a boat as the water gently laps the hull scanning the waters for a sighting of these elusive creatures. So grab a couple of baguettes and pâté sandwiches, hire a boat with a boatman, stock the vessel with your favorite tipple, and head about 10km (6¼ miles) upstream for your aquatic rendezvous. See p. 148.

- **Savoring Kep Crab in Kampot Pepper:** The very faded but formerly grand royal seaside resort of Kep produces some of the most spectacularly delicious seafood in Asia. Coincidentally the nearby town of Kampot produces some of the finest pepper in the world, a product that is exported around the globe. Like the work of a culinary Lennon and McCartney, this geographical accident results in the serving of sublime seafood all along the waterfront. People travel far to sample the Kep crab in Kampot pepper at the source. Once you have tried it you will know why.

- **Biking the Cardamoms:** In 2008, the road between Koh Kong on the Thai border and Srey Ambal on the main road between Sihanoukville and Phnom Penh was completed. It passes through the Cardamom Mountains and is a great road if you like motorcycling. Lots of gentle bends, very little traffic, scenic river crossings, and panoramic scenery. You could equally enjoy it in a jeep or a car.

- **Boating up the Sangker River After the Rains:** The journey from Siem Reap to Battambang can be done by water. It takes you across the Tonle Sap, the heart of the Khmer, and then down the narrow Sangker River. As you chug slowly up the narrow waterway you will be an intimate witness to Cambodian rural life along its bank, with friendly kids waving. See p. 134.

- **Taking in an Apsara Dance Show:** One of the most exquisite forms of dance in the world, the slow, deliberate movements of Khmer classical dance are a wonder to behold. It's elegance incarnate.

- **Taking a Spin Through the Rice Paddies Around Battambang:** Acquire professional two-wheeled transportation and head out from Battambang to the countryside. A real taste of rural Cambodia and village life awaits.

2 FAVORITE LAOS EXPERIENCES

- **Riding a Slow Boat Down the Mekong:** Traveling from Huay Xai in the north of Laos on the Thai border to Luang Prabang by slow boat takes 2 days, with a stopover for the night in Pakbeng. It's a great and relaxing way to see the dramatic scenery of northern Laos. Depending on the quality of your shipmates (because you can't change them once you have boarded), it can also be quite social. See p. 199.

- **Gibbon Spotting in Bokeo:** In northern Laos, the indigenous gibbon has been under threat from slash-and-burn agriculture and deforestation. Now it is protected within the Bokeo Nature Reserve, 123,000 hectares (303,810 acres) of mixed-deciduous forest in a mountainous terrain ranging from 500 to 1,500m (1,640–4,920 ft.) in elevation. Under expert direction you are allowed to hide out and observe these fascinating creatures going about their business in their natural habitat. See p. 290.

- **Driving Rte. 13:** This route between Vang Vieng and Luang Prabang is one of Asia's most spectacular roads. Only 10 years ago, driving it solo was complicated by a problem of armed bandits. Those days are long gone and whether by motorcycle, jeep, or car it is one of the world's most rewarding journeys. Amazing limestone mountains, interesting villages, and a road surface that is no longer a bone-jarring nightmare all contribute to a blissful road trip.

- **Tubing down the Nam Song River in Vang Vieng:** This silly but fun activity has become a bit of a trademark selling point in Vang Vieng. Backpackers consider it a rite of passage. Basically, you're driven a few miles upriver (all guesthouses provide the necessary transport) and then float back to town on the inflated inner tube of a tractor tire. There are little shops along the way selling food and beer. Some people get so hooked on this experience that they do it day after day, wallowing in a lazy, aquatic existence. See p. 250.

- **Traveling on the Nam Ou:** The Nam Ou River is different in character to the Mekong—narrower, steeper on each side, and more intimate. A journey by boat, heading either north or south yields some of the most spectacular scenery in Asia.
- **Riding an Elephant in Luang Prabang:** Laos is called the "Land of a Million Elephants and the Parasol." Going for a ride on just one of these magnificent and symbolic beasts is a pleasure not to be missed. See p. 282.
- **Climbing to Wat Phou:** This Angkorian Khmer temple is built on the side of a mountain, so the climb may be sweaty, but the views are spectacular and the sense of history is palpable. See p. 315.

3 BEST SMALL TOWNS & VILLAGES

- **Battambang:** This is actually Cambodia's second city, but you wouldn't know it by the tranquil pace of life. While Phnom Penh is eaten by traffic and Siem Reap is defined by the pressures of mass tourism, Battambang thrives on its own terms. It is an affluent town, the center of the "rice bowl" of Cambodia. While it is increasing in popularity, it is still a wonderful place to see the real Cambodia. See p. 133.
- **Kompong Chhnang:** This beautiful little town on the main road between Battambang and Phnom Penh retains a sleepy colonial grandeur. It is also a bustling fishing town peopled by ethnic Vietnamese. It is a fine lunch stop, or even an overnight if you want to break up the long journey. If you do stop for the night, get up before dawn and head to the riverfront, which buzzes with activity at a very early hour. It's a great site for shutterbugs. See p. 145.
- **Kampot:** For a laid-back stint of restful hammock swinging, you can't beat Kampot. This little riverine gem has it

all when considering doing absolutely nothing. If you want to splash out a tiny bit, book a bungalow at Les Manguiers, one of Asia's most blissful venues. See p. 167.

- **Tha Khek:** Part of a series of towns strung out along the Mekong through Laos, Tha Khek has been recently restored. It's now a lovely place to contemplate the might of the Mekong to your front and the splendor of the Khammouane Mountains to your back. See p. 302.
- **Nong Kiaow:** This small town boasts one of the most beautiful settings in Asia. It is surrounded by towering limestone mountains fronting fantastic river views. See p. 286.
- **Vieng Xai:** Once the headquarters of the Pathet Lao, this stunningly scenic area is tinged with sadness. Although Communist victory was planned and executed from here, it was also a place where many internees of the previous regime perished through neglect. See p. 294.

4 BEST LUXURY ACCOMMODATIONS

- **Raffles Hotel Le Royal, Phnom Penh** (© 023/981-888; www.raffles.com): Oozing colonial charm, Le Royal is a taste of prewar Indochina at its most authentic. It offers relaxed luxury in elegant Art Deco surroundings. See p. 64.
- **Amansara Resort, Siem Reap** (© 063/ 760-333; www.amanresorts.com): Aman junkies fly around the world just to stay at these transcendent resorts, and it is easy to see why. Prices are stratospheric, but you get what you pay for: The tranquillity and service are unparalleled. The brand-new **Amantaka** resort in Luang Prabang, set to open as this guide went to press, promises more of the same. See p. 97.
- **Raffles Grand Hotel d'Angkor, Siem Reap** (© 063/963-888; www.raffles. com): As a base from which to explore the splendors of Angkor, the Grand Hotel d'Angkor is unrivaled for its languid tranquillity complemented by excellent customer service. See p. 99.
- **Victoria Angkor Hotel, Siem Reap** (© 063/760-428; www.victoriahotels-asia.com): This classy hotel has every modern convenience, and seamlessly merges the practical with the elegant. See p. 100.
- **Settha Palace Hotel, Vientiane** (© 021/ 217-581; www.setthapalace.com): This gem of a hotel is unique in every way with an unruffled, leafy calm that makes it one of the finest hotels in all of Southeast Asia. It is beautifully eccentric. See p. 214.
- **La Residence Phou Vao, Luang Prabang** (© 071/212-530; www.residence phouvao.com): Set on a hill overlooking Luang Prabang, this splendid offering could best be described as a palace. The majesty of the views is matched only by the luxury from which you survey them. See p. 259.
- **Mekong Riverview Hotel, Luang Prabang** (© 071/254-900; www.mekongriverview.com): Stylish but cozy, the Mekong River View is a new hotel situated near the beautiful Wat Xieng Thong. It is the perfect place from which to make excursions to the nearby architectural glories of Luang Prabang while enjoying the peace of the Mekong. See p. 260.

5 BEST MODERATELY PRICED ACCOMMODATIONS

- **Villa Lanka Hotel, Phnom Penh** (© 023/726-771; www.villalangka. com): Intimate and leafy, Villa Lanka is a haven at the heart of this busiest of cities—a place to recharge your batteries by the pool. It is also a great choice if you have kids in tow. See p. 69.
- **Golden Banana, Siem Reap** (© 012/ 855-366; www.golden-banana.com): The gay-friendly, everyone's-welcome Golden Banana is a favorite among Frommer's staffers. The friendly, relaxed vibe is contagious, and the beautiful pool and rooms come at a very affordable price. See p. 102.
- **Viroth's Hotel, Siem Reap** (© 063/ 761-720; www.viroth-hotel.com): This boutique affair is an airy and modern alternative to the predominantly retro style of many hotels in Siem Reap. See p. 103.
- **Le Manguiers, Kampot** (© 012/330-050): A unique and blissful hideaway, the property resembles a small village

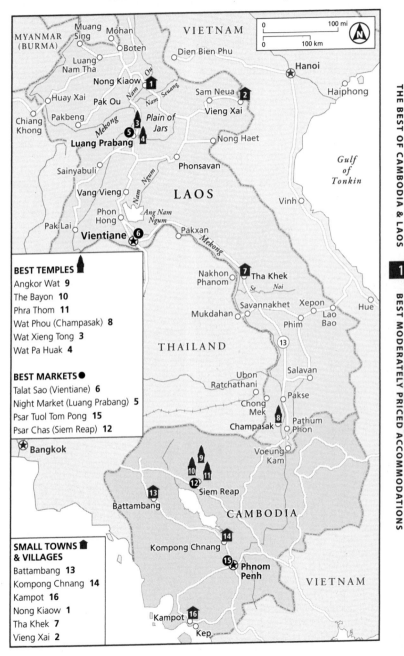

BEST TEMPLES 🏛

Angkor Wat **9**

The Bayon **10**

Phra Thom **11**

Wat Phou (Champasak) **8**

Wat Xieng Tong **3**

Wat Pa Huak **4**

BEST MARKETS ●

Talat Sao (Vientiane) **6**

Night Market (Luang Prabang) **5**

Psar Tuol Tom Pong **15**

Psar Chas (Siem Reap) **12**

SMALL TOWNS 🏠
& VILLAGES

Battambang **13**

Kompong Chnang **14**

Kampot **16**

Nong Kiaow **1**

Tha Khek **7**

Vieng Xai **2**

THE BEST OF CAMBODIA & LAOS

1

BEST MODERATELY PRICED ACCOMMODATIONS

with a series of beautiful bungalows fronted by rice paddies. The stunning beauty of the location and its restful ambience make Les Manguiers a legend among expats in Cambodia. See p. 170.

- **Inter City Hotel, Vientiane** (© 021/ 242-843): Wacky, weird, and wonderful, the Intercity combines an excellent riverside location with some of the oddest decor in Southeast Asia. It's a place where dotty eccentricity oozes from the woodwork. See p. 218.

- **The Elephant Crossing Hotel, Vang Vieng** (© 023/511-232; www.the elephantcrossinghotel.com). Away from the buzz of the backpacker center of Vang Vieng, the Elephant Crossing has a fantastic riverside location with wonderful views of the nearby limestone mountains. It is artfully furnished and the staff is charming. See p. 244.

- **Inthira Champanakone Hotel,** Champasak (© 031/214-059; www.inthira hotel.com): The Inthira is a cozy and sparkling renovation of an old French villa that fits in perfectly with its sleepy surroundings. See p. 315.

6 BEST ECOFRIENDLY HOTELS & NATURE RETREATS

- **Terres Rouges Lodge, Banlung** (© 075/974-051; www.ratanakiri-lodge.com): Luxurious but rustic, Terres Rouges makes a great base from which to explore the wilds. See p. 149.

- **Treetop Eco-Lodge, Banlung** (© 012/ 490-333): Another choice spot in Banlung, these quiet bungalows are run by friendly people. See p. 149.

- **Nature Lodge, Mondulkiri** (© 012/ 230-272; www.naturelodgecambodia. com): The Israeli/Khmer ownership at the Nature Lodge has created a casual haven reflecting the beauty of the surroundings. See p. 151.

- **Rainbow Lodge, Koh Kong** (© 012/ 160-2585; www.rainbowlodgecambodia. com): Tricky to reach but worth the trek, the Rainbow Lodge is right in the heart of the Cardamoms. Come here to experience this region of natural beauty. See p. 166.

- **Lotus Villa Hotel, Luang Prabang** (© 071/255-050; www.lotusvillalaos. com): Luang Prabang is a UNESCO-protected World Heritage Site. At Lotus Villa they have been environmentally conscious with a series of well-thought-out measures to keep their carbon footprint low. See p. 262.

- **The Quay, Phnom Penh** (© 023/992-284; www.thequayhotel.com): An environmentally friendly hotel in hazy and chaotic Phnom Penh? Believe it. This riverside gem strives to be Cambodia's first carbon-neutral hotel, accomplished through a combination of environmental initiatives and purchasing offsets—and it has a great mod setting to boot. See p. 64.

- **Khoun and Khone Guest House, Luang Prabang** (© 020/770-7665; www.khounandkhone.hrorbit.com): A cheerful rural retreat, Khoun and Khone offers a taste of countryside living a few miles outside of Luang Prabang. Half guesthouse and half working farm, it is a perfect place from which to explore the beauty of the area. See p. 264.

- **The Gibbon Experience, Bokeo** (© 084/212-021; www.gibbonx.org): Head deep into the forest, and live in the treetops. This is close to nature as you can get without actually being a gibbon. See p. 290.

7 BEST TEMPLES & WATS

- **Angkor Wat** (Siem Reap): Angkor Wat is the largest religious building in the world and is a highlight of any trip to Cambodia, or indeed the whole of Southeast Asia. It is deservedly considered one of the greatest man-made wonders. See p. 113.

- **The Bayon** (Siem Reap): Eerie and majestic, these huge carved faces of an ethereal god-king survey the world. There is nothing else quite like clambering through it, surrounded by stone faces and bas-reliefs. See p. 116.

- **Ta Prohm** (Siem Reap): Ta Prohm remains a perennial favorite for many visitors to Angkor. It is largely reclaimed by the jungle, as marauding roots of trees intertwine with stonework and sculptures. It was deliberately left as it was found by the French and gives an awesome sense of place and history. See p. 121.

- **Wat Phou** (Champasak): One of a series of Khmer temple sites across Thailand and Laos, Wat Phou was built high up on a hill and is imbued with atmosphere. See p. 315.

- **Wat Xieng Thong** (Luang Prabang): This is the most beautiful temple in a town that is full of them. Wat Xieng Thong is the quintessential example of the Lao temple style and is simply exquisite. See p. 278.

- **Wat Pa Huak** (Luang Prabang): A gorgeous, crumbling temple near the center of Luang Prabang, Wat Pa Huak contains some fascinating murals portraying historical scenes from long ago. See p. 277.

8 BEST RESTAURANTS

- **Frizz** (Phnom Penh) (✆ 012/524-801; www.frizz-restaurant.com): Frizz is one of the best places to sample Khmer cooking and also learn about the details of its preparation. See p. 75.

- **Khmer Surin** (Phnom Penh) (✆ 023/993-163): Head to this old standby for excellent Thai and Khmer food in traditional surroundings. See p. 78.

- **Angkor Palm** (Siem Reap) (✆ 063/761-436; www.angkorpalm.com): This is one of the best Khmer restaurants in Siem Reap—great care is put into preparing the food and it shows. See p. 109.

- **Pomme d'Amour** (Battambang) (✆ 012/415-513): The "Apple of Love" serves excellent French food in some distinctly odd, flamboyant surroundings. It's a lot of fun. See p. 141.

- **Amphone** (Vientiane) (✆ 021/212-489): At Amphone, local dishes from Vientiane are artfully prepared. If you're looking for a Lao culinary adventure, this is it. See p. 222.

- **The Cote d'Azur Pizzeria** (Vientiane) (✆ 021/217-252): This excellent restaurant is deceptively called a pizzeria. It is, more accurately, a riverfront restaurant serving the finest French provincial cuisine. See p. 224.

- **La Cave des Chateaux** (Luang Prabang) (✆ 071/212-100): La Cave des Chateaux is effortlessly elegant. It has a lovely setting overlooking the Mekong River, with superb traditional French food. See p. 266.

- **The Tamarind Café** (Luang Prabang) (✆ 020/777-0484): Come here for light breakfasts and lunches, and a range of Lao delicacies. They've just begun offering cooking classes, too. See p. 269.

- **Vieng Kheam Khong** (Luang Prabang) (© **071/212-726**): This is one of a number of great riverside restaurants in this most beautiful of cities. Try the Luang Prabang sausage. See p. 269.
- **The Dao Savanh** (Savannakhet) (© **041/260-888**): Housed in a converted villa in the crumbling remnants of the old French quarter, the beautiful architecture complements the excellence of the food. See p. 300.

9 BEST MARKETS

- **Psar Toul Tom Poung** (Phnom Penh): Known as the Russian market, this is the place to buy everything from ornate carved Angkorian heads to DVDs, shoes, and car parts. See p. 87.
- **Psar Chas** (Siem Reap): The focus of Siem Reapthis market does a roaring trade in souvenirs. There's plenty on offer, but be prepared to haggle. See p. 128.
- **Talat Sao** (Vientiane): At this market in Lao you can find whatever you need, including practical necessities, gifts, and souvenirs. See p. 236.
- **Night Market** (Luang Prabang): Fabric, handicrafts, jewelry, and more, this market starts at 6pm in the center of town and is a pleasant place to wander as well as shop. See p. 283.

Cambodia in Depth

If ever a country could be in possession of charisma, then this troubled but fascinating Southeast Asian kingdom has it in droves. Where for 3 decades misfortune and war have obscured a rich history and vibrant culture, for the last decade that perception of the country as a place of unmitigated darkness has been in a state of constant revision. It is a nation at peace, no longer a proxy battleground for world superpowers. Historically, Cambodia was home to one of the most glorious and influential civilizations in Asia. The Khmers ruled from what is now Cambodia, all across Laos, Thailand, and large parts of Vietnam. A homogenous race, their art, language, and architecture helped influence every region their empire touched. Subsequent history saw all those glories diminish and implode, culminating in some of the most horrific episodes of savagery in the history of mankind. It may be a cliché, but in the case of Cambodia one is justified in using the phrase "a country of extremes." Very few walk away from Cambodia with simple indifference.

As a tourist, you will be witness to this regeneration of Cambodia as it happens. With the war long since finished, Cambodia is now easy to visit and get around. Infrastructure is vastly improved and accommodations in every category are plentiful. Blessed by some of the most fascinating and beautiful sites Southeast Asia has to offer, Cambodia is finally welcoming visitors on an industrial scale.

1 CAMBODIA TODAY

Just over a decade ago, Phnom Penh was lawless, guns were commonplace, and checkpoints from different political factions leveled "contributions" on all roads out of the city. At night the streets were dark and potholed, and you would be taking a risk by venturing down them at night. Those days are gone and Phnom Penh is reemerging as a boomtown, leaving behind the pressures of the Cold War that drew it into the years of absolute darkness. It is a city that has seen a brand-new economic explosion over the last 3 years.

The mysteries of Angkor Wat are once again being explored by the numbers of tourists it deserves. Rather than being the quiet dusty village of 10 years ago, Siem Reap is thriving as it develops far enough to cater to this never-ending procession of visitors.

Not long ago, traveling around Cambodia was an obstacle course and there were areas where it was dangerous to venture. Now most roads are surfaced and sealed. There is regular bus service to pretty much anywhere you might want to visit. There are good accommodations at often incredibly reasonable prices in every town you would want to visit. New restaurants, serving cuisine from every continent of the planet, spring up daily across Phnom Penh, Siem Reap, and Sihanoukville. New border crossings open all the time and in many ways Cambodia is transforming from one of the most difficult countries to travel into one of the easiest and most welcoming.

Cambodia may be booming, but that is not to say that all the country's past problems are history. Although there is a new generation looking forward to taking its place in a globalized world, there is also a trauma and collective confusion that will take more than one generation from which to recover. There is also a deep and brooding anger building, as the rich get so much richer and the poor stay the same. Cambodia is still one of the poorest nations of the world and infant mortality is high. Corruption is endemic and accepted at every level of authority. It may be publicly questioned but it is a billion miles from being eradicated or even seriously challenged. There is a phrase in Khmer, "Mien loi, jeut l'or. Ot mien loi jeut ot l'or." This translated means "If you have money you have a good heart. If you are poor you have a bad heart." This karmic perversion explains some of the attitude to power, money, and corruption. Wealth, however corruptly or brutally acquired, is seen in some way as being its own cosmic reward and something to be displayed.

In the light of the swift and massive changes, development in Cambodia should be seen as a mixed blessing if not properly charted. There is development all over the country, but a great deal of it is driven by carpetbaggers, hedge funds, and criminals. Cambodia is often described as a country for sale. There are new natural resources of oil and natural gas lying offshore and about to be tapped, but there is no guarantee that the riches they bring will benefit any more than a handful of people. If the destruction of the high-canopy rainforest and the billions of dollars generated by the trade in hardwoods is anything to go by we can be sure that it won't be. Foreign speculators and investors are pumping billions of dollars into developing Cambodia's coastal areas. The central government in Phnom Penh had, in the '90s, designated the entire coast and its islands as state public land that could not be bartered or developed. Now local communities live in fear of the relentless land grabs. As a nation, Cambodia remains

precarious and underpinned by debt and foreign aid, and it has recently found itself a refuge for money and speculators fleeing paralyzed Western financial markets.

Even though not all is rosy by any means, collective experience has taught the Khmers to treasure the stability of the last decade. Although they share many of the qualities that characterize Southeast Asia, particularly in the importance of the concept of "face," they also have a way of interacting that is peculiarly Khmer. They have a casual and warm sense of humor that will be apparent as soon as you arrive. Thigh-slapping jokes intersperse a lot of conversation. Even with all the horror that has befallen them, the Khmers still love a joke and a laugh. Khmers also have a genuine fascination with things foreign. They are intensely nationalistic, but that does not mean that they disdain knowledge of other places or other cultures. That is unless you are Thai or Vietnamese, where a historical and persistent mixture of resentment, hatred, dependence, and jealousy colors the Khmer view. It mostly comes out as pointless racism and sometimes erupts into violence.

While Cambodians are often relaxed and very good company, this does mask a less pleasant reality. They have the reputation for being the most violent people in Asia, and when that side of them is stirred, especially in a crowd, you don't want to be near it.

Family is the absolute and immutable foundation of Cambodian society. Even the direct attacks on the notion of family perpetrated by the Khmer Rouge in the '70s did not destroy its importance. When traveling in Cambodia, people will be interested in your family and will see no problem with you being interested in theirs.

Starting in 2009, the long-awaited process of putting some of the surviving KR leaders on trial by a mixed Cambodian and international court got underway in

Phnom Penh (see p. 83 for more on the trials). It remains a controversial process, since many see it as too little too late and as a token and cosmetic attempt to address only the superficial issues, while ignoring the realities of ordinary people in living with the Khmer Rouge legacy in the country as a whole. Others see it entirely differently as a process providing genuine justice even if it is so many years on. The issues remain fraught with controversy to this day.

Cambodia may be booming, vibrant, and heading toward the future in one way. It may remain vulnerable, troubled, and traumatized in another. It is always complicated. Sometimes it is infuriating, exhilarating, and occasionally horrifying. One thing that it never can be is boring. Whichever side of it you may wish to emphasize, Cambodia remains one of the world's most compelling destinations.

2 LOOKING BACK

EARLY YEARS

The history of what is now Cambodia is largely about the roller-coaster sweep of empire across the whole of the region including Thailand, Laos, and Vietnam. They are all related.

The earliest recognizable national entity in what is now Cambodia was the Indianized kingdom of Funan. This trading nation flourished from the 1st to the 6th century A.D. and probably existed between Prey Veng Province in Cambodia and Kien Giang Province in Vietnam. As most Khmers will tell you, they still regard southern Vietnam, or "Kampuchea Krom," as rightfully Cambodian and historically they have a pretty strong case. Although Cambodia was at the time a patchwork of small fiefdoms sometimes at peace and sometimes at war with one another, it was through its position as a major seaport that Funan imported the Indian religion and culture that would be so important in shaping the future of the region. At its height Funan and its related states stretched across Vietnam, Laos, and as far as the Malay Peninsula. The kingdom is said to have employed Indians in the administration of the state. Sanskrit was the court language, and the Funanese advocated initially Hindu and, after the 5th century, Buddhist religious practice. Hindu deities Shiva and Vishnu were the

focus of worship and the Lingam (or Indian phallic totem and temple focus) seems to have played a central role in religious practice.

By the 6th century, Funan was weakening as trade diminished due to historical shifts in faraway places. The population largely shifted from the coastal areas inland to the Mekong and Tonle Sap rivers, moving from oceangoing trade to wet rice production. Power shifted from the Kingdom of Funan to the more specifically Khmer rebel entity of Chenla. Chenla later divided into separate north and south, referred to by contemporary Chinese sources as "Chenla of the Land" and "Chenla of the Sea," respectively. What is now Champasak in Laos was the center of the north, while the lands around the Mekong Delta and the coast belonged to the south. By the 8th century, Chenla too was weakening as various vassal states broke away.

THE RISE OF ANGKOR

Jayavarman I was the first king of what historians consider to have been the Khmer empire. It emerged from the Kingdom of Kambuja, after which Cambodia is named. He ruled from approximately 657 to 681 but died without an heir. Over the course of his reign, he consolidated power over the lands around him. However, Jayavarman left no male heirs, which led to a return to the chaotic conditions that previously held sway.

These events preceded the rise of the mightiest empire in all of Southeast Asia. It was Jayavarman II, the "god-king" or devaraja, who set off the train of events that would lead to Khmer rule encompassing all of what is now Cambodia, most of what now makes up Thailand and Laos, and large parts of present-day Vietnam. The physical remains of this empire are dotted around the region as far west as Kanchanaburi and as far north as Sukhothai in Thailand, and as far east as the South China Sea. Most historians concur that Jayavarman II rose to power in about A.D. 802. Inscribed on the sacred temple of Sdok Kak Thom on Phnom Kulen Mountain north of Angkor is an account of how Jayavarman had himself made "chakravartin" or universal monarch. It was this dawn of the age of god-kings that saw the creation of Angkor.

Although Hinduism had arrived, original feudal and animist practices survived. One such belief was the blurring of definition between God and feudal lords. This feudal reverence is imbued in the Khmer psyche and in mutated forms continues to this day. Through alliance and conquest, Jayavarman first subjugated nearby Khmer local warlords. He then turned his attention further afield. Not much is actually known about Jayavarman II except the fact that he consolidated the lands that are now Cambodia and laid the groundwork for the empire that was to follow.

Angkor is the surviving representation of hugely ambitious construction. Indravarman I (A.D. 877–89) initiated incredible irrigation projects (an obsession with irrigation was revisited under Pol Pot's Khmer Rouge centuries later, inspired by Angkorian supremacy). These projects were vastly complex and allowed the production of up to three rice harvests a year. Angkor was a power built on water and rice. Indravarman also presided over a flowering of the arts.

THE DECLINE OF ANGKOR & BATTLES WITH SIAM

By the end of the 10th century, the empire was in trouble. A usurper, Suryavarman, pushed the boundaries of empire further by annexing Lopburi in what is now central Thailand. The town is still home to some impressive Khmer ruins (largely inhabited by monkeys). The rise and fall of Angkor was not one unified process. It ebbed and flowed with periods of near collapse followed by triumphal renewal, with new additions as a symbol of triumph.

One of these periods of renewal was under the reign of Suryavarman II (1112–77), ending a period of disunity marking military victory against the Kingdom of Champa in what is now Vietnam. Above all, Suryavarman will be remembered as the man who initially commissioned the building of Angkor Wat itself as a devotion to the god Vishnu. He was killed in a retaliatory strike by the maritime forces of Champa, who fought their way up the Mekong and the Tonle Sap Lake and took the Khmers by surprise.

Their triumph was not to last long. Suryavarman's cousin Jayavarman VII was crowned in 1181 and defeated the Chams decisively. This king was a Buddhist and it was under his rule that much of what one now sees at Angkor was constructed. It is likely his face that you see serenely staring out of the walls of the Bayon on such an amazingly impressive scale. The bas-reliefs around Angkor show a Buddhist king immersed in Buddhist practices. Other sculptures display an image of warlike ferocity and relentless and brutal killing. This undertaking probably involved a huge amount of suffering for the laborers. His motivation was partly political in an insecure world of war and dispute. It was also partly evangelical. His was the desire to spread the word of Buddhism in a predominantly Hindu world (although he was Mahayana, not part of the Theravada line that dominates in Cambodia today).

Jayavarman VII died around 1215 and by this time, even though the Khmer empire was at its zenith, cracks were beginning to appear and signs of a permanent decline were beginning to show. The massive construction projects were taking a heavy toll on resources. The god-kings destroyed themselves by the effort of maintaining their own physical glory in water and in stone. The Thai empire of Ayutthaya was growing in strength as the Angkorian empire wore itself out. Their raids on the Khmers became ever more successful and ever more aggressive. In 1431, Siam attacked the city of Angkor itself, sacking it wholesale. It was around this period that the Khmer empire started to shrink and the area of what is now Phnom Penh grew in importance, as Angkor came under repeated attack from the warlike Siamese. For the next 150 years, conflict with the Thais largely dictated the agenda. It didn't all go the Thais' way. At one point, Khmer soldiers got very nearly to the walls of Ayutthaya only to discover the Burmese had beat them to it, vanquishing the Thais and occupying their capital. Ayutthaya recovered, however, and the Khmers were crushed by their armies in 1594.

YEARS OF CHAOS & THE ARRIVAL OF THE FRENCH

From this time on, Cambodia was largely a power vacuum. Weak kings looked to both Vietnam and Siam for protection. The whole of southern Vietnam including the Mekong Delta was ceded to the Vietnamese, including the village of Prey Nokor—a place now called either Ho Chi Minh City or Saigon. The Thais took the northwestern provinces of Battambang and Siem Reap, a bitter historical irony since the name Siem Reap means "Defeat of Siam." By the late 18th century, Siam was in total control. The only reason that Cambodia survived at all was because the Thais became preoccupied with fending off the ever-aggressive Burmese and the Vietnamese created their own problems of internal strife.

Then there was a colonial intervention. France had initially established and consolidated its rule in Vietnam as part of a move to protect its valuable trade interests. In 1867, French gunboats made their way up the Mekong and King Norodom I was forced to sign a treaty making Cambodia a protectorate of France. For the king at the time, the choice was one of dominance by either the French or the Thais, and the French were the preferred choice. This move actually reinforced the territorial integrity of Cambodia, since it halted Thai and Vietnamese appropriation of territory. In 1887, Cambodia became a part of the newly formed Federation of French Indochina with the Vietnamese provinces of Annam in the north and Cochin in the south. Laos was ceded to France after the Thai-Franco War of 1893. In Cambodia, Norodom remained on the throne, but it was the French who called the shots as they remained aggressively predatory, making a further series of land grabs against the Thais over the following years.

Cambodia remained very much a backwater and a buffer. The French made their money in Vietnam. The Khmers were also heavily taxed, but all the money was used to develop the neighboring provinces of what is now Vietnam. Cambodia remained undeveloped, even in Phnom Penh where most positions of authority in the colonial administration were held by Vietnamese. The French were clever in that they actually exalted the Cambodian monarchy in a way not seen since the days of Angkor, thus diffusing a lot of anti-French sentiment.

Norodom died in 1904 and was succeeded by King Sisowath, who reigned until 1927. He was followed by King Monivong. On Monivong's death, a 19-year-old named Sihanouk was placed

The Rebirth of Nationhood

Curiously, it was the French who re-created a lost sense of Khmer nation-hood—something that had been eroded in the previous centuries by the disintegration of the Khmer empire and centuries of domination by neighboring powers. The French "discovered" Angkor, a place abandoned by the Khmers to slumbering and powerful spirits for 600 years. They resurrected and encouraged the arts, including the Royal Ballet, but adapted it to their own tastes (the Thai ballet is far more authentically Angkorian, since they did not tamper with its borrowed moves). The virulent Khmer nationalism you see today was largely contrived by the French to create a psychological buffer between themselves and the Thais, who were seen as being in the British sphere of influence. It was Theravada Buddhism, the backbone of Khmer culture and society, that often inspired protest against the French, and the monkhood was seen as vulnerable to Thai influence.

on the throne by the French governor, Admiral Decoux. His life remains intimately intertwined with every step of the following decades of drama.

During World War II, Japanese forces rampaged through all of Southeast Asia. Vichy French cooperation with the Axis powers ensured that the actual physical presence of the Japanese was not that great in Cambodia, although the Cambodians did have to hand over much of Battambang and Siem Reap to Thailand, which was an Axis ally. When Paris fell to Allied forces, the Japanese took more direct control of Cambodian affairs. Once the Japanese were defeated, De Gaulle was very insistent on re-claiming French Indochina, bulldozing aside any claims for independence tacitly agreed to by the U.S. Pacific command in return for active resistance to Japanese occupation on the part of Ho Ch Minh and his allies. The British also acquiesced for fear of setting a precedent with regard to India. Sihanouk sneakily welcomed back the French for fear of being engulfed by the old enemies, Thailand and Vietnam. By this time, however, the independence genie had been let out of the bottle and no European colonial power

was in a position to reverse that in the long term. Guerrilla movements demanding independence, such as the Khmer Issarak and the Khmer Serei, grew up in the countryside and battled French control. The French fought back with immense brutality.

INDEPENDENCE

At this point, King Sihanouk confounded the French who put him on the throne. In 1953, he dissolved parliament and declared martial law in aid of what became known as the "Royal Crusade" for an independent Cambodia. Independence arrived in Indochina in 1954, though this was just the beginning of brand-new conflicts as the whole region became tragically sucked into the vortex of the Cold War.

In 1955, Sihanouk abdicated the throne in order to pursue his aims as a bona fide politician. For better or worse, he was to directly dominate Cambodian politics until his overthrow in 1970 and continues to be a major player until this day—an ambitious "god-king" who has endorsed tragedy and sanctioned horror, he sees himself as the deliverer of his nation.

During the 1960s, Sihanouk walked a diplomatic tightrope as he maneuvered to keep Cambodia neutral in the conflict raging in Vietnam. He feared the North Vietnamese Communists who had always taken a fairly patronizing and threatening view of Cambodia. He also deeply distrusted the Americans, breaking diplomatic ties in 1965 in the belief that Washington was plotting his removal. He might well have had cause.

He was, however, shortly to fall off the tightrope. In tilting toward Ho Chi Minh, Sihanouk allowed North Vietnamese forces to use Cambodia as a base and for transit. He didn't really have much choice. The Hanoi-based Communists had enough military power to do what they wanted. Sihanouk's rule became increasingly brutal as dissent grew. Opponents "disappeared." The right-wing forces gained more and more power. The army grew resentful and rebellious. The nascent left wing felt pushed to ever greater extremes as the ravages of a corrupt regime seemed to become ever more totalitarian. Cambodia was sliding toward an abyss.

Rebellion broke out in Samlot in the remote western jungles near the Thai border in 1967, and it was brutally suppressed. Photographs still exist of Royalist soldiers brandishing the severed heads of vanquished rebels. At this point, Sihanouk went for the left wingers and even moderate leftists, and fled to the jungle to organize resistance.

THE SPIRAL OF WAR

Things came to a head in 1970. While Sihanouk was at a conference in France, an American-sponsored coup deposed him. Defense minister Lon Nol took power, a move that had terrible reverberations. An occultist right-wing "Buddhist," he was in many ways a mirror of his nemesis, Pol Pot. Like Pol Pot, he was a plodder professionally. He had reached his exalted position through being Sihanouk's enforcer and hatchet man as head of the army, yet as a soldier and tactician he was to prove disastrous, breaking his own army with bizarre campaign strategies that went against all the rules of good generalship. Like Pol Pot, he was also a deranged xenophobe, particularly against the Vietnamese. He had Vietnamese living in Cambodia massacred on a fairly industrial scale, even though his sponsor at this time was largely the U.S.-backed South Vietnamese government.

Sihanouk went to Beijing. Up to this time there had been a tacit agreement with Hanoi that in return for Cambodia not supporting America, North Vietnam would not actively sponsor the increasingly radical Cambodian left. That agreement was now in shreds and the group that Sihanouk had derided as the "Khmer Rouge" (Red Khmers) became the recipients of massive infusions of military aid and support from Hanoi and China, Sihanouk's previous allies. Effectively, a beast was let off the leash. No one could have guessed the intentions of Pol Pot and his accomplices. The horror to come was unprecedented in the wars of Indochina.

In April 1970, South Vietnamese and American forces invaded Cambodia to root out North Vietnamese forces. Yet the North Vietnamese just retreated farther inside Cambodia. The North Vietnamese and the Khmer Rouge acolytes soon controlled vast areas of the countryside. In these "liberated zones," there was a total disregard for human life as the Khmer Rouge started to implement their horrific ideology. These were dark portents for the future.

Just before Sihanouk's overthrow, the U.S. had begun a secret campaign of bombing Cambodia and Laos to try and interdict the NVA and Viet Cong on the Ho Chi Minh trail and destroy their Cambodian bases. It failed to do either. What it did do was kill thousands upon thousands of innocent villagers and send their relatives rushing to join the fight against the American aggressor or scramble for refuge in Phnom Penh—a city that was increasingly bloated with suffering. Nixon and Kissinger were Pol Pot's greatest friends in terms of recruitment. After 1970 Sihanouk, following the dictum that "my enemy's enemy is my friend," disastrously and naively threw in his lot with the Khmer Rouge, visiting the liberated zones and being photographed with the Khmer Rouge leadership. He was under pressure from China (as was Pol Pot) and his bitterness knew no boundaries. This was a disaster. Even with all the wriggling and squirming that Sihanouk had done to remain in power, he was still revered by Khmers in the countryside and now the Khmer Rouge had his blessing. In his arrogance, Sihanouk thought he could control the Khmer Rouge. It was to prove to be very much the other way around. By 1973, the whole of Cambodia was engulfed in savage fighting, and Phnom Penh was bloated with refugees and was effectively under siege. Pressure continued to build, and the bombs continued to fall. Meanwhile, the Lon Nol government didn't aid its own survival as the practices of brutality and corruption became amplified to operatic proportions.

AN UNBELIEVABLE HORROR: THE KHMER ROUGE YEARS

In April 1975, the Khmer Rouge won the war and entered Phnom Penh. What was to follow was one of the most brutal and evil episodes in the history of Cambodia and, indeed, the history of the whole of mankind. On entering the city the Khmer Rouge emptied Phnom Penh completely and drove the entire population, including the sick and the dying, into the countryside. This was proclaimed to be "Year Zero."

The Khmer Rouge turned Cambodia into one large, starvation-driven, terrorized work camp. Anyone thought to be remotely associated with the old regime was murdered. The Khmer Rouge would torture and kill for acts as subversive as wearing glasses or speaking in a foreign language. Up to two million people died as the result of torture, starvation, and wholesale purges. People were interned and slaughtered on an industrial scale. "Confessions" were extracted from people who generally had no idea why they had been arrested in the first place. The enemies of "Angkar"—or "the Organization"—were tortured, starved, beaten, and killed all over the country.

As the movement became more fractured, more paranoid, and more collectively delusional, the killing got worse. The whole of the "Eastern Zone" became suspicious to "Angkar" and thousands were deported to the seemingly loyal Southwestern Zone. The Easterners were issued with blue kramas (traditional Khmer checked scarves), with everyone wearing a blue krama marked for death.

Today historians, journalists, and commentators are still trying to understand this horror. No one really does. The movement was led by a clique of committed leftists, the head of which was a soft-spoken former teacher with royal connections. His real name was Saloth Sar, but he is known to the world now as Pol Pot (see box on p. 18 for more about him). Many of these leftists had been educated in Paris and became part of a wider Communist movement known as the "Circle Marxiste." As Sihanouk's regime became more brutal this group became more consolidated and, after the Lon Nol coup, better equipped and more effective. Their philosophy was a weird mixture of mangled Maoist thinking and traditional Khmer xenophobic arrogance.

Some blame their brutalization on the American bombing of the countryside. This is far too simple and trite. The Americans bombed Laos and Vietnam as well, yet neither of those countries descended into the carnage that ravaged Cambodia. No one knows why, and although there are UN trials in process, that doesn't mean the surviving Khmer

Rouge leaders will be prompted to start telling the truth.

This particular episode in the Cambodian collective nightmare was ended in 1979. Pol Pot and his gruesome henchmen had been increasingly attacking the old enemy and their former sponsors, the Vietnamese. The North Vietnamese had won their war as the Khmer Rouge had won their own at roughly the same time. By 1978, Pol Pot was sending Khmer Rouge soldiers into South Vietnam where, not content with murdering Cambodian innocents, they perpetrated massacres of Vietnamese villagers. The Vietnamese had had enough and invaded Cambodia, successfully evicting the Khmer Rouge in a blitzkrieg. This may have ended one episode of horror, but the nightmare was certainly not ended.

A VICTIM OF THE COLD WAR: THE '80S

Cambodia was to suffer 2 more decades of war and suffering, a hopeless pawn in Cold War politics. Vietnam may have gotten rid of a regime where inhumanity was honed to a fine art, but in the mind-set of America and its allies this masked an uncomfortable reality. The Vietnamese were pro-Soviet Communists and their invasion of Cambodia marked a major extension of Soviet power. What to do? The answer that the U.S. came up with was to arm and support the Khmer Rouge in the full knowledge of what this movement had done to its own people.

The Khmer Rouge continued to fight under the not very convincing guise of a royalist alliance, with Sihanouk continuing to provide the endorsement (this despite the fact that the Khmer Rouge had confined him and come close to killing him during their rule). They carried Chinese guns largely paid for with American money, but they carried on killing Cambodian people in huge numbers. Historians ask themselves how this could have

happened. Who should now be on trial? The answers remain complex and certainly have little to do with justice.

The Vietnamese installed a pliant, puppet government in Phnom Penh consisting mainly of former Eastern Zone Khmer Rouge rebel defectors headed at first by Heng Samrin (a man who remains justifiably popular even among his political opponents) and then Hun Sen. The war continued and there was a massive exodus of refugees to both Thailand and Vietnam, and as the rice fields went untended people began to starve on a massive scale. Huge permanent refugee camps came into existence in Thailand as the agendas of outside players were forced upon a people for whom war had become the never-ending and tragic norm.

Amazingly, the UN still recognized the Khmer Rouge as the legitimate government of Cambodia, and it was a Khmer Rouge representative who held the Cambodian seat at the UN. The war sputtered on through the '80s, the refugee camps became cities, and all this only diminished with the advent of Perestroika in Russia, the collapse of Soviet support for satellite states, and Vietnamese withdrawal from Cambodia in 1989. There was no longer an imperative for the West to support the Khmer Rouge and they were left only with Chinese support. The government of Hun Sen was forced to look to the outside world now that their Soviet and Vietnamese patrons had quit the scene. The Khmer Rouge adapted their game but not their capacity for the murder of their own people. They continued to plant mines (as did the Vietnamese-backed government forces) around the mountains and forest areas where they continued to hold sway and launch new offensives every year.

UN INTERVENTION

With the Cold War imperative gone, diplomatic efforts to put a stop to the fighting started to become effective in 1990 with

Who Was Pol Pot?

Pol Pot (aka Saloth Sar) was the enigmatic and chillingly ruthless leader of the Khmer Rouge. He took the name Pol Pot upon coming fully to power in 1975. It most likely comes from a phrase translated into French that the Chinese leadership used to describe him, "*Politique Potentielle*," though that is only a theory. Pol Pot and his equally despotic cronies—Nuon Chea, Khieu Samphan, Son Sen, Ieng Sary, Ieng Thirith, Ta Mok, and a host of others—were the architects of a horror so total that the world is still reeling at man's capacity to be so inhumane to his fellow countrymen. Torture was an everyday tool employed by this regime. Toddlers and infants were as callously killed as adults were. The killing was run like a mundane bureaucratic procedure, and Pol Pot was the chief executive calling the shots.

Born in 1925, Saloth Sar was part of the tiny Phnom Penh middle class and he had royal connections. His sister was a palace concubine, while he was sent to Paris to be educated as an electrical engineer. He wasn't very good, repeatedly failing his exams and returning to Phnom Penh in 1954. While in Paris he fell in with a group of committed Cambodian leftists dubbed the "Cercle Marxiste." At this time, Saloth Sar was not in any way the leader of this group and people such as Ieng Sary, who later became Khmer Rouge foreign minister, were far more important.

Saloth Sar may not have been very successful academically, but by the mid-'60s as leftists fled the increasingly repressive Sihanouk regime, he was showing a considerable talent for organization and had an utterly ruthless ambition. Over time, he came to be the de facto leader of the movement. His actions in that role set the tone for the brutality, the arrogance, and the intense paranoia that marked out the Khmer Rouge regime. Although other Khmer Rouge leaders such as Khieu Samphan and Ieng Sary were far more academic ideologues and theorists for this poisonously lunatic bunch, Pol Pot remained very much in control. This was until international support for the Khmer Rouge waned, the movement fractured, and he was toppled by Ta Mok, one of the few of his longtime lieutenants who had not either defected or been murdered on his orders. His death in 1998 was an ignominious one: He is said to have been interned in a seedy shack deep in the jungle, and his body burned atop a pile of car tires.

the Paris peace accords, implemented by the five permanent members of the UN Security Council. A deal was hammered out that suited both Hun Sen's government and the forces of the Sihanouk "alliance." The United Nations Transitional Authority in Cambodia (UNTAC) would create and oversee the conditions under which elections could be held. Sihanouk was rewarded for all his years of politicking and plotting by being put back on the throne.

There was a merciful break in the fighting, but the period saw an influx of foreign troops and money into the country. Phnom Penh became a Wild West–like boomtown awash with money, four-wheel-drives, and rampant prostitution.

As Hun Sen darkly quipped years later, UNTAC should really stand for "United Nations Takes AIDS to Cambodia." Originally the Khmer Rouge were included in the peace process following the delusional and criminal logic that caused the international community to support them through the '80s. They soon realized that this would not suit their ends (largely because no one would vote for them) and they returned to their jungle bases and went back to what they knew best—killing and war.

The election took place in 1993 and Sihanouk's FUNCINPEC party very narrowly won the vote. This didn't suit Hun Sen, who remains to this day a Machiavellian strongman. The UN, in its wisdom, caved in to Hun Sen, appointing him and FUNCINPEC's Prince Norodom Ranariddh as joint prime ministers. They both had armies, they both wanted exclusive power, and they both hated each other with a vengeance.

Meanwhile, the UN left town thinking Cambodia was now a job well done. All that effort and money left Cambodia in continued chaos, and once again the wider world had failed ordinary Cambodians. The inevitable happened—conflict between the two prime ministers worsened and the Khmer Rouge went on the offensive yet again.

THE END OF THE KHMER ROUGE

The key to the beginning of the end came from the Khmer Rouge itself. In 1996, Ieng Sary, former head of the Cambodian Cercle Marxiste and Pol Pot's foreign minister, broke with Pol Pot's center. Ieng's forces were in the Western town of Pailin where they were becoming very rich as a result of logging and gem mining. Pol Pot's center was based in the northern area of Anlong Veng, and they felt that not enough of the money was making it their way. In the end, what broke this murderous Marxist movement was a squabble about cash. The issue of Khmer Rouge defections exacerbated the already fragile peace between the two prime ministers as both attempted to attract enough former Khmer Rouge forces to their own cause and wipe out their rival.

This came to a head in 1997 when Hun Sen seized absolute power in what was wrongly called a "coup," but was actually simply a stand-up fight and settling of scores. FUNCINPEC forces were defeated and Prince Ranariddh fled.

Meanwhile things started to look bleak for Pol Pot. He murdered his old and close friend, Son Sen (and his wife and children) by having them run over by a tank. Pol Pot was in turn ousted by his own brutal one-eyed lieutenant, Ta Mok, dubbed "The Butcher." Ta Mok, quite rightly, probably thought he was next and decided to get in his retaliation first. Pol Pot was convicted in a Khmer Rouge show trial and put under house arrest. He died in a malarial jungle hovel in 1998 and his body was burned on tires with no autopsy being done. A long and painful era of Cambodian history died with him.

A MEASURE OF STABILITY

There were elections in 1998 and in 2003. Hun Sen and the CPP won both times and his grip on power remains almost total. Whether that's a good thing or not is often a point of debate, but the fact is that since 1998 the hard-won stability that now exists has benefited ordinary Cambodian people.

There have been problems. In 2003, an enraged mob torched the Thai embassy over a misquote from a Thai soap opera star claiming that Angkor Wat was Thai. She never said it, but the Thai ambassador had to flee for his life as the mob rampaged through Phnom Penh, burning anything that smacked of Thailand. The Thais simply closed their borders and

Who's Who in Cambodian Politics?

Cambodian politics remains an affair of shifting sands, Byzantine alliances, and Mafia-like power plays. The prime minister, Hun Sen, has ruled the country for 3 decades. He heads the **Cambodian People's Party,** successor to the People's Revolutionary Party of Kampuchea. He was a midlevel Khmer Rouge commander from the Eastern Zone. Initially under So Phim (purged and killed on the orders of Pol Pot in 1978) the Eastern Zone cadres were always fairly strong on their own account. They came under the paranoid suspicion of the "Center" of Angkar in 1978 and were forced into the arms of the Vietnamese. Hun Sen and many others fled to Vietnam after the bloody purges of their people.

When the Vietnamese liberated Cambodia from the Khmer Rouge, Hun Sen was one of the Vietnamese-backed returnees installed in power. Under Heng Samrin, prime minister of the People's Republic of Kampuchea, he served as foreign minister, becoming prime minister himself in 1985. He has been the main power in Cambodia ever since, through turbulent times, winning the last two elections in 2003 and 2008.

FUNCINPEC was formed as a political front, built around Sihanouk's opposition of the Vietnamese after they liberated Cambodia in 1979. This alliance included the Khmer Rouge as the backbone of their fighting force. Following the withdrawal of the Vietnamese in 1979, Sihanouk's son, Prince Norodom Ranariddh, served as co–prime minister from 1993 to 1997 and led the party until October 2006. In 1997, the FUNCINPEC rivalry came to a head and Ranariddh was evicted from government in violent military clashes across the country. This was not unexpected, given that the UN had left in place two competing prime ministers. Ranariddh fled but returned later on to rejoin politics in a reduced role. In reality, he was already finished. He has since been forced out of the party and formed a new one of his own, the **Norodom Ranariddh Party (NRP).** Current leader Keo Puth Rasmey succeeded Ranariddh. Both FUNCINPEC and Ranariddh's new party took a hammering in the 2008 elections, from which they are unlikely to ever recover.

The SRP, or **Sam Rainsy Party,** first formed by the politician of the same name, is a mercurial mix of pro-Western liberal sentiment and violently racist, anti-Vietnamese rhetoric. Sam Rainsy himself was a FUNCINPEC finance minister in the '90s, but quit as a result of what he saw as unbridled corruption. While he highlighted an issue that is central to Cambodia's progress, he has confronted Hun Sen's undoubted thuggery with a political demagoguery of his own. As things stand now, SRP is the second-largest party in the National Assembly but has an increasingly diminishing chance of ever seeing real power.

Khmers suffered the devastating economic effect. There has also been simmering tension around the temples of Preah Vihear (or Khao Phra Viharn in Thai). In 2008,

the two countries came close to war as soldiers of both nations died in firefights.

The general trend, however, is positive. Having had two elections that have taken place largely without violence, Cambodia is now politically stable. From 2001 to 2004, the economy grew at a rate of 6.4%. In 2005, oil and natural gas deposits were found beneath Cambodia's territorial waters, representing a new revenue stream for the government if drilling begins. Arrivals in tourism topped two million in 2008. Cambodia's garment industry employs more than 350,000 people and contributes to more than 70% of Cambodia's exports. The major challenge for Cambodia over the next decade will be creating an economic environment in which enough jobs can be created to handle Cambodia's demographic imbalance. Rural poverty is still a major concern, as the infrastructure in the countryside remains patchy or nonexistent. Levels of education are also woeful and that inevitably holds the country back.

In 2004, the mercurial King Sihanouk abdicated in favor of his son, Norodom Sihamoni, who has gained respect for his quiet dignity in the way he fulfills his duties, although Sihanouk, or "Papa" as many Cambodians refer to him, remains a seminal figure.

3 THE LAY OF THE LAND

Cambodia borders Thailand to the west and the north, Laos to the north, and Vietnam to the east and south. It is slightly smaller than Oklahoma at 181,035 sq. km (69,898 sq. miles). It has a coastline of 443km (275 miles) along the gulf of Thailand. It is largely, although not exclusively, flat and is bisected by the mighty Mekong River, which flows north to south from Laos, through Cambodia and then on to Vietnam. The Tonle Sap, a tributary of the Mekong, feeds the Tonle Sap Lake, the largest in Southeast Asia. The Tonle Sap is a geographical anomaly, since it is the only river in the world that actually changes direction twice a year. From November to May, Cambodia's dry season, the Tonle Sap drains into the Mekong when it reaches Phnom Penh. In June, when heavy monsoon rains begin, the flow reverses to form the enormous Tonle Sap Lake. The Tonle Sap then drains the Mekong and flows into the lake.

There are mountains in the northeast around Ratanakiri, the Dangrek range in the north and the Cardamoms in the southwest. Most population concentrations are around the fertile river valleys or on the coast.

Cambodia used to be largely blanketed by high-canopy rainforest but logging, both legal and illegal, has seen that diminished to almost nothing. The flatlands of the river basin remain incredibly fertile and the countryside is largely dominated by rice production.

Land mines are still found in the areas surrounding the mountain and jungle areas, particularly along the Thai border where the Khmer Rouge had their bases, though this is only a basic rule of thumb.

4 CAMBODIA'S ART & ARCHITECTURE

ARCHITECTURE

Cambodia yields some of the most spectacular sites in Asia. Yet most traditional Cambodian houses are simple structures made of wood and built on stilts raising them from the ground. They vary in size, measured by the number of vertical posts used in their construction. Walls are of woven bamboo. Cambodians generally live communally in one large room, with a

very different concept of privacy than is customary for families in the West. Often the whole village will cooperate to build (although not to pay for) a family's new house, and the effort will later be reciprocated. Livestock and the family motorbike are found underneath the home.

In the towns the French influence is readily evident. Towns like Battambang, Kratie, Kampong Chhnang, and Kampong Cham are all marked by colonnaded streets, ocher walls, and elegant villas. Much of the grandeur is faded, crumbling, and sometimes squalid, but it remains very impressive.

In Phnom Penh development is rapid, but thankfully many (although not all) of the developers are attempting to maintain the feel of the city. Cambodian cities remain distinctly low-rise since development has for so long been held back, but that is certainly changing. Developers using Korean money are in the process of putting up the first skyscraper (the $240-million Gold Tower 42) right in the center of Phnom Penh. Though at the time of writing the project is on hold because of the world economic downturn, this development marks a major change in Cambodian urban planning. Phnom Penh is changing fast, and this is not the only planned highrise. Others are in the advanced planning stages. Not everyone is happy about this change, and some analysts predict that high-rise residential developments will flop, even though there is a need for more office space. What is certainly true is that in a city that did not even have traffic lights 10 years ago, things are happening at lightning speed.

PAINTING & SCULPTURE

The Khmer Rouge attempted to destroy the arts in all forms. They spared Angkor as a symbol of past national glory. Anything else they got their hands on, they tended to smash. A great deal was lost that can never be regained.

There has also been a mass plundering of architectural sites, feeding a lucrative but illegal trade in smuggled artifacts. Thankfully, plenty also survived. If you go to Street 178 (now known as "Art Street") in Phnom Penh, there are a series of art galleries selling paintings and sculptures. They are a mix of old and new, and the Royal University of Fine Arts is right across the road.

The markets of Phnom Penh and Siem Reap are full of magnificent sculptures. Generally, they are imitations of ancient religious pieces and are very popular with tourists. The very Khmer slightly flat face of the Bayon represents a recurring theme. The earliest known Cambodian sculptures were generally images of Hindu gods. To see the real thing, the National Museum in Phnom Penh is where sculpture from the 6th century onward is displayed.

Today, art scenes have sprouted up in both Phnom Penh and Siem Reap. A lot of Cambodian artists who fled abroad during the bad years also absorbed a lot of Western influences, so there is a whole new school of Cambodian artists essentially practicing a synthesis. Recently there has been an interesting initiative by a collective of young Cambodia artists under the guidance of English sculptor Sasha Constable to recycle all the confiscated weaponry from the years of war and recycle it into modern sculptures (see the box "Munitions into Art" on p. 88).

MUSIC

The Khmer Rouge killed musicians as they killed other types of artists and performers including Sin Sisamuth, the much loved and revered Cambodian singer. It is said they made him sing the Khmer Rouge national anthem before they bludgeoned him to death. As with so much else, a lot was lost, but music remains a very integral part of the Cambodian soul.

Generally much traditional music is based around religion and ritual using an array of traditional instruments. Some Cambodian folk music often has a bluesy and deeply melancholy feel. This is particularly true of *chapaye,* which sounds like a cross between sounds from Asia and the Mississippi Delta. It is sung (or wailed) accompanied by a two-stringed lutelike instrument. Cambodian TV often offers late-night performances, which are well worth looking out for.

Traditional music is performed by a small orchestra playing a variety of instruments such as a *ching* (cymbal), *roneat* (bamboo xylophone), *pia au* (flute), *sralai* (oboe), *chapey* (bass banjo), *gong* (bronze gong), *tro* (fiddle), and different kinds of drums. It is often haunting and atmospheric.

In the '60s and '70s, there was a thriving garage rock scene in Phnom Penh with a mixture of pop, R&B, and rock, all with a Cambodian slant. Although the musicians were murdered by the Khmer Rouge, recordings still survive and you can buy CDs in the major markets. The one to look out for is called "Cambodia Rocks."

Today, many returnees to Cambodia have bought their own brand of music, often a mix between Western and Khmer. These days this is often manifested in Khmer rap, which is enormously popular among the young.

And of course, there is karaoke. Whether machine fed or accompanied by a live band and live singers, karaoke is hugely popular with Cambodians. If you head over the Japanese Bridge in Phnom

Who Are the Khmers?

Cambodia is one of the most ethnically homogenous nations in Asia, with 96% of its population being ethnically Khmer. Apart from that there are communities of Vietnamese, Chinese, Cham (both Muslim and Buddhist), plus animist hill tribe groups in Ratanakiri and Mondulkiri. The Khmers have been in this area since the start of recorded history, long before the Thais or Vietnamese migrated here. This fairly straightforward story of Khmer ethnicity gives the Khmers a strong sense of collective self, despite all the upheavals they have undergone. Even 1,000 years later, a pride in the cultural achievements of Angkor is central to Khmer identity. There are also many Khmers living in the northeastern Thai provinces of Buriram, Surin, and Sisaket as well as in Vietnam's Mekong Delta. Ethnically these provinces were Khmer but were dislocated as a result of the ebb and flow of empire.

Penh to the area of Prek Leap, you'll find a number of very lively music and karaoke joints often interspersed with live comedy. People go to eat food, drink beer, and sing their hearts out. It's a very Cambodian experience.

DANCE

Cambodian classical dance is breathtakingly elegant. Related to the palace and the court, this ancient art was an integral part of Cambodian royal ritual. Although the skills declined after the wane of Angkor, they were resurrected by the French as part of a policy of fostering Khmer national pride. It is related to dance in Thailand and although Khmer dance came first, Thai dance is purer and closer to the Angkorian ideal since it is in more direct line without the influence of the French.

The slow, elegant hand movements, the exquisite costumes, and the ethereal music all contribute to creating what feels like an otherworldly experience. Many of the themes come from Hindu epics such as the Ramayana. The Khmer Rouge nearly killed off this ancient art, yet a few trained practitioners survived. In 1981, the School of Fine Arts was reopened in Phnom Penh and the knowledge salvaged from the skills of the few has been taught to many.

Cambodians love to dance in general, whether that's the traditional *ramvong* (a slow dance where people walk around slowly in a circle making traditional hand movements) or a Saturday night out where Dad, Mom, and the kids head down to the local hop and get down in one glorious family boogie to whatever dance music the DJ or band is offering.

THEATER

Cambodian classical theater consists of highly stylized tellings of the Hindu epics such as the Ramayana. The art form is called *lakhaon kaol,* a dance-drama performed by men and based on tales from the Ramayana. This seminal Hindu epic, in which gods and monkeys battle demons and ogres and show supernatural powers as they triumph over evil is a part of Cambodian national consciousness and remains a source of inspiration for Cambodia's artists.

5 CAMBODIA IN POPULAR CULTURE

RECOMMENDED FILMS

The recent trauma of Cambodia has been visited over and over again in both literature and film. Roland Joffe's 1984 movie, *The Killing Fields,* chronicles the lives of foreign journalists covering the fall of Phnom Penh and the subsequent experiences of Cambodian journalist Dith Pran at the hands of the Khmer Rouge during the darkest of periods. It is an excellent introduction to recent history, looking at it through both Cambodian and Western eyes.

These days, Cambodia is a tempting backdrop for filmmakers from both Asia and farther away. *Lara Croft: Tomb Raider* with Angelina Jolie used Angkor as a set. In 2002, Matt Dillon made the indescribably complicated *City of Ghosts,* using locations from all around the country. The plot may be convoluted but the cinematography is superb, and the film used many real local characters in cameos, including Michael Hayes, the then-editor (and founder) of *The Phnom Penh Post.*

Cambodian director Rithy Pran made an extraordinary documentary about Tuol Sleng, the improvised Khmer Rouge prison where thousands upon thousands of people were tortured and killed. In *S21: The Khmer Rouge Killing Machine,* one of the only survivors of Toul Sleng, the artist Vann Nath, actually confronts the prison guards who did the torture and killing. It is moving beyond belief as with immense dignity Vann Nath questions the men who did these inhuman and terrible things to him and thousands of others. There are no real conclusions, but it is an astounding and historic marker.

RECOMMENDED BOOKS

There are many books about Cambodia, plenty of them touching on the years of turmoil. Jon Swain's *River of Time* is a very affecting story of his lifelong love affair with Indochina and his journalistic experiences in covering the Cambodian story. Nic Dunlop, a British photographer who quite by chance discovered the Khmer Rouge torturer in chief, known as Duch, writes a compelling story about that incident but touches on many of the wider implications in *The Lost Executioner*. It is beautifully written and a page turner. One of the best biographies of Pol Pot is by Philip Short and is called *Pol Pot. The Pol Pot Regime* by Ben Kiernan is a very academic but very inclusive historical analysis of the whole era and what made the Khmer Rouge tick. Francois Bizot was a French ethnographer who was captured and imprisoned by the Khmer Rouge in 1973. His account, *The Gate,* gives some insight into their maniacal thinking in the days before they took Phnom Penh. *When the War Was Over* is an immensely thoughtful account of the Khmer Rouge years by *Washington Post* journalist Elizabeth Becker. She covered Cambodia from the early '70s on and actually toured Democratic Kampuchea and interviewed Pol Pot when he was still in power. *Lost Goddesses: Denial of Female Power in Cambodian History* by Dr. Trudy Jacobsen is the first study to address the place of women in Cambodian history. It is a narrative and thoughtful tour de force, revising accepted perspectives on history and posing deep questions about modern Cambodia in the light of history reexamined. There has also been a series of autobiographies by Khmer Rouge survivors who were children at the time. *Stay Alive My Son* by Pin Yathey, *First They Killed My Father* by Loung Ung, and *When Broken Glass Floats* by Chanrithy Him are among them, but there are many others. *Angkor* by George Coedes is the premier read on the temples of Angkor. *Khmer: The Lost Empire of Cambodia* by Thierry Zephir makes a good guide and intro for a visit to Angkor.

6 EATING & DRINKING IN CAMBODIA

Cambodian cuisine does not have the breadth or depth of either Thai food or Vietnamese food, although it has some similarities with both. It is certainly less spicy than you will find in Thailand. Rice is, of course, the staple and most dishes are cooked in a wok. Given the number of rivers and the dominance of the Tonle Sap, it also comes as no surprise that freshwater fish figures quite large at the Cambodian meal table. This includes the very Cambodian ingredient of *prahoc,* or fermented fish paste, that is beloved by Cambodians but which many foreigners find a little too pungent.

Breakfast for Khmers is usually the ubiquitous rice soup. Main meals will consist of a number of dishes served simultaneously, almost always including a soup of some kind. Cambodia's signature dish is *amok*—fish cooked in banana leaves with turmeric and coconut milk. Like many Cambodian dishes, it has a mildly lemony taste. Another biggie is *lok lak.* It consists of diced, fried beef served with fried eggs, salad, and french fries or rice. A common condiment that gives *lok lak* and many other dishes a bit of added taste is pepper mashed in with squeezed lime. It works with chicken, beef, and pork.

There are five principal ingredients in Cambodian cooking. Apart from *prahoc,* lemon grass adds a distinctively balmy flavor to many dishes, and you'll often see it growing in gardens. Kaffir lime leaves are ground into paste and used like bay leaves to flavor soup or sliced into thin threads as a garnish. Galangal, a cream-colored root, resembles ginger but has a more subtle flavor. Again it is either ground into a paste or added sliced to give a slightly roasted flavor. Tamarind paste is the dark pulp from inside the flat pods that grow on tamarind trees. It was introduced as an ingredient by Indian traders.

Khmers use it to darken soups and give them a characteristic mixture of sweet and sour.

The southern coast around Kep and Sihanoukville is the place for magnificent seafood. Kep crab in Kampot pepper is a real treat but there is also steamed fish, lobster, squid, and much other delicious seafood. They will be cooked right in front of you or even at your table.

Cambodians love fruit. Papaya, rambutan, pomelo, melon, bananas, pineapple, jackfruit, durian, and many others all play a major and very healthy part in the Khmer diet.

The imperialist legacy left its mark on cuisine in Cambodia. As in Laos and Vietnam, breakfast can be a fresh baguette and delicious filtered coffee. Also popular are baguette sandwiches with pâté and salad. These can be bought from roadside vendors pushing glass-sided carts.

While Cambodia has yet to see chain restaurants on a larger scale, international cuisine has come to its cities over the last 20 years. You will find Vietnamese-style noodle soup pretty much everywhere and Chinese food is also an integral part of the scene. There is suki soup from North Asia, burgers from everywhere, and lots of Thai food. Phnom Penh and Siem Reap (but particularly Phnom Penh) have some of the best selections of restaurants serving international cuisine in the entire region. Whether you want Mexican tacos or Spanish tapas on the riverfront, a perfect *steak au poivre* in the shadow of Wat Phnom or English fish and chips by Central Market, Phnom Penh has it. This is partly a legacy of the days when the UN was in Cambodia and businesses opened up, catering to the multiplicity of nationalities involved. The last 10 years have seen an explosion of new dining options and the competition keeps standards very high.

Wherever you are, stick only to bottled water. You can also get cold fizzy drinks in most places, but they tend to be sickly sweet. You are also relatively safe with the fruit shakes sold at stalls and in markets. They are popular and very refreshing. Beer both local and imported, and brewed under license, is available everywhere. Angkor is the original Cambodian beer and is not bad, though it will give you a headache if imbibed in quantity. A good alternative is the similarly named Anchor. Pronounce it "Antchor" if you don't want them to give you Angkor by mistake.

7 ETIQUETTE IN CAMBODIA

Cambodia is a very conservative country where modesty is the order of the day. You can dress skimpily, but it won't do you any favors in terms of the Khmers' perception of you. Likewise, openly public displays of affection will embarrass people, so don't do it.

As with other countries in the region the concept of "face" governs social interaction on every level. You will get things done faster if you go out of your way to make sure that you don't cause someone to lose face. If you get angry, try not to show it. Another thing to remember is that a

The Krama: A Scarf for All Seasons

Everywhere you go in the Cambodian countryside, you will see the checkered pattern of the *krama*. This ubiquitous cotton scarf performs many functions. It shades a weary head from the sun. It keeps dust out of the eyes and mouth. It is a carryall, whether that be fruit, money, or babies. It is a skirt, a sarong, a tablecloth, a towel, and a hammock. I have even seen them used to temporarily fix the loose undercarriage of an aging Toyota Camry.

The krama is also, to some extent, the symbol of being Khmer and being a farmer. When Prime Minister Hun Sen (no privileged kid he, Hun Sun is from tough peasant stock in Kompong Cham Province) canvasses in the countryside he dons a krama, puts on the khaki cargo pants, and stands in rice paddies, reminding his constituents that he is the same as them.

There have also been very sinister uses of the krama in Khmer history. In 1978, Pol Pot ordered the Eastern Zone purged. The people of the east were transported to the "loyal" Southwestern Zone run by Pol Pot's brutal one-eyed henchman, Ta Mok. Each deportee was issued with a brand-new blue krama. Maybe they thought he was looking out for their physical well-being. In reality, Ta Mok ordered that anyone seen wearing the blue krama be marked for death.

Kramas do not come only in rough, practical cotton. There are also patterned silk versions with intricate stripes and patterns. The origins of the krama most likely lie in ancient Angkorian times when a simple cloth was used to cover the upper body. Variations of the krama are also worn by rural people in Laos and Thailand, but only in Cambodia is this simple piece of cloth an affirmation of identity.

Cambodian reaction to uncertainty or embarrassment is to giggle or laugh. So if you ask a moto-taxi driver to take you to a destination and it turns out he has absolutely no idea where he is going and giggles when you point it out, don't get angry. He is not laughing at you; it's just the Cambodian way of diffusing tension.

Smile and joke as much as you can. It's the Cambodian way and people will be more willing to help you.

When you beckon someone, don't do it the Western way. Flap your whole hand downward with your palm flat. If you do it with your hand or finger pointing up, it is interpreted as either very rude or as a sexual gesture.

As in all Buddhist countries, the head is considered holy while the feet are considered dirty. Don't go around touching people's heads, even if it's just patting a child on the head. Likewise, don't point the soles of your feet at anyone and certainly not at a Buddha image. Cambodians tend to sit on the floor with their feet tucked to the side. Don't step over someone and don't step over food. It's considered very rude.

If you are in a temple, dress modestly. Have respect for monks in general. Women should never touch them.

Planning Your Trip to Cambodia

With the vast increase in tourism over the last few years, Cambodia is becoming a country that is easy to get around with good facilities. Paperwork has been simplified (you can even get your tourist visa online), and the old image of a difficult country where roughing it was obligatory is now outdated. Buses now go everywhere, when less than a decade ago you traveled by pickup with reinforced suspension over potholed dusty roads. New hotels pop up everywhere, cellphone coverage gets ever better, and minimarts and ATMs are becoming the norm in towns. McDonald's has yet to arrive, but that may be just a question of time. All this doesn't mean that Cambodia is always a breeze—some roads are still bad, and Phnom Penh is chaotic and can be intimidating. This chapter provides plenty of resources and tips for plotting your Cambodia adventure.

1 WHEN TO GO

Located 10 to 13 degrees north of the Equator, like most of Southeast Asia, Cambodia varies from warm to very hot throughout the whole year. There are four annual seasons: cool and dry between November and February; hot and dry between March and May; hot and wet between June and August; and cool and wet between September and early November. The best time to visit is the cool season, when the weather usually benefits from a pleasant dry heat and the countryside is still green from the rains. As February turns into March, the heat begins to build until April and May, when it can be quite oppressive and uncomfortable. In May and June, the rains come and bring a measure of relief. It rarely rains all day, and mostly it will rain for an hour or two in the afternoon or evening. By early September, the heat begins to dissipate and the evenings are cooler. Through October, the frequency of the showers slows and the humidity starts to lower. Although the wet season is low season for tourism throughout most of the region, visiting at that time does have its advantages. It is when the Angkor complex is at its most beautiful, the vegetation is lush, and the crowds are relatively thin.

Average Temperatures & Rainfall (in.) in Phnom Penh

	Jan	Feb	Mar	Apr	May	June	July	Aug	Sept	Oct	Nov	Dec
Temp. (°F)	79	81	83	85	84	83	83	83	82	81	80	78
Temp. (°C)	26	27	23	29	29	28	28	28	28	27	27	26
Rainfall (in.)	0.3	0.4	1.4	3.1	5.7	5.8	6	6.1	8.9	9.9	5.5	1.7

Note that these numbers are daily averages, so expect temperatures to climb significantly

CAMBODIA CALENDAR OF EVENTS

For an exhaustive list of events beyond those listed here, check http://events.frommers.com, where you'll find a searchable, up-to-the-minute roster of what's happening in cities all over the world.

JANUARY

International New Year's Day. Your standard countdown and party, sans Dick Clark. January 1.

Liberation Day. This holiday commemorates the fall of the Khmer Rouge in 1979 and honors those lost during the regime's rule and subsequent wars. January 7.

Chinese New Year. Chinese New Year is not an official holiday in Cambodia but is widely celebrated anyway, primarily by those of Chinese descent and ethnic Vietnamese. February 14, 2010; February 3, 2011.

FEBRUARY

Meak Bochea Day *(Magha Puja Day)*. Takes place on the full moon to commemorate the speech given by the Lord Buddha to 1,250 enlightened monks who had gathered with no organization or prior warning. In the evening, people visit the temple to make offerings. February 21, 2010; February 19, 2011.

MARCH

International Women's Day. This day is significant in Cambodia, and raises awareness concerning gender issues. There are often parades with floats in major towns. March 8.

APRIL

Khmer New Year *(Chaul Chhnam Thmey)*. Along with *Ph'chum Benh* and the Water Festival, Khmer New Year is one of the most important and popular holidays of the year, celebrated for 3 days in mid-April. The festival is all about water in daily life, and during this festival you will experience the reality of water over and over again (though unlike in neighboring countries, the Cambodian authorities have controlled it from becoming too out of hand). April 14 to April 16, 2010; April 13 to April 15, 2011.

MAY

International Labor Day. This is a relatively quiet holiday, where labor unions will sometimes organize events. May 1.

Birthday of the King. Born in 1953, this day celebrates the birthday of the present king who has been on the throne since 2004 when his father, King Sihanouk, abdicated in his favor. May 13 to May 15.

Royal Plowing Ceremony *(Bonn Chroat Preah Nongkoal)*. This marks the start of the rainy season and the planting season. In a ceremony led by the king, elaborately decorated sacred cows plow a symbolic furrow and are then led to trays containing rice, corn, beans, and other foods. These ceremonies are held next to the Royal Palace. May 23, 2010; 2011 dates to be confirmed by astrologers.

Visaka Bochea Day. This festival celebrates the birth, enlightenment, and death of the Lord Buddha. It is held on the 15th day of the sixth lunar month. Candlelit processions take place in the evening. Late May.

JUNE

Birthday of the Former Queen. Celebrates the birthday of the Queen Mother, Norodom Monineath Sihanouk, wife of the former king who abdicated in 2004. June 18.

SEPTEMBER

Constitution Day. In 1993 the new constitution was adopted on this day. September 24.

Bonn Pchum Ben. During this period, Khmer people make offerings to the monks in order to gain merit. It is a time to honor the spirits of ancestors. People travel to pagodas to make offerings of food, incense, and money to help ease the burden of the spirits. Late September to early October.

OCTOBER

Coronation Day. Anniversary of the coronation of King Norodom Sihamoni. The palace is lit up beautifully at night. October 29.

Birthday of the King Father, Holiday for His Majesty King Father Norodom Sihanouk. October 31.

NOVEMBER

November Water Festival. This celebrates the reversing of the current in the Tonle Sap River and marks the beginning of the fishing season. Dramatic longboat races are held in Phnom Penh with teams coming from all around the country. The city fills up with droves of visitors from the provinces. Dates are subject to change. November 19 to November 21, 2010.

Independence Day. Marking independence from France, on this day the king makes a visit to the Independence Monument on Norodom Boulevard. November 9.

DECEMBER

Human Rights Day. In a country where human rights abuse has been an issue, this day observes the Universal Declaration of Human Rights. Cultural events are held at the National Stadium in Phnom Penh. December 10.

2 ENTRY REQUIREMENTS

PASSPORTS

A passport valid for at least 6 months is necessary for entry to Cambodia.

VISAS

All non-Cambodian citizens (except citizens of Laos, Malaysia, Philippines, Singapore, and Vietnam) require a visa. Visas can be obtained at any Cambodian embassy or consulate overseas. Visas are also available on arrival by either land or air. Two photos, a valid passport, and $20 are required for a month-long single-entry tourist visa. This can be extended within the country, and is most easily done through travel agents. Business visas are also available. They cost $25, and can be extended for up to a year, with multiple entry.

The simplest way to apply for a visa is online, using the e-visa scheme launched by the Cambodian Ministry of Foreign Affairs and International Cooperation in 2006. Instead of applying through a Cambodian embassy, you simply complete the online application form and pay with your credit card. After receiving your visa through e-mail, print it out and bring it with you for your arrival. To apply for an e-visa, applicants need to have a passport valid for at least 6 months, a recent passport-size photo (JPEG/PNG format), and a valid credit card (Visa/MasterCard). The visa costs $20 and there is a $5 processing fee. It is important to note this visa is only good for arrival at Siem Reap and Phnom Penh international airports and by land from Thailand at Poipet/Aranyaprathet and Koh Kong/Had Lek, and Vietnam at Bavet/Svay Rieng. It is not valid for any other border crossings. To apply for an e-visa, go to www.mfaic.gov.kh.

If traveling overland, be aware that some border posts are run very much as income-producing concerns by those staffing them. There are often superfluous

> **Warning!** **Fake Visas at Poipet**
>
> On the Thai side of the Poipet border you will be harassed by a legion of touts offering to make your Cambodian visa for you. They will charge you more than if you get your visa at the allotted office before Cambodian immigration. In recent months that harassment has turned to veiled menace. Whoever these people are (and they are Cambodians), there is obviously money in what they are doing since they could not operate without the tacit permission of the Thai border police and the Cambodian immigration officials. When I approached the border, they had actually set up an official-looking checkpoint and flagged down my motorcycle as if they were police. All this is a scam. It is perfectly normal and legal to get your visa on arrival at Cambodian immigration once you have exited Thailand. Anyone who tells you otherwise is lying. Many tourists I saw were visibly upset at the intimidation even before they had set a foot on Cambodian soil. Ignore the touts, however insistent they may be.

touts pushing to help you complete the process for a fee. You don't need them. The process is simple. At some borders with Thailand, Cambodian immigration will insist you pay in Thai baht because they can make money on the differential on the exchange rate. There is not much you can do about this if you want to get into the country.

Although Cambodia issues visas on arrival at most if not all entry points, the same cannot be said if you are traveling the other way to a neighboring country. Vietnam requires that you have a visa before you travel whether you enter by land or by air, and at the time of writing a visa on arrival is not available when crossing from Cambodia to Laos by land. Thailand allows most nationalities to stay as tourists in the country for 30 days on arrival. At press time this was still true if you arrive by air. In 2008, they reduced the period to 15 days only if you arrive by land. Check with the Thai Embassy or a reputable travel agent if you are traveling on to Thailand

from Cambodia and you want to stay in Thailand longer than the allotted time. Requirements are changeable.

CUSTOMS

Visitors who are 18 years or older are allowed to bring into Cambodia 200 cigarettes or the equivalent amount of tobacco, and one opened bottle of liquor and perfume for personal use. Currency in possession must be declared on arrival. Cambodian Customs on the whole are not too fierce.

MEDICAL REQUIREMENTS

There are no vaccination requirements on entering Cambodia, but for your own well-being it is wise to get certain vaccinations including hepatitis A, hepatitis B, typhoid, Japanese encephalitis, cholera, rabies, and tetanus. It is also advisable to update your childhood vaccination series for polio, measles, mumps, rubella, and so on, if you are likely to be around children.

3 GETTING THERE & GETTING AROUND

GETTING TO CAMBODIA
By Plane

There are two international airports: Phnom Penh International Airport (PNH) and Siem Reap (REP). Both are served by flights from all neighboring Asian destinations although the airlines flying the route change often. When coming from Europe, Australia, or America it is usually best to book a flight to Bangkok or Singapore and make your travel arrangements for the short distance to Cambodia from there. International carriers flying into Phnom Penh include: Air Asia (www.airasia.com), Asiana (www.flyasiana.com), Bangkok Airways (www.bangkokair.com), China Airlines (www.china-airlines.com), China Southern (www.flychinasouthern.com), Jetstar (www.jetstar.com), Korean Air (www.koreanair.com), Lao Airlines (www.laoairlines.com), Silk Air (www.silkair.com), Thai Airways (www.thaiair.com), Malaysia Airlines (www.malaysiaairlines.com), and Vietnam Airlines (www.vietnamairlines.com).

It's worth noting that if flying directly to Siem Reap to visit Angkor Wat, Bangkok Airways has a monopoly on all direct flights between Bangkok and Siem Reap. If you're on a budget, it is cheaper to fly to Phnom Penh and to then take the bus or boat to Siem Reap, or travel overland from Bangkok via Poipet/Aranyaprathet.

Important: When leaving Cambodia by air, there is a $25 departure tax.

Getting into Town from the Airport

Taxis make the 30-minute journey into Phnom Penh from the airport for a flat rate of $9. They are monitored and ticketed on entry and exit to the airport and you pay at a desk in the arrivals area. Tuk-tuks (motorcycles with a trailer attached) cost $7 for the same trip and can be booked at the same desk. Motorcycle taxis are not allowed to pick up passengers within the airport complex.

BY LAND

It seems that every year another border crossing from a neighboring country is opened up and another road is built or improved. Now with the road from Koh Kong completed and the border crossing with Vietnam open at Ha Tien (Xa Xia in Vietnam to Prek Chak in Cambodia), it is possible to travel the coast road from Trat and Koh Chang in Thailand all the way to Vietnam. Although Cambodian visas are officially available at the border, some travelers have reported problems and it is safer to have a Cambodian visa in advance. Here are some of the major border crossings.

From Laos

From Voeung Kam in Laos to Dom Kralor in Cambodia There are actually two border crossing points, relatively close to one another. The first crossing is at Koh Chheuteal Thom on the Mekong River. The second is the road crossing at Dom Kralor to Ban Nakasang. If traveling from Laos to Cambodia, you are strongly advised to book a through tour with a travel agent in Pakse since the border crossings here are complicated and subject to change.

From Thailand

From Aranyaprathet in Thailand to Poipet in Cambodia This was the first crossing to open in the late 1990s and these days it still remains the principal crossing point from Thailand. Open 8am to 8pm, this is the main route to get to Siem Reap and Angkor from Bangkok as well as to Battambang and Phnom Penh.

From Had Lek in Thailand to Koh Kong in Cambodia via Cham Yeam Checkpoint Now that the brand-new road from the Cambodia/Thai coastal border to both Sihanoukville and Phnom

Penh is completed, this border crossing is set to become more and more important. An hour away from Trat and only a couple of hours from Koh Chang, this is the gateway to all things south including the Cardamoms themselves, Sihanoukville, Kampot, Kep, and indeed a through route to Vietnam and the Mekong Delta. The border is open between 7am and 8pm.

From Vietnam

From Bavet Checkpoint in Moc Bai, Vietnam, to Bavet in Cambodia This is the main route from Phnom Penh to Ho Chi Minh City (Saigon) on Rte. 1. There is a river crossing at Neak Loeung and when the road is busy there can be a long line for the ferry.

From Kaam Samnor, Cambodia, to Ving Xuong in Vietnam This is the crossing on the Mekong River to the delightful riverine town of Chau Doc in Vietnam. A slow river trip is one of the most interesting and beautiful ways to travel from Phnom Penh to Vietnam. Chau Doc is the gateway to Vietnam's Mekong Delta.

From Xa Xia in Vietnam to Prek Chak in Cambodia This crossing takes you from the Ha Tien in Vietnam's Mekong Delta directly to Kep, Kampot, and on to Sihanoukville in Cambodia. It completes the coastal route from Thailand to Vietnam.

Le Tanh in Gia Lai Province in Vietnam to O'Yadaw in Ratanakiri, Cambodia This is a newly opened international border crossing.

BY BUS
From Laos

Traveling overland to Cambodia from Laos involves several legs pieced together. It can be done one of two ways. First, take a boat from Voeung Kam in Laos to Stung Treng in Cambodia, crossing at Koh Chheuteal Thom. The boat should cost $10. You can also take a shared minibus to the crossing at Dom Kralor, which is becoming the easiest and most popular way to do it. Stung Treng is then served by buses on Sorya Transport, and a ticket to Phnom Penh costs 42,000 riel.

Although a Cambodian visa on arrival exists in principle, there have been some reports that it is not as straightforward as at other entry points. To be on the safe side you should get your Cambodian visa beforehand. There are no Lao visas on arrival if traveling the other way.

From Thailand

Getting from Bangkok to either Siem Reap or Phnom Penh by bus is very easy and straightforward. Take a standard bus from Morchit Northern Bus Terminal in Bangkok (near either Morchit BTS Skytrain or Chatuchak MRT subway stations). Buy a ticket to Aranyaprathet. The trip takes about 5 hours. Once in Aranyaprathet, take a tuk-tuk for between 50 baht and 100 baht to the border. You can also take a minibus direct from the Khao San Road area, which is faster but very uncomfortable. Once you have completed immigration formalities and are in Poipet on the Cambodian side of the border you have the option of taking a regular bus, a shared or private taxi, or a seat in a crowded pickup truck to your destination in Cambodia. There is a free shuttle bus from the border to the place where the buses and taxis are parked.

Given that the journey is a long one and the lines at immigration can be long and dusty, it is advisable to break the journey with a night in Aranyaprathet. There are a number of serviceable hotels in town. The **Aran Garden 2 Hotel** (200 baht without fan, 250 baht with fan and TV, 370 baht with A/C and TV) is right in the center of town. Tuk-tuk drivers will know it. Expect to pay about 50 baht to get there from the station. Reception staff will be able to hail you a tuk-tuk to take you to the border in the morning. There are also a number of resorts and hotels between town and the border. Expect to pay approximately 500 Thai baht. You could spend the night in Poipet, but this is not recommended because it is utterly charmless. It takes between 2 and 3 hours to get to Siem Reap, 4 hours to Battambang, and 9 hours to Phnom Penh.

From Vietnam

Buses connect with neighboring Vietnam at the Moc Bai border area at the town of Svay Rieng on the Cambodian side. From Saigon in Vietnam, contact **Saigontourist** (✆ **08/829-8914**) or **Sinh Café** (✆ **08/ 369-420**) for direct connection to Cambodia—Sinh Café and Capitol Tour (also called Capitol Guesthouse) are in cahoots and one carrier takes up your transport at the border. Going in either direction (to or from Cambodia), you'll cross the border around noon and the $6 bus drops you at your destination sometime after 3pm. The overland border procedure into Cambodia is quick and easy. You just have to fill out some forms and pay the 2,000 VND tax (payable in any currency). The Capitol/ Sinh office is just across the border. Going from Cambodia to Vietnam, ask at any travel agent, hotel, or the Capitol Guesthouse (see above) and be sure that you have a prearranged visa for Vietnam. Visa is available on arrival at any land crossings in Cambodia.

BY TRAIN

There are no international train routes into Cambodia.

BY BOAT

There is a border crossing to Laos on the Mekong, 90 minutes north of Stung Treng at Veun Kham/Dom Kralor. The rules there change often at very short notice and the border officials there a have a reputation for being fairly unscrupulous when it comes to soliciting unofficial contributions. Although a Cambodian visa is officially available on arrival, it is advisable to obtain one beforehand to ensure you won't encounter difficulties, given the frequent changes in the rules.

There are no ferry services from Thailand to Cambodia. Daily boat connections run between Chau Doc in Vietnam and the town of Neak Loeung, some 2 hours east of Phnom Penh in Cambodia. You can arrange the trip through any budget travel agent in Vietnam, and many include the boat connection to Phnom Penh as part of a multiday Mekong Delta trip. *Note:* Budget tour operators Sinh Café (✆ **08/369-420** in Ho Chi Minh City) and Capitol Tour (No. 14 Rd. 182, Phnom Penh; ✆ **023/217-627**) are now working together, so when you cross borders, the other company adopts you. It's an all-day journey in a diesel-belching tour boat, but views of life on the wide, lazy Mekong are worth it. *Note:* A visa is available on arrival when entering Cambodia, but you have to have a prearranged visa for entry to Vietnam. If you want to cross from Chau Doc to Phnom Penh in luxury, contact the Victoria Chau Doc Hotel (✆ **076/865-010**) for a pricey private transfer on a speedy runabout boat.

GETTING AROUND
By Plane

The Thai carrier, Bangkok Airways (www. bangkokair.com), and its subsidiary, Siem Reap Airways (www.siemreapairways. com), are the only domestic operators. The company has a monopoly on all flights to Siem Reap from Bangkok and internally and charges accordingly. The only domestic route now running is between Phnom Penh and Siem Reap.

By Car or Motorcycle

It is possible to hire a car with a driver. The best way to do this is through your hotel or a travel agent. It will cost between $20 and $30 a day.

Another way to get around is by motorcycle, although you should be an experienced motorcyclist if you choose to do this and it's important to drive slowly. Bikes generally range from step-throughs to 250cc dirt bikes. The most established

Pointing the Way with a Rhinoceros

At major junctions and roundabouts in Cambodia, you will often see giant figures of animals, or familiar gods. They are there for a practical reason. Many Cambodians are illiterate and can't read road signs, so these provide easy markers. So for instance when a Cambodian is giving directions he might say "Drive straight for a mile until you reach the white horse, then turn right and continue past the elephant god until you get to the rhinoceros and then turn left."

place in town to rent is Lucky! Lucky! (413 Monivong Blvd.). The quality of the bikes varies so it is important to check them first, and don't be afraid to insist on a different bike if you have been given a bad one.

If you are driving yourself, whether on two wheels or four, be aware that the traffic is very unpredictable and often lethal. The accident rate increased by 35% from August 2008 to August 2009, according to government figures. Driving is chaotic and fast with all the dangers that brings.

By Motorcycle Taxi

Motorcycle taxis (or *motodups* as they are termed in Khmer) are everywhere in Cambodia and often the quickest way to get around. Just hail one from the sidewalk. Most restaurants and hotels will also have a stand of affiliated drivers. If you find one you like, write down his phone number and use him again. Most trips around town will cost less than a dollar during the day. At night, you normally double the fee. Most people don't wear a helmet, but they should, given the dubious quality of both the motorcycles and the driving.

By Cyclo

A gentler but slower way to see the sites, the cyclo, a tricycle with a front carriage propelled by a person cycling behind it, operates under the same rules and pretty much the same rates as the motorcycle taxis. Cyclos take a lot of the stress out of

getting from point A to point B. They are also good in the rain since the cyclo driver will bring out plastic sheeting to shelter you from the elements.

By Tuk-Tuk & Samlor

The tuk-tuk and samlor are relatively new arrivals in Cambodia. They are motorcycles with a trailer attached using a fairly ingenious adaptor. As long as you have more than two people, the tuk-tuk is actually the cheapest mode of transport. When in Siem Reap, you can hire a tuk-tuk for the day to tour the temples. The cost is between $5 and $10 for the day.

By Train

There was in the past a train that made the journey from Phnom Penh to Battambang on alternate days, although at the time of writing it has been suspended. Passenger services running to Sihanoukville and Kampot have also been axed. Though there is talk of reviving the creaky Cambodian rail, nothing has yet been done.

By Bus

Long-distance buses now go to all major towns in Cambodia. They tend to operate from the central market area in most towns. In Phnom Penh, different companies leave from different parts of town, although across from **Psar Thmei (Central Market)** is where you will find the departure points for both **Sorya** and **GST Express.** They are reasonably priced but can be cold due to excessive air-conditioning. **Mekong Express** (leaving from Sisowath Quay on the corner of St. 102) buses are a bit more expensive, but offer bigger seats and are worth the extra dollar or two to use them. Travel remains cheap, with journeys from Phnom Penh to Siem Reap or Sihanoukville costing under $5. Unlike elsewhere in Southeast Asia, there are few night buses and most departures leave in the early hours of the morning, with the last ones leaving midafternoon. The easiest way to buy tickets is through your hotel or guesthouse, or a travel agent.

Main routes run from Phnom Penh to Siem Reap, Sihanoukville, Kampot (stopping in Kep), Koh Kong, Battambang, Kratie, Kompong Cham, Stung Treng, Banlung, Sisophon, and Poipet. Buses also run from Siem Reap to Battambang, and Sihanoukville to Kampot.

By Boat

With the improvement in roads, river travel is diminishing in importance. Ferries do still ply many of the major waterways, however, including from Phnom Penh to Siem Reap and Siem Reap to Battambang. Boats are not as fast as buses and pickups, and charge more money and often appear overloaded. Yet they allow visitors a unique way to experience the country including the Tonle Sap, which is very much at the heart of the Khmer soul.

The boat from Phnom Penh to Siem Reap leaves the pier on Sisowath Quay (near St. 104 opposite the River View Guest House) at 7am. It costs $30 to $35 and takes between 4 and 6 hours. The boat from Siem Reap to Battambang is very much a slow, expensive, and awkward option, particularly at the height of the dry season from April to May when the waters are low and one often has to transfer to lighter and smaller vessels in the middle of the journey. What it does afford is a fascinating glimpse of the everyday life of the people along the banks of the Tonle Sap and the Sangker River. The ferry leaves Siem Reap at 7:30am, costs $16, and takes between 8 and 10 hours.

The open-air boat journey from Koh Kong to Sihanoukville is presently suspended. Going from Phnom Penh to Chau Doc in Vietnam is a great way to make it to the Mekong Delta. The boat leaves at 9am, costs $15, and takes 4 to 5 hours. See the information on getting to Vietnam by boat on p. 35.

4 MONEY & COSTS

Frommer's lists exact prices in U.S. dollars or local currency, both of which are widely used. The currency conversions quoted above were correct at press time. However, rates fluctuate, so before departing consult a currency exchange website such as **www. oanda.com/convert/classic** to check up-to-the-minute rates.

When visiting Cambodia you can spend enormous amounts. Since 2007, prices have started to rise sharply and most things such as food, hotel rooms, and transport have risen by about 40%. On the whole, however, most things remain moderately priced. Very little tourism money reaches ordinary Cambodians. Sadly, poverty is still very much a daily reality in Cambodia for the majority of people.

You can get a hotel room for as little as $3 a night in Siem Reap or Sihanoukville (though we certainly won't vouch for the quality). On the other hand, you can drop $1,000 on the whole luxury package. Cambodia has a wealth of options in the midrange. For between $15 and $80, you can find some excellent accommodations even in expensive Phnom Penh. Battambang is particularly blessed with wonderful

Riel	US$	Can$	UK£	Euro(€)	Aus$	NZ$
5,000	$1.20	C$1.25	£.75	€.80	A$1.30	NZ$1.65

hotels at good prices. In Siem Reap, pricing is heavily seasonal. High-season prices can be as much as 30% to 40% higher than low season. In all these places, a good local meal will set you back about $2. A main course in a tourist-orientated restaurant will cost between $4.50 and $7 at a moderately priced place. A small can of beer averages at about $1.50 and bottled water is more expensive than in London or Paris.

There is no shortage of banks in all provincial towns of any size, including Phnom Penh, Siem Reap, Sihanoukville, Battambang, and Kampot. They offer the usual banking services: cash advances on credit cards (most accept MasterCard and Visa), international currency exchange, telegraphic transfers, and cashing traveler's checks. ANZ Royal Banks, Canadia, and SBC Banks offer ATMs with international access. Canadia Bank levies the lowest transaction charges. Most banks are open from around 8am to 3 or 4pm from Monday to Friday. Some are also open on Saturday mornings until 11:30am. ATMs are available 24 hours and are popping up everywhere. See the "Fast Facts" section in each chapter for bank locations.

The currency in Cambodia is the riel, though for anything over the smallest of amounts the U.S. dollar reigns supreme. Riel is what you use for small change. In the towns of the west, the Thai baht is also used. There are no coins in Cambodia, only notes. Cambodian riel notes come in 50, 100, 500, 1,000, 2,000, 5,000, 10,000, 50,000, and 100,000 denominations, but the red 500 riel note and the blue 1,000 riel note are the most useful and common. Wads of 100 riel notes mount up and are best distributed to beggars in handfuls. Be aware that the slightest tear on a dollar note of any denomination will render it useless. Check the condition of your change.

The use of credit cards is increasing in tourist areas, though Cambodia remains very much a cash economy. Visa and MasterCard are accepted at most upscale hotels, shops, and restaurants. Some midrange places and a growing number of other businesses are following suit. Most businesses charge a 2% to 4% fee to accept credit cards.

5 HEALTH

STAYING HEALTHY

Staying healthy is largely about keeping your eyes open and practicing good hygiene. Some rules of thumb: Drink only bottled water, and also use bottled water to clean your teeth. Wash your hands before eating. If soap and water are not available, use an alcohol-based hand gel (with at least 60% alcohol). Always try and use restaurants that look clean, and make sure that all food is properly cooked. Avoid dairy products, unless you know they have been pasteurized. Avoid eating street food if you can. Fruit and vegetables should be washed or peeled. Put ice in your drinks only if it's cubed or tubed (crushed ice may have been chipped off a big block that has been kept in unsanitary conditions).

While no vaccines are presently required, you may choose to take extra precautions. Many of the other big health threats are borne on the wings of the whining, pesky, hovering mosquito. Protecting yourself

> **(Tips) Come Armed with Singles**
>
> We recommend coming to Cambodia with a large stack of dollar bills. You'll blow through them quickly while zipping around towns on tuk-tuks and motos, and the lower cost of food and drink means they'll come in handy. Larger bills dispensed by ATMs can be harder to break.

against mosquito bites is crucial to preventing a variety of diseases, including malaria. This means using an effective repellent (with DEET, or one of the newer eucalyptus-based products) day and night, and sleeping under a net or in a screened or sealed room. Wear long trousers and a long-sleeved shirt if you are in a risky area.

Another problem in Cambodia can be the heat and the sun. Use a good sunscreen, cover your skin, try to stay out of the sun during the hottest part of the day, and keep up your fluid intake. If you can't avoid being in the sun, make sure you wear a hat. Keep properly hydrated with water (beer, soda, or tea does not do the job). It's a good idea to carry rehydration salts with you.

There are big problems with hepatitis and HIV in Cambodia (an estimated 40% of commercial sex workers are HIV-positive). If you are determined to put yourself in harm's way, then be sure to practice safe sex.

AILMENTS IN CAMBODIA

Like many poor tropical countries, Cambodia is a host to a variety of ailments that with proper attention to hygiene and preventative measures the traveler will avoid getting.

WORMS & OTHER INTESTINAL PARASITES These can be a problem due to poor hygiene. Be careful where you eat and what you eat (especially if it is street food). Watch out for any meat that looks uncooked.

GIARDIA, DYSENTERY, & SALMONELLA These are contracted as a result of infected food and poor hygiene. **Giardia** is a parasite that, if you are infected, causes some fairly unsociable symptoms of flatulence with the odor of rotten eggs. It is treated through a course of prescription drugs, notably metronidazole (brand name Flagyl).

DYSENTERY Dysentery is an unpleasant condition involving stomach cramps, diarrhea (with blood and mucus in the stool), and fever. In **amoebic dysentery,** the parasites that cause it are dealt with through a course of metronidazole. **Bacillary dysentery** can be treated with antibiotics if very severe, but normally one gets through it in 1 to 2 weeks, during which remaining well hydrated is vital. **Salmonella** is also bacterial and symptoms begin with nausea and vomiting and progress to abdominal pains and diarrhea. Additional symptoms include fever, chills, and muscle pains, and it can last anywhere from several days to 2 weeks. There is no treatment, and you just have to get through it by making sure you stay hydrated.

HEPATITIS A Hepatitus A is a viral infection of the liver, also contracted from bad food or water. The best way to avoid it is (if over 2 years old) to make sure you are vaccinated, stick to bottled water, and keep a good eye on what you eat. Symptoms include fatigue, fever, abdominal pain, nausea, diarrhea, loss of appetite, depression, jaundice, weight loss, and itching. Inoculation takes the form of a single shot and a booster after 6 months.

HEPATITIS B Hepatitus B is contracted through contamination by infected blood. As with HIV, it is mostly contracted through sexual contact, blood transfusion, and contaminated needles. Other more everyday objects such as a razor or a toothbrush can also be a conduit. Vaccination, which takes the form of three shots over a 6-month period, is highly recommended.

TYPHOID Typhoid is bacterial and transmitted through contaminated food. Typhoid can be life-threatening, particularly to children and the elderly. Early detection and a course of antibiotics will usually prevent complications. Symptoms include sustained fever, sweating, gastroenteritis, nonbloody diarrhea, and, in some cases, a rash of flat rose-colored spots. Antibiotics are commonly used to treat the disease. Vaccinations are available but are only 50%-to-80% effective. Nevertheless, the vaccine is recommended.

JAPANESE ENCEPHALITIS This is a mosquito-borne disease that is endemic to Southeast Asia. Symptoms include headache, fever, nausea, upset stomach, and malaise. Vaccination is recommended, particularly if traveling in rural parts of the country.

CHOLERA Cholera is a food- and waterborne disease. The main symptoms of infection are diarrhea and intense dehydration. Occasionally there are outbreaks in some parts of the country and vaccination is recommended.

RABIES Rabies is a disease transmitted through bodily fluids, mainly by a bite or contact with the saliva of an infected animal. In Cambodia, there is no shortage of ill-disciplined dogs, monkeys, and bats, all of which may transmit the disease. The symptoms of rabies are malaise, headache, and fever, while in later stages it includes acute pain, violent movements, uncontrolled excitement, depression, and the inability to swallow water or hydrophobia. If you get any kind of puncture wound from a potentially infected animal, it is important to seek treatment immediately. This consists of a series of vaccinations over a 1-month period. If you are planning to spend a lot of time in high-risk areas, you might want to consider preexposure vaccinations. These make postexposure treatment far simpler, reducing the number of shots required as well as preventing the need for rabies-immune globulin (which may not be available and would therefore require evacuation to Thailand). A vigilant eye should be kept on children, given that most of them have an abiding fascination with all creatures four-legged.

MALARIA This is a biggie in Southeast Asia and still a serious threat. There are four strains of malaria and all are life threatening, cerebral malaria being the most serious. Malaria is caused by a one-cell parasite transmitted by the Anopheles mosquito. The parasite travels into the liver, lies dormant, and grows. Then symptoms occur when it enters the bloodstream. Symptoms include high fever, headaches, nausea, vomiting, dizziness, and confusion. Initial symptoms may appear the same as for a number of other conditions, including flu. If experiencing any of these symptoms, seek medical help immediately.

It may be advisable to take a prophylactic such as mefloquine (Lariam), the antibiotic doxycycline, or atovaquone/proguanil (Malarone). The problem is that all these drugs have quite severe side effects. Larium can cause severe and distressing mood swings. Malarone can cause diarrhea, insomnia, dizziness, headaches, loss of appetite, nausea, stomach pain, vomiting, and weakness. Doxycycline may cause the skin to have an intense sensitivity to sunlight, nausea, vomiting, upset stomach, and loss of appetite. The best thing you can do is to simply not get bitten. This means covering all exposed areas of skin, especially at dawn and dusk when the malarial mosquitoes are at their most active. Use a good mosquito repellent with DEET (or one of the newer eucalyptus-based products) in areas where malaria is a problem. Sleep under a mosquito net. If you have air-conditioning make sure your room is properly sealed.

Malaria is not a problem in major towns and cities, and is restricted to remote jungle areas. Unless you are traveling to these areas you are unlikely to have a problem. There is a very low malaria risk in the more remote quarters of the Angkor Wat complex, but not in Siem Reap town. Though you are not allowed to be around the temples at night (when malaria is a threat), you should be protected with repellent during your visit. As with land mines, malaria is mostly a problem in areas of former conflict such as Samlot or Phnom Malai. Most places that tourists visit are safe.

TETANUS Also known as lockjaw, tetanus is a disease contracted through contamination of wounds. It manifests itself through muscle spasms. You should be vaccinated against this and make sure your booster is up to date.

DENGUE FEVER Like malaria, dengue fever is a mosquito-borne disease. It is found in some parts of Laos, particularly at certain times of year. No vaccination or prophylactic is available. Again the answer is simply to avoid getting bitten.

HIV/AIDS AIDS is a very serious problem in Cambodia, especially among commercial sex workers. Some educated estimates put the percentage of sex workers infected as high as 40%. Since the early '90s, it has reached epidemic proportions. Transmittal occurs through infected blood, which primarily occurs from sexual contact, blood transfusions, or shared syringes. Avoid blood products unless absolutely necessary and practice sexual abstinence at best and safe sex as a next best.

WHAT TO DO IF YOU GET SICK AWAY FROM HOME

Medical care in Phnom Penh, Siem Reap, and Sihanoukville is rudimentary, to say the least. Most hospitals are not very good. There are private hospitals in Phnom Penh and Siem Reap, and if you are not in a major town you should head there. In both Phnom Penh and Siem Reap, there are a number of GPs and small clinics with a good reputation. They are very familiar with all the ailments common to Cambodia. You will have to pay upfront, but they will provide receipts for your medical insurance. Before your trip, make sure that you have adequate medical insurance that includes evacuation. Medical care in Cambodia is quite medieval and often overstretched, and you really don't want to be on the receiving end of it for very long. If something seriously untoward happens to you, then you will need to get to a hospital in Thailand. Medical care in Thailand is excellent and cheaper than the U.S. or Europe. Even so, for anything serious, bills can mount up to thousands of dollars quite quickly and you will need to be able to cover that. See the "Fast Facts" sections in each chapter for specific hospital information.

6 SAFETY

Cambodia has a reputation for violence and lawlessness. Some of that reputation is well deserved, while some of it is simply history. Only a decade ago, guns were everywhere, city streets were dark at night, and robberies were commonplace. Cambodia has moved on vastly since then, but robberies still happen. Practice common sense and take the same precautions you would anywhere else.

The Khmer Rouge may be finished, but the land mines left over from the decades of conflict are still there. The good news is

A Dark Side of Cambodia

Sex tourism is a serious issue in Cambodia. Prostitution is endemic in every town and village, with all the attendant issues of trafficking, bonded labor, violence, coercion, and child abuse. In Phnom Penh and Sihanoukville, there are also districts modeled on the Thai sex tourism resort of Pattaya, with hostess bars and gaggles of rural Khmer women trying to make a buck. AIDS is prevalent here among sex workers, though the safe sex message has finally begun to sink in as the sheer prevalence of the virus caused many to see friends or family members die.

What is even more tragic is the reputation that Cambodia gained for pedophile tourism and the stark reality it represents. Children were and are bought and sold to both indigenous and foreign pedophiles. Sihanoukville gained a real reputation for this. It is alleged that organized pedophile rings paid off the police for their full cooperation.

These days, however, they often get jailed when caught and foreign governments are proactive in prosecuting those convicted of child molestation, even when they return home. The reality is found on billboards in Phnom Penh and Siem Reap: "Abuse a child in this country. Go to jail in your own." There are quite a number of foreign pedophiles serving sentences in Cambodia for the abuse of children. Cambodian jails are very unpleasant places indeed. The battle, however, is not yet won.

If you have founded suspicions of child abuse, call the confidential Childsafe Hotline on ℂ **011/312-112** (www.childsafe-cambodia.org). There is also a national police unit hot line at ℂ **023/997-919**. Childsafe's advice is, "Whenever possible, we ask the caller to stay near the child until our team arrives to take appropriate action to protect the child." Do not contact the local police and do not confront the possible offender, however strong your feelings.

that unless you choose to go to more remote regions, particularly near the border with Thailand, then you will not be in mined areas (though Kompong Speu close to Phnom Penh remains a problem area). The area around Angkor Wat is cleared. If you do see the red "Danger. Mines!" sign, take it very seriously. Do not cross into an area fenced off by CMAC (Cambodian Mines Action Center), MAG (Mines Advisory Group), or the Halo Trust. The mines will take decades to clear, but the areas that are afflicted are now fairly well defined. As a general rule, when in the countryside stay on the path and don't wander into the fields or undergrowth.

Street robbery is still a problem in the cities of Cambodia, as it is elsewhere. Bag snatchings have been increasingly frequent. This is dangerous if you are pulled off the back of a motorcycle. If you are confronted by thieves in a potentially violent situation, do not attempt to resist. Simply do as they ask. The adage of the old days in Cambodia, "don't carry it unless you are prepared to lose it" still has some value at night. It is a bad idea to walk long distances by foot after dark. Don't leave valuables hanging from your shoulder where they can be easily seen or snatched. If you are in a tuk-tuk, keep your bag in the center of the vehicle. If you are riding on a motorcycle, keep your things wedged between you and the driver to avoid being pulled off the back of the bike if you are subject to a snatching. Stay on main roads at night if possible.

You might just get a taste of old-style Cambodian gun violence in certain nightclubs (particularly the Heart of Darkness in Phnom Penh; see p. 90). There have been a number of cases of well-connected young men going to nightclubs and starting trouble for recreation. If you smell trouble, back away or be conciliatory.

Last, be aware that the police are not your friends. They can be massively corrupt, so if you are in trouble contact your embassy first.

---

7 SPECIALIZED TRAVEL RESOURCES

GAY & LESBIAN TRAVELERS

Although Khmer society is very traditional and conservative and the subject of homosexuality has long been taboo, there is also a real measure of tolerance toward gay and lesbian people. Flaunting sexuality in general, gay or straight, will invite certain negative reactions, but rank homophobia is rare toward foreigners. In February 2004, then-King Sihanouk wrote on his website that he believed that God views homosexuals, as well as transvestites, as equal because "[God loves] wide range of tastes." The former king also supports gay marriage. That remains his personal view, but it is an indication of acceptable thinking. On the other hand Hun Sen, the longtime ruler and hard man of Cambodia, disowned his own adopted daughter in 2007 because she came out as a lesbian. Cambodia held its first gay pride event in 2003 and it now takes place annually. There is a low-key gay scene in Cambodia with some gay bars in Siem Reap and Phnom Penh.

The International Gay and Lesbian Travel Association (**IGLTA**; ℂ **954/630-1637**; www.iglta.org) is the travel trade association for gay- and lesbian-friendly tour operators. They have an online directory of relevant businesses. **Out Adventures** (ℂ **416/583-2680**; www.out-adventures.com) based in Ontario, Canada, offers tours of the whole region. Another operator offering gay-friendly tours is **Purple Dragon,** based in Thailand (ℂ **+66 2238-3227**; www.purpledrag.com).

SENIOR TRAVEL

Respect for elders is an integral part of Khmer culture and family values. Yet in Cambodia, senior travelers will not find the sort of discounts and deals that are found in the West. When booking your flights and accommodations it's worth mentioning if you are a senior since there may be discounts available.

The most important issues for senior travelers are the potential rigor of the heat in Cambodia and the paucity of adequate healthcare. Both these factors should be taken into account by senior travelers. It is also beginning to compete with Thailand as a retirement destination.

For general information on senior travel, **AARP** (ℂ **888/687-2277**; www.aarp.org), is an organization with over 40 million members that is dedicated to helping the over-50s improve their lives. Membership brings some discounts on international travel and they produce a magazine and a monthly newsletter.

Elder Treks (ℂ **800/741-7956**; www.eldertreks.com) offers tours to those over 50 to both Angkor Wat and the wider region.

The organization **Elder-hostel** (ℂ **800/454-5678**; www.elderhostel.org) arranges worldwide study programs, including their popular "Journey into the Heart of Asia" tour, which covers both Cambodia and Laos.

Overseas Adventure Travel (© 800/493-6824; www.oattravel.com), based in Boston, offers a tour called "Ancient Kingdoms: Thailand, Laos, Vietnam & Cambodia," as well as optional Cambodia add-ons to their other Thailand, China, and Vietnam tours.

FAMILY TRAVELERS

Cambodia is not a particularly child-friendly country. It can be a real experience overload for young kids fresh to this part of the world. What may be fascinating can also be frightening, and families will need to make sure that children are eased into this new environment very gently. They will be confused by the poverty, especially the obvious poverty of kids their own age, many of whom live on the street and lead a very hard life. Cambodia may induce your children to ask a lot of questions that may be hard to answer. You must think carefully about what you take them to see given the recent horror of Cambodia's past—a thing Cambodians cannot explain to their own children because they have no answers.

There are also the normal health concerns, of course, and a constant eye needs to be kept in terms of hygiene rules. Make sure children wear sunblock and remain properly hydrated.

Tricky as it might be for families, Angkor Wat alone is a good reason to take your children to Cambodia. It looks and feels like the set of a movie and indeed it has been used as the set for quite a number of them. They are ancient standing history, far more thrilling than Disneyland ever could be. Impressive as the temples are, touring them can be hot and tiring, so any schedule should incorporate plenty of rest time. Apart from Angkor, the place in Cambodia most suitable for family visits is Sihanoukville. All that white sand is likely to be very much appreciated by the youngest generation.

Your children will attract a lot of positive attention, especially if they are blonde. That is no bad thing, but sometimes they might be confused or overwhelmed by it. Phnom Penh particularly can be very busy and claustrophobic, and children will need to be shielded while they become accustomed to it.

Breast-feeding in public is very common in Cambodia, so there is no need to worry about breaking a taboo.

The main worry throughout Cambodia is keeping an eye on what strange things young children are putting in their mouths. Their natural curiosity can be dangerous in a country where dysentery, typhoid, and hepatitis are commonplace.

WOMEN TRAVELERS

There are no particular safety concerns for women that don't affect men as well. What trouble there might be is nondiscriminatory. What you will find is that you are asked a lot of questions about your marital status and your children, even if you don't have any. Cambodians generally have a fairly conventional view of marriage and children, and if your story diverges from that, they may well be curious. The curiosity is genuine and good-natured, and all explanations will be avidly absorbed. They too will be more than willing to answer your questions about family and children. It is, most certainly, a two-way street.

Dress conservatively, since Cambodia is a conservative country. You should also take a supply of your own tampons. Sanitary pads are the norm for Cambodian women.

TRAVELERS WITH DISABILITIES

Cambodia presents considerable challenges to travelers with disabilities, but they are not insurmountable. Some smaller guesthouses and hotels will not cater to travelers with disabilities, but the bigger and more established ones will. In any case, it is a good idea to check in advance. In Angkor Wat, some parts of the temples are inaccessible to wheelchair-bound visitors because of the irregular paving and simply the nature of the temples. Plenty of it is accessible, however. In the towns and cities, what sidewalks there are usually heavily pot-holed and irregular. Newer buildings such as the airport and top-end hotels will have ramps for wheelchair access, but that is about as far as it goes.

The fundamental key to a successful rip to Cambodia if you are disabled is a lot of planning in advance. Useful organizations include Mobility International USA (🕿 **541/343-1284**; www.miusa.org); Royal Association for Disability and Rehabilitation (🕿 **020-7250 3222;** radar.org. uk); and Society for Accessible Travel & Hospitality (SATH; 🕿 212/447-7284; www.sath.org).

STUDENT TRAVEL

Cambodia is very firmly on the backpacker's Asia circuit. They were coming to Cambodia years ago, when the war was still raging and better-heeled tourists stayed away. As a result there is a plethora of guesthouses, restaurants, bars, and travel agents catering specifically to this market. Now with so many open borders across what was the Bamboo Curtain, the enterprising budget traveler can wander at will all across Southeast Asia in pretty much any direction. Siem Reap and Phnom Penh both have a thriving backpacker scene, and Sihanoukville is fast catching up as it begins to rival the beaches of Thailand as a beach for chilling out. Kampot is the kind of relaxed hammock-swinging venue beloved of the budget traveler and Battambang is in the throes of being discovered. While traveling on a budget in Cambodia, you will inevitably run into many like-minded souls.

8 SUSTAINABLE TOURISM

Sustainable tourism means taking responsibility for your own actions and the impact they might have on the environment as you travel. It means paying attention to the environments you find yourself in and respecting the communities you visit. The **International Ecotourism Society (TIES)** defines eco-tourism as responsible travel to natural areas that conserves the environment and improves the well-being of local people. One thing you will notice in Cambodia is that respect for locales is low. Rubbish and plastic bags are simply thrown out onto the street. Heavily polluting vehicles often create a thick haze over towns and cities. You don't have to join in. Dispose of your own waste, don't use detergents or shampoo in lakes and rivers, and don't use electricity wastefully.

The environment in Cambodia has taken a real beating over the years. It is considered one of the most vulnerable countries in Asia by environmental activists and experts. High-canopy rainforest that once covered much of the country has been decimated by legal and illegal logging. To give you an idea of the scale of this, in 1970 Cambodia was 70% primary rainforest. By 2007, it was 3.1% primary rainforest. The soil erosion resulting from the mass deforestation is also a long-term problem. What hasn't been achieved by active plunder has been achieved by population growth in a country where subsistence-level living is the norm and resources are not used in a sustainable or renewable way.

A lot of the wildlife has also been poached or trafficked. Three-fourths of

Cambodia's wildlife areas have disappeared as a result of the ravages of logging. Endangered species in Cambodia include three species of gibbon, several species of wild dog and wildcat, leopard, tiger, Asian elephant, Sumatran rhinoceros, Thailand brow-antlered deer, kouprey, giant catfish, Indian python, Siamese crocodile, and estuarine crocodile. As of 2001, 23 of Cambodia's mammal species and 18 of its bird species were endangered. Cambodia has a problem with the illegal hunting of rare species, something to keep in mind when shopping in the markets.

There has been some progress in environmental tourism and attempting to preserve what is left. In Kratie, for instance, fisherman no longer use grenades to fish, thereby killing the endangered river dolphins. Yet there is also a lot to be worried about, including the rapid development of Cambodia's coastline and nearby islands, particularly around Sihanoukville. There is a great deal being built there, and the developers are almost entirely unregulated.

ECO-TOURISM IN CAMBODIA

With the construction of the brand-new road from the Thai border at Koh Kong-Hat Lek (near Trat), the Cardamom Mountains, one of the last areas of forest wilderness in mainland Southeast Asia, is set to become the scene for eco-tours, with Koh Kong as its base. This is something that will have to be managed very carefully, if it is to do more good than harm. Hoteliers have also begun to adapt to the ecofriendly trend, opening ecoretreats and a few carbon-neutral options. See "Best Ecofriendly Hotels & Nature Retreats" on p. 6 for a few of our top picks.

In Ratanakiri and Mondulkiri, there are more and more opportunities to enjoy one of Cambodia's most remote areas. The heavy jungle is home to 12 different *Khmer Loeu* ethnic minority groups. On the way, you can stop in Kratie and go dolphin spotting on the Mekong (p. 148). The rare freshwater Irrawaddy dolphins break the surface every now and then, but they remain powerfully shy.

Wild Asia (www.wildasia.net) is a social enterprise working to support the conservation of natural areas and the communities dependent upon their resources. They have a big presence in Cambodia and their website is an up-to-date source of on-the-ground environmental initiatives across the country. **Buffalo Trails** (www.buffalo trails-cambodia.com) operates tours on the Tonle Sap Lake and in the surrounding countryside. Based in Siem Reap, they specialize in sustainably run day trips where they aim to let tourists discover the beauty of the countryside and daily lives of local families. **Pepy Tours** (www.pepy tours.com) is actually part of a wider NGO and environmental education project (PEPY stands for "Protect the Earth, Protect Yourself"). They run a variety of

---

Tips **"Heritage Friendly" Establishments**

Much of Cambodia's ancient history has been lost, thanks to its violent past and the continued looting and trafficking of Khmer artifacts. To help prevent this, look for the "Heritage Friendly" logo. This logo was created by the Heritage Foundation (www.heritagewatch.org), an organization working to preserve Khmer antiquities and culture. The presence of the logo indicates that a business or organization has met certain standards that help protect Cambodian heritage. Travel to Cambodia is good, but responsible travel is even better.

General Resources for Green Travel

In addition to the resources for Cambodia listed above, the following websites provide valuable wide-ranging information on sustainable travel. For a list of even more sustainable resources, as well as tips and explanations on how to travel greener, visit www.frommers.com/planning.

- **Responsible Travel** (www.responsibletravel.com) is a great source of sustainable travel ideas; the site is run by a spokesperson for ethical tourism in the travel industry. **Sustainable Travel International** (www.sustainable travelinternational.org) promotes ethical tourism practices, and manages an extensive directory of sustainable properties and tour operators around the world.

- In the U.K., **Tourism Concern** (www.tourismconcern.org.uk) works to reduce social and environmental problems connected to tourism. The **Association of Independent Tour Operators (AITO;** www.aito.co.uk) is a group of specialist operators leading the field in making vacations sustainable.

- In Canada, **www.greenlivingonline.com** offers extensive content on how to travel sustainably, including a travel and transport section and profiles of the best green shops and services in Toronto, Vancouver, and Calgary.

- In Australia, the national body that sets guidelines and standards for eco-tourism is **Ecotourism Australia** (www.ecotourism.org.au). **The Green Directory** (www.thegreendirectory.com.au), **Green Pages** (www.thegreen pages.com.au), and **Eco Directory** (www.ecodirectory.com.au) offer sustainable travel tips and directories of green businesses.

- **Carbonfund** (www.carbonfund.org), **TerraPass** (www.terrapass.org), and **Carbon Neutral** (www.carbonneutral.org) provide info on "carbon offsetting," or offsetting the greenhouse gas emitted during flights.

- **Greenhotels** (www.greenhotels.com) recommends green-rated member hotels around the world that fulfill the company's stringent environmental requirements. **Environmentally Friendly Hotels** (www.environmentally friendlyhotels.com) offers more green accommodations ratings. The **Hotel Association of Canada** (www.hacgreenhotels.com) has a Green Key Eco-Rating Program, which audits the environmental performance of Canadian hotels, motels, and resorts.

- **Sustain Lane** (www.sustainlane.com) lists sustainable eating and drinking choices around the U.S.; also visit **www.eatwellguide.org** for tips on eating sustainably in the U.S. and Canada.

- For information on animal-friendly issues throughout the world, visit **Tread Lightly** (www.treadlightly.org). For information about the ethics of swimming with dolphins, visit the **Whale and Dolphin Conservation Society** (www.wdcs.org).

- **Volunteer International** (www.volunteerinternational.org) has a list of questions to help you determine the intentions and the nature of a volunteer program. For general info on volunteer travel, visit **www.volunteer abroad.org** and **www.idealist.org**.

adventure and cultural tours, which help fund their aid work. **Asian Adventures** (www.asia-adventures.com) is a Phnom Penh–based company offering a huge variety of tours all over the country under their guiding ethos of responsible tourism.

In Koh Kong, the **Oasis Resort** (© 016/ 331556; www.oasisresort.netkhmer.com) offers local excursions to mangrove forests, waterfalls, sites for dolphin-watching, and secluded beaches.

9 STAYING CONNECTED

CELLPHONES

Cellphones are plentiful in Cambodia as are available networks. The situation is chaotic, however, with many networks that don't always connect well with each other. Dropped calls, endless bleeping, and "network busy" notices are the norm. Until recently, it was hard to buy a local SIM card without proof of residency (this was to reduce the incidence of kidnappings, according to the authorities). That is now changing, although the rules remain confused and different dealers will

say different things. You can buy a SIM card for about $2, and $5 top-up cards are available everywhere all over the country as scratch cards. The main providers are M Phone code 011, MobiTel code 012, Bee Line code 090, Smart Mobiel 010, Star Cell code 098, Cube code 013, and Metphone code 097. MobiTel is the most widely used. Some foreign networks are roaming-enabled in Cambodia. It not advised to use them though, unless you plan on remortgaging your house. The roaming rates are ludicrously high.

(Tips) Telephone Dialing at a Glance

- **To place a call from your home country to Cambodia:** Dial the international access code (011 in the U.S. and Canada, 0011 in Australia, 0170 in New Zealand, 00 in the U.K.), plus Cambodia's country code **(855),** the city code (**23** for Phnom Penh, **63** for Siem Reap), and the six-digit phone number (for example, 011 855 23 000-000). *Important note:* Omit the initial "0" in all Cambodian phone numbers when calling from abroad.
- **To place a call within Cambodia:** Dial the city or area code preceded by a **0** (the way numbers are listed in this book), and then the local number (for example, 023/000-000). Note that all phone numbers are six digits after the city code.
- **To place a direct international call from Cambodia:** To place a call, dial the international access code **(00),** plus the country code, the area or city code, and the number (for example, to call the U.S., you'd dial 00 1 000/000-0000).
- **International country codes are as follows:** Australia, 61; Canada, 1; Hong Kong, 852; Indonesia, 62; Laos, 856; Malaysia, 60; Myanmar, 95; New Zealand, 64; the Philippines, 63; Singapore, 65; Thailand, 66; U.K., 44; U.S., 1; Vietnam, 84.

INTERNET

In Cambodia, where you find tourists you find Internet cafes. Standards vary. Phnom Penh has a few near the riverfront that would not be out of place in London. Sihanoukville wins the prize for the worst of the worst—computers here are so riddled with viruses that they are virtually unusable. In smaller towns you might hunt harder to finder a cybervenue but there will generally be a shop or a restaurant with a couple of computers set up at the back that you can use. Rates vary between 50¢ to $1 a minute. Wi-Fi, usually free, is becoming increasingly common in hotels and restaurants. It is not always properly set up, but in Phnom Penh, Siem Reap, Battambang, Kampot, and Sihanoukville it is not hard to find a place to get connected.

4

Suggested Cambodia & Laos Itineraries

The days when both Cambodia and Laos were countries where you could travel only by plane, unless you were an adventurer, are long gone. Roads are improved, buses are regular, and as a result the internal flight network is vastly reduced. Having said that, both countries remain very much in the developing stage, and charging around with a must-do checklist in a short space of time makes little sense. The pace of life, particularly in Laos and rural Cambodia, is slow (though Phnom Penh is frenetic these days), so a more leisurely trip will keep you in tune with those around you. It is a good idea to think of what interests you most before you set off. If you like history and ancient temples, then consider making Luang Prabang and Siem Reap the central part of your trip. If nature is your thing, then river trips and protected areas in the north of Laos should be the priority. For beaches and relaxation, start with the laid-back islands in the Mekong in southern Laos, followed by time spent on the beach at Sihanoukville in Cambodia. The mix-and-match opportunities are wide and varied.

1 THE BEST OF CAMBODIA IN 1 WEEK

If time is limited you are best off doing fewer things well than tearing around Cambodia doing everything badly. On a first visit, Cambodia can be a bit overwhelming, so the best way to ease into it is to fly to Siem Reap and start your trip with the Angkor Wat complex. Angkor is an overwhelmingly spectacular experience, but Siem Reap is a small town with good facilities where most things are walkable. Once you have arrived and checked into your hotel, head over to the Psar Chas area. Here you have the market, the antiques shops, souvenir stalls, and restaurants and cafes of every type. It's a very compact area and a wander, a meal, and maybe a glass of wine or a cup of coffee is a gentle way to kick off your explorations.

Day ❶: Angkor Wat

Get up before dawn and see the sun rise over **Angkor Wat** (p. 113) itself. As the sky glows red, this spectacular structure will reveal itself first in silhouette and then in all its immense glory. As the first major site you see in Cambodia, you're off to a pretty good start. After this curtain opener, a close-up tour of the temple itself is best undertaken in the afternoon, when its facade is no longer backlit and the afternoon sun begins to wash the carvings, towers, and reliefs in a softer direct

light. After your bleary-eyed but dramatic sunrise experience it is time for you to charge over to one of the world's most enigmatic structures while the light is still soft: the **Bayon** (p. 116). Clambering over this astonishing structure will continue the high-impact start to your journey. There are four gates to **Angkor Thom** where the Bayon is situated, but the south gate is most impressive. Some 200m (656 ft.) to the northwest of the Bayon is the **Baphuon,** the central structure of Angkor before the rest of

Temples of Angkor — **1-2**
Phnom Penh — **3-5**
Sihanoukville — **6**
Optional Kampot — **7**

Angkor Thom was built. Afterward, take in the **Terrace of the Leper King.**

By now you will be very tired, very hot, and in need of something cold and refreshing with lunch. Get your driver to take you the short distance back to town to recharge your batteries.

Early afternoon is a good time to see **Ta Phrom.** This temple, wonderfully overgrown by roots, is a favorite for most visitors. By now it should be about 2pm and the perfect time to head back to Angkor Wat itself and see the spectacular basreliefs and the soaring towers, and to test just how practical your shoes are when negotiating the steep and uneven steps.

In the evening you could take in some classical dancing or simply enjoy the lively restaurants, cafes, and nightlife of Siem Reap.

Day ❷: Temple Hopping

In the morning, take in some more temples. **Preah Khan** is a large and important complex full of intriguing passages lined with carvings (p. 120). The temple mountain of Pre Rup rises out of the flatlands, and if you climb it you not only get to see detailed and richly preserved carvings, you also get good views of the surrounding countryside. After that, you have the option of returning to the temple you liked most for further exploration, whether that's Angkor Wat itself, the Bayon, or Ta Phrom.

The markets and boutiques of Siem Reap are stuffed with all kinds of goodies, so now's a good time to head back for some shopping. Hand-woven Cambodian silks, stone carvings (including replicas of those mesmerizing Bayon heads and the shapely serene apsaras that you have just spent so many hours viewing), woodcarvings, contemporary Cambodian art, handicrafts and traditional musical instruments, temple rubbings, silver betel containers, colored gems, and wickerwork—you will find all these around town.

Day ❸: Phnom Penh

In the morning, fly to Phnom Penh. If you arrive in time for lunch, head to the riverfront around Sisowath Quay where you can eat while adjusting to the frantic bustle of the city.

After you have finished your food wander the few yards to Street 178, have a peek at the art galleries and boutiques, and take a look around the stunning collection of Angkorian and pre-Angkorian sculpture in the **National Museum** (p. 82). The **Royal Palace** (p. 82) just next door is your next port of call. Then take a moto up to **Wat Phnom,** the namesake heart of Phnom Penh (p. 84). Since you are already near the river, head back to Sisowath Quay for some well-deserved refreshment. Look out for Phnom Penh's only elephant, the much-loved and delightful Sambo.

Phnom Penh is replete with restaurants, bars, and nightlife of all sorts. Plan your evening according to your tastes.

Day ❹: History & a Mekong Cruise

Cambodia is a country of incredible history, but some of it is simply horrific. If you are to have any understanding of this place, you will need to visit **Tuol Sleng** or S21 (p. 83). You may leave the building weeping at the thought of the fate of all those faces staring out of the fading black-and-white photographs, but you will come away with a greater understanding of Cambodia. Equally you can follow that with a trip to **Choeung Ek,** the Killing Fields where the terrified victims of S21 met an undeserved oblivion (p. 80). If you are with younger children, then of course these places should be skipped. With older children, it's a tough call and should be handled carefully, because it is all very real.

After lunch, take a cruise down the Mekong. You can find boats near the Royal Palace. You can see how different the city looks from the water and you will also pass traditional fishing villages.

In the evening, cross the Japanese Bridge to Prek Leap and have dinner at one of the popular traditional Khmer restaurants. Some of these have music and even stand-up comedy, which is slapstick enough that you will probably laugh, even if you don't understand a word.

Day ❺: Haggling at the Market

If you aren't all shopped out from Siem Reap, take a swing around **Psar Toul Tom Poung,** often referred to as the Russian Market (p. 87). You will be amazed at what you find. Bargaining here is a tough and time-consuming game. If you want a reasonable price it is necessary, but do it with a joke and a smile.

After lunch take the bus to Sihanoukville, arriving in the late afternoon in time for an aperitif while watching the sun sink over the Gulf of Thailand.

Day ❻: Sihanoukville

Today your only goal is to relax on the beach. You can eat crab or lobster cooked right in front of you by passing vendors.

Day ❼: More Relaxing or Optional Kampot

Either continue to relax on the beaches of Sihanoukville, or head the short distance over to Kampot to enjoy the languid atmosphere of this small riverside town before taking the bus back to Phnom Penh for your flight out.

2 THE BEST OF LAOS IN 1 WEEK

Although infrastructure in Laos is vastly improved, traveling can still be a little rough. If you have only a week, it is probably best to confine yourself to Vientiane, Vang Vieng, and Luang Prabang.

Day ❶: Vientiane

After arriving in Vientiane, start the day by visiting the city's oldest temple, **Wat Si Saket** (p. 231). Check out the thousands of miniature Buddha statues. Then head for the former royal temple of **Haw Pha Kaeo** (p. 228), which previously housed the famous emerald Buddha image that is now in Bangkok. On the way to the famous and sacred structure of **Phra That Luang** (p. 230), you can stop to take a look at the imposing **Patuxai Monument** (p. 230), a huge structure very closely echoing the Arc de Triomphe in Paris. As the sun goes down, make your way to the Mekong for a relaxing drink before enjoying a meal at one of the many superb restaurants the city has to offer.

Day ❷: Vang Vieng

Travel by road to Vang Vieng, possibly making a stop at the 11th-century archaeological sight of **Vang Xang**. Upon arrival at Vang Vieng, you can cross the Nam Song River, and then enjoy a short walk or trek through the breathtaking and eerie karsk scenery to Tam None cave and the nearby hill villages. Today ends with a glorious view of the sunset over the Nam Song River. Enjoy a quiet dinner in one of the restaurants in town, although in all honesty Vang Vieng is a little disappointing on the food front. Pick one by the river, near the hospital unless you like noise.

Day ❸: Tubing on the Nam Song River

Have a relaxing and watery day drifting down the Nam Song river on inflated tractor-tire inner tubes. This has become a must-do in Vang Vieng over the years.

Day ❹: Driving on Rte. 13

Travel by road on the truly spectacular Rte. 13 to Luang Prabang. It is one of Asia's most beautiful drives. You will need to start early. The scenery is unrivaled, with a mixture of steep terraced fields and hill-tribe villages, and there are some interesting stops along the way.

Day ❺: Luang Prabang

Spend the day wandering the spellbinding city of Luang Prabang, enjoying the faded colonial charm of the place including the city's oldest temple, the magnificent **Wat Xieng Thong** (p. 278). In the afternoon, take a cruise on the Mekong River, enjoying the special tranquillity of the area, and visit the mysterious **Pak Ou Caves,** crammed with thousands of gold Buddha statues (p. 280). Along the way, make a stop at the village of **Ban Xang Hai,** known as Lao Whiskey village for their local moonshine (p. 281). Once back in Luang Prabang, take a short drive to **Ban Phanom,** well known for its hand weaving (p. 280). In the evening, wander through the night market where handicrafts, jewelry, and souvenirs of all sorts amount to a shopper's nirvana.

Day ❻: More Highlights of Luang Prabang

Visit the **Royal Palace Museum** (p. 270), which houses a superb collection of Lao cultural artifacts dating from the days of the early kings right through to the last one. Then take a look at the impressive stupa of **Wat Visoun** (p. 278), the shrine of Wat Aham, then climb up to the top of Phousi Hill for an exploration of the sacred, gilded stupa, and a beautiful sunset view of the city and the Mekong River.

1 Vientiane
2–3 Vang Vieng
4 Route 13
5–6 Luang Prabang
7 Vientiane

Day 7: Back to Vientiane

Take a morning flight back to Vientiane. Drive the 24km (14 miles) out of town to Buddha Park (p. 227). Enjoy the strange creation of a philanthropic eccentric, whose vision is realized in this bizarre collection of Buddhist and Hindu sculptures. To finish off your trip, take a leisurely afternoon stroll along the Mekong, watching life on the river go by and stopping at one of the many cafes along the banks.

3 THE BEST OF CAMBODIA & LAOS IN 3 WEEKS

With 3 weeks to play with, you can start in the north of Laos entering at Huai Xai and then have a leisurely journey down the Mekong to Luang Prabang. Fly from Bangkok to Chiang Rai in north Thailand and from there take a bus to Chiang Kong from where you can cross over into Laos. From there, let the Mekong be your guide.

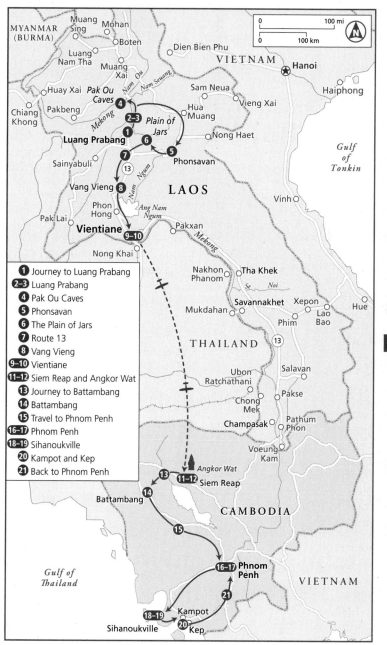

1 Journey to Luang Prabang
2–3 Luang Prabang
4 Pak Ou Caves
5 Phonsavan
6 The Plain of Jars
7 Route 13
8 Vang Vieng
9–10 Vientiane
11–12 Siem Reap and Angkor Wat
13 Journey to Battambang
14 Battambang
15 Travel to Phnom Penh
16–17 Phnom Penh
18–19 Sihanoukville
20 Kampot and Kep
21 Back to Phnom Penh

SUGGESTED CAMBODIA & LAOS ITINERARIES

4

THE BEST OF CAMBODIA & LAOS IN 3 WEEKS

Day ❶: Journey to Luang Prabang

Once you have completed immigration formalities in Huay Xai, walk down to the left of the immigration building to where the slow boats to Luang Prabang are moored. These used to be commercial vessels for which you had to haggle hard to get a decent price for passage, and you shared the journey with farmers (and often their livestock). Now there are boats specifically assigned for tourists. The journey to Luang Prabang is 2 days of scenic views, sticky rice, and if you are lucky with your fellow passengers, convivial chitchat. You will stop for the night in Pakbeng. Be on the lookout for scams (and this, sadly, includes the children). Don't let people carry your bags for you when you get off the boat. This once very basic little one-street town situated on a rocky bend of the river is now fairly developed. There are a number of guesthouses and even some midrange hotels and chichi cafes.

Day ❷: Arrival in Luang Prabang

Continue your slow trip down the Mekong. Enjoy the dramatic forested limestone mountain scenery, the passing rapids, and the village life along the riverbank. You will arrive in Luang Prabang at about 4pm. Once you have checked into your hotel, have a wander and take in the tranquil beauty of this most beautiful of towns. Enjoy the coffee, the baguettes, the wine, and the sunset.

Day ❸: Luang Prabang

Tour the area's temples and sights. Try a bowl of Vietnamese pho for lunch. Have a gander around the central market in the daytime and the night market in the evening.

Day ❹: Pak Ou Caves

Visit **Pak Ou Caves** and see the massed Buddhas (p. 280). In the afternoon enjoy a herbal sauna and massage—Luang Prabang has become famous for them. Once suitably relaxed, head to where the long-distance ferries stop and watch the sunset

as the sun glows red behind the mountain on the opposite bank of the river.

Day ❺: Arrival in Phonsavan

Take the bus to Phonsavan. It will be your base from which to explore the Plain of Jars. It's a grueling 10 hours but the incredible scenery is worth the slog. Phonsavan is not a very interesting town (in fact, it's downright dreary). Get fed and watered and call it an early night.

Day ❻: The Plain of Jars

The best way to see the **Plain of Jars** is by booking a tour with one of the guesthouses in town (p. 294). Most of them offer a package, costing about $14 per person. You can do it on your own, but it's not recommended—since the jars are spread out in a number of groupings you might miss something significant.

Day ❼: Rte. 13 to Vang Vieng

Take the bus to Vang Vieng. This is an 8-hour drive where once again you are treated to some fantastic scenery along Rte. 13.

Day ❽: Vang Vieng

Cross the Nam Song River and spend the morning wandering around the limestone outcrops on the other side. After heading back to town for lunch, enjoy the pointless but fun activity of "tubing"—drifting down the river on an inflated tractor inner tube.

Day ❾: Arrival in Vientiane

Take a bus or minibus to Vientiane (about 3 hr.). After lunch, take in some of the sights such as **Wat Pha Kaeo** and **Wat Si Saket** (p. 231). Have dinner in one of the big Lao riverside restaurants by the Mekong.

Day ❿: Vientiane

Spend the morning visiting the **National Museum** (p. 228) and then take a drive around the city, being sure to pass the impressive but very Gallic **Patuxai Monument** (p. 230). In the afternoon, visit Talat

Sao Market to shop for special Lao fabric and jewelry, or even DVDs and computer games if that's what you fancy.

Day ⑪: Flight to Siem Reap

You could easily spend another week in Laos exploring the south of the country, but if you don't want to be hurried in Cambodia (and you really don't want to be hurried in Cambodia), it is time to employ aviation. Your destination is Siem Reap in Cambodia (both Lao Airlines and Vietnam Airlines fly this route). Arriving at lunchtime, once you have dumped your bags in your hotel head to the center of town around Psar Chas. Here you can kick back in any of the many restaurants, cafes, or pubs and get a feel for the place. Take a look around the market stocked with all kinds of handicrafts, clothing, and much more.

Day ⑫: Angkor Wat

Get up early and see the sunrise over **Angkor Wat** (p. 113). It's a photographer's dream and a moment you won't forget. Then head over to **Angkor Thom** and the **Bayon** (p. 116). There is nothing in the world quite like the glorious enigma of the Bayon. Check out the other sites around Angkor Thom and then head back into town for lunch. In the afternoon go to **Ta Prohm** (p. 121), an overgrown and atmospheric place that makes the set of *Raiders of the Lost Ark* look pedestrian. As the sun starts to lower in the sky at about 2pm, head back to Angkor Wat to explore its many splendors. Don't forget to look out for the spectacular bas-relief sculptures and endless apsaras.

Day ⑬: Journey to Battambang

Today you're heading to the western town of Battambang. You can do this in one of two ways—either by boat (p. 134) or by road. The boat journey is a bit of an adventure, especially in the dry season when the water is low, but the views of life along the banks of the Sangker River are fascinating. The bus is straightforward.

Check in and relax at your hotel and in the evening, get a *motodup* to take you to the Riverside Balcony Bar, an atmospheric wooden building on the river with a huge veranda. After your riverside aperitif, head over to La Pomme d'Amour for dinner. It's an excellent place for hearty French provincial cooking.

Day ⑭: Battambang

There is not a lot to do in Battambang, but nevertheless it's a nice place to spend a day wandering down the old colonnaded streets and exploring the central market, which, unlike in Siem Reap, is a practical Cambodian affair with few concessions to tourists.

Day ⑮: Travel to Phnom Penh

Travel by bus to Phnom Penh, arriving about 4pm. Once you have checked in to your hotel head over to Sisowath Quay on the riverfront. Enjoy a margarita at Cantina, something tasty and French at La Croisette, or something overpriced but with a beautiful view at the FCC. When it comes to dining, Phnom Penh has a dizzying choice of venues serving food from every corner of the globe. Why not start with Khmer food? Malis on Norodom Boulevard serves artfully prepared Cambodian dishes from the kitchen of celebrated Cambodian chef Luu Meng (p. 78).

Day ⑯: Phnom Penh

Take in some of Phnom Penh's numerous sites. Start with the **Royal Palace** (p. 82) and the **National Museum** (p. 82). Then move on to **Wat Phnom** (p. 84). In the afternoon, check out the **Psar Toul Tom Poung,** also known as the Russian Market (p. 87). This vast complex sells just about everything you can think of and some things you never could. In the evening, cross the Tonle Sap to the Prek Leap district where you will find a succession of large traditional Khmer restaurants by the river. Many of them also have bands and singers playing often-melancholic traditional songs.

Day ⓱: History in Phnom Penh

To understand Cambodia's present, you have to understand the horrors of its recent past. Do not expect to enjoy your morning. First take a moto-taxi or tuk-tuk to the south of the city where you will find the **Tuol Sleng** or S21 Genocide museum (p. 83). This is an overwhelming but necessary visit to make. It was here that the Khmer Rouge tortured and then slaughtered thousands of men, women, children, and infants. They photographed their victims meticulously before they killed them and thousands of the fading portraits are on view. The range of expressions is heartbreaking. You can then go to **Choeung Ek,** the Killing Fields, which was the principal place where these thousands upon thousands of people were systematically killed (p. 80). In the afternoon, you can relax and be alone with your thoughts on a boat trip down the Mekong, watching life unfold along the riverbanks.

Days ⓲ & ⓳: Sihanoukville

Take the bus to the beaches of Sihanoukville, find a peaceful place to your liking, order a cold drink, break out the paperbacks, and relax.

Day ⓴: Kampot & Kep

Take a trip along the coast to Kep and Kampot. Sample the tasty seafood while in Kep. A well-known local specialty is Kep crab in Kampot pepper. It is a must-try.

Day ㉑: Back to Phnom Penh

Head back to Phnom Penh by bus and try to work out which restaurant, of the many superb and varied choices on offer, you will go to for your last supper. If you like genuine Spanish tapas and paella, try Pacharan (p. 77) near the Royal Palace. It is in a wonderful old French colonial building, with views of both the river and the Silver Pagoda.

Phnom Penh

Founded in the mid–14th century by the Khmers as a monastery, Phnom Penh replaced Angkor Thom, a city at the Angkor temples, a century later as the country's capital. The city has long been a vital trading hub at the confluence of three rivers: the Mekong, Tonle Sap, and Bassac. In the 1950s and 1960s, Phnom Penh was considered the most beautiful city in Asia. Wide, lazy boulevards shaded by trees and French-built villas set among prewar Art Deco monoliths set the city apart. In the 1960s, when war raged in Vietnam but had yet to engulf its neighbor, Phnom Penh was the R & R destination of choice for those involved in the continuing horror. Perhaps the city's most noted period was actually when it lay vacant; following an eviction order from Pol Pot, the city was deserted in a period of hours, and almost all of Phnom Penh's residents moved to the countryside in 1975, not to return until 1979 under the authority of Vietnamese troops.

It has been a long road to the peaceful and growing Phnom Penh of today. There were many years of frontier-style anarchy after the city was repopulated in 1979.

Today, the city is absolutely frenetic and intense. There has been a massive increase in vehicles and population over the last 5 years and Phnom Penh is now very much a boomtown. In many ways, the city is overtaking Bangkok and Manila for the prize of having the most congested and claustrophobic city streets in Asia. It is smaller than either but far more unpredictable in that everything goes in all directions at once. Yet it was only under a decade ago that the first traffic lights were installed, and the first escalator in Phnom Penh (at the Sorya Center shopping mall) was switched on for the first time at the end of 2001 and became in an instant recreational attraction.

Phnom Penh enjoys its own kind of harmony of opposites and offers visitors peaceful moments of a sunset at riverside as well as its dusty, motorbike-choked labyrinthine alleys and busy markets. The city is an incongruous cluster of crumbling French colonials, and the central riverside area has a pace all its own that's great for wandering. It is easy, although sometimes slightly hair-raising, to get around. Expect delays at peak hours.

1 ORIENTATION

CITY LAYOUT

Phnom Penh lies north to south along the Tonle Sap River and the river provides a natural marker. Your major reference points are the Tonle Sap itself (and the Royal Palace), Wat Phnom, Central Market, Independence Monument, and Boeung Kak Lake.

Along the river is Sisowath Quay. It is here that you will find the Royal Palace, the ceremonial heart of the city. Just near the Palace and the National Museum is one of the primary restaurant and cafe districts. Virtually the whole riverfront is now a series of eateries interspersed with hotels, Internet cafes, and travel agents.

Heading a few blocks west and running parallel to Sisowath Quay is the major artery of Norodom Boulevard. The two major landmarks along this road are Democracy Monument to the southwest of the Royal Palace and Wat Phnom where it ends at the northern end of Central Phnom Penh.

Heading west again across the parallel intersections with Street 51 and Street 63, one arrives at Monivong Boulevard. This is the city's main thoroughfare and is very hectic during the day. Along Monivong, you will find many of the major banks and airline offices. At the northern end of Monivong is the area around Boeung Kak Lake (although the lake itself now represents prime real estate and there are plans afoot to fill it in). This has for a long time been the main backpacker area. Ringing the lake (at present) is a series of very cheap guesthouses and restaurants. To the north, Monivong ends at a large round-about. This place has historical significance since the nearby French Embassy was where foreigners sheltered in 1975 after the city fell to the Khmer Rouge. Heading east from the roundabout will take you to the Japanese Bridge that crosses to Prek Leap.

Phsar Thmei, or the Central Market, is a huge and eccentric French Art Deco land-mark in the center of town between Norodom and Monivong.

Circling the central part of Phnom Penh is Mao Tse Tung Boulevard. Three major arteries radiate out from Monivong to Mao Tse Tung: Confederation de la Russie (Air-port Rd.) heading due west passing the southern side of Boeung Kak Lake; Kampuchea Krom Boulevard, which parallels it 4 blocks south; and Charles de Gaulle (turning into Monireth), which takes you southwest out of the city. Sihanouk Boulevard is a kind of inner ring road partially echoing Mao Tse Tung Boulevard to the west and south starting at Independence Monument and Norodom and ending at Confederation de la Russie just south of Boeung Lak Lake.

A lot, but by no means all, of the hotels and restaurants are situated in the area between the Tonle Sap and Monivong, south of Wat Phnom and north of Victory Monument. Between Monivong and Norodom south of Sihanouk Boulevard is a leafy and relatively quiet residential network of streets, called Boeung Keng Kang, where many expats live, and NGOs and international organizations are housed in former French vil-las. There are also many restaurants and cafes and it is in many ways the most pleasant part of town.

GETTING THERE

BY AIR   All major airlines in the region connect here. **Phnom Penh International** (formerly Pochentong) Airport is about a 20-minute drive from the city center (if the traffic is thin). A cab costs $9, while a tuk-tuk costs $7. Vehicles entering the airport are monitored. You pay at a counter in arrivals and hand the voucher to the driver waiting in the queue at the front. Motorcycle taxis are not allowed into the airport compound, but if you wish you can walk past the airport gates and hail a *motodup* from the side of the road. The fare will be about $3, but be prepared to haggle. This is all probably a bad idea if this is your first time in Phnom Penh, and you are better off sticking with the approved taxi.

BY BOAT   Hydrofoil riverboats connect Phnom Penh with Siem Reap and leave early every morning from the main dock on the north end of town. Tickets are available from both travel agents and hotels or you can purchase directly at the quay. The price is in the region of $35. Now that the road to Siem Reap is completely perfect, boats have lost much of their popularity. This is not surprising as they are often overcrowded and uncomfortable, and their safety record is dubious. The boat route up the Mekong to

The Tonle Sap: The Heart of a Nation

The Tonle Sap is the only waterway in the world that changes direction halfway through the year and starts to flow in the opposite direction according to the season. From November to May, Cambodia's dry season, the Tonle Sap flows into the Mekong River, the two waterways converging at Phnom Penh. However, when the monsoon rains begin in June, the Tonle Sap backs up the other way to form what is essentially an enormous natural reservoir. The direction of the Tonle Sap is decided by the pressure of the water from the Mekong, either forcing it back into the Tonle Sap Lake when the river is high or drawing it into its own flow when the river is low. It is a natural safety valve, giving the Mekong natural elbowroom to flow through the delta and on to the sea. Most of the year, the Tonle Sap Lake is relatively shallow. During the rainy season, it increases in area to 16,000 sq. km (6,240 sq. miles) and its depth can reach up to 9m (30 ft.), flooding surrounding fields and forests. The Tonle Sap is the beating heart of Cambodia. It has traditionally provided abundant irrigation for rice while yielding plentiful amounts of fish—the central sustenance of life for Cambodians.

Kratie has been discontinued altogether. Earlier this century, all the passengers on the Siem Reap ferry were held up at gunpoint and robbed by fellow passengers. The culprits turned out to be hospitality students!

BY BUS Different companies leave from different parts of town, though outside of Psar Thmei (Central Market) is where you will find the departure points for both **Sorya** (© 023/210-359) and **GST Express** (© 023/355-379) bus services. They are comfortable and reasonably priced, but often very cold because of excessive air-conditioning. **Mekong Express** (© 023/427-518), leaving from Sisowath Quay on the corner of Street 102, is generally reputed to be the most comfortable and swift, but you will pay slightly more. It is worth it. Sorya (or Ho Wah Genting as they used to be called) and GST offer a slightly cheaper but less salubrious option. Travel remains cheap, with journeys from Phnom Penh to Siem Reap or Sihanoukville costing under $5. Unlike elsewhere in Southeast Asia, there are few night buses. Most departures leave in the early hours of the morning with the last ones leaving in midafternoon. The easiest way to buy tickets is through your hotel, guesthouse, or a travel agent.

Buses run in both directions from Phnom Penh to Siem Reap, Sihanoukville, Kampot, Koh Kong, Battambang, Kratie, Kompong Cham, Stung Treng, Banlung, Sisophon, and Poipet.

GETTING AROUND

With the increase in crowds and traffic that has occurred in the last few years, getting around Phnom Penh can be a fairly wild experience. The good news is that there are plenty of modes of transportation, and hailing a *motodup*, a cyclo, or a tuk-tuk is very simple since they are everywhere.

BY MOTORCYCLE TAXI Motorcycle taxis are all over town and are often the quickest way to get around. Just hail one from the sidewalk. Most restaurants and hotels will also have a stand of affiliated drivers. If you find one you like, take his phone number and hire him again. Most residents of Phnom Penh will have their own recommendation for good drivers or *motodups,* as they are called in Khmer. The dups are even thought to be mystically "all knowing" by Phnom Penh residents. Most trips around town will cost less than a dollar during the day. At night you normally double the fee. Most people don't wear a helmet, but they should, given the dubious quality of both the motorcycles and the driving.

BY CYCLO   A gentler but slower way to see the sights is by cyclo (p. 36). They operate under the same rules and pretty much the same rates as the motorcycle taxis. Cyclos take a lot of the stress out of getting from point A to point B. They are also good when it rains, since the cyclo driver will bring out plastic sheeting to shelter you from the elements. You will always find lots of cyclos around Psah Thmei (the Central Market), as people use them to transport bulky or heavy goods. As the traffic chaos of Phnom Penh's streets increases, the experience of touring the city by cyclo becomes harder as these gentle vehicles are forced out by land cruisers and trucks. At the moment, however, it remains feasible.

BY TUK-TUK   Tuk-tuks are a fairly new development in Phnom Penh and are readily available. The name is taken from the Thais, but these tuk-tuks have little in common with the noisy, Bangkok two-stroke three-wheeler. Cambodia's tuk-tuks are a two-wheeled cart pulled by a standard motorbike, attached through a fairly ingenious coupling device. They are shaded, and the padded seat seats two (or three if you are thin). There is often a small shelf at the front of the cart, usually with laminated maps and advertisements, and, in a pinch, you can seat two more, but it's not very comfy. It costs between $2 and $3 for trips around town, while a ride farther out to places like the Killing Fields will set you back $15.

BY TAXI   Metered cabs have now made an appearance on the streets of Phnom Penh, though they are limited. **Global Taxi** (✆ **011/311-888**) is generally reserved only by phone, though occasionally you might see one waiting for a fare near a tourist spot late at night. The flag fall is 4,000 riel for the first 2km and then 400 riel per kilometer. **Taxi Vantha** (✆ **012/855-000**) is unmetered and reached by phone only. Expect to pay around $4 to $5 for a short journey.

Enterprising taxi driver **Yinn Vannak** (✆ **016/639-852;** www.cambodiadriver.com) has his own website for bookings and is available for hire on a long- or short-term basis.

There are many unofficial cabs. All guesthouses and hotels will be able to get you are a car within half an hour. A ride to the airport costs between $5 and $7.

BY MOTORCYCLE   Driving in Phnom Penh is not for the fainthearted. In fact, unless absolutely necessary, it is best avoided. If you don't heed this call, you can hire motorcycles at a number of places including **Lucky! Lucky!,** at 413 Monivong Blvd. (✆ **023/ 212-788**), which has been in the business a long time. You can get a step-through type 100cc-to-125cc scooter for $5 a day. Some of them are good, but some of them are unsound in the extreme and you should examine them and refuse them if you have doubts. They also rent bigger 250cc bikes for touring at $9 as well as jeeps and even luxury cars. Driving a motorcycle in Phnom Penh requires experience. It is a chaotic, aggressive, and often nerve-racking experience with traffic going in all directions, often straight at you. Keep space around you, drive slowly, and wear a helmet (if not available when renting, you can buy one for $10–$20 from a shop at Monivong or Kampuchea Krom).

There is a huge choice of accommodations in Phnom Penh, ranging from old, upscale gems to budget minihotels, to even a few small boutique properties. Although the choice is large, so is the disparity in quality within the same price range. While there are hotels and guesthouses scattered all over the city, the main concentrations are in the streets around the riverfront stretching from the Cambodiana to the boat pier for Siem Reap. The crisscross of streets stretching between here and Monivong Boulevard is home to dozens and dozens of places of varying prices and quality. Those on or near the river tend to be more expensive with the area around 178 Street and the Royal Palace forming the fashionable epicenter. The problem with this area is that although it is very central, it also suffers from the increasing insanity of traffic on the streets of Phnom Penh. It is unbelievably hectic as soon as you step out of your hotel. Boeung Keng Kang, the area south of Sihanouk Boulevard, with 51 Street as its central thoroughfare, offers a vastly more relaxed environment if you find your nerves jangling uncontrollably around the center of the city. You will find a whole slew of restaurants and midmarket hotels set in quieter surroundings than farther uptown. Increasingly there are boutique offerings springing up in this area, adding to the many midrange options. Whichever district you choose to explore, it pays to look around. Always ask about seasonal rates.

RIVERFRONT TO MONIVONG
Expensive

Amanjaya Hotel ★★ Near the riverside at Sisowath Quay and the National Museum, this three-story corner building is a true house of style. The porous laterite walls of the lobby and the Buddhist statues throughout contribute to a cool boutique vibe. Though sparse in services and amenities, rooms are spacious, done in rich red silk hangings and bedspreads in bold contrast with dark-wood trim and floors. All rooms have king-size beds. For the same price as the standard suites The Quay (see below) nearby, Amanjaya's deluxe suites are far more spacious and come with a small balcony. All bathrooms are immaculate affairs done in wood and tile, with neat tub/shower units in deluxe suites and separate shower and tub in the more expensive suites, delineated by unique large-stone gravel paths in concrete. Rooms vary in size and shape; best are the corner suites with panoramic views of the river and busy street below. Noisy traffic is the only drawback.

No. 1 St. 154 Sisowath Quay. ✆ **023/214-747.** Fax 023/219-545. www.amanjaya.com 21 units. Apr–Sept $120–$175 deluxe suite; $220 suite; Oct–Mar $155–$215 deluxe suite; $250 suite. MC, V. **Amenities:** Restaurant; room service. *In room:* A/C, TV, fridge, minibar, Wi-Fi.

Hotel Cambodiana ★★ They've got it all at the Cambodiana. With a convenient location, atmosphere, and all the amenities, this is a good jumping-off point for the sites downtown. The building looks like a giant gilded wedding cake, and its vaulted Khmer-style roofs dominate the sky in the southern end of downtown. The lobby is abuzz with activity, whether it's visiting dignitaries or disembarking tour buses, but the helpful staff handles it all with grace. The large riverside pool is great, and there are some fine choices in international dining. Rooms are priced according to their view of the river, and executive floors are of a fine standard. Everything is tidy, but decoration is a chain-hotel style in plain wood and office carpet; it's a bit dull, and some floors reek of pungent deodorizers. Deluxe river-view rooms are the best bet. The high-end suites are richly decorated and unique, and executive privileges on the top floors are luxe. They have wireless Internet (with prepaid cards) available in all public spaces. All rooms have picture windows and good views of town or the river.

313 Sisowath Quay. ✆ **023/218-189.** Fax 023/426-392. www.hotelcambodiana.com. 230 units. $170–$180 double; $400–$500 suite. AE, MC, V. **Amenities:** 4 restaurants; bar; concierge; executive-level rooms; small health club; Internet; Jacuzzi; outdoor pool; room service; sauna; tennis court. *In room:* A/C, TV, fridge, minibar.

The Quay ★★ This chic riverside hotel is giving nearby Amanjaya a run for its money. They advertise "carbon-neutral luxury," and that's what you get at the Quay. They call themselves Cambodia's first carbon-neutral hotel, done through a combination of ecofriendly materials and purchasing carbon-offsets (which provide rural villages with fuel-efficient wood-burning stoves). It is best advised to skip the small, windowless (though admittedly still very stylish) standard rooms and book yourself into a panorama suite. For the extra $50 you get a room twice the size with large balconies with unobstructed views of the river and a cozy sitting area with swan chairs. The decor of light wood, champagne color textiles, and cream walls and furniture create a truly soothing escape from the chaos of Phnom Penh. Bathrooms in all units are sleek and outfitted with stylish sinks and shower cubicles; suites come with large stone tubs. The rooftop Jacuzzi is luxurious, if a bit uncomfortable, as there is also a popular rooftop bar so you may have to shimmy your way past patrons for a soak.

277 Sisowath Quay. ✆ **023/992-284.** Fax 023/224-893. www.thequayhotel.com 16 units. $130 standard suite; $185 panoramic suite. AE, MC, V. **Amenities:** Restaurant; rooftop Jacuzzi; room service. *In room:* A/C, TV, fridge, minibar, Wi-Fi.

Raffles Hotel Le Royal ★★★ This is the best high-end hotel in Phnom Penh. Built in 1929, it is the city's most atmospheric hotel, an authentic Art Deco and colonial classic. Everything from the vaulted ceilings in the lobby to the classic original central stairs breathes history and charm. Walking down the arched hallways, with sunlight bouncing off the black-and-white floor tiles and streaming in through stone columns, is like walking smack into the extravagance of prewar Indochina. Rooms are done with fine tiled entries, high ceilings, indirect lighting, a sitting area with inlaid furniture, and ornate touches like antique wall sconces and fine drapery. Landmark rooms, just one step above the standard, are a good choice in the old wing and are larger, with nice appointments like claw-foot tubs and Art Deco faucets. The Raffles is luxury with a price tag, but it is all well worth it. There are some interesting theme suites named for famous visitors, including Charles de Gaulle and W. Somerset Maugham. Even Jacqueline Kennedy has a room dedicated to photos and memorabilia from her 1967 visit. The central pool area is a tranquil oasis divided by a unique pavilion, and the amenities throughout, such as the fine spa facility, are luxe. The staff is attentive and very professional.

92 Rukhak Vithei Daun Penh (off Monivong Blvd.), Sangkat Wat Phnom. ✆ **023/981-888.** Fax 023/981-168. www.raffles.com. 172 units. $300–$340 double; $390–$2,500 suite. AE, MC, V. **Amenities:** 3 restaurants; 2 bars; babysitting; kids' club; concierge; health club; Internet; Jacuzzi; 2 outdoor pools; sauna; room service. *In room:* A/C, TV, fridge, hair dryer, minibar, Wi-Fi.

MODERATE

Almond Hotel ★★★ This slick new addition to the Phnom Penh hotel scene raises the bar. The emphasis is very much on the modern with plenty of shiny tiles and picture windows. This is tempered by boutique touches such as rattan furniture and silk awnings. The rooms are light with picture windows. The deluxe rooms sport balconies with decent

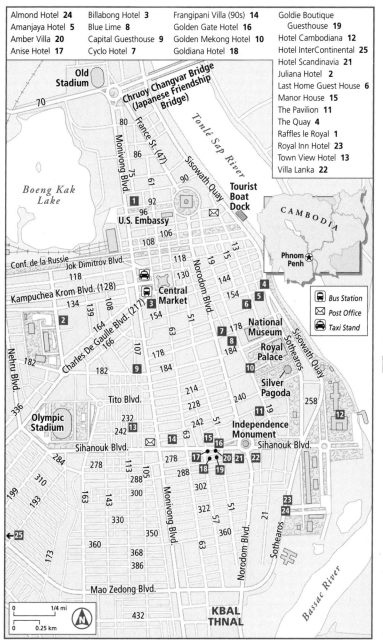

Almond Hotel **24**
Amanjaya Hotel **5**
Amber Villa **20**
Anise Hotel **17**

Billabong Hotel **3**
Blue Lime **8**
Capital Guesthouse **9**
Cyclo Hotel **7**

Frangipani Villa (90s) **14**
Golden Gate Hotel **16**
Golden Mekong Hotel **10**
Goldiana Hotel **18**

Goldie Boutique
  Guesthouse **19**
Hotel Cambodiana **12**
Hotel InterContinental **25**
Hotel Scandinavia **21**
Juliana Hotel **2**
Last Home Guest House **6**
Manor House **15**
The Pavilion **11**
The Quay **4**
Raffles le Royal **1**
Royal Inn Hotel **23**
Town View Hotel **13**
Villa Lanka **22**

Old Stadium

70

Chruoy Changvar Bridge
(Japanese Friendship Bridge)

80

France St. (47)

Monivong Blvd.

86

75

61

90

Tonlé Sap River

Sisowath Quay

Boeng Kak Lake

92

96

U.S. Embassy

Tourist Boat Dock

CAMBODIA

Phnom Penh

108

106

Conf. de la Russie

Jok Dimitrov Blvd.

118

Kampuchea Krom Blvd. (128)

118

130

144

154

19

15

13

Norodom Blvd.

134

139

108

164

166

Charles De Gaulle Blvd. (217)

Central Market

154

63

51

107

178

178

184

National Museum

Royal Palace

184

Silver Pagoda

Nehru Blvd.

182

182

Tito Blvd.

214

228

240

Sisowath Quay

Sothearos

258

Olympic Stadium

336

232

242

Sihanouk Blvd.

284

278

242

51

Independence Monument

Sihanouk Blvd.

19

Bus Station

Post Office

Taxi Stand

310

199

193

113

105

278

288

288

302

Monivong Blvd.

163

143

300

330

350

360

368

386

322

302

57

51

360

21

Sotheoaros

Norodom Blvd.

63

173

Mao Zedong Blvd.

0   1/4 mi
0   0.25 km

N

432

KBAL THNAL

Bassac River

views—a place to contemplate chaos and sunsets from a comfortable height and distance. If you are in town on business, the Almond Hotel is well equipped to cater to your needs, with free Wi-Fi Internet and a business center. The staff is up to speed on their language skills and things do get done. Once the working day is over you can rejuvenate at the spa and beauty salon, which offers treatments and massage from skilled therapists. There are two attached restaurants serving both Western and Asian fare. Their Cantonese chef makes glorious creations in the Yi Sang Chinese restaurant.

No. 128F Sotheeros Blvd. (*) **023/220-822.** Fax 023/220-722. www.almondhotel.com.kh. 56 units. $55 superior single; $65 superior double; $65 deluxe single; $75 deluxe double; $75 deluxe balcony single; $85 deluxe balcony double. MC, V. **Amenities:** 2 restaurants; bar; Internet; room service. *In room:* A/C, satellite TV, fridge, minibar.

Blue Lime ★★   Blue Lime is the latest oasis from the group that brought Phnom Penh the Pavilion (see below). The entire hotel has an industrial-chic decor—there is granite and finished concrete throughout, with brightly colored silk curtains or pillows softening everything up. Plenty of sunshine filters in from windows and vaulted sky-lights. Rooms here are spacious, especially if you bump up to the superiors, and the extra $5 also gets you a nice private balcony. Bathrooms are a good size with stylish sinks and separate rain-shower areas. The hot water comes from solar panels, so there is a bit of waiting involved. The outdoor pool is surrounded by four-poster daybeds and tall, leafy tropical trees. Staff here is friendlier than at Pavillion, and extremely efficient and thoughtful. A room on the top floor offers lovely views of the curved rooftop of the National Museum in the distance. Blue Lime is already very popular among travelers in the know, so book far in advance.

No. 42 St. 19Z (in the alley off St. 19; btw. 181Eo and No. 179B St. 19). (*) **023/222-260.** www.bluelime. asia. 14 units. $40–$50 double (Dec–Jan add $10). MC, V. **Amenities:** Restaurant; bar; outdoor saltwater pool. *In room:* A/C, TV, fridge, hair dryer, minibar, Wi-Fi, no phone.

Manor House   This former ambassadorial residency is in a quiet area between Norodom and Monivong. It is gay-run and certainly gay-friendly but everyone is welcome. The elegant design of the original house is complemented by the thoughtful decor and tasteful but muted furnishings. The rooms at the front are airy and light while those at the back have windows facing on to the corridor. They are quite dark, though equally well appointed and appropriately cheaper. All the rooms are huge with high ceilings. There is a small garden at the back with a surprisingly large and inviting swimming pool.

No. 21 St. 262. (*) **023/992-566.** www.manorhousecambodia.com. 12 units. $43 double. MC, V. **Amenities:** Restaurant; bar; Internet; pool. *In room:* A/C, TV, fridge, minibar.

The Pavilion ★   This is a very popular boutique hotel, so make sure to book ahead and get confirmation of it in writing or by e-mail. The Pavilion—hidden behind big heavy wooden doors and long white walls—is an absolute oasis in this city of honking, jostling tuk-tuks, and motorcycles. Stepping into the central courtyard garden is incredibly calming. Daybeds with overstuffed pillows and a compact outdoor pool offer much-needed comfort after touring the city. Double rooms are basic, with firm beds and a few silk decorations. The bathrooms are a real plus in this price category, as they come with separate shower cubicles, stylish sinks, and Art Deco tile. For a splurge, book one of the pool rooms, which come with nice private toe dippers. *Note:* The Pavillion's sister hotel, the **Kabiki** ((*) **023/222-290;** No. 22 St. 264), was built specifically for families. It has a very similar ambience and level of service.

No. 227 St. 19. ✆ **023/222-280.** www.thepavilion.asia. 20 units. $40–$75 double; $85 suite or pool rooms. MC, V. **Amenities:** Restaurant. *In room:* A/C, TV, fridge, minibar, Wi-Fi.

Royal Inn Hotel ★★   This is a tasteful option decorated in a muted colonial Indo-china style with plenty of dark wood and silk. The rooms have picture windows and large balconies, and are well designed in terms of light and space. They are equipped with a television and minibar, as well as an elegant writing desk. The stylish en suite bathroom offers hot water shower and bathtub. The floors are gleaming polished wood. There is a pleasant rooftop terrace ideal for breakfast or to watch the sunset. There is also Wi-Fi throughout.

No. 128D8 Sothearos Blvd. ✆ **023/214-824.** Fax 023/214-972. www.royal-inn.net. 30 units. $28 standard double; $38 superior double; $48 deluxe double; $66 junior suite; $70 executive suite. MC, V. **Amenities:** Restaurant; bar; Internet; room service. *In room:* A/C, TV, fridge, minibar.

Inexpensive

The Billabong ★   This hotel attracts a laid-back group of travelers who want something a little more luxe than the basic $15 backpacker deal. Everything is done in navy blue and white and feels a bit like an old-fashioned cabana or low-key country club. Rooms are basic, with navy sheets and red silk bed throws. Bathrooms do not have a separate shower unit, but they are clean and tidy. Staff is ultra-friendly here and the outdoor pool is an excellent little oasis after a day of touring the city. Spring for a room with a poolside view—it's worth the extra $3.

No. 5 St. 158. ✆ **023/223-703.** Fax 023/998-472. www.thebillabonghotel.com. 10 units. $36–$39 double; $58 superior; $62 deluxe. MC, V. **Amenities:** Restaurant; Internet. *In room:* A/C, TV, fridge, minibar.

Cyclo Hotel ★★   This spacious and friendly place near Psar Thmei has been conceived with some thought to the building it is in. It is a '60s-style house and indeed a '60s-style concept in its spare but tasteful decor. Nothing is fancy or labored, and the overall feel is one of space and light. It is firmly aimed at the lower end of the midrange market, but with style and imagination. The rooms are large and the deluxe rooms have excellent balconies from which you may view the vivid streets below. Jean-Pierre, the owner, is provincial French and the place has the homey feel of a French country home. The bar/restaurant next to reception is beautifully decorated with ocher tiles and dark wood. With a very Provençal feel, it's a good place to enjoy a glass of pastis. They do not accept credit card payment as yet.

No. 50E St. 172. ✆ **023/992-128.** 10 units. $25 double; $35 deluxe double. **Amenities:** Restaurant; bar; Internet. *In room:* A/C, TV, fridge, minibar.

Golden Mekong Hotel   This newly opened hotel at the back of the Royal Palace is modest, tasteful, and well situated. The building is an old French town house and has been converted with care. The rooms are plain in a pleasingly uncluttered fashion, but what there is in the way of furnishing is well thought out. Being an old building, the rooms are slightly dark. There is a small terrace at the front of the hotel although it is hardly relaxing since one simply becomes witness to the ever-increasing madness of Phnom Penh traffic.

No. 205A St. 19. ✆ **023/211-721.** www.goldenmekonghotel.com. 12 units. $17 double; $20 double deluxe. MC, V. **Amenities:** Restaurant; bar; Internet. *In room:* A/C, TV, fridge, minibar.

The Last Home Guesthouse   This long-running budget guesthouse is very much a family affair. It is basic but clean, and the TV has all the channels you might need. The downstairs restaurant is very good, and there is often a peppering of frugal-minded expats chowing down, content in the knowledge that their wallets remain almost entirely intact. Many of the rooms face the corridor, so there is a shortage of light. For the very low price, however, it remains a viable option.

No. 21 St. 172. ✆ **012/831-702.** 13 units. $7 single fan cold water; $15 double A/C; $20 double A/C daylight facing. **Amenities:** Restaurant; bar. *In room:* A/C, TV, fridge.

BOEUNG KENG KANG
Moderate

Amber Villa This spacious and well-laid-out hotel offers large, light rooms with cool tiled floors. They have all the facilities you might need including Wi-Fi, in-room safe, and free breakfast. There is a restaurant attached. Some of the rooms are a little small, but manage not to be claustrophobic on account of the intelligent design.

No. 1A St. 57. ✆ **023/216-303.** www.amber-kh.com. 7 units. $35 double 1 occupant; $45 double 2 occupants. MC, V. **Amenities:** Restaurant; bar; Internet. *In room:* A/C, TV, fridge, minibar.

Anise Hotel This excellent and really quite funky little place has tastefully decorated rooms and is situated on a pleasant and quiet street. The staff is helpful in an understated way and the atmosphere is warm and welcoming. It has an attached restaurant serving a mixture of Khmer and Western dishes. It is also well set up for business travelers incorporating all the facilities they might need.

No. 2c St. 278. ✆ **023/222-522.** Fax 023/222-533. www.anisehotel.com.kh. 18 units. $35 double 1 occupant; $45 double 2 occupants. MC, V. **Amenities:** Restaurant; bar; Internet. *In room:* A/C, TV, fridge, minibar.

Frangipani Villa (90s) ★★ There are two Frangipani Villa hotels and both are conceived along the same lines. They are named according to the decade in which the original houses were built. As you can imagine, the Frangipani Villas 90s is better than the Frangipani Villas 60s, though both are very good options. The Frangipani Villa 90s has leafy grounds on a surprisingly quiet and scenic street, conveniently close to Monivong Boulevard. They have gone for a boutique style, but with brushed concrete rather than the usual dark-wood and silk route. The garden restaurant is a pleasant haven from the bustle of the city. The rooms in both hotels are more the size of minisuites, with a divided living area separate from the bedroom. The actual suites are larger versions of the same. Staff are hired through an NGO helping street kids (*"Pour un Sourire d'Enfant,"* translating as "For a child's smile") and it seems to be a policy that works on business lines as well as ethical lines since they are absolutely delightful.

No. 20R St. 252. ✆ **023/212-100.** www.frangipanihotel.com. 15 units. $40 double; $60 suite. MC, V. **Amenities:** Restaurant; bar; Internet. *In room:* A/C, TV, fridge, minibar.

Goldie Boutique Guesthouse This is a new Thai-owned boutique guesthouse. It is stylishly decorated with all amenities. Some rooms have a balcony and those on the upper floors are particularly good, with decent views of the southern part of the city. The rooms have picture windows, flooding them with light. They have gone for boutique styling and carried it off with some aplomb. They have, however, neglected the floors in the course of the makeover—they are incongruously covered in '70s-style linoleum. This blemish actually adds a bit of character and is a cute imperfection. There is also an attached spa and massage facility.

No. 6 B-C-D St. 57. ✆ **09/998-6222.** www.goldieguesthouse.com. 15 units. $20 single; $25 junior suite balcony; $30 double. No credit cards. **Amenities:** Restaurant; bar; Internet. *In room:* A/C, TV, fridge, minibar.

Hotel Scandinavia ★   This relaxed offering is firmly aimed at the boutique market but does not take the aesthetic to extremes. The rooms are large, though the ones on the ground floor are a little dark. The decor is simple but tasteful. It has a small swimming pool with pleasant surroundings. The staff is relaxed but helpful. If you pay with a credit card they add a 3% charge.

No. 4 St. 282. ☏ **092/791-449.** www.hotel-scandinavia-cambodia.com.16 units. $42 single; $53 double; $66 double royal lower; $77 double royal upper. MC, V. **Amenities:** Restaurant; bar; Internet; outdoor pool. *In room:* A/C, TV, fridge, minibar.

Villa Lanka Hotel ★★★   A leafy hideaway, the Villa Lanka has a rustic style that really works, especially considering it is right in the heart of the city. Warm ocher floor tiles, draped muslin, and dark wood give it a feel that is half Mediterranean and half old Indochina. It has a minimal but traditional interior, combined with an abundance of light. This successful formula is topped off by a swimming pool large enough to swim laps. It is also a pleasant environment for a cup of tea or cocktail, whether day or evening. The restaurant at the Villa Lanka is excellent, with a chef who is decidedly French.

No. 14 St. 282. ☏ **023/726-771.** www.villalangka.com. 27 units. $44 single; $66 double; $88 deluxe; $121 suite. MC, V. **Amenities:** Restaurant; bar; Internet; pool; room service. *In room:* A/C, TV, fridge, minibar.

Inexpensive

Golden Gate Hotel   For a rock-bottom price, you get rooms that are basic but clean and quite livable. The Golden Gate also offers deluxe rooms that are larger but just as plain. This is a popular spot for long-staying expat business visitors and NGO folks, and the suites, with kitchenette and small living room, are like one-room apartments. Rooms are done in either tile or office carpet and have mismatched but tidy cloth and rattan furniture. The best choice is a deluxe room on a higher floor (with view). Be sure to ask to see the room first, as they really vary.

No. 9 St. 278, Sangkat (just south of the Independence Monument). ☏ **023/427-618.** Fax 023/721-005. www.goldengatehotels.com. $20 standard single; $28 standard double; $35 deluxe; $45 suite (monthly rates available). MC, V. **Amenities:** Restaurant; room service; Wi-Fi. *In room:* A/C, TV, fridge, Internet (deluxe and suite only), minibar.

Goldiana ★   A labyrinthine complex, the result of many construction phases, the Goldiana is one of the best budget choices in the Cambodian capital. It is also another top choice for NGO workers and those working in diplomatic circles. The hotel is just south of the Victory Monument and a short ride from the main sites. It's low-luxe but squeaky-clean. Rooms are very large and have either carpet or wood flooring. The hotel's maintenance standard, unlike similar hotels in town, is meticulous. Although that new-car smell is long gone, it's low on the mildew and musty odors of similar standards in town. Bathrooms are smallish but comfortable, with a tub/shower combo and granite tile. The third-floor pool is a real bonus in this category. The lobby is a designer muddle of heavy curtains, large pottery with fake flowers, mirrors, and bright-colored carved wood, but there's a certain appeal to it all once it becomes familiar. The staff is kind and helpful and is used to the questions and concerns of long-staying patrons, tourists, and business clients. A stay of any length will feel like you're at home.

No. 10–12 St. 282, Sangkat Boeng Keng Kang 1. ☏ **023/219-558.** Fax 023/219-490. www.goldiana.com. 148 units. $48 double; $68–$98 suite. MC, V. **Amenities:** Restaurant; gym; Internet; outdoor pool (rooftop); room service. *In room:* A/C, TV, fridge, hair dryer, Internet, minibar.

OTHER NEIGHBORHOODS

Expensive

Hotel InterContinental Phnom Penh ★   The InterContinental is the place for business travelers. This luxury behemoth has every amenity and every in-room convenience—from wireless and in-room Internet to fine fitness, health, and beauty services. The downside is the location; the self-contained hotel is a long way from the city's action in a fairly dreary part of town. Rooms are done in tidy carpet, dark-wood furnishings, patterned couches, striped raw silk curtains that match the spreads on the king-size beds, and marble detailing in the entryways. Everything is large and luxe and beds are fluffy and comfortable. Well-appointed bathrooms have separate showers and tubs with Art Deco faucets. Oak desks and floor-to-ceiling windows give guests that "power broker" feel (even if you're just a small fish). The large outdoor pool has an Angkor Wat water-park theme to it; there are stone carving decorations, and a red stone fountain of three elephant heads is the centerpiece. There is, however, an elegant water-level bar, and the fitness center is the best in town.

296 Blvd. Mao Tse Toung. ✆ **023/424-888.** Fax 023/424-885. www.ichotelsgroup.com. 346 units. $150–$190 double; $300 Executive/Regency suite; $3,000 Regency/Royal suite. AE, MC, V. **Amenities:** 2 restaurants; bar; 2 snack bars; babysitting; children's playroom; concierge; great fitness center; Internet; outdoor pool; room service; sauna; spa. *In room:* A/C, TV, fridge, minibar, Wi-Fi.

Juliana Hotel   The Juliana is a good distance from the center of town, near the Olympic Stadium. It is popular with group tours. Rooms are situated around a luxurious central pool shaded by palms and with a terrace and lounge chairs: a bright spot in an otherwise dull landscape. The hotel is Thai-owned and managed and popular with regional businessmen. Standard rooms aren't especially attractive and have aging red carpet and the nicks and scrapes of heavy use. That said, superior and deluxe rooms are large and well appointed in tidy carpet and light wood trim. Regal headboards top large beds, and there are nice rattan furnishings throughout. Be sure to request a nonsmoking room and check it out before checking in. Billing as a "city resort" kind of comes up short, but the Continental restaurant is inviting and the pool is a standout, even if rooms don't quite pass muster.

16 Juliana 152 Rd., Sangkat Vealvong. ✆ **023/880-530** or 885-750 www.julianacambodia.com. 82 units. $60–$70 double; $200 suite. AE, MC, V. **Amenities:** 2 restaurants; lobby bar; babysitting; small health club; Internet; outdoor pool; room service. *In room:* A/C, TV, fridge, minibar.

Moderate

Town View Hotel (Value)   There are two Town View hotels very close to each other and they are both orientated very efficiently to the business traveler. Sparkling, clinical, and bright, they are actually a little antiseptic in a city that is anything but. The rooms are large and airy with TVs and every convenience you might need. The staff is also very helpful. They have meeting rooms, a business center, and a conference hall, and the location is convenient both for the airport and the offices around Monivong Boulevard. For Phnom Penh, the Town View amounts to a high-rise and the views from the upper floors give a good view of the city and its astonishing pace of development. The place is lacking in atmosphere, but its efficiency makes it a fantastic deal.

No. 53 St. 113. ✆ **023/991-139.** Fax 023/991-139. www.townviewhotel.com. 56 units. $19 double with bathtub; $17 double with shower. MC, V. **Amenities:** Restaurant; bar; Internet; meeting rooms; room service. *In room:* A/C, TV, fridge, minibar.

Capitol Guesthouse   The Capitol is a Phnom Penh institution as a guesthouse, restaurant, and travel agent. The Capitol has built its considerable budget empire largely on the consistent delivery of sound travel advice founded on a very crisp basis of Chinese business know-how and just simple hard work. There are absolutely no frills at the Capitol but it remains a solid value. The walls are plain white, the tiles are scrubbed, and it feels a bit like a sanatorium for the insane (which may suit some of the guests). It remains a place with some history, surviving the turbulent years and delivering consistently. For travel information, it still remains unsurpassed all these years on.

No. 14AE0 St. 182. ✆ **023/217-627.** Fax 023/214-104. www.capitolkh.com. 60 units. $6 double fan bathroom cold water; $12 double A/C. No credit cards. **Amenities:** Restaurant; bar. *In room:* A/C, TV, fridge.

3 WHERE TO DINE

Between remnants of French colonialism and the more recent influx of humanitarian-aid workers, international cuisine abounds in the Cambodian capital. Along with Vientiane, it is one of the best cities for dining in all of Southeast Asia. Some restaurants themselves are actually NGO (nongovernment organization) projects designed to raise money for local causes or provide training. Ask Khmers where to eat and you'll certainly be pointed to any of the street-side stalls or storefront Chinese noodle shops south of the Central Market, but good eats can also be had from one of many options along Sisowath Quay or among the alleys of the town center. There are simply hundreds of restaurants in Phnom Penh of all cuisine types. The riverfront, from the Royal Place to the Siem Reap boat pier, is one long strip of eateries. Around the residential area of Boeng Keng Kang south of Sihanouk Boulevard and centered around 51 Street are a number of restaurants set in quiet streets, with the long-running **Khmer Surin** really standing out. For a true local Khmer experience, cross the Cambodian-Japanese Friendship bridge on the Tonle Sap River in the north end of town and follow the main road a few short clicks to the town of **Prek Leap.** The large riverside restaurants here are always crowded with locals on weekends. They are usually in big groups of family and friends and the atmosphere of celebration is palpable. There are karaoke, bands, and even variety shows using the universal language of slapstick. It's a good chance to eat, talk, and laugh with locals. All the restaurants serve similar good Khmer and Chinese fare. Go by tuk-tuk and pick the most crowded place; the more, the merrier.

RIVERFRONT TO MONIVONG
Expensive

Foreign Correspondents Club (FCC) ⟨Overrated⟩ CONTINENTAL   This restaurant, in truth, doesn't have much to do with the actual FCC—those ties were severed a decade ago. Ten years ago, this place was often deservedly listed as one of the best restaurants in Asia. The decline in quality since then has been shocking—the food is uninspired Western and very overpriced. The pizza is particularly bland (no tomato sauce and bad cheese), although snacks like nachos and enchiladas are acceptable. It is still worth dropping by for a drink at happy hour to enjoy the ambience and the views, which are wonderful especially during monsoon season when you can see the storms sweeping up the river. Where the FCC does still excel is in its role as an exhibition space and gallery. There are regular exhibitions here both photographic and artistic, and they also have a permanent collection. It is an astonishingly good body of work with amazing photos by such celebrated photographers as Al Rockoff and Roland Neveu, who have chronicled this country over many decades in both war and peace.

363 Sisowath Quay. ✆ **023/724-014.** Main courses $4–$12. MC, V. Daily 7am–midnight.

La Résidence ★★ FRENCH   If you splurge on only one meal in Phnom Penh, do it here. Housed in a former imperial mansion, this is fine dining at its best. Waitstaff is discreet and attentive, the setting is romantic without being stuffy, and the food is fantastic. Book ahead to get one of the tables by the garden window. The ambience is nicer here than at rival 112 Restaurant. The chef previously worked in two- and three-Michelin star restaurants. The menu consists of classic and modern French food. Anything from the foie gras list is rich and decadent, to the stuffed ravioli with duck liver in Parmesan cream sauce, a dish worthy of the zillion-calorie intake. A three-course dinner will likely set you back at least $50; if money is tight, opt for a more frugal three-course set lunch menu.

No. 22–24 St. 214. ✆ **023/224-582.** Main courses $8.50–$80 (average is about $25). AE, MC, V. Mon–Fri 11:30am–2pm and 6:30–10pm. Dinner only Sat–Sun.

112 Restaurant ★ FRENCH   You found it—the new French restaurant highly favored by the expats in this area of town. The decor is a bit busy, with brown-and-white embroidered table settings and chairs, wrought-iron lamps and light covers everywhere, and tall potted trees curving around the arched ceilings. Music is also hit-and-miss—one moment it's Ella Fitzgerald and *My Funny Valentine,* the next moment it's the Carpenters' *Yesterday Once More.* But the food, what really matters, is excellent. They have signature French dishes such as steak tartare, and an impressive salad menu. The green salad with goat cheese on toast and walnuts is crisp and tangy, and a meal unto itself.

No. 1A St. 102 (Colonial Mansions). ✆ **023/990-880.** Main courses $12–$27. AE, MC, V. Daily 11am–2pm and 6-10pm.

Origami ★★ JAPANESE   Sushi in Cambodia? Go figure. There are a number of Japanese restaurants in town, in fact, but Origami serves fine sushi and all manner of good, authentic Japanese that'll have you saying *"Oishi!"* From *tonkatsu* (deep-fried pork over rice) to real Japanese ramen (noodle soup), Ms. Kimura, the genial proprietor, covers all the bases. Essential ingredients are imported from Japan, and everything is priced accordingly. The sushi is the real deal, and the presentation and decor of this little parkside gem could have been lifted straight out of Tokyo. Popular for the many Japanese expats on humanitarian assignment, the restaurant is itself an NGO (nongovernment organization) offering Khmer kids training in Japanese language and culture.

No. 88 Sothearos St. (near the main downtown sites). ✆ **012/968-095.** Main courses $3–$12; set menu $10–$20. V. Mon–Sat 11:30am–2pm and 5:30–9:30pm.

River House ★★ FRENCH/CONTINENTAL   One of many along the riverside, this bar and restaurant stands out by virtue of size and style. A classic corner colonial, with quaint cushioned chairs under canvas umbrellas; there's now an elegant air-conditioned dining room. Classy rattan chairs, two stately bars in wood and glass, and the fine linen and silver presentation are luxe far beyond the price tag. The food is excellent, characterized by fine French specials such as duck prepared as you like, coq au vin, and

Where to Dine in Phnom Penh

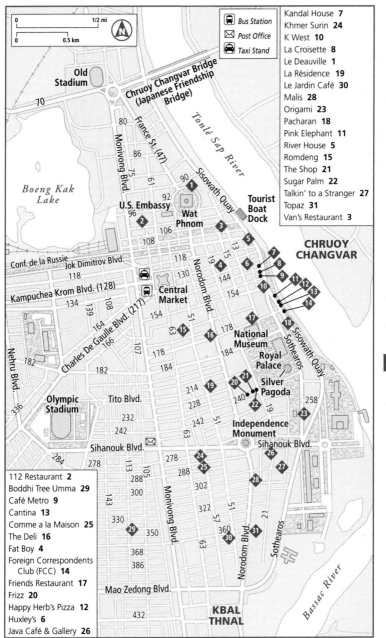

Kandal House **7**
Khmer Surin **24**
K West **10**
La Croisette **8**
Le Deauville **1**
La Résidence **19**
Le Jardin Café **30**
Malis **28**
Origami **23**
Pacharan **18**
Pink Elephant **11**
River House **5**
Romdeng **15**
The Shop **21**
Sugar Palm **22**
Talkin' to a Stranger **27**
Topaz **31**
Van's Restaurant **3**

Bus Station
Post Office
Taxi Stand

Old Stadium
70
80
Chruoy Changvar Bridge (Japanese Friendship Bridge)
France St. (47)
Monivong Blvd.
86
75
61
90
Tonlé Sap River
Sisowath Quay
92
U.S. Embassy
96
Wat Phnom
Tourist Boat Dock
106
108
2
1
3
5
CHRUOY CHANGVAR
Conf. de la Russie
Jok Dimitrov Blvd.
118
118
130
144
154
Norodom Blvd.
13
15
19
4
6
7
8
9
10
11
12
13
14
Kampuchea Krom Blvd. (128)
134
139
108
164
166
107
Charles De Gaulle Blvd. (217)
Central Market
154
51
63
178
15
16
178
184
National Museum
17
18
Sothearos
Sisowath Quay
182
Nehru Blvd.
182
184
Royal Palace
Silver Pagoda
19
20
21
22
23
240
258
19
Olympic Stadium
Tito Blvd.
214
228
232
242
242
51
63
Independence Monument
Sihanouk Blvd.
336
278
284
278
288
113
105
288
288
302
322
Monivong Blvd.
300
143
330
350
368
386
29
Mao Zedong Blvd.
432
Sihanouk Blvd.
24
25
26
27
28
51
57
63
360
30
31
Norodom Blvd.
Sothearos
KBAL THNAL
Bassac River

112 Restaurant **2**
Boddhi Tree Umma **29**
Café Metro **9**
Cantina **13**
Comme a la Maison **25**
The Deli **16**
Fat Boy **4**
Foreign Correspondents Club (FCC) **14**
Friends Restaurant **17**
Frizz **20**
Happy Herb's Pizza **12**
Huxley's **6**
Java Café & Gallery **26**

Boeng Kak Lake
0   1/2 mi
0   0.5 km
N

PHNOM PENH   5   WHERE TO DINE

a popular chateaubriand with morels. The signature dish of Australian beef tenderloin comes highly recommended. Come for a romantic dinner and stay for dancing.

No. 6 St. 110 (corner of Sisowath). ☎ **023/212-302.** Main courses $7–$32. AE, MC, V. Sun–Thurs 10am–11pm; Fri–Sat 10am–1:30am.

Topaz ★★ FRENCH/CONTINENTAL   Good, familiar food and atmosphere that's sophisticated but not stuffy are the hallmarks of Topaz, an 8-year-old French bistro. In air-conditioned comfort, diners choose from informal booth seating near the comfortable bar or at elegant tables with fine linen, silver, and real stemware in a formal dining room unrivaled in town. The menu features great steaks, pasta, and salad. The Caesar salad is noteworthy. Daily lunch sets are popular with the business crowd, and daily specials are contingent on the day's imports of fish or fine steaks. Wine racks line the dining-room walls, with some great choices. Everything here is good.

182Eo Sothearos Blvd. (near the downtown sites). ☎ **023/221-622.** Main courses $10–$35. MC, V. Daily 11am–2pm and 6–11pm.

Van's Restaurant FRENCH   Set in the former Banque de l'Indochine, Van's serves French haute cuisine in truly glorious surroundings. Traditional French fare such as *filet de beouf au poivre* (beefsteak with heavy pepper sauce) or *lapin en gibelotte* (rabbit in a heavy stew with white wine) is unlikely to do wonders for your waistline but is undoubtedly part of the overall experience of this splendid place. Although the glories of the food do not quite match the glory of the surroundings, Van's has only been open a year and this may be the result of growing pains. The main dining room is a series of beautifully laid out tables, the tablecloths and napkins gleaming white, the wineglasses sparkling. It is all very grand and very, very French. There is a wraparound balcony on the corner, where you can dine closer to the buzz of the city below. Van's also offers private function rooms for groups. Upstairs is a small cocktail area dubbed "Le Boudoir" with comfortable bright red cushioned seating and a spacious tiled balcony.

No. 5 St. 102. ☎ **023/722-067.** www.vans-restaurant.com. Main courses $7–$13. AE, MC, V. Daily 11am–2:30pm and 5:30–11:30pm.

Moderate

Café Metro ★ ASIAN/INTERNATIONAL   This stylish, contemporary restaurant serves excellent food in a corner-side location overlooking the river. The menu of mostly seafood and Australian beef is excellent. They've got a nice selection of "small plates" for those who want lighter portions. On the large plate menu, the grilled tenderloin served with a side of fries will knock out any hunger pangs. There's free Wi-Fi access and an extensive martini menu to boot.

No. 271 St. 148 (on the corner of Sisowath Quay). ☎ **023/222-275.** Main courses $8–$17. MC, V. Daily 7am–1am.

Cantina ★★★ MEXICAN   There are many restaurants and cafes along the riverfront, but Cantina stands out for the quality of both the food and the conversation. In the early days of tourism development, many places copied the pizza parlor formula of Happy Herb's—Phnom Penh's first and most original pizza joint. Cantina (next door to Happy Herb's) completely shattered the mold offering tacos, tostadas, and burritos using plenty of fresh ingredients and genuine masa flour imported from Mexico. The originator of this delightfully convivial watering hole is Santa Barbara native Hurley Scroggins.

Phnom Penh's Much-Loved Pachyderm

If you spend any time on the riverfront in Phnom Penh you will at some point catch site of Sambo, Phnom Penh's beloved and only resident elephant. As a baby, Sambo survived a Khmer Rouge attack at the farm of her owner, Sin Son. All four of Sambo's relatives were murdered with machetes. Sambo barely escaped, but in the end managed to flee into the jungle nursing her wounds. No one is sure what happened after that, but she turned up in the Cardamom Mountains and was taken in by a Khmer Rouge cadre. Amazingly (and some say mystically) Sambo was eventually reunited with her handler, who made it his life's purpose to track down the one remaining elephant from his family's farm. Sin Son and his "sister," Sambo, arrived in the capital in 1980. Sambo has been a fixture in Phnom Penh ever since, loved by Khmers and foreigners alike, a gentle reminder of grace and survival. She is also a symbol of so much that is lost in a country that historically revered these amazing animals. Since the country's first UN-organized elections in 1993, civil society groups and political groups have made Sambo the amiable focal point of their public demonstrations. She has marched to protest against global child labor, to raise awareness about UN's Millennium Development Goals, and to promote children's vaccinations. There was total outrage in Phnom Penh in 2009 when a local restaurant (which shall remain unnamed) actually adorned her with crass commercial advertising. The fury was short-lived when the desecration was swiftly removed. Many restaurants along the riverfront serve Sambo a meal when required. These days she seems to have a real fondness for the food at La Croisette.

He is also an amiable source of useful information and perspective on Cambodian politics and history. In addition to the truly superb Mexican food, the cocktails are legendary. Cantina serves some of the best margaritas in Southeast Asia. While enjoying one, check out the photos on the walls—there's stunningly good work by great photographers such as Al Rockoff, Roland Neveu, and Tim Page.

347 Sisowath Quay. ℭ **023/222-502.** www.cantinacambodia.com. Main courses $4.25–$6.50. Fri–Sun 3–11pm.

Frizz ★★★ KHMER   Frizz is a modest and bright little place on 240 Street in the heart of the boutique shopping district. Plenty of clean, white, soft furnishings; rattan furniture; and ocher floor tiles create an atmosphere that is very relaxing in this dusty, crowded city. The specialties are Khmer and they also run a small cooking school that garners respect from chefs both international and local (p. 86). They also serve Western food, delicious baguette sandwiches, and healthy breakfasts. Frizz is a place of maximum quality without pretension in either presentation or price. Some say that Frizz makes the best amok in Phnom Penh, and they may be right. Others would say that Frizz makes the best amok in Cambodia. This would be pushing it, but it is fair to say that it is a contender.

No. 67 St. 240. ℭ **012/524-801.** www.frizz-restaurant.com. Main courses $3.50–$5. No credit cards. Daily 10am–10pm.

Happy Herb's Pizza ★ WESTERN/INTERNATIONAL   The first of the famous "Happy" Phnom Penh pizza joints has a great location overlooking the river. It serves Khmer food, salads, pasta, and, of course, pizza. "Happy" Pizza is sprinkled with marijuana, just so you know. Happy Herb's has been much copied but never bettered. The feta salad is superb and the regular pizza, with absolutely no marijuana, remains the best in Phnom Penh by a long shot.

No. 345 Sisowath Quay. ✆ **012/921-915.** Main courses $3.50–$5.50. No credit cards. Daily 11am–midnight.

Huxley's INTERNATIONAL   Huxley's may not actually be a brave new world, but it certainly is a leap in the right direction. It is a surprisingly authentic English pub with long stretched hardwood stairs, complemented by a waterfall, wood paneling, and smatterings of British knickknacks. Although a few Cambodian-fare items are sprinkled in, Huxley's menu is distinctly English, offering daily specials such as scotch egg (an English delicacy, despite its name, consisting of a hard-boiled egg wrapped in pork sausage meat, breaded, and lightly fried), bangers and mash, and steak and stout pie. Their cottage pie is also excellent although the signature dish is, not surprisingly, fish and chips. On Sundays, Huxley's serves a traditional English roast dinner of either pork or beef. The downstairs bar is a little small and cramped but the upstairs area sports rattan chairs, balconies, and sports on big-screen TVs. They do not accept credit cards but there is an ATM in the pub.

No. 30–32 corner of sts. 136 and 5. ✆ **023/986-602.** Main courses $5–$10. No credit cards. Daily 11am–1am.

K West ★★ WESTERN/KHMER   In the lobby of the Amanjaya Hotel, one of Phnom Penh's coolest boutique properties (p. 63), is this chic little international bar and bistro. It is French owned and managed, and the menu covers all the bases. They feature an array of savory salads. Fine pastas are made fresh and cooked to order, and there are seafood specials and a host of good Khmer dishes, as well as snacks and sides. Dessert includes a lime-and-lemon torte, banana splits, and a dish called "The Colonel" with lemon sherbet and vodka. The air-conditioned double-height interior has cozy wooden booths for privacy and is flanked by a long wooden bar area, popular among expats. The place is a busy catwalk in the evening.

No. 1 St. 154, Sisowath Quay, Phnom Penh. ✆ **023/214-747.** Main courses $5–$30. MC, V. Daily 6:30am–midnight.

Kandal House ★★★ WESTERN/KHMER   This small eatery exudes understated elegance. The food ranges from British fish and chips to Italian pasta and American burgers. Where it really excels, however, is in the quality of its excellent traditional Khmer dishes. The amok here comes highly recommended. They also have a good handle on Thai food and do a good job with both green curry and yellow curry. A friendly atmosphere prevails, making this a popular gathering place, especially for breakfast and lunch. You can also call for free delivery if you want to spend a night in.

239BEo Sisowath Quay. ✆ **016/800-111.** Main courses $4.50. MC, V. Daily 9am–11pm.

La Croisette ★ WESTERN   This slick, air-conditioned haven offers an eclectic menu with a French/Khmer slant, though they also branch out into Italian and more exotic fare. Try the Persian fried shrimp with ginger. The fresh pumpkin soup is also very good, and the ham and cheese croissant is food for the gods. It is quite expensive and you're certainly paying a little more for its excellent riverside location, though the prices are not completely punitive. They also have free Wi-Fi at decent speeds and during working hours you will see many people sunk in labor.

241 Sisowath Quay. ✆ **023/220-554.** Main courses $6.50. MC, V. Daily 7am–1am.

Le Deauville ★ FRENCH   This open-air French bar and brasserie is a good, mellow choice. On the north end of the Wat Phnom roundabout, Le Deauville serves fine, affordable French and Khmer dishes. The atmosphere is unpretentious and cozy, with a large open bar at its center, and tables scattered in the street-side courtyard that is shielded from the traffic by a wall of potted greenery. Daily lunch set menus give you a choice of salad and entree, and you can choose from local specialties like filet of Mekong fish with lime or fine medallion *de boeuf.* The restaurant serves good pizzas and spaghetti and has a wine list that fits any taste and budget. Be sure to ask about Le Deauville II, the large dining barge that makes regular city cruises or can be chartered; aboard the ship, you can enjoy similar fine French cuisine as in this casual bistro. Le Deauville is a popular spot for a relaxed drink in the evening.

St. 94 (just north of Wat Phnom). ✆ **012/843-204.** Main courses $4.50–$12. V. Daily 11am–10pm.

Pacharan ★ SPANISH   This is a hip place serving reliable tapas. They've got all the favorites: patatas bravas, cured meats, Spanish tortillas—the list goes on. In keeping with tapas spirit, portions are small and you're meant to order many different plates to share among friends. The calamari is excellent, but I advise you to skip the lackluster chicken croquettes. They also have a fine selection of Spanish wines.

389 Sisowath Quay. ✆ **023/224-394.** Tapas $2–$10. MC, V. Daily 11am–11pm.

Pink Elephant ★ WESTERN/THAI/KHMER   Founded by an amiable and soft-spoken Yorkshire man named Dave in the mid-'90s, the Pink Elephant remains a place to sample English cooking at its stodgy best. The original owner is, sadly, no longer with us, but the present Khmer management does a great job of keeping alive the flame in the shape of pies, chips, baked beans, and tea. They also serve excellent pizzas and Thai food. The green curry is very good indeed. Their Khmer food is very much up to speed. The lok lak stands out.

343 Sisowath Quay. No phone. Main courses $4.50. Daily 9am–midnight.

Romdeng ★★ KHMER   Romdeng serves tasty Khmer food in an atmospheric French colonial house. Run by the same NGO as Friends Restaurant (see below), the menu is similar, but the decor is a bit cozier with small, separate dining areas, and alfresco seating set around a small outdoor pool and garden. Try the fish and pumpkin curry in coconut sauce—a delicious savory dish that packs just the right amount of spice and is big enough for two. If you're feeling game, they also serve deep-fried tarantulas (yes, as in the spider) with lime sauce.

No. 74 St. 174. ✆ **092/219-565.** www.mithsamlanh.org. Main courses $4.50–$6.25. V. Daily 11am–10pm.

Inexpensive
Friends (Mith Samlanh) Restaurant ★★ KHMER/INTERNATIONAL   Not to be missed is this friendly little gem, an NGO (nongovernment organization) project where Khmer street kids are given shelter and taught useful skills for their reintegration into society. It's a unique opportunity to meet friendly mentors and young folks who've found a new lease on life. The food is great, too, an ever-changing tapas menu of local and international favorites like spring rolls, fried rice, good salads, and a host of desserts. This is a great spot to cool off and have a light bite while touring the city center (it's right

across from the "must-see" National Museum). The place is a cozy open-air colonial in a courtyard, done up in primary-color murals of the kids' drawings. The name of the restaurant means "good friends," and you might meet some here as you find yourself giving English lessons, laughing, and smiling with these young survivors.

No. 215 St. 13 (across from the entrance to the National Museum). © **023/426-748.** www.mithsamlanh. org. Main courses $2.50–$4.75. V. Daily 11am–9pm.

BOEUNG KENG KANG
Expensive

Malis ★★ KHMER   Malis is Phnom Penh's premier gourmet Cambodian dining experience at a price. Contemporary and traditional Khmer cuisine is artfully prepared in the kitchen of the hugely renowned Cambodian chef, Luu Meng. The surroundings are stylish and elegant, with Angkorian-inspired pools that mosquitoes love as much as the ancient god-kings loved the Bayon. The presentation of the dishes is superb. The Battambang steak in Cambodian spices and the roast chicken are their signature dishes (the former comes in at a hefty $68, which amounts to about 3 months' wages for a qualified schoolteacher in Battambang itself). Try one of the more modest but interesting dishes such as *mak mie,* crispy fried noodles topped with stir-fried mince pork and fresh herbs with chili sauce.

136 Norodom Blvd. (near Independence Monument to the south). © **023/221-022.** Fax 023/221-121. www.malis-restaurant.com. Main courses $6.50–$68. AE, MC, V. Daily 7am–11pm.

Moderate

Comme a la Maison WESTERN   Part restaurant, part patisserie, and part cafe, Comme a la Maison is set on a giant leafy veranda. At the back is the bakery and delicatessen serving takeout fresh baguettes, quiche, and pastries. The atmosphere is very relaxing with classical arias wafting across the garden. It is best for light lunches. The chèvre chaud salad with croutons, walnut, apple, and pesto comes highly recommended, but there are many other tasty options. Although Comme a la Maison is certainly very Gallic, the light fare here is in contrast to many of the more traditional French restaurants in town with their heavy saturated sauces. Follow up with fresh yogurt, fruit, and good desserts. The quiet courtyard area is at the top of the list for escaping the chaos of busy Phnom Penh.

13 St. © **023/360-801.** www.commealamaison-delicatessen.com. Main courses $4–$8. Daily 6am–10:30pm.

Khmer Surin ★★★ KHMER/THAI   This long-running Khmer and Thai restaurant simply gets better and better. Set in a large Khmer traditional–style building on leafy 57 Street, the restaurant has beautifully rustic decor featuring dark wood and silk. It has recently doubled in size since they built a new annex. If you want a more rural style of dining head upstairs, where floor cushions are arranged around low tables with balcony views of the street below. It serves a fantastic range of regional dishes, with separate Thai and Khmer menus (Surin is an Isan province of Thailand bordering Cambodia to the north that is almost entirely ethnic Khmer). The dishes range from the simple Thai *rad na gai* (large flat noodles with chicken in gravy) to Khmer favorites such as *dtrey dom rai* (whole fish fried with tamarind sauce). Try the *dtrey chhlounh,* or deep-fried peacock eel direct from the Tonle Sap. The crowning glory of the Khmer Surin is the astonishingly reasonable prices it charges for these wonderful offerings. It remains one of the best places in central Phnom Penh to sample Khmer cuisine.

No. 9 St. 57. © **023/993-163.** Main courses $3.50–$6. No credit cards. Daily 10am–10pm.

Le Jardin Café ★ WESTERN   As its name in French suggests, the Jardin Café is as much garden as it is cafe. It is set up specifically with families in mind. In a city as wild and hectic as Phnom Penh where you have to keep a close eye on the little ones at all times, it serves as a refuge where the children can run riot in the sand pit or charge about waving something plastic with wheels on it from the large collection of toys on offer. You, meanwhile, can order herbal tea or a glass of chilled chardonnay while gently perusing the menu listing a fine selection of tapas and barbecue. After dark the place takes on an atmosphere of rural calm bathed in gentle, leafy lighting. The food is light. The "Tartine de Terrine de Chèvre a la Sicillienne" is particularly delicious. Given the makeup of its daytime clientele it is no surprise that Le Jardin Café serves excellent homemade ice cream.

No. 16 St. 360. ✆ 011/723-399. Main courses $3.50–$5. Daily 8am–10pm.

Talkin' to a Stranger ★★ WESTERN/KHMER   This garden bar and restaurant is quite hard to find but well worth the effort when you arrive. It is deservedly a very popular after-work meeting venue for many expats. The Australian management is delightful and the place is now a Phnom Penh institution. The relaxed garden setting is often the scene of musical and art events. They serve excellent food, with a menu that changes often. The food is always superb, generally offering a fusion of gourmet European and traditional Khmer. You might arrive here a stranger, but the convivial nature of the surroundings and the other people around you mean that you won't remain a stranger for very long. Talkin' is closed on weekends.

No. 21b St. 294. **012/798-530.** Main courses $6. No credit cards. Mon–Fri 5pm–midnight.

OTHER NEIGHBORHOODS
Inexpensive
Boddhi Tree Umma ★ ASIAN/KHMER   Include lunch here with a trip to nearby Tuol Sleng Museum (see "Phnom Penh Attractions," below), a sight that doesn't inspire an appetite, really, but the Boddhi Tree is a peaceful oasis and not a bad spot to collect your thoughts after visiting vestiges of Cambodia's late troubles. Named for the tree under which the Buddha "saw the light," this verdant little garden courtyard and roughhewn guesthouse has comfy balcony and courtyard seating and seems to serve up as much calm as the coffee, tea, and light fare that make it so popular. There are daily specials and often visiting chefs. All the curries are good, and they have great baguette sandwiches. Established in 1997 as a way to drum up funds and support to help Khmer kids and families in challenging circumstances, the folks here welcome your suggestions and invite visitors to get involved in their important work.

No. 50 St. 113, Beong Keng Kong (across from Tuol Sleng Museum). ✆ **023/211-397.** www.boddhitree. com. Main courses $2–$4. No credit cards. Daily 7am–9pm.

SNACKS & CAFES
Java Café and Gallery, 56 Sihanouk Blvd. (✆ **023/987-420**), is a good spot in town to relax and escape the midday heat. Just south of the main sights (near the Independence Monument), this popular second-story oasis has casual seating on a large balcony and an open gallery interior. They serve real coffee, cappuccino, good cakes, and other baked goods; they sometimes feature live music in the evening. It's open daily from 7am to 10pm.

    Fat Boy at No. 124 St. 130 (✆ **012/704-500**) is a submarine sandwich shop that is making waves. It serves up the best American-style subs in town, generously made-to-order on fresh baked just-like-home breads and rolls. Good choices include the Italian sub and imported roast beef sub, and all subs come with a big selection of sauces and add-ons. The Fat Boy sub packing 2 pounds of meat is for real aficionados of the sub at its finest and indeed its largest.

The Deli at No. 13 St. 178 (© **012/851-234**) is a favorite among the expats in town for a good sandwich and excellent pastries.

The Shop ★★ is a stylish cafe on popular Street 240 (© **023/986-964**) and now has a new location on the north end of Sisowath Quay. Come here for baked goods (try the raspberry chocolate tart), filling panini, fresh soups, tea, and coffee in a friendly and comfortable storefront at each location. There are neat details like butcher-block tables and fresh flowers, and they can arrange picnic lunches for day trips from Phnom Penh. Chocoholics *must* visit **Chocolate by The Shop** ★ (No. 35 St. 240; © **023/998-638**) next door, which serves fantastic truffles and bonbons all for reasonable prices. The fiery chocolate sprinkled with pepper from Kampot makes a great gift.

Sugar Palm (No. 19 St. 240; © **023/220-956**) serves good Khmer dishes at streetside or from their upstairs balcony. It's a gallery that features good local crafts and a good place to relax and enjoy real Khmer atmosphere and good treats.

---

4 PHNOM PENH ATTRACTIONS

Phnom Penh is fairly compact and most sights are not far from the central riverfront area. You can walk, but be prepared for a fairly nerve-racking time dealing with the traffic. Alternatively, you can hire a tuk-tuk or *motodup* for the day. The **Russian market** is in the south of town away from the center. **Tuol Sleng** and the **Killing Fields** can be visited together, and arrangements can be made at any hotel lobby. For information on companies that run tours, see p. 86.

Central Market   This Art Deco (called Psar Thmei in Khmer) behemoth, built in 1937, is a city landmark and, on any given day, a veritable anthill of activity. The building is a towering cruciform rotunda with four wings. The eastern entrance is the best spot to find T-shirts, hats, and all manner of trinkets and souvenirs, as well as photocopied bootlegs of popular novels and books on Cambodia. Goldsmiths and watch-repair and -sales counters predominate in the main rotunda, and you can find some good deals. Spend some time wandering the nooks and crannies, though, and you're sure to come across something that strikes your fancy, whether that's a chaotic hardware shop, a cobbler hard at work with an awl, or just the cacophony and carnival-barker shouts of salesmen and haggling shoppers. Be sure to bargain for any purchase. The Russian Market or Psar Toul Tom Poung (p. 87) is actually far better for shopping, unless you are after luxury goods, in which case stick with Psar Thmei.
Btw. sts. 126 and 136 in the town center. Daily 5am–5pm.

Independence Monument   Built in the late 1950s to commemorate Cambodia's independence from the French on November 9, 1953, this towering obelisk is crowned with Khmer Nagas and was designed to deliberately echo Angkorian architecture. The area is at its most majestic when all lit up at night.
South of the town center at the intersection of Norodom and Sihanouk.

The Killing Fields & Choeung Ek Memorial ★★   This was originally a Chinese cemetery before becoming an execution ground for the Khmer Rouge during their maniacal reign under Pol Pot from 1975 to 1979. Choeung Ek is one of many mass

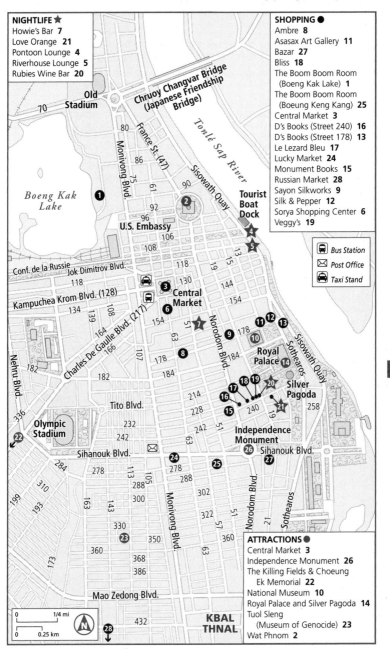

NIGHTLIFE ★
Howie's Bar **7**
Love Orange **21**
Pontoon Lounge **4**
Riverhouse Lounge **5**
Rubies Wine Bar **20**

SHOPPING ●
Ambre **8**
Asasax Art Gallery **11**
Bazar **27**
Bliss **18**
The Boom Boom Room
(Boeng Kak Lake) **1**
The Boom Boom Room
(Boeung Keng Kang) **25**
Central Market **3**
D's Books (Street 240) **16**
D's Books (Street 178) **13**
Le Lezard Bleu **17**
Lucky Market **24**
Monument Books **15**
Russian Market **28**
Sayon Silkworks **9**
Silk & Pepper **12**
Sorya Shopping Center **6**
Veggy's **19**

🚌 Bus Station
✉ Post Office
🚕 Taxi Stand

Old Stadium
70
80
86
75
61
90
92
96

Chruoy Changvar Bridge
(Japanese Friendship Bridge)

France St. (47)
Monivong Blvd.

Boeng Kak Lake

Tonle Sap River

Tourist Boat Dock

U.S. Embassy

Sisowath Quay

Conf. de la Russie
Jok Dimitrov Blvd.
Kampuchea Krom Blvd. (128)
118
118
134
139
108
164
166
107
182

Charles De Gaulle Blvd. (217)

Nehru Blvd.

106
108
118
130
144
154
154
51
178
184
182
178
184

13
15
19

Central Market

Norodom Blvd.

Royal Palace

Sisowath Quay
Sothearos

Silver Pagoda
258
240
19
214
228
242
63
51

Tito Blvd.

Olympic Stadium
336
284
199
310
193
163
143

Independence Monument

Sihanouk Blvd.
278
232
242

Sihanouk Blvd.

Monivong Blvd.

278
288
300
330
350
368
386
360

288
302
322
360

Norodom Blvd.

51
57
63

Sothearos
21

Mao Zedong Blvd.

0   1/4 mi
0   0.25 km

432

KBAL THNAL

PHNOM PENH

5

PHNOM PENH ATTRACTIONS

ATTRACTIONS ●
Central Market **3**
Independence Monument **26**
The Killing Fields & Choeung
Ek Memorial **22**
National Museum **10**
Royal Palace and Silver Pagoda **14**
Tuol Sleng
(Museum of Genocide) **23**
Wat Phnom **2**

graves all over the country dating from the days of Democratic Kampuchea. This particular site is a collection of innocuous-looking mounds, near a towering monument of cataloged human skulls. The monument is 17 stories high, reminding visitors of April 17, 1975, the day the Khmer Rouge took over Cambodia. As a sign of respect, you take your shoes off before mounting the steps to view the monument up close. Human skulls, arranged by age and gender, are set at eye level, while other bones are placed on higher levels. The Killing Fields are often visited in conjunction with a tour of Tuol Sleng (see below).

15km (9¼ miles) south of Phnom Penh. Arrange a private car or motorbike. Admission $3. Daily 7:30am–5:30pm.

National Museum ★★★   What the British Museum is to the Elgin Marbles of Greece's Parthenon, the National Museum of Phnom Penh, opened in 1920 by King Sisowath, is to the statuary of Angkor Wat. This important storehouse holds artifacts and statuary from all regions of Cambodia and is housed in a beautiful building built in the 1920s. The sad fact is that many pieces didn't make it here—they were plundered and smuggled out of the country. Nevertheless, this grand red-sandstone edifice has a beautiful and informative collection of Khmer pieces displayed around a pretty central courtyard. From the entrance, begin on your left with a room of small prehistoric artifacts. A clockwise loop around the central courtyard walks you through time, from static, stylized pieces of stiff-legged, standing Buddhas, to contra-posed and contorted forms in supplication. There are good accompanying descriptions in English, but this is not a bad place to have a knowledgeable guide (ask in the lobby). The central courtyard features a Shiva lingam and large temple fragments. Near the more significant works, the statue of Jayavarman VII for example, elderly women, looking like museum docents, hand out incense and flowers and instruct visitors to place them on makeshift altars. Don't feel obliged—kind of off-putting to some—but feel free to do so if you wish.

Just north of the Royal Palace at St. 178, and a short walk from the river. Admission $3. Daily 8–5pm.

Royal Palace and Silver Pagoda ★★★   Don't miss this glittery downtown campus, the ostentatious jewel in the crown of Cambodia's monarchy. Built in the late 1860s under the reign of Norodom, the sight is comprised of many elaborate gilded halls, all with steep tile roofs, stupa-shape cupolas, and golden temple nagas denoting prosperity. The grand **Throne Hall** at the center is the coronation site for Khmer kings and the largest gilded cathedral in the country. Don't miss the many royal busts and the gilded umbrella used to shade the king when in procession. The French built a small exhibition hall on the temple grounds, a building that now houses the many gifts given to the monarchy, among them cross-stitch portraits of the royal family and all manner of bric-a-brac. Just inside the door, don't miss an original by Cézanne that has suffered terrible water damage and hangs in a ratty frame like an unwanted diploma: a shame. The balcony of the exhibition hall is the best bird's-eye view of the gilded temples. The facade of the neighboring **Royal Residence** is just as resplendent and is still the home of the now abdicated King Sihanouk and his son and successor.

The **Silver Pagoda** is just south of the palace and entrance is included with the same ticket. The floors of this grand temple are covered with 5,000 blocks of silver weighing more than 6 tons. The temple houses a 17th-century Buddha made of Baccarat crystal, and another made almost entirely of gold and decorated with almost 10,000 diamonds. That's not exactly what the Buddha had in mind perhaps, but it's quite beautiful. The temple courtyard is encircled by a covered walkway with a contiguous mural of Cambodia's history

The Khmer Rouge on Trial

As this book is being researched and written the director of S21, Duch (pro-nounced *Doik*), is on trial in a distant suburb of Phnom Penh under the aus-pices of a UN tribunal. He was discovered purely by chance in 1999 by British photojournalist Nic Dunlop in the wild and western province of Samlot. Duch was working incognito for a Christian NGO and claimed to be "born again." He confessed to his role in the horrors of S21 and has been detained ever since. Duch is the first and the most junior of the accused to go before the court. They include Khieu Samphan, the public face of the Khmer Rouge; Nuon Chea, Pol Pot's brutal henchman and second in command; and Ieng Sary, the slippery foreign minister of the regime, who are also lined up for the dock. So is Ieng Sary's wife, Ieng Thirith, who was minister of social affairs and a key figure in the Khmer Rouge from the early days. This is nearly 4 decades after the perpetra-tion of their murderous activities, and they are very old at this point.

Why has it taken so long and why is it happening now, and why is it just these few up for trial? The Khmer Rouge fought on until 1998. Through the '80s they were supported and funded by a coalition of Western powers, China, and Thailand. If the international community and the UN recognize the horror of what the KR did, legitimate questions of why they were endorsed by the very same powers need to be asked and those questions are awkward. Second, the present regime in Cambodia does not have clean hands. It is true that present prime minister Hun Sen was a Khmer Rouge officer in the '70s, but that is a red herring. He was part of the dissident Eastern Zone and basically a simple sol-dier. What is true however is that in the '90s when the KR started to surrender, faction by faction, many deals were made, including those concerning busi-ness over lucrative natural resources. There are many secrets surrounding the surviving members and few are innocent. To put them on trial could also put their benefactors on trial by proxy. What of the Khmers? Feelings are mixed. Some just see it as pointless and want to move on. Others see no justice since former Khmer Rouge live in their towns and villages and in some cases still terrify them. Others see a little justice as better than no justice at all. As ever in Cambodia, the water remains very muddy indeed.

and mythology. On the southern end of the complex is a small hill covered in vegetation and said to model the sacred Mount Meru; there's a large Buddha footprint and a small temple that provokes very devout practice in Khmer visitors.

Btw. sts. 240 and 184 on Sothearos. The entrance is on the east side facing the river. Admission $6.50. Daily 7:30–11am and 2–5pm.

Tuol Sleng, Museum of Genocide ★★ It is important to visit this profoundly disturbing place if you wish to understand modern Cambodia. It is an experience that brings you close to the darkest depths of mankind's capacity for brutality. The grounds of this former high school are just as they were in 1979 at the end of Cambodia's bloody genocide. During the violent recent history in Cambodia, the two-story compound became one of the most notorious concentration camps, essentially a torture chamber before people were slaughtered in the Killing Fields. It was called S21 by the Khmer Rouge and it was by no means the only facility of this sort in Democratic Kampuchea. S21 was one part of a larger organized killing apparatus. From 1975 until 1979, an estimated 17,000 prisoners were tortured at Tuol Sleng and died, or were executed in the nearby Killing Fields. A great number were actually Khmer Rouge themselves accused of disloyalty by the increasingly paranoid leadership. Many were just ordinary Khmer citizens required to confess to crimes they would never have known to exist.

If you don't come with a guide, you'll certainly want to hire one at the entrance, although you're free to roam the grounds on your own. Local guides often have personal experience of the Khmer Rouge years and are vital sources of oral history. The prison population of Tuol Sleng was carefully cataloged; in fact, the metal neck brace employed for holding subjects' heads in place for the admitting photograph is on display. There are some written accounts in English and paintings made by a survivor called Vann Nath. Vann Nath was saved only because the Khmer Rouge used his talents to create paintings of Pol Pot (in July 2009, he testified against "Duch," the prison director and the first Khmer Rouge cadre put on trial). In addition to his artwork there are also gory photos of the common torture practices in the prison.

Perhaps what is most haunting is the look in the eyes of the newly arrived; one wing of the buildings is dedicated to these very arrival photos. Thousands upon thousands of people staring at you across history—some terrified, some bewildered. Children and infants did not escape the savagery and the carnage. This sight is overwhelming, so be prepared. The upper galleries contain the roughly constructed cells, the manacles, and the small metal boxes used for defecation that were part of daily life for all inmates before they were taken away and murdered. To the left as you enter is a series of former classrooms used for torture. There are grisly pictures of what the Vietnamese found when they arrived. Victims still chained to the metal beds on which they had been tortured and then murdered before their persecutors made a hasty exit to save their own skins from the invading Vietnamese army. As the trial of the camp commandant, Duch, continues, more information continues to emerge. The horror here is recent, and the depth of suffering truly unfathomable.

South of town at the corner of sts. 350 and 113. Admission $2; guide fees vary (usually $2–$3 per person). Daily 8am–noon and 1–5pm.

Wat Phnom ★★   This is one of the city's defining landmarks. Legend has it that sometime in the 14th century, a woman named Penh found sacred Buddhist objects in the nearby river and placed them here on the small hill that later became a temple. The rest is history. *Phnom,* in fact, means, "hill," so the name of the city translates to "Penh's Hill."

The temple itself is a standard Southeast Asian *wat,* with Naga snakes on the cornered peaks of the roof and didactic murals of the Buddha's life done in Day-Glo allegories along interior walls. Don't miss the central ceiling, which, unlike the bright walls, is yet to be restored and is gritty and authentic. The area around here is leafy and quiet. It has in the past been a place notorious for robberies at night, but during the daytime it's fine if a little chaotic with beggars, hawkers, and drink sellers competing for your attention. You're sure to meet with some crafty young salesmen here who'll offer you the chance to show your Buddhist compassion by buying a caged bird for a dollar and letting it go; if you stick around long enough, you'll get to see the bird return to the comfort of the cage.

Intersection of St. 96 and Norodom Blvd.

SWIMMING & FITNESS

Many top hotels have pools. If you wish to get wet in opulent surroundings, try the **Raffles Hotel Le Royal** (p. 64). This beautiful place charges $20 weekdays and $30 weekends for nonguests to use the pool, sauna, and gym. The **Villa Lanka** (one of Phnom Penh's best midrange hotels; see p. 69) has a pool in gorgeous leafy surroundings that is free of charge if you are eating or drinking. If you are not they charge $5 for adults and $3 for children during the week. This goes up to $8 for adults and $5 for children at the weekend. **Parkway Health Club** (113 Mao Tse Tung Blvd.; ✆ 023/982-928) has an indoor pool, sauna, and gym. **Paddy's Sports Center** (635 National Rte. 5 near the Japanese Bridge; ✆ 012/217-877) charges an affordable $3 for the gym. They have weights, treadmills, exercise bikes, and all the usual sweat-inducing contraptions.

GO-KARTING

You can find **Kambol Go-Karting** (National Rte. 4; ✆ 012/232-332) just past the airport. It can be great fun but carries the usual risks of the sport. If you go in rainy season, you may well find yourself aquaplaning in a spin. They also have a fully equipped bar and restaurant with a view from which you can watch your friends bashing into each other gleefully.

GOLF

Given what a world-famous place nearby Thailand is for golf, engaging in the sport in Cambodia on expensive and inferior courses makes little sense. If you can't do without a round, head to the **Cambodia Golf and Country Club** (National Rte. 4; ✆ 023/363-666). It costs $35 per round and club rental costs $10.

BOWLING

The **Superbowl at Parkway Square** (Parkway Sq., Mao Tse Tung Blvd.) is the only bowling alley in town. Bowling is something of a chic activity among young Khmers. It costs $9 per hour per lane, and $1 to rent shoes.

MASSAGE, SAUNAS & SPAS

There are massage places all over Phnom Penh, and all the bigger hotels have massage, spa, and sauna facilities.

Amret Spa This international boutique spa is located in Boeung Keng Kang 1 district. They offer massage, aromatherapy, body scrubs, wraps, facials, treatments, and Jacuzzi tubs. Daily 9am–9pm. No. 3 St. 57. ✆ 023/997-994.

Blue 7 Massage Offering a full range of massage services including foot and full body massage in clean air-conditioned rooms. Powder and oil massage are both available. Daily 9am–9pm. No. 10 St. 278. ✆ 011/955-567. www.blue7massage.com.

La Cigale Bleue This traditional Khmer massage shop has three branches. They offer oil, powder, body, foot, and four-hand massage. The facilities are air-conditioned. Call-in hotel service. Daily 24 hr. No. 22 St. 94; ✆ 016/789-618. No. 43A5 St. 86 (Boeung Kak Lake); ✆ 016/789-618. No. 33 St. 294 (in Boeung Keng Kang); ✆ 016/789-618.

Sawasdee Massage The Sawasdee offers a wide selection of massage styles and types including Thai, French, Japanese, Khmer, Hong Kong, oil, powder, body, foot massage (reflexology,) health massages, and aromatherapy. They also have wraps, scrubs, Jacuzzi, manicure, pedicure, and facials. Daily 9am–11pm. No. 6B St. 57; ✆ 023/996-670.

Unwinding (and Helping Out) with a Blind Massage

Cambodia has one of the highest rates of blindness worldwide with an estimated 1.25% of the population being afflicted. Chickenpox, measles, traffic accidents, acid attacks, unexploded ordinance, and insufficient healthcare have all exacerbated the problem. Being such a poor country, the lot of the blind is harsh because of the lack of education or employment opportunities. About a dozen blind massage shops, usually called "Seeing Hands," have opened in Phnom Penh, Siem Reap, and Battambang in the last few years. They are run as cooperatives and offer a better life to the blind as well as empowering them, often providing training in Braille and computers as well as massage itself. A massage costs in the region of $5 and it is a win-win experience. You get a great massage and help a group of people who have traditionally led a very difficult existence to prosper. In Phnom Penh, Seeing Hands can be found at No. 6 St. 94, near Wat Phnom.

COOKING CLASSES

Many understandably fall in love with the subtle and delicious flavors of Cambodian food and want to learn how to create something similar back home. **Frizz Restaurant** (No. 67 St. 240; ⓒ **012/524-801;** www.cambodia-cooking-class.com) runs an excellent **cooking school** ★★, with the option taking their course for half a day or a full day (we recommend the full). The course begins with a market tour to find ingredients, with explanations of some of the market's bizarre offerings. A tuk-tuk then takes you back to the roof of the restaurant, where you'll prepare classic Khmer dishes such as fish amok and salad with banana flower (the amok was one of the best dishes I've ever made). They also throw in an informative free booklet once you have completed the course. The course costs $20 for the full day, and considering how many friends you will make back home when they taste homemade Khmer cuisine for the first time, this is a steal. Classes take place Monday to Saturday and start at 9am. Reservations can be made via the website.

COLONIAL ARCHITECTURE TOUR

Phnom Penh was famed as the most beautiful city in Asia before it was plunged into tragedy and destruction. Underneath the grime and the dust are many stunning examples of beautiful colonial French architecture. **KA Tours** (www.ka-tours.org) are the town's architecture specialists, running a number of city tours using a variety of transportation methods including cyclo. They take in not only the beautiful colonial structures but also modernist '60s architecture. They also publish an excellent map on their website, outlining a do-it-yourself walking tour of major architectural sites in Phnom Penh.

OUDONG

Following defeat at Angkor by the Thais, the Khmer capital moved to Oudong, and kings ruled from there for more than 100 years until the power center shifted to nearby Phnom Penh in 1866. The area was a monastic center, and the 13th-century temples, like most others, pale in comparison to those of the Angkor complex. Still, the hills of Oudong offer breathtaking views. It's 1 hour west of Phnom Penh and is best reached by rented vehicle.

PHNOM CHISOR & TONLE BATI

If you've been or are going to Angkor Wat, these temples will pale in comparison, but the ride through the countryside and among rural villages makes for a good day. Tonle Bati (33km/21 miles south of Phnom Penh) is a small collection of Angkor-style temples. Entrance costs $3. Nearby Phnom Chisor is a group of 10th-century ruins atop a picturesque hill. Phnom Penh travel agents can make all the arrangements.

6 SHOPPING & GALLERIES

The best shopping in town, for everything from souvenirs and trinkets to the obligatory kitchen sink, is at any of the large local markets. The **Central Market** (see "Phnom Penh Attractions," earlier in this chapter) shouldn't be missed, but the **Russian Market** between streets 440 and 450 in the far south of town is where the real deal on souvenirs can be had (go by moto or tuk-tuk). It takes hard haggling to get the good deals on items like opium paraphernalia, carvings, and ceramics. It's all authentic looking, even if made in China. Given Cambodia's large garment industry for export, it is no surprise that some goods "fall off the back of the truck" in transit and end up here. It's a good place to buy brand names at a fraction of their normal retail price.

Shops and galleries are growing in ever-increasing numbers in the developing capital. All along Street 178, interesting little outlets are springing up and include a few affordable silk dealers like **Sayon Silkworks,** just west of the National Museum on Street 178. **Asasax Art Gallery,** No. 192 St. 178 (✆ **012/217-795;** www.asasaxart.com.kh), features unique local works. **Silk & Pepper** at No. 33Eo St. 178 (✆ **023/222-692**) has some great silk accessories and kimonos. Take a stroll along Street 240, which is home to a fantastic cafe culture and a few antiques shops and boutiques like **Bliss,** No. 29 St. 240 (✆ **023/215-754**), which sells some unique beaded and embroidered cushions and quilts; or **Le Lezard Bleu** (No. 61 St. 240; ✆ **023/986-978** or 012/406-294), which features traditional and contemporary artwork and top-notch framing.

Bazar, at 28 Sihanouk Blvd., near the Independence Monument (✆ **012/776-492**), has a small but refined collection of Asian antiques and furniture.

For upscale, original clothing look no further than **Ambre** ★ at No. 37 St. 178 (✆ **023/217-935;** closed Sun). This two-story store carries the whimsical, beautifully cut designs of Cambodian-born, France-raised Romyda Keth. Keth has a love affair with jersey and often layers clothing with funky embroidery or gorgeous swaths of organza.

For CDs, MP3 recordings, DVDs, and cool T-shirts and hip-hop fashions, stop by the **Boom Boom Room,** on Street 93 in the backpacker area near Boeung Kak Lake or at

Munitions into Art

As armed conflict drew to a close at the end of the last century, Cambodia remained awash with weapons of war. Even the *motodups* were often armed back then. Programs to disarm the populace were quickly put into place. AK47s, mortars, and rocket launchers soon started to pile up. In 2003, Sasha Constable, a quietly spoken British artist, trained in London, teamed up with an organization with the unwieldy title of the "European Union's Assistance on Curbing Small Arms and Light Weapons program," or EUASAC.

The cooperation provided the opportunity to channel a vision. Young Khmer artists (from the Royal University of Fine Arts) were aching to express their feelings about the end of war and their hopes for the newfound peace. Under the auspices of EUASAC, Sasha cofounded the Peace Art Project Cambodia, and with expert help from within Cambodia and from around the globe, her students took all these rusting metal piles of misery and transformed them into sculptures reflecting their anger at conflict and their desire for peace. There are giant dragonflies fashioned from machine-gun barrels, huge angry metal figures breaking apart an AK47, the ubiquitous and potent symbol of casual murder across Cambodia. Sculptures include delicately poised ballet dancers, birds of prey with wings soaring, and other more prosaic and typically Cambodian rural themes: A woman carrying water, two buckets slung across her shoulders with a bamboo pole, echoes the etiolated figures of Giacometti. A water buffalo bows its head and a small, sparky guard dog sniffs the air.

In many venues around Phnom Penh you might spot the work of PAPC. Sometimes it is a bar stool, sometimes an ornament. There's a sign and clock made from AK47s at Cantina (p. 74), and a huge "Bird of Peace" sculpture, commissioned by the Australian Embassy, at Sanderson Park near Wat Phnom. There are also large municipal sculptures across Cambodia, particularly in Battambang and Kompong Thom. Although the PAPC program is over, the idea lives on. A group of Cambodian artists is turning land mines into art under the auspices of the Cambodian Mine Action Art Project. With support from UNDP, the artists spend time in the countryside with both local people and working de-miners, and then create paintings and collages to express how Cambodians are positively addressing the challenge of land mine and explosive remnants of war and the effects. The work is shown both within Cambodia and is being shown abroad as well in celebration of the 10th anniversary of Cambodia's ratification of the Anti-Personnel Mine Ban Treaty.

their new location just across from the Golden Gate Hotel at No. 1C St. 278 (© 012/ 709-096).

For essentials and Western groceries, stop by the **Lucky Market,** No. 160 Sihanouk Blvd. (© 023/215-229), the most popular shopping center for Phnom Penh's many expats. The main branch of "the Lucky" is just west of the Victory Monument traffic circle, and there's also a branch on the ground floor of the Sorya Shopping Center (see below). For fresh, organic produce and fine canned goods, **Veggy's** is at No. 23 St. 240

(© **023/211-534**) and carries a similar line of familiar comfort foods from back home, whether home is Arkansas, Tokyo, Paris, or Seoul.

Monument Books, No. 111 Norodom Blvd. (© **023/217-617**), has a great selection of new books; it's a good spot to find books on the Khmer language and culture. Upstairs you'll find Monument Toys for the kiddies. There are also stores at No. 53 St. 426 (© **023/217-617**) and in the airport at the international departure level. For second-hand books and exchange, **D's Books** (No. 12 178 St. and No. 79 240 St.; © **023/221-280**) has a good selection. Also check out the **Sorya Shopping Center** (© **023/210-018**) just south of central market, which has seven stories of brand-name international goods as well as discount copies.

---

7 NIGHTLIFE

Phnom Penh has a reputation for booming nightlife. Booming it is, but a large part of that is actually pretty seedy. As in Thailand, in some parts of town you may see Khmer girls from the countryside, waiting for large white men with fat wallets. There are, however, a number of classier options. Most restaurants are also bars and those along the riverfront will be open as late as midnight. **Cantina** (p. 74) is convivial and very popular. **Talkin' to a Stranger** (p. 79) is a bastion of social relaxation, and **Kandal House** (p. 76) is also cozy and friendly. The nicest Phnom Penh nightlife is largely found in its restaurant scene.

There are a number of large discos you can visit if you feel a boogie impetus coming on. They are not your best bet, however, since they are expensive and not very pleasant. Better to head to one of the bars with a dance floor. Avoid the Heart of Darkness because it is dangerous (see below). Upstairs at the **Riverhouse** (see below) is the best since it is relaxed, not overly peopled with commercial sex workers, and has great music.

BARS & CLUBS

Howie's Bar   Howie's is an all-night joint next to the Heart of Darkness. Being a late, late kind of place it is rough and ready, but has a good atmosphere. Howie, the American Khmer owner, is a good sort who has seen a lot. Howie's is billed as "Way Cool!" and that is a pretty accurate description. It closes when the last person leaves. Daily 6pm–late. No. 32 St. 51.

Love Orange Club   If you want to see how the vibrant privileged youth of Phnom Penh enjoy themselves, head to the Love Orange Club. Anyone over 22 will feel a little out of place, but Cambodian kids now often speak good English and you will be made welcome. The music is largely heavy dance and Khmer rap. During the day it is a Khmer restaurant and coffee shop. 7am–late. No. 32 St. 240. © **023/221-818.**

Pontoon Lounge   People genuinely rock the boat to state-of-the-art DJs at this bar on the Tonle Sap. It is Phnom Penh's hippest late-night venue right now. This is reflected in the prices, which are very high for Cambodia. The hipness is somewhat qualified by the fact that the river itself can sometimes be malodorous. 9pm–late. Sisowath Quay opposite St. 108. © **012/572-880.**

Riverhouse Lounge ★★★   Upstairs at the Riverhouse is the coolest disco in town. The setting is marvelous, with the river glittering before you as you sip one of their fine cocktails on the balcony. They have special guest DJs every weekend, and the music is

---

(Warning!) **Heart of Darkness**

The story of this once wonderful place is one of sad decline, mingled with greed and violence. In the '90s, the Heart of Darkness (at 213 Sisowath Quay) was often described by visiting travel writers (including this one) as the best bar in the world. It was a hole-in-the-wall haven from a city that was then a dark and often risky place at nighttime. The music was brilliant, and the mixture of journalists, NGO workers, diplomats, and mercenaries made for interesting conversation. It was a dark and funky dive with real atmosphere.

Then it started to change. It got bigger. Then it got even bigger again. Then they put in a dance floor and the place filled up with prostitutes. By 2001, the old Heart had ceased to exist and a monster was born. It became a place where fights and violence became the norm as privileged sons of the ruling elite arrived with their armed minders. Gunfire became frequent, and someone got murdered. The bar got security, but the security searched everyone except these scions of the elite, since moonlighting soldiers are loath to offend their commanding officers.

Today, the reputation of the old Heart feeds this beast and on weekends it is packed. You can take your chances, but be aware that it is dangerous and many embassies put out a warning and forbid their staff to visit.

---

great. It serves half as a bar and half as a nightclub, and performs both roles well so you can slip from the dance floor to a table to rest whenever you wish. Daily 4pm–2am. No. 6 St. 110 (corner of Sisowath). (C) **023/212-302.**

Rubies Wine Bar ★★ This sophisticated little place is on the corner of Street 240 among the upmarket boutiques. It wouldn't be out of place in Greenwich Village or the West End of London. It has an impressive array of wines and spirits and is utterly convivial. Tues–Sun 5:30pm–late. No. 13 St. 19. (C) **092/319-769.**

RIVER CRUISES

In the evening, you will see a number of boats lit up like Christmas trees chugging slowly up and down the Tonle Sap. Cruises taking in great views of the Royal Palace, National Museum, and floating villages along the banks are becoming ever more popular as is dinner afloat. You can find these boats of many different sizes and quality along the waterfront between Street 178 and Street 130. They are also at the ferry terminal opposite Street 104. They have small signs up and may also hail you as you walk by. Costs start at about $10 an hour. **Kanika** ((C) **012/848-802**) runs a unique catamaran for parties and dinner cruises. Proceeds go to Seametrey NGO projects. **Experience Mekong Boat** ((C) **012/432-456;** www.cambodiabyboat.com) offers tours of various sorts, including a look at how the boats are built and general life on the river.

DANCE

The **Bopha Penh Titanic Restaurant** (Sisowath Quay near the boat pier opposite St. 104; (C) **092/646-361;** www.bopha-phnompenh.com) stages nightly performances from 7 to 9pm.

The excellent **Sovanna Phum Art Association** (No. 111 St. 360; ✆ **023/221-932;** www.shadow-puppets.org) runs shows of classical performance every Friday and Saturday at 7:30pm. Dance alternates with other disciplines such as shadow puppetry and theater.

The **Veiyo Tonle Restaurant** (237 Sisowath Quay; ✆ **012/847-419**) hosts traditional dance performances by kids from the New Cambodia Children's Life Association. They take place at 8pm.

ART & FILM

The art exhibition center and media lounge **Meta House** (No. 6 St. 264; ✆ **023/224-140;** www.meta-house.com) hosts art shows celebrating contemporary art in Cambodia, and also plays host to foreign films and lectures. Check out their website to see what's available.

Fast Facts   Phnom Penh

ATMs   ATMs are everywhere now in Phnom Penh and accept all internationally recognized cards. Those of the **Canadia Bank** levy the lowest transaction charges. All ATMs dispense U.S. dollars.

American Express   For basic American Express services, contact Diethelm Travel (No. 65 St. 240, P.O. Box 99, Phnom Penh; ✆ **023/219-151;** www.diethelmtravel.com).

Banks & Currency Exchange   **ANZ Bank** has many reliable international ATMs in town, the most convenient being at their riverside branch, 265 Sisowath Quay (✆ **023-726-900**) **Canadia Bank,** at No. 265–269 St. 114 (✆ **023/215-286**) and **Mekong Bank,** at 1 St. 114 (✆ **023/217-112**) are also in the downtown area and can cash traveler's checks and give cash advances. A **Western Union** office is at 327 Sisowath Quay (✆ **023/990-688**).

Business Hours   Stores are generally open between 7am and 7pm from Monday to Friday. Markets close earlier and generally shutter by 5pm.

Doctors & Hospitals   The **International SOS Medical and Dental Clinic,** at No. 161 St. 51 (✆ **023/216-911**), is the best place to handle minor emergencies. **Naga Clinic,** at No. 11 St. 254 (✆ **011/811-175**), is another. For any major emergency or injury, however, you'll want to arrange medical evacuation.

Embassies & Consulates   **U.S.:** corner of Street 96/51, ✆ **023/728-000; Canada:** Represented by Australian Embassy; **Australia:** Villa No. 11 St. 254, ✆ **023/213-470; Ireland:** Represented by U.K. Embassy; **New Zealand:** There is no New Zealand Embassy in Cambodia; **U.K.:** No. 27–29 St. 75, ✆ **023/427-124.**

Emergencies   For police, dial ✆ **117;** for fire, dial ✆ **118;** and for the expat hot line, dial ✆ **023/724-793.**

Internet Access   Internet outlets line riverside Sisowath Quay. Hourly access starts at $1. **Friendly Web,** near Capitol Guesthouse, has good access from its office at No. 199 EO, St. 107 (at the corner of Rd. 182; ✆ **012/843-246**). **Sunny Internet Cafe** has several flatscreen computers with fast ADSL connections in a bright location at 351 Sisowath Quay (✆ **023-986-629**). **KIDS** is an NGO where American owner Bill Herod brings Internet technology to Khmer students. They have good, inexpensive access in their offices at No. 17A St. 178 (☎ **023/218-452;** kids@camnet.com.kh). Many hotels and restaurants have free Wi-Fi. The best and most practical is **La Croisette** on Sisowath Quay.

Maps   There are plenty of free maps available from bars and restaurants all over town. One of the best is the 3D Lets Go! Map.

Magazines & Newspapers   Two English-language dailies are available. The ***Cambodia Daily*** carries plenty of local and national news and contains good analysis, and is the best of the two. The once internationally renowned paper of record, the ***Phnom Penh Post,*** which for many years ran as a biweekly, has now been relaunched as a daily. The ***Bangkok Post*** is also widely available. Locally produced magazines come and go in Cambodia. The best of the bunch at present is the ***Southeast Asia Globe.*** Bookshops stock a range of foreign and international magazines.

Pharmacies   There are pharmacies all over town, but many are unreliable with outdated drugs that might do you more harm than good. The best pharmacy by far is **Pharmacie De La Gare** (81Eo Monivong Blvd.; ☎ **023/430-205**). This is a very professional outfit run to French standards.

Post Office   The post office is in the north end of town on Street 13, east of Wat Phnom. It's open daily from 6:30am to 5pm and has standard delivery service and an international phone. **DHL** has an office on No. 28 Monivong Rd. (☎ **023/427-726**), and **FedEx** is at No. 701D Monivong (☎ **023/216-712**). There's also a post office at the airport in the outdoor archway between arrivals and departures (across from the Dairy Queen).

Safety   The main hazard is traffic. Wear a motorcycle helmet when on the back of a moto. When walking around or crossing the road, stay watchful—since all vehicles are unpredictable, anything can happen. Bag snatchings and robberies do happen. Don't leave bags dangling and don't display expensive items that might attract the wrong kind of attention.

Telephone   The local code for Phnom Penh is **23.** International direct dialing is available in most hotels and at the post office. Storefront Internet cafes along Sisowath do inexpensive Internet calls or direct dialing. Cellphones are very popular in the city, and you'll find street-side stalls on wheels where you can make local and international calls for next to nothing, with a good cellular connection.

Tourism Information   Look out for the excellent free **Canby Visitors Guide to Phnom Penh.** It is available in most cafes, restaurants, and hotels, and provides very comprehensive information. The **Phnom Penh Pocket Guide,** also freely available around town, is up to date with information on bars and restaurants.

Siem Reap

The ruins of the ancient city of Angkor, capital of the Khmer kingdom from A.D. 802 until A.D. 1295, are one of the world's greatest marvels. The "City of God-Kings," Angkor boasts some of the largest religious monuments ever constructed. Angkor Wat itself, the largest religious building in the world, represents Mount Meru. In Hindu mythology this was the home of the gods and the kings of Angkor were gods. Angkor was created from a fusion of feudalism, animism, and Hinduism that impelled the god-kings to create celestial glory on earth to honor their own divinity.

Angkor is a vast and mysterious complex of soaring towers, mysterious faces, and exquisite sculptures. The location was unknown to the outside world until French naturalist Henri Mouhot literally stumbled onto it in 1861. The half knowledge and half rumor of Angkor existed for centuries only as a myth. Although Angkor was abandoned for 600 years, the Khmers knew exactly where it was and had no wish to disturb the power of slumbering spirits. After Mahout made his discovery, archaeologists flocked here. With war and conflict after 1970, Angkor was once again often lost and more often damaged. Many temples were pillaged. Once the wars subsided tourists became the invaders. Today the sight is totally mobbed, but you might still find those quiet moments to contemplate the awesome eeriness of this amazing man-made wonder.

The temple complex covers some 97 sq. km (60 sq. miles) and carries the remains of passageways, moats, temples, and palaces that represent centuries of building. Originally the stone would have been interspersed with wooden buildings and all the bustle of a living city. A millennium

later what there was is gone, eaten by the fierce, humid jungle, and what remains is a magnificent stone skeleton.

The temples are served by the nearby town of Siem Reap, some 6km (3½ miles) to the south. Siem Reap means "Siam Defeated" and refers to the 16th-century victory that solidified the Khmer kingdom, even though the Thais were to triumph once again as empires ebbed and flowed. Animosity between the two neighbors remains to this day. All of western Cambodia was once under Thai control, and Khmer people are very proud of their survival in the face of so many invaders, the very reason that an image of Angkor Wat graces the national flag.

Siem Reap, not long ago a quiet, dusty town of rutted roads and dark nights, now supports a host of large five-star hotels and resorts, numerous restaurants, and the kind of goods, services, shops, galleries, and spas that make the little city a new island of luxury in parched western Cambodia. The town's markets have become a great stop for souvenir purchases as well as more traditional fare such as pig's heads and car parts, and the nearby downtown area is throbbing.

A 3- or 4-day visit will suffice (though many do it in less time) to come away with a newfound love for mystery, religion, and some of the most spectacular sunrises known to man. The sunrise over Angkor Wat itself is often stunning and justifiably famous—a blaze of red and orange silhouetting the central towers. It is a photographer's dream, although these days you will have an awful lot of other photographers in the frame. There are good options for visiting more far-flung temple ruins, and the Bayon always remains sublime.

1 ORIENTATION

Originally a collection of separate villages based around separate pagodas, Siem Reap town is still a rambling place. The Siem Reap River runs north to south with National Rte. 6 (the road to Phnom Penh) running east to west along the north end of town. The center of town is around Psar Chas in the southern end of town, west of the river and east of Sivatha Boulevard, the main north-to-south thoroughfare. Psar Chas itself is on the river and remains your most important reference point. Heading away from the river are a number of parallel streets packed with restaurants, cafes, travel agents, and Internet cafes. The busiest of these is appropriately named Pub Street (St. 8). At night this area becomes frantic with blaring music, crowds of tourists, hordes of raggedy children, and hawkers of all things. In between and parallel to Street 8 and Street 9 is a smaller alleyway with plenty of restaurants and bars, but it is far more relaxed and quiet. Hotels and guesthouses are spread throughout the town on both sides of the river.

GETTING THERE

BY PLANE   **Bangkok Air** (© **023/426-624** in Phnom Penh, or 063/380-191 in Siem Reap; www.bangkokair.com) is currently the only airline running the 1-hour connection to Siem Reap from Phnom Penh. One-way fares are $70.

If you just want to see the great temples at Angkor, the process is simplified with international arrivals: **Vietnam Airlines** (www.vietnamairlines.com) flies directly from Ho Chi Minh City; **Bangkok Air** flies directly from Bangkok. **Lao Airlines** flies (www.laoairlines.com) in from Vientiane. **Air Asia** (www.airasia.com) and **Malaysia Airlines** (www.malaysiaairlines.com) fly from Kuala Lumpur. **Silk Air** (www.silkair.com) flies from Singapore. *Note:* The international departure tax (from both Phnom Penh and Siem Reap) is $25; the domestic tax is $6.

Siem Reap airport is 7km (4⅓ miles) out of town. Taxis cost $5 while a tuk-tuk will be around $4. Many hotels offer free pickup.

BY BOAT   A ride on the 5-hour boat connection between Phnom Penh and Siem Reap costs $30 to $35. Contact any hotel or travel agent (they all sell the same tickets at the same price). The trip connects to Siem Reap via the great Tonle Sap Lake. It is getting less and less popular since the roads have been improved. The buses are cheaper and more comfortable. Siem Reap also connects with Battambang, to the south and west, via the Tonle Sap and the Sangker River. The trip reveals life in fishing villages along the river as you pass the banks. In the rainy season when the water is high, the ride is relatively straightforward, but in the dry season (Feb–May) it can take 8 hours or more and isn't recommended. Book your ticket at any tour agent or the front desk of your hotel or guesthouse. The price is $14.

BY BUS   Your hotel front desk can arrange bus transportation for you at no additional cost. **Mekong Express** (© **023/427-518**) connects Phnom Penh and Siem Reap with daily luxury buses ($11 for the 5½-hr. ride). *Tip:* Earplugs are your friend on this bus ride (and any bus ride really), as the buses play Khmer karaoke songs and various Asian pop music videos. **Capitol Tour** (No. 14 Rd. 182; © **023/217-627**) also runs daily minivans along ($5 for the 5-hr. ride) as well as destinations farther afield like Battambang or Poipet at the Thai border. **Neak Krorhorm Travel and Tour** (© **023/219-496** in Phnom Penh, or 063/964-924 in Siem Reap near the Old Market) provides similar services. The road from Siem Reap to Poipet on the Thai border, which was appalling for

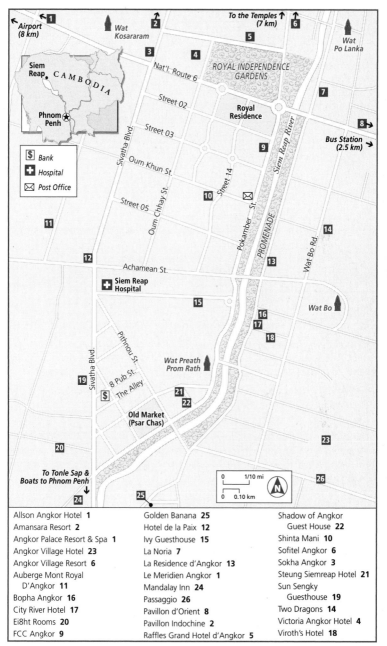

Allson Angkor Hotel **1**
Amansara Resort **2**
Angkor Palace Resort & Spa **1**
Angkor Village Hotel **23**
Angkor Village Resort **6**
Auberge Mont Royal
    D'Angkor **11**
Bopha Angkor **16**
City River Hotel **17**
Ei8ht Rooms **20**
FCC Angkor **9**

Golden Banana **25**
Hotel de la Paix **12**
Ivy Guesthouse **15**
La Noria **7**
La Residence d'Angkor **13**
Le Meridien Angkor **1**
Mandalay Inn **24**
Passaggio **26**
Pavillon d'Orient **8**
Pavillon Indochine **2**
Raffles Grand Hotel d'Angkor **5**

Shadow of Angkor
    Guest House **22**
Shinta Mani **10**
Sofitel Angkor **6**
Sokha Angkor **3**
Steung Siemreap Hotel **21**
Sun Sengky
    Guesthouse **19**
Two Dragons **14**
Victoria Angkor Hotel **4**
Viroth's Hotel **18**

Give of "Yourself" in Siem Reap

They want your blood in Siem Reap. Many humanitarian-aid agencies use Siem Reap as a base for raising funds and treating rural peoples. The Kantha Bopha Hospital, on the main road to the temples, and the Angkor Hospital for Children (contact them through ⓒ **063/963-409** or www.fwab.org) are always looking for blood donors to help young patients through the most trying periods of acute dysentery and hemorrhagic fever. Patients often make it to these centers from rural areas in dire circumstances and need immediate blood transfusions to make it through their first days. Just show up at either clinic to make a donation of blood, time, and/or money—all of which are desperately needed.

years, has now finally been improved and is perfect. Once into Thailand, you can travel on to Bangkok by minibus from the crossing or you can travel on into Aranyaprathet by tuk-tuk and catch a regular bus from the bus station. Any all-inclusive fares either from Bangkok to Siem Reap or the reverse are not recommended as they come rife with scams and rip-offs.

GETTING AROUND

Navigating central Siem Reap around Psar Chas is easy because it is compact (though the town as a whole is very spread out). There is no shortage of willing drivers available.

BY TAXI   One generally hires cars and taxis by the day. They cost around $20 to $25 per day. This is your best bet if hitting the temples farther afield, but if you're just doing the main temple circuits, tuk-tuks or motos represent the best way to get around.

BY TUK-TUK   Tuk-tuks are readily available everywhere. Pay between $1 and $3 for trips around town or $15 to rent one for the whole day.

BY MOTORCYCLE TAXI   Motorcycle taxis are everywhere and are often the quickest way to get around. During the day expect to pay between 50¢ and $1 for most short trips in town. Double that at night. Hiring one for the entire day (to take you to the temples), should cost around $7 to $10 per day.

BY MOTORCYCLE   Foreigners are not allowed to rent motorcycles in Siem Reap.

BY BICYCLE   Many guesthouses and hotels offer bicycles for rent at $1.50 to $4 per day, depending on the quality and sophistication of the bike. Don't forget to wear a helmet.

2 WHERE TO STAY

Not surprisingly, the accommodations scene in Siem Reap has exploded since peace came to Cambodia at the end of the last century, and now the number of places to stay is astronomical in all categories. Even so, high-end hotels often fill up in the high season, so be sure to book ahead. In low season, be sure to ask for a discount. For midrange hotels (below $100), there are a handful of nice boutique choices in town. Most hotels levy a

10% VAT. Budget travelers are also amply catered to, but again in high season you may have to try a few different guesthouses before you find a room.

VERY EXPENSIVE

Amansara Resort ★★   Aman means "peace" in Sanskrit, and the suffix "sara" refers to Khmer Apsara dancers. Set in an old downtown guest villa once owned by King Siha-nouk, the suites of the Amansara are each done in a cool contemporary minimalist design of white stucco and dark timber, all surrounded by shade trees. The outside world melts away when you step into this complex. Large bedrooms with adjoining sitting areas lead to a private outdoor courtyard area. Decor is simple; the bedroom wall has a white stone bas-relief of a banyan tree, while the courtyard has a lotus pond with goldfish. The services at Amansara are unrivaled: private driver and guide, personalized excursions to the temples and town, high tea with freshly baked cookies and cake, stocked bar, wine and cheese cellar . . . the list goes on. The idea is that Amansara is your home, so you can wander into the central house and mix yourself a gin and tonic or grab a cookie whenever you fancy. Unfortunately, the compulsory daily $100 "half-board charge" per person *on top* of the rather steep room fees feels like you're being nickel-and-dimed (or Benjamin Franklin-ed!) here. Still, service is in its own category here and it is a remarkable experience for Siem Reap.

Road to Angkor, Siem Reap, Kingdom of Cambodia. 🕜 **063/760-333.** Fax 063/760-335. www.aman resorts.com. 24 units. $750 suite; $950 pool suite. AE, MC, V. **Amenities:** Restaurant; bar; complimentary bikes (with or without guide); library; 2 large outdoor salt pools; luxurious Aman spa; room service. *In room:* A/C, TV, bar, fridge, hair dryer.

Angkor Palace Resort and Spa ★★   The acres and acres of open space afforded by the Angkor Palace Resort's location—far from the action—wins this one kudos. Plenty of elbowroom, fine gardens, a large pool, and unique tennis courts in a town where real estate is at a premium are quite unique. This high-end resort offers a friendly and casual atmosphere, again unique in a town of more and more haughty, high-end addresses. The pool area is large, open, and inviting, with bridges connecting walkways; the spa is tops, and you'll find extensive services, including a fine Italian restaurant, in-house Internet services, and any kind of tour services or vehicle rental you might need. Rooms are enormous and done in dark wood with white silk spreads on the beds and fine local hangings on the walls. First-floor rooms have direct access to the pool area. Bathrooms are large, with wood floors connecting the main bedroom to a small dressing area, then large Italian tile covers the bathroom floor, where rosewood and granite accent every inch of the walls and counter. The resort's spa is just up and running with a host of fine massage and facial treatments, but planning and construction are underway for a much larger project. You will, however, find a good sauna and steam area as well as a Jacuzzi at poolside. A top getaway.

No. 555 Phum Kruos, Khum Svay Dang Khum, Siem Reap. 🕜 **063/760-511.** Fax 063/760-512. www. angkorpalaceresort.com. 259 units. $350–$400 deluxe; $600 suite; $1,500 villa. AE, MC, V. **Amenities:** 2 restaurants; babysitting; concierge; driving range; health club; outdoor pool; tennis courts; room service; smoke-free rooms; fine spa facilities. *In room:* A/C, TV, fridge, Internet, minibar.

Hôtel de la Paix ★★★   This chic, modern hotel is the height of cutting edge. The original design—a sort of Art Deco meets minimalist meets Khmer decor—is a refreshing change from the colonial-heavy influence of popular hotels like the Raffles or Victoria (see below). This is not a chain hotel (the private owner is Cambodian-Thai), so the place has a personal and flamboyant feel to it. Staff is incredibly friendly and appears invested in providing a wonderful experience for guests. Spacious deluxe rooms come with black-and-white color schemes, accent pillows in deep purple, and silver wall hangings and lamps. A white marble bathtub lies a couple of feet away from the foot of the bed. Around the corner is the funky stone shower console with tropical shower head. If you decide to splurge on the two-story spa suite, get the corner unit (room no. 346), which comes with a huge balcony equipped with a private stone tub, lounge chairs, a love seat with a pretty bodhi tree bas-relief carving behind it, and a cozy dining table. There's a large, partially outdoor pool with an indoor enclave at one end. If you are around at noon, make sure to glance at the marble Apsara statue in the main lobby—a single ray of light filters through a cleverly placed hole in the ceiling and shines on the statue's head. The moving design is a good indication of the thoughtful touches throughout the hotel that pay tribute to the architecture found at nearby Angkor Wat.

Sivatha Blvd. ✆ **063/966-000.** Fax 063/966-001. www.hoteldelapaixangkor.com. 107 units. $300 double; $420–$650 suite. AE, MC, V. **Amenities:** Restaurant; lounge; cafe; babysitting; concierge; fitness center; Jacuzzi; nice outdoor pool; sauna; spa. *In room:* A/C, TV, DVD (suites), iPod/MP3 docking station, fridge, hair dryer, minibar, Wi-Fi.

La Résidence d'Angkor ★★

Formerly the Pansea, La Résidence d'Angkor is a stylish, self-contained sanctuary managed by luxury Orient-Express. Cross a small moat to enter the cool interior of the steeply gabled, dark wooden lobby with its grand Angkor-inspired reliefs. The tranquil central courtyard is lined with palms and dominated by a small but stylish pool fed by the font of stylized Shiva-lingam. The resort area is small, but everything from the gardens to the room decor is tidy and designed for quiet privacy. Rooms are large, well appointed, open, and elegant, with cloth divans, retro fixtures, and nice local touches. Large bathrooms connect with bedrooms by a unique bamboo sliding door, and another glass slider opens to a small private balcony with cool lounges and views of the courtyard. All is stately and comfortable, and if you're guarded from the cares of reality behind these walls, you're reminded of local culture in all the many fine details throughout. The lobby restaurant offers good fine dining, and there are some great open sitting areas for drinks as well as a library with books, chess, and a conference table.

River Rd., Siem Reap. ✆ **063/963-390.** Fax 063/963-391. www.residencedangkor.com. 62 units. $218–$406 deluxe double; $330–$642 suite. AE, MC, V. **Amenities:** Restaurant; bar; saltwater outdoor pool; room service. *In room:* A/C, TV, fridge, hair dryer, minibar, Wi-Fi.

Le Meridien Angkor ★★

The massive monolith of the Le Meridien looks as if a spaceship landed on the road running north to the temples. Three stories and square, the building is beveled, with the larger edge at the top, and is surrounded by a moat and large open areas, all stylistic nods to the temple architecture nearby. Catering mostly to Japanese and Korean groups, the stylish Le Meridien displays accents of culture including fine Apsara sculptures in each room and tinted photos of the temples. Done in dark wood, rooms are clean and elegant, with silken comforters on the beds, cane matting on the floors, and Khmer-style contemporary divans near the window. Deluxe and superior rooms differ only slightly in size. Bathrooms connect to the main bedroom via a shuttered window, and all are done in a sparkly black tile, with granite counters and glass showers separate from tubs. Dining options range from buffet to a fine Italian restaurant, all set in large, glassed-in spaces overlooking a lush central courtyard where a many-headed Ganesha statue holds court. The pool is an unusual esplanade of smaller, tiered pools connected with waterfalls and traversed by interlocking raised pathways and Greek-style colonnaded arches. Staff wear starched jackets and snap to it like they really mean it.

Vithei Charles de Gaulle, Khum Svay Dang Kum, Siem Reap (on the temple road, just north of town and the Kantha Bopha Hospital). (C) **063/963-900.** www.lemeridien.com or www.angkor.lemeridien.com. 223 units. $270 superior; $300 deluxe; $410–$520 suite. AE, MC, V. **Amenities:** 2 restaurants; bar; concierge; health club; outdoor pool; room service; spa. *In room:* A/C, TV, high-speed Internet, minibar.

Raffles Grand Hotel D'Angkor ★★★   Right in the center of town, this is simply the best hotel in Siem Reap; it remains unrivaled for luxury, charm, and service. The imposing colonial facade gives way to a marble lobby, connected by Art Deco black-and-white tile halls to the many rooms and fine services. If arriving by air, hotel staff will pick you up and escort you to a waiting limo while your visa, immigration, and luggage issues are magically taken care of. At the hotel, a doorman outfitted in the old hat and uniform of the Royal Guards whisks you past the cool lobby and into the Conservatory, a bright, alcove restaurant overlooking the expansive outdoor pool. Their State rooms, in the new wing of the hotel, are large, with classic French doors and windows, beautiful black-and-white tile entries, and most come with a balcony. Landmark rooms, the next higher standard, have four-poster beds, a balcony, and nice touches like porcelain bathrooms. Personality suites are gems, and each has a unique theme, color, and decor. The courtyard pool (lit by fairy lights and tiny candles in the evening) is large and inviting and the nearby spa facilities are indulgent.

1 Vithei Charles de Gaulle, Khum Svay Dang Kum, Siem Reap. (C) **063/963-888.** Fax 063/963-168. www.raffles.com. 131 units. $360–$410 double; $510 suite; $2,500 2-bedroom villa. AE, MC, V. **Amenities:** 4 restaurants; 2 bars; concierge; health club; Jacuzzi; kids' club; big outdoor pool; spa; 2 tennis courts; Wi-Fi. *In room:* A/C, TV, fridge, hair dryer, minibar.

Sofitel Royal Angkor ★★   Sofitel is famed in the region for bringing life back to classic hotels of old Indochina, but in Siem Reap, they started fresh, with a project limited only by the designer's imagination. The lobby is an old-world Indochina replica with antique Khmer pagoda and a menagerie of overstuffed European furniture. Design and decor throughout nicely marry Khmer and French styles, with vaulted Naga roofs high above the sculpted central garden and tranquil pond area. The courtyard pool with swim-up bar is large, open, and fun—great for kids, with a short river meander crossed by a small bridge. The spa is tops, and the private massage areas are uniquely resplendent with private bathrooms. Rooms are spacious, with dark-wood floors and rich touches like designer throw rugs and elegant built-in cabinetry. All bathrooms are large, with tubs and large granite counters. Spring for a superior room with a balcony and a view of the central courtyard: It's worth it. There's an Angkor theme throughout, but the statuary is not overdone and is quite pleasing in both common areas and sleeping quarters (unique in a town of gaudy reproductions of the sights). Be sure to take a moment, preferably near the magic hour of sunset (but any time will do) and take it all in from the island pagoda in the central pond.

Vithei Charles de Gaulle, Khum Svay Dang Kum, Siem Reap. (On the way to the temples, just north of the town center.) (C) **063/964-600.** Fax 063/964-609. www.sofitel.com. 238 units. $340–$360 double; $420–$605 suite. AE, MC, V. **Amenities:** 5 restaurants; 3 bars; concierge; 18-hole golf course; health club; Jacuzzi; large outdoor pool; room service; sauna; smoke-free floor; spa; banquet facilities. *In room:* A/C, TV w/in-house movies, fax, fridge, hair dryer, minibar, Wi-Fi.

Sokha Angkor   Maybe this is what Angkor Wat would have looked like if it was a pleasure resort rather than a place of worship. The lobby is gigantic, with big columns framing a bronze and sheer glass chandelier. A blown-up photograph of a Banteay Srei temple is plastered over the elevator doors. In the courtyard, a large stone pediment with a waterfall empties into the outdoor pool. Big stone lions at the back and lingams at the front are mini fountains, spitting out streams of water that also empty into the pool. Rooms are, thank goodness, more subtle. Blond wood furniture gives things a light feeling and a floral spritzer gives everything a springtime-fresh smell. Bathrooms are reasonable size with tallow stone tubs and separate glass shower consoles.

Rd. No. 6 and Sivatha St. © **063/969-999.** Fax 063/969-992. www.sokhahotels.com. 276 units. $250–$300 double; from $500 suite. AE, MC, V. **Amenities:** 3 restaurants; bar; lounge; concierge; health club; outdoor pool; room service; spa. *In room:* A/C, TV, fridge, hair dryer, high-speed Internet, minibar.

Victoria Angkor Hotel ★★ The Victoria expands its empire of fine hotels (mostly in Vietnam) to Cambodia. Victoria Angkor is a tasteful replica of a French colonial–era hotel, but with all of the amenities and functionality of a modern resort. Public spaces are done in earth tones, rattan and wood accents, and Art Deco floor tiles in mustard yellow tones. A large central atrium with period-piece elevator and towering courtyard staircase greets the visitor to this downtown campus, just a stone's throw from the Raffles (see above). The central pool is a private oasis surrounded by a mini jungle, with open-air massage areas nestled in the flora. Rooms are large, luxurious, and decorated with retro oil paintings of peaceful jungle scenes and framed photographs of everyday life in Siem Reap. Floors are wood with a border of fine tile that matches luxurious woven bedspreads. All rooms have balconies. Colonial suites have individual themes and the best ones are the corner suites with large, covered outdoor balconies. Fine dining at their Le Bistrot (p. 106) is tops.

Central Park, P.O. Box 93145, Siem Reap. © **063/760-428.** Fax 063/760-350. www.victoriahotels-asia.com. 130 units. $328–$368 double; $494 colonial suite (breakfast is an additional $18–$20). AE, MC, V. **Amenities:** 2 restaurants; bar; babysitting; bike rentals; children's center; concierge; Jacuzzi; spacious outdoor saltwater pool; room service; spa. *In room:* A/C, TV, fridge, hair dryer, minibar, Wi-Fi.

EXPENSIVE

Allson Angkor Hotel ★ Of the many hotels along the airport road, Rte. 6, the Angkor Hotel is the best (and only slightly more expensive than the rest). Popular with group tours, the hotel is large and ostentatious, with high, Khmer-style roofs and large reproductions of temple statuary in the entry. Everything is clean and comfortable, if a bit sterile. Ask for a room in the new building in the back. Guest rooms are bland but large, with crown molding, clean carpet, and good, familiar amenities like a minibar and safe. The bathrooms are a little small. This is a good, comfortable step down from the glitzier hotels in town, and the best choice if they're full. The lobby is always busy with tour groups, but the staff remains friendly and expedient. The hotel is sufficiently self-contained, with good basic amenities, an outdoor pool in the courtyard, a good restaurant, and all necessary services. The two caged bears in the hotel's garden are enough to make you cry, though.

Rte. 6, Phum Sala Kanseng. © **063/964-301.** Fax 063/964-302. www.angkor-hotel-cambodia.com. 193 units. May–Sept $70 double; $74 deluxe; $150 suite. Oct–Apr $75 double; $85 deluxe; $160 suite. AE, MC, V. **Amenities:** Restaurant; bar; basic gym; Internet; outdoor pool. *In room:* A/C, TV, fridge, hair dryer, minibar.

Angkor Village Hotel ★★ In a quiet neighborhood not far from the main market, this peaceful little hideaway is a unique maze of wood bungalows connected by covered boardwalks surrounding a picturesque ivy-draped pond. Rooms are rustic wooden affairs with high bamboo catay ceilings, wood beams, built-in cabinetry, comfortable beds, and decorative touches like traditional Khmer shadow puppets and statuary. Top units have balconies overlooking the central pond. Bathrooms are all large, with a tub/shower combo and sinks set in unique oversize ceramic cauldrons. The central lobby is a series of platforms and private sitting areas, a good place to rest after a day at the temples. The staff is very welcoming. The pool is small but picturesque in a verdant courtyard at the rear. The Auberge de Temples Restaurant is on a small island in the central pond and serves fine French and Khmer cuisines. The hotel's **Apsara Theater Restaurant,** just outside the gate, has Khmer-style banquet dining and performances of Khmer Apsara dancing nightly. The whole place is infused with Khmer culture and hospitality, and so popular is the original that they've expanded (see **Angkor Village Resort** below). Angkor Village is often full so be sure to book ahead.

Wat Bo Rd., Siem Reap. ℂ 063/965-561. Fax 063/965-565. www.angkorvillage.com. 52 units. $169 (off-season discounts available). AE, MC, V. **Amenities:** Restaurant; bar; Internet; outdoor pool; limited room service; small library. *In room:* A/C, TV, fridge, minibar, Wi-Fi.

Angkor Village Resort ★   This campus of luxury rooms is located a few steps closer to the temples (it all counts when you're racing for the sunrise). The resort offers the same standard of comfort and style as its sister hotel (see above), but with a fun pool as well as large ponds of Japanese koi, fountains, and lush landscaping. The resort does a good job of creating a sanctuary far away from town, but unfortunately the loud music from nearby developments occasionally overpowers the tranquil buzzing of cicadas. Rooms are set in two-story blocks of Khmer-style peaked roofs, two rooms on each floor. Rooms are stylish but lean more to the cozy than to the austere. A Naga (snakelike temple decoration) adorns the one desk; old prints of Angkor scenes hang on the walls; and four-poster firm beds complete the cozy effect. All rooms have balconies overlooking the pool. Bathrooms are large with raised shower units open to a tile room with a one-piece wooden counter set with two bright, free-standing porcelain sink bowls; pale-green tile and cool indirect lighting are quite pleasing. The toilet area is separate. The staff is as friendly as they come. Breakfast of fresh breads and crepes by the pond is a treat (and the kids will love feeding the fish).

Phum Traeng (on the north end of town nearer the temples), Siem Reap. ℂ 063/963-561. Fax 063/963-363. www.angkorvillage.com. 40 units. $199 double. AE, MC, V. **Amenities:** Restaurant; bar; Internet; outdoor pool; limited room service; small library. *In room:* A/C, fridge, minibar, Wi-Fi.

FCC Angkor   This hotel is located beside the restaurant of the same name (p. 108). Located behind high walls and shaded by towering tropical trees, the FCC has an excellent location. All the rooms have names (Basil, Lychee, and so on), not numbers, to give things a personal feel. Rooms have low beds on wooden frames and modern amenities like flatscreen TVs and hip furniture. The decor is similarly cool, with pale-yellow tile floors paired with fun block color paintings hang on the walls. The long and narrow outdoor pool is great for an afternoon cool-off.

Pokambor Ave. (next to the Royal Residence and just north of the post office). ℂ 063/760-280. Fax 063/760-281 www.fcccambodia.com. 31 units. Low season $130–$150 double, $280 suite; high season $170–$190 double, $340 suite. MC, V. **Amenities:** Restaurant; bar; outdoor saltwater pool. *In room:* A/C, TV/DVD, fridge, minibar, Wi-Fi.

Pavillon d'Orient ★★   Another Art Deco colonial hotel arrives in Siem Reap, but this one stands out for its newness and boutique charm. Pavillon is a great choice in this price range as it comes with nice perks like free tuk-tuk transportation to the temples. Rooms are large and all have private balconies overlooking the central garden. Bathrooms come with tubs and rain showers. This buzz-worthy place is often full so make sure to

102 call ahead; if it's booked, you'll find similar standards of service and friendliness at its sister hotel Pavillon Indochine (see below).

Rd. 60, Siem Reap (on the new road to the temples). ☎ **063/760-646.** www.pavillon-orient-hotel.com. 18 units. $85–$110 double. AE, MC, V. **Amenities:** Restaurant; bar; nice outdoor pool; room service; spa. *In room:* A/C, TV, fridge, minibar.

Shinta Mani ★ A member of the Sanctuary Resorts group, a Hong Kong–based hotel organization dedicated to sustainable tourism, environmental stewardship, and holistic practices, Shinta Mani is both a small boutique hotel and a school of hospitality—creating opportunities in health, beauty, and hospitality for the next generation of underprivileged kids in Siem Reap. While public spaces are done on a small scale—the pool is quite tiny—fine rooms and cool minimalist decor set this hotel apart. Each unit is stylish, with cool tile and buff-polished wood features. Lower-priced rooms (and their bathrooms!) are quite compact so if you need your space, I strongly suggest upgrading to a deluxe. Bathrooms connect to the main room via large sliding doors. The overall effect is chic, clean, and luxurious. Their dining space has won international awards.

Junction of Oum Khum and 14th St. (near the FCC). ☎ **063/761-998.** Fax 063/761-999. www.shintamani. com. $100–$110 double; $125–$140 deluxe. MC, V. **Amenities:** Restaurant; bar; small outdoor pool; room service; spa. *In room:* A/C, TV, fridge, minibar, Wi-Fi.

MODERATE

Bopha Angkor With their popular nightly dance show and Khmer restaurant, there's a certain "cultural theme park" vibe to this place, but Bopha Angkor is tidy, affordable, and genuinely offers a culturally infused visit to Siem Reap. Rooms are arranged in a U-shaped courtyard around a lush central garden. Private spaces are large but not luxe and feature fun local accents like mosquito nets and souvenir-shop trinkets on the walls. The staff is friendly and the hotel is close to the old market area.

No. 0512 Acharsvar St. (across the canal from the market). ☎ **063/964-928.** Fax 063/964-446. www. bopha-angkor.com. 38 units. $55–$87 double; $180 suite. MC, V. **Amenities:** Restaurant; bar; outdoor pool. *In room:* A/C, TV, fridge, minibar, Wi-Fi.

Golden Banana ★★★ **Finds** The gay-friendly, everyone's-welcome Golden Banana is tucked away in a side alley, across the river from the town center. It is a full complex that includes a bed-and-breakfast, boutique hotel, and Khmer restaurant. The new boutique hotel has rooms clustered around a saltwater pool and waterfall. Accessed from two flights of steps, my room felt like a treehouse; it was filled with light (my bedroom alone had six windows) with high cathedral ceilings. All rooms feature artwork by Chinese artist Yue Minjun and incorporate local materials such as sugar palm. The highlight was taking a bath in the stone tub on my balcony, a decadent and relaxing end to a day spent hiking around temples.

Phum Wat Damnak, Siem Reap. ☎ **012/855-366.** www.golden-banana.com. $23–$25 double; $15–$20 fan room. MC, V. **Amenities:** Restaurant; pool. *In room:* A/C, Wi-Fi.

Pavillon Indochine ★ This converted traditional Khmer house and garden is the closest you'll get to the temples and is quite peaceful, even isolated, in a quiet neighborhood. The upscale guesthouse is charming and surprisingly self-contained, with a good restaurant and a friendly, knowledgeable French proprietor whose staff can help arrange any detail in the area. Rooms are large, clean, and airy, in terra-cotta tile and wood trim, but they're not particularly luxe. There's a fine line between rustic atmosphere and necessary comforts, like hot water and air-conditioning (though many choose to go with a fan). The courtyard area is a picturesque garden dotted with quiet sitting areas with chairs or floor mats and comfy pillows.

On the back road to the temples, Siem Reap. ☎ **012/804-952.** www.pavillon-indochine.com. $60–$65 double; $85 suite. 24 units. AE, MC, V. **Amenities:** Restaurant. *In room:* A/C (cellphone available upon request).

Viroth's Hotel ★★ (Value)   This hotel is super chic and very affordable. A small boutique affair, this spot provides a private, intimate experience. The rooms have cool gray stone floors, and the shelves, entertainment unit, and bed frames are built into the white walls. One corner is painted a contrasting maroon color and marks the shower console. It is minimalist and modern with sleek geometric furniture, but soft touches like a floor vase filled with large pieces of dried palm leaves, dark brown leather desk tops and coffee-colored coverlets and accent pillows keep it warm and inviting. Most rooms have private balconies. The best room in the house is room no. 3, on the ground floor. It comes with a large, poolside corner terrace equipped with cozy lounge beds. There's a small outdoor pool surrounded by cream-colored sun beds. Breakfast is served on the rooftop restaurant. It's lit with fairy lights at night and is an excellent place to spend the evening, looking out over the rooftops of Siem Reap.

0658 Wat Bo Village (behind City River Hotel) ☎ **063/761-720.** Fax 063/760-774. www.viroth-hotel.com. 7 units. $75–$80 double. AE, MC, V. **Amenities:** Restaurant; bar; rooftop Jacuzzi; saltwater outdoor pool; room service; small spa. *In room:* A/C, TV, Wi-Fi, no phone.

Steung Siemreap Hotel ★★ (Finds)   This brand-new hotel in two separate buildings in a pretty square does a great job of looking aged. Although this is not a new or even an uncommon concept, at the Steung Siemreap they manage it rather well. Downstairs, attractive checkered red and cream tiles that appear to have been purloined directly from the south of France (and may well have been) are complemented by muted dark-wood furnishings. The rooms are large and very bright with floor-to-ceiling French windows facing on to the balcony, shaded by crisp curtains. The furnishings are uncluttered and the feel is spare but not spartan. The space, light, and location make this hotel a real contender in the higher echelons of the midrange category.

St. 9, Psar Chas. ☎ **063/965-169.** Fax 063/965-151. www.steungsiemreaphotel.com. 76 units. $80 superior double; $90 deluxe single; $100 deluxe double; $130 triple; $180 junior suite; $200 colonial suite; $250 Steung Siemreap suite. MC, V. **Amenities:** Restaurant; bar; concierge; small health club; Internet; outdoor pool; room service. *In room:* A/C, TV, fridge, minibar.

INEXPENSIVE

The downtown area of Siem Reap, on either side of the main road, is brimming with budget accommodations.

Auberge Mont Royal D'Angkor   Down a lazy lane just to the west of the town center, Auberge is a cozy choice for budget travelers. This comfortable hotel is Canadian owned and managed. Terra-cotta tile covers all open areas and rooms, and there are atmospheric touches like canvas lamps, carved wood beds, cushions, and traditional hangings, curtains, and bedspreads. The walls could use a fresh coat of paint, but the hotel is neat and tidy overall. The traditional decor is pleasant and inviting. Bathrooms are done in clean tile and have tiny bathtubs. Pool villa rooms are well worth the upgrade.

West of the town center. ☎ **063/964-044.** www.auberge-mont-royal.com. 26 units. $30–$50 double; $60 pool villa. AE, MC, V. **Amenities:** Restaurant; bar. *In room:* A/C, TV, fridge, minibar, no phone.

City River Hotel   Here are simple accommodations near the town center. Popular with bus tours, the tidy new City River Hotel handles it all with ease. Shiny lacquered wood in the lobby is as bright and airy as the friendly staff, who snap to in their starchy uniforms, quite a rarity in this category. As the name suggests, you're right on the Siem Reap River, a short walk from the popular Old Market area. Rooms are spartan, with no real decoration to speak of, but are clean and quiet; the bus tours haven't had at them yet, so this is one to get to before it falls victim. And the price is reasonable, though there are few amenities. They do, however, offer guests access to the nearby Bopha Angkor hotel (p. 102) with use of the pool.

No. 0511 Achasva St., Wat Bo, Siem Reap. ✆ 063/763-000. Fax 063/963-963. www.cityriverhotel.com. 60 units. $68–$99 double; $150 suite. AE, MC, V. **Amenities:** Restaurant; limited room service; tour services. *In room:* A/C, TV, fridge, hair dryer, Internet, minibar.

Ei8ht Rooms   This is a very unique guesthouse that actually has 12 rooms. This confusion aside, they have attempted to create a boutique experience at a very affordable price. The two buildings themselves are very standard, large concrete houses. It is what they have done with them that sets it apart. Muted yellow wash on the walls, modernist (almost Dalí-like surreal) fixtures and fittings, oddly shaped but pleasing furniture, and plenty of dark silk all contribute to the urban chic atmosphere. The staff are exceedingly trendy and very friendly. Some will appreciate the artsy flow; others will find it twee. We just liked the fact that it is so different.

138/139 Streoung Village. ✆ 063/969-788. 12 units. $25 double. MC, V. **Amenities:** Internet. *In room:* A/C, TV, fridge, minibar.

Ivy Guesthouse   The Ivy Guesthouse represents cheerful, basic backpacker territory at its best—a leafy, willowy cove that looks as though hobbits may appear. There are no hobbits though, only little pockets of budget travelers nestling in the foliage. The downstairs restaurant and surrounding garden is convivial if a little in need of an actual gardener. The upstairs tiled balcony is a peaceful place to loll about rustically in hammocks. The basic rooms are very basic indeed and at $6 this should be no surprise. If you start flinging your cash around wildly and splurge for the $8 room, you will get a wooden cabinlike space of decent size and sleep on a wooden dais. These rooms are strange but have a lot of character. The Ivy is a mixed bag, but for the budget-minded it is a good option as long as you pick your room carefully. The staff is smiley and charming.

Just off Pokambor Ave. ✆ 012/602-930. 20 units. $8 fan double. **Amenities:** Restaurant; bar.

La Noria ★   La Noria is a mellow group of bungalows connected by a winding garden path. The guesthouse is near the town center but you wouldn't know it in the hush of this little laid-back spot. Rooms are basic but have nice local touches. Terra-cotta floors, wooden trim, and small balconies are all neat and tidy, and fine hangings and details like shadow puppets and authentic Khmer furniture round out a pleasing traditional decor. Bathrooms have no separate shower consoles, but are small and clean. The place is light on amenities but has a small pool and makes up for any deficiency with gobs of charm. The open-air restaurant is a highlight, serving good Khmer and French cuisine. The hotel is affiliated with Krousar Thmey "New Family," a humanitarian group doing good work, and there's a helpful information board about rural travel and humanitarian projects.

Down a small road off Rte. 6, to the northeast of town. ✆ 063/964-242. Fax 063/964-243. www.lanoria angkor.com. 28 units. $39 with fan; $49 with A/C. No credit cards. **Amenities:** Restaurant; outdoor pool. *In room:* A/C (optional).

Mandalay Inn One of the first things that strikes you on entering this Burmese-owned guesthouse is the truly remarkable design of the reception telephone. It is antique, ornate, and beautiful and dates, no doubt, from some time before the first moon landings. The staff is quite happy to let you use it, making you instantly feel like Marlene Dietrich. Even discounting that highlight, the Mandalay Inn holds its own within its category. The rooms are large and decorated in a muted dark-wood style. The staff is super friendly and the Mandalay accepts credit cards and has fast Wi-Fi, which is unusual at this end of the range. Don't pick one of the rooms on the top floor, since this is a relatively tall building with no elevator. It actually has a gym on the roof. Half the workout is just getting there up all those stairs.

Psar Krohm St. ⓒ **063/761-662.** www.mandalayinn.com. 33 units. $8 single fan; $16 single A/C; $10 double fan; $18 double A/C; $15 family room fan; $20 family room A/C. MC, V. **Amenities:** Restaurant; bar. In room: A/C, TV, fridge.

Passaggio This unpretentious hotel is convenient to downtown and adjoins its own helpful travel agent, Lolei Travel. Rooms are large and tidy but not much more; the three floors here are something like a motel in the U.S., complete with tacky art. The one suite has a bathtub; all others have stand-up showers in bathrooms that are nondescript in plain tile but are neat and new. The friendly staff can arrange any detail and is eager to please.

Watdamanak Village (across the river to the east of town). ⓒ **063/760-324.** Fax 063/760-163. www.passaggio-hotel.com. 17 units. $35–$45 double. AE, MC, V. **Amenities:** Restaurant; free airport transfers; free Internet. In room: A/C, TV, fridge, minibar, Wi-Fi, no phone.

Two Dragons ★ Two Dragons is the best budget spot for picking up good information on the temples and onward travel and meeting up with other travelers. Run by American Gordon Sharpless, the guesthouse hosts many young backpackers who read Gordon's popular Tales of Asia website (www.talesofasia.com), which is packed with useful information about the rigors and rip-offs of crossing overland with Thailand regional travel. Rooms are spartan but very clean and with either air-conditioning or fans. A little patio area is on the second floor, and free tea and coffee are available 24 hours a day. Good camaraderie pervades this place. The restaurant serves terrific Thai and Khmer cuisine. The staff is as friendly as they come and can help arrange good guides to the temples. It's an uphill battle with the electricity company, but Gordon is hoping all rooms will have A/C by the time you read this.

1 Wat Bo Area (on the east side of the river adjacent to the post office). ⓒ **063/965-107.** http://talesofasia.com/cambodia-twodragons.htm. 14 units. $17–$27 double. AE, MC, V. **Amenities:** Restaurant; bar; bike rental. In room: A/C, fridge (some rooms), Wi-Fi, no phone.

Shadow of Angkor Guest House ★★ Although this little place is far away from Angkor's actual shadow, it does have a very pretty locale overlooking the river. It is also set in a colonial building that has genuine atmosphere. There is also a Shadow of Angkor 2, which is still a good deal but doesn't have as good a location as here. Given its price range and the location of this place, it is not surprising that it is very popular. The colonnaded restaurant is quiet and relaxing, set back far enough that you will not be bothered by the hawkers and beggars but still allowing you to contemplate the river in front of you in peace. The rooms range from very basic (and cramped) to spacious riverfront chic. The surrounding verandas are a great place to sit and chill after a long day of slogging around the temples.

No. 353 Pokambor Ave. ☏ **063/964-774.** www.shadowofangkor.com. 35 units. $20 river balcony A/C; $15 double A/C; $8 double fan. MC, V. **Amenities:** Restaurant; bar. *In room:* A/C, TV, fridge.

Sun Sengky Guest House   This is a no-nonsense clean, bright, and well-run option with secure parking right near Psar Chas on Sivatha Road. There are few frills (just TV, fridge, and air-conditioning) but the rooms are large and new with an outside veranda. The wide, white tiled corridors are certainly not going to win any prizes for subtlety of decoration, but they might win some for light, bright functionality. It is the equivalent of a good motel in Missouri after a long drive across the Midwest. The staff is relaxed but precise and efficient, and the security guard stays wide-awake all night.

No. 15 Sivatha Rd. ☏ **063/964-034.** 27 units. $10 double fan; $15 double A/C. **Amenities:** Restaurant; bar. *In room:* A/C, TV, fridge.

3 WHERE TO DINE

Dining in Siem Reap is not a pricey affair. The major hotels all have fine upscale eateries, and there are also several good free-standing spots. The area around the Old Market is a cluster of storefronts, most of little distinction from one another, but all are affordable and laid-back.

EXPENSIVE

Le Bistrot de Siem Reap ★★ FRENCH   The atmosphere in this restaurant is wonderfully charming, with old French music playing lightly in the background, light gray walls with the ceiling trim and accent walls painted warm maroon, and black lacquer tables with mixed wooden and rattan chairs. The walls are adorned with old posters advertising voyages to the Far East, but the cuisine is a superb culinary trip to France. The wine list is a work in progress, so ask for a recommendation. They also have a good selection of Cuban cigars. It's a wonderful, tasty slice of old Indochina.

Central Park, P.O. Box 93145, Siem Reap. ☏ **063/760-428.** Main courses $15–$26. AE, MC, V. Daily 6:30am–midnight.

Meric ★★ KHMER   This is a slick, trendy restaurant located in the equally stylish Hôtel de la Paix. The Western dishes are stronger than the Khmer menu, though both are constantly changing with the latter often offering off-the-beaten path specials such as mashed snake or frog. The steaks here are the best in town and service is tops. There is outdoor dining around a stately bodhi tree in the central courtyard, or indoor tables near the open kitchen.

Sivatha Blvd. ☏ **063/966-000.** Main courses $18–$26. AE, MC, V. Daily 6–10:30am, noon–3pm, and 6–10:30pm.

MODERATE

Abacus ★ ASIAN/FRENCH   This restaurant, set in a traditional Cambodian stilt house, is a refreshing change from the eateries along Pub Street. There is a central bar made of volcanic stone and a few tables with rattan chairs on the first floor, underneath the house. Terrace seating upstairs is divided among various small, cozy rooms. The menu is written on a chalkboard and you can choose from a good selection of either Asian rice bowls or Western mains with a couple of side dishes.

Oum Khun St. ☏ **012/644-286.** Main courses $5–$17. No credit cards. Daily 11am–late.

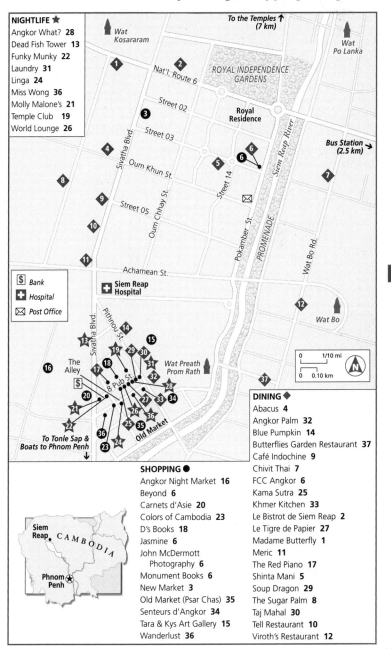

NIGHTLIFE ★
Angkor What? **28**
Dead Fish Tower **13**
Funky Munky **22**
Laundry **31**
Linga **24**
Miss Wong **36**
Molly Malone's **21**
Temple Club **19**
World Lounge **26**

To the Temples ↑
(7 km)

Wat Kosararam

Wat Po Lanka

Nat'l. Route 6

ROYAL INDEPENDENCE GARDENS

Street 02

Royal Residence

Street 03

Siem Reap River

Bus Station →
(2.5 km)

Oum Khun St.

Street 14

Siwatha Blvd.

Street 05

Oum Chhay St.

Pokamber St.

PROMENADE

Wat Bo Rd.

Achamean St.

$ Bank

✚ Hospital

✉ Post Office

Siem Reap Hospital

Wat Bo

Pithnou St.

Siwatha Blvd.

The Alley

$

8 Pub St.

Wat Preath Prom Rath

0   1/10 mi
0   0.10 km

Old Market

To Tonle Sap & Boats to Phnom Penh ↓

SIEM REAP

6

WHERE TO DINE

SHOPPING ●
Angkor Night Market **16**
Beyond **6**
Carnets d'Asie **20**
Colors of Cambodia **23**
D's Books **18**
Jasmine **6**
John McDermott Photography **6**
Monument Books **6**
New Market **3**
Old Market (Psar Chas) **35**
Senteurs d'Angkor **34**
Tara & Kys Art Gallery **15**
Wanderlust **36**

DINING ◆
Abacus **4**
Angkor Palm **32**
Blue Pumpkin **14**
Butterflies Garden Restaurant **37**
Café Indochine **9**
Chivit Thai **7**
FCC Angkor **6**
Kama Sutra **25**
Khmer Kitchen **33**
Le Bistrot de Siem Reap **2**
Le Tigre de Papier **27**
Madame Butterfly **1**
Meric **11**
The Red Piano **17**
Shinta Mani **5**
Soup Dragon **29**
The Sugar Palm **8**
Taj Mahal **30**
Tell Restaurant **10**
Viroth's Restaurant **12**

Siem Reap ●

CAMBODIA

Phnom Penh ★

Cafe Indochine ★★ ASIAN   On the north end of the busy central road that leads to the temples, Cafe Indochine is a cool, old Indochina throwback. Set in an old wooden building that's been newly renovated, this little wooden perch is a cool place to watch life go by on the busy street out front and unwind from a busy day at the temples. The menu is an eclectic list of Thai, Cambodian, Vietnamese, and French dishes: true Indochina. Start with some fine, light spring rolls, either fried or fresh. Salads are savory, and they serve good Thai spicy soups like tom-yam as well as French bouillabaisse. Try a shared set menu for $9 per person and get a short course in local cuisine such as beef done in savory *lok lak* style; fine curries; amok fish; a number of whole-fish dishes; and beef, chicken, or vegetable stir-fries. Follow up with good ice cream or coffee.

44 Sivatha Rd. Ⓒ **012/804-952.** Main courses $5–$9. AE, MC, V. Daily 10am–3pm and 5–11pm.

FCC Angkor (Foreign Correspondent's Club) INTERNATIONAL   This glowing white, modern cube would be at home in a nouveau riche California suburb or a Jacques Tati film, but is a bit jarring canal-side in the center of Siem Reap. The first floor is boutique shopping and the second floor is an elegant open space with high ceilings. There's an Art Deco bar, low lounge chairs at the center, and standard dining space on the balcony. The main room is flanked on one end by an open kitchen. The FCC is the town's runway and holds numerous functions and hosts live music. The menu is the same as the original FCC in Phnom Penh, with the same dichotomy between the enormity of the prices and the rather low quality of the food, which includes soups, salads, pasta, steaks, and wood-fired pizzas. The staff can't seem to believe they work here, and service is hot and cold but very friendly. Even if just for a drink, it is worth swinging by at least once. The first-floor compound continues to expand, and now supports some of the finest shopping in the city. Also, check out their cool billiards room, which is like a modernist installation behind glass, or their big-screen television surrounded by large lounge chairs at poolside.

Pokambor Ave. (next to the Royal Residence and just north of the post office). Ⓒ **063/760-283.** Main courses $8–$22. AE, MC, V. Daily 7am–midnight.

Madame Butterfly ★ THAI/KHMER   Serving the finest authentic Khmer- and Thai-influenced cuisine in town, the setting is very pleasant and alone makes it worth a visit. In a converted traditional wooden home, seating is in low rattan chairs, and the decor is characterized by a tasteful collection of Buddhist and Khmer artifacts. Candlelight mingles with mellow indirect lighting, and the whole effect is casual and romantic. There are daily specials, and the menu is heavy on good curries and hot-pot dishes. Try the poached fish in coconut sauce with sticky rice. The Masaman curry is excellent and the *mchou pous,* a chicken-and-shrimp bisque, is rich and tasty. Great for a leisurely evening.

A short ride west on No. 6, airport road. Ⓒ **016/909-607.** Main courses $6–$15. V. Daily 6am–11pm.

The Red Piano ★ INTERNATIONAL   Angelina Jolie and cast and crew of the film *Tomb Raider* made this atmospheric bar their second home while filming at the temples. Imported steaks, spaghetti, sandwiches, salads, and international specialties like good Indian samosas or chicken *cordon bleu* round out a great menu of familiar fare. Everything is good, and this place is always hoppin' late into the evening. Due to popular demand (it's sometimes hard to get a seat and they take no reservations), they've expanded onto a second floor and renovations throughout give the place a tidy, upscale charm.

50m (164 ft.) northwest of the Old Market. Ⓒ **063/963-240.** Main courses $4–$6. No credit cards. Daily 7am–midnight.

Shinta Mani ★★ INTERNATIONAL   Shinta Mani is uniquely refined for Cambodia. Dining indoors is cool, referring to both the air-conditioning and the decor: dark-
wood furnishings against a minimalist backdrop of peach pastel walls and simple,
modern artwork. Outdoors is a small open bar area and a few tables set under a heavy
wooden lattice thatched roof. Candlelight and a single white lotus flower, with its exterior petals bent into origami shapes, complete the effect. Service is professional, but the
staff seems slightly nervous, often worrying over the details a bit too much, and you
might even catch yourself rooting for them. Prices are high for this part of the world, but
everything that comes out of the kitchen has panache. Elegant presentations on white
china enhance the experience of fine Khmer and Western dishes made with the best of
local ingredients. Popular entrees include a fine beef sirloin, a savory stuffed chicken
breast, and comfort foods like spaghetti and fried rice (which are a bit easier on the
budget). In a town where you can eat for so cheap, Shinta Mani is carving its own niche
and attracting rave reviews from international critics, but the backpackers are kept at bay.
The wine list is exhaustive, the drink list doesn't stop, and whether dining in the cool,
intimate inside or among the humming cicadas outdoors, this is the place to enjoy a
slow-paced savory meal with good conversation.

Junction of Oum Khum and 14th St. (near the FCC). ⓒ **063/761-998.** Main courses $8–$20. AE, MC, V.
Daily 6:30am–10:30pm.

INEXPENSIVE

Angkor Palm ★★ TRADITIONAL KHMER   This gem stands out from the crowd
by a mile. It serves Khmer food at its finest in elegant surroundings that put some of its
more expensive rivals to shame. Light, bright traditional Khmer furnishings and comfortable rattan chairs in a beautiful colonial villa in a central location set the scene for an
operation that is both professional and elegant. Monsieur Bun Try, the owner, spent
much of his life in Paris and has combined traditional Khmer values with French
panache. The *lok lak,* a simple and universal Khmer dish of diced beef with a simple
sauce, is superb, coming with the very Khmer pepper and lemon dip one finds in the
simplest of villages. The starters are the size of main courses. The staff is charming and
superb, being attentive without being obsequious. The prices are far lower than pretty
much any of its rivals, leading to a consistently full restaurant with a consistently satisfied
clientele.

Pithnou St. opposite the northern end of the Alley. ⓒ **063/761-436.** www.angkorpalm.com. Main
courses $3–$6. MC, V. Daily 10am–10pm.

Chivit Thai ★ THAI   Authentic Thai is served in this atmospheric street-side restaurant, with both air-conditioning and outdoor dining. The food is great, the price is low,
and there's casual floor seating and a rustic charm to the place, quite romantic in candlelight. Name your favorite Thai dish, and they do it here. The *tom yum* (sweet, spicy Thai
soup) is excellent, and they have good set menus comprised of many courses that are
much finer than their low price tag.

130 Wat Bo Rd. (across the river from the FCC, near the intersection of Rte. 6 going out of town). ⓒ **012/
830-761.** Main courses $2.50–$5. No credit cards. Daily 7am–10pm.

Kama Sutra ★ INDIAN   This restaurant serves excellent Indian food in the heart of
Pub street. It has covered outdoor seating so dining is informal and there's the option of
refreshing A/C seating upstairs. The fare is hearty, and the atmosphere is loud and happy.

E161 Pub St. ⓒ **063/761-225.** Main courses $2.50–$7.50. No credit cards. Daily 11am–late.

Khmer Kitchen Restaurant ★ KHMER This busy little storefront hides itself down an alley on the north end of the Old Market, but draws a nightly crowd for big portions of simple, delicious Khmer fare. Good curries and stir-fries share menu space with unique dishes like baked pumpkin. It's about the food here, not the service, but these folks are friendly enough considering how busy they usually are.

Down an alley just north of the Old Market. ✆ **063/964-154.** Main courses $2–$3. No credit cards. Daily 10am–10pm.

Le Tigre de Papier ★ KHMER/INTERNATIONAL Since Le Tigre de Papier is part of a business empire of restaurants and hotels, you might think this would render it impersonal. Surprisingly, this is not the case. It is a long, thin building with openings both onto Pub Street and the alley. During the daytime, the Pub Street end is pleasant with comfortable seating (they haven't made the mistake of cramming in too many tables) and partially traditionally decorated interior. In the evening it is fine until the music starts pumping from the surrounding venues and it gets uncomfortably loud. The Alley end of the restaurant is deliberately more subdued (as is the Alley itself) and there is no music. Given that they have free Wi-Fi it is a good place to surf in peace and quiet. The food is patchy. The Khmer food is excellent (since the restaurant runs affiliated cooking classes, it needs to be), and the spring rolls are very light and crispy. If you like chili, try the spicy shrimp salad. The pizzas are also very good, though some of the Western dishes don't make it. The merguez sausage tastes like sawdust.

No. 198 St. 8 (Pub St.). ✆ **063/966-100.** www.letigrepapier.com. Main courses $3.25–$7. MC, V. Daily 24 hr.

Soup Dragon VIETNAMESE/KHMER This is a longtime popular Pub Street cafe now with three floors and excellent views of the Old Market area. It is a place of noodles and soup. Authentic Vietnamese staples such as pho (noodle soup), fresh spring rolls, and all manner of wok-fried dishes are the mainstays. There are two floors of open-air dining overlooking the busy street in the center of town and they are always packed. There is also a large rooftop area. The place opens into a casual bar in the late evening and, whether to just escape the heat at noontime or to talk late into the night, Soup Dragon is a good place to enjoy cool drinks and a fine Sinitic meal. Try the Soup Ch'nang Dae.

Corner of 2 Thnou St. and St. 8 (Pub St.). ✆ **063/964-933.** Main courses $2.50–$9. No credit cards. Daily 6am–late.

The Sugar Palm ★★ TRADITIONAL KHMER This is the place where food and beverage managers from nearby five-star hotels come to feast. Co-owner Kethana serves old-fashioned, flavorful, and hearty Khmer food. The Siem Reap restaurant is on the second floor of a spacious house. The restaurant has a warm and inviting ambience with subdued, covered lighting, a wall painted in sunny yellow, and vaulted ceilings. The furniture and bar are done in dark sugar palm wood. Staff walks around barefoot on spotless wooden floors. Most of the seating is on the wraparound balcony, partially covered from the outside world with roll-down bamboo blinds. On the menu, the pomelo salad is excellent. Fleshy pomelo tendrils are played off the sharp taste of dried shrimp and crunchy chopped peanuts, and strips of spicy red pepper give it an extra kick. For mains try the chicken stir-fried with ginger. The meat is tender and the sauce is loaded with equally tender slices of sautéed ginger. It is quite a treat.

Ta Phul Rd. (400m/1,312 ft. south of the Caltex gas station). ✆ **063/964-838.** Main courses $4–$6. MC, V. Daily 11am–3pm and 5–10pm. Bar till late.

Taj Mahal ★★ NORTHERN INDIAN   It has become almost obligatory where young tourists gather to have an Indian restaurant be the flame for the travel-weary and empty-bellied moths, and Taj Mahal is in fact a bright light. It serves a range of northern Indian cuisine—from heaping *talis* with curries, lentils, and rice to delicious tandoori, fiery curries (unless otherwise specified), and good nan breads to sop it all up, plus beer to wash it down. Cozy and clean Taj Mahal is an old Siem Reap standby and packs 'em in nightly. Seating is best at street-side as you face the north end of the market with its many, busy street stalls. Ask for your samosa cooked to order and you'll be bowled over. Everything is good.

North Old Market. ✆ **063/963-353.** Main courses $1.50–$4.50. No credit cards. Daily 8am–11pm.

Tell Restaurant ★★ GERMAN/INTERNATIONAL   Tell Restaurant serves hearty German fare, catering to the many expats and travelers longing for a bit of home (mostly a German and Scandinavian home). Savory entrees like goulash and Vienna schnitzel, German sausages, *cordon bleu,* stroganoff, great steaks, and a signature raclette special or enormous cheese fondue (priced at $27 and expected to be shared by two or more) are quite impressive. You walk away with a bit of a heavy belly into the steamy Khmer evening, but after a day touring the temples (and usually another one planned), a hearty meal might be just the ticket. They also have a whole roster of good salads and lighter fare, from Mexican to Indian and Italian, as well as good Khmer entrees. The menu reads like one from a U.S. diner, with just about everything you can imagine. Don't miss the choice of "Hangover Breakfasts," comprised of a shot and a beer and a pile of good fried food, great after sampling the many and exotic cocktails available. The restaurant is just a busy storefront on central Sivatha Road alongside the likes of Dead Fish Tower, a popular bar, and lots of small storefronts catering to backpackers, but Tell is a real standout.

No. 374 Sivatha Rd. (200m/656 ft. north of the Old Market). ✆ **063/963-289.** Main courses $3–$9. V. Daily 10am–2pm and 5:30–10pm.

Viroth's Restaurant ★★ KHMER   Like its sister hotel two streets down (p. 103), Viroth's Restaurant boasts a sleek and stylish interior. The French and Khmer were the original owners of popular Angkor Café (see "Dining at the Temples" below). Unlike the hotel, which is still a secret among those in the know, the restaurant is well known and much loved. The food is traditional Khmer cuisine and is very tasty. The amok fish is a perfect blend of coconut milk and lemon grass and, unlike at other restaurants, the fish is completely deboned. The spacious dining area is on a raised wooden platform and is flanked on one side by a wall of bamboo rods. Ceiling and floor fans keep a cool breeze going and send ripples through the strips of sheer saffron sheets suspended from the ceiling and hanging between tables.

246 Wat Bo St. (behind La Résidence Hotel). ✆ **063/760-774.** Main courses $3.30–$7. MC, V. Daily 10:30am–2pm and 5:30–10pm.

SNACKS & CAFES

Blue Pumpkin   This stylish, all-white cafe is a longtime local favorite, serving great pastries, coffee, and entrees like burgers and sandwiches. They'll pack you a lunch for the temples, too. Wi-Fi access is available. Located at the northeast end of the Old Market, it's next door to Kokoon, a fine shop for trinkets and souvenirs.

365 Mondol 1. ✆ **063/963-574.** Main courses $1.50–$5. MC, V. Daily 6am–11pm

Butterflies Garden Restaurant ★   Don't miss this netted enclosure with a butterfly farm and meticulous menagerie of local flora and fauna, including a pond filled with Japanese carp. There are detailed descriptions of all plants and some individual butterflies. They serve Khmer and international cuisine. Vegetarians will also enjoy an extensive selection here.

Just across the Siem Reap River north of the Old Market. Main courses $3–$10. Entrance costs $2. No credit cards. Daily 8am–5pm.

DINING AT THE TEMPLES

Across the busy parking lot closest to Angkor Wat, you're sure to spot the snazzy **Angkor Café** (✆ **063/380-300**). This little gallery and souvenir shop serves, for a mint by Khmer standards, good coffee, tea, and sandwiches, all of which is provided by the folks at **Blue Pumpkin** (see "Snacks & Cafes," above). It's the best thing going on the Angkor compound, and, apart from the good food, the building is air-conditioned, great for a break at midday. Don't miss their attached boutique, with high-end silver and stone reproductions of the temples as well as silk and other souvenirs. Open daily from 8am to 5:30pm. No credit cards.

Among all the major temples, you'll see lots of small, **thatch-roofed eateries,** and all will implore you to enter. The competition means that you have more leverage when haggling: "Are you sure this Coke is $2? Someone over there said it was . . ." You get the picture. You'll be swarmed by vendors when you approach these restaurants. Just pick one quickly and the rest will split. Prices are slightly inflated, but it's a tourist sight and people need to make a living (and probably have to pay some heavy kickbacks). A few bucks will get you fried rice, noodles, or vegetables. Most of these places have shaded hammock areas out back (mostly for drivers, but a good place to rest) and basic toilets. Carrying your own antiseptic hand sanitizer is a good idea.

---

4 SIEM REAP ATTRACTIONS

Angkor Wat is one of the most astonishing structures built by humans. The temple complex covers 97 sq. km (60 sq. miles) and requires at least a few busy days to get around the major sights thoroughly. Everyone has their favorite, but there are some generally recognized highlights that you will not want to miss. Be sure to plan carefully and catch a sunrise or sunset from one of the more prime spots; it's a photographer's dream. *Note:* The temples are magnificent themselves, and days spent clambering around the temples are inherently interesting, but be careful not to come away from a visit to ancient Angkor with a memory of an oversize rock collection or jungle gym. There's much to learn about Buddhism, Hinduism, architecture, and Khmer history; it's useful to hire a well-informed guide or join a tour group. There are also subtleties to temple touring, and a good guide is your best chance to beat the crowd and catch the intricacies or be in the right place for the magic moments of the day. Contact any hotel front desk or the tour agencies listed above. Hiring a guide for 1 day costs $20.

THE TEMPLES

Entrance fees for Angkor Wat are as follows: A 1-day ticket is $20, a 3-day ticket is $40, and a 1-week ticket is $60. The tickets were recently restructured, extending the validity of 3-day passes to 1 week instead of 3 consecutive days. Similarly, 1-week passes are now valid for 1 month. Tickets are good for all sights within the main temple compound, as well as Banteay Srei, to the north, and the outlying temples of the Roluos Group. Other

Some Guidelines When Visiting Angkor

When you arrive at the temples of Angkor you will soon realize just how many people visit this place every year. These are some tips on how to keep your footprint as low as possible.

- Accept the restrictions placed on the temple complex (for example, do not touch, do not photograph, do not enter).
- Avoid touching—every small touch becomes harmful when repeated by 1,000 people every day.
- Wear appropriate footwear—avoid high heels and studded soles.
- Mind your backpack—you could brush up against the walls and damage the carvings and bas-reliefs.
- Avoid climbing unnecessarily on the statues and monuments. If you must take a photo on top of a monument, be selective and choose to climb only one.
- Shop responsibly—beware of buying objects of unknown origin. Looting of temples has been a problem.
- Don't litter—take everything with you.
- Respect peace and silence—allow others to enjoy what you are enjoying in peace and tranquillity.

sights like Beng Melea or Ko Kur require an additional fee. The temples open at dawn and you can buy a ticket as early as 5am to get there for sunup. At dusk, around 6pm, temple attendants start gently nudging visitors out of the park.

It is highly recommended to hire a guide, for at least for 1 day of temple touring. A guide provides not only the most useful information that will serve as a background for your further exploration, but makes the logistics of that first day much easier. Contact any hotel front desk or tour office and they can arrange something for you. The cost of a guide is $20 per day. Guides are certified and come from the same school and so dispense nearly the same information, but, of course, some are better than others. Ask around for recommendations.

Important note: The temple sites listed below are more or less in the usual order you might visit them on tour. A visit to Angkor is now a noisy romp among large Korean, Thai, Chinese, and European groups. An average guide will take you along in the heart of the herd, following the standard temple routine, but a good guide knows how to get you out of the pack. Insist on it.

The Angkor complex is currently undergoing massive restoration. Most of the temples noted below are included in the extensive project and as such certain sections are hidden behind scaffolding or closed off to visitors. While it is disappointing, the restoration is not so invasive as to warrant canceling your trip here. Work should wrap up sometime in 2010.

Angkor Wat ★★★   The symbol of Cambodia, the five spires of the main temple of Angkor are known the world over. In fact, this is the most resplendent of the Angkor sites, one certainly not to miss even in the most perfunctory of tours.

Built under the reign of Suryavarman II in the 12th century, this temple, along with Bayon and Baphuon, is the very pinnacle of Khmer architecture. From base to tip of the highest tower, it's 213m (669 ft.) of awe-inspiring stone in the definitive, elaborate Khmer style. The temple moat is 1.5×1.3km (1×¾ mile) around, and some 90m (295 ft.) wide, crossed by a causeway with long naga statues on each side as railings from the west; in fact Angkor is the only temple entered from the west (all others from the east). Angkor Wat is also the only Angkor monument that is a mausoleum—all others are temples or monasteries. Angkor's main temple is dedicated to Vishnu.

Approaching the temple, you'll first cross the causeway over the main moat—restored in the 1960s by the French. Enter the compound across the first gallery, the Majestic Gallery, with some carvings and Brahma statuary, then pass into the large, grassy courtyard housing the main temple. This next causeway is flanked on either side by two small library buildings as well as two small ponds. (**Hint:** Hop off the causeway and take a photo of the temple reflected in the pond on the right.)

An outdoor staircase sits at the approach to the main temple. From there, you'll enter the richest area of statuary, galleries, and bas-reliefs. The famous bas-reliefs encircling the temple on the first level (south side) depict the mythical "Churning of the Ocean of Milk," a legend in which Hindu deities stir vast oceans in order to extract the elixir of immortality. This churning produced the apsaras, Hindu celestial dancers, who can be seen on many temples. Other reliefs surrounding the base of the main temple show Khmer wars, and corner towers depict Hindu fables.

The most measured and studied of all the sites, Angkor Wat is the subject of much speculation: It's thought to represent Mount Meru, home of Hindu gods and a land of creation and destruction. Researchers measuring the site in *hat,* ancient Khmer units of measure, deduce that the symmetry of the building corresponds with the timeline of the Hindu ages, as a map or calendar of the universe, if you will. The approach from the main road crosses the baray (reservoir) and is an ascending progression of three levels to the inner sanctum. The T-shirt hawkers are relentless, and the tricky steps and temple height are a challenge to those with vertigo, but the short trip is awe-inspiring and the views from the top are breathtaking. *Note:* There's a guide rope on the southern face (and often a long line up).

It's a fair walk up to the second level, a flat, open space that overlooks the main temple square, the famed Angkor *prangs* or parapets on each corner. From here, it's a steep climb (use the staircase with roped handrail on the south side of the temple) up to the third and final level (at time of writing, this level was closed to visitors). There are four large courtyards surrounded by galleries, and balcony overlooks from the base of the prangs at each corner. These high perches are great spots for watching the sunset over Bakeng Hill (though lately, the guards try to get more people down earlier and earlier).

Angkor Wat is the first temple you pass when entering the temple complex, but depending on your guide, you might save it for the evening and head directly to nearby Angkor Thom.

Bakeng Hill ★★ Just past Angkor Wat, Bakeng Hill is meant to resemble Mount Meru, the center of the earth in the Hindu cosmology. The hill makes a great spot for sunrise or sunset viewing and gets crowded like a mosh pit in high season. The hike up is a good way to limber up and break a sweat pre-dawn, but the crumbled steps and slippery mud are a bit much for some. Consider taking the trek in style high up on an elephant's back in a houda. Elephants for hire start at about $20 and wait at the bottom of the hill.

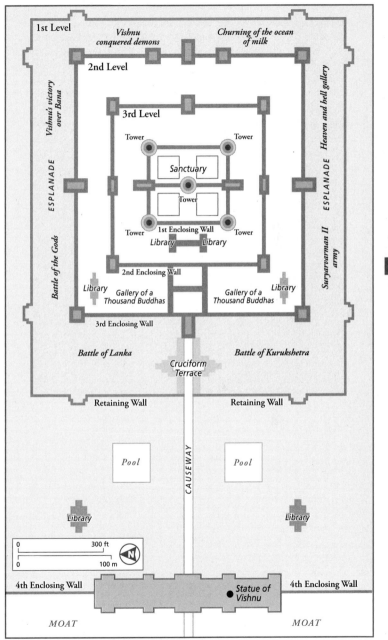

1st Level

Vishnu conquered demons

Churning of the ocean of milk

2nd Level

Vishnu's victory over Bana

Heaven and hell gallery

3rd Level

ESPLANADE

ESPLANADE

Tower

Tower

Sanctuary

Tower

Tower

Tower

1st Enclosing Wall

Library

Library

2nd Enclosing Wall

Battle of the Gods

Suryarvarman II army

Library

Gallery of a Thousand Buddhas

Gallery of a Thousand Buddhas

Library

3rd Enclosing Wall

Battle of Lanka

Battle of Kurukshetra

Cruciform Terrace

Retaining Wall

Retaining Wall

Pool

Pool

CAUSEWAY

Library

Library

0   300 ft
0   100 m

N

4th Enclosing Wall

Statue of Vishnu

4th Enclosing Wall

MOAT

MOAT

Angkor Thom ★★★   The temple name means "the great city" in Khmer and is famed for its fantastic 45m (148-ft.) central temple, **Bayon** and nearby **Baphuon.** The vast area of Angkor Thom, over a mile on one side, is dotted with many temples and features; don't miss the elaborate reliefs on the Bayon's first floor gallery or of the **Terrace of the Leper King** and the **Terrace of Elephants.** The **Angkor Thom Gates,** particularly the south gate, are good examples of the angelic carving of the Jayavarman head, a motif you will find throughout the temple sites. The bridge spanning the moat before the south entrance is lined with the gods and monsters said to have been in competition to churn the proverbial sea of milk that would cause creation of the world. The line of statues with the gate in the background is a classic Angkor scene.

The Bayon ★★★   The **Bayon** is the very centerpiece of the larger Angkor Thom city, and with its classic carved faces is one of the best loved of the Angkor temples. A magical, eerie, and mysterious place. Bayon is a Buddhist temple built under the reign of prolific Jayavarman VII (A.D. 1190), but the temple was built atop a previous Hindu site and adheres to Hindu cosmology and, with its central tower depicting Meru and its oceanic moat, can be read as a metaphor for the natural world. The Bayon is famous for its huge stone faces, usually set in groups of four around a central *prang*, or tower, and each face indicating an ordinal direction on the compass. The curious smiling faces are done in deep relief at Bayon, and you'll also find them in different forms at the entrance gates to Angkor Thom, at Ta Prom, and Banteay Kdei. Their expression is as enigmatic as the Mona Lisa. Representing compassion and equanimity, they are also said to depict Jayavarman VII, the temple's very builder and benefactor, himself. You approach the Bayon along a forested area at the city center, cool and misty, where streams of light come through in visible rays and the drone of cicadas is deafening (you might even see some monkeys). Elephant trekkers also line the road to the temple.

The three-level Bayon is nearly square. The first level is surrounded by an intricate **bas-relief gallery** depicting stories of Khmer conquests and battles, as well as daily life and ritual among the early Khmers. A good guide can lead you to the juicy bits of the fun story, and you can spend a good bit of time sorting out the details for yourself too (kids love it). Look for the unique pairs of Apsara dancers on columns near the gallery (Apsaras usually dance alone). On the South Wall, find three tiers depicting Khmer battles with the Cham from 1177 to 1181, a battle that took place on the waters of the Tonle Sap Lake in boats—look for the grisly images of crocodiles eating the carcasses of the fallen. Also note the Chinese figure with beard, top knot, and lance on a horse. Khmer soldiers ride elephants and have short hair, a spear, and a magic string for invincible fighting; they also carry shields and banners. A good guide can point out details like a lady crouching and getting burned on a fire and a man handing a turtle to a chef, as well as a scene of a cockfight and soldiers sacrificing a buffalo to ensure good luck in battle. There's a real sense of humanity to these images.

The second level has some Apsara reliefs and porticos with lingam, but the third level is the most interesting, the place where you can get up close with the many **Apsara Faces** thought to resemble a serene Jayavarman. Each of the 54 small towers is adorned with a face, or a number of faces, and you can have a ball with your zoom lens. There are a number of porticos with small lingam statues, and elderly matrons sell incense sticks and a chance to make merit by making an offering. The large central tower, or Prang, is 25m (82 ft.) in diameter with 16 small coves for meditation of kings and high priests. In 1933, French archaeologist George Groslier excavated the main prang only to find a massive

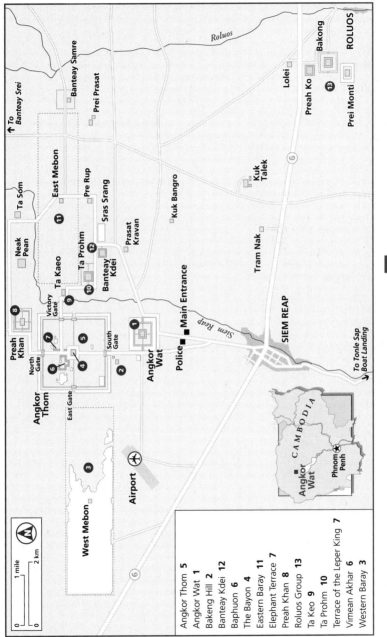

Angkor Thom **5**
Angkor Wat **1**
Bakeng Hill **2**
Banteay Kdei **12**
Baphuon **6**
The Bayon **4**
Eastern Baray **11**
Elephant Terrace **7**
Preah Khan **8**
Roluos Group **13**
Ta Keo **9**
Ta Prohm **10**
Terrace of the Leper King **7**
Vimean Akhar **6**
Western Baray **3**

statue of Jayavarman hidden underneath. The statue, called **Jaya Bot Mohania,** is a seated Jayavarman with a seven-headed naga snake looming over him; it is now on display at a small temple near the **Victory Gate** (just east of the Bayon).

One of the greatest views of the many faces of the Bayon is from the ground at the northern end of the temples, just before a large snack, refreshment, and shopping area. Stop here on your way to the Baphuon (reviewed below) by foot.

Baphuon   Just north of the Bayon is the stalwart form of the **Baphuon,** a temple mount built in 1066 and an important Khmer capital. Early French archaeologists sought to restore the crumbling mount, and began to disassemble the temple block by block, but their efforts were interrupted by war, and it would be some years before archaeologists would return to find a confused jigsaw puzzle of a dismantled temple. The plans were lost. Bilateral efforts are underway to solve the puzzle and put the temple back together, and these ongoing efforts give visitors an idea of what original temple construction might have been like. The Baphuon was the last capital in the Angkor period.

The east gate of the Baphuon is the only remaining part of what was once a large laterite wall. A narrow causeway with moats on either side connects the gate with the main temple. The temple has five levels that are all the same height, which makes the site more like a pyramid and quite unique among Angkor temples. *Note:* From the Baphuon you can make a clockwise loop, first to Vimean Akhar, then to the Terrace of the Leper Kings and the Terrace of Elephants (all on foot) before you return to the vendors' area and your awaiting chariot to go on to Preah Khan or via the east gate to Ta Prohm.

Pre Rup ★   With its three central spires, **Pre Rup** looks a bit like a mini Angkor Wat. Prerup was built by King Rajeindravarmen II in 961 and was dedicated to Shiva. The best views are from the Hindu temple's south side. It is made of gray sandstone, which is a less durable material than the pink sandstone of Banteay Srei. As such, time and weather have had its way with the temple and many of the intricate carvings and detail have been worn away by rain and erosion. It's a crumbling edifice but still completely awesome in size and structure. Plants have begun to grow on the central towers and you can see their bright green leaves working their way through the gray stone. You'll be scrambling over the fallen rock and debris near the bottom of the temple and you still feel like a humble, insignificant mortal. Climb to the top of the temple and look west; on a clear day, you can see Angkor Wat's spires (roughly 12km/7½ miles away) peeking out over the treetops.

Vimean Akhar ★   Continuing north of the Baphuon—and still within large Angkor Thom—you reach the "Palace of Air," or **Vimean Akhar,** which was a royal palace built by three successive kings, Jayavarman II and V as well as Suryavarman I, between 944 and 1045. This Hindu temple dedicated to Shiva is some 12m (40 ft.) high with three levels; each of the three levels represents one of the kings who helped build it. Each side has steep steps and the shallow moat is full in rainy season. The top of the temple is a narrow pillared gallery. The steep climb is best attempted to the left (west) when approaching from the Baphuon (there's a handrail). Have a drink or a fresh coconut in a shaded area at the bottom of the other side.

Adjacent to the Baphuon are two large ponds: the biggest is 125m (410 ft.) long and was where the king himself bathed; the smaller ponds were for the king's courtiers.

Note: The eastern entrance of the Vimean Akhar has a Sanskrit inscription with a brief history of construction and orientation. Most are in museums and this is one of just a few that you can still find on the temple site.

(Moments) **The Magic Hours at Angkor Wat**

The skies over Angkor always put on a show. With just a bit of prior planning, you can see the dawn or the day's afterglow framed in temple spires, glowing off the main wat or reflected in one of the temple reservoirs. Photographers swoon. Here are a few hints for catching the magic hours at the temples.

The sunrise and sunset views from the upper terraces of Angkor Wat, the main temple, are some of the best, though it's a tough climb for some. At dusk, temple staffers start clearing the main temple area just as the sun dips. Smile; avoid them; and try to stay for the afterglow.

For the classic photographer's view of the main temple, Angkor Wat, at sunset—with the image reflected in a pool—enter the first wall of the temple compound, walk halfway down the front gangway and then take a right or left down the set of stairs and out into the field. The view from the water's edge, with warm light bouncing off the temple, is stunning. The pond on the right nearly disappears in dry season, but has natural edges, not stone, and makes for a nicer shot.

Okay, so it's a bit crowded, but the views from Phnom Bakeng (Bakeng Hill), just a short drive past the entrance to Angkor Wat, are stunning at both sunrise and sunset. It's a good climb up the hill, and those so inclined can go by elephant for about $20.

The open area on the eastern side of Banteay Kdei (see map, earlier in this chapter) looks over one of Angkor's many reservoirs, Sras Srang, which serves as a great reflective pool for the rising glow at sunrise. See the "'Getting High'" at Angkor" box, below, for other options.

If money is no object, contact **Helicopters Cambodia Ltd.** ★ at their office just north of the Old Market at No. 217 (✆ **012/814-500**). For a fee, you can see the sights from any angle you choose. Be sure to specify your needs and interests and they can create an itinerary that suits.

More affordable is a ride with Angkor Balloon. Just $15 gets you a 10-minute ride up to 250m (820 ft.) above the ground. The balloon basket is large, good for walking around and taking in the view from different sides. The balloon is controlled from the ground by tether, a very sophisticated contraption brought to Cambodia by French developers. It's a bit like an amusement park ride really. The takeoff is 1km (½ mile) west of the main entrance to the temples (you're sure to see them from afar throughout the day). Flights start at 5:30am and end at 6pm, and the prime sunrise and sunset spots fill up quickly. Call them at ✆ **012/520-810** to book a ride. In the middle of the day, it's first-come, first-served.

The Terrace of the Leper King ★★ Built by Jayavarman, this section is the northern half of a long north-south shelf (the Elephant Terrace, below is the southern half) of what was supposedly a main viewing stage for the king and his entourage to watch elaborate shows in the open area out front. Approach the terrace from its most northern point. Outside, you'll find an image of the guardian of hell because the area site was a crematorium. The top of the terrace is a statue of the king with leprosy (a copy of the original). The long terrace is made of two walls and visitors pass through a shaded walkway on the interior. The whole site is lined with rich relief carving and has been lovingly restored and propped up with a new concrete wall that maintains the integrity of the original. ***Note:*** There are portable toilets at the far north end of the Terrace of the Leper King.

The Elephant Terrace   This terrace is the south end (near the Bayon) of a long performance terrace of the king, so named because of its elaborate reliefs of elephants, whose trunks make decorative columns. The long concourse (about 350m/1,148 ft.) depicts scenes of circus acrobats, wrestlers, and images of hunting elephants in the wild.

Preah Khan   Built by Jayavarman VII in 1191, the name of the temple means "Sacred Sword." It's rumored that this was where Jayavarman called home during the building of the Bayon. You approach the Preah Khan through a walkway lined with low lantern towers (note that the Buddhist reliefs were changed to divine vultures during the iconoclastic period). The compound is surrounded by wall and moat. The moat represents the ocean, the wall is a mountain, and the temple is Mount Meru—the mother mountain of Hindu creation. Four gates face the ordinal directions, and each gate has a God and Demon statue like entry to Angkor Thom but just a tower, no Apsara face. Stop in at the small visitor center for information about preservation. The temple is a monastery, like Ta Prohm and Banteay Kdei, and is thought to have been built in homage to Jayavarman's father. The site plan is much like Ta Prohm. The temple passage has lots of meandering galleries and side rooms with statues (most broken or missing) and Shiva Lingam. Many Buddha reliefs here have been chiseled off. Interior walls are lined with cross-legged, bearded forest hermits in relief. The central tower is a stupa for ashes of a later king, dating from the 16th century and replacing a large Buddha statue of Jayavarman VII that was found by the French in 1943, then summarily lost. The many empty pedestals and lintels are courtesy of the Khmer Rouge and many tomb raiders.

"Get High" at Angkor

Like many of the world's great monuments, the temples of Angkor are laid out over massive spaces, with miles of temple wall on the side of each temple, as if a sign to the gods. Visitors approaching temples on foot experience the temple like Khmers of the Angkor period would have, in procession from one side to the other, but we see only one section of the main gate, for example, or experience only the inner sanctum of the temples without being able to see the whole. It is important to remember that the Angkor temples were each self-contained cities or large monasteries, with populations in the hundreds of thousands. Now choked with jungle, these wider areas are best appreciated from above, where the scope of the building at Angkor is best understood. The rule is that there's a 1km (half-mile) "no fly" radius around the temple compound, and the tour operators know just where that is and can take you as close as they are allowed.

Enter the temple from the west, then make the long and winding walk along the central axis, exiting through the east gate where you'll see a massive spoong tree (like a banyan tree). From here, make your way back through to the west entrance and your transport.

Ta Prohm ★★★   The jungle foliage still has its hold on this dynamic temple, which was left in a ruinous state when early archaeologists freed the temples from the jungle. Ta Prohm is a favorite for many; in fact, those very ruinous vines appeal to most. As large around as oak trees, the Khmer Spoong tree is something like a banyan tree, and it's often encased in the wandering tendrils of the *charay,* a thick vine. The powerful spoong and the charay vines cleave massive stones in two or give way and grow over the top of temple ramparts. It's quite dynamic, and there are a few popular photo spots where the collision of temple and vine are most impressive. Sadly, Ta Prohm was looted quite heavily in recent years, and many of its stone reliquaries are lost. The temple was originally built in 1186 by Jayavarman VII as a monastery dedicated to the king's mother and spiritual teacher. There are 39 towers connected by numerous galleries. The exterior wall of the compound is 1km×600m (½ mile×1,969 ft.), and entrance gates have the classic Jayavarman face. Most visitors enter from the west gate—and some drivers will come and pick you up on the other side. A line of small open-air eateries is just outside the main entrance to Ta Prohm, popular places for a snack or lunch.

Ta Kaeo ★   What's most interesting about Ta Kaeo is that it was never completed. Legend has it that the temple was struck by lightning during its construction, and all work was abandoned at a stage where the main structure was complete, but no adornment had been added; as such it serves as "Temple Structure 101." Also unique is the fact that Ta Kaeo is made of a rich green sandstone (elsewhere it's a deeper brown or grayish color). Built in the 10th century by Jayavarman V, the temple was dedicated to Shiva. The central prang once housed a lingam, and the three levels are all encircled by sandstone galleries. The climb to the top is very steep, but the view is well worth it.

Banteay Kdei   The first temple built by Jayavarman VII in 1181, Banteay Kdei is just opposite the large **Sra Serang Reservoir,** a lovely lily pond that is 300×700m (984×2,296 ft.) and surrounded by sandstone steps of Khmer Vintage—the reservoir is a popular place to watch the sunset gleaming off the water's surface. Sra Serang once housed a small island temple where the king liked to meditate—now locals bathe here or steer the water to local rice farms. The four gates of Banteay Kdei have Jayavarman's iconic smiling face—like those at the famed Bayon. The east entrance brings you past an area lined with lions and nagas along an open terrace once used for performances. There's a moat around the second interior gate. The Buddha at the entrance is an original, intact statue, quite unique to the Angkor compound where so many pieces have been stolen or destroyed (beheaded).

Some portions of the main interior temple area are held together with strong rope and cable. Look for a small offering house with columns just inside on the right used to gain merit through gift giving. Also keep your eyes open for the refined Apsara carvings on the main temple. Exit via the west gate—look for more Jayavarman heads—and walk the verdant fields around the side of the temple back to the east gate and your wheels, or take a short walk, through a gauntlet of young hawkers, to the Sra Serang Reservoir.

ATTRACTIONS FARTHER AFIELD

Banteay Srei ★★   True temple buffs won't want to miss this distinct complex. Some 32km (24 miles) north of the main temples, the 10th-century buildings of Banteay Srei are done in a style unique to the high spires of Angkor. The collection of low walls surrounds low-rise peaked structures of deep red sandstone. It is the only building to have been built with pink sandstone, a high-quality mineral that can withstand tougher elements. As such, the carvings and bas-reliefs on this temple are some of the most intricate, best preserved carvings you'll find in Angor. Translated as "The Citadel of Women," it has relief carvings on the squat central buildings and intricate tellings of ancient Hindu tales. Walking through the temple, there's a real feeling of "work in progress." Some of the doorways flanking the central pathway were originally framed in wood and have weakened with age. As such, the sandstone pediments that once stood on top crashed to the ground and broke into large pieces. They've since been reassembled and lie at the foot of the doorways like some ancient jigsaw puzzle. After the first gate and walkway, you'll come to a small entranceway that has a square pedestal with a round piece in the middle that used to hold a lingam (it was stolen some years ago). Look at the frame of the square. It isn't smooth and straight, as you would expect, but completely warped and oddly worn away. The Khmer Rouge used to sharpen their knives here. The hallmarks here are the three temples; the middle one is dedicated to Shiva and it is flanked by temples honoring Vishnu and Brahma. I highly recommend you go with a guide who can explain the finer details of temple inscriptions. *Tip:* The colors are best before 10am and after 2pm, but there are fewer visitors in the afternoon.

Beng Melea ★★ Truly the temple aficionado's temple, Beng Melea is where to go if the Angkor temples seem tame, if you are longing to go "Tomb Raider" and clamber around the crumbling stones of a temple that has been reclaimed by the jungle. Squint or use your imagination and you can feel like Indiana Jones. The kids will love it. Beng Melea is 60km (37 miles) east of Siem Reap and often arranged as a day trip after a stop at the Roluos Group. The road is paved and smooth until just after the Roluos Group where you turn north at the town of **Dom Dek,** which has a local market that's worth a stop. From there, follow a dusty, bumpy road. If you go by motorbike—good luck—wear a krama or a good mask. The temple has three gallery walls and a moat at entry. No one has ever found the Sanskrit inscription on the temple, but Angkor Wat's builder, Suryavarman, supposedly put it up in the 12th century. The interior temple area is a big, fun pile of rubble. The area has just been cleared of mines, and the temple, long a secret enclave for temple buffs, is now attracting more visitors. There was a film recently produced on the temple site, and the filmmakers have left their handy ramps, making it a bit easier to get around. The east entrance is closed because of the many rocks fallen here, but enter just to the right of this main entrance and look for the relief images of the god of fire over the first door as you approach the gallery by the first ramp, then an image of a three-headed elephant born of the mythical churning of the ocean of milk Hindu creation legend. A small library is inside this first gallery area. From here, plunge into the temple center. The platform path takes you through a covered, dark gallery. Between sections, you'll have to do some clambering and rock hopping. *Warning:* Be careful of the slippery moss. The path exits the opposite (west) side of the temple, and from there you can either wend your way back through, following a different course to the rocks, or walk around the outside. Get here as early in the morning as you can and you'll have the place to yourself. The ride is 1 hour by car at a cost of about $50 with a driver, and about 1½ hours by motorbike, about $20 to $25 with a driver. North of Beng Melea is **Koh Ker,** another popular off-the-map temple.

Kabal Spean ★★ (Finds) Known as the "River of a Thousand Linga" (a lingam is a phallic symbol representing the Hindu god Shiva), Kabal Spean lay undiscovered by

Westerners until a French researcher stumbled across it only recently. Dating from the early 11th century, the relief carvings that line the streambeds are said to purify the water before it fills the reservoirs (called *barays*) of Angkor. It's the journey here that's really interesting—on some rough roads through rural villages north of Banteay Srei—and there's a fun forest hike (about 30 min. to the first waterfall). Khmers come here to picnic, and it's a good spot to swim or follow the path that trips along at brook side; from there, you can view the many carvings in relief on the banks and creek bed.

5km (3¹/₂ miles) north of Banteay Srei. Entry fee $3.

Roluos Group   About 13km (8 miles) east of the town center, these three are best viewed in context of Angkor architecture's progression, as the forefathers of the more dynamic of Angkor's main temples. A visit to these temples is included in the temple ticket but will cost you a bit extra for transport.

Land Mines Museum   You won't find signs leading you to this seemingly impromptu museum; Cambodian officials prefer their own rhetoric to that of the owner and curator, Mr. Akira. The museum itself is just a corrugated-roof area stacked high with disarmed ordnance and detailed data about the use, effects, and statistics about UXO (unexploded ordinance) in the country. Most interesting is the small grove out back, an exhibit of how mines are placed in a real jungle setting. The museum is a call to action for de-mining in the country. Resist any temptation to volunteer (unless properly trained), but you're sure to have a chance to chat with Mr. Akira, peruse his recent book on the subject, and sign a petition (he's hoping to achieve NGO status). It's an interesting visit.

On the main road to the temples, just before the checkpoint and a few miles east. Go by motorbike or taxi. www.cambodialandminemuseum.org. Entry $1. Daily 7am–5pm.

Tonle Sap Lake   Day trips on the Tonle Sap Lake fall into two categories, so be careful what you're signing up for. First, avoid the 1½-hour tours out of the boat ferry jetty, Chon Khneas. These trips sound like fun, and for just $15 per boat or $10 per person, you can go with a driver and guide out onto the Tonle Sap. You do glimpse a bit of river life, the net-twirling fishermen, floating schools donated by Korean NGOs, and the commercial boat traffic on the Tonle Sap's main inlet, but once out on the water of the lake you get a quick ride among ethnic Vietnamese, Khmer houseboats, and fisherman, then stop at a large tourist-trap barge with crocodile pits, small fish farms, perhaps an aquarium with some sickly looking turtles, snakes, and fish choking on dirty water. It's all about the $1 Coke or souvenirs you might buy. Not worth the trip, so be sure to avoid rides to just Chong Khneas. The only exception to this is the fine upmarket evening cruises along this same route through the company **Terre Cambodge** (see below). The cost is $20 per person and doesn't include the good cocktails you might enjoy while watching the sun dip into the cool lake.

The best day trips are one of the many full-day options that take you to far-flung floating villages like **Kampong Phluk** in canoes among low mangrove or to a lush bird sanctuary, called **Preak Toal.** Following these routes with the larger tour operators comes with a hefty price tag for Cambodia, from $80 or so per day, but it's worth it.

Contact **Terre Cambodge** (www.terrecambodge.com) or talk with any of the budget tour operators in town (or your hotel's tour desk). All services are consolidated through the same providers so you get the same trip wherever you buy it. Be sure and specify the exact sights you want to see and any inclusions you'd like, such as lunch. One unique find is the folks at **OSMOSE** (www.osmosetonlesap.org), whose main focus is conservation but who run fine tours as well.

These trips are best in rainy season because the mangrove swamps are dried up at other times. The birds at the bird sanctuary are best viewed from December to April. The Tonle Sap basin is lush and green when the water recedes in the dry season, but the water is so low that getting around on the lake, which drops from 12m (39 ft.) down to 4m (13 ft.) in depth, and falls to a third of its rainy-season size, is quite difficult.

If you're connecting onward with Siem Reap or Battambang by boat, you'll get a glimpse of life along the aquatic byways of Cambodia. The road heading south to the lake follows the Siem Reap River and gives you a glimpse into communities of precarious stilt houses that look ready to totter any second, and farmers herding groups of domesticated ducks along canals. Getting to the boat, you'll follow a long dirt causeway lined with shanty houses and elbow among trucks overloaded with minnows and small fish caught in the lake, squishing and leaking and bouncing precariously. Once out on the open water on the speedboat to or from Phnom Penh, it's just hot sun and blue water— not an especially picturesque ride, but fun when the water is high in the rainy season.

IN SIEM REAP TOWN

Angkor National Museum   This brand-new museum beckons visitors from the main road to the temples. It houses an impressive collection of artifacts from Angkor, many of which are on loan from the National Museum and the Conservation d'Angkor, a treasure-trove that was heretofore closed to the public. Highlights include a room displaying 1,000 Buddhas and an Angkor Wat exhibition with a model of the famed temple. It's a good place to see carvings and statue details up close and with decent explanations on hand. But only visit if it is pouring rain or you need a respite from walking around in the blistering heat; otherwise your time and money are better spent at the temples. Historians and conservationists have criticized the lack of history (most of the "1,000 Buddhas" date from the 20th c. only), and local Cambodians are smarting at the fact that the private Thai company behind the museum (to be fair, it has agreed to transfer control to the Cambodian government after 30 years) appears to be profiting from national treasures—the museum is unfortunately housed in a sterile retail mall that looks like it was beamed in from the suburbs of America.

968 Vithei Charles de Gaulle, Khrum 6. ℂ 063/966-601. Admission $15. Daily 8:30am–6:30pm.

SPAS & MASSAGE

After a day of scrambling, sweating, and climbing the temples, there's nothing like a bit of pampering to round things out, and with the tidal-wave rise in tourism in Siem Reap, all kinds of services are popping up. On the high end of the scale, contact the **Sofitel Hotel** (on the way to the temples on Vithei Charles de Gaulle; ℂ 063/964-600), the **Raffles Grand Hotel D'Angkor** (at the very town center; ℂ 063/963-888), and the **Angkor Palace** (ℂ 063/760-511).

In town, try **Visaya Spa** at the plush FCC complex (Pokambor Ave. just north of the post office; ℂ 063/760-814), which has three stylish treatment rooms and a roster of high-end services including body scrubs, wraps, facials, aqua therapy, and massages, all at high prices for this part of the world (a 90-min. massage is $40) but worth it. Contact them to make a reservation or just stop in. Open daily from 10am to 10pm.

Frangipani, a small storefront spa just down a little alley opposite the Blue Pumpkin in the area north of the Old Market, offers a fine roster of treatments, from facials and aromatherapy to oil massage and traditional massage. A good, little find with a professional staff offering services starting at just $18 per hour for a traditional massage. For booking, call ℂ 012/982-062.

Body Tune Spa, in the very heart of Pub Street (btw. the Red Piano and the Soup Dragon restaurant; © 012/444-066), is in the midmarket range (about $10) with good affordable services and some burgeoning style.

On the lower end of the scale, where you can expect to pay as little as $6 for an hour of massage, try any of the small storefronts just north of the Old Market, in the popular tourist area. Services vary at these little storefronts, now numbering five and growing. For good Khmer massage, similar to Thai massage, try **Islands Traditional Khmer Massage** (north of Psar Chas; © 012/757-120). The most affordable massage in town, and a great way to support local enterprise, is at one of the many massage schools for the blind. Trained by international volunteers, blind masseuses—who in Khmer society might have little other chance in life—are able to make a comfortable living. There are a few different sights; one that's convenient and very professional is **Seeing Hands IV** (© 012/286-316 or 286-317) on central Sivatha near the Tell Restaurant and the Dead Fish Tower Bar. Trained by Japanese and endorsed by Aus Aid and the Blind Care Foundation, masseuses are professional, and for only $5, you can't go wrong. Most folks tip heavily here and come away with a unique connection. Call or just stop in.

The newest trend in Siem Reap is fish massage, where hundreds of tiny fish feed on your feet to remove dead skin cells and increase circulation. To try it, head to Pub Street or the night market where you will find pools set up.

ORGANIZED TOURS

Siem Reap is full of helpful traveler services and information. In fact, most hotels and guesthouses can help you arrange all of the essentials. Below are a few service providers we'd recommend among the many others you'll see in the area.

Expensive

- **Diethelm,** House No. 470, Krous Village, Svay Dangkum Commune, Siem Reap (© 063/963-524; fax 063/963-694; DT_Cambodia@kh.diethelmtravel.com). Providing all local and regional services, Diethelm is a top international tour operator, offering classic tours in Angkor as well as anywhere in the region.
- **Exotissimo,** New Bldg. B, 2021 St. 60MK, Siem Reap (© 063/964-323; fax 063/ 963-621; www.exotissimo.com). Like Diethelm, above, Exo is a large conglomerate, with offices throughout the region, with a wide range of options including luxury, volunteering, and cycling tours. Mostly for larger budgets.
- **Osmose,** at Sam Veasna Center for Wildlife Conservation (© 063/963-710; www. osmosetonlesap.net). Offering high-end tours to the far-flung coastal areas of the Tonle Sap Lake, Osmose levies high fees for its popular eco-tours in order to maintain high standards of low environmental impact, and to fund its efforts at encouraging sustainable development and preservation in the region.
- **Terre Cambodge,** 668 Hup Guan St. (© 092/476-682; www.terrecambodge.com). Catering to many of the French tourists who flock to Siem Reap and have deeper pockets, Terre Cambodge arranges adventure trips to the farther-flung reaches in the area, ranging from off-the-map destinations along Tonle Sap to little-known jungle temples far from Angkor.

Budget

Here are just a few of the more reliable companies that come at a cheaper rate. Hotel or guesthouse front desks can, for free or a small fee, arrange tickets with one of the companies listed below. In fact, popular **Capitol Guesthouse** and more upscale **Mekong**

Express Tours don't even have offices in town, and must be booked through hotel front desks.

- **Neak Krorhorm Travel and Tours,** just adjacent to the Old Market (east side; ℂ **063/964-924**), is a good one for onward bus connections to rural stops like Battambang. In fact, book with one of the other operators and you'll likely end up waiting for the bus out in front of these offices.
- **PTM,** right in the heart of the bar street near the Old Market (ℂ **063/964-388;** fax 063/965-486; www.ptm.com.kh) offers basic bus services and can book flights.

---

5 SHOPPING

Shopping in the Angkor temple town has boomed, and new boutiques pop up daily. The old standbys, like the market and smaller boutiques, are also benefiting from increased numbers of tourists and expats.

You can find good **reproductions of temple statuary** anywhere in town, but it's a pretty cumbersome buy unless Siem Reap is your last stop before, say, Bangkok and a flight home. **Rubbings** of temple bas-reliefs can be found anywhere and are easily transported, best in a light poster tube. Original artwork and photography are available at every turn. Silk hangings and clothing are on sale in many boutiques, but "buyer beware" of price and quality before making a big investment. The vendors below are the best of many, and the Old Market area, where most are concentrated, is all within easy walking. Don't miss the chic FCC compound and its many upmarket shops and galleries.

You'll find lots of small convenience stores in and around town. Star Mart is a familiar convenience store open 24 hours (on the airport road), though just one among many. It's not a bad idea to stock up on a few snacks before a day of temple touring.

ARTS & CRAFTS

Beyond   This place is indeed "beyond," and parents should certainly heed the warning at the door that within they will find explicit material. The artwork of owner Jerry Swaffield, an Irishman and longtime expat, is wonderfully bizarre. A pastiche on Asian travel and the state of the world in pen and ink drawings (like refined political cartoons), they are odd and sometimes a bit vulgar. He also prints his own comic book about the typical visitor in Cambodia (check the website at www.cheapcharliecomics.com). Swaffield also has a collection of extreme photographs, set in a chaotic yet stylistic display, in the back room. Images of Khmer Rouge cannibalism and atrocities as well as diseased figures are a bit much for some. It's a very unique collection not to be missed (but maybe just stay in the front room). Open daily from 9am to 9pm. MasterCard and Visa accepted. At the FCC Angkor, Pokambor Ave. ℂ **063/760-609.** beyondart@online.com.kh.

Carnets d'Asie   Bookstore, boutique, gallery, and tea shop all in one, Carnets d' Asie features some rare finds, including works by local artists as well as fine temple reproductions and statuary. The large, tinted photographs of **Pier Poretti** (also see his gallery in Siem Reap; ℂ **012/925-684**) features large in the collection, with some classic views of the temples as well as scenes of life in rural Cambodia. The large, open tea area at the back of the gallery is a good place to meet with friends and have a look at your finds. Open daily from 10am to 10pm. No. 333 Sivatha. ℂ **063/746-701.** www.carnetsdasie-angkor. com.

Lindenhurst Memorial Library

Library Hours:
Monday - Thursday 9 am - 9 pm
Friday 9 am - 6 pm
Saturday 9 am - 5 pm
Sunday 1 pm - 5 pm (Sep - May)

02/10/2020

Checked out to: p45458856

Title: **The pearl / John Steinbeck ; with**
BRCD: 3 1801 00313 6581
Due Date: **03-02-20**

Title: **Frommer's Cambodia & Laos /**
BRCD: 3 1801 00464 9376
Due Date: **03-02-20**

Total items checked out: 2

**You just saved an estimated $30 by
using the Library today.**

Thank you for visiting!

Colors of Cambodia Here's a fun one. A project set up to fund Cambodian schools, the shop sells framed artwork of young Khmer kids who visit the temples or depict their daily life in Technicolor crayon. Some of the work is quite expressive and a purchase here certainly goes a long way to helping out. Open daily from 8am to 7pm. No credit cards. House No. 270, Mudull 1 Village (northwest side of the Old Market). ✆ 063/965-021. colorsof cambodia@yahoo.com.

John McDermott Photography Just next door to the FCC, American John McDermott displays his stunning silver gelatin prints, some very classic images of the temple, in a cool, tiled contemporary space. The gallery is inspiring for more amateur photographers shutter-bugging at the temples, and these fine prints make great gifts. Small postcards are available for $2, larger reproductions just $35, and poster-size prints start at $300. Due to popularity, a beautiful two-story second gallery has opened in the heart of the backpacker district. The second floor features exhibitions by other artists. Both open daily from 10am to 10pm. MasterCard and Visa accepted. On the north end of the FCC compound on Pokambor Ave. ✆ 012/615-695 and on the Passage, near the Old Market. ✆ 012/274-274. www.mcdermottgallery.com.

Senteurs d'Angkor Carrying good contemporary Khmer arts and crafts, statuary copied from Angkor's greats (a good place to pick up that Jayavarman VII bust), traditional leather shadow puppets, silver jewelry, Khmer silks, kramas (Khmer scarves), traditional local spices (pepper and lemon grass), potpourri, local teas, rice brandy, and fragrant handmade soaps, Senteurs d'Angkor is a good stop to satiate your shopping appetite before a flight back home. It has great souvenirs at reasonable prices. Open daily 7am to 9:30pm. No. 275 Psaa Chas, cater-cornered to the northeast end of the busy Old Market. ✆ 063/964-801 or 012/954-815.

Tara and Kys Art Gallery A stunning collection that ranges from comically stylized caricatures of Khmer and Vietnamese life (they also have a gallery in Ho Chi Minh City) to expressive paintings and prints from the temples, Tara and Kys gallery is a fun visit. Open daily 9am to 9pm. 105 Mondol 1, opposite the Provincial Hospital north of the market. ✆ 012/679-011.

BOOKS

D's Books Conveniently located on Pub Street, D's Books stocks a good selection of fiction and nonfiction including a fairly complete range of titles on Cambodia and Southeast Asia. Open daily 9am to 10pm. Pub St.

Monument Books An expansion of the popular Phnom Penh outlet, Monument Books carries the best in new volumes about the temples, from coffee-table tomes to guidebooks and histories, as well as international newspapers. Their new Old Market–area location is large and carries an extensive collection. Open daily 8am to 8:30pm. Inside Angkor National Museum. MC, V. Also inside Lucky Mall on Sivatha St.

CLOTHING

Jasmine This is a popular boutique with original, feminine designs made of silk and plenty of organza. Open daily 9am to 10pm. Pokomobor Ave. (FCC Bldg.). ✆ 063/760-610.

Wanderlust This new boutique was opened in late 2008 by Elizabeth Kiester, an expat who in a former life was an editor at several fashion magazines in New York. Her shop sells vibrant clothes and accessories, bright pillows, and other stylish trinkets. Kiester works in conjunction with an NGO called Coalition for Financial Independence to help villagers in Takeo, south of Phnom Penh, grow their own businesses. There is also a brand-new branch of Wanderlust in Phnom Penh (on No. 21 St. 240). Open Mon-Sat 11am-10pm; Sun 2-10pm. Alley West. ☏ **063/965-980.** www.wanderlustcambodia.com.

MARKETS

Angkor Night Market   Entering this market, you may think that you've arrived in Thailand. Neat thatched roofs cover stalls selling an array of silks, statuary, souvenirs, clothing, jewelry, and art. You won't find any bargains here, but it is a relaxed place to shop with little of the hassle one finds elsewhere. You can check it out beforehand by looking at their website. Daily 3pm to midnight. Off Sivatha Rd. ☏ **092/654-315.** www. angkornightmarket.com.

New Market   Recently rebuilt, the New Market is distinct from the old in that it caters more to local tastes, which makes it good for a wander and for taking some photos. Open daily from dawn to dusk. On the north end of Sivatha St.

Psar Chas, the Old Market   The very heart of tourist Siem Reap, this is the best place to find Buddhist trinkets and souvenirs such as T-shirts, as well as good books on the temples. The market is a fun wander and friendly folks here are used to foreign visitors so you can easily haggle in English (or by passing a calculator back and forth to display your offer on an item). The many food stalls on the north end of the market are a good way to sample local cuisine for next to nothing. Most businesses in town give their address in relation to the Old Market address, so it's a good place to know for orientation purposes. Open daily from dawn to dusk. Riverside in the south end of town.

6 NIGHTLIFE

Siem Reap is a town where most visitors are up with the sun and out visiting the temple sites, but there are an increasing number of good evening options.

BARS & CLUBS

Pub Street is now beginning to resemble the party towns of Thailand with throbbing music, wandering crowds, boisterous backpackers, hawkers, prostitutes, and touts. It is amazing how quickly these developments have taken place. There are now quite a number of bars open into the small hours.

The **Angkor What?** (Pub St., 1 block west of the Old Market; ☏ **012/490-755**) was the first—and still the most popular—one here, more or less where it's at in Siem Reap. Sign your name on the wall and say hi to all those you met that day at the temples or on highways elsewhere. **Easy Speaking Café and Pub,** just next to the busy Angkor What? (above), handles the spillover. A similar crowd stays late. **World Lounge** (☏ **012/865-332**), in the same area, also rocks late and has a free pool table.

At **Miss Wong** (The Lane behind Pub St.; **855/92-428-332**) you'll leave Cambodia behind and time-travel to Old Shanghai. This bar, with deep red walls, leather booths, and excellent cocktails, adds some welcome class to Siem Reap's after-dark scene.

Dead Fish Tower (☏ **063/963-060**), on the main road heading toward the temples, is set up like the rigging of a tall ship, with precarious perches, funky nooks, and unique drinks.

Laundry (☏ **016/962-026**) is the funky side of Siem Reap. When the temple town gets psychedelic and stays up really late, this is where it happens. On a side street to the

A Dance for the Divine

The royal classical dancing of the Khmers was the moving spirit of Angkor and many cite it as the purest form of classical dance in Asia, although the reality is that the French had a hand in adapting it to their needs. The dance forms originated in India and came to Cambodia over 1,000 years ago as re-creations of Hindu epics. Thailand's form is a copy dating from the days when the empire of Ayutthaya sacked Angkor, when the Khmers were seen as the guardians of the purest forms of culture by the Siamese. The reality today is that experts say that the Thai version is purer "Khmer" than the Khmer version, since it didn't suffer from the meddling of the French in their attempts to reconstruct a Khmer identity in the 19th and early 20th centuries. In ancient Angkor the ballet dancers were considered heavenly apsaras come to earth. Only the deva-raj or god-king could touch them. When the Khmer Rouge took over, most of the dancers and musicians were murdered, and with them died centuries of accumulated poise and grace.

After the Khmer Rouge was evicted, there were attempts to reconstruct these nearly lost arts from the minds of the few survivors. The Royal Ballet is now, once again, world famous. To watch one of these performances is to see something so exquisitely graceful it is enough to stop your breath. Slow, contorted movements of immense refinement and exquisite beauty are performed by dancers in elegant silks and gold (they actually have to be sewed into these elaborate costumes). It reaches a point of tension and crescendo all in incredible slow motion. When visiting Angkor, taking in a classical dance performance is an unmissable experience and will help bring history alive. See p. 131 for performance information.

north of the Old Market, it's open nightly, but usually hosts special events that you'll see promoted all around town.

Linga (North of Old Market; ✆ 012/246-912) is a gay bar that attracts a decent mixed crowd to its two-story corner location overlooking the small side street and the traffic on Mundul 1 Village St. The walls have psychedelic paintings of Buddhist monks.

Molly Malone's (Pub St., across the street and west of Red Piano Bar; ✆ 063/965-576) is the hippest pub in town. They've got local expats playing live music, a mix of original songs and covers of crowd pleasers like old Beatles and Roberta Flack numbers. The bar is fully stocked with a fine selection of Irish whiskey and they've got a good stock of imported beer.

Temple Club (Central Pub St.; ✆ 063/965-570) is many things to many people. During the day it is an open-air bar and restaurant. They have traditional Apsara dance performances between 7:30 and 9:30pm. Then, at around 10pm the sound system kicks in, blasting out techno pop at maximum volume. If you want to boogie until 4am, you can do it here. They also have live sports on TV and three pool tables.

Funky Munky (corner of Pub St. near the Old Market; ✆ 092/276-751). It's open from noon until the wee hours of the morning, there are over 50 cocktails to choose from here, and during high season the place is packed.

The Remote Temple of Preah Vihear

Known as Preah Vihear to the Khmer and Khao Phra Wiharn to the Thais, this beautiful temple dramatically situated 1,700 feet up on the top of a cliff along the Dangrek range of mountains, is one of the most spectacular Angkorian temples. Part of a chain of Angkorian temples stretching across Laos and north-ern Thailand, the temple is 200km (124 miles) from Angkor, near the border with Thailand.

One has to travel terrible roads through one of Cambodia's most scarred and wild provinces to reach Preah Vihear. It is a trip only for the adventurous. It is possible to take a shared taxi from Siem Reap to the town of Sra Em (about 3 hours, $7.50) which is 19 miles from the temple; then a motorcycle taxi up the mountain to Preah Vihear (about $3.75). Roads are at their worst during the rainy season, from June to October.

Work started on Preah Vihear in the early 9th century and it ended up being a bit of a mishmash of styles, since it was altered and added to a number of times over the centuries. Appropriately dedicated to Shiva the Destroyer (given the destruction that has subsequently surrounded it), the earliest surviving parts of the temple date from the early 10th century. The bulk of it was con-structed during the reigns of kings Suryavarman I (1002–50) and Suryavarman II (1113–50). Like Angkor Wat itself, Preah Vihear is a representation of Mount Meeru—the abode of the gods.

During the years of war, Preah Vihear proved to be a formidable fortress. In 1975, it was the last place held by Lon Nol troops before they were driven out by the Khmer Rouge. After that, Preah Vihear Province and the Dangrek Moun-tains were Khmer Rouge heartland. Many of the Khmer soldiers garrisoning the temple area today are former Khmer Rouge soldiers.

The temple has long been claimed by both the Thais and the Khmers. In 1962, the International Court of Justice in the Hague definitively awarded the temple to Cambodia, according to maps drawn up by the French and previ-ously not disputed by the Thais. The land surrounding it is still in dispute, and battles have been fought over it recently with casualties on both sides. Due to its strategic importance, Khmers won't permit Preah Vihear to be Thai. It is a point of supreme military advantage, and a natural artillery platform from which an enemy could target positions deep within Cambodia. The reality is a military one as much as a historical or cultural one.

In July 2008, Preah Vihear was designated a UNESCO World Heritage Site. This drew a storm of protest from Thailand because perceived Khmer encroach-ments on surrounding territory in the Thai province of Sisaket were yet to be resolved, along with calls for joint heritage status. At the time of writing, border crossing from Thailand was closed. Preah Vihear has become a political football for both sides, useful for raising nationalistic feelings and anger when there is an election looming. If planning to visit, be sure to read local papers to check the political climate first.

Having spent the day looking at the stone variety of Apsaras, why not spend an evening checking out the living ones? A number of places around town hold shows of **Apsara Dance.**

Angkor Village. Dancers in traditional gilded costume practice their slow elegant art. This comes combined with a fine set Khmer menu in the traditional indoor banquet-house theater. To make reservations for the nightly show call ✆ **063/963-561.** Dinner begins at 7pm, and the show starts at 7:30pm (tickets cost $22).

The **Raffles Grand Hotel D'Angkor** has a similar show in an open pavilion on the lawn at the front of the hotel ($32 including dinner). Times and performances vary so be sure to call ✆ **063/963-888** in advance. Most hotels have a performance space, and many small restaurants have shows of varying quality.

Okay, admittedly this one is pretty kitschy, but the kids might like it: **Cambodia Cultural Center,** far west of Siem Reap on the airport road (Svay Dongkum; ✆ **063/963-836**) holds a host of shows and all-day events, including a mock Khmer wedding and Apsara dance. Call for current offerings, as the program varies. If you don't like the performance, take heart that you can walk the grounds, set around a large central pond, spend some time in Cambodia's only wax museum, walk among all of Cambodia's sights done in miniature, or visit various exhibits of village life and rural skill. You can even get around in an electric car. This one's most popular with Asian tour groups.

Dr. Beat (Beatocello) Richner plays the works of Bach and some of his own comic pieces between stories and vignettes about his work as director of the **Kantha Bopha Foundation,** a humanitarian hospital just north of the town center. Admission is free, but donations are accepted in support of their valiant efforts to serve a steady stream of destitute patients, mostly children, who suffer from treatable diseases such as tuberculosis. Dr. Richner is as passionate about his music as he is about his cause. You're in for an enjoyable, informative evening. Performances are every Saturday at 7:15pm just north of the town center on the road to the temples.

SIEM REAP · **6** · **FAST FACTS: SIEM REAP**

ⓕ Fast Facts   Siem Reap

ATMs As with Phnom Penh, ATMs are springing up at a fast pace in Siem Reap. There are many around Psar Chas and they accept all major cards. Canadia Bank is the kindest in terms of fees charged.

Banks & Currency Exchange **Canadia Bank,** on the western side of the Old Market (✆ **063/964-808**), and **ANZ Royal Bank** (566–570 Tep Vong St.; ✆ **023/726-900**) are the best options for services. **ANZ** has several ATMs around town including one at the central branch and two 24-hour ATMs in the heart of the backpacker district just south of Red Piano Bar. You can change traveler's checks in some hotels and in any bank.

Doctors & Hospitals **Royal Angkor International Hospital** (No. 6 Airport Rd.; ✆ **063/761-888;** www.royalangkorhospital.com) provides 24-hour emergency care, ambulance, translation, and evacuation. Check on their website before departure to make sure your insurance covers you under their terms and conditions.

Emergencies There's a tourist police station near the entrance to the temples. For local police, dial ✆ **117.** In the event of a medical emergency, contact **International SOS Clinic** in Phnom Penh (✆ **023/216-911**).

Internet Access   Small storefront offices surround the central market area. On the main street, try **E-Café**, No. 011 Siwatha Blvd., an air-conditioned facility with speedy connections, for just over $2 per hour, by far the best in town. **Phsar Chas Netweb,** on the northwest corner of the Old Market (© **012/461-849**), is typical of the many others in the Old Market area. It's just $1 per hour for relatively speedy dial-up service, and they can connect you to your home country with Internet phone for next to nothing, or you can borrow a cellphone for in-country calls. Almost all Internet shops can burn CDs if you need to empty your camera's memory card. Also try the shops just adjacent to the Red Piano. Most are open early to late (7am–midnight). If you have a Wi-Fi capable laptop, you can connect using prepaid PIC cards at the **FCC** restaurant, the **Raffles Grand** and **Sofitel** hotels, as well as at the **Angkor What?** bar among others. **Le Tigre de Papier,** the **Blue Pumpkin,** and **Molly Malone's** offer free Wi-Fi access to customers.

Post Office   The post office is on Pokambor Avenue at riverside near the town center (next to the FCC; see "Where to Dine," earlier in this chapter). It's open daily 7am to 5:30pm and can handle foreign and domestic regular and parcel post.

Telephone   The city code for Siem Reap is **63.** Most hotels have international direct dialing (IDD), but many of the Internet cafes around the Old Market have better rates and offer callback service or Internet phone services.

Battambang & Northern Cambodia

From laid-back Battambang in Cambodia's far northwest to Ratanakiri in the northeast, there are riches to discover in Northern Cambodia in addition to the glories of Angkor Wat (see chapter 6).

Atmospheric, French colonial architecture in Battambang and Kratie, the wild natural beauty of the highlands bordering Vietnam, or a meal of deep-fried tarantulas in Skuon all offer a fresh perspective.

1 BATTAMBANG

Until recently, Battambang was considered an undiscovered gem among those who ventured farther afield than Siem Riep, Phnom Penh, and Sihanoukville. It remains a gem, but it is also now being discovered in a big way. There are hotels, cafes, and restaurants in numbers. Not so long ago there were limited options, and your fellow diners would generally be NGO field workers, Scandinavian de-miners drinking copious amounts of beer while not on the job, and the occasional journalist heading to the former Khmer Rouge stronghold of Pailin in an attempt to unlock dark secrets (none have yet succeeded). As it stands at present, Battambang is in that precarious period of grace where what made it special has not been swamped by a tourist influx, but the comforts and facilities you might want to make it a comfortable stay are all in place. It may well stay that way given that Battambang will never see the same kind of flood of visitors justifiably attracted by the wonders of Angkor.

Battambang does not have major sites like Angkor Wat (where else does?), nor does it have the buzz of a capital city like Phnom Penh. In fact considering that it is Cambodia's second city it could still best be described as somnambulant. What Battambang does have is wonderful French colonnaded architecture and a relaxing riverside atmosphere. It is an elegant place in a slightly dusty and chaotic Cambodian way. In the surrounding countryside are temples, Angkorian ruins, and rich scenery. This is the "rice-bowl" of Cambodia, and if you are here when the paddies are green and the sun is shining, you are witness to a quintessential vision of Cambodian rural life. Many fall for its intangible grace. After a day spent exploring the jungled temple ruins in the countryside around the city, followed by a gin and tonic in the Riverside Balcony Bar with the sound of the Tropics gently drifting up from the trees and the river below, it is easy to see why.

ORIENTATION
Arriving

Battambang is small and the center is easy to navigate by foot. If you want to venture farther afield, *motodups* are plentiful until after 8pm when you might consider hiring one for the duration of the evening to save the hassle of tracking one down on the dark and leafy outskirts.

The city runs along both banks of the Sangker River north to south. The city center and pretty much everything you need is on the west bank. The only three numbered streets in the city run parallel to the river. These are the blindingly complicated Street 1 (by the river), Street 2 (the first parallel), and Street 3 (the second parallel). All run from the two-lane crossroad near the post office and the Teo hotel to Phsar Nath (the "Meeting Market"). Street 3 is the town's main street with shops (an incredibly high proportion of which are devoted to mobile phones), hotels, and restaurants. Phsar Nath is very much the town hub. Banks and travel agents are all situated around here. There is a cluster of hotels around this area and an increasing number of tourist-focused eateries.

To the south of the central district and largely hugging the river are a number of administrative and municipal offices and some glorious colonial-era villas on leafy grounds.

On the east bank of the river there a number of hotels and restaurants on the old route NH#5, heading toward the main road that takes you to Phnom Penh.

Crossing the river south to north are the "New Iron Bridge" and the "Old Stone Bridge" (which is actually concrete and restricted to motorcycles and pedestrians), both linking up with Old NH#5 taking you to the main Phnom Penh Road. There's also the "Old Iron Bridge" linking the east bank directly to the center of town and the "New Stone Bridge" linking the north end of town to the main road to Phnom Penh via the new NH#5. In reality, it doesn't matter too much where you cross, since most roads on the east side will take you to the Dambong Roundabout and all other roads radiate out from there, and on the west side the grid system is simple to navigate both north and south.

Getting There

BY PLANE   There are no flights to Battambang at present, although the airport is still there and this may change. Until relatively recently there were flights to and from Phnom Penh on decaying prop planes run by a number of fairly dubious outfits. Those companies are no more and it does not seem to be in any airline's financial interest to run the route at present.

BY BOAT   Daily ferries leave in each direction to and from Siem Reap at 7am. This is becoming a major tourist draw in Cambodia. The fare is $19 to $25 per person. It's a beautiful, 7- to 9-hour journey across the Tonle Sap and along the Sangker River in the wet season, but can take a lot longer in the dry season due to low water levels—rarely under 8 hours at any time of year. Passengers also get dropped off along the way and the stops can slow up the trip. Ask about current conditions. The boats are not incredibly safe but it's not far to swim to the bank in a worst-case scenario, and the water is mostly quite shallow. It can become very uncomfortable on the wooden seats after many hours, so bring a cushion. There is no direct boat to Battambang from Phnom Penh.

BY BUS   The road from Battambang to Siem Reap around the west side of the lake is now finally in excellent condition the entire way. It takes about 4 to 5 hours. Bus companies running the route are **Neak Krorhorm, Mekong Express,** and **Rith Mony.** There are frequent air-conditioned buses daily. Tickets can be bought from the company offices for $4 or $5, just north of Psar Nath on Rte. 5.

Making Your Shared Taxi Bearable

For more comfort, pay double and keep the whole front seat to yourself. You won't regret it.

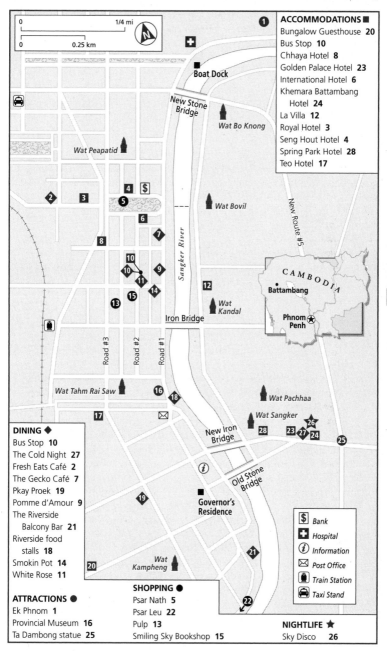

Boat Dock

New Stone Bridge

Wat Bo Knong

Wat Peapatid

Wat Bovil

New Route #5

Sangker River

CAMBODIA

Battambang

Phnom Penh

Wat Kandal

Iron Bridge

Road #3

Road #2

Road #1

Wat Tahm Rai Saw

Wat Pachhaa

Wat Sangker

New Iron Bridge

Old Stone Bridge

Governor's Residence

Wat Kampheng

ACCOMMODATIONS ■
Bungalow Guesthouse **20**
Bus Stop **10**
Chhaya Hotel **8**
Golden Palace Hotel **23**
International Hotel **6**
Khemara Battambang
   Hotel **24**
La Villa **12**
Royal Hotel **3**
Seng Hout Hotel **4**
Spring Park Hotel **28**
Teo Hotel **17**

DINING ◆
Bus Stop **10**
The Cold Night **27**
Fresh Eats Café **2**
The Gecko Café **7**
Pkay Proek **19**
Pomme d'Amour **9**
The Riverside
   Balcony Bar **21**
Riverside food
   stalls **18**
Smokin Pot **14**
White Rose **11**

ATTRACTIONS ●
Ek Phnom **1**
Provincial Museum **16**
Ta Dambong statue **25**

SHOPPING ●
Psar Nath **5**
Psar Leu **22**
Pulp **13**
Smiling Sky Bookshop **15**

$ Bank
✚ Hospital
ⓘ Information
✉ Post Office
🚉 Train Station
🚖 Taxi Stand

NIGHTLIFE ★
Sky Disco **26**

0   1/4 mi
0   0.25 km

In the past, the 291km (180-mile) journey from Battambang to Phnom Penh on Rte. 5 was fearsomely bumpy—today it is superb. Several bus companies (including Phnom Penh **Sorya, GST, Neak Krorhorm, Mekong Express,** and **Capitol Tours**) run frequent daily buses between Phnom Penh and Battambang. The first bus leaves at 6:30am and the last at 2:30 or 3pm. It costs 17,000 riel to 20,000 riel and the trip takes 5 hours. In Battambang, buses depart from the various different transportation company offices around town.

BY TAXI From Siem Reap, a private taxi to Battambang costs $40 to $50 and takes 3 to 4 hours. A shared taxi will be $7. From Phnom Penh, a taxi all to yourself costs $35 to $45. A seat in a shared taxi costs 25,000 riel per person and the ride takes 4 hours. Be aware that they cram in the riders.

Getting Around

As with most other towns in Cambodia, your choices include the cheery *motodup*, renting a car with a driver, or renting out a motorcycle (without a driver). Your hotel can arrange

An Evil Harvest

The war may have officially come to an end in Cambodia in 1998, but its legacy lives on and continues to claim the lives and limbs of ordinary Cambodians every day. During the years of conflict, all sides used land mines indiscriminately. They didn't keep maps of where the minefields were laid, and when the war ended vast swathes of the country were left littered with these murderous devices. Most of the minefields are around the border areas with Thailand, where offensives ebbed and flowed throughout the '80s and '90s. Once the war finished, many desperately poor families moved to these areas to claim land and to farm. The fact that the fields presented the ever-present possibility of setting off unexploded ordinance was seen as the lesser of two evils. There have been 63,000 recorded injuries and deaths due to land mines since 1979. Thousands of Cambodians now live as amputees, one of the highest rates in the world. Thousands more again simply have died in the bush, too far from help to make it through. Some 38% of injuries result from people tampering with ordinance, usually to try to get the scrap metal to sell. And 56% of injuries occur when people are trying to earn a living; farming, carrying water, collecting wood, collecting forest products, and so on. The costs of laying mines are low, about $3 per mine, but the costs of removal are very high, up to a $1,000 per mine according to expert estimates. Although the minefields have been cleared around the areas you are likely to visit (particularly Siem Reap and Battambang), the problem should last for decades, even assuming that mines continue to be cleared at the rate they are being cleared now. The situation is improving, with 271 casualties registered in 2008 as opposed to thousands in the mid-'90s (such as 4,320 in 1996). This change is partly due to clearing and partly due to increased awareness and education. If you do find yourself in an environment where you see the little red markers with DANGER MINES! fencing off a specific area, take those markers very seriously.

either a car with a driver or a motorcycle. **Cars** cost around $20 per day and **motorcycles** **137** rent from $5 to $8 per day. The *motodups* are everywhere during the day, but seem to evaporate at night. If you are going any distance for the evening it may be a good idea to hire a *motodup* for the evening at about $5. A ride in town should range 500 riel to 1500 riel, while crossing a bridge to the east bank hikes up the fare. Double those rates at night. Many hotels rent out **bicycles** for $1.50 a day. There are now **tuk-tuks** in Battambang, and if there are a few of you they make a sensible alternative to the *motodup* convoy.

(Fast Facts Battambang

ATMs There are a number of bank offices ringing Psar Nath, and each bank has an ATM. Canadia Bank has the lowest charges.

Banks & Currency Exchange Canadia Bank (𝄐 053/952-267; open Mon–Fri 8am–3pm, Sat 8–11:30am), **UCB** (𝄐 053/952-552; open Mon–Fri 8am–3pm), and **ANZ** (𝄐 053/953-830; open Mon–Fri 8:30am–4pm) are situated around Psar Nath. **ACLEDA Bank** (𝄐 053/953-171; open Mon–Fri 7:30am–4pm, Sat 7:30am–noon; Western Union and traveler's checks only) is on the east bank of the river just over the Old Iron Bridge. All of these banks cash traveler's checks, exchange major foreign currencies, and issue advances on Visa and MasterCard. There are also money-changers in Psar Nath itself. There is no real reason to use them unless you are caught cashless out of banking hours and you don't have an ATM card.

Business Hours Business hours are generally between 7am and 7pm from Monday to Friday. In the center of town some shops may stay open a little later.

Doctors & Hospitals The **Polyclinique Visal Sokh** (junction of St. 3 and NH#5 north of Psar Nath; 𝄐 053/952-401) is your first stop if you need medical attention. They have a pharmacy and an ambulance and some English is spoken. If it is anything serious, your second port of call is Thailand. The closest Thai hospitals are in Aranyaprathet and Sa Kaeow, but it's best to head to Bangkok.

Internet Cybercafes are plentiful on Street 1 and the adjoining roads. They cost about $1.50 an hour and speeds are variable. The **Bus Stop Guesthouse** on Street 2 has free Wi-Fi with a fast connection. The **Gecko Cafe** also has swift Wi-Fi. Many hotels also now have Wi-Fi.

Pharmacies The Polyclinique Visal Sokh (see above) has a pharmacy. There are also a number of others around Psar Nath.

Post Office The main post office is situated near the river where Street 1 forks after the museum, near the main junction between the Old Stone Bridge and the Old Iron Bridge. It is open Monday to Friday 6am to 5pm and Saturday 8am to noon.

Telephone Internet cafes are equipped for long-distance calls. There are also scores of shops selling mobile SIM cards and phones all over the center of town. A new SIM card costs as little as $2 and is your best option if you want to make local calls.

Tourist Information The **Tourist Office** (St. 1; 𝄐 053/730-217; open Mon–Fri 7–11am and 2–5pm) is situated in a very swish French villa, but the actual information they provide is a little thin.

In times past the only acceptable hotel in Battambang was the Teo. That has all changed and now the range and quality of accommodations are very impressive. For $15 a night you can find yourself a palace. Establishments are cash only unless specified.

Bungalow Guesthouse   If you wish to stay a little bit out of town, the Bungalow Guesthouse is a great choice. It is in the southern part of town on the west bank of the river. It is very pleasant with two huge rooms with very shiny floors in the house itself and three less impressive bungalows at the back. The rooms in the house are far and away the better choice, and cost the same as the bungalows. There is a good restaurant on the site with Thai and Khmer food. The place is hard to find, but its website includes a map and all the *motodups* will know where to take you.

144 Phum Kamakor Sangkat Svay Por. ⓒ 012/916-123. www.thebungaloweb.com. 5 units. $15 double. No credit cards. **Amenities:** Restaurant; Internet. *In room:* A/C, TV, fridge

Bus Stop ★   This is an excellent guesthouse run by an Australian-Khmer couple with constructive contributions from their boisterous 2-year-old son. The owners have put a lot of thought into the facilities. Rooms are small but light with gleaming tiled floors, and are very well equipped with reliable Wi-Fi throughout. There is a big-screen TV in all of the rooms and the rate includes a hearty breakfast and free laundry. They also organize tours of the local sites and can rent you out a motorcycle or bicycle. The downstairs restaurant also serves as the local pub of choice for the small expat community (p. 140).

149 St. 2. ⓒ 053/730-544. www.busstopcambodia.com. 6 rooms. $9 fan double; $12 A/C double; $18 deluxe balcony double. **Amenities:** Restaurant; Internet. *In room:* A/C, TV, fridge.

Chhaya Hotel   Conveniently situated near Psar Nath, the Chhaya Hotel has had a major makeover and rebranded itself as the number-one choice of the newly arrived backpacker collective. It is absolutely enormous, and a 17-floor extension at the back of the hotel is in the works, so soon the Chhaya will rival the Pentagon in Byzantine architectural complexity. The rooms are absolutely spotless and newly tiled, grouted, and furnished. They also rent out bicycles and motorcycles, and sell bus and boat tickets. Mr. Lee, the manager, is a cheery soul and is a font of local information. If you are a budget traveler, this is the place to hook up with your compadres.

St. 3. ⓒ 012/733-204. 100 units. $5 double fan; $10 double A/C. **Amenities:** Internet. *In room:* A/C, TV, fridge.

Golden Palace Hotel ★   Like the Spring Park, the Golden Palace is pretty monstrous from the outside but the impression changes once at reception. This clean, functional hotel is aimed largely at the business traveler and is of a very high standard if a little antiseptic. Rooms are large, light, and functional. They have Wi-Fi throughout as well as LAN satellite Internet connections in the rooms. The newly located Cold Night Restaurant is on the hotel grounds and is a good option for breakfast, lunch, and dinner.

East bank of the river, Old NH#5. ⓒ 053/953-901. Fax 053/953-903. www.goldenpalacehotels.com. 50 units. $15 double; $20 superior. MC, V. **Amenities:** Restaurant; Internet. *In room:* A/C, TV, fridge.

International Hotel ★   This newly renovated hotel is in a superb location near both the market and the river. Everything is sparkling and unlike many of their competitors they haven't renovated only the rooms, they have also renovated and decorated the corridors giving the hotel a unified feel. What the renovation has not been able to achieve is to change the layout of the hotel itself. Half the rooms have windows and are very pleasant indeed with casual but smart furnishings and plenty of light. The other half have exactly the same furnishings but no windows and no light at all and feel like a mausoleum. The rooms with windows are superb value. Pay the extra two bucks and embrace the sun.

St. 2. © **053/953-999.** 29 units. $13 double without window; $15 double with window. *In room:* A/C, TV, fridge

Khemara Battambang Hotel ★ This is a solid businesslike option with four stories built around a courtyard with parking. They call themselves "boutique," but that is delusional on their part although that fact actually does not detract from what the Khemara has to offer. The rooms are palatial, spotless, and airy. At present they do not accept credit cards but they hope to change that.

East bank of the river. Old NH#5. © **053/732-727.** Fax 053/737-979. www.khemarahotel.com. 50 units. $15 double. No credit cards. **Amenities:** Restaurant; Internet. *In room:* A/C, TV, fridge.

La Villa ★★★ La Villa continues to reign as the top luxury option in Battambang. The luxury is packaged with immense style, in a beautiful colonial French villa on the east bank of the river. The villa has been extended but in such a way that it is hard to tell the old from the new. The beauty of the building is complemented by muted but tasteful Art Deco period furnishings. All the rooms are different—we particularly liked the loft-style room on the top floor with its rustic wooden beams and scattered floor cushions. The rooms have sturdy four-poster beds with draped mosquito netting and faded black-and-white photos on the walls. The casual and slightly vague Francophone management go out of their way to be helpful without getting in your hair. The newly added swimming pool is a godsend in the hot season and is a great place to enjoy an early evening drink. If you're not staying here (and it is an expensive option, even though it is worth every dollar) it is worth dropping by for a meal or some refreshment just to soak up the atmosphere.

185 Pom Romchek. © **053/730-151.** www.lavilla-battambang.com. 7 units. $60 standard; $85 suite. MC, V. **Amenities:** Restaurant; bar; Internet; outdoor pool; room service. *In room:* A/C, TV, DVD player.

Royal Hotel ★ This hotel next to Psar Nath is part of a small chain. They have an eclectic range of rooms and will happily let you pay less if you don't want to use the air-conditioning, the TV, or the fridge. It is a sort of modular, do-it-yourself, go ahead and assemble your own hotel room approach. The rooms themselves are large with balconies and a real touch of style. It is in no way boutique, but they have borrowed some boutique flourishes with silk cushions, traditional wall hangings, potted plants, and the perennial plastic flower placed artfully on the bedspread. The staff are helpful and speak English. It is a very good choice at a very acceptable price. They have a slightly scruffy but very convivial rooftop restaurant if you are up to the vertical hike. If booked up, the nearby **Asia Hotel** (near Psar Nath; © 053/953-522) and **Star Hotel** (near Psar Nath; © 053/953-522) are identical in facilities to the Royal Hotel and part of the same chain (the Star Hotel also offers suites).

Near Psar Nath. © **053/953-522.** 42 units. $6 double bathroom, fan, and TV; $8 double bathroom fan, TV, and fridge; $10 double A/C; $13 large double A/C; $20 king-size double. MC, V. **Amenities:** Laundry service. *In room:* A/C, TV, fridge.

Seng Hout Hotel ★★★ (Finds Even by the excellent standards of Battambang, the Seng Hout stands out for both quality and value. This brand-new hotel is filled with light and has a well-proportioned sense of space. Best of all, there are a number of very pretty outside sitting areas. The terrace on the fourth floor is particularly pleasant, with potted plants and comfy rattan chairs. There is also a shaded rooftop restaurant from which you can survey the red tiled roofs of Battambang below you. The prices for all this thoughtful design are astonishingly low. The A/C single and the fan single are the same—they just disable the A/C if you don't need it and bring up a fan.

1008B St. 2. ✆ 092/530-293. www.senghouhotel.com. 35 units. $15 A/C double; $20 A/C double superior view. V. **Amenities:** Restaurant. *In room:* A/C, TV, fridge.

Spring Park Hotel ★ From the outside the Spring Park looks simply awful, having been built in the weirdly blocky architecture that blights so much of Thailand. But once inside, you find yourself facing an incongruously very well-designed interior. Once you make your way to the bedrooms, the surprises continue. The rooms are large and airy, and furnished with brightly colored bedspreads and tasteful silk cushions. All the facilities are state of the art and the hotel is also set up for business travelers with Wi-Fi throughout and conference rooms equipped with audiovisual aids. The staff is friendly and attentive. It is an immensely good value, even by Battambang's high standards.

East bank of the river. Old NH#5. ✆ 012/849-999. Fax 053/730-999. 78 units. $8 fan double; $11 standard double; $13 superior double; $20 deluxe. MC, V. **Amenities:** Restaurant; Internet. *In room:* A/C, TV, fridge.

Teo Hotel The Teo holds a special place in the hearts of those journalists, de-miners, and NGO workers who knew Battambang when the Khmer Rouge were still just up the road. The good news (apart from the war being over) is that years later it is still gleaming. The spotless cleanliness of the Teo is a site to behold, and during the day you may trip over a legion of blue-shirted women scrubbing, polishing, and mopping. Any clothes thoughtlessly discarded on the floor will be returned to you within hours all washed and pressed. If all this sounds slightly fascistic, it is not—the staff at the Teo is supercasual and friendly. The rooms are on the small side but include a fridge and TV. Despite the recently arrived competition, the Teo's rates are actually lower than they were a decade ago. The Teo claims to have free Wi-Fi, but this is not quite a reality since it is very rarely working and doesn't penetrate the walls of the guest rooms.

St. 3. ✆ 053/952-288. 87 units. $13 double; $25 VIP. MC, V. **Amenities:** Restaurant; Internet. *In room:* A/C, TV, fridge.

WHERE TO DINE

Battambang may not rival either Phnom Penh or Siem Reap for choice, but it certainly has a few eating options that stand up in terms of quality. All establishments are cash only.

Bus Stop ★ WESTERN This Australian-style restaurant/pub serves huge portions of fantastic home cooking. The sausage and mash is particularly good. The pork chops are delicious with lots of thick, tasty gravy, and when it comes to a full English breakfast the Bus Stop is in master class territory. The beers are super cold and the draft Angkor beer is a very reasonable 75¢. The Bus Stop's pub is a meeting place for expats and has a full range of spirits.

149 St. 2. ✆ 053/730-544. www.busstopcambodia.com. Main courses $5. Daily 6:30am–10pm.

The Cold Night KHMER/WESTERN Like the Teo Hotel, the Cold Night is an establishment that dates from the days when Battambang was a much rougher place than it is today. The restaurant has actually moved in the intervening years but it still retains its relaxed, open-air charm. The typical Khmer and Western food has never stood out but it was always adequate and, in keeping with its name, the beer is always cold.

East bank of the river. Old NH#5. ✆ **012/994-746.** Main courses $4–$6. Daily 6am–11pm.

Fresh Eats Cafe WESTERN   This is a good place for snacks, pastries, pizza, pies, Western breakfasts, and an excellent selection of coffee and tea. It is conveniently situated near many of the hotels around Psar Nath and is affiliated with an NGO that helps families affected by HIV/AIDS.

West of Psar Nath past the Royal Hotel. ✆ **053/953-912.** Main courses $1–$3. Mon–Sat 6:30am–9pm.

Gecko Cafe ★ (Finds WESTERN/ASIAN   Right in the center of town on Street 3 is this wonderful old French colonial building, with a new cafe on the second floor. Most of the Gecko Bar takes up the surrounding balcony, furnished with comfortable wicker furniture and cushions. The food is light with a combination of pasta, great burgers, and sandwiches, and they also do some Khmer signature dishes such as amok. With some dishes the logistics are way off—after ordering the battered and fried fish with french fries, the two constituents of the meal arrived half an hour apart. If you're a tea drinker, skip the tea here, which is orange and virulent-tasting. They also offer foot and shoulder massage. All in all, the Gecko cafe is a fine addition to Battambang's dining scene just for the ambience alone.

St. 3. ✆ **092/719-985.** www.geckocafecambodia.com. Main courses $4.50. Daily 8am–10pm.

Pkay Proek ★★ KHMER/THAI   This Thai and Khmer restaurant has been around a long time and was a favorite of the expat/NGO crowd, largely because there wasn't much else around and also because it is very good. It remains very good. With spicy Thai and lemony Khmer, the Pkay Proek serves fresh curries, river fish, and amok. It is popular with locals and visitors alike. If you want an authentic Khmer meal in the company of local diners, this is the place to visit.

St. 3. ✆ **089/888-819.** Main courses $2.50–$4. Daily 9am–10pm.

Pomme d'Amour ★ FRENCH   This newcomer to the Battambang scene serves excellent French provincial food in quirky but tasteful surroundings. It is not the place to go if you are on a diet since it is a palace of blood-red beefsteak with heavy creamy sauces accompanied by a wide range of red wine. If you are in the mood for something Gallic, rich, and delicious this should be your first stop. It is furnished with lots of billowing silk and muslin. The tables are artfully decorated, again with rich dark silk. It could almost be called boutique but it isn't, simply because it all feels a little bit too crazy, but in an engaging and fun way. It is no surprise to hear that the "patron" is a lifelong circus performer. It is situated in the small street between Street 2 and Street 3 running parallel to both at the northern end near Psar Nath.

63 St. 2¹/₂. ✆ **012/415-513.** Main courses $6–$15. Daily 8am–10pm.

The Riverside Balcony Bar ★★★ WESTERN   The Riverside Balcony is quite simply one of the best bars in Cambodia. It is found in an all-wooden Khmer house right on the river 1km (½ mile) south of the Teo Hotel. It used to be a private house for the Battambang program director of the United Nations High Commission for Refugees. Now it is Australian owned and has become a central part of the Battambang experience. The restaurant's giant dark-wood veranda exudes an atmosphere of relaxed grandeur. The food is not the main draw here, though the burgers are very good and they have a good

Food Stalls by the Riverside

On both the east and the west bank of the Sangker between the Old Iron Bridge and the New Iron Bridge are lots of stalls selling local food. Fried chicken, steaming soup, and other staple dishes are served under florescent tubes. It is a jovial Khmer scene and you will be made welcome. Learn a few words of Khmer and you will become popular as you are questioned in depth about your family members and financial liquidity. Open daily 5 to 9pm.

selection of Tex-Mex offerings and pasta. Come here for the perfect place to enjoy a gin and tonic, soda water, or glass of wine as the light fades, the crickets chirp, and the tropical night begins to fall.

St. 1. ✆ 053/730-313. Main courses $3.50. Tues–Sun 4pm–midnight.

Smokin' Pot KHMER   This is a cooking school as well as a restaurant (p. 143), and a great place to sample authentic Khmer cuisine. They serve all the Cambodian classics such as amok or stir-fried beef with morning glory and peanuts. The fried chicken is delicious. Eat it the Khmer way with a simple dip of pepper mixed with lemon juice. Don't come here for the ambience, since the restaurant has a functional feel to it.

Btw. St. 1 and St. 3 opposite the White Rose Restaurant. ✆ 012/821-400. Main courses $1.50–$3. Daily 7am–11pm.

White Rose ASIAN   The popular White Rose is a no-nonsense Khmer restaurant with an encyclopedic menu embracing Chinese, Thai, and Vietnamese, as well as Cambodian. The soups are excellent and they also offer delicious baguette sandwiches crammed with pâté, omelets, or cream cheese. The White Rose also serves decent Lipton tea as well as the Cambodian and Chinese varieties. The Terrace at the front of the restaurant on the corner is a good place to sit and watch the world go by (this being Battambang, it goes by slowly).

St. 2. ✆ 012/536-500. Main courses $1.50–$4. Daily 6:30am–10pm.

ATTRACTIONS

A wander among Battambang's classic crumbly colonials, all of which are colored a deep yellowish tan that lights up in the morning and evening light, makes for nice city walking. There are a few Buddhist temples scattered around town, and south of the city is the large statue of a kneeling **Ta Dambong,** the legendary founder of peace and stability in the region, holding the "Disappearing Stick" for which Battambang gets its name.

The real sights in this area are the rural temples and beautiful countryside. A 1-day trip can get you to all of them, and as much fun are the rural stops in between, a visit to a farmer's field perhaps or to roadside juice stands; you will see real rural Cambodia in all its richness and variety. There are rice paddies in shades of deep green, flocks of kids cycling home from school, old folk pottering about their business, their heads swathed in kramas, their baggy black pants billowing around their legs. A trip to Wat Phnom Sampeou and Wat Banang is a good circuit, beginning at Rte. 10 on the west end of town and then returning along the river. For $5, most motorbike drivers will try to talk you into a trip back on a small metal-and-bamboo, motor-driven platform that sits on top of the train tracks, a common form of transport considering that the train only passes once each day. A visit to Wat Phnom Ek is an additional trip in the other direction.

Bamboo Train The bamboo train is an improvised form of transportation that follows the now-defunct railway tracks. It is made up of a small bamboo cart powered by a motorcycle engine that rides the railroad tracks picking up and dropping off passengers, cargo, animals, motorcycles, and pretty much anything else along the way. When two of these contraptions meet, one (the one carrying less cargo) is whipped off the rails in a minute or two while the other is allowed to pass. You can find these marvels of invention at various intersections around town. The *motodups* will know where they are. Times vary.

Cooking School at the Smokin' Pot There is no better way to understand the depth and complexity of a country's cuisine than to cook something for yourself. The Smokin' Pot Restaurant offers a very popular cooking course that covers many of the bases. The day starts at the market, where you'll pick up ingredients such as piles of fresh herbs, tubs of pungent prahoc (fermented fish paste), and a selection of meat both white and red. With six students and one teacher in a class, the Smokin' Pot (p. 142) offers an intimate hands-on learning session. You get busy chopping chilies and lemon grass, pounding galangal, kaffir leaves, and garlic, creating an authentic curry paste. Then you put it to good use. Amok is the signature dish here and if you get to master this then you are looking at big praise if you serve it at dinner parties in Europe or the States. It is delicious. The cooking class costs a very reasonable $8 for the day, which usually includes three dishes.

Class daily 9am–1:30pm.

PPS Circus *Phare Ponleu Selpak,* meaning "the brightness of art," originated during the civil war in 1986 in Site 2 Refugee Camp on the Thai border. The idea of a creative association, which would use art and expression to help young refugees overcome the trauma of war, emerged from drawing workshops held for children in the camps. This original idea continued after the refugees returned to their homeland, and PPS was formally founded in 1994 by a group of former Site 2 children. They have weekly circus shows (every Thurs at 8pm unless you are Khmer, in which case it's free) mixing different disciplines, live music, choreography, tremendous technique, poetry, and burlesque. Through the performance of all these artistic outlets, these teenagers and young adults give to the audience their vision of modern Cambodia. Contact the Phare Ponleu Selpak office for the schedule. Be aware that the circus is in a fairly poor suburb. Make sure you already have transport back to your hotel since tuk-tuks and *motodups* will be scarce.

Rte. 5 about 1km (¹/₂ mile) west of town. © **053/952-424** or 012/890-360. www.phareps.org.

Ek Phnom This atmospheric Angkorian pile dates from the 11th century and was constructed as a Hindu temple under Suryavarman I and is really quite impressive. The temple consists of prasats on a platform with some bas-relief carvings in very good condition. You can climb up to the main sanctuary although you may have company from the local contingent of beggars. Some of the stone doorways are semi-collapsed in a very aesthetically crooked way. There is a modern pagoda next to the temple of no distinction. The river road drive to Ek Phnom from Battambang passes through small villages and rice paddies, and it is an absolutely stunning little journey, a real slice of genuine rural Cambodia.

Admission $2.

Phnom Banan   This mountaintop temple dates from the 11th century and consists of five prasats or towers. Its elevated location gives good views in all directions. It is quite a daunting climb up to the ruins, but you can buy drinks once at the top. The opening times vary, but it's generally open from 7am to 6pm.

Phnom Sampeou Mountain   This hilltop temple on the road to the old Khmer Rouge stronghold of Pailin affords fantastic views of the surrounding area. There are still two government artillery pieces in place pointing to the former Khmer Rouge positions. About halfway up the hill are the "Killing Caves." This was an execution ground during the years of Democratic Kampuchea. Victims were bludgeoned to death and thrown into the caves. There are kids at the base of the mountain, some of whom speak good English and act as guides for a small fee. There are two ways to the summit. One by steep stairs, the other by a far easier track around the sides of the mountain. Phnom Sampeou is best visited in either the early morning or the late afternoon when the light is best and the views are best lit. It's generally open from 7am to 6pm.

Provincial Museum   The Battambang Provincial Museum is on the riverfront in the center of town and houses a large collection of Angkorian and pre-Angkorian statues and carvings. Magnificent carved lintels (similar to those in Ek Phnom) and ornate pedestals, heads of Hindu gods, and a huge urn are some of the highlights. A visit here complements a day spent looking at some of the nearby ruins.

St. 1. Mon–Fri 8–11am and 2–5pm. Admission $1.

Boat Trip on the Sangker River   Gecko Cafe (p. 141) offers an afternoon cruise lasting about 1½ hours on the Sangker River. If you have not taken the boat from Siem Reap this will give you a chance to see village life along the banks. The cruise costs $8 to $12 per person depending on the numbers, and you get a cocktail thrown in free.

SHOPPING

Psar Nath in the center of town is the main market and is geared toward locals. You can find all kinds of practical goods and foodstuffs—fruit, vegetables, meat, clothing, kramas, shoes, hats, food stalls, and so on. Gem dealers, photo shops, and money-changers line the streets that surround the market. **Psar Leu,** just south of town, is the place to buy produce such as oranges and pomelos. The oranges are said to be the best in Cambodia. The **Smiling Sky Bookshop** (St. 2; ✆ **012/298-005**) sells secondhand English-language books including Cambodia-related titles, novels, and popular literature. They also trade books. **Pulp** (btw. St. 2 and St. 3; ✆ **012/178-3584**) is a new secondhand bookshop. They also sell snacks and coffee. There are a few **souvenir shops** on streets 1 and 2 selling local goods such as **woodcarvings** and some **cotton and silk accessories.** Compared to Phnom Penh and Siem Reap, though, the options are limited. The main commodity on sale in the center of town seems to be cellphones—Battambang must have more cellphone shops per capita then anywhere else on the planet.

AFTER DARK

Battambang is very quiet after 9pm. There are karaoke joints, restaurants, and a few bars but they hardly make a dent in the town's general sleepiness. The **Bus Stop** (p. 140) stays open until midnight if there are customers and it can get quite busy. The **Riverside Balcony Bar** (p. 141) also caters to a crowd if one is around. Until 2001, there were a number of fantastic discos on Street 3 where a live band would get the crowd going with a mix of traditional Khmer ballads and '70s soul. Whole families would come down on a Sunday evening and boogie together. Sadly these are now gone and the main nightspot dancing venue is the **Sky Disco** (℗ **012/862-777;** open daily 8pm–1am) near the Khemara Hotel and Cold Night restaurant on Old NH#5. This is much more of a modern Thai-influenced affair with some pretty strange playlists. It can get busy on weekends and is a good place (well, the only place) to expend energy and work up a dance-induced sweat.

2 KOMPONG CHHNANG

Kompong Chhnang is a great place to break up the road journey from Battambang to Phnom Penh, whether you stop only for lunch or stay the night. It is a quiet, elegant town distinguished by some beautiful Colonial French architecture and a bustling riverfront that begs out for shutterbugs to do their thing. The word Chhnang means earthenware pot and it is the production of these that gives the town its name. It has long been one of the most prosperous towns in Cambodia and that is echoed in the laid back charm of the place. Apart from fishing, the main activity here seems to be petanque, or the French equivalent of bowls.

GETTING THERE & GETTING AROUND

The ferries going from Phnom Penh to Siem Reap pass by Kompong Chhnang. If this is where you fancy being put ashore, ask the operator when you buy your ticket and make sure that the request has been relayed to the crew. Kompong Chhnang is right on National Highway 5, so all buses between Phnom Penh and Battambang also pass through town. You can also get a seat in a shared taxi for $3 from Phnom Penh 2 hours away, and $9 from Battambang 4 hours away.

(Fast Facts   Kompong Chhnang

Banks & Currency Exchange   **Acleda Bank** (NH5; ℗ **026/988-748**) changes travelers checks and has an ATM. **Canadia Bank** (Street 33. ℗ **026/770-017**) provides the same services.

Internet Access   A number of mobile phone shops near the bus station have one or two computers hooked up to the internet and can be used for $1 per hour. Do not expect speedy connections.

WHERE TO STAY & DINE

Sokha Guesthouse (southwest of the central square; ℗ **012**/762-988. $5 double fan, $13 double A/C) has been around a while, catering to NGO workers as well as those aimlessly passing through. It is clean, efficient, and friendly. The Sovannphum Hotel (NH5 towards Phnom Penh; ℗ **011/886-472;** $10 double) is a brand new business-orientated hotel where everything works smoothly. It is a good alternative to Sokha, though it lacks its style and warmth. The **Somrongsen Hotel** (Phsar Krom Road; ℗ **026/989-011;** $10 double) is a new place with large, airy rooms around a courtyard.

As a stopover point on the main East-West Highway, Kompong Chhnang has a number of restaurants strung out along NH5, largely serving the same kind of Khmer fare to those on buses whistling through. **Mitthapeap Restaurant** (NH5; ℰ 012/949-397; main courses $1.50) is probably the best, but it is still fairly pedestrian.

ATTRACTIONS

Kompong Chhnang is a serene and quiet town. The main interest of the place, apart from contemplating the ochre buildings left by the French or watching the local kids play petanque, is the bustling riverfront. In the morning it is very busy. The people who work and live here are largely ethnic Vietnamese and you will hear their musical and slightly frantic sounding tones as much as Khmer. Their haggling is great to watch. Get there early.

3 KRATIE

Most people stop in Kratie for one reason only—to catch a sight of the bottle-nosed Irrawaddy dolphins. With the overland route to southern Laos becoming more and more popular, Kratie is also increasing in popularity as an overnight stay before moving on elsewhere. The town itself is very pleasant. It was pretty firmly Khmer Rouge throughout the war in the '70s so it was never a battlefield. The pretty riverine colonial architecture remained intact and the waterfront remains a pleasant place to sit with an ice-cold drink and watch the sun go down.

GETTING THERE & GETTING AROUND

This used to be a place best reached by boat from Phnom Penh. The boat is no longer running as the road is now perfect. The bus station is in the northwest part of the town within walking distance of the center. Regular buses run the 350km (217-mile) trip from Phnom Penh and it takes about 5 hours. The onward trip to Stung Treng and the Lao border is 141km (87 miles) and takes 3 hours. There is now a daily bus from Siem Reap to Kratie changing at the town of Skuon (the place where people famously eat tarantulas). It leaves at 7:30am and costs $10. You can also get a seat in a shared taxi in either direction. It costs $7 to Phnom Penh and takes about 4 hours. Kratie is small, so navigating the town on foot is very easy. Should you want go a bit farther afield there are plenty of *motodups* hanging around, and some guesthouses also rent out bicycles.

(Fast Facts Kratie

Banks & Currency Exchange There is an **Acleda Bank** (Rue Preah Sihanouk; ℰ **072/971-707;** open Mon–Fri 7:30am–4pm) that exchanges cash and traveler's checks. There is now also an ATM but it does not accept all cards, so it would be risky to rely on that alone.

Internet Access For the Internet, head to the **You Hong Guesthouse** (p. 147).

WHERE TO STAY & DINE

The scene here is firmly in the realm of backpackerdom, so both food and accommodations are cheap and cheerful. There are quite a number of guesthouses, all of which also

The Spiders of Skuon

In the town of Skuon at the junction between highways 6 and 7, people eat big, juicy tarantulas with relish. They are hairy, large, and they move alarmingly quickly (when not yet fried). Originally unearthed by starving Cambodians in the dark days of Khmer Rouge tyranny, Skuon's spiders have been transformed from vital sustenance of desperate refugees to a national delicacy. Black, hairy, and packing vicious, venom-soaked fangs, the burrowing arachnids common to the jungle around Skuon do not appear at first sight to be very delicious at all. For local people, the "a-ping," as the breed of palm-size tarantula is called in Khmer, is a source of fame and fortune in an otherwise impoverished region. At around 300 riel a spider, the eight-legged snack industry provides a tidy income in a country where around one-third of people live below the poverty line of $1 per day. Conservationists and vegetarians might recoil at the relentless pursuit of so many spiders for the sake of a snack, but locals are confident the arachnid population will hold up. According to aficionados, the best spider is one plucked straight from its burrow and pan-fried with lashings of garlic and salt over a traditional wood fire until its skin turns a deep red-brown color. Crispy on the outside, gooey on the inside, it should then be served piping hot. Many Cambodians also attest to its medicinal properties, especially when mixed in a rice wine cocktail. It is said that with the wine, it's very important the spiders still have their fangs, or the medicine loses its power.

serve food. The British-run **Star Guesthouse** (west side of the market; ✆ **072/971-663;** $4 single, $5 double) is the most established place in town and the management is very knowledgeable about things to do and onward travel arrangements. The **Balcony Guesthouse** (Rue Sumamarit on the riverfront, 350m/1,148 ft. north of the bus stop; ✆ **016/604-036;** $4 double shared bathroom, $6 double attached bathroom) is a new addition to the Kratie guesthouse scene and is jointly Australian and Khmer managed. It has large, light, clean rooms with good-quality furnishings. There is a relaxing restaurant/ bar on the balcony overlooking the Mekong, and a communal area with a large collection of DVDs. The **Heng Heng Hotel** (Rue Sumamarit; ✆ **072/971-405;** $12 double, $5 single) offers nice riverfront rooms, and the restaurant is a good dining option. The **Oudom Sambath Hotel** (Rue Sumamarit; ✆ **072/971-502;** $15 double, $8 single) is by Kratie standards veering toward opulence. The **Santepheap Hotel** (Rue Sumamarit; ✆ **072/971-537;** $15 double, $8 single) is another more mildly upmarket option with TV. The **You Hong Guesthouse** (north of the market; ✆ **012/957-003;** $3 double) is a popular budget option. They have Internet (on standard computers) and the management is experienced in dealing with most questions you might need answered.

In addition to guesthouse restaurants, the place to be as the afternoon turns into evening is along the riverfront where stalls set up selling grilled chicken, soup, and other Khmer staples. Don't expect anything grand. The **Red Sun Falling** (Rue Preah Sumarit; main courses $1–$4) is the liveliest place in town (which of course means it is actually quite quiet).

Irrawaddy Dolphins   These shy creatures found near Kratie are highly endangered, the casualties of hunting for their oils and collateral damage from dynamite fishing. Forty years ago, it's estimated that the dolphins here numbered in the four figures. Now there are estimated to be fewer than 100. There was some hope that the ban on net fishing in these waters and an increase in conservation awareness was beginning to have a positive effect on dolphin numbers. It is certainly true that local people now realize it is very much in their interest to see the dolphins preserved since they are a valuable tourism resource and a source of income. Pollutants in the river, however, are driving the dolphins to extinction. The dolphins can be found at Kampi about 15km (9½ miles) north of town and your guesthouse will be able to point you in the direction of a *motodup* for the afternoon. The trip costs about $4. Once at Kampi, a boat out to view the dolphins costs about $4 per person. Both the Star Guesthouse and the You Hong Guesthouse run an all-inclusive package. Once you're on the water, get the boatman to switch off his engine. You then simply sit there and relax, scanning the waters waiting for these elusive creatures to break the surface. It becomes a fairly mesmerizing experience and very satisfying when you catch sight of a few dolphins.

---

4 RATANAKIRI

Cambodia's remote northeast is a mixture of wild and unforgiving jungle, rolling cultivated hills, and red, red earth. It is home to a mosaic of indigenous peoples collectively dubbed the *Khmer Loeu* ("high Khmer"), a reference to the area's geography, not their historical or social status. They have their own culture, history, and languages and have historically been far removed from the lowland Khmer. The physical and environmental character of the province is made up of an impressive range of high land with undulating hills and mountains, a level plateau, watershed lowlands, crater lakes, rivers, and waterfalls. Forest cover varies from area to area, from the dense impenetrable forest in the northern reaches, which are still rich in wildlife, to the drier and sparser forest, found in the southwest. Similarly, the soil types present range from rich volcanic soil to the sandy soil found near rivers. Rapacious logging is taking a heavy toll here. Ratanakiri has also long been an area of profitable gem mining some although the whole district is on the edge of being totally mined out.

It was to this region that Pol Pot and his henchmen fled in the '60s when Sihanouk decided to crack down on those he dubbed with contempt the Khmer Rouge. In many ways these men on the run found a willing and loyal audience among the tribal peoples of this remote region. They had often been discriminated against and bonded into slavery.

These days this region is emerging as a very popular eco-tourism destination and facilities, while still basic, are improving with each passing year.

BANLUNG

Banlung is the capital of Ratanakiri Province and is the base from which you can explore the surrounding countryside with waterfalls, lakes, and villages.

Getting There & Getting Around

It is possible to travel directly by bus to and from Phnom Penh to Banlung, the capital of Ratanakiri, stopping in Kratie. Several minibuses offer the service, which costs about

$10 but can be more during high season. The road is mostly new and surfaced, but it does disintegrate into dirt past Stung Treng, 100km (62 miles) before you reach Banlung. The companies running this route are **Bung Rung** (✆ 012/684-041), **Bona Transport** (✆ 012/567-161), and **Ly Heng Express** (✆ 023/991-726).

You can also travel by regular bus leaving Phnom Penh at 6:15am and Banlung at 7am going the other way. It is a 600km (372-mile) journey and costs $12. **Rith Mony, Phnom Penh Sorya,** and **GST Express Bus Company** all run this route.

Motorcycle taxi *(motodup),* rental motorcycle, and bicycle are the primary options for exploring the immediate area. You can hire a *motodup* for the whole day for about $8. If they speak good English they might ask for more. A 100cc motorcycle costs $5 a day. A bicycle costs $1 a day. Ask at your guesthouse. You may also be able to rent four-wheel-drives for $40.

(Fast Facts) Banlung

Banks & Currency Exchange There is one bank, the **Acleda Bank** (near the market. ✆ 075/974-220; open Mon–Fri 7:30am–4pm). They change traveler's checks. There is an ATM but at present it does not accept international cards.

Internet Access There is Internet access at a number of places around the center of town but prices are relatively high ($3 per hour) and speeds are excessively slow. Try **Srei Mom's Internet,** on the road west to east close to the market and bus stop.

Post Office The **Post Office** is on the road east heading toward Vietnam. It offers international phone calls, although there are cellphone kiosks from which it is cheaper to call.

Where to Stay & Dine

Terres Rouges Lodge (Boeung Kansaign; ✆ 075/974-051; www.ratanakiri-lodge.com; $35 double, $40 twin, $65 deluxe, $85 suite) is a beautiful old wooden house with leafy gardens and even a small swimming pool. It is real luxury for this part of the world, and there is even an attached spa. The rooms are rustic but stylish with plenty of dark-wood furnishings. The restaurant and bar serves both Khmer and French food, though the harder to prepare dishes need to be ordered a day in advance. It is the best restaurant in town. **Treetop Eco-Lodge** (Hillside district; ✆ 012/490-333; $10 double) opened in early 2009. It offers beautiful bungalows with wraparound verandas that hang from the side of a verdant hillside. The bungalows are well appointed for the location with electricity, vaulted ceilings, and an en suite bathroom. The restaurant has a nice atmosphere while the food is nothing to write home about. The **Yaklom Hill Lodge** (10-min. drive in dry season east of Banlung past the lake; ✆ 012/644-240; www.yaklom.com; $10 single, $15 double, $20 triple, $45 deluxe bungalow) is an ecolodge that is set in the middle of the woods 6km (3¾ miles) out of town, with wooden bungalows interspersed among the trees. You'll find yourself completely removed from the world outside (this impression is advanced by the lack of electricity during the day). During wet season the proximity of all that foliage ensures that the atmosphere is also one of constant damp. The restaurant serves both Khmer and Thai food. The **Lakeside Chheng Lok Hotel** (far side of the lake; (© **012/957-422;** $10 double A/C; $5 double fan; $20 bungalow) is set on the other side of town among leafy surrounds. The rooms come with hot water and TV so you can enjoy modern amenities in tandem with great lake views, all at a very reasonable price.

Most guesthouses have attached restaurants, but there are other options with one or two pleasant surprises. **Gecko House** (© **012/422-228;** main courses $1–$4) is rather trendy for an area so remote. The thatched building is furnished with hanging plants and bamboo furniture with a pebble-strewn floor. The Khmer dishes receive good reviews and there is also a reasonable range of Western meals, including pizzas and burgers. **Sal's Restaurant and Bar** (© **012/284-377;** main courses $1.50–$5) is located in a small wooden house near the edge of town. They serve a pretty good mix of Western and Khmer food, and you can call ahead to order pizza since waiting times can be quite long.

Attractions

Yak Lom Lake is Banlung's number-one attraction. It is a volcanic crater filled with fresh water, surrounded by a trail that takes about an hour to walk. The lake has mystical significance to local people. There is a pier from which you can swim and inner tubes are available to rent. The entrance fee is $1. There is also a visitor center, which displays some local handicrafts and has information on local tribes and some good walks in the area. Yak Lom Lake is 5km (3 miles) from Banlung heading east. It is an hour's walk or you can hire a moto for $1 each way plus a tip if you make him wait any length of time.

There are a number of waterfalls around Ratanakiri, some of which are easily accessible from Banlung. **Chha Ong waterfall** is west of Banlung on National Rd. 78. It is purported to be the highest in Ratanakiri at 30m (98 ft.). You can swim at the foot of the falls. Entrance is 2,000 riel. **Katieng waterfall, Kah Chhang waterfall,** and **Bai S'rok waterfall** are other nearby waterfalls worth a stop. Katieng is often considered to be the most fun because you actually clamber under a rock shelf and behind the flow of the water a bit like Daniel Day-Lewis in *The Last of the Mohicans.*

At Bai S'rok there is still a lot of gem-mining activity although that might be diminishing since the whole area is getting pretty much mined out. You can combine a visit with an **elephant ride** and a **village home stay**—ask at your guesthouse.

Lumkut Lake is another beautiful cratered lake situated in dense forest near Borkeo district about 30km (19 miles) north of Banlung. You can swim here, but not in rainy season when the dirt path that leads there is virtually impassable. With a guide, the trip should cost about $15 per person for a half-day trip and can include a stop in a Tampuan minority village.

Virachey National Park is a wild area teeming with wildlife that has yet to be fully explored. All trips to Virachey have to be arranged through the park service and accompanied by an approved guide. You can sort this out through your guesthouse or you can go directly to the ranger's office and arrange the trip with them. The park headquarters is located 3 blocks north of the post office. The most popular trek is the 3-day trip, which includes spending 1 night inside a hut adjacent to an ethnic Brou village just outside the park, and 1 night spent in a hammock about 20km (12 miles) inside the park boundary. It is about a 30km (19-mile) walk total and costs $107 per person, though the price can come down with groups that have more than two people.

The central market of **Psar Banlung** is the place to see Khmer Loeu people arrive early in the morning carrying "back strap" baskets laden with vegetables, fruit, and forest products, which they sell at the market. It can be a fascinating and photogenic scene. It is

Exploring Mondulkiri

The remote eastern region of Mondulkiri is Cambodia's largest, yet it's the most sparsely populated province and traveling there is difficult. There is only one dirt road that takes you to the tiny provincial capital of **Sen Monorom,** a 10-hour trip from Phnom Penh. The initial part of the trip, to **Snuol,** is on well-surfaced roads. Once past Snuol, you hit mud in the rainy season and flying dust in the dry season. Like Ratanakiri, Mondulkiri is set on a plateau, making it different from the lowlands in both climate and vegetation. It gets very cool in winter. Mondulkiri is lined up for massive and controversial rubber cultivation. Logging has already ravaged this part of the world and the hills are largely bare. What remains is still alluring, with a unique beauty. Sen Monorom is very quiet, with just a few dirt tracks and one roundabout in the middle of a series of grassy rolling hills. There are two main streets in Sen Monoram and where they meet is the de facto center of town, where you will find guesthouses and restaurants. When your bus arrives there will be plenty of *motodups* to ferry you to your guesthouse of choice.

Mondulkiri's main attraction is its waterfalls, and it's worth hiring a *motodup* to take you to the main ones rather than trying to negotiate the dusty tracks yourself. **Bousra Waterfall** is the largest waterfall within easy reach, about 35km (22 miles) from Sen Monorom. It takes 1 bumpy hour to get there. The falls are on two levels and the main rest area is between the two. On the upper level the falls are wide and swift. There are a couple of places to swim. The lower falls a far more narrow, but at 25m (82 ft.) they are far higher. If you cross the falls and take the path to your left you will reach a very uneven set of rough stairs that takes you to the base of the lower set of falls. A *motodup* will charge $10 for ferrying you about for the day, or you can hire your own bike for $7. Heading the opposite way out of town you will find are several smaller water-falls near ethnic Phunong villages. **Sen Monorom falls** and **Kbal Preah Water-fall** make a nice afternoon excursion. **Elephant treks** cost $25 per person for the day and enable you to reach falls not accessible by vehicle. The trips usually start in a local Phnong village, and take about 2 hours. If you haven't traveled by ele-phant before, be warned it is hard work as the movements throw you around a bit. **Sunset Hill** is a good place to catch the sunset. You can also stop at **Phnom Doh Kromom Pagoda,** giving you a fine view of the rolling hills beyond.

The **Long Vibol Guesthouse and Restaurant** (past the airstrip; ✆ **012/944-647;** $10 double) is an established favorite with visiting NGO workers. Rooms have TVs, and the food is good though the service is extremely relaxed. **Nature Lodge** (✆ **012/230-272;** www.naturelodgecambodia.com; $10 double) is an ecolodge that gets rave reviews and the Israeli/Khmer ownership has created a homey atmosphere. You will need to hire a *motodup* to find it.

Southern Cambodia

When you think of Cambodia, visions of tranquil beaches probably aren't the first thing that come to mind, which is a shame. It isn't much when compared with the quality and quantity of beach living in nearby Thailand, or even along the coast of Vietnam, but the southern coast of Cambodia boasts some fine sandy stretches worthy of putting your feet up for a few days, especially after some heavy-duty temple touring or bouncing around the roads of rural Cambodia.

Rte. 4, which connects Phnom Penh with Cambodia's only port at Kompong Som, or **Sihanoukville** after the former king, was built by the United States to facilitate Cambodian trade and the influx of aid starting from the mid-1960s. Just adjacent to the busy Sihanoukville port,

you can find some lovely little beach areas, most of which are speckled with budget bungalows and groovy bars owned by Western expatriates. The town of **Kampot** is a lazy little river town, just a grid of mostly colonial-style houses along a quiet, lazy river, but another good place to kick back. You might also visit nearby **Kep,** which was a French colonial vacation spot whose 1950s/1960s-era villas lay in ruin. It's also a seafood mecca, and worth visiting just for its Kep crab in Kampot pepper. Connections by bus with Sihanoukville are convenient, and many choose to do this region in a rented vehicle or even by affordable local taxicab. So, if you're stuck in Phnom Penh for a few days waiting out a Vietnam visa, hit the beaches. You'll be surprised.

1 SIHANOUKVILLE

Also called Kompong Som, Sihanoukville was first founded in the '50s as a deep-sea port. The town itself is a mess of dusty concrete and grubby shop fronts. The main beach areas are where the action is, particularly around **Ochheuteal Beach.** This beach and the district behind it are now replete with any number of hotels, guesthouses, restaurants, and nightlife venues. It is a pleasant place, though the beach at the north end can get pretty crowded. The other side of town around **Victory Beach** is developing in an entirely incongruous fashion. The beach itself has seen an influx of Russian money which has led to some bizarre venues, including a disco with a real airplane in it and a restaurant you share with snakes and crocodiles. Behind the beach around Victory Hill is a small district that has a couple of fine restaurants. The area is blighted by an increasing amount of sleaze, so you may want to keep your distance.

ESSENTIALS
Orientation
Sihanoukville is set on a wide peninsular area jutting south and east into the Gulf of Thailand. The peninsula is shielded by islands—Koh Rong, Koh Rong Sam Leuem, Koh T Kiev, and Ko Ses are among the many. Starting on the north end of the peninsula, you'll find the busy and dusty port area, just south of which, tracing the coast, you'll find Victory Beach, Independence Beach, Sokha Beach, and Ochheuteal Beach to the far

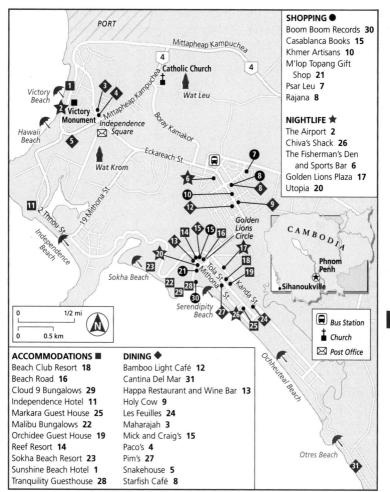

SHOPPING ●
Boom Boom Records **30**
Casablanca Books **15**
Khmer Artisans **10**
M'lop Topang Gift
  Shop **21**
Psar Leu **7**
Rajana **8**

NIGHTLIFE ★
The Airport **2**
Chiva's Shack **26**
The Fisherman's Den
  and Sports Bar **6**
Golden Lions Plaza **17**
Utopia **20**

Bus Station
Church
Post Office

ACCOMMODATIONS ■
Beach Club Resort **18**
Beach Road **16**
Cloud 9 Bungalows **29**
Independence Hotel **11**
Markara Guest House **25**
Malibu Bungalows **22**
Orchidee Guest House **19**
Reef Resort **14**
Sokha Beach Resort **23**
Sunshine Beach Hotel **1**
Tranquility Guesthouse **28**

DINING ◆
Bamboo Light Café **12**
Cantina Del Mar **31**
Happa Restaurant and Wine Bar **13**
Holy Cow **9**
Les Feuilles **24**
Maharajah **3**
Mick and Craig's **15**
Paco's **4**
Pim's **27**
Snakehouse **5**
Starfish Café **8**

south. Ekareach Street turns inland at the terminus of Rte. 4, just past the busy port, and cuts a path across the peninsula to the downtown market area before ending at the Golden Lion Monument near Ochheuteal Beach. Signs point the way from Ekareach to the beaches along its length.

The most popular beach area comprises **Ochheuteal** to the south of town and a short 5- to 10-minute ride away. It comprises 4km (2½ miles) of white sand and gently lapping waves. The northern end of the beach is called **Serendipity** and is largely the haunt of the budget-minded, though there is a pleasant range of resorts and guesthouses for all. Behind Ochheuteal are three parallel roads where you will find hotels, restaurants, and the odd rather ropey Internet cafe. To the south of Ochheuteal is Otres Beach, in many ways the nicest beach of all since you get the white sand and the azure sea without the crowds or, in the evening, the ever-blasting sound systems. Directly north of Serendipity is **Sokha Beach,** entirely appropriated by the Sokha Resort and Spa. This is a good option if you want peace, quiet, and unmatched safety and are prepared to pay for it. North of Sokha past a large promontory is **Independence Beach** and north of that again is **Victory Beach.** There are a number of beachside resorts along both as well as some large Khmer restaurants. The south end of Victory Beach is largely a Russian enclave (Victory Beach as a whole is owned by a Ukrainian speculator), while the north end takes you on to the port.

Getting There

BY PLANE   Commercial flights to Sihanoukville were terminated in 2007 after a plane crash. The small airport is situated 17km (11 miles) to the east of the town. It is not certain if and when commercial flights will resume.

BY BUS   The bus station is located in the northeast of the downtown area next to Psar Leu. It is essentially a large, dusty parking lot. You will be greeted by platoons of motos and tuk-tuks. A ride to Ochheuteal Beach costs between $1 and $2 by motorbike and $3 to $5 by tuk-tuk.

Traveling from Phnom Penh, National Rte. 4 has long been one of Cambodia's best roads. It was constructed in the '60s and for a long time was virtually Cambodia's only decent road. **Sorya** and **GST** run services from the bus station at Psar Thmei (Central Market) in Phnom Penh. The journey takes about 4 hours and costs $4.50. You can book through a guesthouse or just buy your ticket at the station itself. The first bus leaves at 7:15am, the last one at 2:30pm. **Mekong Express** also runs two buses a day for $6, and if you are tall it might be worth considering since the seats on Sorya and GST buses since Mekong Express buses are a little roomier. Mekong Express buses depart from their office in Phnom Penh at No. 87 Sisowath Quay, on the corner of Street 102 near the riverfront.

Rith Mony and **Virak Buntham** run buses from Sihanoukville to Koh Kong and the Thai border ($6–$8) with an 8:30am departure time. There are also minibus services running this route (4 hr.). There are no regular bus services from Sihanoukville to Kampot but there are minibus services leaving at 8:30am. The journey takes 2 hours, and are best booked through your guesthouse. Alternatively, you can get a seat in a shared taxi. This costs $5, but you are better off paying $10 for the whole front seat. All services from Sihanoukville arrive and depart from the central bus station downtown next to Psar Leu.

BY TAXI   Taxi is the fastest and most comfortable way to get to Sihanoukville from Phnom Penh. To charter the whole vehicle costs about $40. You can pick them up on the south side of Psar Thmei.

BY BOAT   There used to be a hydrofoil service from Koh Kong to Sihanoukville, a dangerous trip that is now suspended. If it does reappear, be aware that the vessels are not designed for the open sea and storms blow up quickly on those waters.

BY TRAIN   There is no longer train service to Sihanoukville although the tracks remain in place.

Getting Around

Sihanoukville is very spread out. There are plenty of motos and tuk-tuks. A moto from the beach to town or vice versa costs $1 in the daytime and $2 at night. A ride from

Ochheuteal Beach to Victory Beach costs $3. A tuk-tuk costs double that, though they struggle up the hills. You can hire a small motorcycle from most guesthouses for $5 a day. Wear a helmet. Even better, buy your own (you can buy a good one downtown for $17). The helmets provided by guesthouses are thin plastic with loose straps, and will not protect you in the event of an accident. Taxis cost $5 around town and your guesthouse can call one for you.

(Fast Facts Sihanoukville

ATMs There are ATMs all around Sihanoukville. They take all international cards. The best one to use is the **Canadia Bank,** since they have the lowest charges.

Banks & Currency Exchange **Canadia Bank** (197 Ekareach St.; ℂ **034/933-490;** open Mon–Fri 8am–3pm, Sat 8–11:30am), **UCB** (195 Ekareach St.; ℂ **034/933-833;** open Mon–Fri 8am–3pm), **ANZ** (215 Ekareach St.; open Mon–Fri 8:30am–4pm), and **ACLEDA Bank** (135 Ekareach St.; ℂ **034/320-232;** open Mon–Fri 7:30am–4pm, Sat 7:30am–noon) are all situated downtown. They all cash traveler's checks, exchange major foreign currencies, and issue advances on Visa and MasterCard.

Business Hours Business hours are generally between 7am and 7pm from Monday to Friday. Nightlife in parts of Sihanoukville runs 24 hours.

Doctors & Hospitals Medical care in Sihanoukville is woeful. The **CT Clinic** (47 Boray Kamakor; ℂ **034/934-222;** open 24 hr.) should be your first stop if in need. Apart from that, you should head up to Phnom Penh and on to Thailand for anything complex or serious.

Internet Access There are Internet cafes scattered around all areas where there are tourists. Many of the machines are so badly maintained and so riddled with viruses that they do not function. The excellent **Beach Club Resort** (p. 156) has Wi-Fi in the restaurant by the pool.

Pharmacies The **CT Clinic** (see above) has a pharmacy that you can trust. Other more dubious ones can be found downtown.

Post Office The main post office (Ekareach St. at the intersection of Mittapheap and Kampuchea-Soviet St.) is open Monday to Friday 6am to 5pm and Saturday 8am to noon.

Telephone Internet cafes are equipped for long-distance calls. There are also scores of shops selling mobile SIM cards and phones all over the center of town. A new SIM card costs as little as $2 and is your best option if you want to make local calls.

Tourism Information The best source of information is from guesthouses and hotels. They will book trips to the islands and onward travel.

WHERE TO STAY

There are good accommodations in Sihanoukville at very attractive rates. The best area to stay is around Ochheuteal Beach. The town itself is grim and unpleasant.

The Independence Hotel ★   This restored hotel has an excellent location on a private strip of sand on Independence Beach. The hotel used to be a showpiece of the royal family and once played host to elite dignitaries. Former King Norodom Sihanouk himself was responsible for the interior design of the hotel back in the 1960s, but don't expect royal appointments. The rooms have a musty smell and bland decor. Furniture is polished blond wood and chintzy, pink upholstered chairs. Floors are boring white tile. The layout of the deluxe rooms is awkward, there's a large entranceway, but the bed is tightly crammed between two walls—you may have to turn sideways to get into bed. The views, however, are amazing; many rooms overlook the ocean. There's also a beautiful garden walkway at the base of a rocky outcrop along Independence Beach. Staff is also very friendly and very eager to please.

St. 2 Thnou, Sagkat No. 3, Khan Mittapheap. *C* **034/934-300.** Fax 034/933-660. www.independence hotel.net. 52 units. $140–$160 double; $250–$450 suite. MC, V. **Amenities:** Restaurant; bar; concierge; Internet; outdoor pool; room service; spa. *In room:* A/C, TV, fridge, hair dryer, minibar.

Sokha Beach Resort ★   Where the Independence is all cool and modern architecture, Sokha Beach Resort is finely executed kitschy Khmer. You can see the traditional, winged red-tile roofs from a good distance, and the public spaces are decorated with carved stone reliefs and Khmer statues. Room decoration is functional, with bamboo rattan chairs and tables, and terra-cotta floors. Club suites have swanky '70s-style circular beds and all suites come with an ocean view. If you're looking for something special, rent one of their 10 villas. The villas bear '50s/'60s box-style architecture and were originally military housing units. The exterior is done in unfinished gray brick and white stone walls, and a small driveway leads to a private entrance. The bedrooms have the same decor as those in the hotel. Each villa has a small living room and a separate garden space, so you're really set apart from other hotel guests.

Tip: If you're on a luxe budget, book a room at the **Sokha Inn.** It lies at the northern end of the property, about a 2-minute walk from the main entrance, but golf carts will shuttle you back and forth. Rooms are $85. Sure, it kind of feels like you're staying in the "servants' quarters," but you have access to all the hotel's amenities for about a third of the price.

St. 2 Thnou, Sangkat 4, Mittapheap District, Sihanoukville. *C* **034/935-999.** Fax 034/935-888. www. sokhahotels.com. 166 units (Sokha Inn: 24 units). $250–$300 double; $350–$380 villa; from $500 suite. MC, V. **Amenities:** 2 restaurants; 3 bars; babysitting; bike rentals; children's play area (jungle gym) and planned activities; health club; room service; spa; tennis courts; watersports equipment rentals; Wi-Fi. *In room:* A/C, TV, fridge, hair dryer, minibar.

Inexpensive

Beach Club Resort ★★   Light, bright, and thoughtfully conceived, this spacious Australian-owned resort near Ochheuteal Beach is a bit of a gem. Built around a central pool, the whole feel is one of space and comfort. The open-air restaurant is relaxed with excellent food and zipping Wi-Fi Internet. There are a number of shaded areas around the pool to read, and all in all it is one of those holiday venues that one is loath ever to leave. The staff is charming although they can only speak in a good-natured yell, garnished by a friendly cackle. The rooms have large windows and are light and airy, in keeping with the atmosphere of the resort as a whole.

St. 23 Tola. *C* **034/933-634.** www.beachclubcambodia.com. 33 units. $35 standard; $39 superior; $60 deluxe; $65 family. MC, V. **Amenities:** Restaurant; Internet. *In room:* A/C, TV, fridge.

Beach Road Hotel ★ Covering both the low midrange and the budget categories, Beach Road is central to the emerging nightlife area on the road to Serendipity and is a place that aims to tick all the boxes and succeeds with style. The rooms are sparkling and disarmingly fashionable in a way that doesn't cloy. There is a nod to the boutique aesthetic with a touch of draped traditional silk and vessel washbasins but it is in no way overdone. The rooms are situated around a courtyard with a pool in a slightly alarming amphitheater style, but it does have a quiet and sheltered feel. There is a lively attached restaurant and bar, and you are also next to the weirdly wonderful Top Cat Cinema if you fancy watching a movie or playing X-box on a truly enormous screen.

Road to Serendipity. ✆ **017/827-677.** www.beachroad-hotel.com. 80 units. $10 double fan; $15 double A/C; $25 deluxe. MC, V. **Amenities:** Restaurant; Wi-Fi. *In room:* A/C, TV, fridge.

Cloud 9 Bungalows The urge to greet the management of this charming, jungly option with the words "Me Tarzan. You Jane" is tempered only by the fact that he is German and has a handlebar mustache. The property gives will make you feel like you're deep in the jungle and roughing it in the wildlife, yet while providing all modern conveniences and friendly, family service. The rustic bungalows in leafy surroundings afford good views of the ocean. They are equipped with mosquito nets and fans. Eats are a gentle stroll down the hill to the beachside restaurant.

Serendipity Beach. ✆ **012/479-365.** www.cloud9bungalows.com. 7 units. $10–$35 double. No credit cards. **Amenities:** Restaurant; Internet; Wi-Fi.

Markara Guest House ★ This is one of the best budget options in Sihanoukville and is often full. Even the cheaper fan rooms are large and spotless and have a brand-new large-screen TV. The staff is very helpful and run a smooth travel agency operation without being on the sell or in your face. The manager speaks very good English and very elegant French. They rent out well-maintained motorcycles and also have an Internet cafe with machines that are not totally consumed with spyware and viruses—unusual for Sihanoukville. The beach is just across the road and the Markara offers free beach mats. All in all the Markara is a very friendly and well-run operation.

14 Mithona St. (south end of Ochheuteal Beach). ✆ **034/933-448.** 41 units. $7 double fan; $10–$15 double A/C; $22 double with balcony. **Amenities:** Restaurant; Internet; Wi-Fi (not in rooms). *In room:* A/C, TV, fridge.

Malibu Bungalows ★ Owned and operated by the friendly Ms. Lina, Malibu is a cool collection of beach bungalows on a steep hillside overlooking the beach. There's also a small hotel block farther back. Beautiful orchids line the balcony. There's a cozy little sitting area near the entry, and the hotel's restaurant offers great views of Sokha Beach below and the sea beyond. There's a central dining area, the breakfast buffet is delicious, and Ms. Lina can, upon request, arrange for a unique Khmer-style royal meal. The rooms are simple, free-standing bungalows lining the precipitous steps along a verdant hillside path. They are a little small and pokey, but have rustic charm. Electricity can be erratic here. At the bottom is a bar area and small private beach. There are also air-conditioned apartment blocks near the entry at the top of the hill. Mosquito nets and bamboo furnishings give the place a certain Robinson Crusoe feel.

Group 14, Mondol 4, Sangkat 4, Khan Mittapheap, Sihanoukville (on a small rise above the Sokha Beach Resort). ✆ **012/733-334** or 016/770-277. www.malibu-bungalows.com. 19 units. $40–$45 double; $35–$45 bungalow. No credit cards. **Amenities:** Restaurant. *In room:* A/C (in rooms only, bungalows have fans), TV, fridge, minibar, no phone.

Orchidee Guest House ★ This excellent guesthouse is popular with expats and many returning guests. Simple rooms have air-conditioning and satellite television, but very basic tile bathrooms with a shower-in-room setup. It's affordable and a fun party vibe prevails. The $30 standard rooms are big with white tiles and the best choice (better than the red-carpet rooms). Bathrooms are large, plain affairs with tubs. Get a room next to the pool and you're likely to make lots of friends over oversize drinks with umbrellas.

23 Tola St. (1 block back from Ochheuteal Beach), Sihanoukville. ℭ **034/933-639** or 012/380-300. www. orchidee-guesthouse.com. 72 units. $13–$28 double; $30–$40 family room. No credit cards. **Amenities:** Restaurant; outdoor pool; car and motorbike rentals. *In room:* A/C, TV, fridge, minibar, IDD telephone.

Reef Resort ★ This small hotel is casual and laid-back. Rooms are neat and tidy, and the bamboo furniture, silk lamps, wall hangings, and knit blankets give the place a very charming appeal. Each room comes with a small poolside terrace. The bar has a proper pool table and a large flatscreen TV for movies or sports events. It is airy with the beating of ceiling fans and muted rattan furniture giving it a relaxed semicolonial atmosphere. They also have a good selection of Mexican food. It is a great place to while away the evening with a couple of beers.

Road from Golden Lion to Serendipity. ℭ **012/315-338.** www.reefresort.com.kh. 11 units. $35–$65 double; $70–$80 family room. MC, V. **Amenities:** Restaurant; bar; small outdoor pool. *In room:* A/C, TV, DVD (family rooms), fridge, minibar, Wi-Fi, no phone.

Sunshine Beach Hotel This is the best of the resorts lining Victory Beach. It is a whole beachside complex with a large restaurant and shaded beachside salas in which to enjoy your crab or lobster. The rooms themselves are ocher tiled with white cotton furnishings. Given the hotel's generally pristine look, some of the furniture is quite weirdly tatty. The more expensive rooms look directly on to the beach and the sea is only a short leap away.

Krong St., Victory Beach. ℭ **034/933-708.** 28 units. $30 standard not facing sea; $40 standard sea facing; $60 deluxe. **Amenities:** Restaurant; bar; room service; Wi-Fi. *In room:* A/C, TV, fridge, minibar.

Tranquility Guesthouse Given the spread of sound systems across Ochheuteal and Serendipity, tranquillity is in increasingly short supply; however, this beachside guesthouse is one of the better beach options. It hovers between backpacker and flashpacker and is a pleasant option if that is your scene. There is a range of rooms from basic to relatively luxe. If you fancy living with the sand between your toes but value your creature comforts, Tranquility fits the bill. It offers TV, DVD player, Wi-Fi, and (important for a beach bungalow) a safe.

Serendipity Beach. ℭ **016/463-492.** www.tranquility-sihanoukville.com. 14 units. $12–$25 double fan; $35 double A/C; $45 deluxe. MC, V. **Amenities:** Restaurant; Internet. *In room:* A/C, TV, fridge.

KOH RONG BEACH

Lazy Beach ★ On the isolated island of Koh Rong lies Lazy Beach, with a series of basic wooden bungalows set on a beautiful private stretch of sand. To reach it, boats for the island leave every day at noon from Ochheuteal Beach, and the trip there takes about 2 hours and costs $10. The grounds include a bar and restaurant, with fresh seafood caught daily from local fishermen. Snorkeling and fishing gear are available to guests. Frommer's staff rave about this pristine tropical paradise, perfect for a true getaway, and friendly British proprietors. You can book a night at their office at Serendipity Beach (on the dirt track leading to Serendipity).

WHERE TO DINE

Dining in Sihanoukville means mostly good seafood for little cash, and there are lots of ocean-side budget stops. They mainly serve the same seafood barbecue with barracuda, shrimp, and baked potato or rice for a standard $3. It may be uniform, but it is also delicious. Other eateries of all sorts are spread around town and near all the beaches.

Bamboo Light Café ★ SRI LANKAN   Like their popular restaurant in Kampot, the people at Bamboo Light serve great Sri Lankan fare including hot curries (or tempered to your taste) with chapatti or nan bread, as well as Sri Lankan Kottu roti, a dish of roti pancake mashed up with potato, curry, and vegetable. Everything is delicious, and they can even put together a good packed lunch for any day trips.

78 Ekareach St., in the downtown area. ☏ **012/925-707.** Main courses $2.50–$4. No credit cards. Daily 7am–10pm.

Cantina Del Mar ★★★ MEXICAN   Sister to the riverfront Cantina in Phnom Penh, Cantina del Mar offers delicious fish tacos and tostadas in a beachfront house on glorious Otres beach. The road to Otres is a rough one from nearby Ochheuteal, but is worth the trek. The central recipe at Cantina de Mar consists of beautiful white sand, gleaming blue sea, a glorious sunset, and one of the best margaritas you will find in Asia. This is a total winner. That is before you have even ordered your food, when it all gets even better. Expect delicious seafood using the freshest of ingredients. Cantina Del Mar is the perfect complement to the most exquisite of tropical sunsets.

Otres Beach. ☏ **023/222-502.** www.cantinacambodia.com. Main courses $4.25–$6.50. Fri–Sun 3–11pm.

Happa Restaurant and Wine Bar JAPANESE   Serving teppanyaki-style cuisine (the Japanese art of cooking on the iron skillet), Happa's iron skillet sits centrally in the restaurant where you can see your food being prepared. You can order full meals or order a la carte small, very reasonably priced portions of meats, veggies, and tofu prepared in a selection of mouthwatering special sauces: miso-sesame, garlic-ginger, teriyaki, apple-onion, and a Cambodian sauce called *kroeng*. The lamb kabobs in rosemary are absolutely delicious and best accompanied by an icy Asahi beer. There is also a good wine selection by the glass and bottle.

Road to Serendipity. ☏ **034/934-380.** Main courses $4–$7. MC, V. Daily 5:30pm–midnight.

Holy Cow WESTERN/KHMER   Situated in an old Khmer house on the busy road from Ochheuteal to town, Holy Cow is a laid-back restaurant/cafe serving a mixture of European and Khmer dishes. This restaurant houses a bar on the first floor with a relaxed and friendly feel. The upstairs dining area features balconies overlooking the garden bordering the busy road beyond. The dishes are thoughtfully presented, though portions are not huge. The chicken in Kampot pepper with mashed potatoes is good, as are the sandwiches. The music played is eclectic—when we were there it went from traditional Khmer sounds to the Mississippi blues of Robert Johnson (oddly enough, they have quite a lot in common).

Ekareach St. btw. Ochheuteal and town. ☏ **012/478-510.** www.holycowcambodia.com. Main courses $4–$6. Daily 9:30am–11pm.

Les Feuilles FRENCH   Les Feuilles is set 2 blocks back from the southern end of Ochheuteal Beach and prepares excellent provincial French food. The beefsteak is highly recommended. Les Feuilles is also a popular meeting place for Sihanoukville's large French expat community—a place to shrug shoulders in the nicest of surroundings.

23 Tola St. (south end). ☎ 034/933-910. Main courses $4.50–$7. V. Daily 7:30am–10pm.

Maharajah INDIAN   Situated right next door to Paco's, Maharajahs offers an array of excellent Indian food—particularly the delicious South Indian *tali*. This staple meal of rice, dal, chutneys, chapatti, curd, and curry is light, wholesome, Indian food at its best. The North Indian *palak paneer,* or spinach curry with cheese, is also a surefire winner and, importantly, is not too oily. Their menu is a reasonably comprehensive culinary journey from Kashmir at the start of the Himalaya, to Kanyakumari in the deep south of Tamil Nadu. What a delicious journey it is.

Weather Station Hill on Ekareach St. ☎ 015/966-221.. Main courses $2.50–$4. Daily 11am–11pm.

Mick and Craig's ★ WESTERN   These guys are the real originals in Sihanoukville, and backpackers and expats alike flock here. Some of the best food in town is here, served in a casual open-air setup with good tunes, a busy bar, and a billiards area. You can sign up for trips with their in-house eco-tour company, pick up a book in their casual book corner, or even stay in their new guesthouse. They offer lots of favorites from home: pizza, sandwiches made with bread baked on-site, snacks like nachos and potato skins, steaks, bangers and mash (sausage with mashed potatoes), grilled fish, and good veggie offerings, including an excellent veggie burger, as well as lots of good Khmer dishes. Dessert is apple crumble or ice cream. Extensive breakfasts are the best cure for that Sihanoukville hangover: muesli and fruit or the full-on greasy fry-up so beloved by the English.

Just adjacent to the Golden Lion Traffic circle at the head of the road leading to Serendipity Beach. ☎ 012/727-740. Main courses $5–$9. No credit cards. Daily 7am–11pm.

Paco's ★★ SPANISH/VIETNAMESE   What do Spanish and Vietnamese food have in common? The answer, of course, is absolutely nothing—except that here at Paco's the owners are a Spanish/Vietnamese couple who decided to pool culinary resources to good effect. Situated in the now slightly run-down and sleazy area of Victory Hill, Paco's is worth the journey even if you are staying over on Ochheuteal. The seafood paella is fantastic, but you'll need at least two to enjoy. There are plenty of tapas options, and a mixture of two or three comprises a pretty good meal in itself. The range of Vietnamese dishes on offer may make a potentially anarchic combination if you already got talked into the Rioja, but it is very, very good. The spring rolls stand out.

Weather Station Hill on Ekareach St. ☎ 092/673-911. Main courses $4–$8. Daily 9am–11pm.

Pim's ★ (Kids) WESTERN   Run by a very friendly Dutch couple, Pim's is the perfect place for a family meal. There is plenty of space for the kids to run around in a safe environment. Meanwhile, you can test your putting skills on the minigolf course in the back (or, indeed, play table tennis or petanque—it's all here). The food is a delicious mix of Western barbecue and some Khmer. The fall-off-the-bone spareribs are delicious and the slow-roasted beef is sublime. It is a meaty kind of place.

23 Tola St. (north end). ☎ 017/969-023. www.pimssihanoukville.com. Main courses $4–$7. No credit cards. Daily 8am–1:30am.

Snakehouse INTERNATIONAL   Here's a fun night out. It's part restaurant, part jungle menagerie with snakes, turtles, and crocs. The snakes are all correctly labeled and range in size from tiny, venomous little beasts to mighty, murderous pythons acting ever so languid. The food is good (the animals are for viewing, not eating). Russian owned and managed (this being the Russian enclave), Snakehouse serves a good selection of local dishes and standard international fare, anything from spaghetti to steak and sandwiches. The place is up on a hill above town and makes for a fun evening.

Soviet St., on the hilltop near Victory Beach. *Ⓒ* **012/673-805.** Main courses $4–$9. No credit cards. Daily 8am–11pm.

Starfish Café INTERNATIONAL   Set up as an NGO to train and employ people with physical disabilities, many of whom are victims of land mines, the Starfish Café gives hope to a group of people who are systematically shunned by Khmer society. The place has been around since 2001 and offers a time-tested formula of good sandwiches, baked goods, and light local fare. The place funds local literacy programs and serves as a drop-in point for clients of the Starfish Project (see their website for more information). The friendly counter staff can offer good information about local tours and travel. There's an upstairs reading area as well as a shaded courtyard. They sell popular T-shirts advertising the cafe as well as products from the Snar Dai Project, which sells goods made by mothers of street kids.

Just behind the Samudera Market at the town center. *Ⓒ* **012/952-011.** www.starfishcambodia.org. Main courses $3–$4.50. No credit cards. Daily 7am–6pm.

WHAT TO SEE & DO
Diving & Snorkeling

There are excellent diving opportunities around Sihanoukville and the surrounding islands. Reefs encrusted with coral are a feature of nearby islands, supporting an abundance of marine life including stingrays, moray eels, dolphins, and even the odd whale. The waters off Sihanoukville are warm (consistently 81°F–88°F/27°C–31°C) and though visibility can be quite low during the height of rainy season, in the diving season from October to June it ranges from 10 to 25m (33–82 ft.). First-rate dive sites can be found around the islands such as Koh Rung Samloem and Koh Kon, all within a 2-hour boat journey. The very best sites are at Koh Tang, Koh Prins, and Condor Reef and are 4 to 6 hours away. There are now a number of dive shops in Sihanoukville, including those that are PADI authorized. In addition to organized dives they offer introductory courses for beginners. Most of the islands have uninhabited sandy beaches where divers can relax between outings.

Two hours away, **Koh Rung Samloem** is the best nearby island to Sihanoukville and can be done as day trip. The island is made up of a small fishing village, three principal beaches, and several minor ones, all of which are almost completely uninhabited, including some sheltered ones on the north side close to **Koh Kon.** Both islands feature rocky reefs and go to depths of 18m (59 ft.). As with all of the nearby islands, the best diving and visibility is on the west side. **Koh Kon** is a small island to the north of Koh Rung Samloem and is home to rocky, coral outcrops. **Koh Tang, Koh Prins,** and **Poulou Wai** to the southwest of Sihanoukville offer some of the best scuba diving waters in the area and take 4 to 8 hours to reach, requiring an overnight stay. The area has reefs with depths of 15 to 40m (49–131 ft.) and much better visibility than reefs closer to land. Koh Prins also has two shipwrecks to the northwest. Koh Tang was the scene of "Mayaguez

Incident" in 1975 when American marines battled the Khmer Rouge to regain control of a captured ship and its crew—the last American fight of the Indochina wars in which the U.S. Marine Corps suffered high casualties.

The **Dive Shop** (road to Serendipity Beach near the Golden Lions; ☎ **012/161-5517;** www.diveshopcambodia.com) is a PADI Dive Center offering courses on Introductory Discover Scuba, PADI Open Water, Advanced Open Water, and Rescue and Dive Master. Other options include fun dives, overnight trips, and custom tours.

EcoSea Dive (225 Ekareach near Ochheuteal Beach and the Golden Lions; ☎ **012/654-104;** www.ecoseadive.com) is a dive center offering authorized PADI and SSI Dive Courses. EcoSea provides daily fun dives and $10 snorkeling on their custom dive boat. They also have beachside accommodations for divers and snorkelers on Koh Rung Samloem.

Scuba Nation PADI 5 Star Dive Center (Mohachai Guesthouse on Serendipity Beach Rd.; ☎ **012/604-680;** www.divecambodia.com) is Cambodia's first PADI five-star National Geographic Dive Center, offering daily trips and live-aboards to the islands, plus PADI dive courses in English and other languages. All dives include food, PADI diver insurance, and the only custom-made dive boats in Cambodia.

Fishing & Boat Trips

There are lots of angling opportunities in the waters around Sihanoukville. The best fishing is in the dry season when the weather is fair. A variety of game species swim in the local waters, including the much-prized barracuda. If you want to take a day trip, you can get a tourist boat right off of the beach, or you can arrange it through your guesthouse or a tour operator. Prices start at $6 to $10. The standard tour will take you to one to three islands for snorkeling, swimming, and lunch. The **Fisherman's Den Sports Bar** (downtown, alongside the Star Mart; ☎ **034/933-997**) offers fishing and other kinds of boat trips on a 16m (54-ft.) Western-style fishing boat with shower, toilet, wet bar, and all necessary equipment. The skipper is a very experienced professional fisherman from New Zealand.

Ream National Park

Sihanouk National Park is more commonly called Ream National Park, for the district in which it is located. It was established in 1993. It encompasses a large portion of the coastal area, including sandy beaches, mangrove forests, the **Prek Tuk Sap Estuary,** offshore coral reefs, and two islands (**Koh Thmei** and **Koh Seh**). It is also the habitat of elusive creatures such as macaques, sun bears, dolphins, mouse deer, pangolin, and over a hundred species of birds; and some say that it is also home to a tiger although there are no proven sightings. Guesthouses and tour operators in Sihanoukville offer a number of different tours of the park including jungle trekking and riverboat trips along the Prek Tuk River through the jungle and mangroves and on to the sea. The river trip is the most popular tour and is also the most likely to yield sightings of wildlife. Most tours are less than a half-day. The nearby **Kbal Chhay waterfalls** are spectacular and refreshing in wet season, although in dry season they virtually cease to exist. It is a good place for a picnic. Tours may be arranged through a tour operator directly through the Park at the **Park Office** (located 23km/20 miles north of Sihanoukville, 500m/1,640 ft. off Rte. 4 on Airport Rd., opposite the entrance to the airport; ☎ **012/875-096** or 215-759). The park office is open daily from 7am to 5pm.

Cooking Courses

If you want to learn how to create Khmer cuisine yourself, **Traditional Khmer Cookery** (335 Ekareach St.; ✆ 092/738-615) offers courses for $25 per person starting at 10am. They teach you how to create a range of dishes including amok, banana flower salad, beef *lok lak,* fish soup, and pumpkin custard. Book a day in advance.

Cinema

The delightfully odd Top-Cat Cinema (road to Serendipity; ✆ 011/617-799) is a great way to polish off a day spent baking on the beach. This large air-conditioned cinema is furnished with comfy furniture and loungers. Movies cost $3 per person or a group of five or more can rent the whole cinema for 2 hours for $15. You can also play video games on the giant screen—a fact best kept from children if you ever want them to see daylight again.

SHOPPING

Sihanoukville is not a particularly good place for shopping compared to Siem Reap or Phnom Penh. **Khmer Artisans** (downtown; Ekareach St.; ✆ 012/615-111; open daily 8am–8pm) offers quality silks, tailor-made clothing, handicrafts, carvings, and statues. **M'lop Tapang Gift Shop** (road to Serendipity; 8:30am–8pm) is a nonprofit NGO-based operation offering homemade products created by young women "committed to learning skills to empower themselves." It features handicrafts, silks, and a range of products made from recycled drinking straws. **Rajana** (✆ 012/789-350; www.rajanacrafts.com; daily 8am–6pm), above the Starfish Café (p. 161), is another NGO-based operation offering local arts and crafts. **Boom-Boom Records** (Ochheuteal Beach; ✆ 097/666-6409) is the place for music and beach clothing. **Casabalanca Books** (road to Serendipity; ✆ 012/484-051; daily 8am–10pm) has a selection of new and used books. It is next to Mick and Craig's restaurant (p. 160). **Q&A** (downtown at 95 Ekareach St.; ✆ 012/342-720; daily 7:30am–7:30pm) is a used bookshop and cafe.

Psar Leu, in the center of town, is very much a replica of the Russian Market (Psar Toul Tom Pong) in Phnom Penh, with many similar goods for sale. Clothes, DVDs, bags, shoes, handicrafts, and silk are all available in their own part of the market complex. The hassle levels and the stress levels are lower than Phnom Penh, but don't expect the bargaining to be much easier.

NIGHTLIFE

Sihanoukville is a late-night party town, though venues are spread out and the streets are dark. Be aware that in some places there is an underlying vibe of either serious drug abuse or prostitution or both. The sound systems along **Ochheuteal Beach** blast late into the night and often early into the morning and there are often beachside parties. **Chiva's Shack** is Ochheuteal's first beach bar and restaurant and serves great food, drinks, and unique sunset happy-hour cocktails right on the beach. They have beach parties every Tuesday and Friday. More bars are concentrated at the north end of the beach around Serendipity. **Golden Lions Plaza,** on Kanda Street a few blocks from the beach, is home to a number of late-night drinking dens, the most popular of which is the **Shipwreck**— a place where one encounters interesting characters of all sorts. One gets the impression that it would be a good place to make shady foreign deals while being lulled by the rich baritone of Johnny Cash. The downside of this place is the breathtaking rudeness of the bar staff. **Utopia** on the road to Serendipity is a very late-night bar and disco. The bar staff here is made up of young Western backpackers, and the place has a kind of unpleasant and druggy vibe. Avoid **Victory Hill,** now home to a slew of depressing and sleazy "hostess" bars. One of the best and most bizarre places to party in Sihanoukville is at the **Airport** on Victory Beach. This Russian-owned place is a disco hangar in which there is a real Antonov 24 prop plane. Until very recently these dubious machines were in service flying to Siem Reap and Battambang—the ramshackle airborne shower that was President Airlines. It is a welcome sight to see this one firmly decommissioned and grounded. They serve a full range of cocktails and it gets hopping only after 10pm. It is a beach bar during the day. It is place that could be truly called bizarre beyond bizarre. The **Fishermen's Den and Sports Bar** downtown is the place to catch the game of your choice. They show a full range of sports.

2 KOH KONG

Koh Kong was long a strange kind of place. Better reached from Thailand than Cambodia, it was isolated from the rest of the country by the Cardamom Mountains. One could reach Sihanoukville on a dangerous hydrofoil—a boat designed for rivers unleashed on the open sea and crewed by men with no maritime skills who couldn't swim. The town gained a reputation among Khmers for being a place where "the bad people go to find money" and indeed its reputation for drugs, prostitution, gambling, smuggling, and crime was not unfounded. With the opening of the border crossing to Thailand, tacky casinos mushroomed catering to Thais, since gambling in Thailand is illegal. That image is now changing. The bridge across the Kah Bpow River to Thailand was completed in 2003 and National Rte. 48 to Srey Ambal and on to Phnom Penh was finally finished in 2008 when the last bridges became operational. This is Cambodia's most scenic road (built by the Thai army) and it winds majestically past wonderful mountains and forests kept pure and pristine by decades of war. With these recent improvements Koh Kong is no longer a sleazy transit point pinioned by hills and rivers; it is now coming into its own as a prime location for eco-tourism on one of Asia's most important highways conveniently near the roaringly popular Thai resort island of Koh Chang. As makeovers go, the one now transforming Koh Kong looks to be pretty dramatic.

GETTING THERE & GETTING AROUND

From both Phnom Penh and Sihanoukville there are regular bus services. From Phnom Penh, **Virak Buntham Express Travel (012/322-302)** departs at 8am from Street 106 on the waterfront (the return trip also departs Koh Kong at 8am). If you are coming from Thailand, you can take a minibus (costing 100 Thai baht and leaving from right in the center of town next to the market) from the town of Trat to the border at Had Lek on the Thai side crossing to Cham Yeam on the Cambodian side. From there it is a 10-minute motorcycle ride (costing 50 Thai baht) to Koh Kong itself. The ferry service to Sihanoukville has been discontinued and is unlikely to reemerge (if it does, it will no doubt resume being both overpriced and dangerous, so it's best avoided).

Koh Kong itself is small and easily walkable. It is set out on a very simple grid stretching back from the river. If you need a ride, there are plenty of *motodups* hanging about. Usual rates of between 1,000 riel and 2,000 riel apply.

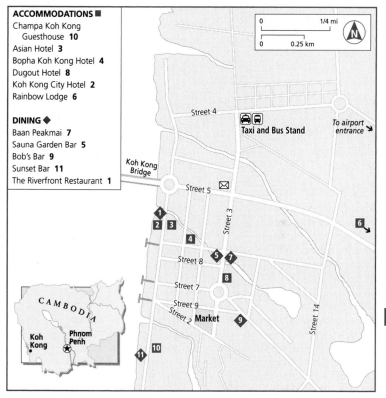

ACCOMMODATIONS ■
Champa Koh Kong
  Guesthouse **10**
Asian Hotel **3**
Bopha Koh Kong Hotel **4**
Dugout Hotel **8**
Koh Kong City Hotel **2**
Rainbow Lodge **6**

DINING ◆
Baan Peakmai **7**
Sauna Garden Bar **5**
Bob's Bar **9**
Sunset Bar **11**
The Riverfront Restaurant **1**

Street 4

Taxi and Bus Stand

To airport
entrance

Koh Kong
Bridge

Street 5

Street 3

Street 8

Street 7

Street 9

Street 2 **Market**

Street 14

CAMBODIA

Koh
Kong

Phnom
Penh

(Fast Facts Koh Kong

Banks & Currency Exchange   Koh Kong is firmly in the Thai baht zone, although U.S. dollars will be accepted. There is an **ACLEDA Bank** (St. 48; 🕐 **035/936-693**) that performs Western Union transfers and currency exchange, and cashes traveler's checks. It also has an **ATM** with Visa card access only. It would be a bad idea to rely on it.

Hospitals   If you have medical problems, cross the border to Thailand where medical care is good. If they are really minor, head to the **Visal Sok Clinic** (St. 3; 🕐 **011/988-586;** daily 6am–9pm).

Internet Access   There are a few Internet cafes in the center of town with fairly sluggish connections.

Tourism Information   Most guesthouses double up as travel agents and they are the places to go for tourist information.

The **Champa Koh Kong Guesthouse** (St. 1 north of the ferry dock; ℭ **035/393-912;** $7–$17) is a good riverside option. They also have a restaurant and organize tours and scuba diving. The **Asian Hotel** (riverfront; ℭ **035/936-667;** $15–$20 double) is a new riverfront hotel offering clean, large air-conditioned rooms with all the amenities. Rooms have cable TV, minibar, and en suite bathroom, most with hot water. It has some rooms with a balcony overlooking the river. The restaurant next door serves Khmer, Thai, and Western food. The **Bopha Koh Kong Hotel** (off the riverfront very near the Sihanoukville ferry dock; ℭ **016/350-123;** $5–$20 double) is a newish hotel offering large air-conditioned rooms with cable TV, fridge, and en suite bathroom with hot water. The restaurant serves Khmer, Thai, and Chinese dishes. The rooms are very clean, though the lurid nylon bedspreads might give you a headache. They organize tours to surrounding beaches and mangrove forests. The **Dugout Hotel** (St. 1; ℭ **016/650-325;** $6–$12 double) is a popular full-service guesthouse, bar, and restaurant with both fan and air-conditioned rooms. They also have a restaurant, swimming pool, and Internet access, and they organize tours. The **Koh Kong City Hotel** (St. 1; ℭ **012/901-902;** $15–$35 double) is a large, comfortable, new, midrange hotel right on the riverside with a great sunset view of the river and Koh Kong Bridge. It offers clean, nicely furnished rooms with all-modern amenities including A/C, cable TV, minibar, and hot water. There is Internet access in the lobby and a riverside seafood restaurant serving Khmer, Thai, and Chinese food.

A short way outside of Koh Kong lies the ecoresort **Rainbow Lodge** (20km/12 miles south of Koh Kong on National Rte. 48; ℭ **012/160-2585;** www.rainbowlodge cambodia.com; $35–$80 double). You can reach it only by boat after driving 20km (12 miles) along the road to Phnom Penh and then taking a 10-minute boat trip upriver. Buses run from Phnom Penh to the nearby town of Tatai; see their website for further directions. It is set in peaceful surroundings right in the Cardomom Mountains. Here you can experience firsthand the sights and sounds of the jungle from the comfort of a traditional Khmer-style bungalow. Kayaks and rowboats are available for guests free of charge and all meals are included in the tariff. You can book either via e-mail or by phone and they will send a boat to pick you up when you arrive.

All the guesthouses and hotels in Koh Kong double up as restaurants. In addition, **Baan Peakmai** (St. 6; ℭ **035/393-906;** main courses $2; daily 7am–10pm) is a pleasant Thai-style garden restaurant serving good seafood. The **Sauna Garden Bar** (St. 3; ℭ **015/601-633;** main courses $2; daily 7am–10pm) is a similar operation. **Bob's Bar** (St. 9; ℭ **016/326-455;** main courses $2; daily 9am–10pm) is Australian owned and serves a range of Western dishes. **Sunset Bar** (St. 1; ℭ **016/326-455;** daily 8am–9pm) is tucked down an alleyway and is on the water's edge. As its name suggests, it is a good place to watch the sun sinking to the west. The **Riverfront Restaurant** (St. 1; ℭ **011/943-497;** main courses $3–$4.50; daily 7am–9pm) offers similarly fantastic views, this time accompanied by excellent Thai soup enjoyed in a shaded sala.

WHAT TO SEE & DO

Koh Kong is very much a fresh destination as far as tourism is concerned, as it shakes off its shady past. The thickly jungled nearby **Cardamom Mountains** and rivers to the northeast, and the beaches and islands to the south, are presenting brand-new opportunities for eco-tourism. The waterfalls and beaches may soon supplant the casinos as the primary attraction for foreigners staying here. Eco-tours include treks in the nearby mangrove forests or taking a boat upstream to spectacular waterfalls. Alternatively, you can take a motorcycle or car into the Cardamom Mountains. In addition, Koh Kong now has serious PADI-licensed **dive shops,** and diving has become a central attraction of the region. Most of the guesthouses and hotels can offer advice and organize tours to the nearby destinations.

Beaches & Islands

There are a few beaches only a short journey from town. **Koh Yor Beach** near Ba Blong Village on the ocean is a long, narrow, secluded, white-sand beach. There are a number of small shacks serving seafood. These include the Barracuda Beach Bar, run by Koh Kong Divers. To get to Koh Yor Beach, cross the bridge and turn left at the first junction, and head south on the dirt road for about 10 minutes.

Koh Kong Island is in the Gulf of Thailand, about an hour boat ride from town. It has several unspoiled and completely deserted beaches with good white sand. All guesthouses can organize a boat and snorkeling gear.

Koh Kong Safari World

This animal theme park puts on shows featuring dolphins, crocodile feeding, and orangutan boxing (something we find highly disturbing). Safari World is open every day and is situated 500m (1,640 ft.) from the Thai border.

Scuba Diving

Impian Divers Activity Center (✆ **035-313-912;** www.impiandivers.com) is a dive operator offering snorkeling, fun dives, scuba diving, introduction dives, reef cleaning, and environmental projects. They include free accommodations at Champa Koh Kong Guesthouse for those doing dive courses. They also organize mangrove forest and waterfall tours and organized motorcycle trips.

Koh Kong Divers (✆ **017/502-784;** www.kohkongdivers.com) is the first PADI scuba diving operation in Koh Kong. They have a range of courses to suit all levels of skill and organize dive trips to local islands and reefs as well as multiday excursions. They also offer snorkeling and island tours, waterfall trips, and jungle adventures. Their office is located on the riverfront road next to the Koh Kong Guesthouse. They can also be contacted through the **Barracuda Beach Bar** on Koh Yor Beach.

Waterfalls

There are many waterfalls and rapids surrounding Koh Kong, as rivers flow from the Cardamom Mountains. Some are close to town and some are farther upstream; you can reach them by motorcycle taxi or your own rented motorcycle. Many of the falls are only a trickle in the dry season and not worth a visit. In the wet season, many of them roar. The **Ta Tai Waterfalls** are the nearest to town and are the most visited. They are situated close to the main road about 20km (12 miles) to the east. The Tai Tai falls are wide and on two levels dropping by about 6m (20 ft.). There are others farther away such as **Koh Por Falls, Tuo Kokir Rapids,** and the rugged jungle gorge **Kbal Chhay Falls,** located farther upriver.

3 KAMPOT

Kampot is a great place to spend a couple of days winding down. A neat grid of French colonial villas and houses line the Kampong Bay River, on the opposite bank of which are low mountains making for beautiful lingering sunsets. A strip of small cafes, restaurants, and guesthouses line the riverfront. The main attraction here is the eerie and decayed old French colonial hill station of Bokor. At the time of writing, access to Bokor is either not allowed or highly restricted as the inevitable renovation of Cambodia's only real place in the cool gets underway. Don't let that put you off a visit to Kampot and the surrounding area—there is more to it than Bokor. The surrounding countryside is some of the prettiest in the country with the usual flat, deep green rice paddies, this time interspersed with steep limestone outcrops and crisscrossed with inlets and rivers.

GETTING THERE

From Phnom Penh, there are two routes to Kampot, National routes 2 and 3. Neither remotely matches National Rte. 4 to Sihanoukville. Both are bumpy but adequate. Rte. 3 is the more direct route, but also in slightly worse condition. The best way is to take Rte. 2 from Phnom Penh until Sambout halfway through Takeo Province. Then take a right on Road 22 that takes you the short distance onto Rte. 3 for the rest of the journey. The road from Sihanoukville is good and takes 2 hours by car.

BY BUS   **Sorya Transport** leaves Central market (Psar Thmei) in Phnom Penh and takes 4 to 5 hours. From Kampot buses leave from the central bus stand. The first service is at 7:30am, the last one at noon. It is a long journey since the bus has to take the long way round, making a stop at Kep, because of vehicle restrictions on bridges on the more direct routes.

There are no scheduled buses from Sihanoukville. Your guesthouse can book you a seat in a shared taxi costing $5. You can also go to the bus stand at Psar Leu, from which they depart, and negotiate the ride yourself.

BY TAXI   From or to Phnom Penh, a seat in a shared taxi costs $7 each way. Better to pay double and book the whole front seat. In Phnom Penh, the taxis leave from a stand near the InterContinental hotel (p. 70). In Kampot, your guesthouse can organize one for you. Make sure that they don't organize one that is empty apart from you, or you will be driven back to the taxi stand and might have to wait awhile for it to fill up. If the guesthouse knows what they are doing, they will contact a driver who has a full taxi already but has been informed to reserve the front seat for you, hours before your departure time.

GETTING AROUND

Kampot is tiny and you can walk everywhere. If you wish to explore, you can rent a motorcycle. Many decide to stay in Kampot and do Kep as a day trip since Kampot is a friendlier place to overnight, unless you actually want the evening isolation that Kep offers. The countryside around Kampot is delightful and well worth a day's two-wheel pottering, even though Bokor is off-limits. There are a couple of places near the main traffic circle that rent out bikes, **Sean Ly Motor Rental Shop** (No. 27 D Soeng Ngoc Rd.; ℂ **012/944-687**), just south of the central traffic circle, and **Cheang Try** (ℂ **012/974-698**) next door. Renting a small step-through, 100cc machine costs $5 a day. A 250cc dirt bike costs $11 to $12 a day. You can also arrange this through your guesthouse, which keeps your passport for security (instead of the rental shop). The same offices also rent cars or even four-wheel-drive vehicles for $20 per day. The dirt bikes have spent their days being plowed up to Bokor and they have suffered accordingly. Check the brakes, lights, and above all check the horn—it is your friend.

If you don't want to drive yourself, you can take a motorbike with a driver to Kep for just $10 per day trip, or $5 one-way if you stay in Kep overnight. For more extensive tour services, contact **Art Suriya Travel** (ℂ **012/501-742**), sponsored by the owners of the

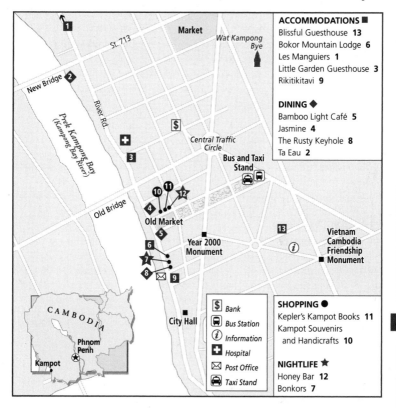

ACCOMMODATIONS ■
Blissful Guesthouse **13**
Bokor Mountain Lodge **6**
Les Manguiers **1**
Little Garden Guesthouse **3**
Rikitikitavi **9**

DINING ◆
Bamboo Light Café **5**
Jasmine **4**
The Rusty Keyhole **8**
Ta Eau **2**

SHOPPING ●
Kepler's Kampot Books **11**
Kampot Souvenirs
  and Handicrafts **10**

NIGHTLIFE ★
Honey Bar **12**
Bonkors **7**

$ Bank
🚌 Bus Station
ⓘ Information
✚ Hospital
✉ Post Office
🚕 Taxi Stand

SOUTHERN CAMBODIA

8

FAST FACTS: KAMPOT

Champey Inn in Kep, which offers custom tours of the surrounding area or other parts of the region. Costs are higher than the storefront tour offices, but you get the full custom treatment here. Or contact **Mr. Sok Lim** at his tour offices on the north end of Kampot (at riverside, north of the central bridge; ℂ **012/719-872**) for adventure trips and jungle-trekking tours.

(*Fast Facts*   **Kampot**

ATMs   Both ACLEDA and Canadia banks have 24-hour ATMs accepting all major cards.

Banks & Currency Exchange   **Canadia Bank** (one block northwest of the central traffic circle; ℂ **033/932-392;** Mon–Fri 8am–3pm, Sat 8–11:30am) and **ACLEDA Bank** (Ekareach St.; ℂ **033/932-880;** Mon–Fri 7:30am–4pm, Sat 7:30am–noon) cash traveler's checks, exchange major foreign currencies, and issue advances on Visa and MasterCard.

Business Hours Business hours are generally between 7am and 7pm from Monday to Friday. Kampot closes down early in the evening, though a few bars stay open late. They are hard to miss since they have lights on.

Doctors & Hospitals There is no medical care in Kampot. Head straight to Phnom Penh if you have medical problems.

Internet Access There are Internet cafes scattered along the riverfront. Both Bokor Mountain Lodge (see below) and Rikitikitavi have free Wi-Fi for customers at respectable speeds.

Post Office The main post office (River Rd. toward the south of town) is open Monday to Friday from 6am to 5pm and Saturday 8am to noon.

Telephone Internet cafes are equipped for long-distance calls.

Tourist Information The best source of information is from guesthouses and hotels.

WHERE TO STAY

Blissful Guesthouse An old, colonial villa fashioned with heavy wooden beams, Blissful Guesthouse has hammocks swinging from every veranda and under every tree, a quiet upstairs sitting area, and lots of cozy cushions and couches to curl up with a book and rest. Rooms are guesthouse basic, with hard beds and small shower-in-room bathrooms, but everything is clean. Angela, the friendly Danish owner, is a font of local information. The bar hops late and this is a great place to meet up with other travelers, perhaps arrange a taxi share, or get metaphysical late into the night.

Just a short walk east of the river, past the "2000" monument. ✆ **012/513-024.** www.blissfulguesthouse. com. 10 units. $4–$8 double. No credit cards. **Amenities:** Restaurant; bar; helpful car and motorbike rental. *In room:* Fan only, no phone.

Bokor Mountain Lodge This old colonial building lined with cool travel photos on the riverside has the best location in town. Open colonnaded walkways overlook the quiet street below and river beyond. Breakfast is included and there's a good in-house tour company that can arrange excursions. The rooms at the front with a river view are definitely worth the little bit extra since they are larger than the rooms at the rear and far more pleasant. They also have good Wi-Fi access throughout.

Riverfront Dr. (riverside at the center of Kampot). ✆ **033/932-314.** www.bokorlodge.com. 6 units. Oct–Apr $35–$45 double, $60 family suite; May–Oct $30–$40 double, $50 family suite. Rates include breakfast. MC, V. **Amenities:** Restaurant; bar. *In room:* A/C, TV, Wi-Fi.

Le Manguiers ★★★ (Kids) This riverside gem (which translates as "the Mango Garden") is legendary among resident expats in Cambodia. It is popular with NGO types, UN wallahs, and embassy staff. There is a good reason for this awed and hushed popularity. Les Manguiers is simply a superb experience—so much so that they do not need to do any advertising at all. It is situated 2km (1¼ miles) north of Kampot up a rough dirt road. A complex of beautiful stilted wooden houses overlooking one of the most scenic locations in Cambodia, it is a place to kick back with friends, keep an eye on the kids swimming in the placid waters of the river, and enjoy a place that manages to be truly rustic (they even have their own working rice paddies in front of the bungalows) while also feeling eminently sophisticated. The bungalows range in size and shape and there is also a more straightforward house with three rooms available. They serve a selection of Khmer food on demand (though a big group dinner requires a day's notice). They have canoes and bicycles for guests to use. Les Manguiers is the ultimate place to kick back in style.

Riverside on the eastern bank 2km (1¼ miles) from town. ℭ 012/330-050. www.mangomango.award space.com. 9 units. $8–$18 double main house depending on view; $22–$40 garden bungalows depending on size. **Amenities:** Restaurant; bar; Internet.

Little Garden Guesthouse The place is just that, a little garden area with an upstairs block of clean, basic, affordable guesthouse rooms. Go for a top-floor unit adjoining a cool open sitting area shared by a few rooms. The rooftop terrace has wonderful views of the river (on clear days you can see neighboring Vietnam's Phu Quoc Island) and is a terrific place to collapse on hot days. The management are involved with the local orphanage so there are often crowds of kids about. They are very polite and respectful though, so they won't disturb you. They are also good with tours here and the reception desk is very efficient at catering to all your travel needs, including onward tickets and bike hire.

River Rd. (just north of the bridge). ℭ 012/256-901. www.littlegardenbar.com. 15 units. $10–$25 double. Long-term rates available. No credit cards. **Amenities:** Restaurant; tour information and rentals. *In room:* TV, A/C and fan rooms, no phone.

Rikitikitavi Located in a converted rice barn, this is a stylish but rustic little place. The rooms are muted and tasteful in terms of furnishings and decoration, and the beds are equipped with spring mattresses. Breakfast is included in the tariff. It is just a few short steps up to the rooftop balcony restaurant, where you can enjoy both the sunset and a cocktail. The rooms are equipped with DVD players, and there are over 100 DVDs to choose from at reception.

River Rd. ℭ 012/235-102. www.rikitikitavi-kampot.com. 5 units. $25–$35 double. No credit cards. **Amenities:** Restaurant; bar; Wi-Fi. *In room:* A/C, TV, DVD player, minibar.

WHERE TO DINE

The Sri Lankan **Bamboo Light Café** (River Rd. near the bridge; ℭ 012/681-530; main courses $2.50–$4; daily 7am–10pm) offers cheap and quality eats, and curries that are red or yellow, mild or fiery, prepared to your tastes. The mutton dishes are especially good, as are the special Sri Lankan Kottu roti dishes (pancakes cut up and mixed with potato and curry). The very clean interior has cool, indirect lighting in bamboo stanchions. The balcony area out front is where you're most likely to run into the groovy dudes you saw out on the road in the day. There are also great breakfasts of bacon and eggs, as well as good sandwiches, and Western meals are served all day. With an Internet cafe upstairs, this is a good place to beat the heat.

The **Bokor Mountain Lodge** (see above) and the **Rikitikitavi** (see above) represent higher-end dining in Kampot. The **Bokor Mountain Lodge** is patchy and very expensive, albeit with a wonderful view. The **Rikitikitavi** offers an eclectic menu with cuisine from around the world, including French, Indonesian, Italian, and Mexican dishes. The signature dish is the Trencherman, an enormous breakfast costing $12. It includes a half-pound steak, 10 slices of bacon, 5 sausages, 3 eggs, a baguette, mushrooms, hash browns, and tomatoes. Nobody has ever actually yet finished one, according to the management. There are also more modest options. The chicken yogurt wraps are very popular with Kampot's expats, and the Indonesian chicken is another signature dish, with the sauce made from real peanuts rather than peanut butter. **Jasmine** (River Rd.; ℭ 012/927-313;

main courses $5; daily 10am–10pm) is a stylish riverfront cafe with a mildly Italian slant. They serve a mixture of Khmer and Western dishes and there is also a good selection of interesting photo books to glance through. The **Rusty Keyhole** (River Rd.; © 012/679-607; main courses $2.50–$4.50; daily 4pm–midnight) is a popular Western-run cafe and restaurant serving good-value Western and Asian food at a very reasonable price. The daily seafood specials come recommended. For tasty crab done a dozen different ways, we highly recommend the open-air **Ta Eou** (© 012/820-832), an affordable local joint jutting out on the river, right next to the New Bridge.

After dinner and a brief walk around town, you'll find that there are a number of little bars. They are easy to find, since they are the only things with lights ablaze on the otherwise dark streets. The **Honey Bar** (just back from the river on the left side of the road that goes to the central roundabout) stays open late, as does **Bonkors** (a pun on the slang word for crazy and the nearby mountain) on the riverfront. The bar at **Blissful Guesthouse** is popular with backpackers and gets busy in high season. In general, Kampot is an early-to-bed kind of place.

WHAT TO SEE & DO
Bokor Mountain

This is the main attraction in and around Kampot. Unfortunately at the time of writing it is largely closed to visitors as the road is being repaired. Bokor hill station was built by the French as a high-altitude complement to the fashionable seaside resort of Kep across the bay. Both are now faded and crumbling in a very atmospheric fashion. Bokor was also the scene of fierce fighting in the '80s, with Khmer Rouge and Vietnamese troops battling it out across the mountaintop for control of the buildings and the rest of this strategic area of high ground. After you've spent some time in Cambodia navigating overcrowded Phnom Penh and the tourist rush at Angkor, you might see why the French sought out quiet, cooler climes, building this sanctuary to privilege on a mountaintop far from the madding crowds. Bokor Mountain is part of the larger Bokor National Park, a thick jungle sprawl of giant ferns and thick vegetation. Tigers may exist and if so are rare (and very shy), as well as leopards, Asiatic black bears, and slow lorises and other monkeys, as well as a unique grouping of jungle birds, snakes, crawlies, and even a small population of Asian elephants. To get down-and-dirty with the local flora and fauna and do some trekking, contact **Mr. Sok Lim** at his tour office **Sok Lim Tours** on the north end of Kampot (at riverside north of the central bridge; © 012/719-872).

Note: At the time of writing Bokor Mountain is closed to visitors, with the occasional exemption for an organized tour. If that can be negotiated, although the rules change frequently, be prepared for a 3-hour hike up the hill and then a 3-hour hike down again. By the time you read this, the situation may have changed and the road may be open and brand-new. It is not clear at present what renovations are planned for the hill station itself, although it looks like the words "luxury" and "resort" may figure prominently. It is a prime and unique location. Ask at your guesthouse or contact **Sok Lim Tours** (see above) to get the latest updates before heading out for this trek.

If you manage to get up this mountain, you'll be rewarded with beautiful views; be sure to stop along the way at the few landslide areas where the trees have been cleared. The top of the mountain is a large plateau and, after tracing its length, you'll reach the crumbling hulks of the **Bokor Palace Casino and Resort,** now stripped bare and covered in moss and graffiti. On the approach, you'll first pass a few villas worth a look, as much for their vantage point over the flatland as the sea below. Next, you'll pass a small temple and a turnoff to a small waterfall (not worth it in dry season), and another leg leading to the main hotel compound.

One can only imagine what life was like in this opulent little casino. You can climb to the top of the old colonial edifice for great views. Ask for a map when you pass through the entrance gates at the bottom. There's a small church, a school, post office, and other minor residential buildings, as well as an old worn-out Vietnamese gun emplacement. There are rustic accommodations available, too. Ask park officers for information.

The entrance fee was $5 before closure and the gate was open from dawn to dusk. This too may change. The whole trip takes half a day. The turnoff to the mountaintop is 8km (5 miles) from Kampot to the east and 95km (59 miles) from Sihanoukville. The road up to the top from the main road is 32km (20 miles) of twisting and turning.

Caves & Waterfalls

The whole area around Kampot is dotted with limestone mountains rising steeply out of the deep green of the rice fields. Some of these contain caves with bizarre rock formations and Buddhist shrines. Caves require good shoes and a flashlight. **Phnom Chhork** is a place of stalactites and stalagmites and small religious structures from the pre–Angkorian Funan era. There are two caves. If you look closely at the entrance of **Cave One,** you will see limestone formations resembling elephants. The entrance to **Cave Two** is about 300m (984 ft.) from Cave One. There are fewer formations, but it is quite deep, requiring quite a lot of clambering if you choose to attempt it. **Phnom Sla Ta'aun** contains a less interesting cave but it is worth it for the climb, which is interesting. **Phnom Sasear** is known as the "White Elephant Cave" because of the shape of a rock formation at the base of the mountain. It is next to a pagoda, and once up the steps on the outcrop you will get some good views of the countryside, especially during the rainy season when the vistas will be lush and green. If you cross the river and drive north for 3.2km (2 miles) you reach the scenic area of **Tek Chhou falls.** They are not really spectacular since they don't fall very far, but it is a very pleasant area by the river to enjoy a sandwich and a cold beer. It is very popular with locals on a Sunday afternoon when the sun is shining. To see the caves and waterfalls, hire a guide or a *motodup* who knows where he is going; they are tricky to find on your own.

Rabbit Island

Twenty to 40 minutes by local boat from Kep is Rabbit Island. A place of white sandy beaches and coconut palms, it is an idyllic day trip from either Kampot or Kep. Although the waters are clear there is no coral, but don't let that put you off donning a mask and flippers. Rabbit Island is a place of psychedelic fish. There are some beach bars in which you can stay the night for about $10, though conditions are very basic. Seafood here is great. Most likely when you order crab on Rabbit Island, your restaurateur will wade out into the tepid ocean and haul your lunch directly from one of the crab pots. It doesn't come fresher than that. A boat for the return trip costs $20. Guesthouses offer a package for $7, but you won't get to pick your own boat, beach, and crab buddies.

SHOPPING

Kampot is a place with next to zero shopping opportunities, but there is one very good bookshop run by a very friendly Khmer couple. **Kepler's Kampot Books** (open daily 8am–8pm) is situated next to the Old market near the Honey Bar. They have some titles on history and culture in Indochina that others around the country seem not to. In the same area is the new **Kampot Souvenirs and Handicraft** shop (open daily 8am–8pm). Their selection of goods is growing and they are worth a browse.

4 KEP

Only a half-hour's drive from Kampot is the place that was once considered the Cambodian Riviera in the time of the French, continuing under the rule of Sihanouk. Indeed, Sihanouk's old seaside villa still stands, though he never actually stayed in it since the area became unstable before the curtains were chosen and the place was furnished. Now it is crumbling and pocked with bullet holes, but one can easily imagine how grand it once could have been. Kep (and indeed much of southern Cambodia) was a fierce battleground over the years of war and the derelict feel still remains, although developers are moving in fast and things are changing. There is very little beach at Kep and what there is remains pretty scruffy and stony. There are some secluded resorts that appeal to some, but at present facilities are limited. Kep is better done as a short, relaxed day trip from Kampot, unless it provides the particular kind of seclusion you crave. It is a pretty drive from one to the other.

Where Kep is a world beater is when it comes to seafood. They fish some of the best crab in the world off Kep, and Kampot is renowned for producing the best pepper on the globe. The killer recipe doesn't take much working out and Kep crab in Kampot pepper lives up to anyone's expectations. There is a strip of restaurants right on the beach road coming from Kampot (it is signposted) where the crab is unloaded. This place is called, not surprisingly, the crab market.

GETTING THERE & GETTING AROUND

Kep is situated around a loop in the main road from Kampot to Vietnam. Approaching Kep from Kampot, you turn right off the main road (Rte. 33) at the roundabout with the "White Horse Monument" at its center. The diversion takes you first past the crab market, then on to the main beach. It is a one-way road once in town, with an inner loop that takes you up the hill behind the beach and following on round the back, returning to the crab market. If you continue on the wider loop along the beach and the seafront you pass Sihanouk's former villa, continuing past the boat dock and the market until the loop reunites you with the main road heading east. Resorts and guesthouses are situated along the beach road coming from the White Horse Monument turnoff and scattered among the hills behind the main beach. From Kampot, take a tuk-tuk, a moto, or a taxi. Alternatively, hire your own motorcycle (p. 35) so that you have the freedom to stop where you like and explore. If you are staying in Kep, you can rent a motorcycle from a guesthouse just back from the seafront near the main roundabout called **Ratanak Kongkea** (© 099/791-679) for $5 a day. **Cheak Chit Guesthouse** (© 016/770-277) right next door and **Sovan Sakor** (© 012/608-345) a little farther up the road also rent out bikes.

Buses (Sorya Transport) from Phnom Penh to Kampot pass through Kep and drop off and pick up near the beach.

Ⓣ **Tips** **Feasting in Kep**

The restaurants at the Kampot end are a little more expensive and not as good. The best one is the farthest along toward Kep. On the weekend you will see more cars parked outside this restaurant than any other.

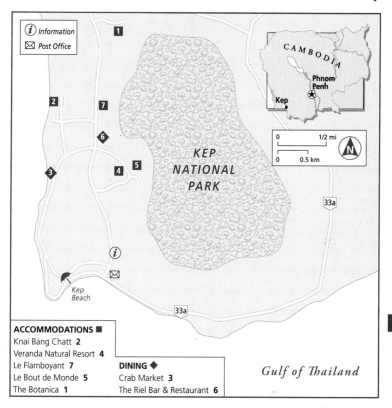

ⓘ Information
✉ Post Office

CAMBODIA

Phnom Penh

Kep

| 0 | 1/2 mi |
| 0 | 0.5 km |

KEP NATIONAL PARK

33a

33a

Kep Beach

ACCOMMODATIONS ■
Knai Bang Chatt **2**
Veranda Natural Resort **4**
Le Flamboyant **7**
Le Bout de Monde **5**
The Botanica **1**

DINING ◆
Crab Market **3**
The Riel Bar & Restaurant **6**

Gulf of Thailand

Ⓒ**Fast Facts Kep**

ATMs The nearest place for banks and ATMs is Kampot.

Doctors & Hospitals There are no medical services in Kep, and you'll need to head to Phnom Penh if you're sick.

Tourism Information There is a Department of Tourism Office just near the central circle. It is in a fine building but is rarely open. Your hotel or guesthouse remains your main source of information if staying in Kep.

WHERE TO STAY

There has been something of an explosion in accommodations in Kep, no doubt in anticipation of development to come. While there are many places of a good or even excellent standard, unless it is real quiet and seclusion you seek, nearby Kampot remains a more practical option.

Botanica Guest House   Those on a budget might want to consider the Botanica, a pleasantly rustic series of bungalows surprisingly well turned out with good amenities. There is a Belgian flavor here, particularly when it comes to the beer. They serve a selection of top-notch Belgian brews such as Leffe and Hogaarden in the well-equipped and comfortable bar in addition to a selection of "inventive mixes" of nonalcoholic refreshments. The restaurant serves an astonishingly eclectic range of dishes from India to Spain via Cambodia with the emphasis on fresh salads and cold platters.

Beach road before the crab market turnoff. ✆ **016/562-775.** www.kep-botanica.com. $8 single; $10 double. No credit cards. **Amenities:** Restaurant; bar.

Knai Bang Chatt   This is the finest luxury option in Kep. This seaside property is made of one new and three renovated villas, built in what was called the New Modern Khmer style of the 1960s. Rooms are spacious and done in mellow, neutral colors. Everyone gets a huge, private terrace overlooking the garden or ocean. The outdoor infinity pool faces some stiff competition from the nearby ocean, where you can take a midnight dip among phosphorescent plankton.

Phum Thmey Sangkat Prey, Thom Khan Kep. ✆ **012/879-486.** www.knaibangchatt.com. $200–$450 double. MC, V. **Amenities:** Restaurant; bar; outdoor pool; spa. *In room:* A/C, TV, fridge, minibar, Wi-Fi.

Le Bout du Monde   With a name meaning the "end of the world," this place lives up to its name in rustic Gallic style. One of the first Kep operations to open, it offers beautiful bungalows with stone bathrooms open to the outdoors. It has an old-fashioned feel whether you pick a modest, simple bungalow for $15 or the "Tradition and Prestige" suite for $85. The restaurant menu is made up of French and Cambodian cuisine based exclusively on fresh produce from the garden or from the local market whether fish, shellfish, salads, or vegetables, and is great place from which to enjoy majestic views of Bokor wreathed in cloud.

Near the ASPECA orphanage and far up the hillside overlooking town. ✆ **011/964-181;** www.leboutdu mondekep.com. $15–$85 double. MC, V. **Amenities:** Restaurant; bar. *In room:* Minibar, safe.

Le Flamboyant   Le Flamboyant offers unique bungalows, with outdoor showers and lounging beds on rooftop verandas. They have a reasonably sized swimming pool with a bistro beside it serving a mixture of Khmer and Asian fare (main courses $5). Because it is lower down the hill, Le Flamboyant misses out on the ocean views of its competitors.

Beach road before the crab market turnoff. ✆ **012/230-357.** www.flamboyant-hotel.com. $35–$80 double. No credit cards. **Amenities:** Restaurant; bar; outdoor pool. *In room:* A/C, TV, fridge, minibar, Wi-Fi.

Veranda Natural Resort   This resort is located on a hilltop overlooking town. On stilts overlooking the sea far below, the rustic thatch-and-wood units are compact but tidy. Rooms are connected by raised boardwalk. The bar is a popular spot for sunset views over Bokor Mountain across the bay. The restaurant serves good faux-Western and Khmer (expect to pay btw. $5–$10 for main courses), and it's a good thing they have tasty food, because you're pretty much stranded up here. If it is seclusion you want, this is a good place for it.

Opposite ASPECA orphanage and far up the hillside overlooking town. ✆ **012/888-619.** www.veranda-resort.com. $30–$75 double; $195 villa. MC, V. **Amenities:** Restaurant; bar; car and motorbike rentals. *In room:* A/C, TV, Wi-Fi.

All the hotels and guesthouses double up as restaurants (see above), but the real Kep dining experience comes with the fresh seafood served on the seafront. Both the crab market and the esplanade in town in front of the beach are places to enjoy this wonderful aquatic bonanza. If you're at the crab market, there is a series of wooden restaurants with sea-facing verandas serving the Kep signature dish, among others. If directly on the beachfront, just take a pew on one of the empty wooden platforms and the vendors will come to you. Most places have menus in English these days. On a weekend in good weather expect crowds (almost all of who will be locals), with a good time being had by all. After dark many of the Crab Market stalls stay open until 11pm.

The **Riel Bar and Restaurant** (© **017/902-771;** open daily 7–10am, 6pm–midnight) on Crab Market turnoff is the main place to go for evening entertainment and it often stays open late. The Dutch/Khmer management is trying to promote the use of the Cambodian riel as opposed to the U.S. dollar, so the prices are cheaper if you use local currency.

ATTRACTIONS

Being so close to Kampot most excursions are doable from both locations including caves and Bokor Mountain (if and when it is open to the public). See p. 172.

SOUTHERN CAMBODIA

8

KEP

Laos in Depth

Wherever you have traveled from, arriving in Laos involves slowing down. For many years, Laos remained a forgotten land and wasn't considered by many to be a viable travel option. Part of this ignorance is a result of the shroud of Laos's Communist government, which became politically and economically isolated after taking power in 1975. An air of mystery then drifted over the country.

In recent years, more light has shined on Laos, and the world is slowly discovering what the country and its people have to offer. Following in the footsteps of its more prosperous neighbors, Laos is making a concerted effort to build its fledgling tourism industry. Laos is one of the poorest countries in the world. Its designation by the United Nations as a "least-developed country" ensures an influx of money from both foreign governments and nongovernmental organizations (NGOs) alike. In the last 10 years, the level of development and interaction with the outside world has been extremely rapid. These days, it is fast becoming the crossroads of the region as infrastructure is developed connecting China, Vietnam, and Thailand. There are now two bridge crossings over the Mekong, and the Golden Triangle is becoming a pivotal junction for all the countries it encompasses. The days of Cold War isolation are now a very distant memory, as tourists flood into Laos to enjoy the cultural riches of Luang Prabang, the laid-back charm of Vientiane, and the enigmatic mysteries of the Plain of Jars. Only just over a decade ago, crossing from Thailand to Laos was like crossing a bridge in time. Thailand was looking forward to the 21st century, draped in neon, fast food, and six-lane highways. Lao people, still recovering from war and living in the aftermath of 20 years of Vietnamese and Soviet sponsored isolation, sat in their intermittently lit, crumbling, colonial French built towns staring across the Mekong at a different age. The gap is narrowing fast.

Yet the essential appeal of Laos remains intact. It remains very much a land of misty mountains, beautiful French colonial–built towns, and glittering Buddhist temples. Vientiane, a perennial candidate for the "sleepiest capital in the world" crown, may be shocking to some. But a few days spent wandering the streets and watching the sun set over the Mekong makes a good introduction to "Lao time." A few hours north of Vientiane, **Vang Vieng** has become a hideaway for the backpacker-hippie crowds who gather in the shadow of the spectacular limestone outcrops that line the Nam Song River. Farther north lies Luang Prabang, ancient capital and UNESCO World Heritage Site. With its almost three dozen temples, French colonial architecture, and rich history, Luang Prabang is a magical town and not to be missed. In the far north, the Nam Ha Biodiversity Conservation Area, in Luang Namtha, offers off-the-beaten-path adventures. The pre-Angkorian temple Wat Phou sits in the southern province of Champasak. Finally, remnants of an even older civilization are in evidence at the mysterious Plain of Jars, in the heart of Xieng Khouang province.

Sixty percent of Lao people are practicing Buddhists, and that fact colors every facet of life. Temples and stupas dominate the architecture of even the smallest village, and you're sure to spot groups of monks in colorful robes on their early morning pintabat, or alms rounds, especially in Luang Prabang. Buddhist acceptance and compassion play an important part in Lao culture; arguments are the exception, and the sangha, or monastic community, fosters a strict moral code. Even the shortest visit to Laos offers unique insight into Buddhist culture.

Laos is a place to tread lightly, but foreign travelers are made quite welcome and encouraged to do their part to preserve and participate in cultural practices. The beauty of Laos exists not only along the Mekong at sunset, but also in smiles at the market or impromptu Lao lessons on the street corner, things that are easily missed if you're in a hurry. It's an enchanting land that demands you slow your pace to match its own, and even the shortest visit might add tranquillity to your travels.

1 LAOS TODAY

Despite its mineral resources, Laos is one of the least developed countries in Asia. The vast majority of Lao people, approximately 75%, depend on subsistence agriculture. Traditionally there is only one rice harvest a year, compared to the three that one often sees in Vietnam. For most people life tends to be simple. It's early to rise, planting or harvesting rice or fishing, then maybe a drop of rice whiskey and fairly basic food which will almost certainly center around sticky rice. Families tend the fields together. Men plow and prepare the ground, control the irrigation to the paddies, and thresh the crop; women perform the transplanting of the seedlings, weeding, and carry the harvested rice to be threshed.

Villages consist of collections of basic wooden houses, stretched along one street. Education is very basic. In the evening, families will often gather around the communal TV to watch Thai soap operas or premier league football (that's if the village has electricity, which many don't).

Buddhism and Theravada Buddhist ritual is central to life in Laos. The Communist Pathet Lao wisely never made any attempt to suppress the religion after taking power in 1975, and from the 1950s actually attempted to co-opt the Buddhist clergy to their cause. Almost every Lao male will spend some time as a monk at some point in his life. Monks remain revered and anywhere near a wat or temple you will see people making their early morning food donations as the monks go on their alms round. Unlike in neighboring countries, in Communist Laos monks are required to work, taking on the role of physicians and teachers.

Laos is very much a one-party state, ruled by an all-powerful and largely aging elite with absolute power to crush any dissent. The Lao People's Revolutionary Party (LPRP) is led by President Chummaly Sayasone as the head of state, while Bouasone Bouphavanh is the prime minister and head of government presiding over the National Assembly, elected with no legal opposition in 2006. The real power is the 10-member Politburo, and to some extent the 52-member Central Committee, all of whom are appointed and operate behind firmly closed doors.

Foreign aid, whether European, Japanese, or Chinese, is what funds development here. There is no taxation since the country is too poor to afford it or implement it. The politics of donor countries and the concessions they try to wring out of the recalcitrant Politburo—be that trade, human rights, or future access to natural resources—remains a dance of competing agendas at which the Lao authorities have become very adept. The more they interact politically and commercially with the outside world, including other ASEAN (Association of South East Asian Nations), the more sophisticated they are forced to become in ensuring they maintain what they see as social order. They have had a lot of success, as dissent in Laos is rarely seen.

There are big hydroelectric projects afoot in Laos to dam the Mekong, which would free Laos from donor control to some extent. This move is causing regional panic since it would severely affect other countries farther downstream.

Laos today is a curious mixture of the ancient and the modern and the deprived and the fortunate. Although the cities are modernizing fast and infrastructure all over the country is improving, education levels remain low to nonexistent while rural poverty remains high. Laos is certainly moving into the 21st century in its cities along the Mekong, while many remoter areas have yet to experience electricity.

2 LOOKING BACK

EARLY YEARS

Until the advent of European colonialism, the history of Laos and its neighbors was largely defined by the ebb and flow of empires. Like the tides of the sea played out over the centuries, one ruling civilization broke the power of its predecessor, leaving its mark on culture, language, and buildings.

The earliest defined kingdom or state in Laos was Chenla, based in what is now Champasak in the south. There were other kingdoms, such as Sri Gotapura in central Laos around what is now Tha Khek and Chanthaburi in what is now Vientiane. The original Thai, Shan, and Lao people were migrants from southern China. They all practiced wet rice cultivation and they tended to settle along river valleys. Their gods in the form of powerful snakes called *ngeuk* were believed to live in these rivers. Many rural Lao people still believe in them.

Laos can trace its history as a unified state to the Kingdom of Lane Xang Hon Khao ("one million elephants under a white parasol"). Formed in 1353 by an exiled prince named Fa Ngum, its capital was Xiang Dong Xiang Thong, later renamed Luang Prabang, or "Great Prabang," in honor of a gold Buddha image (prabang) given to the kingdom by the

court at Angkor. Fa Ngum ran into trouble with local nobles both because of his loyalty to Angkor and his habit of trying to seduce their wives and daughters. He was deposed in favor of his son, Samsenthai, and went into exile, dying 5 years later in the northern Thai town of Nan in what was then the Kingdom of Lanna. Samsenthai made overtures to the Thai kingdoms of both Lanna and Ayutthaya (the emerging power that supplanted Sukhothai), marrying princesses from both, thus reducing dependence on Angkor and consolidating independence within the dynastic shifts. Samsenthai was on the throne for 42 years and after he died the kingdom was less stable, with Queen Mathevi successfully murdering a procession of young kings before taking power herself. She was then deposed by nobles and finally drowned in the Mekong as a sacrifice to the snake god. After these dramatic events, Samsenthai's youngest son took the throne, modestly naming himself *Xainya Chakkaphat,* which means "Universal Ruler." To be fair he did live up to his name, and turned out to be a wise and decent monarch.

At the end of the reign of Xainya Chakkaphat, Lan Xiang suffered invasion at the hands of the Vietnamese under their emperor Le Thanh Tong. The Vietnamese forces captured and sacked Xiang Dong Xiang Thong. Xainya Chakkaphat took to the mountains and jungles with his remaining forces and, in a precursor to modern events, mounted a successful guerrilla campaign against the invaders who were beaten not only by the force of arms but also by malaria.

Renewal came under the rule of King Visoun, who arrived on the throne in 1501 having previously been governor of Viang Chan. This renewal gained momentum under his son Pothisarat, and reached its peak under his grandson Setthathirat. It was his reign that saw construction of Laos's most beautiful wats, including Wat Xieng Thong in Luang Prabang.

LAND IN TURMOIL
Around this time, the Burmese became a new and predatory power on the scene and the region was plunged into turmoil. King Setthathirat had cultivated ties with Lanna and Ayutthaya, both of which came under attack from the Burmese. He moved his capital to Vieng Chan in 1560. War against the Burmese was to be his downfall, eventually bringing in an era of defeat and turmoil for the next 60 years. Lan Xang became resurgent in 1638, with the ascent to the throne of King Suriya Vongsa. His 57-year reign marked a golden age of Lao history during which Lan Xang was not only politically and militarily powerful but also a center of Buddhist learning and the arts.

In 1695, toward the end of Suriya Vongsa's reign, a succession crisis ensued. His son and heir was found guilty of adultery and the king made no effort to prevent a sentence of execution being carried out. After the king died, the fact that there was no heir caused Lang Xang to fracture into three disempowered kingdoms. All of them eventually came under the suzerainty of the now all-powerful empire of Ayutthaya. The Burmese sacked Ayutthaya in 1767, but under General and then King Taksin, they were driven out. By 1779, all the Lao king-

doms were once again paying fealty to the Siamese. In 1826, the new king of Vieng Chan, Chao Anou (who was originally Siamese educated and Siam sponsored), attacked the Siamese but was quickly driven back. Chao Anou died a captive in Bangkok and Vieng Chan was sacked while its population was driven into exile en masse east of the Mekong to Siam, large parts of which remain heavily Lao in character to this day. All of Laos was now under the Thai thumb, but there was also a new factor to be considered: the French.

THE FRENCH STEP IN
In 1863, France declared Cambodia a protectorate and shortly afterward the new colonial power sent boats up the Mekong on an exploratory expedition. Twenty years later, Luang Prabang became the epicenter of an anarchic battle between Chinese warlords, Siam, and the French. The town was looted and burned by these Chinese interlopers and their allies in 1887. The King fled further into the arms of the French and they offered him their protection. At this time, confrontation between French colonial interest and Siamese power got nasty. The French sent gunboats to Bangkok. The Thais ceded all the lands east of the Mekong River to France and thus Laos became part of a new empire.

As with Cambodia, the French were most interested in using Laos as a buffer state to insulate their lucrative interests in Vietnam. They established their capital in Viang Chan, which they changed to the Francophone name of Vientiane. They certainly had their eyes set on further conquest, but that was checked by the buildup to World War I and a realignment in their old colonial rivalry with the British. Over the next 5 decades, the French built many of the things that give Laos so much of its character today. It also saw an influx of Vietnamese who actually outnumbered locals in some places and still define the character of towns along the Mekong.

The Emergence of French Indochina

In this modern age, rampant imperialism is something that we would find very hard to justify. Good coffee, however, is not. France's interest in the Indochina region began in the 17th century with the mission of the Jesuit priest, Father Alexandre de Rhodes. Involvement was confined to trade during the 18th century. The French became more proactive during the 19th century, aiding Catholic missionaries in Vietnam who were under pressure from the ruling Nguyen dynasty. In September 1858, 14 French gunships, 3,000 men, and 300 Filipino troops provided by the Spanish under the command of Charles Rigault de Genouilly attacked the port of Tourane (present-day Da Nang), causing a lot of damage, and occupying the city. Heading south, De Genouilly then attacked and occupied the poorly defended city of Sai Gon (present-day Ho Chi Minh City). On April 11, 1862, the Vietnamese government was forced to cede the territories of Biên Hòa, Gia Dinh and Dinh Tuong to France. In 1862, France obtained further concessions from Vietnamese Emperor Tu Duc, ceding huge amounts of territory to this newly rapacious aggressor. In 1863, the Cambodian King Norodom had requested the establishment of a French protectorate over his country. French Indochina came into being in October 1887, consisting of Annam, Tonkin, Cochinchina (which together form modern Vietnam), and the Kingdom of Cambodia following the Sino-French War of 1884. Laos was added after the Franco-Siamese War of 1893. The union continued until 1954, when the French were forcibly ejected by the heroic efforts of the forces of Ho Ch Minh under the command of military genius General Giap at Dien Bien Phu. Although the French occupation of Indochina was short and often brutal, they left their mark in culture, food, language, and architecture. It was the French who recognized the beauty of Luang Prabang and enhanced it. It was they who rebuilt Vientiane after its was destroyed by the Thais, and it was they who attempted to restore many ancient monuments. Above all, it was the French who bought the humble baguette sandwich to Asia and some of the best coffee in the world. The Lao call baguette Khao ji, and this French legacy of superb breakfasts continues to this day.

WORLD WAR II & AFTER

With the advent of World War II, Siam was allied to Japan and went for an opportunistic land grab, taking western Cambodia and Xainaburi and Champasak in Laos. In response, the French actively encouraged Lao nationalism (even though Vichy France was pro-Axis after the fall of Paris), thus letting a genie out of the bottle that they would never be able to return. It prompted a massive and punitive response from the Japanese in 1945. After the defeat of the Japanese, there was turmoil as King Sisavang Vong veered wildly between independence and supporting a return of the French. After sacking his prime minister and cousin, Prince Phetsarath, he was deposed by the National Assembly. The French were largely behind this as part of De Gaulle's push to regain the lost colonies of Indochina. The British who were administering these countries acquiesced, not wishing to create a precedent in terms of their own colonial upheavals, particularly in India.

There had been contacts between the Lao freedom movement, or Lao Issara, and the Communist Viet Minh since 1945. In

1950, an offshoot of pro-Vietminh Issara came into being. It was dubbed the Pathet Lao. The main figure behind this was Lao Prince Souphanouvong, who became the focus of Lao resistance to the French and president of the Naeo Lao Issara or Free Laos Front. The real power, however, lay with hard-core Communists Kaysone Phomivane and Nouhak Phoumsavan. In 1953, the Vietnamese revolutionary forces of Ho Chi Minh entered northern Laos in a drive to take Luang Prabang, although they were stopped by the French. It was to prevent this happening again that the French built a remote military base at Dien Bien Phu in the mountains of North Vietnam and it was here that they were to meet their nemesis in Indochina. Surrounded by the Viet Minh under the military genius from Hanoi, General Giap, pounded by heavy guns dragged over incredibly rough terrain, supplied by intermittent airdrops, the French were beaten and surrendered.

INDEPENDENCE

Under the Geneva conference of 1953 France granted independence to the countries of Indochina, including Laos, with the Franco-Laos Treaty of Amity and Association. This set up the scene for conflict between the Pathet Lao and the newly formed Royal Lao Government. They came increasingly to rely on American support while the Pathet Lao retained close ties to, and were sponsored by, North Vietnam. The government was led by Prince Souvanna Phoumma while the Pathet Lao was led by his half bother, Prince Souphanouvong. They patched up an agreement on joint government, but it fell apart in 1958.

Phomvihane, the Gentle Revolutionary

Kaysone Phomvihane was a very low-key revolutionary. Born Nguyen Cai Song in what is now Savannakhet Province in southern Laos, his father was Vietnamese and his mother was Lao.

He went to law school in the 1940s in Hanoi, but dropped out early in order to join the struggle against the French. In 1955 he was an important figure in the creation of LPRP at Sam Nua in northern Laos, and he then went on to serve as the Pathet Lao leader, although Souphanouvong, known as the "Red Prince," acted as the figurehead.

In the following years, it was Kaysone who led the Communist forces against the Kingdom of Laos and the Americans. The old regime fell without the same degree of bloodshed seen in Cambodia and Vietnam, a result of both his military and diplomatic skills. After the Pathet Lao victory, he served as Prime Minister from the founding of the Lao PDR in 1975 until 1991, when he became president.

Although Kaysone was a lifelong committed old-school Communist, he was also a pragmatist. It was he who initiated the necessary economic reforms at the end of the Cold War when Soviet power in the region ceased to be. Though revered in Laos, Kaysone has failed to receive the kind of posthumous international fame that sees the image of Ho Chi Minh and Che Guevara printed on T-shirts. If you want to find out more about him, the National Museum in Vientiane (p. 228) displays plenty of black-and-white photos of him in action, both young and old.

BOMBING & WAR

The Americans installed a right-wing proxy regime and the Pathet Lao returned to war. The following years were marked by confusion, uncertainty, and conflict. In May 1961, a second conference was held in Geneva to hammer out a solution. Eventually the three protagonists, Sovanna Phouma for the neutralists, Souphanouvong for the Pathet Lao, and Prince Boun Oum of Champasak for the right wing, came to an agreement that established a government that balanced all factions. This quickly started to crumble as the pressures of increasingly ferocious conflict in Vietnam took its toll. As with Cambodia, North Vietnam used Laos as a place from which to arm and supply its army. And as previously for the French, the Plain of Jars was the Achilles' heel of Hanoi and it became a fierce battleground. While the fiction of neutrality was maintained, in 1964 the U.S. started a campaign of mass carpet-bombing and air-to-ground attacks on the Plain of Jars. This was soon repeated all up and down the Ho Chi Minh Trail. From 1964 to 1973, the U.S. Air Force dropped more ordinance on Laos than it did on Germany in World War II; more than 2 million tons of it involving over 600,000 missions. No one knows just how many Lao villagers were killed or incinerated in this brutal but secret war, but what is certainly known is that North Vietnamese supply lines to the Viet Cong in the south remained intact. One-third of Lao people became internally displaced. By 1968, there were an estimated 40,000 North Vietnamese troops on Lao soil with an added 35,000 Pathet Lao. The Lao government fielded 70,000 soldiers supported by 30,000 U.S.-sponsored hill tribe Hmong mercenaries under the command of General Vang Pao. The battles raged until the Americans pulled American forces out of the Vietnam War in 1973.

THE PATHET LAO TAKE OVER

April 1975 marked the fall of both Saigon and Phnom Penh. The Pathet Lao instigated mass street protests against the Lao government and the Americans. After peacefully "liberating" town after town across the country, Pathet Lao forces marched into Vientiane in August 1975 and Souvanna Phouma stepped down to prevent bloodshed. This was essentially a North Vietnamese victory. Many prominent figures from the old regime, and many less prominent, were sent to remote camps for long periods of what both the North Vietnamese and the Pathet Lao termed "reeducation." Many Lao people voted with their feet and crossed the river to Thailand, while King Sisavang Vatthana was forced to abdicate and died 3 years later in a Pathet Lao prison camp. On December 2, 1975, the victorious Communists established the Lao People's Democratic Republic and the institutions that exist to this day.

Although by no means cuddly, the new regime was far more flexible than those in Vietnam or Cambodia. Its final victory was achieved by pressure and negotiation rather than direct military conquest. Although rigorously Communist, the Pathet Lao did not challenge Buddhism or the respect for the Sangha (the Buddhist clergy). The former Hmong mercenaries of Vang Pao were hunted down and continue to be persecuted, though they have also become a regional and international political football. The Lao government has also been relatively nimble on economic reform, instituting the "New Economic Mechanism" in 1986 to counter a crisis of lack of investment and foreign aid. With the death of the original leader, Kaysone Phomvihane, the party did not falter in maintaining its grip on power. It has successfully followed the Chinese model of

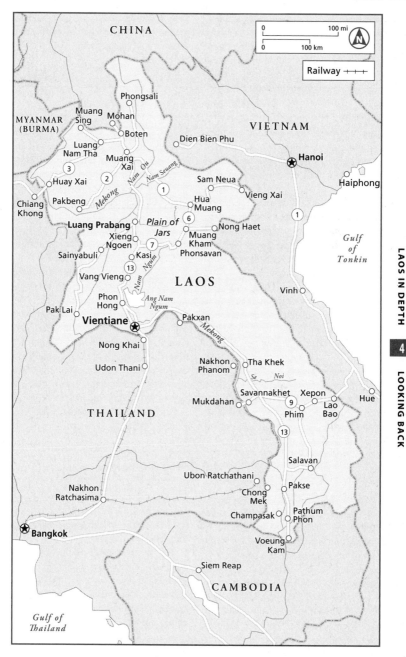

liberalizing in terms of economic freedom and making the country more open, while still keeping an iron grip on political power. Close relations with Vietnam have been maintained but have become more balanced by a closer relationship with the Thais (who are, after all, ethnic cousins). There has been occasional dissent with some bombings and shootings, which the government blamed, almost certainly spuriously, on Hmong rebels.

3 LAY OF THE LAND

Laos is a landlocked nation that covers 236,800 sq. km (92,352 sq. miles), roughly the size of the state of Utah or Great Britain. The country is divided into 16 provinces. It is bordered by Burma to the northeast, Cambodia to the south, China to the north, Thailand to the west, and Vietnam to the east. Its location has often made it a buffer between neighboring states and empires, as well as a crossroads for trade and communication.

Laos is mostly mountainous, with steep terrain, narrow river valleys, and little agricultural potential. Seventy percent of its land is mountain ranges and plateaus. These mountains extend across most of the north of the country, except for the plain of Vientiane and the Plain of Jars in Xiangkhoang Province. The south of the country contains large level areas in Savannakhet and Champasak provinces that are well suited for extensive wet rice cultivation and livestock. Much of Khammouane Province and the eastern part of all the southern provinces are mountainous. Together, the alluvial plains and terraces of the Mekong and its tributaries cover only about 20% of the total land area. Only about 4% of the total land area is classified as arable. Forests have declined dramatically in the last 40 years due to logging and slash-and-burn agriculture.

With an estimated population of nearly 5.7 million, Laos is one of the most sparsely populated countries in Asia. Natural landmarks include the Annamite Mountains along the border with Vietnam, as well as the Mekong River, which flows from China and along Laos's border with Thailand. About 55% of the landscape is pristine tropical forest, sheltering such rare and wild animals as elephants, leopards, the Java mongoose, panthers, gibbons, and black bears.

4 ART & ARCHITECTURE

ARCHITECTURE

Architecture in Laos is a real mix. In the countryside and villages, people live in wooden houses simply constructed. In the flatlands these house tend to be on stilts (as in Cambodia). Structures in larger towns are much different. There are exquisite temples built in a number of styles that are very close to that of North Thailand. Generally with Lao wats, the roof reaches very low—almost to the ground in an elegant arc. There is also plenty of dark wood and gold. A wander around Luang Prabang is a rewarding experience if you have an interest in Buddhist temples. They are simply stunning.

The other element to the mix that makes Luang Prabang and Vientiane so beautiful is the French factor. Whether they did it intentionally or not, the French created beautiful buildings all over Indochina, and Laos is no exception. In Vientiane or Luang Prabang, these buildings look cared for and preserved. In other less visited places such as Savannakhet, the opposite is true and there is a real sense of decay. It's a very elegant decay, but there is a real worry that the old French buildings will fall down if they are not knocked down first.

It is a subjective view, but when it comes to Lao architecture the real challenge is the buildings created during the Soviet era, when the words "bombastic" and "concrete" became the order of the day. Thankfully, buildings of that sort are no longer being built and in areas of conservation there is a real effort to make new construction fit in with the existing structures.

PAINTING & SCULPTURE

There is no real strong tradition of painting and sculpture apart from that concerned with religion. Impressive religious art and architecture are created in a singular Lao style, particularly the "standing" or "praying for rain" Buddha, upright with hands pointing straight down at the earth. The bas-reliefs, murals, and wooden inlay on many temples are breathtaking. As with architecture, styles are very close to that of Northern Thailand, echoing such temples as Wat Phumin in Nan or Wat Lampang Luang in Lampang.

FABRIC & JEWELRY

Laos is renowned for its silk and fabrics. Markets in both Vientiane and Luang Prabang abound in silk, brocade, and cotton. Intricate and beautiful designs are produced by village women on simple wooden framed hand- and foot-operated looms. Silk thread is still hand-spun and dyed too in the outer villages, but due to the lack of availability of enough raw silk, Chinese and Japanese thread is being used increasingly. The fabrics are woven from hand-grown spun and dyed cotton or silk thread. Quality varies and not all the hand-woven items seen in the markets are pure silk. There are various different

regional styles. There is also a lot of seriously satisfying chunky silver jewelry, much of which originates from hill tribes.

MUSIC

Music and dance are integral to the Lao character, and you'll get a taste of them during your stay. Folk or khaen music is played with a reed mouth organ, often accompanied by a boxed string instrument. Don't miss a Baci ceremony, in which a circle of celebrants chant and sing to honor or bless an event.

Classical music is another art form where the Lao share almost identical cultural roots with the Thais. The Lao orchestra is defined by two forms, one large and the other small, or *Sep Nyai* and *Sep Noi*. The *Sep Nyai* is ceremonial and consists of two sets of gongs (kong vong), a xylophone (lanat), an oboe (pei or salai), two kettle-drums, and cymbals (xing). The *Sep Noi* is more relaxed and popular in feel and includes two bowed string instruments, the *So U* and the *So I*. These instruments, probably Indian in origin, have a long fret board and a small sound box made from bamboo and coconut. Both instruments have two strings and are played with a bow.

Lao pop music is the same as in the northeastern Isan provinces of Thailand. It is bluesy, often melancholic, and the rhythms are relentless, pushing along haunting melodies often in minor keys. As with American blues, the stories told are of everyday life, hardship, and love lost. The very distinctive sound that a lot of this music has is as a result of an instrument called the *Khaen* (or *Khene* in French). If you encounter a folk band, they will often be performing something called *morlam*. As with Thailand and Cambodia the singers, often one man and one woman, will be doing a routine of call and response and improvising a banter that can be irreverent or even bawdy. Even if you don't understand the language, it's great fun to watch.

The large population of Lao people living in France and the USA means that there are also singers playing hybrid forms of Lao and western music, be that genres as international as rap or heavy metal. This is a relatively new phenomenon in Laos itself since until as recently as 2003, "modern" music was virtually against the law since the seriously unhip ruling politburo thought it was a capitulation to decadent Western values.

There is a vibrant live music scene in Vientiane. Bars such as **The Wind West** (p. 239) feature very skilled musicians playing both Western covers, Lao pop, and traditional music.

DANCE

Although Laos shares traditions of classical dance with both Thailand and Cambodia, it is not an art form that has been particularly nurtured over the last 40 years. This is largely as a result of relentless conflict and a population generally prioritizing survival rather than the arts. Unlike in Cambodia where dance was very nearly dramatically and murderously wiped out, the Lao government has been largely indifferent to the slow decline of some traditional arts. That doesn't mean that all dance is dead. The lamvong, the national folk dance in which participants dance in concentric circles, remains very popular.

5 A PATCHWORK OF ETHNICITY

The people of Laos are ethnically diverse, though a truly authoritative survey of all ethnic groups has never been conducted. Before the wars in the '60s and '70s, more than 60 different groups were commonly identified. The 1985 census listed 47 groups. Some of these were made up of only a few hundred people. A lot of this huge variation in estimated numbers was a result of disagreement about what actually represents a separate ethnic group. The 1985 census also defined three general ethnic group classifications defined by origin and language. Defining ethnicity in Laos still remains an inexact science.

The lowland Lao, or Lao Loum, make up the majority of the population, 66% in total. In turn they are made up of a number of different sub groups. All Lao Loum speak languages of the Tai-Kadai family; Lao, Lue, Tai Dam (Black Tai), and Tai Deng (Red Tai). They stay in the river valleys and engage in wet rice cultivation. The distinction between Thai and Laos is a political one rather than an ethnic one. The vast majority of people who could be classified as Lao actually live in the northeastern provinces of Thailand.

The Lao Theung, or midland Lao, account for about 24% of the population of Laos; they were originally displaced to higher ground by the migrations of the Lao Loum. The cultural and linguistic variation among the numerous Lao Theung groups is more pronounced than those of the Lao Loum or Lao Sung, or upland Lao. Groups range from the Khmu and Lamet in the north, to the Katang and Makong in the center of the country, to the Loven and Lawae farther south.

The Lao Sung, often called hill tribes, make up about 10% of the population. These groups are Miao-Yao or Tibeto-Burmese speaking peoples who migrated relatively recently from Southern China. In Laos most highland groups live on the upper slopes of mountains in the north farming rice on steeply stepped terraces. Some of these groups have been resettled in lowland areas since the 1970s. The Hmong are the most numerous of these hill tribe groups, with villages spread across all the Northern provinces. Mien (Yao), Akha, Lahu, and other related groups are fewer in number and tend to be located in more restricted areas.

There have been some tensions along ethnic lines although this is more an issue of political vendetta than genuine racial friction. Over a millennia lowland Tai-Lao migrants pressured the Lao Theung groups forcing them to move to higher ground. They also dominated them politically. The Lao Theung were frequently referred to as *Kha,* a derogatory term meaning "slave" since they were historically often forced into being indentured labor.

French colonial rule tended to favor lowland Lao by granting them access to education and putting them in a position of authority. In the early 1900s, Lao Theung and Lao Sung groups mounted several insurgencies against the French and the Lao-Thai. The rebellions were easily suppressed, but the tensions lived on. During the 1950s, significant numbers of Lao Theung and Lao Sung fought for the Pathet Lao. After 1975, the number of Lao Theung and Lao Sung in positions of government and social responsibility increased, but even in the 1990s they were still underrepresented.

The unresolved issue of Hmong resistance to Communist rule persists. There were about 30,000 Hmong recruited by the CIA to fight against the Pathet Lao and North Vietnamese in during the '60s and '70s. When the Americans left, remnants of this force (with their families) remained stranded in the jungle and carried on the war. There is a continuing refugee problem for Thailand, Laos, and the U.S. Some would say that for the situation not to be solved suits certain political vested interests. In 2003 Bangkok-based Australian photographer Philip Blenkinsop was the first foreigner to find these beleaguered groups. Their situation was one of intense distress.

6 LAOS IN POPULAR CULTURE

RECOMMENDED BOOKS

One of the most interesting books about Laos (and indeed Vietnam and Cambodia) is *A Dragon Apparent* by the celebrated English travel writer Norman Lewis. Written before Indochina was plunged into Cold War conflict, it takes a look at the end of French rule and is both insightful (although very opinionated) and entertaining. *A Short History of Laos: The Land in Between,* by Grant Evans, published in 2002, is a good introduction to Lao history. *Ant Egg Soup* by Natacha du Pont de Bie is a foodie's tour of the country. It chronicles the author's adventures and describes the people she meets, the places she visits and, of course, the food she eats. *Another Quiet American* by Brett Dakin is a subjective look at the expatriate community in Vientiane at the start of this century and lays out the author's struggles with the issues of poverty. *One Foot in Laos* by Dervla Murphy is a quirky piece of travel literature and a good light read. *The Spirit Catches You and You Fall Down* by Anne Fadiman portrays the struggle between a Hmong refugee family and their American doctors over the care of their epileptic daughter. It is a tragic tale of cultural misunderstanding and disconnection. *Voices from the Plain of Jars: Life under an Air War* compiled, with an introduction and preface by Fred Branfman, is written by a former volunteer in the '60s and addresses the secret war that killed so many. *The Politics of Heroin in Southeast Asia* by Alfred W. McCoy was so controversial the CIA tried to have it banned. It's a book that really packed a punch when published.

RECOMMENDED FILMS

Laos has not appeared too much on the big screen or indeed the small one. In 2008, *Good Morning, Luang Prabang* was released to critical acclaim. It was the nation's first privately funded movie, a love story between a Thai photographer and a Lao tour guide. *The Most Secret Place on Earth* is a documentary by filmmakers Marc Eberle and Tom Vater, uncovering the history of covert American involvement in Laos during the '60s. The film interviews key players of the secret war including former CIA agents, American pilots, Lao fighters, and war reporters taking the viewer on a journey into the physical heart of the conflict. Information on this film can be found on the filmmaker's website, www.tomvater.com

7 EATING & DRINKING IN LAOS

As with so much in Laos, it comes as no surprise that the food is closely affiliated to that of Thailand. It is, however, a lot more basic and lacks the huge variety of Thai cuisine. The basic ingredients are the same, with lots of lemon grass, coriander, basil, galangal, and, of course, the very pungent fish sauce. Like Thai food, it is often lemony and tangy, using fresh ingredients swiftly prepared.

The staple for lowland Lao is sticky rice, though many highland groups don't eat it at all. In fact, Laos boasts more than 3,000 traditional rice varieties, with colors ranging from black and purple to red and brown. It is eaten steamed or boiled, with a wide range of meats, vegetables, poultry, and fish, all well spiced and flavored. Lao cooking uses an astounding array of flavorings including garlic, chilies, tamarind, sugar, lime juice, and fermented fish sauce. Fresh salads, native sausages, and noodles are other common ingredients. Most food is dry and spicy, and often watered down with fruit juices, beer, or plain water. Grilling, boiling, stewing, and steaming all come into play in a Lao kitchen. Stir-frying is now also very common, but actually considered to be a Chinese influence. Stews are often green because of the many fresh vegetables used. Soups you will encounter include *tom cheut, keng,* and *keng soua. Keng* is characterized by ginger and padek, and *keng soua* is *keng* that contains both galangal and ginger. *Tom cheut* is a mild soup with tofu and no spices.

Ping is grilled food, be that chicken, pork, or field rat (everything that is healthy and edible in the rice field will eventually go into the pot). *Laab* is a spicy salad that is very popular. You will also find restaurants serving the "cook-it-yourself" steam boat and grill. A fire is lit under a large metal grill, surrounded by a trough at the side for boiling vegetables and noodles.

Since Laos is landlocked, it will come as no surprise that fish tends to be freshwater. You will also find a lot of Vietnamese food and Chinese food. *Pho* (pronounced "fur") is the ubiquitous Vietnamese noodle soup. It contains pork or beef, plenty of fresh vegetables, and fragrant fresh mint.

As with elsewhere in Southeast Asia, the French influence remains. Fresh baguette *(khao ji),* strong filtered coffee, and pâté sandwiches *(khao ji pâté)* are all available on the street. Laos is also a major coffee producer, so if caffeine is your thing you are in for a treat. Ask for *"kah-fe Lao"* to make sure you don't get served a cup of instant granules rather than the real thing. Both Vientiane and Luang Prabang boast superb French restaurants with authentic Gallic fare and great wine. Both places are a gourmet treat and have gotten better over the years as competition has forced up quality. The food in both towns is world-beating in terms of both quality and price.

Water in restaurants is safe to drink since it is purified. Apart from that, stick with bottled water. There are also the usual soft, sweet fizzy drinks available. Then there is Beer Lao. This used to be the only beer on the market—now in tourist areas you can also get Heineken, Carlsberg, and Tiger, although Beer Lao is still by far the cheapest and most popular. Beer Lao has achieved high international status and is now widely exported. People rave about it as if they had joined a religious cult. It's hip, it's fashionable, and it's popular. Laos is a country that is very proud of its national beer, though there is serious dissent. Some people describe it as a flat, overrated, chemical brew. If you like beer, you will have to decide for yourself whether you wish to be a Beer Lao evangelist. The other thing that Lao people drink in quantity is *"lao-lao."* It is an astonishingly cheap, brutally strong white rice liquor and is really best avoided unless you are a supremely confident hangover adventurer. The stuff is lethal. As with French food, Laos is also a great place for French wine in the major towns and it is also very reasonably priced.

8 ETIQUETTE

Laos is a very conservative place on a tight social leash. Education is low and generally people are not very worldly and are easily shocked. Dress modestly. You will see that people of both sexes dress conservatively, showing little skin above the elbow or midcalf. You as a foreigner can get away with shorts and T-shirts, but if they are excessively short or dirty you will garner a fairly negative reaction.

It's all about respect in the end. Avoid open displays of affection. The usual rules of respect for religion apply. Take your shoes off when entering a temple (and indeed a private home). Women should never make any physical contact with a monk. It is also important not to point the soles of your feet at another person and certainly not at a Buddha image. Never step over food or people. The feet are seen as being dirty while the head is sacred. Don't pat people on the head, even if it is meant as a gesture of affection.

The traditional greeting is called the *"nop"* or *"wai,"* and if you can master it you will be considered very polite. You don't do it to waitresses or children. It is a sign of respect for your equals and social superiors. To perform a *nop,* place your hands together at chest level as if you are praying, bow your head to your hands, and your upper body slightly. In a business setting, a handshake is also appropriate. When you beckon someone, do not do it the Western way. Flap your whole hand downward with your palm flat. If you do it with your hand or finger pointing up, it is interpreted as either very rude or a sexual gesture.

As in neighboring countries, the concept of "face" is pivotal, and even if it means things take longer try and engineer things so that no one loses face. Lao people take a gentle approach to human relationships. A person showing violence or ill temper is regarded with surprise and disapproval. A calm approach will take you further. Patient persistence and a smile always win out, especially when haggling. It is important to haggle, of course, but just one or two go-rounds are usually enough, and no means no.

Planning Your Trip to Laos

Only a decade ago, Laos was a very difficult country to get around. When there were roads, they were usually dreadful. The domestic airline, then called Lao Aviation, had a reputation for plummeting as much as flying horizontally. Anywhere outside of the most touristed areas, facilities were often reduced to a level of cold water, no electricity, and food that could flatteringly be described as basic. In short, it was an adventure.

That era seems like a different age when you travel in Laos today. In one short decade, almost all the main roads have been paved and sealed. Planes are now less likely to fall out of the sky and buses are now frequent (though it would be a lie to call them comfortable). Fresh hotels and guesthouses spring up every month in every category. In the major towns, one can sample high-quality French cuisine, while Lao food is distinctive and delicious. Laos also remains a cheap country for travel. The slow pace of life has been complemented by change rather than destroyed by it, and Laos's tranquillity now comes with a great deal less physical discomfort than was once the case. There are exceptions, Vang Vieng being the glaring example.

Having said all this, it is still a good idea to factor in plenty of time when traveling in Laos, since levels of efficiency are still not high.

1 WHEN TO GO

High season for tourism in Laos is November through March and the month of August, when weather conditions are favorable, plus the Lao New Year in the middle of April. Accommodations run at full capacity and transportation can be overbooked at these times.

Laos's tropical climate ushers in a wet monsoon season, lasting from early May to October, followed by a dry season from November through April. In Vientiane, average temperatures range from 71°F

(22°C) in January to 84°F (29°C) in April. The northern regions get chilly from November to February and can approach freezing temperatures at night in mountainous areas. Beginning in mid-February, temperatures gradually climb, and April can see temperatures over 100°F (38°C). In order to avoid the rain and heat, November through February is the best time to visit southern Laos. In the mountains of the north, temperatures are still comfortable from May through July.

Average Temperatures & Rainfall (in.) in Vientiane

Month	Jan	Feb	Mar	Apr	May	June	July	Aug	Sept	Oct	Nov	Dec
Temp. (°F)	73	77	82	85	84	84	83	83	82	81	78	72
Temp. (°C)	23	25	28	29	29	29	28	28	28	27	26	22
Rainfall (in.)	0.1	0.7	1.1	2.2	6.6	8	8.3	9.3	8.7	2.1	0.3	0.2

Note that these numbers are daily averages, so expect temperatures to climb significantly

LAOS CALENDAR OF EVENTS

For an exhaustive list of events beyond those listed here, check http://events.frommers.com, where you'll find a searchable, up-to-the-minute roster of what's happening in cities all over the world.

JANUARY

New Year's Day. The worldwide holiday is celebrated in Laos. January 1.

Pathet Lao Day. This holiday celebrates the victory of the Pathet Lao against the royalist Western-backed government of the time. January 6.

Army Day. This celebrates the founding of the Lao People's Army in 1949 by Kaysone Phomvihane in the former revolutionary stronghold of Huaphan province. January 20.

Boun Khoun Khao. This holiday is celebrated after the rice harvest. A ceremony takes place to give thanks to the spirits of the land and make good luck for the next harvest. Late January to early February.

FEBRUARY

Chinese and Vietnamese New Year's (*Kud Chin* and *Kud Viet*). These are celebrated with a bang—fireworks, parties, and merit making take place at Chinese and Vietnamese temples. February 14, 2010; February 3, 2011.

Boun Makha Bousa. As in Cambodia and Thailand, this holiday takes place on the full moon to commemorate the speech given by the Lord Buddha to 1,250 enlightened monks who had gathered with no organization or prior warning. In the evening, people visit the temple and circle the wat three times with candles in a ceremony known as *vien tian*. February 21, 2010; February 19, 2011.

Boun Khao Chi. Special offerings of sticky rice coated with eggs are made to monks. It is associated with Mahka Bousa. Late February.

MARCH

International Women's Day. This public holiday honors women in Lao society, with celebrations at homes and in offices. March 8.

Day of the People's Party. This day celebrates the ruling Lao People's Revolutionary Party and all its works. March 22.

Boun Pha Vet. Lasting 3 days and 3 nights, this religious festival celebrates Buddha's previous incarnation before being born as Prince Siddhartha. Late March.

APRIL

Lao New Year (*Boun Pi Mai*). Celebrated for 3 days, this is the most important celebration of the year. The Pi Mai festival is all about water in daily life, and no one is spared the bucket. Dress is casual. In Laos, the festival still retains more of its original gracious character. The best place to experience it is in Luang Prabang. The Luang Prabang festivities include a procession, a fair, a sand-castle competition on the Mekong, a Miss New Year pageant, folk performances, and cultural shows. Make sure you're booked and confirmed in hotels before you go. April 14 to April 16, 2010; April 13 to April 15, 2011.

MAY

Labor Day. The international day celebrating workers. May 1.

Rocket Festival (*Boun Bang Fai*). This is essentially an animist rainmaking and fertility festival, held just before the start of the rainy season. Huge homemade rockets are fired into the air to prompt the gods to create rain for the upcoming rice-growing season. This is a wild and happy ceremony with music, dancing, performances, and processions. Mid-May.

Boun Visakha Bousa. This festival celebrates the birth, enlightenment, and death of the Lord Buddha. It is held on the 15th day of the sixth lunar month. Candlelit processions take place in the evening. Late May.

JUNE

Children's Day. Lao people adore kids and this is a day to remember the little ones. June 1.

JULY

Boun Khao Phansa. At local temples, worshipers in brightly colored silks greet the dawn on Buddhist Lent by offering gifts to the monks and pouring water into the ground as a gesture of offering to their ancestors. Lent begins in July and lasts 3 months. Monks are required to stay within their wat during this time, to meditate and focus on dharma studies. Lao men are traditionally ordained as monks during this time. Mid-July.

AUGUST

Day of the Free Laos (*Lao Issara*). A celebration of the Issara, the freedom fighters who gained victory in Laos in the 1970s. August 13.

Haw Khao Padap Din. During this festival, respect is paid to the dead. Late August or early September.

SEPTEMBER

Boun Khao Salak. At this time, Lao people make offerings to the monks. These include practical items such as books, pens, sugar, and coffee. Laypeople also give wax flower candles to the monks in order to gain merit. Mid-September.

OCTOBER/NOVEMBER

Day of Liberation. This is the day the long war ended in Laos in 1975 and the Pathet Lao achieved victory. October 12.

Bun Ork Phansa. Buddhist Lent and the rainy season both end in this joyous

holiday, and monks are liberated to perform their normal community duties. It is celebrated with boat races (see below) and carnivals. In the evening of Van Ork Phansa, a beautiful ceremony is held throughout the country in which people launch small, candlelit banana-leaf (*heua fai*) floats on the rivers, decorated with offerings of incense and small amounts of money to bring luck and prosperity. Mid-October.

Dragon Boat Races (*Bun Song Hua*). Held at different times in late summer and early fall in every riverside town, these races celebrate the end of Buddhist Lent. Teams of 50 paddle longboats in a long sprint, and winners parade through town. The Vientiane Boat Race Festival (Vientiane and Savannakhet) is held the second weekend in October. The Luang Prabang Boat Races are held in early September along the Nam Kan, with a major market day preceding the races and festivities throughout the night on race day.

That Luang Festival (*Boun That Louang*). This major Buddhist fete draws the faithful countrywide and from nearby Thailand to the sacred That Luang Stupa in Vientiane. Before dawn, thousands join in a ceremonial offering and group prayer, followed by a procession. For days afterward, a combined trade fair and carnival offers handicrafts, flowers, games, concerts, and dance shows. Full moon in early November.

Hmong New Year. Although this is not a national holiday, it is celebrated among this northern hill tribe. End of November/beginning of December, in the north.

DECEMBER

Lao National Day. The entire country celebrates this public holiday, commemorating the establishment of the Lao People's Democratic Republic in 1975. In Vientiane, you'll find parades and dancing at That Luang temple. December 2.

PASSPORTS

A passport with at least 6 months validity remaining is necessary for entry to Laos.

VISAS

A tourist visa for Laos with 30 days validity can be issued via a travel agent or by applying to a Lao embassy or consulate. The visa will cost between $30 and $42, depending on your nationality and in which city you apply.

Getting a visa on arrival is easily done at most overland crossings between Thailand and Laos, including the entry points at Huay Xai, Vientiane, Savannakhet, Tha Khek, and Vieng Tao. It is also available at Vientiane, Luang Prabang, and Pakse airports, costing $37, in cash only. You will need one passport-size photo. Visas are also available at the Boten crossing with China and at the main international crossings from Vietnam. Visa on arrival is not available at the Paksan crossing at present, nor the southern road or river crossings from Cambodia. That may change shortly but at the time of writing, if you are planning a trip overland from Cambodia to Laos make sure you get a visa in Phnom Penh before making your way up the Mekong.

You can extend a tourist visa either through the immigration office in Vientiane or through a travel agent. The cost is $2 a day if you do it yourself (Vientiane only). It's a fairly relaxed process. It will be closer to $3 per day if you use a travel agent, which is a necessity if you are outside Vientiane. All tourist visas are single entry only. If you want to stay in Laos longer than a month, it's no problem to cross to Thailand and come back into Laos on a new tourist visa for another 30 days. If you do overstay your visa, you will be fined a fairly hefty $10 a day, which mounts up pretty quickly. If you're calculating an overstay of anything over than a day or two, then you are better off leaving within the expiration date of your visa and crossing over to Thailand to enter on a fresh one.

There is no departure tax if leaving by land on either a bridge or a boat, though one is occasionally asked for an illicit but small "fee" of some sort, particularly after dark or on a weekend. If you're flying out of either Vientiane or Luang Prabang international airport, there is a departure tax of $10, but since early 2009 this fee was being incorporated into the price of the air ticket at the point of sale.

CUSTOMS

Being very much still a Communist country, what you can and can't take into Laos remains of some importance. Any traveler arriving at either an international airport or any other international land crossing can bring in free of import duties and taxes 1 liter of spirits and 2 liters of wine; 200 cigarettes or 50 cigars or 250 grams of tobacco; and 50 grams of perfume.

A wide variety of goods are subject to prohibitions and restrictions. These goods are defined as products that affect national stability and security, public health, wildlife, endangered species, environment, archaeology, and the artistic, cultural, and historical heritage of Laos. Import and export of articles of national heritage, which include antiques and artifacts such as Buddha statues and images, bronze drums, spears, swords, and bracelets shall be made after the approval of the Ministry of Information and Culture.

MEDICAL REQUIREMENTS

The only required inoculation is for yellow fever, if you have come from a country where it's prevalent. While not required, it is wise to get vaccinations for hepatitis A, hepatitis B, typhoid, Japanese encephalitis, cholera, rabies, and tetanus. It's also advisable to update your childhood vaccination series for polio, measles, mumps, rubella, and so on, if you are likely to be around children. For other health-related recommendations, see "Health" on p. 202.

3 GETTING THERE & GETTING AROUND

GETTING TO LAOS
By Plane
In most cases, to get to Laos you will need to connect in Bangkok in Thailand first, since it is the major regional hub for onward travel all over the region. There are three international airports in Laos: **Wattay International Airport** (VTE; ☏ 021/512-165), **Luang Prabang International Airport** (LPQ; ☏ 071/212-856), and **Pakse International Airport** (PKZ; ☏ 031/212-844). **Savannakhet International Airport** has just reopened and there are planned scheduled flights to Vientiane and an international flight to Udon Thani in Thailand.

Lao Airlines (www.laoairlines.com) is the national carrier and has domestic flights to all airports in the country as well as to Thailand, Cambodia, China, and Vietnam. In addition, **Thai Airways** (www.thaiair.com), **Vietnam Airlines** (www.vietnamairlines.com), and **China Eastern Airlines** (www.chinaeastern.com) serve Vientiane, while **Bangkok Airways** (www.bangkokair.com) and **Vietnam Airlines** (www.vietnamairlines.com) serve Luang Prabang. **Air Asia** (www.airasia.com) runs flights from Kuala Lumpur to Vientiane. There are also flights to Pakse from Siem Reap in Cambodia and also from Bangkok on Bangkok Airways (Wed, Fri, Sun).

By Land Crossing
There are now many international land border crossings into Laos from neighboring countries. At most one is able to get a 30-day tourist visa on arrival. However, this is not always the case and it is important to check the situation before you set off for your intended destination.

From **Cambodia,** there are actually two border crossing points relatively close to one another. The first crossing is at Koh Chheuteal Thom on the Mekong River. The second is the road crossing at Dom Kralor. *Note:* Although Cambodian visas are officially available at the border, some travelers have reported problems. It is safer to have a Cambodian visa in advance.

From **Thailand,** Chong Mek/Vang Tao is the easiest and swiftest access route to southern Laos. Visa on arrival is available. There are good rail, bus, and air connections from Bangkok to the regional capital of Ubon Ratchathani just over an hour from the border at Chong Mek. From Ubon you can catch a scheduled bus to Chong Mek. Once in Chong Mek it takes a few minutes to walk through the border posts (although considerably longer to negotiate the paperwork). Once through to the Lao side *songthaeaws* will run you to Pakse in about an hour.

The second Friendship Bridge connecting Savannakhet in Laos to Mukdahan Province in Thailand was finished in 2006, and this is now the main transit route across Laos to Central Vietnam. Visa on arrival is available. Take a minibus from Mukdahan to the Friendship Bridge (your guesthouse can arrange this). Once through immigration take a tuk-tuk to the bright lights of Savannahkhet.

A simple river crossing connects Tha Khek in Laos to Nakhon Phanom in north-western Thailand. The trip, on a floating vehicle platform, runs about six times a day. Visa on arrival is available. The two towns are right opposite each other and you can virtually exit the restaurant in Nakhon Phanom where you had a late breakfast and step off the ferry into a restaurant on the Lao side for an early lunch.

The mainland entry point from Thailand is at Nong Khai/Vientiane. Visa on arrival is available. The bridge is 22km (14 miles) from Vientiane and 2km (1¼ miles) from Nong Khai. Transport is easy at every stage. Since 2009, this is also where the international rail connection enters Laos with trains running direct from Bangkok's Hualamphong Station to Thanalaeng station near Vientiane (p. 210). There is little point in staying on the train; it is far simpler to disembark in Nong Khai and cross the normal way.

Huay Xai/Chiang Khong is the northern entry point if you are making the river trip to Luang Prabang via Pakbeng. Visa on arrival is available.

If you're coming by land from **Vietnam,** you can cross from Sop Hun to Tay Trang. This consists of the road from the rugged former battlefield of Dien Bien Phu, which has only just recently opened to international travelers. Visa to Laos is available on arrival, but not so if you're going the other way. The road on the Lao side can close in rainy season.

NamCan to Nam Khan is a convenient crossing if you want to travel from Hanoi to Luang Prabang (although its still a bit of a slog from Hanoi to Vinh) and the rest of northern Laos. Visa to Laos is available on arrival, but the same is not true if entering Vietnam from Laos. There are buses covering the 12-hour, 400km (248-mile) trip from Vinh to Phonsavan. You actually can do the through trip all the way from Luang Prabang to Vinh, but it's not advised unless you are in a very great hurry or have tendencies to self harm since it is a fearsomely arduous journey of 690km (428 miles).

Dansavanh to Lao Bao was the first land border to open between Laos and Vietnam in the early '90s, and is now an international highway and the main artery from Thailand to Vietnam. The advantage of going this way is that on the Vietnamese side you are treated to the spectacular scenery around Khe Sanh. The disadvantage is that if you are doing Vietnam from north to south or south to north, this border crossing brings you right to the middle of the country near Da Nang and Hue. Visa to Laos is available on arrival, but a visa to Vietnam is not. Buses run directly from the Savannakhet on the Thai/Laos border to Hue in Vietnam.

If you are coming to Laos from **China,** crossing from Boten to Mengla between Luang Nam Tha province in Laos and Yunnan in China is the only option. Visa on arrival is available for Laos but unavailable for China if heading in the opposite direction.

By Bus

From Cambodia, **Sorya Transport** (**012/631-545;** www.ppsoryatransport. com) runs a bus from Phnom Penh to Stung Treng on the Laos border. It leaves daily at 7:15am from the bus station south of the Central Market (the return trip also departs Stung Treng daily at 7:15am) and costs 42,000 riel. From Stung Treng, you can arrange transport to the border.

Getting from any major Thai town or city to any border crossing with Laos is a very simple task since buses are frequent, cheap, efficient, and ubiquitous. Buses from Bangkok's Morchit Northern Bus Terminal take about 9 hours and usually leave Bangkok in the evening and travel overnight. Tickets are 500 baht to 1,000 baht, depending on the quality of facilities on the bus.

There are also buses to all major cities in Vietnam from both Vientiane and Luang Prabang, Savanakhet and Pakse (direct buses are only from Vientiane to Hanoi and Savanakhet/Dong Ha).

By Train

You cannot reach Laos from Cambodia by train. In 2009, the extension of the railway line from Bangkok to Nong Khai was completed. The railway terminates at Vientiane's Thanalaeng station. It's easy to travel from Bangkok to Vientiane (or vice versa) by train on the daily overnight sleeper train direct from Bangkok to the new international rail terminal, about 13km (8 miles) outside Vientiane. This train uses the new rail link over the Friendship Bridge opened in March 2009, and you can then take a local bus or tuk-tuk to central Vientiane.

Alternatively, you can still travel between Bangkok and Vientiane the old way, using any of the Bangkok-Nong Khai trains, then making your own way by bus or taxi between Nong Khai and Vientiane. At present visas on arrival for Laos are **not** issued at Thanalaeng station, only at the Friendship Bridge, so you can only use the new through train northbound if you already have a visa for Laos. If not, you'll need to get off the train at Nong Khai and use road transport across the Friendship Bridge. From Nong Khai, take a local tuk-tuk from the railway station to Nong Khai bus station. A shuttle bus runs from the bus station across the Friendship Bridge to Laos every 20 minutes throughout the day. It costs about 30 baht. It stops at Thai immigration 5 minutes after leaving the bus station, then crosses the Friendship Bridge to arrive at Lao Customs and Immigration. You now remove your luggage from the bus and go through Lao Customs. Once through, take another tuk-tuk to your hotel. When traveling southbound, leave central Vientiane at least 3 hours before your train leaves Nong Khai for Bangkok in order to allow time for border formalities and the various bus/taxi journeys.

GETTING AROUND
By Air

The national carrier, **Lao Airlines** (Pangkham Rd., Vientiane; © 021/512-028; www.laoairlines.com) is the only domestic airline in Laos. It used to have a very bad reputation for safety, and indeed the United Nations banned its staff from using it. It has improved greatly in the last decade. They fly in both directions from Vientiane to Luang Prabang, Pakse, Phonsavan, Udomxai, Huay Xai, Luang Nam Tha, and Savannakhet; and from Luang Prabang to Pakse and Phonsavan.

Lao Air (© 021/513-022; www.lao-air.com) is small airline based at Wattay Airport serving remote areas in northern Laos. They fly from Vientiane to Sam Nua, Xayabury, and Phongsaly. You can find the full up-to-date schedule on their website. You can pay with a credit card if in Vientiane or Luang Prabang, but if elsewhere you will need cash. Flights can be heavily booked over holiday periods such Lao New Year, so book well in advance. It's recommended that you confirm your flights a day or two in advance.

By Bus

The bus system has vastly improved over the last few years in coverage, speed, and comfort. Nevertheless, taking a long-distance bus in Laos can be an arduous option, and may be very slow and often quite crowded. Quality really varies. Buses can also be packed with other passengers' luggage or great piles of goods being transported from one place to another. Buses are slow, so unless you're in a big hurry it will help your blood pressure to plan trips in short stages.

On major routes, minibuses will parallel the public buses for a few more dollars. They are certainly faster though not any more comfortable, since you will still be crammed in and they swing around the bends in a way that can make your head spin.

Air-conditioned VIP buses (often from the magnificently named company "King of Bus") ply the routes between major towns. On the long journey from Champasak to Vientiane, there are many companies offering sleeper buses with your own curtained-off bunk. The VIP buses are best booked through a travel agent or your hotel. VIP buses vary considerably between air-conditioned luxury to vehicles piled high with luggage and added chaos.

When you are in the mountainous north, whichever of these options you take the driver will most likely be issuing all passengers with a plastic bag or two. That is because these mountain roads bring whole new meaning to the words "travel sick."

Finally, there is that mainstay of Lao transport, the *songthaeaw*. This is a van with a covered rear with two benches (the word means "two rows" in Lao) on either side facing each other. They tend to cover smaller local journeys, though you certainly can take them all the way on longer routes if you are feeling particularly sociable.

By Boat

The river used to be the main means of transport in Laos. That has changed rapidly as the whole country progresses to being sealed and paved, and road transport has undercut river transport in both money and time. Yet for tourists who look forward to the experience of slow river trips through jungled limestone canyons,

it is a different story. The journey down from Huay Xai in the north to Pakbeng remains very popular and a number of companies run vessels of varying luxury. You can book a ticket from a travel agent on the Thai side of the border in Chiang Khong before you cross, though this is not recommended because you won't see what you are getting. For the normal tourist boat, you can simply walk through immigration in Huay Xai and then wander down to where the boats are moored and buy a ticket for $20. The trip can be wonderful unless the boat is too crowded, so that is something to watch out for. The boats leave when they have enough passengers loaded on, and the trip takes about 6 to 8 hours. One tends to leave by about 10am and arrive around 4:30pm. Pakbeng has transformed from the sleepiest of backwaters only a decade ago to a place flooded with tourist money, so people may be pushy. Boat traffic south of Luang Prabang is virtually nonexistent. Elsewhere in the country you can charter your own boat, but that is expensive and logistically complicated.

By Motorcycle & Car

Laos offers an experience only one stop away from nirvana for those who like their scenery served up on two wheels. Not long ago most of the country was strictly dirt bike territory, but now that is ancient history. These days you can tour most of the country on a heavy Harley Davidson or a Triumph Bonneville if you so wish. Most of the main roads are surfaced and there is little traffic, although you want to keep a careful eye out for what there is. The scenery in northern Laos is unparallel—one descends from huge mountains into vistas of limestone karst outcrops that stretch as far as the eye can see. If this is your cup of tea, take Rte. 13 from Vang Vieng to Luang Prabang (p. 252).

> ## Warning! Speedier but Scarier
>
> If you are in a hurry, the quickest way to move is by Lao speedboat—a narrow flat-bottomed skiff with an outsize car engine bolted to the back that skims the surface of the water at 50 mph (80 km/h), shooting rapids and narrowly missing boulders. If you do reach your destination, you will do it very quickly. Huay Xai to Luang Prabang takes about 6 hours and costs $30.
>
> Passengers are required to wear a helmet and a life jacket, with very good reason. These craft are extremely dangerous with a track record of accidents. If you do choose to take your life in your hands, it's definitely an experience for the adrenaline junkie. It is, at turns, both exhilarating and terrifying as you imagine the bottom of the boat being ripped out and yourself disemboweled by the needle-sharp points just below the surface of the churning water. It is worth remembering that medical care in northern Laos is basic to say the least. At the time of writing, speedboat service on the route from Huay Xai to Luang Prabang had been suspended due to noise disruption and accidents. It was still running on the Nam Ou River from Phonsaly to Muong Khua.

In Laos you are required to wear a helmet by law, but you will notice that most people don't. Wear one anyway and make sure it fits well and is of adequate quality. Wear gloves and a jacket, and make sure you have goggles or a visor. Both bugs and dust can be a problem. Above all, ride slowly to give yourself plenty of reaction time. The traffic may be sparse, but dogs, pigs, snakes, goats, water buffalo, and small children are unpredictable and appear out of nowhere. Also be aware that drivers in Lao, particularly Vientiane, are aggressive. Keep space around you. For up-to-date and in-depth info from real motorcycling experts check out www.gt-rider.com. A bike suitable for touring, generally 250cc dirt bikes, costs $25 a day and can be hired in Vientiane (see p. 212 in chapter 11).

If you are pushed for time and want to undertake an organized motorcycle or self-guided tour tailored to your needs, but with expert support, **Remote Asia** (www.remoteasia.com) in Vientiane are the experts. They offer a range of services including motorcycle rental (ranging from well maintained 400cc cruising road bikes to 250cc dirt bikes), equipment rental, plus a flexible range of tour options. They'll design an itinerary that will cater to your needs and ensure you don't waste a precious minute of your motorcycling adventure. They will also keep in touch with you along the way to make sure everything is running as planned and smooth the way if you alter your plans on a whim.

If you want to rent a runaround to see the sites, you can hire a 100cc-to-125cc step-through in most towns of any size for $5 and $15. Some are Thai-made and some are Chinese-made—the Thai-made bikes are better.

You can rent a car to drive yourself if you wish, but generally it costs no more to hire one with a driver who is used to the roads, knows where he is going, and is responsible for any damage or breakdowns. Your hotel or a travel agent will be able to organize a car and driver for about $50 a day. If you want to drive yourself, the most established options are Lao-Wheels (☎ **021/223-663** or 020/550-4604), which provides a very friendly personal service (there's no address; you just call them up), or **Asia Vehicle Rental** (354–356 Samsenthai Rd.; ☎ **021/217-493;** www.avr.laopdr.com), which rents a range of cars, pickups, and bikes.

By Tuk-Tuk & Jumbo

These three-wheeled vehicles are ideal for short journeys around town. Jumbos (found only in Vientiane) are a bit larger than tuk-tuks, and their engine and cabin size mean they can carry more people. Both are generally motorbikes with a trailer welded to the back and cost about 25¢ per kilometer. In both Luang Prabang and Vientiane, you will need to haggle hard.

By Bicycle

For serious cyclists, as with serious motorcyclists, Laos is love at first sight. The good roads, sparse traffic, and fantastic scenery make it one of the best countries for cycling in all of Asia. Most cyclists bring their own bike, but you can rent one in most towns, and companies run organized tours, particularly Green Discovery (www.greendiscoverylaos.com). You should be aware that some of the maps of Laos are a bit far-fetched and they shouldn't be relied on. Gradients can be misleading and in northern Laos that can be a real problem. You will need some preparation for the hills and the heat. You should let others know where and when you are going. In southern Laos it is not too much of an issue, but parts of the north are a little wilder. Getting lifts on the backs of trucks and getting on buses with a bike is no problem, and there's no extra cost.

4 MONEY & COSTS

The Value of Lao Kip vs. Other Popular Currencies

Kip	US$	Can$	UK£	Euro (€)	Aus$	NZ$
10,000	$1.18	C$1.20	£0.75	0.80€	A$1.30	NZ$1.60

Frommer's lists prices in U.S. dollars or local currency, both of which are widely accepted. The currency conversions quoted above were correct at press time. However, rates fluctuate, so before departing, consult a currency exchange website such as www.oanda.com/convert/classic to check up-to-the-minute rates.

Laos in general is still a cheap place to travel, though you can easily spend a great deal on accommodations and food in Luang Prabang, where many hotel rooms will set you back $200 a night and $30 or $40 a meal is average. Yet this all changes once you are in the countryside and

smaller towns, where you can get a room for as little as $3. If you pay $15 then you will enjoy relative luxury for that town. The same is true of dining, and Vientiane is one of the best places in Asia to dine well for little money. For $10, you are in gourmet territory.

The main bank in Laos is the **Bank Pour Le Commerce Extérieur Lao.** They exchange cash and traveler's checks and issue U.S. dollars in all the major towns. They also advance money on MasterCard and Visa and charge 3% commission. The **Joint Development Bank** also changes cash and traveler's checks. Both banks now have **ATMs** in Vientiane, Luang Prabang, Pakse, Savannahkhet, and Tha Khek. ATMs are springing up at a rapid rate, and many accept both Visa and MasterCard. They are not particularly useful if drawing money from a foreign account, since they only issue Lao kip with a daily limit in the region of 700,000 kip and the transaction charges are very high. Bank **exchange booths** are far better. They are rapid and can issue U.S. dollars as well as Lao kip. In Luang Prabang, many travel agents also change money and traveler's checks as well as advancing cash on a credit card.

The official currency is the Lao kip. Notes come in denominations of 500, 1,000, 2,000, 5,000, 10,000, 20,000, and 50,000 (the endless zeros can give you a real headache after a while). There are no coins. Both the Thai baht and the U.S. dollar are also accepted and are used for larger transactions. If you are carrying larger amounts of cash, then it is best to carry dollars or baht. Also bear in mind that the kip is non-exchangeable outside Laos.

Credit cards are accepted by larger hotels, more expensive restaurants, and boutiques. In general, though, their use is restricted and Laos is very much a cash economy.

5 HEALTH

STAYING HEALTHY

Like many poor tropical countries Laos is host to a variety of ailments. It's a good idea to check the most recent information at the Centers for Disease Control (click "Travelers' Health" at www.cdc.gov).

No water in Laos is considered potable, so stick with bottled water. Also, Lao cuisine uses many fresh ingredients and garnishes, and condiments made from dried fish that might have been stored under unsanitary conditions. Exercise caution when eating from roadside and market stalls and smaller local restaurants. You should make sure that the vaccinations you had as a child—polio, measles, mumps, rubella, and so on—are up to date. This is especially true if you plan to be working with children.

In Laos, medical facilities are scarce and rudimentary. Emergency medical facilities exist in Vientiane, but outside the capital you'll require medical evacuation. Contact information is provided in "Fast Facts: Laos," in chapter 16.

Traveling to Laos puts you at risk for many of the same ailments you will find in Cambodia. For a list of these ailments and their symptoms, see p. 39. There was an outbreak of **cholera** in southern Laos in 2008. As in Cambodia, **malaria** is a threat in the jungle areas of Laos, though is not a risk in major cities. If you're in a remote area, sleep under a mosquito net and use a repellent with DEET, especially at dawn and dusk. Note that in Laos the disease has developed a fairly strong resistance to most anti-malarials (particularly the provinces of Bokeo, Luang Nam Tha, Salavan, and Champasak, as well as the areas along the Thai and Burmese borders). **Schistosomiasis** may occur if swimming in the Mekong River. It is a disease caused by a waterborne parasite, generally carried by certain kinds of snails. If left untreated it can cause severe organ damage. Most people show no early symptoms, though they may include rash or itchy skin, fever, chills, cough, and muscle aches

Although levels of **HIV/AIDS** are, at present, relatively low in Laos, its incidence among commercial sex workers is quite high.

WHAT TO DO IF YOU GET SICK AWAY FROM HOME

Medical facilities in Laos are very basic. Most foreigners living in Laos go to Thailand for treatment for all but the most trivial of ailments. The Friendship Bridge connecting Vientiane to Nong Khai in Thailand, is open from 6am to 10pm. If there is a real medical emergency then crossing out of hours is allowed. Many travelers go to AEK International Hospital (© +66-42/342-555) or the North Eastern Wattana General Hospital (© +66-1/833-4262), both of which are in Udon Thani about 55km (34 miles) from the border. Both hospitals have English-speaking staff. For less complex medical procedures, Nong Khai Wattana Hospital in Nong Khai, Thailand (© +66-1/833-4262) is also an option.

Within Laos, the International Medical Clinic operated by Mahosot Hospital is situated on the banks of the Mekong on Fa Ngum Road (© 021/214-022; open 24 hr.). The Australian Embassy also operates a modern medical clinic. It is situated at Km 4 on Thadeua Road in Watnak Village. (© 021/353-840; fax 021/353-841; open Mon–Fri 8:30am–12:30pm and 1:30–5pm). Most doctors and hospitals in Laos require payment in cash, regardless of whether you have health insurance. The Australian Embassy Clinic accepts both MasterCard and Visa.

6 SAFETY

Laos is generally a very safe country in which to travel, with little reported crime and fewer of the scams so often found in other countries in the region. However, the vast influx of tourists and money over the last decade has given rise to petty crime, bag snatchings, hotel burglaries, and low-level scams. Often these kind of things will be more opportunistic than planned and if you are aware of them and use basic common sense, problems are fairly easily avoided. Keep an eye on your things and keep valuables concealed. Keep an eye on your bags when on bus journeys and keep valuables under your clothing. If you ride a bicycle or motorbike in the city, don't place anything valuable in the basket—thieves on bikes have been known to snatch bags from baskets. Also in Vientiane, there have been several reports of women having day packs stolen after they've changed money near the BCEL bank on the riverfront.

It is also worth noting that sexual relations between a Lao national and a foreigner are illegal unless they are married, and marriage requires special permits. There have been some reports of deliberate attempts at entrapment with police involvement. The fine imposed can be up to $5,000.

Drug use in Laos results in heavy fines and expulsion at best, and imprisonment at worst. Drugs are also having a deeply detrimental effect on local communities, and you as a tourist can be instrumental by avoiding them.

Unexploded ordinance is still a major problem in areas of previous conflict. This is particularly true around the Plain of Jars and indeed anywhere that was formerly a part of the Ho Chi Minh trail. As a general rule of thumb, stay on established paths and roads.

Until a decade ago there were cases of armed attacks on buses, particularly on Rte. 13 from Vang Vieng to Luang Prabang.

Buses even used to carry armed men on the roof as a not very convincing deterrent. It was never proved who was doing the ambushing, but what is sure is that they have stopped and this particular kind of attack doesn't happen anymore.

7 SPECIALIZED TRAVEL RESOURCES

GAY & LESBIAN TRAVELERS

Generally speaking, being gay is a nonissue in Laos. It's a deeply conservative country and any kind of overt displays of sexual affection will cause deep embarrassment. Although homosexuality is technically illegal, there is no sense of bigotry or homophobia among the Lao. Some travelers make the mistake of thinking that some of the more dubious social mores that are acceptable in a few of Thailand's racier resorts are also acceptable in Laos. This is not the case. Whether gay or straight, it is simply an issue of common sense in how you behave in order not to cause offence.

The **International Gay and Lesbian Travel Association (IGLTA;** © 954/630-1637; www.iglta.org) is the travel trade association for gay- and lesbian-friendly tour operators. They have an online directory of relevant businesses. **Out Adventures** (© 416/583-2680; www. out-adventures.com), based in Ontario, Canada, offers tours of the whole region. Another operator offering gay-friendly tours is Thailand-based Purple (© +66-(0)2/238-3227; www.purpledrag.com).

SENIOR TRAVEL

Respect for elders is a pivotal part of Lao culture and family values. Even so, elderly travelers to Laos will not find the sort of discounts and deals that are found in the West. When booking your flights and accommodations, it's worth mentioning if you are a senior since there may be discount schemes available. As in Cambodia, the most important issues for elderly travelers are the potential rigor of the heat in Laos and the paucity of adequate healthcare, both of which should be taken into account.

For general information on senior travel, **AARP** (© 888/687-2277; www. aarp.org) is an organization with over 40 million members that is dedicated to helping the over-50s improve their lives. Membership brings some discounts on international travel and they produce a magazine and a monthly newsletter.

Elder Treks (© 800/741-7956; www. eldertreks.com) offers tours for those over 50 to Laos and the wider region.

The organization **Exploritas** (© 800/454-5678; www.exploritas.org) arranges worldwide study programs, including their very popular "Journey into the Heart of Asia" and "Treasures along the Mekong: An Intergenerational Adventure" tours, which include both Cambodia and Laos.

Overseas Adventure Travel (© 800/493-6824; www.oattravel.com), based in Boston, offers an "Ancient Kingdoms: Thailand, Laos, Vietnam & Cambodia" tour as well as optional Cambodia add-ons to their other Thailand, China, and Vietnam tours.

FAMILY TRAVELERS

Laos is not a particularly suitable destination to take young children. Bus travel through the mountains can be quite demanding and kids often get motion sickness. Many of the attractions in Luang

Prabang and Vientiane are geared more for adults. Some of the river excursions from Luang Prabang might amuse them for an afternoon, and elephant rides should really get them going. A combined vacation to Thailand and Laos together can work, with a flight directly up to Luang Prabang from Chiang Mai or Bangkok. There is also a lack of adequate medical facilities.

Inner Journey Expeditions (P.O. Box 2467, Parap, Darwin, Northern Territory, 0804, Australia; ℂ **+61 400/806 039;** www.ije.com.au) offers specifically tailored family expeditions for families with older children.

WOMEN TRAVELERS

There are no particular safety concerns for women that don't affect men as well. What trouble there might be is nondiscriminatory. Being out late at night on your own is not actually particularly dangerous in Laos, but it remains unwise.

It is unusual for a Lao woman to travel on her own, but given your obviously foreign status, all allowances will generally be made for your choice to do so.

The main thing to remember is that Laos is a very conservative country. Anyone who behaves in a loutish or uncouth way, especially if intoxicated, will cause deep shock, worry, and offense. This is doubly true for women. Another thing you will notice is how modestly Lao women dress. No one will stop you from wearing skimpy clothes, but it is likely to embarrass them even if they don't say anything. When bathing or swimming, Lao women remain covered. You don't have to do the same, but if you do wear a T-shirt or even a sarong while bathing in the river, particularly in Vang Vieng, your consideration will likely be noted by local people.

TRAVELERS WITH DISABILITIES

Laos poses severe challenges to travelers with disabilities. Apart from one or two top-end hotels, there is virtually no concept of wheelchair access. Sidewalks are uneven and full of potholes. Local transport is difficult and chaotic. Luang Prabang with its almost pedestrianized nature is easier to navigate than most places once you are there, but realistically any trip to Laos if in a wheelchair would need a lot of planning. The best way to navigate the country is to charter a private minibus or car for the duration of your trip. That way you are not subjected to the fairly hectic restraints of public transport, you can stop when you want, and you can take your time.

Online resources with general information for travelers with disabilities include **Access-Able** (www.access-able.com), **Mobility International** (ℂ 541/343-1284; www.miusa.org), **Society for Accessible Travel and Hospitality** (ℂ 212/447-7284; www.sath.org), and **Royal Association for Disability and Rehabilitation** (ℂ 020/7250-3222; www.radar.org.uk). Tour operators catering specifically to the needs of travelers with disabilities include **Directions Unlimited** (ℂ 800/533-5343 or 914/241-1700) and **Accessible Journeys** (ℂ 610/521-0339; www.disabilitytravel.com).

STUDENT TRAVEL

For students who lack funds, Laos is cheap and spectacular. Since the mid-'90s, this has meant that Laos has become very popular among budget travelers. There is also a whole network of services catering to their needs. Although their footprint tends to be environmentally small, their cultural footprint can be very destructive indeed. This is certainly the case in Vang Vieng, which is now a veritable mecca of young people. The place remains beautiful, but the town itself has a rather desperate air, largely created by the thousands of budget travelers and including illegal drugs.

For the budget traveler, Laos is busy and interesting. You will certainly meet many like-minded souls as you make your way around.

8 SUSTAINABLE TOURISM

Laos has a low population density, unspoiled diverse ethnic lifestyles, and perhaps the richest, most extensive network of ecosystems on the Indochina Peninsula. There are over 800 species of birds and more than 100 large mammals already identified in Laos, with new species being discovered every year. Some of the more exotic species include tigers, clouded leopards, douc langur monkeys, gibbons, the Irrawaddy dolphin, hornbills, peafowls, ibis, crested argus, and silver pheasants. A network of 20 national protected areas was designated to protect and conserve its ecosystem. It is often cited as one of the best designed protected area systems in the world. It covers nearly 14% of the country with large tracts of tropical

Sustainable Travel Tips for Laos

While in Laos, you can make your trip a constructive one by following these simple guidelines:

- Eat Lao food as much as you feel able. Purchasing fresh foods in the market and eating Lao dishes ensures that your money stays local and supports Lao farmers. When on a tour, request to eat in the village instead of taking food with you from town. This will provide villagers with income and you with an authentic Lao meal.

- Purchase local crafts. Purchasing handicrafts in markets or villages directly supports local artisans and their traditional crafts.

- Use local guides. Taking a village guide and/or a local guide from town will make your trip more enjoyable and will help employ local people. Inquire about packaged tours that include local guides, local food, and local accommodations.

- Stay overnight in villages. Staying overnight in a village as part of an organized tour provides a genuine and rewarding experience of Lao culture and Lao people. Remember to compensate villagers for accommodations and for food and to visit villages with a local guide.

- Visit national protected areas. Visiting national protected areas can help generate income and awareness to support the protection of threatened wildlife and forest ecosystems.

monsoon forest, diverse wildlife populations, spectacular karst limestone formations, and a diversity of minority ethnic groups.

ECO-TOURISM

Laos has been fortunate in many ways, because conservation and environmental protection took hold very quickly after the country opened up to mass tourism in the early '90s. Both the government and many tourism-related businesses took the message very seriously and acted on it. This doesn't mean that everything in the garden is rosy, but what it does mean is that Laos

is relatively sophisticated in the support it gives for an ecofriendly infrastructure.

Although most of Laos's protected areas are remote and difficult to reach, there are opportunities for eco-tourism-themed activities such as trekking, kayaking, birdwatching, and camping that allow you to experience firsthand the country's magnificent natural and cultural diversity.

For a list of specifically ecofriendly activities and places to stay all over Laos, visit www.ecotourismlaos.com. This website is maintained by the Lao National Tourism Administration and reflects its enthusiasm in pushing the eco-tourism agenda.

9 ACTIVE TRAVELERS

For those who enjoy the pleasures of nature and the outdoors, Laos is a place to really stretch yourself in the most pristine and interesting of surroundings. For **cycling,** Laos is ideal. You are best off bringing your own bicycle if you can, though, since those for rent tend to be clunkers designed only to get around town. The riding can be tough but the rewards are immense. Getting villagers to understand that you pedal for pleasure even though you could actually afford a vehicle with an engine might take some doing. If you prefer, you can take an organized tour.

Trekking in Laos (particularly the north and the center around Khammouane) is now very popular. It is a good way to get a taste of the real rural Laos. Most tour companies and many guesthouses will be able to organize a trek for you or put you in touch with those who can.

After what happened in Thailand and Nepal in the '80s and '90s, when trekking became an industry that often bought

rapacious operators into delicate ethnic communities, there was real worry that Laos could go the same way. Happily that hasn't happened and operators have acted responsibly to preserve the natural and cultural environment. Ordinarily a day's trekking costs about $20 per person. Bring stout shoes, a hat, and sunblock.

Kayaking and even **white-water rafting** are popular on the northern waterways of the Nam Ou, the Nam Ming, and the Nam Xouang as well as the Ang Nam Ngum reservoir between Vientiane and Luang Prabang. Local tour operators and some guesthouses in Vientiane, Vang Vieng, Luang Prabang, and Luang Namtha will be able to enlighten you as to your potential options.

Looking at all that amazing karst limestone scenery around the country, it is no surprise that **rock climbing** is an increasingly popular activity in Laos. Vang Vieng now attracts world-class climbers and is in the running for Southeast Asia's primary rock climbing destination.

One of the country's principal operators, **Green Discovery** (www.greendiscovery laos.com) is the activity tour specialist with offices in Vientiane, Vang Vieng, Luang Prabang, Luang Namtha, and Pakse. Their website offers a wide range of options for every activity. They also run tours offering a combination of activities. **Remote Asia** (www.remoteasia.com) offers a "Work up a sweat" 11-day activity tour of the north, involving dirt biking, trekking, kayaking, caving, mountain biking, and stays in hill tribe villages.

10 ESCORTED GENERAL-INTEREST TOURS

ESCORTED TOURS

Green Discovery (www.greendiscovery laos.com) offer a range of tours, taking in every site and activity you could want to see in every part of the country. They have offices all over the country so trips can be booked locally or all in one go from Vientiane. They specialize in adventure activities but they also provide a full range of tours covering towns and villages, and historical sites.

For **Remote Asia** (www.remoteasia. com), the flagship activity is motorcycling, with other tours as well. The Laos Heritage and Cultural Expedition is an 11-day experience, taking in all the major sites of interest from Luang Prabang in the north to Wat Phou in the south. They also offer tours tailored to your needs and these can be put together beforehand.

Diethelm Travel (www.diethelmtravel. com) is a Pan-Asian operator offering a whole range of tours both long and short all around the country.

Exotissimo (www.exotissimo.com) is another Pan-Asian tour company offering a range of escorted tours throughout the country.

Inter Lao Tourism (www.interlao.com) was one of the first operators on the scene and has been established in Laos since 1989. It has Lao ownership and all staff is Lao and has very detailed local knowledge.

11 STAYING CONNECTED

CELLPHONES

Laos has bypassed the need to upgrade the land-line system by investing heavily in the cellphone network. There are a number of operators and you can buy a local SIM card for $5. Recharge cards are also cheap and widely available. There are a number of providers. **Laotel** and **ETL Mobile** have the best coverage. **Tigo** has agreements with over 100 International phone networks. They also have a low-cost international rate of 2,000 kip per minute to many countries, if you buy their SIM card and dial "177" instead of "+." Their coverage is still said to be poor away from larger towns. **ETL Mobile** (www.etllao. com) is known to have better coverage in rural and remote parts of Laos. However, in Laos "better" certainly does not mean "everywhere."

INTERNET & E-MAIL

There are Internet cafes in every town of any size at all. Prices vary between 100 kip and 300 kip a minute. Connections are usually fairly slow. Computers are often badly maintained and riddled with viruses, so beware if you are using a thumb drive

ⓘ Tips **Telephone Dialing at a Glance**

- To place a call from your home country to Laos: Dial the international access code (011 in the U.S. and Canada, 0011 in Australia, 0170 in New Zealand, 00 in the U.K.), plus Laos's country code (856), the city or local area code (21 for Vientiane, 71 for Luang Prabang), and the phone number (for example, 011 856 21 000-000). Important note: Omit the initial "0" in all Laos phone numbers when calling from abroad.

- To place a call within Laos: Dial the city or area code preceded by a **0** (the way numbers are listed in this book), and then the local number (for example, 021 000-000).

- To place a direct international call from Laos: Dial the international access code (00), plus the country code, the area or city code, and the number (for example, to call the U.S., you'd dial 00 1 000/000-0000).

- International country codes are as follows: Australia, 61; Cambodia, 855; Canada, 1; Hong Kong, 852; Indonesia, 62; Malaysia, 60; Myanmar, 95; New Zealand, 64; the Philippines, 63; Singapore, 65; Thailand, 66; U.K., 44; U.S., 1; Vietnam, 84.

to transfer information to your own machine. Wi-Fi is becoming more and more common in Vientiane and Luang Prabang, where many hotels and restaurants are hooked up. You can also use a Thai DTAC SIM card to connect to the Net in Vientiane and Savannakhet through GPRS.

Vientiane

Vientiane (Wee-en-chan) is one of the few world capitals that lacks the look and feel of what most Westerners would consider a "city," much less a capital. Quiet, provincial, sleepy: These are terms that come to mind on seeing Vientiane for the first time. And if you drive into town, you might not even realize when you're actually in the city proper, as "metropolitan" Vientiane blends seamlessly with the countryside. Just a short ride in any direction from Lane Xang, the main north-south avenue, will quickly carry you into the beginnings of rural Laos.

But for better or worse, the slow march to modernity seems inevitable, as the massive influx of foreign aid and manpower from both foreign governments and NGOs is bound to reshape the city and dramatically affect those who inhabit it. While recent infrastructure and telecommunications improvements portend greater future transformation, change has still come slowly in Vientiane. Traffic is only a trickle on the city center's beautiful tree-lined boulevard, the people are always armed with their easy and ready smiles, and the city is asleep by 11pm every night.

The city was ransacked by the Siamese in 1828, so it lacks some of the ancient history

you find in the former capital of Luang Prabang, but many of Vientiane's temples have been beautifully reconstructed. That Luang is the preeminent Buddhist temple in the country and the scene of a huge festival every November. The Patuxay Victory Monument is a peculiarly Lao version of the Arc de Triomphe. The Morning Market comprises a full city block of goods to explore. And the Mekong, lined with picturesque colonials and cozy thatched bars, rolls through the very heart of the city and glows pink at sunset—not to be missed. It's worth a stay of several days to take it all in and enjoy Vientiane's relaxed atmosphere—while it lasts.

Vientiane is often described as one of the world's most laid-back capitals. It is small, pleasant, and compact. Although it lacks the splendors of Luang Prabang, it does have its own unique charm. Even though it is a long way from the sea, by this stage in its course the Mekong River is very wide, meandering, and rather mesmerizing. Upon arrival, whether by land or air, make your way **Chanthabuli,** the central district by the river. Here you will find guesthouses, hotels, restaurants, and Internet cafes. Once there most things you want to reach will be within easy walking distance.

1 VIENTIANE ESSENTIALS

ORIENTATION

Vientiane hugs the northern bend of the Mekong River. The city is divided into districts called *bans* or villages. With a population of only half a million people, it is both manageable and small. Most places are easily reached by foot or bicycle.

The covered market of **Talat Sao** marks the center of the city. Nearby are the main post office, the bus station, and tourist information office. There are also a number of banks and government offices in the same area. In addition to Talat Sao itself, there are also plenty of other shops and boutiques worth checking out in this area. Near the southern side of the market beside the post office is the **Ethnic Handicraft Market** where one can find goods from every part of Laos.

The areas of **Ban Mixay** and **Ban Sisaket** are situated next to each other west of Talat Sao, and running through them parallel to each other are the main thoroughfares of Samsenthai Road and Setthathirath Road and Fa Ngum Road running along the riverfront. In this area you will find most of the restaurants, hotels, guesthouses, and cybercafes. A number of side streets connect **Samsenthai** and **Setthathirath** roads, the busiest of which is **Pangkham Street** ending at **Nam Phu Fountain.** The northern part of the city is centered on **That Luang.** Apart from the temple itself, the main points of interest for visitors in that district are **That Luang Market,** the **That Luang Dok Mai Plant Market,** and **Patuxai Monument.**

Wattay International Airport is located 4km (2½ miles) to the northwest of the city. The bus station serving the south of Laos is 8km (5 miles) from the center of the city to the northwest. The bus station serving the north is about 2km (1¼ miles) away in the same direction. The **Thai-Lao Friendship Bridge** marking the border with Thailand is 19km (12 miles) to the southeast.

GETTING THERE

For more information on arriving by plane or by train, see p. 35.

BY PLANE Vientiane is Laos's major international hub for air travel. **Wattay Airport** is situated fairly close to the city. If you are coming from anywhere far away you will fly to Bangkok first and take a connecting flight to Vientiane. (A taxi to town will cost 50,000 kip.. The airlines serving the airport are:

Vietnam Airlines (first floor, Lao Plaza Hotel, Thanon Samsenthai; ✆ **021/217-562;** www.vietnamairlines.com). Open Monday to Friday 8am to noon and 1:30 to 4:30pm, Saturday 8am to noon.

Lao Airlines (Thanon Pangkham; ✆ **021/512-028;** www.laoairlines.com). Open Monday to Saturday 8am to noon and 1 to 4:30pm.

Thai Airways International (Thanon Luang Prabang; ✆ **021/222-527**). Open Monday to Friday 8am to 5pm, Saturday 8am to noon.

China Eastern Airlines (Thanon Luang Prabang; ✆ **021/212-300;** www.china eastern.com).

BY BUS There are three separate bus stations in Vientiane. The **Northern Bus Station** (✆ **021/260-555**) connects Vientiane with northern Laos, China, and Vietnam. The **Southern Bus station** (✆ **021/740-521**) is the port of call if you heading in the direction of Tha Khek, Pakse, or Savannakhet. There is also a bus station at the **Morning Market** (✆ **021/216-507**), which is called Talat Sao in Lao, but which is devoted to local buses around Vientiane province only. There are buses to destinations farther away (such as Vang Vieng) from Talat Sao, but they are best avoided because they are incredibly slow and stop frequently. It is best to head for the long-distance buses from either the Northern or Southern terminals. It is from here that buses also leave to Udon Thani and Khon Kaen in northeastern Thailand.

Note: If coming from Bangkok, a cheaper alternative to flying directly to Vientiane is to take an internal flight to **Udon Thani** 55km (34 miles) away in Thailand and travel on to **Nong Khai** by bus crossing into Laos on the **Friendship Bridge.**

BY TRAIN In 2009, the extension of the railway line from Bangkok to Nong Khai was completed. The railway terminates at Vientiane's **Thanalaeng station.** You can now travel from Bangkok to Vientiane (or vice versa) by train on the daily overnight sleeper train direct from Bangkok to the new international rail terminal some 13km (8 miles) outside Vientiane.

When taking this route, it is generally easier to get off at Nong Khai and negotiate the border in the normal way. The principal **express trains** depart **Hualamphong station** in **Bangkok** at **6:40pm** and **8pm.**

At present visas on arrival for Laos are *not* issued at Thanalaeng station in Laos, only at the Friendship Bridge, so you can only use the new through train northbound if you already have a visa for Laos. It's really not worth it for the final 4km (2½ miles) of the journey. Take any train between Bangkok and Nong Khai, and then use road transport into Laos. From Nong Khai, take a local tuk-tuk from the railway station to Nong Khai bus station. A shuttle bus runs from the bus station across the Friendship Bridge to Laos every 20 minutes throughout the day. It costs about 90¢. It stops at Thai Immigration 5 minutes after leaving the bus station and then crosses the Friendship Bridge arriving at Lao Customs and Immigration. You then remove your luggage from the bus and go through Lao Customs. Once through, take another tuk-tuk to your chosen hotel.

When traveling southbound, leave central Vientiane at least 3 hours before your train leaves Nong Khai for Bangkok, in order to allow time for border formalities and the various bus/taxi journeys.

GETTING AROUND

Most of the things you will want to see in Vientiane are completely accessible by foot. If you want to travel a little bit farther or a little bit faster you can do it by bicycle.

BY BICYCLE Bikes are a great way to get around town. Both bicycle and motorcycle rentals are available at many storefronts along Fa Ngum Road near the river or along Samsenthai. Many guesthouses have a few rattlers available, though don't expect anything too high-tech. The fee varies, but is generally around a dollar a day.

BY BUS If you want to get a bus to an outlying area, go to the local bus station at Talat Sao. You can also catch a bus to the Thai border at the Friendship Bridge from here for 40¢.

CAR RENTAL You can rent a car with driver for $70 per day around town. Trips farther afield will cost between $80 and $90. Call **Asia Vehicle Rental** (© **021/217-493;** www.avr.laopdr.com), or inquire at any hotel front desk. Daily rates for sedans start at $60.

BY MOTORCYCLE Hiring a motorcycle is a popular way to explore both Vientiane and the surrounding area. Rte. 13 from Vang Vieng to Luang Prabang is a legendary road among motorcyclists. There are a number of places that rent out both small step-throughs for about $8 a day and bigger 250cc dirt bikes for $25 a day. If they don't provide you with a satisfactory helmet, then buy your own.

BY TAXI Taxis operate from the airport only and cost $5 for the ride into town. Going the other way, it's easier to take a tuk-tuk for $2.

BY TUK-TUK & JUMBO When taking a tuk-tuk in Vientiane you need to have your wits about you, since all is not as it first appears. There are actually three kinds of tuk-tuks doing the rounds in the city. The tuk-tuks specifically targeting tourists are the most expensive. You will see them lined up near sites and big hotels. The drivers will often have a printed rate card and the rates themselves are double what you pay for a regular tuk-tuk. They can be quite pushy if they see you walking by. You can bargain with them but it's not a very pleasant experience.

The second type is regular tuk-tuks that patrol the city looking for a fare. These are cheaper than the tourist vehicles. Cheapest of all are the fixed-route jumbos (a slightly bigger version of a tuk-tuk), which operate in the same way as buses. You can hail them as they pass or go to Talat Sao and take one from there. For most places around town you will pay about 20¢ to 40¢.

VISITOR INFORMATION & TOURS

There is a tourist information office on Lane Xang Avenue, just north of the Morning Market. Also see "Organized Tours" (p. 235) for tour providers in Laos, all of which have helpful offices in Vientiane. The Vientiane Times (www.vientianetimes.org.la) is the local English-language paper, a fun read with good listings of local events.

2 WHERE TO STAY

Vientiane has some good options that range from luxury rooms to backpacker dives. Book ahead, especially in late November and early December, and ask for a discount if you come during the rainy season (some places post their low-season rates). Hotels accept U.S. dollars, Lao kip, or Thai baht. Be warned that the prices listed below do not always include a government tax of 10% or any additional service charges (sometimes applicable in high season).

VERY EXPENSIVE

Don Chan Palace (Overrated)   "It's on the river. You can't miss it." That's all you need to know to find the Don Chan Palace. While Vientiane has a law banning buildings taller than the seven-story Victory Monument, the 14-story Don Chan brushed aside this inconvenience by being built on an island in the Mekong. Set just south of the city business center (a 15-min. walk or short shuttle-bus ride) and resembling a life-size dollhouse, it really is an awful eyesore. It is enormously ugly and blights the skyline of this most elegant of cities. Constructed in 2004 for the ASEAN conference, it really is a mystery as to why it was allowed to come into being in the first place—the best explanation is a misplaced desire for international prestige. Still, the views of the Mekong and surrounding areas, especially from the rooftop restaurant, are spectacular. With its vast convention hall and extensive business facilities, the Don Chan was clearly designed to cater to the Asian business traveler. Rooms are business-hotel standard, with muted colors and few traditional Lao touches, but they're comfortable nonetheless. While the rooms are large and up to international standards, don't expect any charm here. You may as well be in Chicago or Kuala Lumpur. The real draw here is the unparalleled views, so ask for a room on the Mekong/sunset side, where you can enjoy the scenery from your own small balcony.

Unit 6 Piawat Village, Sistanak District, Vientiane. © **021/244-288.** Fax 021/244-111. www.donchan palacelaopdr.com. 229 units. $160–$190 double; $350–$550 suite. AE, MC, V. **Amenities:** 3 restaurants; bar and disco; bakery; coffee shop; concierge; outdoor gym; indoor pool; spa; sauna; steam room; travel agency; shuttle-bus service (to city center and airport). In room: A/C, TV, hair dryer, Internet access, minibar.

Lao Plaza This luxury hotel is about as central as you can get, which is its main advantage. It has everything you need but it is not very interesting. Every time we have visited, there seems to be some sort of Lao-Vietnam government conference going on involving huge numbers of serious-looking military types. Rooms are either beige or blue, with solid wood furniture, thick rugs, firm beds, and small marble-tile bathrooms with terry-cloth robes. The pool is big and inviting. The May Yuan restaurant has admirable Chinese food, while a cheery cafe has buffet meals and a deli/bakery. The rooms are huge, the fitness center is the best in town, and the staff is very friendly, but it simply can't match either the Settha Palace or the Novotel for style. Maybe because they don't want to—the Lao Plaza fulfills a function and is the main venue for conferences.

63 Samsenthai Rd., P.O. Box 6708, Vientiane. ✆ **021/218-800.** Fax 021/218-808. www.laoplazahotel.com. 142 units. $120–$140 superior single/twin; $150–$170 plaza single/twin; $230–$480 suite. AE, MC, V. **Amenities:** 3 restaurants; bar; popular nightclub; beer garden; bakery; conference rooms; gym; Jacuzzi; nice pool; sauna; travel agency; smoke-free rooms. In room: A/C, TV, hair dryer, Internet access (Plaza rooms free), minibar.

Novotel Vientiane ★★ Just a short ride west of the town center, the Novotel Vientiane is a pleasant oasis from the dusty streets and downtown tuk-tuk clamor. The building itself is from the French era and very stylish. The foyer is cavernous with a sweeping staircase and decorated in a classic Art Deco theme, with stylish woodwork and a domed ceiling painted in a muted pastel yellow. Somehow one expects Humphrey Bogart to emerge from the dining room and say something cynical—it's that kind of a place. Renovated executive rooms have fine wood furniture and marble bathrooms. They also come with perks such as free laundry, a minibar, and Internet access. Standard rooms are done in pastels with cane furnishings and plain tile bathrooms, and suites are enormous with high ceilings and plenty of light. All units feature hangings and artwork that keep your mind in Indochina.

The fantastic pool area is leafy and atmospheric. Adjoining the lobby is a well-appointed Continental restaurant with indoor and outdoor by-the-pool seating. The staff is friendly and helpful, and the hotel offers a wealth of facilities and services, including use of its smart business center and chic executive lounge. It's a bit far from town but has very convenient amenities and good transportation. The busy disco, Dtec, is always a happening spot. Along with the Settha Palace Hotel (below), this is one of the two best luxury options in town.

Unit 9, Samsenthai Rd., P.O. Box 585, Vientiane. ✆ **800/221-4542** or 021/213-570. Fax 021/213-572. www. novotel.com. 172 units. $90 standard; $110 superior; $180 executive; $450 executive suite. AE, MC, V. **Amenities:** Restaurant; 3 bars; babysitting; health club; nice outdoor pool; room service; sauna; steam bath; tennis; free and frequent transport to the town center. In room: A/C, TV, hair dryer, Internet, minibar.

Settha Palace Hotel ★★★ (Moments) Once the distinguished address for visitors from the adjacent colonies of Indochina, this masterfully restored, early-20th-century French colonial mansion traced a long history of decline before its multimillion-dollar face-lift and 1999 reopening. As you walk up the leafy driveway you will be greeted by the site of a genuine London minicab, used to ferry guests to the airport. As you enter this rambling complex, you will then be greeted by friendly staff in a columned marble entry, where light coming through the large windows lends a softness to the lobby that is not unlike stepping into a sepia photograph of a distant time. Rooms are cozy, with antique details, dark-wood reproduction furnishings, and stalwart four-poster beds. If a stay at the Palace is a trip to the past, modern amenities such as in-room Internet access

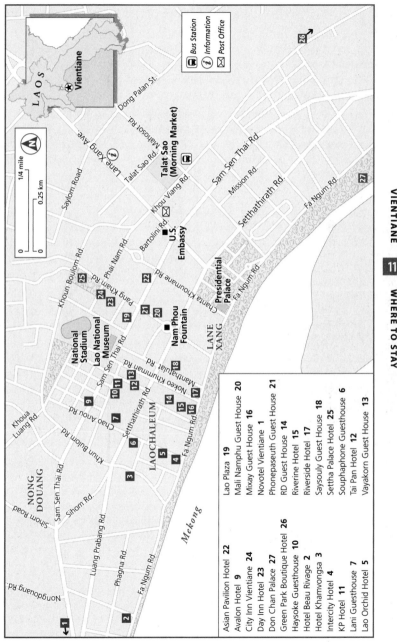

Bus Station
Information
Post Office

Dong Palan St.

Talat Sao (Morning Market)

Saylom Road

Lane Xang Ave.

Talat Sao Rd.

Mahosot Rd.

Khou Viang Rd.

Sam Sen Thai Rd.

Mission Rd.

Setthathirath Rd.

Fa Ngum Rd.

Bartolini Rd.

U.S. Embassy

Chanta Khoumane Rd.

Presidential Palace

Fa Ngum Rd.

Khoun Boulom Rd.

Phai Nam Rd.

Pang Kham Rd.

Nam Phou Fountain

LANE XANG

National Stadium

Lao National Museum

Sam Sen Thai Rd.

Nokeo Khumman Rd.

Manthatulat Rd.

LAOCHALEUM

Khoua Luang Rd.

Chao Anou Rd.

Setthathirath Rd.

Khun Bulom Rd.

Fa Ngum Rd.

NONG DOUANG

Sam Sen Thai Rd.

Sihom Rd.

Luang Prabang Rd.

Phagna Rd.

Fa Ngum Rd.

Mekong

Nongduang Rd.

LAOS

Vientiane

1/4 mile
0.25 km

Asian Pavilion Hotel **22**
Avalon Hotel **9**
City Inn Vientiane **24**
Day Inn Hotel **23**
Don Chan Palace **27**
Green Park Boutique Hotel **26**
Haysoke Guesthouse **10**
Hotel Beau Rivage **2**
Hotel Khamvongsa **3**
Intercity Hotel **4**
KP Hotel **11**
Lani Guesthouse **7**
Lao Orchid Hotel **5**

Lao Plaza **19**
Mali Namphu Guest House **20**
Mixay Guest House **16**
Novotel Vientiane **1**
Phonepaseuth Guest House **21**
RD Guest House **14**
Riverine Hotel **15**
Riverside Hotel **17**
Saysouly Guest House **18**
Settha Palace Hotel **25**
Souphaphone Guesthouse **6**
Tai Pan Hotel **12**
Vayakorn Guest House **13**

and satellite TV will keep you connected in the present. The hotel's elegant restaurant, La Belle Epoque (p. 221), serves excellent Continental cuisine. The pool area is leafy and calm, and an ideal place to relax. While the Settha Place is very expensive (with the most basic single coming in at five times the cost of most rooms in town), its service is unmatched and it offers quality far exceeding its price tag.

6 Pangkham (P.O. Box 161), Vientiane. ☏ **021/217-581.** Fax 021/217-583. www.setthapalace.com. 29 units. $180 deluxe; $280 junior suite; $380 suite. AE, MC, V. **Amenities:** Restaurant; bar; Jacuzzi; outdoor pool (nonguests welcome for $7.50); room service. In room: A/C, TV, minibar, Wi-Fi.

EXPENSIVE

Green Park Boutique Hotel ★   Combining the traditional and contemporary into a seamless whole can be difficult, but the Green Park has succeeded in doing just that. Raised tile pathways set among jar fountains lead from the elegant reception area to the central courtyard, where contemporary Lao-style pavilions surround a lovely swimming pool and adjacent reflecting pool. Stylish guest rooms boast rich wood floors, beautiful Lao silks draped over chic teakwood furniture, and all the modern conveniences, including free wireless Internet access. Cozy balconies have views of the pools and the newly planted frangipani trees that dot the surrounding garden areas. Set next to the undeveloped Nong Chanh Park, Vientiane's largest, and a 15-minute walk to the Morning Market, the Green Park is far enough away to feel secluded but not too far to feel isolated from the city. Add to this tranquil setting an eager-to-please staff that caters to guests' every whim, and you get a hotel that has set the bar extremely high for future boutique properties in Vientiane.

248 Khouvieng Rd. ☏ **021/264-097.** Fax 021/263064. www.greenparkvientiane.com. 34 units. $165 classic double; $175 deluxe double; $350 deluxe suite; $450 executive suite. Internet rates available. AE, MC, V. **Amenities:** Restaurant; lounge; free airport transfers; Jacuzzi; outdoor pool; spa. In room: A/C, satellite TV, hair dryer, minibar, Wi-Fi.

Lao Orchid Hotel   The Lao Orchid is an upscale and comfortable choice. The decoration is muted but easygoing with plenty of beige, ocher, and pastel green. The facilities are top of the range and the rooms are large and well equipped. A few have a good view of the river. It is a bit overpriced when you look at the midrange competition, but not extortionately so.

Chao Anou Rd. ☏ **021/264-134.** Fax 021/264-133. www.lao-orchid.com. 30 units. $45 standard; $65 suite. MC, V. **Amenities:** Restaurant; bar; Internet; room service. In room: A/C, TV, fridge, minibar.

Tai Pan Hotel ★   This hotel combines businesslike practicality with a certain amount of style. It is brand-new, tastefully and efficiently designed, and well equipped, with friendly staff. If you are on business and want to be near the center of town, the Tai Pan will give you everything you need. Neither fancy nor glamorous, it is about getting things done. That does not mean that it is soulless—the designers obviously put a lot of thought into combining functionality and style, and that combination is very successful. The rooms are large and come with all the conveniences you would need. The pool and the business center are state of the art and the foyer has just enough painted-on retro charm to do justice to its old town location.

2–12 Francis Nginn St. ☏ **021/216-906.** Fax 021/216-223. www.taipanhotel-vientiane.com. $64 standard single; $82 standard double; $70 deluxe single; $88 deluxe double; $82 junior suite single; $99 junior suite double; $148 suite. AE, MC, V. **Amenities:** Restaurant; bar; health club; Internet; outdoor pool; room service. *In room:* A/C, TV, fridge, minibar.

MODERATE

Asian Pavilion Hotel   Formerly called the Hotel Constellation, during the '60s and '70s journalists, spies, diplomats, and adventurers slept, drank, plotted, and socialized here. These days, it is not particularly remarkable and a stay here would purely be about soaking up the atmosphere of times past. The hotel is quite central but a bit dingy. The carpet could do with refurbishing and the walls would benefit from a spell of redecorating. However, this is undeniably a place with history.

379 Samsenthai Rd. ℂ **021/213-439.** Fax 021/213-085. www.asianpavilionlaos.com. 40 units. $25 single; $25 double; $35 triple. MC, V. **Amenities:** Restaurant; bar; Internet; room service. *In room:* A/C, TV, fridge, minibar.

City Inn Vientiane ★★ (Finds   This brand-new hotel is a stylish option for downtown Vientiane. The decor is minimalist with a touch of traditional Laos. Double rooms are spacious, with unfinished stone floors, cream-colored walls, and contemporary wood furniture. Cool rattan furniture and traditional Lao silk bed throws round out the look, alongside modern comforts such as flatscreen TVs and American standard tubs and sinks. The large lobby has sparkling white floors and Scandinavian-style furniture mixed with dark-wood accents. This is a great place to check into for a few days. Longer stay/serviced apartments are also available.

Pangkham Rd. (across from Day Inn) Lane Xang Ave., P.O. Box 3925, Vientiane. ℂ **021/218-333.** Fax 021/218-444. 40 units. $55 deluxe; $90–$100 suite. MC, V. Free parking. **Amenities:** Restaurant; bar; sauna; smoke-free rooms. In room: A/C, TV, minibar.

Haysoke Guest House   Right near the central Nam Phu fountain and with a rather grand facade, the Haysoke ranges from modest budget accommodations to muted, mid-range semiluxury. It has a nice homey feel with plenty of rattan furniture and rustic rugs. The basic rooms are very basic but are very clean. The A/C doubles are actually pretty nice. Some of the downstairs rooms smell a bit musty and damp, so it is probably best to look at a few before choosing your room.

83/1-2 Heangboun Rd. ℂ **021/219-711.** Fax 021/219-755. http://haysok.laopdr.com. 22 units. $13 single with shared bathroom; $18 single; $22 double. MC, V. In room: A/C, TV.

Hotel Beau Rivage ★★   You found it! The best riverside mini hotel in Vientiane. Don't let the pink facade send you running—the Beau Rivage offers fun, colorful accommodations in a picturesque location. The Australian owners and hotel staff are extremely friendly, and unlike other hotels in this price range, employees here speak English very well. Superior rooms on the third floor are the best choice—they are painted blue and have excellent views; second-floor superiors are a bit too pink for my taste. This is probably the only riverside hotel where they have really thought about maximizing the enjoyment of the river views, and being a bit up the river it is very quiet. There are also art exhibits scattered around. The bar/restaurant is rustic and very comfortable, and in true boutique style the Beau Rivage has an attached spa.

8–10 Fa Ngum Rd. ℂ **021/243-350.** Fax 021/243-345. www.hbrm.com. 16 units. $57 superior double; $42 standard double; $39 standard single. MC, V. **Amenities:** Restaurant; bar; Internet; room service; spa. *In room:* A/C, TV, fridge, minibar.

Hotel Khamvongsa ★   This brand-new hotel is tastefully located in an old French villa near the river. It is all very old Indochina with black-and-white tiled floors, wicker furniture, plenty of dark-wood furnishings, and high ceilings. The rooms are spacious and airy. The service is relaxed but efficient. There is a restaurant serving breakfast only, which gets very good reviews.

Khun Bulom Rd. © 021/218-415. Fax 021/223-257. 26 units. $25 single; $30 double. MC, V. **Amenities:** Restaurant; room service. *In room:* A/C, TV, fridge, minibar.

Inter City Hotel ★★★ This hotel is quirky beyond belief. It looks as if it was decorated by a slightly color-blind grandmother. In short, it is great fun if you are in the mood for the eccentric. It is in an old French riverside villa, and rooms are aged and feel very "lived in" but they are not ragged at all. It has original wooden floors and big windows. The furnishings are dark wood and silk and along the corridors are rustic looking pillars painted in purple and gold reminiscent of a Buddhist temple. The river-view deluxe rooms are simply superb. The walls of reception are an exhibit in themselves, lined with real pebbles seemingly picked up from the gray beaches of the English Channel. If you like your accommodations on the wacky side, the Inter City will not disappoint. It is a hotel with genuine charm and character.

24–25 Fa Ngum. © 021/242-843. 47 units. $35 standard; $55 deluxe; $75 suite. MC, V. **Amenities:** Restaurant; room service. *In room:* A/C, TV, fridge, minibar.

KP Hotel This hotel is modern, well equipped, and very central. The rooms are a little bit pokey, but not claustrophobically so. It is beautifully furnished with silk bedspreads, muted lighting, and enough boutique touches to be pleasant without being cloying. The management has obviously thought about providing a businesslike efficiency with a casual atmosphere, and they appear to have succeeded. In its price range it is one of the most comprehensively equipped hotels in town, including car rental and traditional massage.

59 Hangboun Rd. © 021/241-616. Fax 021/241-616. 27 units. $35 double. MC, V. **Amenities:** Restaurant; bar; Internet; room service. *In room:* A/C, TV, fridge, minibar.

Lani Guest House This hotel stands out from the crowd simply because they are doing something quite different from everyone else. It is down a shaded lane in a slightly rambling old villa. The place is filled with atmosphere, with statues and handicrafts scattered artfully around both the rooms and the communal areas. The rooms in the house are large, airy, and pleasant. Those in an adjoining annex are bit dark. It is a lovely place but somewhat overpriced. They have, however, done very well to create something special for a niche market. The Lani inspires real enthusiasm among those who stay there often and gets a lot of repeat customers. In keeping with its pleasant but slightly snooty outlook, the Lani Guest House does not have TVs, but it does have wireless Internet throughout.

281 Setthathirath. © 021/214-919. www.laniguesthouse.com. $40 double; $25 single. MC, V. **Amenities:** Internet. *In room:* A/C.

Mali Namphu Guest House ★★★ ⓥ**Value** In the center of Vientiane lies this beautiful French villa. They have gotten the renovation in old Indochina style exactly right and at $25, this place is a steal. Rooms are tastefully furnished. The atmospheric ocher building is constructed around a shaded courtyard with a very Parisian-looking terrace on which you can sit and enjoy your very Parisian-looking coffee. The staff is very friendly. They also have an unusually efficient website operation if you wish to book in advance.

114 Pangkham Rd. © 021/215-093. Fax 021/263-297. www.malinamphu.com. 40 units. $25 double. MC, V. **Amenities:** Restaurant; bar; Internet; executive-level rooms; room service. *In room:* A/C, TV, fridge, minibar.

Riverine Hotel   This old colonial villa right on the river has been converted as a boutique hotel, even having the requisite attached spa. In some ways in fact it seems a little overdone, having checked all the "boutique" boxes without actually thinking about what works. The foyer area does work well, since the retro style is complemented by high ceilings and tasteful fittings. You then walk through a small courtyard to the back of the hotel where you find the rooms in a separate annex, and this is where the lack of imagination starts to niggle. The rooms are small and dark, due to the architecture of the original villa. This would not be a problem if the designers had worked to maximize space—but they didn't. Rather than cooling tiled floors and minimal furniture the rooms are all dark wood, traditional silks, and deep carpets with state-of-the-art flatscreen TVs. This can work well in some cases, but here it just creates a claustrophobic environment. The Riverine is still a pleasant and affordable place to stay, and the location is superb, but it could have been restored with far more thought to the building itself. The hotel offers complimentary fruit.

48 Fa Ngum Rd. ✆ **021/214-643.** Fax 021/216-633. 20 units. $25 single; $30 double; $45 VIP suite. MC, V. **Amenities:** Restaurant; bar; room service; Internet. *In room:* A/C, TV, fridge, minibar.

Riverside Hotel   This is a modern hotel very close to the river. All the rooms are airy, light, and well furnished, although we are not sure about the lime green color scheme. The rooms do vary and it's worth asking to look at a few. The VIP rooms on the top floors are worth that little bit extra and they have just recently installed an elevator—a good idea since potential customers were probably put off by the hike to the fourth and fifth floors.

Nokeo Khoummane Rd. ✆ **021/244-390.** Fax 021/244-391. 32 units. 180,000 kip twin; 220,000 kip triple; 220,000 kip VIP. MC, V. **Amenities:** Restaurant; bar; room service; Internet. *In room:* A/C, TV, fridge, minibar.

Souphaphone Guesthouse ★★ (Finds)   Sparkling new with large, well-appointed rooms with plenty of space, high ceilings, and tasteful furnishings, this is an excellent midrange option. The staff is very relaxed, but also helpful and friendly. If you can get a room with a view of Wat Mixai that is an added bonus. The room style is retro-colonial but it is not overdone. Clean, dark-wood furniture is complemented by muted tones, wood floors, and the occasional silk hanging.

145 Ban Watchan. ✆ **021/261-468.** Fax 021/262-094. http://souphaphone.net. 26 units. $28 double. *In room:* A/C, TV, fridge.

Vayakorn Guest House   "Guesthouse" is a misnomer for this place, which is centrally located and offers nicer digs than many of the more expensive hotels in town. It is spanking new and one of the best deals in Vientiane. Clean, comfortable rooms come with wood floors, soft beds, leafy balconies, and spotless shower-only bathrooms. Amenities, as well as views, are almost nonexistent, but you can't complain at these prices. A deal like this is difficult to keep hush-hush and the word has been out for a while, so be sure to book ahead.

91 Nokeo Khoummane Rd. ✆ **021/241-911.** Fax 021/241-910. 21 units. $27 double; $18 single. MC, V. **Amenities:** Restaurant. *In room:* A/C, TV, minibar.

INEXPENSIVE

Avalon Hotel ★ (Value)   This brand-new mini hotel is the best option in this price range. It's about 2 blocks away from the main tourist drag, which is a good thing or a bad thing depending on your love/tolerance of loud music and chatty travelers. Double rooms are nice, but the corner twins are worth the upgrade—they're bigger and have better views. Each room is named for a flower, and quotations offering pearls of wisdom are pasted to the walls or fridges. Staff is eager to please; some have excellent English, others get an A for effort.

70 Phnom Penh Rd., Ban Anou, Vientiane. ✆ **021/263-597.** Fax 021/263-596. www.avalonbooking.com. 30 units. $30–$35 double/twin; $65 suite. Internet rates available. MC, V. **Amenities:** Restaurant. *In room:* A/C, satellite TV, fridge (not available in single rooms), Wi-Fi.

Day Inn Hotel ★ ⓕ**Finds**　This charming little inn in the shadow of the Lao Plaza was once the Indian embassy, and it retains some of that urban, colonial dignity in its large, airy rooms, with their high ceilings and tall French doors. Though it's all a bit simple, and the bright sea-green color scheme is a little overpowering, you're in an ideal downtown location. Rooms (with orange, blue, or pink walls) are furnished in basic but tidy wicker, with hard beds and clean bathrooms (some with a tub). The Day Inn is like an upscale guesthouse, really, but it has the standard in-room amenities of a proper hotel. Ask for a room in the front, where doors and windows open to small private balconies. The staff is extremely cheerful and helpful, making this an all-around pleasant stay.

059/3 Pangkham Rd., P.O. Box 4083, Vientiane. ✆ **021/223-848.** Fax 021/222-984. dayinn@laopdr.com. 30 units. $40–$45 double/twin; $55 suite. MC, V. **Amenities:** Restaurant; Internet access in lobby. *In room:* A/C, TV, minibar.

Mixay Guest House ★　For those who are used to backpacker accommodations being filthy, run down, slightly shady, and often unfriendly, the Mixay will come as a pleasant surprise. These are some of the cheapest rooms in town, but it is clean and very well run. The neatly uniformed and courteous staff gives the place the air of a youth hostel rather than a guesthouse. It is all slightly institutional. Rarely on the banana pancake circuit will you be treated so well for so little. The rooms are spartan but clean. Above all (as the staff politely pointed out), in the afternoon you are served free cake! The Mixay is a civilizing influence.

54 Nokeo Khoummane Rd. ✆ **021/243-400.** 30 rooms. 50,000 kip single shared bathroom; 40,000 kip dormitory; 80,000 kip double shared bathroom; 90,000 kip double; 110,000 kip double A/C. No credit cards. *In room:* A/C.

Phonepaseuth Guest House　This guesthouse is in a very good location just behind the central fountain, for a very reasonable price. The rooms are largely pale green but don't let that put you off, it isn't entirely institutional. The rooms are all standard, but they will charge less if you don't want to use the air-conditioning—which for 8 months of the year makes it a very good deal indeed.

97 Pangkham Rd. ✆ **021/212-263.** Fax 021/261-395. 30 units. $13 with fan; $18 A/C. No credit cards. *In room:* A/C, TV.

RD Guest House　This is a spick-and-span little place with a quirky atmosphere and very friendly staff. The rooms (dorm rooms only) are very light and clean if a bit peculiar. To get to the stairs one passes what I was solemnly told is the "library." It's a nice touch, being a small common room with lots of floor cushions, books, and no TV, which makes it very unusual for accommodations at the budget end of the spectrum. Another quirky peculiarity is that the entrance to the bathrooms has saloon-style swing doors. That means that you should know your roommate well, since there is no privacy at all. If you should get into a disagreement you can fling each other in and out of the bathrooms in true spaghetti western style.

Saysouly Guest House ★   This is an excellent budget option in a good location. The guesthouse is in an atmospheric old building and the management has put some thought into creating a pleasant environment. The rooms are light and airy with high ceilings, modest but tasteful furnishings, and wooden floors. At the front is a shaded terrace from which you can watch the world go by at your leisure. There is also a pleasant and well-kept garden at the back.

23 Manththatultath Rd. ✆ **021/218-383.** Fax 021/223-757. www.saysouly.com. 28 units. $6 single with fan; $8 double with fan; $10 triple with fan; $9 single A/C; $13 double A/C. No credit cards. In room: A/C.

---

3 WHERE TO DINE

French is very big in the Lao capital, and good international restaurants of this ilk actually outnumber those serving Lao fare. You'll find some great, affordable fine dining. A few local specialties to watch out for are *khao poun,* rice vermicelli with vegetables, meat, or chilies, in coconut milk; *laap,* minced meat, chicken, or fish tossed with fresh mint leaves; or a tasty Lao-style pâté. Try sticky rice, eaten with the hands, as an accompaniment to most Lao dishes (it's a thrice-a-day staple for Laotians). ***Note:*** Restaurants are cash only unless specified.

EXPENSIVE

La Belle Epoque ★★ (Moments) FRENCH/LAO   In the atmospheric Settha Palace Hotel (p. 214), you can't beat the atmosphere of La Belle Epoque—colonial elegance mixed with Vientiane's laid-back charm. The service is efficient, and the menu covers a wide range of Continental specialties, with meat, game, and seafood prepared to order. Imported Australian steaks and salmon top a fine list of specialties, such as grilled lamb with ratatouille or terrine of duck liver marinated in wine. Try one of the creative appetizers, such as the goat-cheese pastry. Don't pass up the crème brûlée. You would pay an arm and a leg for such a meal anywhere but here. The Sunday poolside buffet brunch (11am–2pm) is a steal at $18; price includes pool admission.

6 Pangkham Rd. ✆ **021/217-581.** Main courses $15. AE, MC, V. Daily 9am–10pm.

Le Nadao ★★ FRENCH   Once a little-known eatery of just a few tables, where ordering a soufflé meant a long, languid wait, Le Nadao's Lao-born and French-trained chef and owner, Mr. Sayavouth, is reaching a wider market at his larger location adjacent to the Patuxay Monument, Vientiane's Arc de Triomphe. Le Nadao means "Stars in the Ricefield," and indeed this little star now plays host to Vientiane's best and brightest business folks and dignitaries. The dining room is a converted teak house, very rustic and soothing, with a corrugated metal ceiling showing through rough slats, warm indirect lighting, and live local music. The menu is classic French: no fusion, no foolin'. You might start with calamari pan-fried in cream Catalonian style, followed by roast partridge in a rich gravy with potatoes and a lightly fried Mekong filet with lemon, capers, and local organic brown rice. Dessert is chocolate mousse—so rich you'll melt—or a unique "tulip" of pastry with local fruit and ice cream. Bring someone special and make a long evening of it.

Patuxai (on the west side of the Patuxai Monument circle). ✆ **021/213-174.** Main courses $4–$30. MC, V. Daily noon–1:30pm and 7–10:30pm.

L'Opera ★ ITALIAN   For more than 10 years, L'Opera has been serving "real Italian" cuisine and garnering nothing but praise. It features homemade egg-noodle pasta, fine grilled and broiled entrees, daily specials, and fantastic desserts and espresso. There is also a large selection of pizza Lao, which is a surprisingly good combination of tomatoes, cheese, chilies, Lao sausage, and pineapple. The ambience is a rather formal Italy-meets-Lao, with linen tablecloths, brick walls, and wood-beam ceilings in a large, open setting. Lao staff in fine restaurants often act as if their foreign patrons are armed and dangerous, but here the service is confident and professional. Groups of four or more can try the Opera Menu of nine different special appetizers, pastas, and main courses for $25 per person.

Nam Phu. ✆ **021/215-099.** Main courses $8–$16. AE, MC, V. Daily 11:30am–2pm and 6–10pm.

Le Silapa FRENCH   For cozy atmosphere and authentic French cuisine, this is a find in Vientiane (if you can find it). The effusive French proprietor will make you feel welcome. There's a great wine list to go with tasty meals such as whitefish subtly garnished with capers, lemon, and parsley. The food is a lot more sophisticated than you might expect from such an unassuming storefront. This is a popular lunchtime venue on account of the good-value set menu.

17/1 Sihom Rd. ✆ **021/219-689.** Main courses $5–$12. MC, V. Mon–Sat 11am–2:30pm and 6–10pm. Closed Sun.

MODERATE

Amphone ★★★ LAO   This is one of my favorite restaurants in Vientiane: It's affordable, sticks to classic Lao fare (there's not a dinner knife in sight), and offers a decent wine selection. If you are a serious foodie and want to sample Lao food at its most artistic, this is where your quest might end. A major bonus is the menu's proper explanations of Lao dishes—no guessing around with funny English translations. The outdoor courtyard is an elegant, inviting space with wooden floors, dim lighting, and jazz music piped through the speakers. Order a tasting menu for a quick introduction to Lao cuisine, or otherwise I recommend the Mak P—a savory whitefish steamed in a banana leaf—and sticky rice. You can't go wrong.

34/1 Setthathirath Rd. ✆ **021/212-489.** Main courses 50,000 kip. Daily 11am–2pm and 5–10pm.

Chokdee Café ★★ Ⓜoments BELGIAN   This is an intensely Belgian experience. From the Tin Tin and Asterix cartoons on the wall, to the fridge full of excellent beers brewed by Catholic monks, the Chokdee Café rarely lets you forget the glories of Belgian culture. The food is superb with a real feeling of home cooking. Best of all on Fridays they do a spectacular *moules marinieres* (mussels in white-wine sauce with Belgian fries, cooked the way only Belgians know how). This is a Belgian culinary flagship. Friday "Moules" nights at the Chokdee has become something of a weekly ritual for expats and the place is usually packed. You have to book your meal a day in advance because the energetic young Belgian owner goes all the way to Thailand to purchase the fresh ingredients to-order, list in hand. The one minor drawback of the Chokdee Café is that it is on the riverfront road and there is a real problem with incoming dust if you're sitting on the outside terrace during the day.

19/3 Fa Ngum. ✆ **021/263-847.** Main courses 29,000 kip–50,000 kip. Tues–Sun 11am–10pm.

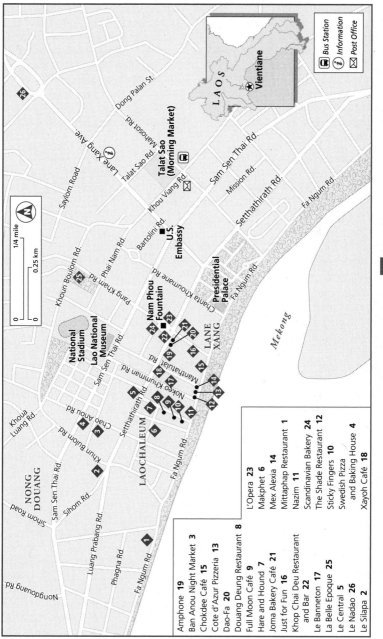

11

Amphone **19**
Ban Anou Night Market **3**
Chokdee Café **15**
Cote d'Azur Pizzeria **13**
Dao-Fa **20**
Douang Deung Restaurant **8**
Full Moon Café **9**
Hare and Hound **7**
Joma Bakery Café **21**
Just for Fun **16**
Khop Chai Deu Restaurant
  and Bar **22**
Le Banneton **17**
La Belle Epoque **25**
Le Central **5**
Le Nadao **26**
Le Silapa **2**

L'Opera **23**
Makphet **6**
Mex Alexia **14**
Mittaphap Restaurant **1**
Nazim **11**
Scandinavian Bakery **24**
The Shade Restaurant **12**
Sticky Fingers **10**
Swedish Pizza
  and Baking House **4**
Xayoh Café **18**

The Cote d'Azur Pizzeria ★★ (**Value**) FRENCH   The Cote d'Azur is misnamed. It is not a pizzeria, although it does sell pizza. This is an extremely traditional provincial French restaurant and the chef is quite obviously a genius. This is real top-range provincial French cuisine at unbelievably modest prices. There is a very regular Gallic crowd who obviously recognize this. Even by the extremely high standards of French restaurants in Vientiane, the Cote d'Azur stands out. Neither the decor nor the atmosphere is particularly inspired (in fact it's a bit gloomy) and the owners are suitably indifferent and shoulder-shrugging in a very French style. This is a place devoted to food and food alone. Every dish we tried here, be it the goat cheese salad, the Mediterranean-style oysters cooked with a delicious and light tomato and herb garnish, or the steak, was superb.

62/63 Fa Ngum. (**C**) **021/217-252.** Main courses 50,000 kip–70,000 kip. MC, V. Mon–Sat 11am–2pm and 5:30–11pm. Closed Sun.

Douang Deune Restaurant ★ ASIAN   This is a tasteful and friendly little place serving excellent Lao, Vietnamese, and Thai food. The ambience is muted with silk hangings and there's a homey atmosphere complemented by the exceptional choice of Western classical music (some excellent renditions of Bach when we were dining). The French host has created a place that is both friendly and relaxing and is rewarded by a loyal local clientele who keep coming back.

Francois Nginn St. (**C**) **021/241-154.** Main courses $2.50–$5. Daily 10:30am–11pm.

The Full Moon Café ★★ WESTERN/ASIAN   Boasting Lao, Thai, Chinese, Vietnamese, and Indian daily specials, this is the place to go if you're not sure which Asian country's cuisine you want to sample. Other places stretch themselves thin through too much variety, but the Full Moon covers all the culinary bases pretty well. The main menu is a mix of tasty Western and Thai staples, while the tapas menu offers a few interesting selections, most notably the "Water Buffalo Wings" and "Pig Between the Sheets." Of course, if I see "Pig Between the Sheets" on a menu, I'm going to order it. And of course, this being Laos, it wasn't quite what I expected (it was a little like French toast), but it was good nonetheless. If you're simply looking for a place to beat the heat, order a frappe/cappu/mocha-cino, sink into one of the oversize cushions lining the dining area, and relax.

Francois Nginn St. (**C**) **021/243-373.** Main courses $3–$6.50. Daily 9am–11:30pm.

Hare and Hound WESTERN   This is an English pub with the requisite English pub grub, dartboard, and slightly heavy wooden atmosphere. It's a good place for homesick Brits serving pie and chips, fish and chips, or just chips.

9 Francois Nginn Rd. (**C**) **020/630-2616.** Main courses 45,000 kip. Mon–Sat 11am–2pm and 5pm–midnight. Closed Sun.

Khop Chai Deu Restaurant and Bar WESTERN/ASIAN   The name means "Thank you very much." No matter how short your stay in Vientiane, you can't miss this place even if you want to. Just south and west of the Nam Phu Fountain and set in a large colonial building, Khop Chai Deu is the crossroads for expats, backpackers, and tourists. Folks come to get connected with the local scene as much as anything. The menu is extensive, with some tasty barbecue and good Lao selections. Consider the Lao Discovery set, which walks you through various short courses of typical Lao dishes. Asian standbys are on the menu, as is Western fare including pizza, spaghetti, and other microwavable favorites from home. They have submenus within the main menu such as "the expatriates relief" and the "backpacker's experience" and have an extensive range of fried insect dishes including crickets and larvae. Sit on one of the many balconies of this multitiered building, pull up a chair in the courtyard or at the bar, get into some NGO shoptalk, or share notes with English teachers and backpackers. Khop Chai Deu is abuzz late into the evening, and the 90¢ draft beer flows freely.

54 Setthathirath Rd. ℂ **021/251-564.** www.khopchaideu.com. Main courses $2.50–$8. Daily 10am–11pm.

Le Central ★★ FRENCH/CONTINENTAL   This is an elegant yet casual addition to the growing stable of French fine-dining options in Vientiane. Le Central scored a coup by stealing one of the chefs from La Belle Epoque. His new twists on Asian favorites (deep-fried spring roll filled with goat cheese and cashew nuts) and a nice selection of French and Chilean wines complement the Continental main menu. The aforementioned spring rolls are excellent; the braised lamb shank is melt-in-your-mouth tender. However, the highlight of the meal will undoubtedly be the chef's specialty: chocolate volcano cake with custard and gingerbread ice cream. Outstanding. Even if you eat dinner somewhere else, the freshly baked cakes and pies are worth a look for dessert.

077/8 Setthathirath Rd. ℂ **021/243-703.** Main courses $5.50–$28. MC, V. Daily 11:30am–2pm and 6:30–10pm.

Makphet ★★ LAO   This restaurant serving gourmet Lao fare is also part of a project providing career opportunities to impoverished street kids. Friends International (which also operates in Phnom Penh) teaches them the skills of the restaurant trade in an attempt to bring a sustainable improvement to their lives. That is actually not the main reason you might want to eat here—the food is superb with traditional Lao dishes presented in a very tasteful and relaxed environment in an old French villa. There is also a shop on-site selling handicrafts. This is another part of the NGO operation bringing funds to otherwise impoverished villagers.

Behind Wat Ong Teu. ℂ **021/260-587.** Main courses $3–$6. Daily 11am–9pm.

Mex Alexia TEX-MEX   If you suddenly get the urge for something mildly Mexican but actually far more American, this Tex-Mex riverside restaurant and bar has all the standard offerings of burritos, enchiladas, and tacos that resemble similar places in London or Budapest but would cause the locals in Cuernavaca or Tuxtla Guttierrez to start scratching their heads. The Mex Alexia is in a great location but rather overpriced. What it does do is provide a refreshing change from Lao, French, Italian, Thai, and Indian food if these main Vientiane staples are making you weary. If not, the Mex Alexia also serves pizza.

Fa Ngum. ℂ **021/241-349.** Main courses 50,000 kip. Daily 9am–11pm.

Sticky Fingers ★★ WESTERN   Started by Australians who came to Laos with the UN and are involved in NGO work, Sticky Fingers serves soups, burgers, sandwiches, and snacks in a relaxed atmosphere. It's got the corner on the casual business lunch and the after-work crowd. The menu includes plenty of light, healthy salads but also has a section of comfort foods for those missing their fish and chips, ribs, or burgers. There is a full range of cocktails including the signature "tom yam martini," an inspired concoction with chili and lemon grass. Be sure to choose from the impressive list of homemade dips and sauces (available for takeout). This is the place to grab a falafel or get your hummus fix and a respite from the afternoon heat.

103/3 Francois Nginn St. ☎ **021/215-972.** Main courses $3.50–$6. Tues–Sun 10am–11pm.

INEXPENSIVE

Just for Fun   Despite the rather cheesy name this a good option for committed veggies. They are also good with tea, offering quite a range of herbal brews plus Lao coffee. It also doubles as a Lao handicrafts store. The colorful menu offers both a variety of vegetarian dishes with a local twist, and helpful bits of information such as "eggplant helps to balance the heat in your body." Nonvegetarians can substitute chicken for tofu in any dish. It is a pleasant and quiet place where you can sit indoors among the handicrafts or outdoors among the plants.

51/2 Phangkham Rd. (opposite the Lao Aviation building). ☎ **021/213-642.** Main courses $1–$3. Mon–Sat 9am–10pm.

Mittaphap Restaurant (Moments) LAO   This huge restaurant by the river serves a wide selection of Lao barbecue and steamboat-style dishes (where you cook the meat in a heated dome over a fire). It is very popular with local people and on the weekend you will see big groups of family and friends stirring the soup or piling meat and fish onto heated metal domes, fired by hot coals right at the table. It is a very Lao family experience.

Fa Ngum (near the Hotel Beau Rivage). ☎ **021/264-444.** Main courses 25,000 kip. Daily 11am–2pm and 5–10pm.

The Nazim INDIAN   There are a number of Indian restaurants around Vientiane, but the Nazim has a legendary reputation among backpackers. For great Indian cuisine at affordable prices, Nazim has cornered the market in Laos and now has branch locations in Vang Vieng and Luang Prabang. Serving everything from biryani to any kind of curry you can imagine, Nazim offers a survey of Indian cuisine (and the beer to go with it) in a no-frills storefront along the Mekong. If you like sweet Indian *masala chai* (tea with milk and sugar boiled together) then the Nazim won't disappoint. The staff can sometimes act as if taking your order is an unspeakable bother, but the food is tasty and the prices are reasonable, making this a popular backpacker spot and an expat standby. There's another location at 9 Francois Nginn Rd. (☎ **020/630-2616;** main courses 45,000 kip; Mon–Sat 11am–2pm and 5pm–midnight, closed Sun).

Fa Ngum. ☎ **021/223-480.** Main courses 25,000 kip. Daily 9:30am–10:30pm.

The Shade Restaurant WESTERN/ASIAN   This is part of a series of cheap eateries side by side facing the river. They are all very similar to each other with simple menus of Thai, Lao, and Western food. The Shade stands out slightly on account of its Middle Eastern kabobs and falafel. It is popular with the resident West African community.

Fa Ngum. Main courses 15,000 kip–30,000 kip. Daily 8am–10pm.

Snacks & Cafes

Joma Bakery Café, across from the fountain on Setthathirath Road (☎ **021/215-265**), is renovated and spruced up, with fine breads and good coffee, as well as wireless Internet access. Next door is the newly opened **Dao-Fa** (☎ **021/215-651**), offering the same fine crepes and pastas as its sister branch in Luang Prabang. Nice toasted baguette sandwiches can be had at **Le Banneton** (Nokeokumman Rd.; ☎ **021/217-321**). The **Scandinavian**

(Finds) **Vientiane's Street Fare**

The busy area of **Ban Haysok** on the western edge of the town center is Vientiane's small **Chinatown** and an excellent place for an evening stroll and some great snacks. One-dish meals of rice or noodles, Lao/Chinese desserts, and super-sweet banana pancakes are sold by street vendors. It's an area that stays up late for sleepy Vientiane, and its charm is in the clamorous chaos. Don't miss it.

The many storefronts along riverside **Fa Ngum Road** are popular gathering spots for travelers, and across the street, on the riverside, is a row of thatched-roof eateries serving all the basics. This is a great spot for viewing the Mekong and neighboring Thailand at sunset.

On the north end of Chou Anou is the **Ban Anou night market** with vendors selling steaming bowls of noodles to hungry locals. It is a real urban Lao experience and can also be quite sociable if you are near a bunch that want to practice their English, of whom there are often quite a few. It's open daily from 8pm to midnight.

Bakery (© 021/215-199), off Nam Phu Fountain Circle, has good fresh bread and is always packed with travelers. It's a good place to pick up a foreign newspaper and people-watch on the terrace. The **Swedish Pizza & Baking House** (Chou Anou; © 021/215-705) is another tasty European option that also serves decent pizza. **Xayoh Café,** just across from the **Lao National Culture Hall** (© 020/612-051), serves pub grub of all sorts and is a good place to relax and have a beer or a coffee anytime. For excellent desserts, including a chocolate and wine sampler, try **Le Central** (see above).

4 VIENTIANE ATTRACTIONS

Vientiane is a pleasant city to explore on foot or by bicycle, because virtually all the sites are in a fairly compact area. Add to that the fact that the streets are wide and often leafy and there is no shortage of cafes and restaurants to keep refreshed, and a few days pottering among the monuments becomes a pleasure. In a couple of days, you can cover most of the sights and intersperse your explorations with the occasional riverside respite.

Buddha Park Buddha Park is a surreal and fanciful sculpture garden full of Hindu and Buddhist statues about 24km (15 miles) out of town heading south along the river. It is a concrete testament to the obsession of Luang Pu, a shamanist priest who conceived and started building the park in the 1950s. He died in 1996. The statues are captivating, whether they are snarling, resting, or saving maidens in distress (or carrying them to their doom—it's hard to tell). Luang Pu gained a big following before the Communist take-over with his message combining Hinduism, Buddhism, and mythology into a pluralistic hodgepodge of beliefs. He moved over the river to Thailand in the mid-'70s where he carried on with his mission, establishing Wat Khaek in Nong Khai. The huge reclining Buddha is outstanding; you can climb on its arm for a photo. There is also a large pumpkin-shaped dome to climb, itself filled with sculptures. The dusty and bumpy bus ride here provides clear views of Thailand across the Mekong. To get there, take a bus from Talat Sao for 40¢ or hire a tuk-tuk for round-trip.

Admission 5,000 kip. Camera fee 5,000 kip. Daily 8am–4:30pm.

Haw Pha Kaeo Constructed in 1565, this temple was built to house the celebrated Emerald Buddha. This was later appropriated by Siam in 1779, and still resides in Wat Phra Kaew in Bangkok. According to legend, the Emerald Buddha was originally found when lightning struck a chedi at Wat Phra Kaew Don Tao in Chiang Rai province, Thailand, in 1434. Discovered inside the chedi was a statue covered in stucco. The stucco was removed to reveal the Emerald Buddha itself. It is actually made out of a form of jade. Later the statue was moved to Lampang where it remained until 1468 when it was moved again to Wat Chedi Luang in Chiang Mai. King Setthathirat bought it with him from Lanna to Luang Prabang (his mother was a princess of the Lanna Kingdom in what is now northern Thailand). He ordered the building of Haw Pha Kaeo when he moved his capital from Luang Prabang to Vientiane and bought the Emerald Buddha with him. Now Haw Pha Kaeo is a museum containing religious art. This, however, is not the original temple. That was destroyed by the Thais in the Siam-Laos war of 1828. This version was rebuilt by the French and completed in 1942. The original wat is unlikely to have very much resembled the present structure, which has a distinctly Thai feel to the architecture rather than the sweeping curves of Lao design. Despite that it still has an impact, largely because it is so large. The surrounding grounds are also very pleasant. It houses some exquisite artifacts including Buddha images dating back as far as the 6th century.

Setthathirath. Admission 5,000 kip. Daily 8am–noon and 1–4pm.

Kaysone Phomvihane Memorial This man was to Laos, in many ways, what Ho Chi Minh was to Vietnam or Fidel Casto is to Cuba. Born in 1920, his father was from Vietnam while his mother was Lao. Kaysone Phomvihane became involved with the Indochina freedom struggle while studying law at University in Hanoi during the 1940s. He left college before completing his studies to join the Pathet Lao. In 1955, he was influential in setting up the Lao People's Revolutionary Party (LPRP) at Sam Nuea in northern Laos, and after that was effectively the Pathet Lao leader, although the "Red Prince," Souphanouvong (p. 183) held the position officially. After the Pathet Lao victory, Phomvihane served as prime minister between 1975 and 1991 and president after that until his death in 1992. This museum was opened in 1996 and is made up of his house with a variety of artifacts and objects from his daily life and a museum (about 1km/½ mile away) built in monumental style with financial assistance from Vietnam. The exterior is designed in traditional Lao style but the interior layout is strongly reminiscent of that of the Ho Chi Minh Museum in Hanoi. There are two stories: the upper story comprises a central statue hall, surrounded by exhibition rooms with dioramas and displays that trace his life and career in the context of the Lao revolutionary history. Outside is a huge bronze statue of the man himself (looking rather self-effacing in a tight-fitting suit) flanked by Soviet-style heroic statues depicting tough revolutionaries doing tough revolutionary things.

Rte. 13 heading 6km (3³/₄ miles) south toward the Friendship Bridge. Admission 10,000 kip. Tues–Sun 8am–noon and 1–4pm.

Lao National Museum ★★ This slightly haphazard museum is housed in an interesting old colonial structure built by the French as the office of the police commissioner.

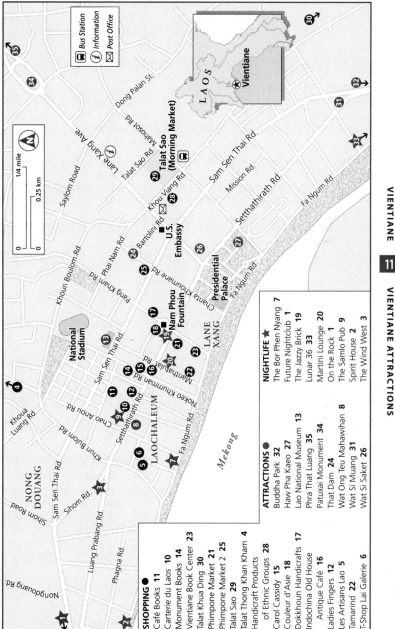

VIENTIANE

11

VIENTIANE ATTRACTIONS

SHOPPING ●

Café Books **11**
Carterie du Laos **10**
Monument Books **14**
Vientiane Book Center **23**
Talat Khua Ding **30**
Phimpone Market **21**
Phimpone Market 2 **25**
Talat Sao **29**
Talat Thong Khan Kham **4**
Handicraft Products
   of Ethnic Groups **28**
Carol Cassidy **15**
Couleur d'Asie **18**
Dokkhoun Handicrafts **17**
Indochina Old House
   Antique Café **16**
Ladies Fingers **12**
Les Artisans Lao **5**
Tamarind **22**
T-Shop Lai Galerie **6**

ATTRACTIONS ●

Buddha Park **32**
Haw Pha Kaeo **27**
Lao National Museum **13**
Phra That Luang **35**
Patuxai Monument **34**
That Dam **24**
Wat Ong Teu Mahawihan **8**
Wat Si Muang **31**
Wat Si Saket **26**

NIGHTLIFE ★

The Bor Phen Nyang **7**
Future Nightclub **1**
The Jazzy Brick **19**
Lunar 36 **33**
Martini Lounge **20**
On the Rock **1**
The Samlo Pub **9**
Spirit House **2**
The Wind West **3**

Legend:
🚌 Bus Station
ⓘ Information
✉ Post Office

Talat Sao (Morning Market)

Nam Phou Fountain

U.S. Embassy

Presidential Palace

National Stadium

LAO S
Vientiane

Mekong

1/4 mile
0.25 km

The Museum of the Revolution has photos, artifacts, and re-creations of the Lao struggle for independence against the French and Americans. The exhibits (firearms, chairs used by national heroes, and the like) are rather scanty, barely scratching the surface of such a complicated subject, but most are captioned in English. The museum features everything from dinosaur bones and sandstone sculptures of the Hindu god Shiva to machine guns and black-and-white photos of the Pathet Lao soldiers in action against the U.S.-backed regime. Archaeological finds and maps presented on the first floor help make a visit here worthwhile. There are also numerous artifacts such as pots, drums, and tools as well as an ethnographic section. Additionally there are some exhibits on cultural and historical sites like the Plain of Jars and Wat Phou, which provide visitors with insights into the rich cultural heritage of Laos. The second floor is divided into a series of galleries, each displaying artifacts and pictures of periods dating from far as 1353, including the history of the Lao kingdom of Lan Xang up to 1707, the division of Lan Xang into three principalities, the rule of the Thais, the French colonial period, the first Indochina War, U.S. intervention, the successful liberation of the country in 1975, and finally the period of national development since 1975. There are a lot of interesting historical photos with captions making it absolutely clear who were the "colonialist" and "imperialist" aggressors.

Samsenthai. Admission 10,000 kip. Daily 8am–noon and 1–4pm.

Phra That Luang ★★   This is the preeminent stupa in Laos, a national symbol that's an imposing 44m (144 ft.) high. It is not the original; the first, built in 1566 by King Setthathirat over the ruins of a 12th-century Khmer temple, was destroyed when the Siamese sacked Vientiane in 1828. It was rebuilt by the French in 1900, but the Lao people criticized it as not being true to the original. It was torn down in 1930 and remodeled to become what you see today. As you approach, the statue in front depicts Setthathirat. After you enter the first courtyard, look to the left to see a sacred bodhi tree, the same variety Buddha was sitting under when he achieved enlightenment. It has a tall, slim trunk, and the shape of its foliage is almost perfectly round. According to the Laotians, bodhi trees appear only in sacred places; legend has it that the site originally housed a stupa containing a piece of the Buddha's breastbone. The stupa is built in stages. On the second level, there are 30 small stupas, representing the 30 Buddhist perfections, or stages to enlightenment. That Luang is the site of one of Laos's most important temple festivals, which takes place in early November.

Admission 3,000 kip. Tues–Sun 8am–noon and 1–4pm.

Patuxai Monument   This monument was completed in 1968 and dedicated to those who fought in the war of independence against the French. Ironically, the monument is an arch modeled on the Parisian Arc de Triomphe. Its detailing is typically Lao, however, with many kinnari figures—half woman, half bird. It's an imposing sight, and you can climb up for a good city view. Once on top, numerous signs forbid the use of cameras (government paranoia, perhaps), but no one seems to take heed. This is the town's main teenage strutting ground and is crowded on weekends.

Lan Xang. Admission 5,000 kip. Mon–Fri 8am–4:30pm; Sat 8am–5pm.

That Dam   The That Dam is a large stupa at the center of a quiet roundabout at the end of Thanon Chanta Khumman. It is believed to be inhabited by a seven-headed dragon that tried to protect the Lao from the raging armies of Siam who invaded in 1827 (if so, it certainly failed the test). That Dam means "Black Stupa," a name that is self-explanatory.

Chanta Khoummane.

Wat Ong Teu Mahawihan   Wat Ong Teu is in a particularly propitious place. It is surrounded by four temples: Wat Inpeng to the north, Wat Mixay to the south, Wat Haysok to the east, and Wat Chan to the west. It is named after a huge bronze Buddha (ongteu) in the sim (ordination hall). It's a mighty 5.8m (19 ft.) high. It is why it is called "Temple of the Heavy Buddha." It is also known for its beautifully carved wooden facade. The temple was first constructed in the early 16th century during the reign of King Setthathirat. Like almost every other temple in Vientiane it was destroyed in later wars with the Thais. The temple was then rebuilt in the 19th and 20th centuries. Wat Ong Teu Mahawihan is also the home base of the Patriarch of Lao Buddhism and serves as a center for Buddhist studies.

Setthathirath.

Wat Si Muang   This temple is more interesting for its story than for its architecture. There are many different versions but all concur that in 1566 when King Setthathirat founded the temple, Si Muang was a young pregnant woman in a nearby village. According to local superstition that held sway at the time, it was necessary to appease the angry spirits with a human sacrifice when the ground was first consecrated and the pillar marking the foundation of the city was built. Si Muang jumped into a hole in the ground before the pillar was lowered and was crushed to death by the rocks thrown on top of her or by the lowering of the pillar itself. To this day, Si Muang is still worshiped as a kind of patron saint, and the wat that is constructed on the place where she supposedly died is named after her, as is the surrounding village or "ban." There is no sign here to recount the story of Si Muang. There is only a pile of old bricks next to a small statue of her at the back of the temple. The reality is that given that Wat Si Muang is built on the site of a previous and far more ancient Khmer temple it is likely that if there is any truth to the legend it occurred far longer ago than the time of King Setthathirat.

The original wat was destroyed in 1828 when the Thais ravaged Viang Chan. This building was constructed under the French in 1915. Both the pillar and a nearby Khmer style chedi probably date from the Khmer era. There is also a Buddha image that may well be from the original structure and survived the destruction wrought by the Thais. It is thought to have mystical powers. All in all Wat Si Muang is considered to be a place of very powerful magic.

Setthathirath, Samsenthai, and Tha Deua Rd. Daily 6am–7pm.

Wat Si Saket ★   Completed in 1818, Wat Si Saket was the only temple in Vientiane to survive the pillaging of the city by the Siamese in 1828, perhaps because the temple was built in traditional Thai style. It is renowned for the more than 10,000 Buddha images, of all shapes and sizes, in every possible nook and cranny. Look for Buddha characteristics that are unique to Laos: the standing or "praying for rain" Buddha; or the pose with arms up and palms facing forward, the "stop fighting" or "calling for peace" Buddha. The pose in which Buddha points the right hand downward signifies a rejection of evil and a calling to mother earth for wisdom and assistance. Lao Buddhas also have exaggerated nipples and square noses, to emphasize that Buddha is no longer human. The sim (chapel or ordination hall) features a Khmer-style Buddha seated on a coiled cobra for protection.

Lan Xang and Setthathirath. Admission 5,000 kip. Daily 8am–noon and 1–4pm.

START:	Patuxai Monument
FINISH:	Mekong at the end of Kun Bulom Road
TIME:	3 to 4 hours, not including eating or shopping stops.
BEST TIMES:	Morning or late afternoon (midday can be hot and dusty)

Vientiane is a terrific walking city. This tour hits Vientiane's highlights, which you can leisurely explore with stops for food and drink. Be sure to read the full listings for each stop, above.

Begin your tour with a climb to the top of:

❶ Patuxai Monument

This structure resembles Paris' Arc de Triumph, with distinctive Lao features. Dedicated to those who fought for independence from France (*patuxai* means victory in Lao), the monument offers panoramic views of the city.

Then stroll down Lane Xang Avenue heading south toward the Mekong staying on the left side of the road. You will soon arrive at:

❷ Talat Sao (the Morning Market)

Located at the eastern corner of Lane Xang Avenue and Khu Vieng Road, Talat Sao consists of many small shops, restaurants, and fruit and vegetable stalls. You can browse through jewelry, silk and clothing, wooden crafts, musical instruments, electronics, appliances, housewares, CDs and DVDs/VCDs, and groceries if you wish. There is also the Ethnic Handicrafts Market next door packed with colorful clothing and heavy ethnic jewelry.

Cross over Lane Xiang Avenue and walk northwest up Bartholomie Road. This will bring you to:

❸ That Dam

The "Black Stupa" is set in a quiet traffic circle with next to no traffic. This is one of the oldest monuments in the city—though it's never been dated, it's estimated to have been constructed in the 15th century.

Walk south down Chant Khammouane Road and turn right. Walk a few minutes up to the Nam Ou Fountain.

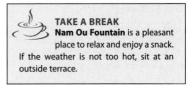

TAKE A BREAK
Nam Ou Fountain is a pleasant place to relax and enjoy a snack. If the weather is not too hot, sit at an outside terrace.

Walk back up Setthathirath Road. On your right, you will see the:

❹ Presidential Palace

The Beaux Arts–styled Presidential Palace was originally built for the French governors, and later housed the monarchy during their reign after Laos gained its independence. It is closed to the public.

Opposite the Presidential Palace is:

❺ Wat Si Saket

This wat is renowned for its *jataka* murals (scenes depicting the lives of Buddha before his final incarnation) and the many Buddha images set in niches in the cloister.

Just a little farther up on the other side of the road is:

❻ Haw Pha Kaeo

This temple was rebuilt in 1942 after the original was destroyed in the Sino-Laos war, and houses a fascinating collection of religious art.

Now head south on Mahasot Road, until you reach the riverfront and Fa Ngum. Stroll along the banks of the Mekong, stopping where you will for a tipple of your choosing until you reach Nokeo Khumman Road. This will take you to:

❼ Temples Along Setthathirath

As you turn left at Setthathirath Road, you'll find a cluster of temples, including

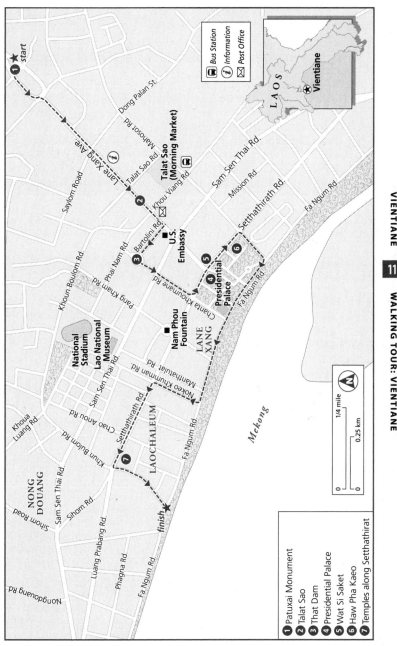

Bus Station
i Information
⊠ Post Office

LAOS

Vientiane

Dong Palan St.

Mahosot Rd.

Talat Sao Rd.

Talat Sao (Morning Market)

Lane Xang Ave.

Saylom Road

i

Khou Viang Rd.

Sam Sen Thai Rd.

Mission Rd.

Setthathirath Rd.

Fa Ngum Rd.

Bartolini Rd.

U.S. Embassy

Phai Nam Rd.

Khoun Boulom Rd.

Pang Kham Rd.

Chanta Khoumane Rd.

Presidential Palace

Fa Ngum Rd.

National Stadium

Lao National Museum

Nam Phou Fountain

LANE XANG

Manthatulat Rd.

Nokeo Khummane Rd.

Sam Sen Thai Rd.

Chao Anou Rd.

Setthathirath Rd.

Khoua Luang Rd.

Khun Buom Rd.

Fa Ngum Rd.

LAOCHALEUM

NONG DOUANG

Sihom Road

Sam Sen Thai Rd.

Sihom Rd.

Luang Prabang Rd.

Phagna Rd.

Fa Ngum Rd.

Nongdouang Rd.

finish

Mekong

1/4 mile

0.25 km

0
0

VIENTIANE

11

WALKING TOUR: VIENTIANE

❶ Patuxai Monument
❷ Talat Sao
❸ That Dam
❹ Presidential Palace
❺ Wat Si Saket
❻ Haw Pha Kaeo
❼ Temples along Setthathirat

Wat Mixay, Wat Impaeng, and **Wat Hay-soke.** Take the time to admire them; each one has its own distinctive features.

Head south down Khum Bulom Road arriving, once again, at the Mekong. Pull up a plastic chair, order something cold and if it's evening, wait for the sunset.

Swimming

There are a number of places to cool off and get wet in Vientiane, ranging from the luxurious to the municipal.

The beautiful pool at the Settha Palace (p. 214) charges $9 a day. It is pleasantly surrounded by French colonial architecture and landscaped gardens. The Tai Pan (p. 216) swimming pool and fitness center is open to the public for a slightly cheaper $7.50 a day and the excellent Novotel (p. 214) charges $8 a day.

The large municipal pool on Ky Houng Road (btw. the National Museum and the Lao Plaza Hotel) is open daily from 8am to 7pm. At $1, it is satisfyingly cheap for doing laps, but it's less good for lounging. There is also the newly opened Nong Chan Water Park with huge slides for the kids. It is situated on Khouvieng Boulevard, near the central bus station.

Massage/Sauna

There are excellent massage places all over town ranging from small shop fronts to luxury hotels. The quality is very good indeed.

There is traditional massage and herbal sauna at **Wat Sok Pa Luang** (Sok Pa Luang Rd.; open daily 1–7pm; sauna 10,000 kip; massage 20,000 kip).

Meditation

There are meditation classes every Saturday led by monks at **Wat Sok Pa Luang.** They take place between 4 and 5:30pm in the gardens of the wat. The instruction is free and there is a translator to answer your questions.

Golf

The 18-hole **Youth Garden Golf Course** (Km 14 on Rte. 13 heading south) was the first one in Vientiane. It is not far from the Friendship Bridge. Nonmembers pay $16 on weekdays and slightly more on weekends. This gets you a caddy but not clubs. You have to either bring your own set or arrange a rental. There is also the quiet 9-hole course (Km 6 on Rte. 13 heading south), which hosts expat tournaments although on the weekend it's very quiet.

Bowling

Ten-pin bowling is now a very popular activity in Vientiane and there is a good choice of places to try and clatter the pins.

Lao Bowling Centre   On the corner of Ky Houng Road and Khou Boulom Road just past the swimming pool is the Lao Bowling Centre near the Novotel. One game costs 10,000 kip per person up until 7pm, and 12,000 kip after that. Shoes are supplied, and socks available for 8,000 kip. The bowling center is open from Monday to Saturday from 9am until midnight. Khun Bulom Rd. *©* **021/218-661.**

Vientiane Bowling Centre   This is at the Lao-ITECC shopping center (about 4km/2½ miles out of town on the northern ring road toward the Friendship Bridge). It's a bit smarter than the one in town, and costs only 6,000 kip a game till 6pm and 10,000 kip after that. Daily 9am–11pm. Chanthaburi District. *©* **021/218-66.**

Organized Tours

Most hotels, guesthouses, and local travel agents will be able to organize a city tour or put you in touch with a company that can.

Diethelm Travel   This major tour company offers a 1-day "City and Temples" tour, and a 1-day excursion to nearby rural areas.

Setthathirath. ✆ **021/213-833.** Fax 021/217-151. www.diethelmtravel.com.

Exotissimo   In addition to their huge range of tours all over Laos and the region, this major tour company also offers a range of shorter tours around the major sites.

4666-06/044 Pangkham St. ✆ **021/241-861-2.** Fax 021/252-382. www.exotissimo.com.

Green Discovery Laos   Although they specialize in activity tours around the country, Green Discovery also provides city tours of Vientiane.

Hang Boun Rd. ✆ **021/264-680.** Fax 021/264-679. www.greendiscoverylaos.com.

Remote Asia   Although Remote Asia specializes in adventure tours far afield they also run a 1-day tour of areas of interest around Vientiane. They can tailor this to your needs in advance if you contact them by e-mail.

Km 5, Thadeua Rd. ✆ **020/202-2139.** www.remoteasia.com.

---

5 SHOPPING

There are many shops in the central district of Vientiane along Setthathirath and Samsenthai, selling a mixture of silks, handicrafts, jewelry, and clothing. They tend to get more upmarket the farther east you get closer to Wat Phu. It is a compact area so it is easy to browse your way along both streets without expending too much energy or shoe leather. We have listed some businesses here, but the best thing to do is just wander by and see what takes your fancy. Virtually all sell a similar mixture of Buddha images, silk, clothing, woodcarving, and jewelry.

The other place to shop is the main morning market of Talat Sao. The days when Vientiane yielded bargains of any kind are long, long gone and if you find yourself bargaining be aware that your interlocutor will have a lifetime of daily experience at the sharp end. Keep smiling and don't be worried about walking away if you suspect you're getting ripped off.

BOOKSHOPS

Café Books   Owned by a longtime resident expat, this shop sells secondhand books. Open daily 9am to 7pm. 053/2 Heng Boun Rd. ✆ **020/689-3741.**

Carterie du Laos   A small selection of books and maps, plus some artfully designed postcards, posters, and souvenirs. Open daily 9am to 7pm. 118/2 Setthathirath. ✆ **021/241-401.**

Monument Books   Monument Books sells a lot of glossy coffee-table books on Laos and Indochina in general. They also sell magazines and newspapers from abroad. It is quite expensive. Open Monday to Friday 9am to 8pm, Saturday and Sunday 9am to 6pm. Nokeo Khoummane Rd. ✆ **021/243-708.**

Vientiane Book Center   Conveniently situated near the Nam Phu Fountain. This shop carries a stock of secondhand books as well as cards and postcards. Open Monday to Friday 8:30am to 5:30pm, Saturday 9am to 4:30pm. Pangkham Rd. ✆ **021/212-031.**

Talat Khua Ding, near Talat Sao Bus Station, is the main market for fresh food. If you get the urge to put together your own meal or feast on bread, cheese, and wine on the balcony of your hotel, head to the **Phimpone Market** (Setthathirath Rd.; open daily 7:30am–9pm) and **Phimpone Market 2** (on the corner of Samsenthai and Chanta Khoummane; open daily 8am–8:30pm). They have entirely different owners and Phimpone 2 has less variety and is more expensive. Both sell a range of wines, cheeses, and other fancy delicacies from far away. They also sell practical items such as stationary and shampoo.

MARKETS

There are a number of covered markets in Vientiane selling everything from handicrafts to car parts. They tend to open early at about 8am and close early at 4pm. By 5pm they are all but deserted.

Handicraft Products of Ethnic Groups   You'll find this shop beside Talat Sao, the main morning market. They sell handicrafts from all over the country. If you aren't traveling farther afield, this is a good place to discover what is on offer in different regions.

Morning Market (Talat Sao) ★★   Full of surprises around every corner, the Morning Market is the hub of local commerce and really where the action is. Here you can find anything from the Thai version of a Britney Spears CD to a Buddhist keepsake from one of the tourist shops or trinket salesmen. Great deals can be found on Lao silks if you bargain hard. This is the Laos version of mall culture, and sometimes the everyday tool department or stationery area gives a special glimpse into daily life. Enjoy a good wander and hassle-free shopping. While we were here the whole place was being renovated. There is also a shopping center to the south of the main market. There are few touts, but, as always in crowded places, mind your valuables.
On Talat Sao Rd., off Lane Xang Ave. Daily 8am–4pm.

Talat Thong Khan Kham   This market is north of the center of the city and like Talat Sao covers all the bases in terms of shopping whether it is silks, pottery, or footwear.

SHOPS & BOUTIQUES

Carol Cassidy ★★   Established in 1990, this is both a textile factory and a shop in an old French villa. The studio and gallery creates woven art. Specializing in 100% handwoven silk, they produce wall hangings, scarves, shawls, and custom furnishing fabrics. The work of this gallery is displayed in a number of museums in the U.S. including the Textile Museum in Washington, D.C., the Philadelphia Museum of Art, and the Museum at the Fashion Institute of Technology in New York. They have established quite a name for themselves exporting worldwide and producing goods to order. The manufacturing goes on in the building and you can witness the weavers at work or take a look at the goods on offer front of house. Open Monday to Friday 8am to noon and 2 to 5pm, Saturday 8am to noon. 84–86 Nokeo Khoummane Rd. © **021/212-123.** Fax 021/216-205. www. laotextiles.com.

Couleur d'Asie   A very upmarket shop and fashion house specializing in high-end silk haute couture, fabric furnishings, and clothing. Open Monday to Friday 9am to 8pm, Saturday and Sunday 10am to 7:30pm. Nam Phu Sq. © **021/223-008.** www.couleurdasie.net.

Dokkhoun Handicrafts   Mainly specializing in antiques and jewelry, this shop also stocks some silk and textiles. Open Monday to Saturday 9am to 8pm. Pangkham Rd. ✆ **021/263-522.**

Indochina Old House Antique Café   A shop where you can enjoy a cup of coffee while looking at the textiles, jewelry, and woodcarvings. Open Monday to Saturday 10am to 8pm. 86/2 Setthathirath Rd. ✆ **021/212-579.**

Ladies Fingers   Specializing in bedspreads, warps, and curtains. They also have some interesting fabric screens. Open Monday to Saturday 10am to 8pm. Phanthong Rd. ✆ **021/263-823.** www.ladiesfingers.net.

Les Artisans Lao ★★★   Les Artisans Laos Centre was created in 2004 to teach job skills to disadvantaged and marginalized persons, the majority of them living with a mild handicap. The center is supported by foundations, private businesses, and international organizations. Open Monday to Saturday 8am to 8pm, Sunday 10am to 6pm. Vat Inpeng St. ✆ **021/223-178.** www.artisanslao.com.

Tamarind   This upscale shop near the river sells the usual mixture of silk, handicrafts, and some clothing. Open daily 9am to 8pm. 55 Manthatourad Rd. ✆ **021/243-564.**

T'Shop Lai Galerie   The owner is dedicated to providing fair-trade products for those interested in both modern and traditional art in a range of mediums, furniture, and interesting handicrafts. Open Monday to Saturday 10am to 8pm. On Paeng Rd. ✆ **021/223-178.**

6 NIGHTLIFE

Vientiane was long known as a city that was firmly shut by midnight. Although it is still definitely a place that tends to close very early, there are now quite a number of venues where you can drink, dance, or talk until 1am, or even quite a lot later if the police are not in the throes of one of their periodic crackdowns. A lot of the restaurants and bars are indivisible. The Khop Chai Deu (p. 224) is most certainly all things to all men and all women. The Mex Alexia (p. 225) is another place that functions on both the bar and the restaurant level. Sticky Fingers (p. 225) is packed on weekends and is a hybrid bar/restaurant/cocktail lounge fulfilling all functions with a superbly stylish aplomb. In addition there are a few new chic cocktail lounges doing good business. It's also something of an open secret that if you want to be drinking and dancing into the wee hours it is now very feasible, although you will certainly have to know your venues. Also be aware that there is a fair aspect of sleaze among one or two of them with a slightly moth-eaten brigade of weary-looking prostitutes patrolling sadly from one to another like a pack of lost and slightly resentful penguins. They are, however, vastly outnumbered by boisterous backpackers loudly trumpeting legends of wild adventures and the joys of Beer Lao while enjoying British Premier League soccer and comparing iPod playlists.

BARS & CLUBS

The Bor Phen Nyang   This is a rooftop bar up four long flights of stairs on Fa Ngum. The views of the Mekong are absolutely superb and there is a bit of a breeze as the lights of Thailand twinkle invitingly from over the water. It has two pool tables and is pretty well laid out. The problem is that it can have a slightly sleazy and threatening atmosphere. A combination of drunk backpackers, ragged commercial sex workers, and some unsavory-looking types on visa renewals from across the river makes it all feel a little rough. They also have a selection of fairly indifferent Western food. The staff is very capable and friendly, however, and given its slightly explosive nature it is very well managed. The view is beautiful and worth the climb. Open daily 10am to midnight. Fa Ngum. © 020/787-3965.

Future Nightclub This is another deafening, thumping nightclub with frenetic lighting situated just past the Novotel. It gets very busy even on weekdays. Like Lunar 6 it follows the Thai format and there is no dance floor. Revelers stand around their table laden with Black Label and Beer Lao and jiggle about madly. Be aware that the Future has an aspect of very marked sleaze about it but not threateningly so. You will not be harassed if you wish to jiggle in peace. It ostensibly closes at 1:30am. In practice they are often open longer. Open daily 5pm to 1:30am. Luang Prabang Rd. (just past the Novotel).

The Jazzy Brick As chic as its name suggests, the Jazzy Brick's rampage to impose good taste means that customers will only be allowed in to sip expensive cocktails if they are properly attired; no shorts or sleeveless shirts allowed. The place is cool (quite literally, given the generous A/C) with lots of dark wood, brass fittings, and laid-back music, but it is also very expensive which may be intentional on their part to further deter those they view as the shorts-wearing riff raff. All said it is a class act. Open daily 11am to midnight. Setthathirath Rd. © 021/212-489.

Lunar 36 On the roof of the monstrous Don Chan Palace Hotel, the Lunar 36 adds to the already tasteless tackiness with wild abandon. It is a booming modern nightclub open 'til late and packed with a fairly wide assortment of customers from well-groomed visiting businessmen, to young clubbers, to a local good-time crowd. It's fun if you are in the mood for a weekend night out bathed in the glow of vulgar neon and deafened by the sound of techno tunes. It remains the most popular disco in town and is open until the small hours. There is, however, no dance floor. People dance about around the tables where they drink in a style borrowed from Thailand. Open daily 6am to 11:30pm. 6 Ban Piawat, Fa Ngum Rd. © 021/244-288. Fax 021/244-111. www.donchanpalacelaopdr.com.

Martini Lounge This is another upscale cocktail bar, and it is pretty relaxing and well thought out if you wish to lounge in the heavily air-conditioned half-light of an acquired international elegance. They have happy hours on Monday and Wednesday between 6pm and 7:30pm when you can get two-for-one cocktails. They also show movies upstairs on Monday, Tuesday, and Wednesday at 8pm. On Thursday they spread the word of salsa dancing. Nokeo Khumman. www.martini-laos.com.

On the Rock This is a lively nightclub with a live band that makes you feel you have been flung back through time to 1982, when big bouffant hairdos, tight stonewashed jeans, and white high-top sneakers were the order of the day. It is a world where the band Toto could actually be fashionable. Once you are over the shock of the time shift, you will have a great time as the young Lao crowd rocks out in a dated but charming fashion. This club is supposed to close at midnight, like everywhere else. It often seems to manage to still be open at 1:30am on weekends. Open daily 7:30pm–midnight. Luang Prabang Rd. No phone.

The Samlo Pub This is probably the latest opening bar or pub in town and as a result attracts an end-of-the-night crowd of the usual backpackers, expat late-risers, and single-minded sex workers. It is one of the oldest pubs in town and fills up after everywhere else has closed, going on until 2am in practice. Packed and smoky with live sports on TV, it is a little bit rough and ready to say the least. Open daily 4–11:30pm. Setthathirath Rd. C 021/222-308.

Spirit House ★   This relaxed bar is part of the chic Beau Rivage Hotel and attracts a lot of expats with its riverside location and quiet rustic atmosphere. It is characterized by comfortable cushions and lots of untreated dark wood. It is divided into two parts: One side is a wooden platform right on the river, while the main part of the bar is a few feet away on the other side of the narrow road, under the hotel itself. Open daily 7am–11pm. 8–10 Fa Ngum Rd. C 021/243-350. Fax 021/243-345.

The Wind West ★★   With a title that sounds curiously like a typing error, the Wind West has very dim lighting, and a superb live band. This is the late-night venue of choice for many expats and you don't see many tourists here. It's very convivial and becomes more so as both the Johnny Walker and the Beer Lao flow. It officially closes at midnight but in reality goes on until about 2am. Open daily 5pm–midnight. Luang Prabang Rd. C 020/200-0777.

LAO TRADITIONAL PERFORMANCE

There are daily dance performances at the **Lao National Theatre** (Nokeo Khoummane Rd. near the junction with Fa Ngum) in high season only. They are about an hour long and include traditional lowland dancing (Lao Loum) in addition to the dance of Laos's other ethnic groups. You can buy a ticket from 5:30pm onward at the theater itself or from a guesthouse or travel agency.

An even better option is the **Phatoke Laoderm** at the **Senglao Hotel** (Chou Anou; shows begin at 7:30pm). They have nightly shows with classical and folk dancing accompanied by some fine traditional Lao dishes.

ⓕ Fast Facts   Vientiane

American Express   Vientiane's Amex representative is **Diethelm Travel,** Namphu Square, Setthathirath Road (C 021/213-833; www.diethelmtravel.com).

ATMs   There are ATMs all over the center of the city, but they are not your best bet for getting cash from home. They only issue kip (with a limit of 700,000 kip). They also levy quite a hefty charge on top of any charges your own bank might levy. If you see a crowd of men in military fatigues carrying AK47 assault rifles milling around an ATM, don't be alarmed. They are hired to top up the cash supply. There's a **Banque Pour Le Commerce Extérieur Lao (BCEL)** ATM on Setthathirath Road (across the street from Joma Café), maximum withdrawal is 700,000 kip. The newly opened **Australia New Zealand Bank Vientiane (ANZV)** has two ATMs at their Lang Xang Avenue branch near the Victory Monument (at Blvd. Khounboulan intersection).

Banks & Currency Exchange   **Banque Pour Le Commerce Extérieur Lao (BCEL)** is on Pangkham Street down by the river, just west of the Lane Xang Hotel (C 021/213-200). At BCEL and most other banks, you can exchange money in all major currencies, change traveler's checks to U.S. dollars, and get cash advances on Visa and MasterCard; commission rates start at 3%. The nearby **Joint Development Bank** (75/1 Lan Xang; ✆ **021/213-535**) also exchanges cash and traveler's checks. You can also exchange money at Banque Setthathirat, near Wat Mixay. All banks are open Monday through Friday from 8:30am to 3:30pm. Other banks line Lane Xang Avenue; exchange counters dot the city.

Business Hours   Generally shops are open from around 9am to 8pm on weekdays with slightly reduced hours on weekends. Cafes tend to run from about 8:30am to 9pm or 10pm. Many restaurants open for lunch and dinner only and will be closed between 2 and 5pm. Government offices generally open Monday to Friday at 8:30am, close for lunch from noon until 1pm and close again at 5pm. Even with the fast-changing nightlife scene in Vientiane, most bars are closed by 11pm or midnight. There are quite a number of clubs and music venues that stay open unofficially past this time. Many businesses are closed on Sunday.

Doctors & Hospitals   Medical facilities in Laos are very basic indeed. Most foreigners living in Laos go to Thailand for treatment of all but the most trivial of ailments. The Friendship Bridge connecting Vientiane to Nong Khai in Thailand is open daily from 6am to 10pm. If there is a real medical emergency then crossing outside of these hours is allowed. Many travelers go **to AEK International Hospital** (✆ **+66-42/342-555**) or the **North Eastern Wattana General Hospital** (✆ **+66-1/833-4262**), both of which are in Udon Thani about 55km (34 miles) from the border. Both hospitals have English-speaking staff. For less complex medical procedures, **Nong Khai Wattana Hospital** in Nong Khai, Thailand (✆ **+66-1/833-4262**) is also an option.

Within Laos the **International Medical Clinic** operated by Mahosot Hospital is situated on the banks of the Mekong on Fa Ngum Road (✆ **021/214-022; open 24 hr.**). The **Australian Embassy** also operates a **modern medical clinic.** It is situated at Km 4 on Thadeua Road in Watnak Village. (✆ **021/353-840;** fax 021/353-841; open Mon–Fri 8:30am–12:30pm and 1:30–5pm). Most doctors and hospitals in Laos require payment in cash, regardless of whether you have health insurance. The Australian Embassy Clinic accepts both MasterCard and Visa.

Emergencies   For police, dial ✆ **991;** for fire, dial ✆ **190;** and for an ambulance, dial ✆ **195.** For medical evacuation, call **Lao Westcoast Helicopter Company** (✆ **021/512-023**).

Internet Access   There are Internet cafes all over the center of town. The ones we found to have the best speeds and biggest monitors were opposite the Joma Café on Setthathirath. Beware of using your own thumb drives to save data though, since virus protection is patchy. Many cafes and restaurants now have free Wi-Fi. Both Sticky Fingers (p. 225) and Full Moon Café two doors up (p. 224) have good connections. Full Moon Café functions as a daytime office for many, largely because of its very comfortable seating; comfortable benches lined with lots of big cushions. More and more places are installing Wi-Fi and it's getting much easier to find a connection in town.

Newspapers & Magazines   Laos is still very much Communist and this means that media is most definitely not free. *The Vientiane Times* is turgid and fairly pointless. You can buy the *Bangkok Post* in some bookshops or find copies to read in cafes and bakeries. You will have to line up to get your hands on them, since many people will be catching up on the outside world with the single newspaper available. Bookshops also sell international magazines such as *Time* and *Newsweek* for a fairly hefty price.

Pharmacies   Laos, like Vietnam and Cambodia, largely replaces proper medicine with self-diagnosis. As a result, there are many pharmacies around town selling antibiotics and other drugs using diagnosis methods that lack rigor or, in fact, any process of diagnosis whatsoever. If you get sick, head to a clinic. If you need something simple, the better pharmacies are to be found on Nong Bon Road near Talat Sao. Try and avoid Chinese-made drugs if you can and go for European and Thai imports and check the expiration date. The Australian Embassy Clinic (see "Doctors & Hospitals," above) also runs a fully equipped modern pharmacy.

Post Office   The general post office is at the corner of Khou Vieng Road and Lane Xang Avenue, opposite the Morning Market. Hours are Monday to Friday 8am to noon and 1 to 5pm, Saturday 8am to noon. EMS and FedEx services are just next door. For international calls, you are better off using one of the many Internet cafes.

Safety   Vientiane is a safer city than most, but it's still a good idea to take all the usual precautions, especially at night. There have been reported cases of bag snatching, so it's best not to leave things lying about or dangling invitingly from your shoulder. Also be aware that some of your fellow travelers might be the ones with light fingers. One aspect where the city can be difficult is on the road on a motorbike or car. Belying the gentle reputation of the country, Lao drivers can be downright aggressive. Keep space about you and take extra care at night when there will be a fair number of drunks behind the wheel.

Telephone   The city code for Vientiane is **021.** For international calls, go to an Internet cafe. It is cheaper, quicker, and more efficient. You can also buy a Lao sim card for your mobile for approximately $5, if you want to make local calls. Calls are cheap and refill cards can be found everywhere.

Vang Vieng & Surrounding Area

When you arrive in Vang Vieng, a visually unappealing town, you'll be faced with a choice: fight or flight. Resist the urge to flee. Fight through the central backpacker ghetto, with its guesthouse restaurants blasting Friends DVDs on a constant, mind-numbing loop, and make your way to the Nam Song River and the breathtaking karst peaks beyond. The surrounding natural beauty more than makes up for the appearance of the town itself—less than a mile across the fast-moving waters rises a complex of karst limestone mountains rippling into the distance to a great height, their summits often wreathed in trails of cloud. A few days spent exploring caves, kayaking, trekking, or just sitting at a riverside bar and enjoying a cocktail while admiring the scenery (a personal favorite) is highly recommended. Vang Vieng also lies at the start of one of Asia's great mountain journeys—the spectacular drive to Luang Prabang.

Beautiful as it is, the development of Vang Vieng is a serious cause for concern and is held up across Southeast Asia as a cautionary tale. It was popular on the hippie trail before the Communist takeover in 1975. After 1990, the stunning attractions of the area, not surprisingly, immediately drew tourists back. Vang Vieng became known as a mecca for those whose main aim was to take drugs and do little else. Sadly the problems have multiplied and Vang Vieng today is hauntingly beautiful but tragically blighted. There is little that is Lao about Vang Vieng town. Many are here simply to party on a circuit that stretches from Sydney to Koh Phan Gan in Thailand to Goa in India. It is rather like the worst kind of spring break on Daytona Beach, except that the theme is tie-dye laced with narcotics. It is often true that budget tourists have a relatively low environmental footprint. Their cultural footprint, however, can be devastating.

1 VANG VIENG ESSENTIALS

ORIENTATION

Vang Vieng is tiny. It lies along the Nam Song from north to south parallel to Rte. 13. The center of town is around the junction on the main street. Turning left (if heading north) you take the road that directly lines the river. There is a small right turnoff there leading to a cluster of cheaper restaurants and guesthouses. If you turn left you arrive at a series of more tranquil hotels and resorts.

Spanning the Nam Song are a number of narrow wooden bridges. The opposite banks of the river are being developed fast and there are already quite a number of restaurants and hotels. In Vang Vieng there are no road or street names. This is no problem, since the town really only has two streets.

GETTING THERE

Vang Vieng is a smooth 3-hour bus ride north on Rte. 13 from Vientiane. There are numerous daily departures from the **Morning Market** (℃ 021/216-507), and tickets are 57,000 kip on a VIP bus and 90,000 kip on a minibus. Bus connection to Luang Prabang is a popular option, a bumpy but scenic 6-hour ride for just 105,000 kip. However, attacks just north of town mean that road travel must be undertaken with caution. Ask around about the current situation, and do not be surprised if there is a bus-company employee toting a machine gun onboard.

The bus station (℃ 023/511-341) is just outside of town on Rte. 13 heading north about 2km (1¼ miles) from the main junction, and there are plenty of tuk-tuk drivers there who can take you to the town center or the guesthouse of your choosing.

GETTING AROUND

Vang Vieng is a very small place and you can walk everywhere. Many choose to do this without shoes, despite the health risks. You can also hire bicycles for $1 a day or motorbikes for $8 a day from many guesthouses.

VISITOR INFORMATION & TOURS

Quite a number of local guesthouses and operators offer tours of various sorts.

Other operators offering the same mixture of outdoor activities are situated on the road that runs down from the main junction to the old market and on to the river. They include **Wonderful Tours** (℃ 023/511-566), **Riverside Tour** (℃ 023/511-091) and **Namthip Tours** (℃ 020/562-3536).

Green Discovery If you are looking for eco-tours and adventure activities, Green Discovery is the acknowledged expert with a full range of kayaking, rafting, caving, climbing, cycling, and motorcycling tours. They have an excellent safety record. They provide tours where you can enjoy a mixture of activities. Their office is right on the main junction next to the Xayoh Restaurant (same company). They will also tailor activity tours to your personal needs. In addition to the potpourri of outdoor activities on offer they also offer a 1- to 3-day tutorial climbing course.

Main junction next to Xayoh Restaurant. ℃ **023/511-230.** www.greendiscoverylaos.com. Daily 8am–10pm.

X-plore-asia X-plore-asia offers a range of caving and trekking tours. They also specialize in kayaking.

Luang Prabang Rd. ℃ **020/255-5176.** www.x-plore-asia.com. Daily 8am–10pm.

⟨Fast Facts **Vang Vieng**

Banks & Currency Exchange The **BCEL** (℃ **023/511-434;** Mon–Fri 8:30am–3:30pm) is on the main street south of the main junction. There is, however, a convenient exchange kiosk (open daily 8:30am–3:30pm and 5–8pm) in the center of town opposite the Dokeun Guesthouse near the main junction. They change cash and traveler's checks and make advances on Visa and MasterCard. There is also an ATM issuing kip only (up to 700,000 kip).

Hospital   A hospital is by the river heading south opposite the Ban Sabi Bungalows.

Internet Access   There are Internet cafes everywhere catering largely to the hordes needing to use Skype. The best by far is **Magnet Internet** (Main Rd., opposite the Nazim Restaurant; ℂ **020/541-7894**). They have fast connections and work to maintain their machines and keep them virus free.

Post Office   A **post office** (ℂ **023/511-434**) is located next to the Old Market.

2 WHERE TO STAY

If you want to avoid the mayhem of Veng Vieng, we recommend that you stay away from the center of town and head south down the river past the hospital. This area is much quieter and you'll find hotels, guesthouses, and restaurants where you can enjoy the amazing scenery in relative tranquillity.

MODERATE

Ban Sabai Bungalow   This quiet collection of riverside bungalows, owned by the same folks who run the Xayoh Café and Green Discovery tours, provides a real lesson in the Lao language. Ban means "house," sabai means "calm and relaxed," and you'll pick up words such as ngiep ("quiet") and baw mi banha ("no problem") if you stay long enough. Rooms are simple, rustic, but clean bungalows. One bungalow abuts the river, while the others form a quiet courtyard area. The riverside restaurant is tops.

Ban Sysavang (along the river just south and west of the town center). ℂ **023/511-088.** 13 units. $28 standard; $30 double; $34 deluxe. MC, V. **Amenities:** Restaurant; bar. In room: A/C.

Bungalow Thavansouk ★   In this prime riverside spot, you'll find a range of neatly fitted, affordable bungalows. Accommodations start at basic guesthouse standards and go all the way up to a unique riverside suite with—get this—a picture window next to the bathtub with views of the river. Rooms vary in age, quality, and mildew smell, so ask to have a peek before checking in. Lounge chairs on the lawn face the breathtaking wall of karst peaks across the river. Riverside rooms here have better views than those at Ban Sabai Bungalow (see above). The attached Sunset restaurant and bar serves good local fare and is a happening spot at dusk.

Ban Sysavang (along the Nam Song just south and west of the town center). ℂ **023/511-096.** Fax 023/511-215. www.thavonsouk.com. 44 units. High season $25 garden view, $45 river view, $55–$75 traditional Lao house; low season $20–$70. MC, V. **Amenities:** Restaurant; concierge can arrange tours and all rentals. In room: A/C, TV, minibar (not available in garden-view rooms).

The Elephant Crossing Hotel ★★   The Elephant Crossing, run by a Laotian/Australian couple, is your best option in Vang Vieng. The hotel boasts friendly staff, fantastic views of the karsts, and spotless mildew-scent-free rooms. Standard rooms are the popular option for their views from the top two floors of the hotel. The decision to place deluxe rooms on the lower floors was based on weight—they have cozy, if heavy, bathtubs with sliding doors so you can enjoy the view while having a soak. The garden fronting the hotel is very quiet and a great place if you have children and want to keep

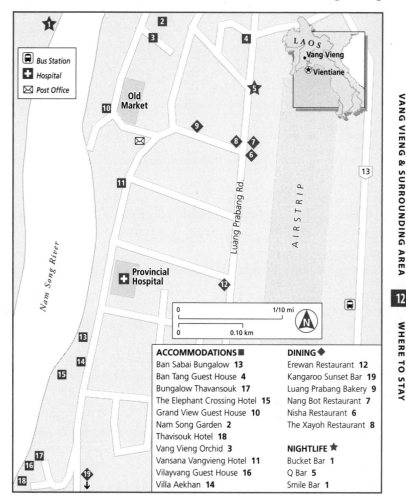

ACCOMMODATIONS ■

Ban Sabai Bungalow **13**
Ban Tang Guest House **4**
Bungalow Thavansouk **17**
The Elephant Crossing Hotel **15**
Grand View Guest House **10**
Nam Song Garden **2**
Thavisouk Hotel **18**
Vang Vieng Orchid **3**
Vansana Vangvieng Hotel **11**
Vilayvang Guest House **16**
Villa Aekhan **14**

DINING ◆

Erewan Restaurant **12**
Kangaroo Sunset Bar **19**
Luang Prabang Bakery **9**
Nang Bot Restaurant **7**
Nisha Restaurant **6**
The Xayoh Restaurant **8**

NIGHTLIFE ★

Bucket Bar **1**
Q Bar **5**
Smile Bar **1**

an eye on them, either from your room or the riverfront restaurant. A leisurely repast at the riverside restaurant is a fantastic way to start and/or end the day.

Ban Viengkeo (along the Nam Song, next door to Ban Sabai Bungalows). ✆ **023/511-232.** Fax 023/511-232. www.theelephantcrossinghotel.com. 31 units. $45–$50 double; $80 suite. MC, V. **Amenities:** Restaurant; bar; concierge can arrange tours. In room: A/C, TV, minibar.

Thavisouk Hotel ★★   This is a well-equipped and very pleasant hotel slightly out of town that combines convenience, luxury, and a fantastic location. The main hotel is modern. The rooms are spacious and light with floor-to-ceiling windows and understated but elegant, traditional decoration. The riverside balconies offer great views on the upper floors. By the river is an attached resort with well-appointed bungalows. They are smaller than the hotel rooms and the approach is entirely different. One gets the impression that they are designed to appeal to Thai tourists, which is no bad thing since their standards can be exacting. There is an attached restaurant on a deck right on the river, which serves Lao and Thai food. The food is excellent, especially the Tom Yam. The view is superb. The one minor drawback is that the restaurant (main courses 15,000 kip–35,000 kip) offers karaoke in the evening, which certainly affects the natural peace of the environment.

Riverside Rd., south of town. (€ 023/511-340. www.thavisouk-hotel.com. 71 units. $25 resort double; $35 hotel double. MC, V. **Amenities:** Restaurant; Internet; room service. *In room:* A/C, TV, fridge.

Vansana Vangvieng Hotel ★   The inviting outdoor pool (nonguests can use it for a 20,000 kip) is what sets this place apart from the other riverside hotels. Stick with the doubles, as the suites are just standards with a couch. Rooms have wood floors and a few Lao fabrics for color. The restaurant is right on the river and is a great place to have a drink and watch the sunset.

Ban Sysavang (along the Nam Song just south and west of the town center). (€ 023/511-598. Fax 023/511-600. www.vansanahotel-group.com. 38 units. $35–$58 double. MC, V. **Amenities:** Restaurant; pool. In room: A/C, TV.

INEXPENSIVE

Ban Tang Guest House   This is a place with some character since it is in an original old all-wood house. The larger A/C rooms are like minisuites with a slightly odd front living room complete with comfy sofas and lurid plastic plants. The beds are oversoft, but that's hardly a surprise since nothing here is very new. Many of the rooms have large wooden balconies. Since it's all wood and quite old, don't be surprised if you should see the odd spider.

Riverside Rd. (€ 023/511-406. 14 units. 40,000 kip fan double; 90,000 kip A/C double. No credit cards. *In room:* A/C, TV.

Grand View Guest House ★★ (Finds)   This is a new guesthouse right by the river at the end of the road leading from the main street. Its courtyard and large entrance make it appear rather grand but it is actually quite modestly priced. This is one of the best budget options in town. If you get one of the upper rooms facing the river you will be faced by views so beautiful that you may never leave the spacious balcony during daylight hours. The rooms are large and airy and well appointed in a rather spartan style. The management is also very friendly and helpful and can put you in the know on most things, including tours and onward transport. Sadly the hotel suffers from evening noise from the "Bucket Bar" across the river.

Riverside Rd. (near the tubing operator by the river). (€ 023/511-474. 22 units. 70,000 kip fan double facing the street; 100,000 kip fan double facing the river; 150,000 kip A/C double facing the street; 250,000 kip A/C double facing the river. No credit cards. In room: A/C, TV.

Nam Song Garden   A modest guesthouse on the river, the Nam Song Garden offers a variety of rooms including the rental of a small house to groups. It is a favorite with rock climbers. They have had some problems with robberies in the past hence each room now has a safe. Best to use it.

Riverside Rd. (€ 023/511-544. 14 units. 90,000 kip river-view double. No credit cards.

Vang Vieng Orchid   This is an excellent riverside option. Balconies are very large in the riverside rooms, which shows some foresight on the part of the builders since the views are superb. The rooms are bright and well equipped. It can be a noisy in the evening though since there are a slew of backpacker bars on the opposite island blasting out techno pop.

Riverside Rd. ✆ **023/511-172.** 19 units. 80,000 fan double; 120,000 kip A/C double. No credit cards. *In room:* A/C.

Vang Vieng Resort   Down a small road, right in the lee of the mountain just across the river about .5km (.3 mile) from town on the way to Tham Jang cave, the Vang Vieng Resort is very peaceful. Separate bungalows set in leafy grounds (frequented by a not very energetic crowd of chickens) make stay here very tranquil. The bungalows are a bit aged but perfectly acceptable if a little dark.

Next to the bridge to Tham Jang Cave. ✆ **023/511-050.** 28 units. 80,000 kip fan double; 120,000 kip A/C double. No credit cards. *In room:* A/C, TV.

Vilayvang Guest House   This a good-value midrange option with rooms inside the main building and bungalows outside. The bungalows are very nice, if slightly dark, but a little far from the river compared to other operations on the same drag. This is reflected in the price, and we are only talking about a few feet. The staff and management are very relaxed and friendly.

Riverside Rd., south of town. ✆ **023/511-673.** 25 units. $18 resort double. No credit cards. **Amenities:** Restaurant. In room: A/C, TV, fridge.

Villa Aekhan   This is a new and slightly peculiar hotel. The whole of the downstairs is a cavernous handicrafts and textiles shop. Upstairs are eight clean, spacious rooms, which are both airy and well appointed. Only two have river views since the building has been constructed perpendicular to the river. They are the same price as all the other rooms, so are a bargain if you manage to get one. There is a balcony at the front of the building.

Riverside Rd. ✆ **023/511-357.** 8 units. 150,000 kip double. No credit cards. In room: A/C, TV.

3 WHERE TO DINE

Whereas Vientiane is memorable when it comes to dining and Luang Prabang can certainly hold its own, Vang Vieng is known for the fairly mundane quality of its restaurants. You don't eat badly in Vang Vieng, it's just that you don't eat very well either. If you have been in Vientiane before enjoying the astonishing range and quality of food on offer, be prepared to lower your standards a little when in Vang Vieng. In the center of town most restaurants are attached to guesthouses and are of the cheap backpacker variety with menus that are all roughly similar. It is the usual mixture of Asian-light, pizza, and pancakes. The Xayoh right on the crossroads is a little more upmarket, but the food is nothing special, being rather dreary and insipid. It is a good place to escape the surreal tyranny of blasting TVs.

Generally when in the center of the town do not order anything on the menu that is termed "happy" unless you actually want to get high. They also put all kind of things in the milkshakes. Some of the restaurants here are really not a place to bring the children, although they might make their own way to them of their own accord when they leave high school. There are restaurants by the river attached to hotels serving some very good Lao and Thai food if you head south toward the hospital. The Thavonsouk Resort, the Elephant Crossing, and the Thavisouk Hotel all have excellent restaurants serving Lao and Thai food in peaceful riverside locations with great views. The Thavisouk fires up the karaoke machine in the evening if they are entertaining a Thai tour group, but if you can survive that, the tom yam is great Note that the restaurants below do not take credit cards.

Erewan Restaurant LAO/WESTERN   A good restaurant with tasty, simple food. This is not a place for gourmet eating but it is a place for wholesome fare in a pleasing atmosphere where blaring TV screens do not figure.

Luang Prabang Rd. ✆ 023/511-093. Main courses 30,000 kip. Daily 8am–11pm.

Nang Bot Restaurant ★ LAO   The Nang Bot is a slight anomaly in the center of Van Vieng since it serves food that is genuinely Lao in an obviously Lao environment. They do not have a TV. The decor is traditional, muted but pleasant, and characterized by Lao silk.

Main Rd. ✆ 023/511-018. Main courses 15,000 kip–40,000 kip. Daily 7am–11pm.

Nisha Restaurant INDIAN   The Nisha is a big rival to the ubiquitous Nizam chain of south Indian restaurants in Van Vieng. The food and service are better on every level. The masala chai is the real thing and the dosa is more than adequate.

Main St. ✆ 023/511-579. Main courses 20,000 kip. Daily 7am–11pm.

Kangaroo Sunset Bar ★★ WESTERN   Past the hospital heading south right near the main bridge to the other side of the Nam Song, the Kangaroo Sunset serves the usual mishmash of vaguely Thai and vaguely European food. Generally it's more edible than the stuff served in town. It is far from the noise of the center of town, the staff is smiley and fun, and the views are superb. Mick, the Australian owner, runs one of the most genuinely friendly operations in town.

Riverside Rd. ✆ 020/771-4291. Main courses 30,000 kip. Daily 9am–11pm.

Luang Prabang Bakery ★ WESTERN   This is an excellent place for breakfast with good pastries, croissants, and coffee in a nicely furnished dark wood atmosphere. They also do main courses and pizza.

Next to the BCEL, main junction. ✆ 023/511-145. Main courses 30,000 kip–40,000 kip. Daily 7am–11pm.

The Xayoh Restaurant LAO/WESTERN   The Xayoh has an inviting environment with an open terrace right on the main junction. It is a very pleasant place to enjoy a glass of chilled chardonnay, but the food is disappointing and resembles the kind of fare you get in airports—intensely average but perfectly edible.

Main junction. ✆ 023/511-088. Main courses 25,000 kip–30,00 kip. Daily 7am–11pm.

4 NIGHTLIFE

Vang Vieng has a number of bars catering to the backpacker crowd. They serve beer in bottles or you can buy cheap spirits in plastic buckets that come equipped with straws so that one bucket may be shared among many. Young people gather around their buckets and guzzle away. The main bar of this sort in town is the **Q Bar** on the main street about

20m (66 ft.) from the main junction heading north. There is an island in the river opposite the Vang Vieng Orchid Hotel where a whole slew of bars have appeared. They are effectively giant shacks with overworked sound systems that do little for the natural evening serenity of Vang Vieng. The aptly named **Bucket Bar** and the longer-running **Smile Bar** seem the most popular but that can change week by week.

5 ATTRACTIONS

ROCK CLIMBING

Between November and May, Green Discovery (p. 243) offers rock climbing among the spectacular limestone karsts on the other side of the Nam Song. They run a 1-day to 3-day tuition course and you can rent all the specialized gear you need. The instructors are skilled and the fee includes all transport costs and lunch. More than 100 routes have been pegged by world-class climbers and along with Krabi in Thailand, Vang Vieng is very much on the Asia climbing circuit. Tham Non (Sleeping Cave) with over 20 identified climbs and the nearby Sleeping Wall are the most popular climbing locations. There are more than 50 bolted routes in the area graded from 5b to 8c according to the French system of grading.

CAVING, TREKKING & KAYAKING

The ethereal limestone karsts that tower over Vang Vieng are riddled with caves. Those who enjoy cave exploring will find themselves in a paradise of sorts. Some caves are very big with stunning formations, and some are tiny, comfortably accessible only to the extremely thin. Many are really covered rivers and small lakes, and one can swim or kayak through. Many also have religious significance, so look for shrines and Buddha images.

You can visit most of the caves, either by yourself or as part of an organized tour. **Most guesthouses** or tour operators can sell you a package that combines caving, trekking, kayaking, and tubing. They will also take you to nearby ethnic villages. You can also buy a **2-day tour,** which includes a visit to the Organic Farm and overnight camping. Meals are generally included.

With the exception of trips organized by **Green Discovery,** all of the tours you go on will actually be part of a Vang Vieng cooperative arrangement run by the same people. Wherever you booked the tour, the same set of guides lead the same set of six trips. You can check with different guesthouses to make sure you get the cheapest price, but essentially they are all part of a cartel. A 1-day trip should cost about $12, a 2-day trip $350, and a half-day trip costs $8. The guides are not uniformly as good as one another and some of the equipment is old.

Green Discovery (which we recommend, p. 243) runs a host of combination tours and can also put together a personalized package. They are a bit more expensive than the cartel, but only by a few dollars. Their guides are better trained, more skilled, and can speak better English. In the end the primary issue is safety.

You can visit the caves on your own. Maps are sold in Vang Vieng. It is best to hire a bicycle or motorbike to cover the 3 to 10km (1¾–6 miles) to the sites, or hire a tuk-tuk, which will take you to the caves for 5,000 kip per person in a party of about six. Make sure the day fee is well established in advance. Some drivers have been known to raise the fee after the fact.

Tham Poukham, 7km (4⅓ miles) from town, is the most popular cave around Vang Vieng. It costs 5,000 kip to enter. The main features are a beautiful, cool lagoon, which will look very inviting if you are feeling damp and sweaty (which you will be since it's a steep and slippery climb to get here) with its shimmering blue and green waters. Apart from swimming the cave is famous for a Thai-style reclining Buddha. Poukham is reached by a pretty but bumpy road to the village of Ban Na Thong, where there are signs showing the way to the cave about 1km (.6 miles) on. **Tham Non** (admission 5,000 kip), or the "Sleeping Cave" is about 4km (2½ miles) north of town. It earned its name because when Vang Vieng was being bombed during the war, people would take shelter there during the night. **Tham Xang** (admission 5,000 kip) and **Tham Hoi** (admission 5,000 kip) are located in the same dramatic limestone outcrop about 15km (9.3 miles) north of town on the road to Luang Prabang. Take a left at the village of Sinsomxai where there is a turnoff to the caves. Tham Xang houses a large Buddha image and is of quite some religious significance to local people. Tham Hoi is a huge cave running at least 7km (4.3 miles) deep. Some locals say it is even deeper. You should only go any distance into the cave if you have an experienced guide. There is a Buddha image at the entrance of the cave. **Tham Chang** (admission 10,000 kip) is close to town and very popular with both Thai and foreign tourists. You go through the grounds of the Vang Vieng Resort (for a 10,000 kip two-way fee!) and cross a small bridge to some manicured grounds on the other side of the river. Tham Chang was used as a fortress against the Chinese Haw invaders in the late 19th century. Its name translates as firm and unwavering. It is by no means the most spectacular cave in the area, but there is a great view of the valley from a bird's-eye perspective. **Tham Phu Thao** (admission 5,000 kip) stretches for 2km (1.2 miles) and the tunnels are lined with huge stalactites and stalagmites. There is a subterranean pool where you can swim in the rainy season. In the dry season, you can continue beyond the pool and explore the cave in its entirety. There is also a Hmong village nearby peopled by returnee refugees from Thailand. They were driven from their homes during the war of the '60s and '70s and ended up in exile but were refused admission to the United States or other Western countries. They were returned to Laos and settled here.

Many combine caving with kayaking, which costs $12 a day and if you wish you can make the trip all the way to Vientiane. Green Discovery runs the safest operation with experienced guides, although there are many other companies that will give you a cheaper deal.

TUBING

Floating down the Nam Song River on an inflated tractor inner tube has become almost a religious ritual for the thousands of people who come to Vang Vieng to go tubing. A whole mini-industry of restaurants and bars has grown up around it, and many local people have become prosperous on the simple activity of floating about. Although it is now associated with Vang Vieng in the minds of many visitors, it is something you will see kids doing all over the country.

All guesthouses will be able to organize tubing trips for you. Wherever you buy the trip, they are all part of the same collective cartel based near the old market. You can also just go directly to this central "depot," next to the old market on the junction next to the riverside road. You can't miss it since there are huge stacks of inner tubes behind the front desk. For 35,000 kip (plus a 60,000 kip deposit), you will be driven about 4km (2½ miles) north of town and issued with your inner tube. From here you will float back to town

The Amazing Mountain Journey to Luang Prabang

The road journey from Vang Vieng to Luang Prabang is one of the most spectacular journeys in Asia. Among aficionados of two-wheeled travel whether self-propelled (and you would have to be a serious cyclist to undertake it) or on a motorcycle, Rte. 13 is famous for its spectacular winding roads and mountain views of simply unbelievable beauty. You start by driving along the banks of the Nam Song River. The jagged karst formations you see in Vang Vieng continue. This area is peppered with caves and if you have time you can stop off and explore. Bear in mind that you still have 250km (155 miles) of winding roads to go. The elevation starts to get higher and the limestone outcrops get bigger. Once past the town of Kasi they are much bigger indeed, jungled walls rising vertically from the valley like a giant tidal wave of solid rock. As you wind your way up to Poukhoun this dramatic scenery is laid out below you: a huge green carpet of natural peaks, abrupt precipices, and sharp ridges wreathed with wisps of cloud, and lit by intense sunshine. Just before Poukhoun itself a viewing platform has been constructed, and it is a great place to get an early lunch and take in this natural amphitheater. Once past Poukhoun the mountain scenery starts to change. Sharp and jagged limestone gives way to huge, rounded mountains stretching far into the distance. You make your way along roads cut into the hillside, each turn revealing yet another astounding view. The whole route is lined with small villages of varying ethnicity where hundreds of children wave maniacally, which you are free to reciprocate if it's safe. In the late afternoon you slowly start to descend into the mountain panorama itself until you reach the valley floor. Again a straight wooded road takes you along the banks of the Nam Khan River and into Luang Prabang.

being treated to some of the finest views Asia has to offer. Along the way are bamboo restaurants, rope swings, and volleyball courts.

Note: Tubing while intoxicated or during inclement weather is dangerous—don't do it. Also, women should not spend too much time wandering around only in a bikini. The Lao are modest and it offends them, however used to it they may seem.

Luang Prabang & Northern Laos

Northern Laos is part of a chain of wild and mountainous country stretching from north Thailand and on to northern Vietnam. Dramatic limestone scenery dissected by rivers sometimes torrid and sometimes tranquil provides the setting for hill tribe settlements, enigmatic remnants of past empires, and vast wild areas of immense ecological worth.

Set among all of this stunning scenery is the jewel of northern Laos and indeed Southeast Asia as a whole—Luang Prabang. Many a traveler's tale in Luang Prabang begins like this: "Well, I was only supposed to stay here for a couple of days, but . . ." The quiet street-side cafes, ancient temples, and laid-back, friendly locals give this town a tranquillity that has sucked many unsuspecting visitors in for weeks (or years) at a time. A visit here feels like a vacation from your vacation.

The town is fed by rivers and a journey up either the Mekong or the Nam Ou will take you through a land of incredible mountains, dense forests, and contorted limestone outcrops alternating between being clothed in mist, grilled by the sun, and pounded by intense monsoon rains.

1 LUANG PRABANG

When talking of Luang Prabang it is hard not to employ superlatives, and pretty much everyone who has spent time in the town does. It is a place where history, atmosphere, and terrain combine to create something of astonishing beauty. Set in the northern mountains where the Nam Khan tributary joins the Mekong, the surrounding hills are rugged, jungle clad, and spectacular. The town itself is a magical mixture of some of the most ancient and exquisite Buddhist temples in the region combined with the sort of intimate French colonial architecture that often makes towns in Indochina so atmospheric.

Start your day at dawn, when the temple drums break the early morning silence and saffron-clad monks walk the misty streets to receive rice from the townspeople for their daily meal. Buddhists believe that by giving rice in this life ("making merit"), they are ensuring that they will not go hungry in their next life. Tourists can also participate in this ancient tradition, but should understand that although it has become an attraction of sorts, it is still a sacred ritual.

The rest of the day can be spent seeing the sights or relaxing and soaking in the atmosphere. The town itself is the main attraction, though, and the timeworn streets will undoubtedly reveal hidden gems and memorable encounters, whether it's a store selling the perfect antique or a temple housing monks anxious to practice their English. Add into this mix of perfect architectural yin and yang the fact that the streets are not crowded with traffic (buses and lorries are not allowed) so noise levels are low and stress levels even lower. Even with all the development of facilities purely designed for tourism, the soul of

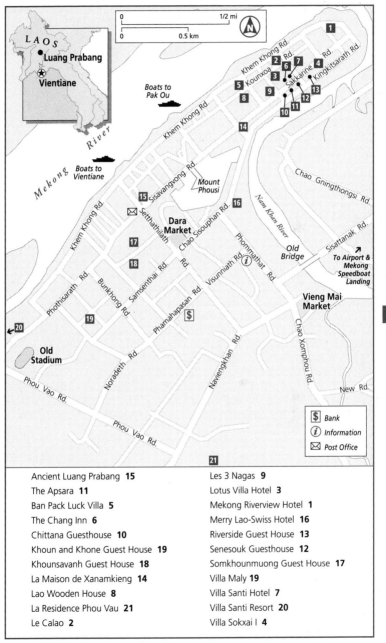

Ancient Luang Prabang **15**	Les 3 Nagas **9**
The Apsara **11**	Lotus Villa Hotel **3**
Ban Pack Luck Villa **5**	Mekong Riverview Hotel **1**
The Chang Inn **6**	Merry Lao-Swiss Hotel **16**
Chittana Guesthouse **10**	Riverside Guest House **13**
Khoun and Khone Guest House **19**	Senesouk Guesthouse **12**
Khounsavanh Guest House **18**	Somkhounmuong Guest House **17**
La Maison de Xanamkieng **14**	Villa Maly **19**
Lao Wooden House **8**	Villa Santi Hotel **7**
La Residence Phou Vau **21**	Villa Santi Resort **20**
Le Calao **2**	Villa Sokxai I **4**

Luang Prabang is intact and the feel of the city has remained unaltered over the last 15 years. The massive increase in restaurants and the introduction of a Thailand-style night market are part of inevitable changes as the city becomes ever more established on the Indochina tourist circuit. Unlike Siem Reap in Cambodia, Luang Prabang accommodates the changes without some of the circus like aspects that have become part and parcel of a visit to Angkor. In Luang Prabang the views remain the same and they are absolutely superb.

For centuries before Luang Prabang was founded, several Thai-Lao principalities flourished in the area around it, in the valleys of the Mekong. It used to be called Muang Sua before it was conquered by a Tai Prince called Khun Lo in A.D. 698. From the 11th to the 14th centuries, there was a city called Xieng Dong Xieng Thong on this site. From 1185 to 1191, Xieng Dong Xieng Thong came under the rule of the mighty Khmer god-king Jayavarman VII.

King Fa Ngum created the first truly Lao Kingdom, called Lan Xang, or Kingdom of One Million Elephants in 1353. At this time, the city was known as Xaxa. In 1357 the name was changed to Meuang Xieng Thong, or Gold City District. After that, King Fa Ngum's successor, King Visoun, received from his Khmer overlords a gift of a Sinhalese Buddha image called Pha Bang. It is from this image that the name Luang Prabang is derived.

In 1545 King Phothisarat moved the capital of the kingdom to Vientiane although Luang Prabang continued to thrive. The kingdom of Lan Xang fractured into three separate entities in 1694 on the death of the heirless King Vongsa. Luang Prabang declined under the grandson of the Vongsa. It didn't get better as time went on. Burmese, Chinese, and Vietnamese marauders imposed their will at various times. In 1887 Chinese "Haw" bandits attacked the city and the Luang Prabang administration invited the French to take the city under its colonial wing. The town developed quite fast under the French, not least because they, like tourists today, took an immediate fancy to the place. They allowed the monarchy to continue and knowingly prettified the already very beautiful city. Through the Japanese ascendancy of World War II and the wars of independence against the French, Luang Prabang was thankfully spared damage. After the 1975 Pathet Lao victory the last Luang Prabang monarch, Sisavang Vatthana, and his family were sent to a remote incarceration where they succumbed to hunger and lack of medical care.

In 1989 after the Vietnamese declared *doi moi,* or their own form of perestroika, Luang Prabang began to emerge from the dilapidation visited upon it by the harsh years of collectivization and a planned economy that drained the city of its entrepreneurs and educated elite. Over the next decade the city rapidly blossomed as the old French colonial buildings were restored, flourishing businesses came into being, and tourists enthusiastically flooded in to enjoy this jewel of Indochina.

LUANG PRABANG ESSENTIALS
Orientation
Luang Prabang is set out on a slightly crooked grid system. Most of the most beautiful parts of the city are on a narrow finger of land extending to where the Mekong joins the Nam Khan River. What could be called the center of town extends up from the long-distance boat pier. Thanon Kitsarat heads southeast, past Phousi hill and the Dara Market on the left to the crossroads where it meets Thanon Mahapatsaman and Thanon Wisunarat. Most of the old French municipal buildings cluster around the beginning of Thanon Kitsarat near the boat pier. To get to both the main cluster of bars and

The Fate of the King

Savang or Sisavang Vatthana was the last king of Laos. He ruled from 1959 after his father's death, until he was forced to abdicate after Pathet Lao victory in 1975. He and all his family were sent to a reeducation camp and after that the truth of their fate becomes unclear apart from the certainty that they died. Educated in France, Prince Savang earned a degree from the École Libre des Sciences Politiques (now called Sciences Po), the elite academy for French diplomats. After a decade, Savang Vatthana came home, but his spoken Lao was now so shaky he had to relearn it. Savang married Queen Khamphoui in 1930, and they had six children, Crown Prince Vong Savang, Prince Sisavang Savang, Prince Savang, Prince Sauryavong Savang, Princess Savivanh Savang, and Princess Thala Savang. The king was devoutly religious and took his role seriously as protector of the Buddhist faith.

Succeeding to the throne in 1959, he was never officially crowned, postponing his coronation until the end of the war. After Communist victory Savang refused to leave the country. He was arrested in March 1977 along with all his family. The new regime feared that Savang Vatthana, who then had lived quietly in the Royal Palace as a private citizen, would become a symbol of popular resistance. As a result, he was suddenly spirited away by helicopter to Houaphan along with Queen Khamboui and Crown Prince Say Vongsavang. Imprisoned in "Camp Number One," the crown prince died on May 2, 1978, and the king 11 days later of starvation. The queen died on December 12, 1981. According to an eyewitness, all were buried in unmarked graves outside the camp's perimeter.

restaurants on Sisavangvong Road head northeast of the boat pier with Phu Si hill to your right. You will soon see the ornate gold decoration and dark wood of some of the most ancient wats in Laos. Sisavangvong Road to the east side of the narrow strip of land between the rivers has become a tourist high street of Internet cafes, bars, and restaurants. The parallel road on the western side of this small riverine peninsula runs directly by the banks of the Mekong. You can do this whole district in a half an hour or so by foot. It remains one of the world's most relaxed and delightful strolls. To take in the often spectacular Mekong sunset, head back to the boat pier. The sun sinks behind a small mountain on the other side of the Mekong in a giant orange ball silhouetting the boats moored to the south of the pier.

The airport and northern bus terminal are to the northeast of the city while the southern bus terminal is to the southwest.

GETTING THERE

BY PLANE **Lao Airlines** (© **021/212-057** or 214-427 for reservations; www.laoairlines. com) has daily flights from Vientiane to Luang Prabang for $76 one-way. Their routes to Thailand are to Bangkok (one flight a day there and back), Chiang Mai (one flight a day there and back) and Udon Thani (two flights a week). To Cambodia they fly only to Siem Reap (two flights a day there and back). To Hanoi in Vietnam (one flight a day there and back). Domestic connections from Luang Prabang are to Vientiane (at least three flights a day) and Pakse (two flights a week). There are also infrequent flights to Phongsali and Xieng Khuang. There are no direct flights to the far north; for that, you'll need to fly directly from Vientiane.

Bangkok Airways (57/6 Sisavangvong Rd.; ✆ **071/253-334** or 253-253; www. bangkokair.com) also flies twice daily between Bangkok and Luang Prabang. You can book online at their website. **Vietnam Airlines** (Luang Prabang International Airport; ✆ **071/213-048;** www.vietnamairlines.com) flies to and from Luang Prabang from both Hanoi and Siem Reap five times a week.

The Luang Prabang International Airport (✆ **071/212-173**) handles international flights from Chiang Mai, Bangkok, Hanoi, and Siem Reap. Visas are available on arrival at the airport. The airport is about 4km (2½ miles) from town, and transport is best arranged through any hotel. Otherwise, you can hire a tuk-tuk for $5. Going the other way, get your guesthouse or hotel to organize a tuk-tuk. It should cost about $3.

BY BUS   The overland route to Luang Prabang from Vientiane's Northern bus terminal takes about 10 hours by public bus, assuming there are no difficulties (breakdowns are common). There are international warnings about travel on this stretch, and though it has been quiet in recent years, you should ask around before hitting the road. The trip is bumpy and winds interminably, and local buses are often packed. If you suffer from travel sickness then be sure to bring the right pills or you are in line for 10 hours of pure, unremitting, queasy, hell. However, the jaw-dropping scenery, past the mountains and limestone formations at Vang Vieng and several Hmong hill villages, is well worth it. The bus costs 150,000 kip and has a few morning departures from Vientiane's Northern Bus Station. Go early to get a seat. Luang Prabang's Naluang (Southern) Bus Station is a 10,000 kip per person shared tuk-tuk ride from the town center. There are also daily connections to Phonsavan (90,000 kip) and the far north.

There are two main bus stations in Luang Prabang. One for traffic to and from the south called Naluang, the other for traffic to and from the north called Kiew Lot Sai Nuan. To get from one station to another, take a tuk-tuk for around 10,000 kip per person. Double that fare at night.

A faster alternative to a public bus is to take a minibus. You can buy a ticket from most travel agents and some guesthouses. The journey on a minibus is faster but they can also be pretty cramped. A minibus from Luang Prabang to Vang Vieng takes 5 hours and costs 60,000 kip. To Vientiane takes about 7 hours and costs $18. In terms of travel sickness the minibuses may well be worse than the regular buses since the drivers swing them round the bends at full speed.

BY BOAT   One of the nicest and most popular ways to get to Luang Prabang is to cross the border at Chiang Khong in Thailand to Huay Xai and take a boat up or down the Mekong through spectacular and scenic countryside. If you take the slow boat (recommended) then it will take 2 days, with an overnight in the small town of Pakbeng, a village with basic accommodations, before arriving in Luang Prabang on the afternoon of the next day (assuming no engine trouble or other delays). In Huay Xai the slow boats leave from a pier just next to Immigration and the 2-day journey costs $20. Slow boats to Huay Xai going the other way leave from the pier at the end of Thanon Khitsarat in the center of town. Arrive early at the riverside quay. There have been complaints in the past of boat operators overloading these passenger boats. If you feel that the boat is overloaded then ask for your money back and find one that isn't. Be prepared for all kinds of

> **(Warning!)** **Lao Speedboat Risks**
>
> Alternatively you can take a Lao speedboat. These are flat-bottom skiffs with an outsize outboard motor attached that propel you at alarming speed over both calm water and rapids, avoiding (with any luck) some of the needle-sharp rocks that occasionally break the surface. You have to wear a helmet on these trips, which is indicative of just how wise it is to get in one of these vessels in the first place. They are best avoided because they are, quite simply, very dangerous indeed. Tickets can be bought at all travel agents and cost 400,000 kip to Huay Xai and 250,000 kip to Pakbeng only. Going from Luang Prabang speedboats leave from the pier at Ban Don, a 15-minute tuk-tuk ride from the center of town. Going to Luang Prabang from Huay Xai they leave from a pier about 2km (1¼ miles) south of Immigration.

discomfort, though you'll have many tales to tell afterward. The chug upriver from Luang Prabang takes up to 3 days and is not recommended.

If you want to spend considerably more money, but enjoy considerably more comfort, you can take a trip with **Luang Say Cruises** (50/4 Sakkarine Rd.; ✆ **071/252-553;** fax 071/252-304; www.luangsay.com), which offers a 2-day or 3-day luxury Mekong jaunt going in both directions. The 2-day cruise leaves Luang Prabang on Tuesdays, Wednesdays, and Saturdays in the high season and only Wednesdays and Saturdays in low season (May–Sept). There is an overnight at the company's own Luangsay Lodge just near Pakbeng. This package costs $243 to $394, depending on the season. The 3-day option departs every Monday, Tuesday, and Friday in the high season, and on Tuesdays and Fridays in low season. It follows the same route with an extra overnight stop at the Khamu Lodge near an ethnic Khamu village. It costs between $343 and $525. The Luang Say Lodge and Kamu Lodge are both charming, rustic ecolodges on the banks of the Mekong. Meals are included as is wine and coffee. The boat has a fully equipped bar, but drinks apart from tea and coffee are not included in the price.

The Lao/German company Mekong Sun Cruise (2/2 Sakkarine Rd.; ✆ **071/254-768;** www.cruisemekong.com) also runs high-end river trips on all navigable stretches of the Mekong and indeed the Nam Ou.

Getting Around

Luang Prabang is easy to cover on foot or bicycle. If you get tired, tuk-tuks and jumbos cost about 5,000 kip per trip (less with more people and some haggling). Note: Citing the many accidents in recent years, local officials have put the kibosh on motorbike rentals (which also ensures work for local transportation providers). Luang Prabang is a town for walking, really, but it is a shame that you can no longer go putt-putting out to the waterfalls.

Vatthanaluck Vehicle Rental, around the corner from the **Villa Santi** (✆ **071/212-838**), covers all the bases for rentals and is the best bet of the many competitors. Bicycles go for just $1 per day; a rented car with driver is $25. For sights outside the city, jumbos and tuk-tuks usually gather along Xieng Thong Road across from the popular cafes and restaurants; prices are negotiable.

> ## (Tips) Where the Streets Have No Names
>
> In Luang Prabang, though you'll see street signs, the same road can change names as it progresses through the city, making things confusing. For example, the main street (I refer to it as "restaurant row" at the town center) is Chao Fa Ngum, Sisavangvong, or Sakkarine Road, depending on where you are. Locals use village names, not streets, to navigate, and villages are commonly named for the local wat. When checking into your hotel, get a business card or ask the name of the local wat to tell taxi and tuk-tuk drivers. Also note that the Western spelling of many street and wat names is very inconsistent. Just sound it out.

Longtail boats are for hire at Luang Prabang's main pier and can take you to adjacent villages and the Pak Ou Caves (p. 280).

VISITOR INFORMATION & TOURS

In addition to the following recommendations, small tour offices with good budget ticket services are chockablock in town, especially on "restaurant row." Try **All Lao Services** (5/7 Sisavangvong Rd.; ✆ **071/252-785;** fax 071/253-523) for ticketing, rentals, and Internet access.

- **Diethelm Travel,** Sakkarine Road, near the Villa Santi (✆ **071/212-277;** fax 071/212-032; www.diethelmtravel.com). The top agent in town, Diethelm arranges city tours and excursions to out-of-town sights.
- **Exotissimo Travel,** 44/3 Ban Vat Nong, Khemkong Rd. (✆ **071/252-879;** fax 071/252-879; www.exotissimo.com).

WHERE TO STAY

Luang Prabang's UNESCO World Heritage status mercifully prevents large-scale construction in the historic center. As a result, developers have renovated existing hotels and completed boutique conversions of old guesthouses. A few resorts have also sprung up on the outskirts of town to keep up with demand. In high season, the town is absolutely stuffed with visitors, so finding a place can be a trial. Book ahead from November through March and during the Lao New Year festivities in mid-April.

The main concentration of accommodations is along the peninsula dissected by Sisavangvong Road on the banks of both the Mekong and the Nam Khan rivers and all the crossroads in between. All prices quoted here are for high season (Nov–Mar). Most operations slash their rates by more than half in low season (Apr–Oct) when it is actually quite nice to visit as long as you manage to dodge the rain. You will certainly be dodging the crowds. Those hotels that take credit cards will generally charge you an extra 4% on top of your bill. Quite a number of the more boutique-style hotels deliberately do not have TVs in the rooms so as to maintain a traditional and tranquil atmosphere.

Expensive

The Apsara   Named after the celestial nymphs in Hindu mythology that grace the frescoes of Angkor Wat, the British-owned Apsara is a stylish choice. Set on the less-developed Nam Khan River side of the Luang Prabang isthmus, its rooms are split between two beautiful colonials. Superior units are like loft spaces with high ceilings, old wood floors, and fashionable room dividers separating the bathroom area from the living space. Modern dark-wood furniture is highlighted by four-poster beds covered with hand-woven silks and plush pillows. Smaller standard rooms are just as airy. French doors leading to either a patio by the road or a second-floor balcony let in an abundance of light, especially in the morning. The bar and restaurant are top-notch, but early-to-bedders beware: Two second-story rooms are immediately above the restaurant and can be noisy until closing time. Large families or groups should inquire about the nearby Villa Savanh, a three-bedroom traditional house that the hotel rents on a nightly basis.

Ban Vat Sene. ✆ **071/254-670.** Fax 071/254-252. www.theapsara.com. 13 units. $70 Standard downstairs; $75 Superior downstairs; $80 Standard upstairs; $120 Superior upstairs. . MC, V. **Amenities:** Restaurant; bar; Internet. *In room:* A/C, fridge.

The Chang Inn   Here they have made a real effort to create luxury but in a very Lao traditional style (although it is actually Thai owned). The rooms are dark wood throughout from floor to ceiling. We found that a little claustrophobic but do appreciate their intensely skillful design imperative. It is a rambling place with lots of little passages and hidden corners all artfully decorated with silk and woodcarvings. In some ways the meticulous attention to detail might start to grate. The Chang Inn is, without a doubt, artful boutique perfection but the very efficiency of the warm atmosphere appears clinically calculating and screams business. Still, the hotel is in a beautiful location, the staff is wonderfully friendly with good English, and the design is genuinely creative. For those reasons, the Chang Inn has done a successful job of separating itself from the crowd.

93, Unit 3, Phoneheuang Village. ✆ **071/253-553.** www.thechang.com. 22 units. $200 deluxe; $220 Khan deluxe; $250 Khan suite. MC, V. **Amenities:** Restaurant; Internet; room service. *In room:* A/C, TV, fridge, minibar.

La Residence Phou Vao ★★★   Luang Prabang's finest hotel offers deluxe accommodations, excellent service, and a lofty perch away from the fray of the busy town center. Rooms are priced accordingly, but worth it. The Phou Vao is named for the hill on which it stands. Shallow ponds trace the courtyards that connect the buildings, and bushes of bougainvillea, palm, and frangipani frame views of Mount Phousi in the distance. The views are especially lovely from the pool area and the balconies of the more choice rooms. The accommodations are like small suites, decorated with a bamboo-and-wood inlaid headboard, fine rosewood furniture, and retro fixtures such as fans and mosquito netting. The large marble bathrooms feature oversize stone tubs and dark-teak sink stands. Private balconies come with low, Lao-style divans. The Phou Vao combines the amenities of a city hotel with a boutique, upscale rustic charm. The recently opened spa, consisting of luxury cottages set around an infinity pool and lily pond overlooking the town below, further solidifies the Phou Vao's position as the premier hotel in Luang Prabang.

Phou Vao Rd. ✆ **071/212-530.** Fax 071/212-534. www.residencephouvao.com. 34 units. $511 Garden View; $554 Mountain View; $510 Mountain Pool View; $569 Suite. MC, V. **Amenities:** Restaurant; bar; concierge; health club; Internet; outdoor pool; room service. *In room:* A/C, TV, fridge, minibar.

Les 3 Nagas ★   This hotel's original structure was built in 1898 as an unofficial reception area for the royal family before being converted into an ice-cream factory in the 1930s. A newer wing across the street was built in 1903 by a counselor to King Sisavang Vong. The inspired recent renovation has just the right mix of style, convenience, and connection with local living and history. That style can be seen in the clean-lined rosewood interiors, contemporary Asian furniture, and Lao touches such as woven floor mats and ladders to upper floors. Bathrooms are done in dark wood, shower and all. Convenience points are earned because the hotel is close to the town center, but far enough from the din to afford some peace. The connection to history comes as the very professional staff welcomes you to a place that provides a glimpse into an aristocratic Indochina of a bygone era. The hotel restaurant (p. 266) is tops, too.

Sakkarine Rd. ℂ **071/253-888.** Fax 071/253-999. www.alilahotels.com. 15 units. $125 superior; $175 junior suite; $225 executive suite. MC, V. **Amenities:** Restaurant; concierge; Internet; room service. *In room:* A/C, TV, fridge, minibar.

Mekong Riverview Hotel ★★   This is the only hotel offering stunning mountain and river views from the balcony of every room. The location is well complemented by the exquisite design. The rooms are beautifully furnished in a French provincial style with dark-wood furniture, rattan chairs, and faded ocher floor tiles. There is a shaded veranda overlooking the river providing a very pleasant place to enjoy your croissants in the morning. The rooms are equipped with every luxury you would expect in a top-line hotel. The beds are "remote controlled" and imported from Sweden. The hotel offers free transfer to the airport and they have a golf buggy to take you uptown. You are also just next to the ethereal Xieng Thong temple, one of the Luang Prabang's major landmarks.

Mekong Riverside Rd. ℂ **071/254-900.** Fax 071/254-890. www.mekongriverview.com. 7 units. $190 double. MC, V. **Amenities:** Restaurant, breakfast only; Internet; room service. *In room:* A/C, TV, fridge, minibar.

Villa Maly ★   The newest super-deluxe option in Luang Prabang (along with the soon to be opened Amantaka), the Villa Maly opened in October 2008. Housed in the former home of Prince Khamtan (built in 1938), it offers 33 rooms in 7 buildings, set among lush gardens. Rooms feature wooden parquet floors and four-poster beds. Le Vetiver restaurant offers dining al fresco, and there is also a spa, pool, and gift shop. The company that owns Villa Maly also runs lunch and dinner boat tours along the Mekong for $35; ask them to book a trip for you. Breakfast is included in the room rate.

BP 78. ℂ **071/253-902.** Fax 071/254-912. www.villa-maly.com. 33 units. $200-$350 deluxe double; $250 standard double; $300 superior double; $200-$350 deluxe double. MC, V. **Amenities:** Restaurant, concierge; Internet; outdoor pool; room service. *In room:* A/C, TV, hair dryer; minibar.

Villa Santi Hotel   For charm and convenience, the Villa Santi is the top in-town residence. Formerly the home of Lao princess Manilay, this low-key villa reopened in 1992. Whether in the original building, in the nearby annex, or at the latest venture some 6km (3¾ miles) from town (see Villa Santi Resort, below), you'll find peaceful elegance and a connection with culture and nature. The decor is deluxe colonial, with overstuffed pillows, fine linens, mosquito netting, local weaving, parquet floors, and rosewood furniture. The tile bathrooms are small but neat. Nice touches include old-fashioned sun umbrellas available for borrowing, plus fresh flowers in every room. The newer annex just across the street has common balcony sitting areas and a charm all its own. Only four rooms have king-size beds, so be sure to specify when you book if that's what you want. The staff is friendly and professional. The downtown location is terrific, right in the thick of things.

Sakkarine Rd. ℂ **071/252-157.** Fax 071/252-158. www.villasantihotel.com. 25 units. $170 deluxe double; $250 suite. MC, V. **Amenities:** Restaurant; Internet; room service. *In room:* A/C, fridge, minibar.

Villa Santi Resort ★★   This resort is a roomier rural companion to the popular downtown Villa Santi and similarly sophisticated, without being stuffy. Tucked among lush rice paddies and picturesque hills, this little Eden has a tranquil stream that tiptoes through the grounds, a placid pond, and an open garden area. The buildings seem at ease with the surroundings, and from the open-air, high-ceilinged lobby to the two-story villas scattered about, there's a certain harmony to the place. Rooms are larger versions of those at the downtown Villa Santi, with similar tile floors, dark rosewood trim, and local decoration. The hotel has laid claim to the largest swimming pool in town and plans to add tennis courts and a fitness center in the near future. The staff is kind and courteous, and will ensure efficient transport to and from town (as with the other resorts, distance is the biggest drawback here).

Santi Resort Rd., Ban Nadeuay, P.O. Box 681 (6km/3³/₄ miles from town, a 10-min. drive), Luang Prabang. ✆ **071/253-470.** Fax 071/253-471. www.villasantihotel.com. 52 units. $110 deluxe double; $185 suite. AE, MC, V. **Amenities:** Restaurant; bar; room service. *In room:* A/C, TV w/in-house movies, fridge, hair dryer, minibar.

Moderate

Ancient Luang Prabang ★ This hotel closed down for 3 years for a top-to-bottom makeover, and the final result is lovely. Lao textiles mix with contemporary comforts such as flatscreen TVs in the rooms and new Mac computers for Internet access in the open-space lobby. Twelve rooms named after Chinese zodiac animals are bachelor style, with dark-wood floors and spacious tubs in most. Staff is friendly if a bit stiff on monetary matters (one guest had to pay to charge his iPod using the lobby computer's USB port, and a complimentary day-old muffin was out of the question for me even though I left before breakfast was served). It's located right beside the night market, so grab a room with a balcony on the top floor and watch the chaos unfurl below. If you're aiming for a bit more peace and quiet, book yourself into the Snake Room, which faces away from the market and has a sleek stone tub in the corner.

Sisavangvong Rd. ✆ **071/212-264.** Fax 071/212-804. www.ancientluangprabang.com. 12 units. $65 double; $60 single. No credit cards. **Amenities:** Internet. *In room:* A/C, TV, fridge, minibar.

Ban Pack Luck Villa The Ban Pack Luck is decorated throughout in a frenzied boutique style. If you like the silk, the knickknacks, the dark wood, and the flowery touches that define this approach then you will like this hotel (if you don't, you might find it a bit cloying). The rooms are thoughtfully appointed although some of them, particularly on the ground floor, are a little small. Guests we spoke to, however, were very happy with their lot. The corner rooms on the second floor are by far the best since they have reasonably sized balconies. The monks from Wat Nong next door may wake you up earlier than you like with their atmospheric but quite loud early-morning prayers.

Ban Wat Nong. ✆ **071/353-373.** 6 units. $30 downstairs; $45 upstairs. No credit cards. **Amenities:** Internet. *In room:* A/C, TV, fridge, minibar.

La Maison de Xanamkieng This very new hotel is different from many in the midrange since it does not even attempt a retro feel. The design is actually quite minimal and urban. Rooms are large and airy with wooden floors and silk furnishings. The foyer area is massive with French windows on all sides, lots of comfy sofas, cushions, and a big TV. It's all very sociable. Staff is very friendly and capable.

Ban Vat Sene. ✆ **071/255-123.** Fax 071/255-789. 7 units. $65 double. MC, V. **Amenities:** Restaurant; Internet. *In room:* A/C, TV, fridge minibar.

Lao Wooden House ★ An elegantly restored wooden villa once owned by a member of the royal family. Not surprisingly all the rooms are paneled in dark wood. Somehow this manages not to be at all claustrophobic and the tone is lifted by the white linen furnishings. The upstairs rooms are carpeted while the downstairs rooms have polished wooden floors. All rooms are fronted by a wooden veranda. Downstairs there is a little bar where they can rustle you up a cocktail or two.

Ban Watnong. ✆ **071/260-283.** Fax 071/260-284. www.laowoodenhouse.com. 6 units. $70 double. MC, V. **Amenities:** Bar; Internet. *In room:* A/C, TV, fridge.

Le Calao ★★ This restored 1904 villa stands near the tip of Luang Prabang's peninsula on the banks of the Mekong. Unique and picturesque, it has a location and style all its own. The second-floor rooms are a nice size, with high sloping ceilings, wood furniture, neat tile floors, and firm beds. Bathrooms have wood cabinetry but are otherwise rather spartan, with no tubs. The staff is, well . . . hey, where did the staff go? What sells these rooms and commands the seemingly high price tag is that each unit has a large private balcony facing the majestic Mekong. The casual ambience at the Calao comes at a premium, but the place is quite popular (be sure to book ahead). The newly renovated downstairs suite (formerly a kitchen and staff room) has two double beds and a private balcony, perfect for a family with kids. The restaurant at the front, also with great views of the river, La Cave des Chateaux, serves excellent provincial French food with a gourmet touch bought to you by staff whose spoken French is as elegant as the surroundings in which they speak it.

Khem Kong Rd. ✆ **071/212-100.** Fax 071/212-085. 6 units. $80 double. MC, V. **Amenities:** Restaurant. *In room:* A/C.

Lotus Villa Hotel ★★★ This is a brand-new hotel that was constructed in exact imitation of the decaying French house it replaced. The approach is boutique but very understated with a creative approach to every detail. The tiled rooms are light, spacious, and airy, with large windows. There are rooms in the main house and also in a block set in the rear among a jungly garden, with seating in the central area where breakfast is served. What makes this hotel special is its real commitment to minimizing environmental impact. The sewage system is a UNESCO-approved, multilevel natural filtration system, where nothing damaging is discharged into the environment or the river. Detergent use is minimized, and they use a nonchemical system for hotel cleaning and have reusable cloth shopping bags for daily shopping. Room soaps are made with essential oil extracts sourced in the region. They recycle all plastic and aluminum cans (the only recycling initiative available at present), and organic waste is fed to livestock outside of Luang Prabang. In addition, they provide education and mentoring for staff.

3 Kounxoa Rd. ✆ **071/255-050.** www.lotusvillalaos.com. 15 units. $62 double; $124 suite. MC, V. **Amenities:** Restaurant, breakfast only; Internet. *In room:* A/C.

Merry Lao-Swiss Hotel ★ Near Mount Phousi overlooking the Nam Khan River this hotel has very airy rooms with check tiled floors and very high ceilings. It feels a bit like a European hotel in atmosphere. If you are not a fan of the dark wood, traditional Lao feel of so many of Luang Prabang's midrange hotels, then the Merry Lao-Swiss provides a wholly different option with its own unique style.

Kingkitsarath Rd. ✆ **071/260-211.** www.freewebs.com\merrylao_swiss. 20 units. $50 double; $60 twin deluxe; $80 VIP. MC, V. *In room:* A/C, TV, fridge, minibar.

Riverside Guest House Advertising themselves with the curious phrase "The unforgotten touch of Luang Prabang," the Riverside Guest House offers all-wood rooms in a great riverside location, although the design of the building means that only one room actually has a riverside view. Rooms are tastefully furnished in an Art Deco style, though they're a bit pokey. It is family run and the family is very relaxed and friendly.

Ban Khili. ☏ **071/212-664.** www.villariverside.com. 7 units. $60 double; $70 triple; $80 VIP Private Balcony River View. No credit cards. *In room:* A/C, TV.

Sala Prabang ★★ ⦅**Finds**⦆   Here's a trendsetter in developing Luang Prabang: an old riverside colonial that's been refurbished and refitted by its architect/owner, the walls reinforced with stone, and good hot-water showers and air-conditioning installed. The renovation was done with some panache, with beams and supports made of rough natural wood, sponge painting, and cool neutral tones throughout. The lobby area is a chic open-air space overlooking the Mekong, and top-end rooms on the second floor are large and have great balcony views. A recent expansion added seven naturally styled rooms in a riverfront villa down the street, as well as Nadao (under construction at press time), an offshoot of the Vientiane favorite Le Nadao, promising the same high-quality French cuisine at its riverside perch. Sala Prabang is a boutique guesthouse at its best, and a model that will likely be copied.

Mekong Riverside Rd., 102/6 Thanon Ounkham, Xieng Mouane, P.O. Box 902, Luang Prabang. ☏ **071/252-460.** Fax 071/252-472. www.salalao.com. 29 units. Low season $50–$60 double; high season $60–$75 double. MC, V. **Amenities:** Restaurant; cafe; airport transfer; Internet access. *In room:* A/C, hair dryer.

Sayo Guest House   This guesthouse isn't trying to be anything more than it is, and that's its charm. Service is nonexistent, and the lobby is just a little hallway, but the rooms on the second floor are enormous. Ceilings are practically barn height, and the rooms are done up with tasteful Lao decorations. Rooms also feature four-poster beds if you are suddenly feeling a little bit like Henry VIII and wish to relax. The upstairs family rooms have a mezzanine area, which is great for children who wish to create their own den. Bathrooms are clean, large, and of the all-in-one variety (shower and toilet together). The rooms in the back are smaller, with exposed brick and unique loft spaces like little crows' nests. Sayo Guesthouse is basic, but it's an eccentric place with a lot of character. The location is convenient to the main street.

Ban Xieng Mouane. ☏ **071/252-614.** 14 units. $40 double; $60 family room. No credit cards. *In room:* A/C, TV.

Senesouk Guesthouse   This is a really pleasant guesthouse decorated in a Franco-Lao style. The furnishing is dark wood and silk. Some rooms are completely paneled in dark wood giving them a very traditional feel. It is not everyone's cup of tea since it is a mite gloom-inducing, but if it is your style then you won't be unsatisfied. The all-wood rooms are not claustrophobic because they are very large indeed with high ceilings. The nonwooden rooms are much smaller.

Sakkarine Rd. ☏ **071/212-074.** 19 units. $30 standard double; $35 standard twin; $40 superior double; $40 deluxe twin; $50 deluxe double. MC, V. *In room:* A/C, TV, fridge.

Villa Sokxai I   This is a basic guesthouse in an attractive colonial that happens to be in one of my favorite spots in town. Clean rooms have wood floors, soft beds, and both air-conditioning and a fan, a real plus for some. Try for an upstairs room overlooking the balcony and Wat Phon Heuang—this is one of the first spots where monks receive their morning alms, and the hotel staff can help you buy sticky rice if you'd like to make merit. At dusk, you can sit on the balcony and listen to the hypnotic chanting drone of the evening prayers. One drawback is the Sokxai's poorly run reservations system; you should confirm your reservation more than once before arriving. If it's full, look for its sister hotel, Villa Sokxai 2, on the other side of Mount Phousi.

Sakalin Rd. (across from Wat Phon Heuang), Ban Kilee, Luang Prabang. ✆/fax **071/254-309.** sokxaigh@yahoo.com. 7 units. $35 double; $50 family suite. No credit cards. *In room:* A/C.

Inexpensive

Chittana Guesthouse   This is a very good value budget option close to the center of town. The rooms are very basic and vary in size and quality so it's best to look at a few before picking one. They have wooden floors and slightly grubby whitewashed walls. There is a pleasant all-wood veranda on which to lounge after temple hopping. The staff is very friendly and casual.

Ban Vat Sene. ✆ **071/212-552.** 10 units. 80,000 kip fan double; 120,000 kip A/C double. No credit cards. **Amenities:** Internet.

Khoun and Khone Guest House ★   If you fancy being a little in the boonies, come to this family-run place set in a small farm 5km (3 miles) out of town. The family is delightful and speaks very good English. They serve meals and many of the ingredients they use are grown on the farm. Khone is a great cook and can rustle up either Lao or Western food depending on your preference. The surrounding garden is beautiful and relaxing and the owners are justifiably very proud of it. Khoun and Khone also run tours of the surrounding countryside and villages, about which they are very knowledgeable. The bungalows themselves are large and rustic with hot water and a small balcony.

Ban Na Dad. ✆ **020/770-7665.** www.khounandkhone.hrorbit.com. 6 units. $25 double. No credit cards. **Amenities:** Restaurant.

Khounsavanh Guest House   This is in a small area with a concentration of budget accommodations to the north of Wat Phousi. This a very good budget option with airy, light rooms set around a courtyard. There are seating areas on the wraparound veranda. The rooms have high ceilings, but they could do with a coat of paint. They have both fan rooms and air-conditioned rooms.

Ban Thongchaleun. ✆ **071/212-297.** 14 units. 100,000 kip fan double; 150,000 kip A/C double. No credit cards. *In room:* A/C (10 rooms).

Somkhounmuong Guest House   This rambling old French villa hosts a warren of corridors with a pleasant veranda at the entrance. The rooms are basic and quite small but do have A/C and are clean. It is a nice environment, given that it is offering very low-budget accommodations.

53 Tomkham Rd. ✆ **071/254-662.** 10 units. 80,000 kip. No credit cards. *In room:* A/C.

WHERE TO DINE

Luang Prabang has its own very distinctive style of cuisine and there are many places in Luang Prabang that can demonstrate just how rich that tradition is. Some are very expensive by Lao standards but are also incredibly good, often combining northern Lao tradition with that of France. New upmarket bistros, many run by foreign restaurateurs, have added to the culinary diversity of little Luang Prabang. There are also very modestly priced places (our favorites are along the Mekong itself), where you can sample the famous Luang Prabang sausage, the delicious fermented fish stew, and many other Lao culinary concoctions. Whatever your cuisine of choice, dining in this sleepy northern burg is a delight.

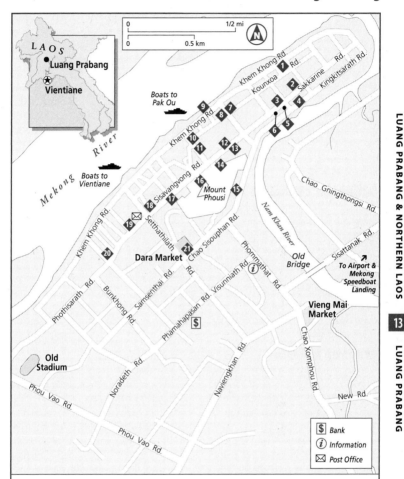

LUANG PRABANG & NORTHERN LAOS

13

LUANG PRABANG

The Apsara **4**
Baguette stands **18**
Blue Lagoon Restaurant **11**
Café Des Arts **13**
Chill Out Café **21**
Couleur Café and Restaurant **7**
Indochina Spirit **20**
Joma **19**
La Cave des Chateaux **1**
Le Café Ban Wat Sene **6**
L'Elephant Restaurant **10**

Les 3 Nagas **3**
L'etranger **15**
Luang Prabang Bakery **16**
Nazim Restaurant **12**
Night Market **17**
Scandinavian Bakery **14**
The Tamarind Café **8**
Tamnaklao-the Three Elephants
    Restaurant **5**
Vieng Kheam Khong **9**
Villa Santi **2**

The Apsara ASIAN/INTERNATIONAL   This is often cited as the best restaurant in town and there is a fair amount of legitimacy behind that claim. The menu is not large but it is very well thought out and beautifully conceived at every level. For a starter the cauliflower soup spiced with roast cumin is simply delicious in an understated way. For something really Lao go for the Luang Prabang buffalo sausages. For a main course try the braised river fish, or if you wish to try something completely left field abandon Asia altogether and try the Moroccan tagine of young goat served with couscous. The wine cellar is suitably impressive. The decor is muted but stylish with Lao silk offset by sparkling white tablecloths with dark-wood folding doors open to the Mekong. Portions are generous and staff is friendly. Apsara's quiet ambience is a lovely getaway from the din of Sisavangvong Road.

Kingkitsarath Rd. ✆ **071/254-670.** Fax 071/254-252. www.theapsara.com/laos-bar-restaurant.html. Main courses $6–$12. MC, V. Daily 7am–10pm.

La Cave des Chateaux ★★★ FRENCH   Situated in the superbly atmospheric Calao Inn, this equally atmospheric French restaurant completes the circle that firmly transports you back to a feeling of uncontrived old Indochina. Many, many restaurants work hard to create the atmosphere that at La Cave des Chateaux simply exists. The slumberous but appropriate decor, combined with prompt but friendly service, all combine to make this place unique. The food is provincial French with a hint of Lao and it is very good indeed although all this reverie comes at a fairly stiff price. Breakfast is good here as well whether it is accompanied by excellent Lao coffee or pastis as one is served on the Côte d'Azur itself.

Khem Kong Rd. ✆ **071/212-100.** Fax 071/212-085. Main courses 110,000 kip. No credit cards. Daily 7:30am–2pm and 5–10:30pm.

L'Elephant Restaurant FRENCH   This stylish bistro is where it's at for fine dining in Luang Prabang. Run by French expats, it has a laid-back, retro-chic atmosphere inside a high-ceilinged colonial. There are daily and weekly specials, and just about everything is good, especially the imported steaks. Tasty cheeses and wines are also imported, though local stock is used whenever possible. Boar and venison specials are popular, for example. The wine list could hold its own in a much larger city, and it's unlikely that you'll stump the bartender. Daily set menus explore the best of what's available in the kitchen. A range of tasty dishes, from coq au vin to grilled buffalo to a vegetarian savory baked eggplant, covers all the bases. The cavernous interior makes it quite popular with high-end tour groups since they can all fit in comfortably. L'Elephant is very expensive for Laos, but more than worth it. Be sure to make a reservation—it's often fully booked.

Ban Vat Nong. ✆ **071/252-482.** www.elephant-restau.com. Main courses 140,000 kip. MC, V. Daily noon–2:30pm and 6–10pm.

Les 3 Nagas LAO/INTERNATIONAL   You can get real Lao cuisine done right at this new open-air spot on the quiet end of "restaurant row." Dining here is as sumptuous an affair as a stay at the connected 3 Nagas boutique hotel (p. 259). Meals are based on the culinary styles of the chef's own hometown, presented on fine china by a meticulous and capable waitstaff (you won't find the bones and gristle of traditional Lao restaurants here). Start your meal with betel-leaf soup before moving on to sautéed local mushrooms (when in season), laap, and grilled delicacies, from chicken satay to whole chunks of hearty river fish, lightly marinated in lemon grass and chilies. For dessert, go for the

Lao-style crème brûlée, a custard of pumpkin and coconut that's divine. Great coffee,

too. Note: 3 Nagas' Lao restaurant sometimes closes during the low season, so call ahead.

Sakkarine Rd. © **071/253-888.** Fax 071/253-999. www.alilahotels.com. Main courses 100,000 kip. MC, V.
Daily 10:30am–2pm and 5–10pm.

Moderate

Blue Lagoon Restaurant WESTERN/ASIAN   If the classic cuisine of La Cave des
Chateaux is not to your taste and you prefer a more modern approach, the nearby Blue
Lagoon Café may just fit the bill. Here Nouvelle cuisine characterized by small but artfully presented portions is the order of the day. The restaurant itself is situated in a
tropical garden with rattan chairs and candlelit dark-wood furniture. A surprisingly
eclectic menu of Asian and European dishes come to you as a feast for the eyes before
you start to chow down.. Both the simmering Indian curry and steak *cordon bleu* are
reported to be exceptional, as is the wine list.

Ban Choumkhong. © **071/253-698.** Fax 071/260-265. www.blue-lagoon-cafe.com. Main courses
100,000 kip. MC, V. Tues–Sun 10am–10pm.

Chill Out Café ★★ LAO/INTERNATIONAL   Situated on the far side of Dara
Market from the Mekong, this elegant new eatery is as it describes itself, stylishly decorated in an airy retro style. It is open on all four sides allowing a touch of a breeze to cool
you after a hard session of shopping among the market stalls. The staff is very friendly if
a little diffident. The food is a delicious fusion of Asian and Western with the emphasis
on light tasty snacks. Both the cheese and bacon panini and the cauliflower soup spiced
with cumin come highly recommended. The house wines are good, the crisp Italian
white being particularly delicious. The Chill Out Café also has very fast Wi-Fi (well, fast
for Laos!) so you will often see people working away on their laptops.

Dara Market. © **071/261-006.** Fax 071/253-418. Main courses 45,000 kip. No credit cards. Daily 7am–8pm.

Couleur Café and Restaurant ★ LAO/FRENCH   This unassuming but atmospheric down-alley bistro features affordable fine dining. Several local expats prefer the
food here to that of L'Elephant (see above). The decor is elegantly sparse, with colonial-
size high ceilings and walls adorned with the work of local artists. Though run by a young
French expat, the bistro has Lao specialties such as steamed fish with coconut in banana
leaf, or perhaps fried prawns in oyster sauce. Both are served with sticky rice, of course.
Eggplant, mushrooms, and crispy green beans are combined in a tasty Casserole Luang
Prabang. Order some Mekong seaweed for an interesting appetizer, and ask about the
fine Lao whiskey and imported wines. It's a quiet little getaway for next to nothing.

48/5 Ban Vat Nong. © **071/254-694.** Main courses 25,000 kip–150,000 kip. MC, V. Daily 11am–2:30pm
and 4:30–10:30pm.

Indochina Spirit ★ LAO/THAI/WESTERN   Housed in a restored 70-year-old
wooden home, Indochina Spirit, as its name suggests, dishes up as much atmosphere as
it does good grub. This gorgeous Lao home has been put to lovely use and now features
traditional Lao music most evenings from 7:30 to 8pm (check the chalkboard in front to
make sure). Indochina Spirit has done a great job with the simple local decor inside and
charming garden dining outside. The menu is an ambitious list of Lao, Thai, and Western dishes. It's a good place to have a drink, enjoy an affordable appetizer plate, and hear
some good music before strolling the city at night.

52 Ban Vat That, opposite the fountain across from Maison Souvannaphoum. © **071/252-372.** Main
courses $5–$10. MC, V. Daily 8am–10pm.

LUANG PRABANG & NORTHERN LAOS

Tamnaklao—the Three Elephants Restaurant ★ LAO   This renovated colonial in the temple district is generally considered to be one of the best places in Luang Prabang to sample expertly prepared authentic Lao cuisine—odd since it is Australian owned and run. For the best variety, try one of the Tamank's three set menus. A sample of two, offering a total of 10 dishes, could include pork casserole in coconut milk, lahp pla (spicy fish salad), and pork stuffed in crispy bamboo shoots. The casseroles are more like stew, with a sweet-and-sour taste that pairs wonderfully with a bowl of sticky rice. If you want to extend your knowledge even further, they also run cooking classes daily where you can learn about ingredients and cooking methods.

Sakkarine Rd. ✆ **071/252-525.** Main courses 20,000 kip–50,000 kip. No credit cards. Daily 8:30am–10:30pm.

Villa Santi ★★ LAO/CONTINENTAL   On the upper floor of the popular hotel's main building (p. 260), this atmospheric open-air perch has just the right angle on the busy street below. Set with linen and silver, a candlelit table on the balcony is hands-down the town's most romantic spot. The food is local and traditional Lao, along with some creative Asian-influenced Continental (on the whole, though, it's a bit uninspired—stick to Lao and Thai specials, and sample one of the fine curries). The daily set menus are always a good choice. The desserts are scrumptious: Try bananas flambéed in Cointreau, or fruit salad in rum. There are more casual offerings for lunch, including burgers. Most evenings feature traditional music and dancing in the courtyard below.

In Villa Santi Hotel, Sakkarine St. ✆ **071/212-267.** Main courses $4–$8. V. Daily 6:30am–10:30pm.

Inexpensive

For good eats and the company of many fellow travelers, don't miss what we've called "restaurant row" (it's hard to miss on any trip to Luang Prabang). It is the only place in town alive past 9pm, though it quickly dies at 11pm. If restaurants are empty, it may close earlier. This fun, affordable place is great for exploring—almost like a Khao San Road.

Café des Arts ★ FRENCH/CONTINENTAL   Pasta, hamburgers, crepes, filet de boeuf, and tartines round out the very appetizing menu here. Breakfast brings omelets galore. Open-air like all the others on "restaurant row," Café des Arts has a better atmosphere than most, with real tables and chairs (not plastic), linen tablecloths, and a gallery of local artwork for sale.

Sisavangvong Rd. (on "restaurant row"). ✆/fax **071/252-162.** Main courses 18,000 kip–75,000 kip. MC, V. Daily 7:30am–11pm.

Nazim Restaurant ★ INDIAN   Just like the other Nazim outlets in Vientiane and Vang Vieng, Nazim serves a fine complement of good curries and halal food. The dining area is kind of grubby, but the food is great and Nazim is always packed. There's another location on "restaurant row," Sisavangvong Road, at the town center (✆ **071/253-493**).

78/4 Ban Visoun, Visounnarath Rd. ✆ **071/252-263.** www.nazim.laopdr.com. Main courses 12,000 kip–28,000 kip. No credit cards. Daily 8:30am–11pm.

Park Houay Mixay ★ LAO   A popular lunch option for package tours, this looks more like a traditional Lao restaurant than the places on "restaurant row." Note the tin roof, beat-up wood floors and tables, and numerous pets and kids running around—but you come here for the food, not the ambience. The large portions of delicious and cheap Lao and Thai dishes are not watered down for Western palates. If you're here for lunch, make sure the ubiquitous tour group has been served already, or else you're in for a long wait.

75/76 Ban Xieng Mouane. ☏ **071/212-260.** Main courses 23,000 kip–45,000 kip. MC, V. Daily 11am–2pm **269**
and 6:30–9:30pm.

The Tamarind Café ★★ LAO   Open only for breakfast and lunch, this excellent
little place offers a range of Lao-style tapas, or little sample plates of many different Lao
tastes. They also serve refreshing and original fruit drinks. They can also cater to groups
to order if you give them a day's notice at about $8 a head. Staff is brisk and not
unfriendly, but nothing special. The kitchen is small, so sit back and enjoy the fine views
of Wat Nong while you wait for your food. They also have begun offering a Lao cooking
class on weekdays and Saturday evenings (from $22–$28) that's become quite popular—
check out their website for more details.

Ban Wat Nong. ☏ **020/777-0484.** www.tamarindlaos.com. Main courses 38,000 kip. No credit cards.
Mon–Sat 11am–6pm.

Vieng Kheam Khong ★★★ Ⓜoments LAO   There are a host of restaurants lining
the Mekong and many are good. The Vieng Kheam Khong is very popular and this is
borne out by the fact that you will see many local people there as well as foreigners. It is
also very reasonably priced. There is an area by the roadside but far nicer is a softly lit
wooden deck overlooking the river where you can contemplate the twinkling lights of the
boats as they glide by silhouetted mountains lit by moonlight on the far shore. The food
is authentically Lao and authentically delicious. The Luang Prabang sausage is interesting
if you have also tasted Chiang Mai sausage in Thailand. It has an almost woody taste,
gently seasoned as compared to its fierier Thai cousin. The Lao stew (whether fish,
chicken, or pork) is also a good option. Beware, although it is not that spicy they do
chuck in whole unseeded chilies and if you accidentally bite into one then you might find
yourself leaping feverishly into the fast-flowing waters of the Mekong to put out the fire.
It does work pretty well as a momentarily distressing cure for blocked sinuses or indeed
the common cold.

549 Ban Xieng Mouane. ☏ **071/212-726.** Main courses 25,000 kip. No credit cards. Daily 9am–10:30pm.

Snacks & Cafes
For atmosphere, there is nowhere better than **L'Etranger Books & Tea** (☏ **020/537-
7826;** booksinlaos@yahoo.com), in Ban Vat Aphay on the back side of Mount Phousi
(the opposite side from the main street and royal palace) near the Nam Khan River. The

Baguettes Near Wat Phousi

At the midtown end of Sisavangvong Road, just in front of Wat Phousi near the
Hmong Market, is a series of stalls selling delicious baguette sandwiches
(baguette being khao ji in Lao). They are served with a variety of fillings, and
plenty of healthy salad and mayo. The ladies assembling these delights are
utterly charming, but they will likely ask you to pay a steep 15,000 kip. If you
point out that anywhere else in the country the same thing would cost 8,000
kip, they'll skip down ever so swiftly to 10,000 kip with an unabashed "you got
me there" smile. The stalls are open daily from 8am to 9pm.

friendly Canadian owners are full of good advice and lend books from their downstairs collection. Have a pot of tea or a cocktail (don't miss the lao-lao margarita) in their atmospheric upstairs teahouse and gallery; it's also a good place on a steamy afternoon to relax on the floor against a cozy Lao cushion while perusing one of the old National Geographic magazines. Young travelers descend for the films, played each day at 4 and 7pm.

A popular restaurant on "restaurant row," the **Luang Prabang Bakery,** 11/7 Sisavangvong Rd. (✆ 071/212-617), serves some good pizza as well as a host of baked goods, plus has an extensive collection of books. Farther east, the **Scandinavian Bakery,** 52/6 Sisavangvong (✆ 071/252-223), and chic, air-conditioned **Joma** (✆ 071/252-292) both serve similar fine coffee and baked goods.

The same team of expats who run L'Elephant (see above) own **Le Café Ban Wat Sene** (✆ 071/252-482), an atmospheric, open-air space. Their desserts and coffee are excellent, as are their light lunch specials of sandwiches and salads. They also offer wireless Internet access. Find them just across from the elementary school.

The best place in town for authentic French crepes, savory or sweet, is **Dao Fa,** on Sisavangvong Road (✆ 071/252-656), also a good spot for people-watching. It has excellent Mediterranean entrees and homemade pastas cooked to order, too.

Vegetarians should be on the lookout for the side-street buffets by the **Night Market,** along Photisarath Road. Only 5,000 kip gets you a bowl and all the nonmeaty goodness you can handle.

ATTRACTIONS

Mount Phousi ★   Rising from the center of town and forming something of a defining feature, Mount Phousi has temples scattered on all sides of its slopes and a panoramic view of the entire town from its summit. That Chomsi Stupa, built in 1804, is its crowning glory. Taking the path to the northeast, you will pass Wat Tham Phousi, which has a large-bellied Buddha, Kaccayana. Wat Phra Bat Nua, farther down, has a yard-long footprint of the Buddha. Be prepared for the 355 steps to get there. Try to make the hike, which will take about 2 hours with sightseeing, in the early morning or late afternoon to escape the midday heat. It is also a great spot from which to watch the sunset.

Sisavangvong Rd. Admission 20,000 kip. Daily 8am–6pm.

Royal Palace Museum or "Haw Kham" ★   This palace was originally built for King Sisavang Vong after the original building was destroyed by Chinese Haw invaders in 1887. Started in 1904, it was completed in 1909. It is also called Haw Kham which means golden hall. The site it occupies was chosen so that visitors could be received directly from the boats in which they arrived. It remained the royal residence until the Pathet Lao takeover in 1975. The last Lao king, Sisavang Vattana, and his family were forcibly relocated to a remote jungle in the northern part of the country where they perished in the late '70s and early '80s. The palace contains exhibits that are interesting if few in number. The architecture of the building is a combination of traditional Lao styles with French neoclassical. The layout is cruciform on a multitiered platform. Over the entrance is an image of the three-headed elephant sheltered by the sacred white parasol that was the original symbol of the Kingdom Lan Xang and the Lao monarchy. Italian marble steps lead up to the colonnaded doorway at the entrance.

To the right of the entrance as you walk in is the king's reception room. It contains busts of the Lao monarchy as well as two large gilded and lacquered Ramayana screens,

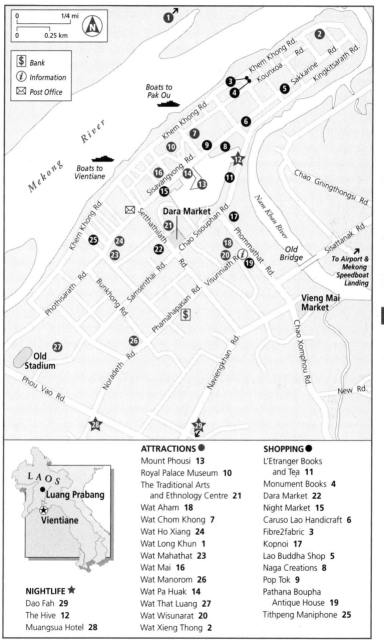

LUANG PRABANG & NORTHERN LAOS

13

LUANG PRABANG

ATTRACTIONS ●
Mount Phousi **13**
Royal Palace Museum **10**
The Traditional Arts
  and Ethnology Centre **21**
Wat Aham **18**
Wat Chom Khong **7**
Wat Ho Xiang **24**
Wat Long Khun **1**
Wat Mahathat **23**
Wat Mai **16**
Wat Manorom **26**
Wat Pa Huak **14**
Wat That Luang **27**
Wat Wisunarat **20**
Wat Xieng Thong **2**

SHOPPING ●
L'Etranger Books
  and Tea **11**
Monument Books **4**
Dara Market **22**
Night Market **15**
Caruso Lao Handicraft **6**
Fibre2fabric **3**
Kopnoi **17**
Lao Buddha Shop **5**
Naga Creations **8**
Pop Tok **9**
Pathana Boupha
  Antique House **19**
Tithpeng Maniphone **25**

NIGHTLIFE ★
Dao Fah **29**
The Hive **12**
Muangsua Hotel **28**

made by the local artisan Thit Tanh. Covering the walls are murals depicting traditional Lao scenes, painted by French artist Alex de Fauntereau in 1930. These were placed so that at the right time of day natural light falls on a corresponding depiction of the same time of day in the painting highlighted.

In the right front corner room of the Palace (you access it from the outside entrance) are many of the museum's top attractions including a replica of a golden standing Buddha that was a gift to King Fa Ngum from Khmer king Phaya Sirichantha in 1359. This is the Phra Bang from which the town takes its name. It translates as "holy image" and the original was cast in Sri Lanka in the 1st century A.D. Twice the Siamese stole the Buddha image—once in 1779 and again in 1827. King Mongkut returned it in 1867. This room also has on display another Buddha image engraved with large elephant tusks and three embroidered silk screens made by the queen herself.

To the left of the entrance hall, the secretary's reception room is filled with a variety of paintings, china, and silver presented to Laos as diplomatic presents from countries the world over. These objects are, quite bizarrely, grouped by their origin—either capitalist or socialist.

What was the queen's reception room is next on the left. There are huge royal portraits of King Savang Vatthana, Queen Khamphoui, and Crown Prince Vong. They were painted by the Russian artist Ilya Glazunov in 1967.

The central throne room is decorated with colorful glass mosaics dating from a renovation in the 1930s. After the throne rooms is a compound of not very lavish bedrooms containing what little finery was left after the last king was evicted in 1975. The bedrooms have been preserved as they were in 1975 when the king departed. There is a dining hall and a room that contain royal seals and medals. There is a wedding cake–like temple at the compound entrance and a large, obviously Soviet-made, statue of Sisavang Vong, the first king under the Lao constitution.

Sisavangvong Rd. Admission 30,000 kip. Daily 8–11am and 1:30–4pm. Informal dress is not allowed. You cannot wear skimpy shorts or have your shoulders exposed.

The Traditional Arts and Ethnology Centre (TAEC) ★★ This museum is a fantastic place to learn about the various ethnic minorities of Laos. The modest-size center is housed in the 1920s former residence of a French colonial judge. Staff is extremely friendly and can answer any questions you have. The handful of exhibits are well curated, displaying traditional clothing, weaving looms, and household wares. Accompanying explanations are in Lao and English. Entry fees and donations go directly toward running TAEC and promoting cultural diversity and preservation. There's a small shop in the back selling textiles and housewares purchased directly from artisan communities.

Photisarath Rd. ✆ **071/253-364.** www.taeclaos.org. Admission 20,000 kip. Tues–Sun 9am–6pm.

Wat Aham This is the "Monastery of the Opened Heart" (Le Monastère du Coeur épanoui) and stands between Wat Wisunarat and the Nam Khan River. It has a somewhat contentious past as it served as a mediating, or perhaps meeting, ground between the animist religion of spirit guardians and Theravada Buddhism. Stylized stucco tigers guard the front entry steps, and statues of temple guardians Ravana and Hanuman (central figures of the Indian Ramayana epic and its Laotian counterpart, the Phalak Phalam) stand at the southern and eastern corners of the frontal porch. There are a number of stupas in the grounds as well as two large and quite large bodhi (banyan or Bo), trees where a shrine of the royal spirit protector Haw Phi Khon is located. The interior of the sim is bright and very colorful. The pillars and beams are painted in reds and gold, while the interior walls are covered with murals depicting Buddhist hell. These are scenes of torture and suffering experienced by those who inflicted evil on others in their lives getting a good karmic going over after death. There are also scenes reflecting the historic past of the city. The wat, does in fact, have an interesting past. The founder of the Lan Xang kingdom, Fa Ngum, established a shrine here for worshiping the guardian spirits of Luang Prabang (devata luang), Pu No, and Na No (Phou Nheu and Nha Nheu). Fa Ngum also made Theravada Buddhism the state religion. Beginning in 1527, however, the devout ruler of the Lan Xang kingdom, King Phothisarat began a concerted attack on the worship of these guardian spirits. He banned religious ceremonies in their honor, smashed their shrines, and erected a Buddhist monastery on the site of the former spirit shrine. Some discrete worship of the guardian spirits continued despite the ban. Shortly after the attacks on the guardian spirits the city was beset by a number of crises, including disease, drought, and crop failure; in the popular mind the destruction of the shrines had brought the disasters. After King Sai Setthathirat moved the capital to Vientiane in 1563, the spirit shrine was rebuilt. The spirit gods and Buddhism lived together until the mid–20th century, when the spirit shrine was destroyed. The spirits of Pu No and Na No by this time had achieved embodiment in the two large banyan trees that stood on the monastery grounds. For much of the 19th century, Wat Aham also served as the residence of the Sangkhalat, or the supreme patriarch of Laotian Buddhism.

Visunarat Rd. Admission 10,000 kip. Daily 8am–5pm.

Wat Chom Khong   The small but attractive Wat Chom Khong Sourintharame means the "Monastery at the Core of the Gong," is located northeast of the Royal Palace. The name comes from the raised boss in the center of a bronze gong, from which it is said the wat's central Buddha figure was partly made.

Choum Khong was founded by Phakhu Keo in 1843, during the reign of King Sukaseum (1836–51). The sim was restored in 1933 and 1951, and its decoration was entirely remade in 1962. It shares a wall with Wat Xieng Mouane, and the sims of the two monasteries have a lot in common in terms of style and decoration. The grounds of the wat are beautiful.

In front of the monks living quarters or *kutis* are two Chinese stone statues. In 1861 these were presented to King Chantharath (1850–72) by the Chinese ambassador from Kunming during his visit to Luang Prabang. They represent the elements of yin and yang, and the Vajra (the lightning or thunderbolt representing masculine principles) and the Ghanta (representing the bell, or feminine principles). These statues had a bit of a rough ride under the French. In the 1890s the interim high commissioner, Joseph Vacle, placed them in front of his residence. After World War I they were placed in the Royal Palace. In the 1930s, the Lao prince and director of culture, Tiao Patasavong Sisouphan, presented them to Wat Chom Kong. They used to guard the central stairway of the sim. Now they flank the doorway of the nearby kuti.

Wat Ho Xiang   Wat Ho Siang Voravihane or the "Lottery Pavilion" is next to Wat That on a small hill southwest of Mount Phousi. There is a naga-flanked stairway going up the hill to the temple. The wat was named in a 1548 ceremony by King Setthathirat. The sim is simple with a central pillarless hall and a single highly decorated doorway. Stylized murals, some of which depict the karmic and really quite brutal punishment visited on evildoers, adorn the entry and the side walls. There have been many reconstructions over the years. The first one was in 1823. The wat was also destroyed by a storm in 1900 and rebuilt once again. The octagonal pediment pillars and the verandas on the northeast and southwest sides of the sim were added in 1952. The octagonal pillars and gilded leaf capitals were added as recently as 1973.

Wat Long Khun Wat Long Khun with the rather uplifting meaning of the "Monastery of the Happy Song" is also sometimes dubbed the "Monastery of the Willow Stream." It is pleasantly situated at the top of a long stairway leading from the river's edge on the far bank of the Mekong almost directly opposite Wat Xieng Thong.

The monastery had important links with royalty and it was tradition that each new king would spend 3 days there in ceremonial bathing and meditative retreat before crossing the river for the preenthronement ceremonies at Wat Xieng Thong. With the end of royalty, Wat Long Khun was abandoned and fell into disrepair, as did the other temples on the right bank of the Mekong. The Lao Department of Museums and Archaeology and L'École Française d'Extrême Orient painstakingly restored the temples during the mid-1990s using traditional materials and techniques.

The Luang Prabang style sim has two sections set on a low platform. The rear and older half is the original sim and dates from the 18th century. It has some interesting interior jataka murals depicting the various lives of the Buddha. Sadly many of them are badly decayed by damp. At the front is an extended portico built during the reign of King Sisavang Vong in 1937. On the facade of the sim are depicted two large, bearded Chinese warriors on either side of the main entry. There some traditional wooden kutis (monks' quarters) in the grounds and a long, narrow structure without windows that served as a royal meditation room.

Wat Mahathat Wat Pha Mahathat or the "Monastery of the Stupa" was founded by King Say Setthathirat in 1548. The king was actually ruling from the Lanna Kingdom of North Thailand at that point. He also erected the imposing Lanna-style stupa, to the rear of the sim. The northern Thai influence can be seen in the golden umbrellas on the top of the stupa.

The staircase leading from Thanon Chao Fa Ngum Road with its silver colored seven-headed naga has echoes of the similar but much longer staircase at Doi Suthep in Chiang Mai. The sim was rebuilt in 1910 by Chao Maha Oupahat Boun Kong to replace the one that collapsed during a storm that struck during evening prayers in April 1900. Many people died in this tragedy. The sim, built in Luang Prabang, was restored in 1963. There are interesting relief murals in the portico at the front and decorations that depict the legends of King Thao Sithoanh and the Nang Manola. Others portray the kinnari (divine half-woman/half-bird renowned for its carefree kindness) and stories from the Ramayana. Within the confines of the wat also are the ashes of the revered Prince Phetsarath (believed by many to have had magically invincible powers as a half-deity), who declared Lao independence after the Japanese surrender in 1945, and Prince Souvanna Phouma, his younger half brother, who served as prime minister before the advent of the Pathet Lao.

Wat Mai ★★★ Wat Mai Suwannaphumaham, or the "New Monastery" is actually one of the oldest surviving monasteries in Luang Prabang. Like Wat Xieng Thong it was spared the ravages of the Chinese Haw invaders of the 1880s. It is also is one of the biggest, most beautiful, and most photographed of all the wats in the city. It is located right on Sisavangvong Road where all the restaurants and Internet cafes can be found.

Tips Make Merit

Picture Sunday Mass at a typical church somewhere: Everyone is seated, ready for the ceremony to begin. The priest and altar boys start to walk down the aisle. Suddenly, visiting tourists rush to the end of the pews and start photographing like paparazzi, flashes and all. Sound crazy? Well that's what happens at Luang Prabang's Tak Bat, or Make Merit, a living religious ritual that occurs at dawn each day. The procession of saffron-clad monks walking down the streets of Luang Prabang to collect the food offerings of devout, kneeling Buddhists is a breathtaking sight. But it is disrespectful to treat it as a tourist show. When I watched, several travelers were chatting while they were giving food and thrusting cameras uncomfortably close to the monks. One man, after he had given away all his sticky rice, hollered across the street to his companions, "All right, should we move on to the outdoor market then?" Monks were still walking past him. Put your best foot forward here and observe these local customs (as laid out by the National Tourism Authority) before you take part in or simply watch the act of Tak Bat.

- Observe the ritual in silence and contribute an offering only if it is meaningful for you and you can do so respectfully.
- Buy the rice at the local market earlier in the morning rather than from street vendors along the monks' route.
- If you are not making an offering, keep an appropriate distance and be respectful. Don't get in the way of the monks' procession or people giving alms.
- Do not photograph the monks too closely; camera flashes are very disturbing for both the monks and those giving alms.
- Dress appropriately; your shoulders, chest, and legs should be covered.
- Do not make physical contact with the monks.

The wat was founded by King Anourout (1795–1817) in about 1796. No one is exactly sure of the exact year. Most of it dates from the 19th century. Restoration of the wooden sim possibly started in 1821 or 1822 during the reign of King Manthatourat (1817–36), when it was given the name of the New Monastery. There were also major restorations in 1943 and 1962, as well as more recently. The sim is built in the traditional Luang Prabang style with a sweeping roof and porches on two sides.

Wat Mai served as a temple for the royal family and long has been the residence of the Pra Sangkharat, the patriarch of Lao Buddhism. In 1887 the Haw spared this temple. Historians say it was because they found it too beautiful to destroy. If so they get zero points for consistency given what they did decide to set fire to. Wat Mai became the repository of the Pha Bang until, in 1947, the gold statue was moved to the royal palace, now the Royal Palace Museum. During Pimai, or Lao New Year, the Pha Bang is ceremoniously brought from the museum to a temporary pavilion in front of the sim and for 3 days there is ceremonial washing of the image and opportunities for the faithful to make offerings.

A previous abbot of Wat Mai also took a part in the opening of Luang Prabang to the world outside of Asia. In 1887 Auguste Pavie, who had a strong admiration for the region, arrived in Luang Prabang as the first French (and European) vice-consul in Laos.

At the time the city and region were under Siamese control. They tried to prevent Pavie and his group from getting access to the king, Oun Kham. The abbot, however, a confidant of the king, served as a courier for messages between the king and Pavie and invited the Frenchman to stay at the monastery. French influence grew and by 1893 Siam was forced to secede Laos to the protectorate of the French. Pavie was also allowed to examine the extensive palm leaf manuscripts of the Wat Mai and used them to write the first history of Lao in a European language.

The sim has a magnificent five-tiered roof. It also contains a superb relief, which actually dates only as far back as the late 1960s. The cement reliefs were first covered with a black lacquer and then gilded. This relief depicts scenes from the Ramayana and the Vessantara-Jataka, the Buddha's penultimate reincarnation, all taking place in countryside that is reminiscent of the surrounds of Luang Prabang. During the 3-day festival of Pimai in April Buddhists outnumber tourists, reinforcing just how important Wat Mai is to the Lao.

Sisavangvong Rd. Admission 10,000 kip. Daily 8am–5pm.

Wat Manorom   Wat Manorom Sattharam is situated just outside the remains of the old city walls to the south. Most experts agree that it is built on the site of one of the earliest Khmer Buddhist sites, although they disagree about the date it was founded. It might have originated with Samsenthai (1373–1416), the son of King Fa Ngum in 1372 or 1375 (either before or after he ascended to the throne). Others suggest in 1491 or 1492, during the reign of La Saen Thai. That it was important is sure since it housed the Phra Bang at one point from 1502 until 1513, when it was moved to Wat Visoun. The sim was rebuilt in 1818, but, like so much else, was destroyed by the Haw in 1887. The present sim, rebuilt in 1972, is one of the tallest in Luang Prabang. In the grounds behind the sim are the remains of an earlier wat—Xieng Kang. Although the sim is fairly modern and pales into insignificance compared to others in Luang Prabang, it does play a significant role in the community. One of its most important features is the great Buddha cast in the 1370s

---

(Moments)   Taking Refuge: Making Friends at the Temple

There is little that's spectacular on the sleepy peninsula of Luang Prabang. Rather, time spent here is about soaking up the atmosphere and taking leisurely walks along dusty roads lined with French colonial buildings. Another great local activity is to stop in at a temple—any temple, really—and meet with the monks or young novices. The monks are great sources of information and insight into Laos culture, Buddhism, and the vagaries of human existence. Language is a big part of their training, and they study Pali and Sanskrit as well as English and French (and even Chinese and Japanese). Novices like to practice their English or even get help with their homework. Women should be careful not to touch or sit too close to monks and novices, but all are welcome in the temple. Don't give in to any pleas for sponsorship (unless you want to); monks live through the generosity of the sangha, or monastic community, and don't need sponsors.

during the reign of Sam Saen Thai. It is in the Sukhothai style rather than Lao or Khmer. The sitting statue weighs over 2 tons and is 6m high. The image is in the "victory over Mara" pose with one hand touching the earth. It is the oldest large Buddhist statue in Luang Prabang and for much of its history it sat outside the sim. It was heavily damaged during the rampages of the Haw in 1887 and also during the Franco-Thai war in the late 19th century, when its arms were destroyed. This piece of wanton theft and destruction was most likely perpetrated by the French although they reaped their karmic reward as their boat sank in the Mekong. They forgot a part of the Buddha's forearm and that can now be seen at the base of the statue in the sim. When the sim was rebuilt in 1972, the statue was enclosed in the sim and the arms were reconstructed from cement. The wat has the largest number of monks and novices of any monastery in Luang Prabang and there is also a primary school. A new wall encircling the grounds of the wat was completed in 1995.

Wat Pa Huak ★★★ (Moments) Wat Pa Huak or the "Monastery of the Thornless Bamboo Forest" was founded in 1861 by Phaya Si Mahanam during the reign of King Chantharath (1850–72) and was named after the bamboo forest that used to be on the site. It is situated to the northeast of Mount Phousi and opposite the Palace Museum. The rather dainty sim is in the Vientiane style. The exterior is of the temple is in dire need of repair. There is a delightful and elaborate carved wooden facade formerly covered in mosaics, although little remains. In the center of the facade there is a depiction of Indra riding Airavata, the three-headed elephant of Hindu mythology. The weathered doors still show traces of what they once were.

The most interesting features of Pa Huak are the quirky 19th-century murals decorating the interior walls. They provide fascinating insights into ordinary life at the time rather than the usual religious themes that one normally finds. Most interesting is the depiction of the story of the Buddha's humiliation or the taming of the haughty King Jambupati, by showing himself as the Buddha King of the world rather than a lowly monk. There are also portrayals of Luang Prabang receiving Chinese, European, and Persian visitors with elephants, horses, and tigers. It's all very lively. If you are a fan of history as told through murals (such as in Wat Phumin in Nan and Wat Phra Singh in Chiang Mai, Thailand), then Wat Pa Huak is a treat.

Sisavangvong.

Wat That Luang Wat That Luang Rasamahavihane is known as the "Monastery of the Royal Stupa." It has long been associated with Lao royalty of Luang Prabang. Legend suggests that an early monastery on the site originated from a visit by Buddhist missionaries sent by Asoka, the 3rd-century-B.C. Buddhist evangelical Indian king. The legend is unsupported by any real evidence however. Relics from the early 12th century have been discovered, though they may have come from a site in northern Thailand.

The present sim was constructed on a small hill south of the city in 1818 during the reign of King Manthaturat (1817–36). It may have been built partly from the branches of a bodhi tree located near Wat Keo Fa. The sim is built in Lao style with gables on both the northeast and southwest sides. There are no porches or verandas, nor are there the sweeping rooflines that you find on so many wats in Luang Prabang. The large bronze-and-gilded Buddha inside the sim was transferred from the now-defunct Wat Aham Mungkhun, located a short distance from That Luang. It weighs about 1,100 pounds.

That Luang has long been one of the important ritual sites for Buddhist, traditional, and royal events; the Festival of the 12th month, or Tat, in particular. In the past it was presided over by the king. There are two large stupas on the grounds. The golden funerary stupa in front of the sim contains the ashes of the king, Sisivang Vong (1904–59). It is the site of annual commemorations. There are also a number of smaller stupas that contain the ashes of other kings, members of the royal family, and a mixture of dignitaries. The wat is home to one of the city's larger communities of monks and novices.

Phu Vao Rd.

Wat Wisunarat (Wat Visoun) ★★ This was another building that was only restored by the French after the Chinese bandit invasions of the 1880s. The original structure was built in 1513 under King Wisunarat (also called King Visoun) and it represents the earliest Lao style, sometimes referred to as Luang Prabang Style I, of Lao temple architecture. It was rebuilt in the late 1890s. It's actually the oldest functioning wat in Luang Prabang, which gives it a slightly different feel from some of the other sites. It's an unusual in that it has a strange, almost European-looking, sloping front roof covering the entrance. The celebrated *Pha Bang* Buddha now in the Royal Palace Museum was housed here from 1507 to 1715 and again from 1867 to 1894. The sim today continues to be a valuable museum of religious art with numerous centuries-old Buddha statues in bronze and gilded and unadorned wood, ordination precinct stones, and other religious objects. It is famous for its lotus stupa. The dome stylistically reflects a Sinhalese influence and is the only stupa of this shape in Laos, or indeed the rest of Indochina or Thailand. Lao people refer to it as the *Makmo* or watermelon stupa. It becomes obvious why when you first see it. It was built in 1515 and was originally packed with small Buddha images made of jade, gems, and gold. Once you have read only a little bit about the history of Luang Prabang it comes as no surprise that the plundering Haw tore the stupa open to steal everything they could. The French restored it in 1895, but they didn't do a very sound job since they had to do it again in 1932 after rain caused it to partially fall down again.

Wisunerat Rd. Daily 8am–5pm. Admission 10,000 kip.

Wat Xieng Thong ★★★ This is considered to be the most magnificent temple in Luang Prabang—the "Golden City" or "Golden Tree Monastery." This is saying something since standards of breathtaking beauty and serenity in temple building in Luang Prabang are very high. Xieng Thong is situated on an embankment above the Mekong near the point where it joins the Nam Khan River and it often served as the gateway to the town. Visitors from Siam, which long controlled the region, would end their journey at Ban Xieng Mene on the right bank and be ferried across to the city. This was also the entry point for the king to be on the eve of his coronation after the customary 3 days of prayer and meditation at Wat Long Khun. It was the site of coronation of Lao kings and also the center of numerous annual festivities. The sim, or ordination hall was first built by King Setthathirat in 1560 and it remained under royal patronage until the Communists broke the link in 1975. The Triptaka library was not added until 1828 and the drum tower as recently as 1961.

Here there is little history of the damage that scarred so much of the city and caused the need for so much renovation and restoration under the French. Wat Xieng Thong was spared the destruction visited on the rest of the town by the rampaging Chinese Haw in 1887. The wat was desecrated but not destroyed. Their leader, a Vietnamese ethnic White Thai from what is now northern Vietnam, had studied there as a novice monk. With Wat Xieng Thong he somehow managed to get in touch with his feminine side, something notable by its absence when he destroyed everything else in sight, and used this temple as his headquarters.

Its name translates as "golden city monastery," echoing a pre-Buddhist era when the area was known as Muang (municipality) Xieng Thong. Wat Xieng Thong is a perfect example of the Lao style with a low, majestic, sweeping roof with stylized naga boards. Inside, there is a magnificent Buddha image and overhead is a naga-shaped wooden channel that carries the water for the new year and ordination ceremonies before it flows out through the trunk of a carved elephant.

Outside, on the rear wall of the temple, there is a "tree of life" in mosaic. Inside the richly decorated wooden columns hold up an elaborate ceiling on which "dharma wheels" are portrayed in gold. Other buildings in the complex include what the French called "La Chapelle Rouge" or the Red Chapel. This contains a rare and beautiful black reclining Buddha that was most likely carved at roughly the same time King Setthathirat ordered the construction of the original sim. This is a very unusual image indeed since it breaks from the predominantly Lanna- and Thai-oriented styles that one normally sees on reclining Buddhas in Laos and was made in a pure Lao classical manner.

Like other Buddha images from Laos that ended up elsewhere, this image is fairly well traveled. The French took it to Paris for the city's 1931 exhibition and, when it was returned to Laos, it stayed in Vientiane before finally being returned to Wat Xieng Thong in 1964.

Another remarkable sight is the imposingly enormous (12m/39-ft. high) funeral carriage that was paraded through Luang Prabang, carrying the ashes of royalty as part of the funeral rites. There are funeral urns containing the ashes themselves. They are protected by yet another fearsome naga.

Khem Khong Rd. Admission 20,000 kip. Daily 8am–5pm.

| WALKING TOUR | LUANG PRABANG |

START:	Wat Phousi
FINISH:	Mekong riverbank
TIME:	3 or 4 hours, not including eating or shopping stops.
BEST TIMES:	Morning or late afternoon

Luang Prabang is a city made for strolling. It's a tiny place, and every few steps you will come across something ancient or fascinating or both. Be sure to read the full listings for each wat, above.

Start with a climb up the hill to:

❶ Wat Phousi

Wat Phousi provides excellent views of the town, with the two rivers that flank it set out before you.

At the foot of the hill is:

❷ Wat Pa Huak

This wat features fascinating murals of life in Luang Prabang in centuries past.

Cross over the road to the:

❸ Royal Palace Museum

This museum allows you to take in some of the atmosphere of the prerevolution royal city. You can also see a replica of the Pha Bang statue that gives the city its name.

Now walk directly northeast up the peninsula of land where most of Luang Prabang's sites are situated. It starts as Sisavangvong Road and turns into Sakkarine Road. Along the way, you will find:

④ Wats at Sisavangvong and Sakkarine

In this area, drop into **Wat Mai** (before the Royal Palace), **Wat Nong, Wat Sene,** and **Wat Khili.** Each of these wats is an absolute jewel.

> **TAKE A BREAK**
> Stop for lunch at any one of the superb restaurants on both Sisavangvong Road and Sakkarine Road when the temples become tiring.

At the end of the peninsula is:

⑤ Wat Xieng Thong

This is the premier wat of Luang Prabang. With its exquisite exterior, typically Lao sweeping roof, and intricately carved doors, it is a cultural highlight.

Exit Wat Xieng and walk up Kingkitsarath Road. Keep Mount Phousi at your right, then turn into Phommathat road and then Visunerath Road where you will find:

⑥ Wat Visoun and Wat Aham

These two magnificent structures feature beautiful statues and stupas (including Wat Visoun's "Watermelon Stupa"), and viewing them is the perfect end to your day of temple hopping.

When you get to Setthathilrath Road, turn right and walk straight down to the Mekong, stopping at:

⑦ Dara Market

Enjoy a cup of coffee at the Chill Out Café (p. 267) and do a little stall browsing at the Dara Market.

Wander down to the boat pier and walk down the steps to the riverbank itself. Here you have a great view of the small mountain on the other side of the Mekong, behind which the sun sinks dramatically, silhouetting the working riverboats as they chug along the waters or sit lethargically at their moorings.

Sights Outside the City

Other sights outside of town include Wat Phon Phao (Peacefulness Temple), a golden stupa on a hilltop about 5km (3 miles) away, best viewed from afar—though the view back to town from its height is worth the trek. From here, visit nearby **Ban Phanom Weaving Village,** a now-commercialized weaving collective where you can find deals on Lao Ikat patterns and hand-woven bags. Just past Ban Phanom and hidden in a jungle riverside area (signs point the way down the embankment), find the Tomb of Henri Mouhot, the 19th-century French explorer credited with the rediscovery of Cambodia's Angkor Wat. He died in Luang Prabang of malaria while hunting the source of the Mekong. Day trips across the Mekong to small temples and villages are also popular and can be arranged with boat drivers at quay-side.

Kuangsi Waterfall ★★ As famous now for its recent collapse as anything, Kuangsi was a tower of champagne-glass limestone formations until the whole structure fell in on itself in 2003. Locals say that tour operators became too greedy and neglected local spirits, called Pi. The falls are still beautiful, but less so. The ride here, however, is quite spectacular. You'll have to travel by songthaeaw (covered pickup) for $5 per person if shared, or by boat and tuk-tuk for the same fee.

Another option, Tad Se Waterfall, is 21km (13 miles) from town and good for swimming, even if it's less spectacular in height than Kuangsi. During the rainy season, the falls are stunning. Hire a driver for about $5 or pay a bit extra for a ferryboat.

36km (20 miles) south of town. Admission 10,000 kip. Daily dawn–dusk.

Pak Ou Caves ★★ The longtail-boat ride on the Mekong is alone a worthy day trip. This stretch of river is lovely—and from the base of the cave entrance, you get a view of

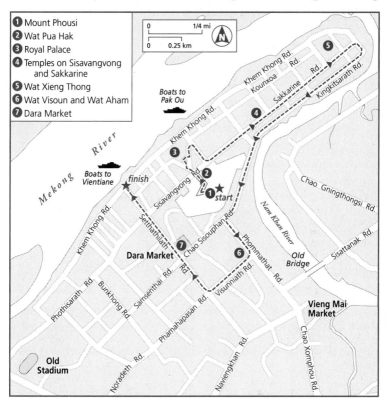

① Mount Phousi
② Wat Pua Hak
③ Royal Palace
④ Temples on Sisavangvong and Sakkarine
⑤ Wat Xieng Thong
⑥ Wat Visoun and Wat Aham
⑦ Dara Market

Boats to Pak Ou

Boats to Vientiane
finish

start

Dara Market

Old Bridge

Vieng Mai Market

Old Stadium

LUANG PRABANG & NORTHERN LAOS

13

LUANG PRABANG

the high cliffs and swirling water of the Nam Ou River as it joins the Mekong. Inside the caves is enshrined a pantheon of Buddhist statuary. A day tour costs $5 per person in a boat shared by many tourists (more for a private charter). Arrangements can be made at any hotel front desk at an inflated rate, or you can just go down along the Mekong and negotiate with boat drivers directly (these guys are sure to find you). The half-day trip often includes a visit to a weaving village or the Lao Whiskey village, where you'll have a chance to try some really potent local brew.

25km (16 miles) from town on the Mekong. Admission 15,000 kip.

Organized Tours

Green Discovery This country-wide eco-tourism orientated outfit offers tours around Luang Prabang such as the 1-day "Luang Prabang Heritage Experience" plus a whole range of adventure tours over the whole of northern Laos involving trekking, kayaking, motorcycling, mountain biking, sightseeing, and combinations of all of the above.

Unit 44/3, Sisavangvong Rd. ℭ **071/212-093.** Daily 7am–9:30pm.

Remote Asia Remote Asia offers a whole range of activities around this region. They differ from other Laos-based operators in two ways. Firstly they are totally online based and your whole trip can be meticulously planned in advance by e-mail with expert advice from the Remote Asia office. That means that when you arrive in Laos not a minute of your time is expended on admin. Secondly, although Remote Asia can offer an already set itinerary, you are also able to devise your own individual trip tailored entirely to your needs and desires. Again they use their on-the-ground knowledge to implement the logistics and provide support once you arrive. An affiliate agent in Luang Prabang is Laos Jewel Land, 02/29 Ounheuan Rd., Ban Chomkong (© **071/253-910**; www.laojewel land.com).

Rte. 13, Km 4, Vientiane. © **020/202-2139.** www.remoteasia.com.

Diethelm Travel This well-established Pan-Asian operator offers a whole range of tours both long and short in and around Luang Prabang as well as all over the north of the country.

7/2 Sisavangvong Rd. © **071/212-277.** www.diethelmtravel.com.

Tiger Trail Outdoor Adventures Tiger Trail offers series of tours and treks around northern Laos with the emphasis very much on sustainable and ethical community-based tourism. The project generates jobs and limits numbers of visitors. Their "Fair Trek" approach also promotes remote areas and makes these low-income areas a new and interesting destination for responsible visitors.

Sisavangvong Rd. © **071/252-655.** www.trekking-in-laos.com.

Luang Say Mekong Cruise This company offers luxury trips either up or down the Mekong with stopovers at ethnic villages plus the luxury company–owned Luang Say Lodge in Pakbeng. Their boats are floating palaces as much as slow boats from which you can explore life along the upper reaches of the Mekong in pampered splendor at an appropriate price.

50/4 Sakkarine Rd. © **071/252-553.** Fax 071/252-304. www.luangsay.com.

All Lao Travel Service This small outfit puts the emphasis very much on elephants. If are enchanted by these creatures, the very symbol of Lao identity, the All Lao Travel Service can bring you the experience of mahout (elephant driver) training, elephant riding, and elephant bathing. They mix these pachydermian pursuits with kayaking, mountain biking, rafting, and trekking.

13/7 Sisavangvong Rd. © **071/253-522.** www.alllaoservice.com.

Spa Treatments for All Budgets

The newly opened spa at **La Residence Phou Vao** (p. 259) is by far the most luxurious in town. Like the hotel itself, treatments are pricey but well worth the money. The **Red Cross of Luang Prabang,** near Wat Visoun to the southeast of the city, offers traditional massage and an herbal sauna to raise money for its education programs. The Red Cross is the cheapest place in town, in addition to funding a good cause. The herbal sauna is open daily from 4:30 to 8:30pm; a 1-hour massage (9am–8:30pm) costs just $3.

SHOPPING

The central area of Luang Prabang is full of places to buy souvenirs, silk, handicrafts, and jewelry. With its royal heritage and the accompanying emphasis on pageantry and tradition it is no surprise that Luang Prabang has a rich tradition of artisanship. This is compounded by its situation at the heart of a mountain region where ethnic minorities forged their own traditions of craftsmanship. Bargains are hard to find these days but there is a lot of competition so you can certainly get a reasonable deal.

Bookshops

L'Etranger Books & Tea   This bookshop stocks both secondhand books plus some new books on Southeast Asia. They also serve a delicious range of tea in the gallery upstairs or on the terrace at the front. Open Monday to Saturday 8am to 10pm, Sunday 10am to 10pm. Kingkitsarath Rd. ✆ **020/537-7826.**

Monument Books   This branch of the Indochina book chain stocks glossy coffee-table books, fiction, and nonfiction. It also sells foreign and international magazines at a fairly hefty price. Daily 9am to 9pm. 2 Thou Gnai. ✆ **071/254-954.**

Markets

Dara Market   This is the central market next to Wat Phousi and until recently it was a rough-and-ready functioning provincial commercial hub selling motorcycle parts, electrical goods, flip-flops, light bulbs, some foodstuffs, and pretty much everything else you might need. That has now changed and it has been rebuilt and gentrified. This was inevitable given its position and Luang Prabang's progress as a major tourist destination. Now it is a pleasant, clean, orderly, and mildly antiseptic tiled market with a series of stalls selling clothes, fabrics, and jewelry as well as more practical things such as shampoo, shoes, bags, and coffee. The sell is notably gentle here, and with a smile you can get people down by about 30% from their asking price. Daily 8am to 5pm.

The Night Market   Every evening from approximately 6 to 9pm, the end of Sisavang-vong Road between the central junction with Setthathirath Road past the Royal Palace to the start of the main shopping area is blocked off and becomes a Thai-style night market. Here you can get fabrics, wall hangings, T-shirts, ceramics, woodcarvings, and a great deal more from legions of grinning old ladies from the hills. Grinning they may be, but you will still need to bargain hard to get a good price. The place has a nice vibe and it's quiet and largely candlelit. In high season there are crowds but they are rarely stifling.

Shops & Boutiques

Caruso Lao Handicraft   Sandra Yuck's inspired collection of housewares, furnishings, and silk. Daily 8am to 10pm. Sakkarine Rd. ✆ **071/254-574.**

Fibre2fabric ★   Fibre2fabric Gallery is a not-for-profit exhibition space that demonstrates the role and function of textiles from different regions and ethnic groups in Laos. Through temporary bilingual exhibitions, visitors and locals have the opportunity to learn about the cultural significance of textiles in local daily life. F2F, situated in a two-story shop house, is a small resource center for those interested in learning about the textiles of Laos's ethnic groups. The ground floor hosts the changing exhibitions while the first floor houses a permanent textile collection representing 12 ethnic groups from Laos. There is also a selection of specialist films and documentaries that can be watched in the upstairs room. Ban Vat Nong, Luang Prabang, opposite Ban Pack Luck Guesthouse and next to L'Elephant Restaurant. Daily 9am to 8pm. ✆ **071/254-761.** www.fibre2fabric.org.

Kopnoi ★★★ At the corner of Phommathat Road and Phousi Road is a warehouse-like shop full of handicrafts of all kinds. Kopnoi is closely associated with an NGO called Stay Another Day. This NGO connects travelers with organizations that help to preserve local culture and heritage, and supports community projects benefiting local people and initiatives that counter tourism's negative environmental impact. Taken from the Lao language, Kopnoi means "little frog," a universal symbol for balance in the environment. The goods are varied and superb, including silk clothing and accessories, designer jewelry, and home furnishings, as well as gift boxes, spices, and delicacies. Working closely with artisans, villages, and nonprofit producers, their collections are created using traditional Lao skills. Kopnoi also has a beautiful boutique-gallery in the village of Ban Aphay, on the other side of Mount Phousi from the Mekong. Daily 9am to 8pm. Junction of Pommattha and Kingkitsarath roads. (❼ 071/260-248. www.madeinlaos.com.

Lao Buddha Shop If you are looking for a Buddha image this is the place to get one. They have all sizes and many positions. They also sell ceramics and heavy silver jewelry. Daily 9am to 9pm. Sakkarine Rd. (❼ 071/260-332.

Naga Creations Right on the main shopping drag, Naga specializes in jewelry for all budgets. You can see the craftsmen at work on the premises. Daily 8:30am to 9pm. Sisavangvong Rd. (❼ 020/777-5005.

OckPopTok ★ This self-financed initiative both produces and designs textile handicrafts. *Ock Pop Tok* in Lao means East meets West. Established in partnership with the Lao Women's Union and rural artisan communities, OckPopTok combines craftsmanship and tradition with artistic creativity and market knowledge. The initiative now provides livelihoods for nearly 200 people in both Luang Prabang and six northern provinces. Their Weaving Center is both a workshop and learning center where visitors can witness the weaving process or participate in a number of classes, workshops, and seminars. The riverside garden comprises a weaving workshop, an area for dyeing, and a Mekong Sala where classes take place. Under the traditional Lao wooden house is a weaving exhibition and cafe featuring the food of **Tamarind Café** (see p. 269). The shop carries pretty, contemporary clothing and silks, and provides significant benefits to Lao communities. Daily 9am to 8pm. Sisavangvong Rd. (❼ 071/253-219. www.ockpoptok.com.

Pathana Boupha Antique House Housed in a beautiful old French mansion, this is a good place to find a range of pretty much everything Luang Prabang has to offer. It is also a handicrafts museum. Daily 8:30am to 7pm. 29/4 Ban Visoun. (❼ 071/252-383.

Tithpeng Maniphone Luang Prabang is famous for its silverware. This is the most famous silversmith in town; they work, among other things, by appointment to the royal family of Thailand. The pieces on offer may be more expensive than those you might pick up in the market, but you are guaranteed that they will be absolutely top quality. Daily 8:30am to 6:30pm. Wat That. No phone.

(*Fast Facts*) **Luang Prabang**

ATMs There are ATMs all over the center of the city, but they are not your best bet for getting cash from home. They only issue kip (with a limit of 700,000 kip). They also levy quite a hefty charge on top of any charges your own bank might levy.

Banks & Currency Exchange   The **Bank Pour Le Commerce Extérieur Lao** (BCEL; Sisavangvong Rd.; Mon–Fri 8:30am–3:30pm) exchanges cash and traveler's checks and issues U.S. dollars. They advance money on MasterCard and Visa and charge 3% commission. The nearby **Lao Development Bank** (Sisavangvong Rd.; Mon–Fri 8:30am–3:30pm) also exchanges cash and traveler's checks but does not advance money on credit cards. All along the main restaurant drag of Sisavangvong Road there are small exchange booths open until 9pm that will change cash and traveler's checks, and make advances on MasterCard and Visa. The one attached to the Luang Prabang Bakery seems to offer the best rates.

Business Hours   Generally shops are open from around 9am to 8pm on weekdays with slightly reduced hours on weekends. Cafes tend to run from about 8:30am to 9pm or 10pm. Many restaurants open for lunch and dinner only and will be closed between 2 and 5pm. Government offices generally open Monday to Friday at 8:30am, close for lunch from noon until 1pm, and close again at 5pm. Many businesses are closed on Sunday.

Bicycle & Motorcycle Rentals   Many guesthouses offer bicycles for rent for between $1 and $3 per day. It is also possible to rent small motorcycles from a few travel agents but they are expensive. They all come from the same place and they cost $20 per day. If you want to rent a larger motorcycle for serious touring then it is better to arrange it in Vientiane. Remote Asia (www.remoteasia.com) can also send larger-capacity motorcycles from the capital to Luang Prabang.

Climate   Between late October and early February, Luang Prabang is pleasantly warm and usually sunny during the day. It can actually be really quite cold at night, however, so bring a pullover. The heat starts to build in early spring and the combination of midday sun and the dust can make it a little oppressive in the middle of the day. The rains break in May and June, when the climate remains hot but also becomes humid. The temperature cools in late summer. The best time to be in the city is between November and February in terms of weather but not in terms of crowds. During the rainy season the town entertains only a fraction of the high-season tourist population and given that rainfall tends to be sporadic rather than constant, it is actually quite a good time to experience Luang Prabang. You will certainly have more of it to yourself. Hotels also cut their room rates massively in the low season.

Doctors & Hospitals   The quality of healthcare in Luang Prabang is low. If you are afflicted by anything serious then you will need to get to Thailand. There are two hospitals in town offering rudimentary healthcare. The **Provincial Hospital** (Setthathirath Rd.; ✆ **071/252-049**) and the **Chinese Hospital** (Ban Phu Mok; ✆ **071/254-026**) can deal with relatively simple and nonserious ailments.

Emergencies   For police, dial ✆ **071/212-453;** for a medical emergency, call ✆ **071/252-049.**

Internet Access   There are Internet cafes all over central Luang Prabang charging 100 kip a minute before 10pm and 300 kip per minute afterward. A few places have free Wi-Fi, the best of which is the Chill Out Café in Dara Market.

Pharmacies   One of the more reliable pharmacies in town is the Boua Phanh Pharmacie (Sakkarine Rd.; ✆ **071/252-252**).

Post Office The post office (Mon–Sat 8:30am–3:30pm) is on the corner Chao Fa Ngum and Kitsarat Road just near the central roundabout by Mount Phousi.

Telephone The city code for Luang Prabang is **071.** If you want to make an international call don't bother with the post office, simply go to an Internet cafe.

Tourism Information **The Provincial Tourism Department** (Sisavangvong Rd.; ℂ **071/212-487;** Mon–Sat 9am–noon and 1–5:30pm) has a selection of brochures available and can help with simple questions.

NIGHTLIFE

Luang Prabang is a morning town, really, but there are a few good spots for drinks and music. Backpackers fill the quiet lanes of Ban Wat That, the old silversmith quarter near the Mekong on the east end of town, and you'll sometimes find folks up late. Take a walk down any alley for budget guesthouses and adjoining bamboo bars.

Dao Fah A modern Thai-style disco where music is played at deafening volume, whether by a live band or a spiky-haired DJ, and where Luang Prabang's young and hip congregate moodily. Daily 9:30am to 11pm. Rte. 13 near Southern Bus Station.

The Hive This bar on the Nam Khan side of Phousi is part of a small stretch where opening hours are later than in the rest of town. The Hive is a favorite of backpackers although it has none of the unimaginative vulgarity that is the curse of similarly aimed places in Vang Vieng. The music is loud and slightly punky. There is an outside terrace and the place is the busiest in town after 10pm. Daily 9am to midnight. Kingkitsarath Rd.

Muangsua Hotel At the back of this hotel is a darkened discothèque where a band plays loud Thai and Lao pop and people emerge from the darkened fringes to engage in the *ramvong* (traditional Lao and Khmer circle dancing) as well as more free-form boogie. When the locals get their en-masse synchronized "thang" together, it is really quite impressive. Daily 9:30am to 11pm. Phu Vao Rd.

SIDE TRIP TO NAM OU RIVER

Heading north from Luang Prabang is the Nam Ou River. Taking a slow boat either up, down, or both ways takes you through areas of breathtaking scenery. Limestone karsts tower over steep river valleys. There are also plenty of villages along the way peopled by a diverse variety of ethnicities. In the upper reaches during hot season when the water is low white sandy beaches are revealed—the perfect place for a swim. During rainy season when the river is high and road transport becomes difficult the Nam Ou still retains its role as a major trade and transport route and, like the Mekong, the water also flows through terrain too mountainous for road construction.

---

2 NONG KIAOW

This small town boasts one of the most beautiful settings in Asia. It is surrounded by towering limestone mountains fronting fantastic river views. There is not much to do in the town itself and facilities are still very basic. At nighttime the town remains unlit, and electricity itself is in short supply. Brace yourself for cold showers in winter.

If you go by road it takes about 3 hours from Luang Prabang, and buses leave twice daily ($3.20). Taking the boat takes twice as long but it is the journey that is the reason to be heading this way. Boats to Nong Kiaow leave infrequently from the ferry pier in Luang Prabang ($12).

There are a number of caves near Nong Kiaow worth a visit. One was the scene of tragedy during the last Indochina war when a bomb struck, incinerating all those sheltering inside. The village temple is also worth looking at since it is 250 years old, making it one the oldest surviving wats in the region.

One of the best things to do here is take the boat tour up the Nam Ou past Moung Ngoi to the canyons. Boat tours can be easily set up riverside.

WHERE TO STAY & DINE

All the accommodations and restaurants in Nong Keaow are clustered around the bridge over the Nam Ou where the boats arrive and depart. The **Nong Kiau River Side** (☏ 020/570-5000; www.nongkiau.com; 320,000 kip double) is the best place in town. It has comfortable rooms, great views, and wireless Internet. The **Chan-a-Mar Resort** (☏ 071/253-939; www.greenheartfoundation.org; $100 double) offers luxury bungalows (at a rather inflated price), in a private setting, surrounded by breathtaking views of five mountains and two rivers. This combined with gourmet Lao cuisine, happy hour cocktails, informative local tours, and an optional traditional Baci ceremony to welcome you, creates a real Lao experience unmatched in northern Laos. The **Sunset Guest House** (Riverside; ☏ 071/600-033; 200,000 kip double, 100,000 kip single) is an excellent option. It is tastefully decorated. A large balcony restaurant overlooks the river serving traditionally prepared Lao food. The **Sengdao Guest House** (☏ 071/600-001; 80,000 kip bathroom, 30,000 kip shared bathroom) offers small and basic bungalows with diminutive balconies overlooking the river. Each room has mosquito nets, electricity all night, a small fan, and a towel supplied. There is also an atmospherically lit restaurant. It may not be luxurious but it is a bargain given that it offers the best views in town.

3 MUANG NGOI NEUA

This is a pleasant, sleepy town with no road access. The lack of motorbikes and pickups gives it a very ethereal feel. Limited electricity means that the day starts at sunrise and the town shuts down by 9 or 10pm at night. No phones and no Internet add to the feeling of being constructively lost. In fact there is no infrastructure at all, so make sure you bring everything you need. It is a taste of what much of northern Laos was like only a decade or so ago. Although it is smaller than Nong Kiaow, Muang Ngoi offers more to see and do and some guesthouses offer **trekking, walking, boating,** or **caving** trips. Almost all guesthouses have hammocks on their balconies, and indeed hammock swinging is an activity approached with relish in this town. Historically Muang Ngoi was part of the Ho Chi Minh Trail so it was quite heavily bombed during the war, and locals often lived in caves to avoid the falling fire from the sky. Some of these caves can now be visited. **Accommodations** here are basic. There is a series of guesthouses offering simple bamboo huts for between $2 and $5 a night. They are all very much the same and they all serve food. The **Ning Ning Guesthouse** has hot showers, which makes it "luxury" in this neck of the woods. Muang Ngoi Neua can be reached by boat from Nong Kiaow ($1.80, 1 hr.).

Three days' travel up the Nam Ou River is the far northern town of Phongsali. This remote mountainous place is home to the greatest variety of hill tribe ethnicities in all of Laos. You will see that in the variety of tribal dress you see around you. There is also a strong Chinese influence. The picturesque Chinese Quarter of cramped, cobblestone streets lined with small, low-roofed houses is really quite atmospheric and decorative in a pleasingly simple style. You feel like you have just leaped through a Hollywood time warp onto a misty film set showing how southern Chinese towns appeared 100 years ago. It also gets pretty cold up here at 4,200m (1,400 ft.) in the winter months so a pullover or a fleece, or both, is a must. The two principal **hill tribe groups** here are **Phou Noy,** whose members wear white leggings, and the **Chinese Ho.** They are descendants of the old Yunnanese traders as well as the bandit *Haw* hordes who ravaged so much of this region in the 19th century. They wear traditional baggy trousers. Chinese is a far more widely spoken language here than Lao, and Phongsali is a Yunnanese town in both feel and culture. It was really only because of the presence of the French that this place remained within Lao borders at all. The town snakes along the top of mountain ridges overshadowed by the **Phou Fa,** or the **Sky Mountain.** The views are spectacular and the air is crisp, damp, and clear. Phongsali is a good base for trekking trips to explore this wild and remote region. It is a tough place to get to, but the rewards are worth the hardship. A visit to the **Museum of Tribes** (Mon–Fri 8–11:30am and 1:30–4:30pm; 20,000 kip) is well worth the effort if you want some background to the patchwork of ethnicities in Phongsali Province. If you are feeling fit, take a stab at hiking up **Phou Fa** itself. It is a mere 400 steps up. The views from the top are spectacular.

> ## (Fast Facts   Phongsali
>
> ***Banks & Currency Exchange***   There is a **Lao Development Bank** here that can change cash only, whether that be U.S. dollars, Thai baht, or Chinese yuan.
>
> ***Electricity***   Electricity is available only between 6 and 10pm.
>
> ***Post Office***   There is also a **post office** and a **Lao Telecom Office** offering card phone facilities within Laos.
>
> ***Tourism Information***   The **Provincial Tourism Office** (℗ **088/210-098;** Mon–Fri 9am–4pm) can fix you up with trekking information and they also organize tours.

WHERE TO STAY & DINE

The **Phongsali Hotel** (℗ **088/412-042;** 50,000 kip double, 30,000 kip single) is Chinese built and austere to a degree that might have you yearning for the cheesiest of Luang Prabang's most mindless boutique offerings. The rooms are reasonably bright and a little grubby. The more expensive rooms have hot water during the hours of electricity. Think functional. The restaurant serves adequate Lao and Thai food although you have to put up with a TV blaring out Chinese soap operas or deafening karaoke. The **Viphaphone Hotel** (℗ **088/210-111;** 80,000 kip double) is the best in town although that does not mean it is actually particularly good in the larger scheme of things. The rooms are big with Western-style toilets and hot showers. They have made some efforts to make them homey. The **Phou Fa Hotel** (✆ 020/569-5315; 50,000 kip double) is built on a hill, used to be the Chinese consulate, and is suitably fortified given the fractious history of the area. The rooms are perfectly well appointed but dark. The views are fantastic from the garden and the restaurant is acceptable.

5 HUAY XAI

If you are entering Laos by land in the north intending to make your way to Luang Prabang by river, the busy little river port of Huay Xai will be your first glimpse of the country. In Bokeo Province at the heart of the Golden Triangle, Huay Xai has long been a busy trading and transit point. Mule caravans passed through here on their way from Yunnan Province in southern China to the northern Siamese capital of Chiang Mai laden with opium and tea. Although most people transit through here jumping directly on a Luang Prabang–bound boat down the Mekong, Huay Xai is worth stopping in for a day or two. With the Mekong at your front and rugged hills at your back you are not far from ethnic minorities and some spectacular and unspoiled natural beauty. It was also recently discovered that Bokeo has one of the last remaining populations of black-cheeked gibbons in Laos. An innovative canopy forest camp, called the Gibbon Experience, has been developed to provide travelers with the opportunity to see and hear the black-cheeked gibbon. From Houay Xai you can make day trips to ethnic Lantaen villages where production of traditional saa paper and other crafts can be seen.

GETTING THERE

Crossing the river from Chiang Khong in Thailand you arrive at Immigration where you can get a visa on arrival if you haven't already got one. Some 500m (1,640 ft.) to the north is the slow-boat landing. From here you can get a boat to Pakbeng and then Luang Prabang, taking 2 days. Boats tend to leave at about 9am. There is a ticket office at the landing or you can book through a guesthouse. If you wish to take a risk with your life (p. 257), you can also get a speedboat from a landing 2km (1¼ miles) to the south of Immigration. It is possible to get buses to Luang Namtha in the north or indeed Luang Prabang from the bus station approximately 3km (1¾ miles) south of town.

(**Fast Facts**   **Huay Xai**

Banks & Currency Exchange   The **Lao Development Bank** (open Mon–Fri 8am–3:30pm) has an exchange booth near Immigration. It will cash traveler's checks and change U.S. dollars and Thai bhat.

Post Office   The **Post Office** (Saykong Rd.; Mon–Fri 8am–10pm) can facilitate international calls.

WHERE TO STAY & DINE

The **Sabaydee Guest House** (Saykong Rd.; ✆ 084/211-503; 70,000 kip double) gets good reviews, although the mattresses are rather wooden in nature. The **Oudomphone Guest House** (Saykong Rd.; ✆ 084/211-308; 50,000 kip fan double, 80,000 kip A/C double) is very clean and businesslike. The **Keoudomphone Hotel** (Saykong Rd.; ℰ 084/211-405. 50,000 kip fan double, 100,000 kip A/C double) is the grandest digs in town although in dusty Huay Xai that means not very grand at all. You do have the option of A/C and TV. It is about .5km south of town. The **Aramid Guesthouse** (Saykong Rd.; ℰ **084/211-040;** 70,000 kip fan double, 140,000 kip A/C double) offers bungalows with their own balconies near the slow-boat pier. It has clean tiled bathrooms with hot water, and the management speaks English.

Huay Xai is very unlikely to ever make it on to anyone's culinary map, but there are some decent places if you like Lao food. The **Riverside Huay Restaurant** (off Saykong Rd.; main courses 14,000 kip; daily 8am–10pm) has a varied menu of Lao and Thai food that you can enjoy along with the Mekong view. The **Nut Pop** (Saykong Rd.; main courses 10,000 kip; daily 11am–10pm) is sited on a pleasant leafy deck. The Lao food here is fiery, traditional, and delicious. The **Muang Neua** (Saykong Rd.; main courses 14,000 kip; daily 8am–10pm) offers interpretations of Western fare as well as Lao.

ATTRACTIONS

Fort Carnot is actually best viewed from across the river in Thailand. It is now a Lao Army barracks and is off-limits. In previous days the black hilltop walls were home to a detachment of French Foreign Legion. **Wat Manilat** is interesting because part of it is constructed in the teakwood Shan style that you will see in northern Thailand. There are jataka paintings (representations of the previous lives of Buddha) decorating the outside walls of the sim (ordination hall) paid for by former Lao refugees on their return from the west. The morning market or **talat sao** is very busy with traders from many different places given Huay Xai's nature as a riverine regional crossroads. There is a traditional herbal **sauna and massage** venue run by the Lao Red Cross (Saykong Rd.; ℰ **084/211-264;** daily 4–8:30pm). A sauna costs 10,000 kip while a 3-hour massage costs 30,000 kip.

Around Huay Xai

The Gibbon Experience ★★★ A good reason to linger in Huay Xai is as a base to enjoy the **Gibbon Experience** (Saykong Rd.; ℰ **084/212-021;** www.gibbonx.org). They have an office in Huay Xai just north of Immigration. The experience itself is situated deep in the Bokeo Nature Reserve, which consists of 123,000 hectares (303,810 acres) of mix-deciduous forest in a mountainous terrain ranging from 500 to 1,500m (1,640–4,920 ft.) in elevation. This conservation project came into being after the discovery in 1997 that the indigenous **black-cheeked gibbons** were not extinct as previously thought. The Gibbon Experience involves two innovative programs centering on a network of canopy huts that provide a rare opportunity to see black-cheeked crested gibbons. It is situated far into Bokeo province, a 3-hour drive and 1-hour trek into the jungle. The project's aim is to conserve the vast nature reserve and raise funds to protect wildlife while also alleviating poverty among local people. The Gibbon Experience allows visitors to experience the rainforest high up at canopy level. With a complex system of zip-lines and treehouses visitors scan the forest, in search of a sighting of the elusive ape. The project has a total of four treehouses grandly stocked with food and the necessities of life. Trekkers choose how to spend their time, and there is no schedule. Food comes when you are hungry and the guides are always around and at your service. The **Waterfall Gibbon Experience** takes trekkers deeper into the reserve with 2 to 3 hours of hiking per day along the Nam Nga River.

If you are taking the slow river trip from Huay Xai to Luang Prabang you will spend 1 night in Pakbeng, the only settlement of any size between the two. It is a fairly unprepossessing place. On the walk up the sharp incline from the boat landing to the one main street, you may be accosted by some fairly insistent kids offering to carry your bags to a guesthouse. Once there, they will ask you for the equivalent of about $10, so if you do want to engage their services agree on a price first. Although Pakbeng has long been a stop for those transporting trade goods, it is only in the last 20 years that it has been dragged out of poverty by the captive market in tourists. As late as the mid-'90s there was only one government-run guesthouse and you washed from a giant jar of cold water at the back. Electricity only ran for 2 hours a day between 6 and 8pm, when people would sit glued to Thai boxing and British Premier League soccer. Evenings were dark and the town was thoroughly basic. These days there is electricity powered by a hydroelectric dam in the Beng River, but it is erratic. There are now fridges, which means that at last the beer is cold. Although the main street is still ramshackle there are a few incongruously fashionable-looking restaurants staffed by waiters with hair gelled in spikily MTV-inspired styles. Pakbeng remains a slightly uncomfortable place both physically and in atmosphere. The sheer numbers of well-heeled tourists passing through for 1 night only in a village that until recently was very poor indeed has created predictable problems inspired by the extremes of poverty and wealth. The locals are not particularly friendly and it is no surprise that greed is rampant. There have been reports of thefts from guesthouse rooms, although whether the perpetrators were Lao or foreign is unsure. Keep your valuables with you. There are also reports that hard drugs have made an appearance here, which is very bad news indeed considering the ravages that have occurred elsewhere in Laos as a result of this evil scourge. Pakbeng is a perfectly agreeable place to stay a night (you don't have a choice anyway), but you wouldn't want to linger.

WHERE TO STAY & DINE

Accommodations in Pakbeng are generally pretty basic wherever you choose to lay your head. The available restaurants in town don't serve the world's best food, but there are some nice views of the river as it carves its way through the rock valley below. All guesthouses and restaurants are on the same street because it is the only street in town.

Villa Salika (© 081/212-306; 70,000 kip double) is minimally less basic than most other accommodations. Large, clean fan rooms constructed from concrete with cold showers make it feel a little like a gulag. That impression is ameliorated by a balcony on the top floor offering stunning views of the Mekong. The restaurant (main courses 7,000 kip–15,000 kip) below also enjoys excellent views. You will be woken very early by the speedboat drivers revving their engines in preparation for the day's forthcoming adrenaline-fueled river antics. That's not a bad thing, though, since you will want to be up early yourself to get your own boat up or down river. The **Phonethip Guest House** (no phone; 40,000 kip double) is typical of most accommodations here. None-too-clean rooms with a bed and a mosquito net. Shared bathrooms are a bit grubby, although the staff is quite cheery. The **Monsaven Guest House** (no phone; 40,000 kip double) is pokey but clean. The rooms are tiny and very basic, with bamboo walls, a bed, a fan, and a mosquito net. The shared bathrooms are newly tiled and reasonably sized. There is a hot shower when the electricity is working. The new **Pak Beng Lodge** (© 081/212-304; fax 081/212-304; $30 double) is the town's only real midrange option (apart from the

Luang Say Lodge, but you need to be on a Luang Say cruise to stay there). For Pakbeng this is the equivalent of the Palace of Versailles. Pretty rooms with shiny wooden floors include a minibar and bathrooms with hot water. The main balcony, made of gleaming dark wood, also affords good views of the river. The **Kopchaideu Restaurant** (main courses 10,000 kip; daily 10am–11pm) specializes in Indian food although they also do some Western and Thai. The dining area is on a deck overlooking the river. In the morning little stalls selling baguette *(khao ji)* sandwiches dot the main street providing you with a lunch option for the final leg of your boat journey.

ATTRACTIONS

Pakbeng is worth a wander about. There are two wats, of which one is quite interesting. **Wat Sin Jong Jaeng** is a 10-minute walk up the only street turning right from the boat landing. The sim (ordination hall) boasts some great murals depicting early European traders or invaders. The views from here are very good. There is also a small **market** in the center of town. Look out for the local delicacies, such as barbecued field rat on a stick.

7 PHONSAVAN & THE PLAIN OF JARS

Phonsavan and the surrounding province of Xieng Khuang has a history that is both mysterious and intensely tragic. As the flattest part of mountainous northern Laos in the very strategic position buffering north Vietnam, the rolling green hills of this area were often the scene of interminable conflict. From the start of the 19th century until 1975 armies and destruction swept back and forth across the Plain of Jars. Although an independent principality, the area was ravaged by the Vietnamese and the rampaging Chinese *Haw* (p. 270). At the end of the century the Xieng Kuang region accepted Thai and then French protection. Any respite was doomed to be short-lived. When the Indochina wars of independence started to rage, the strategic position of the area covering the "back door" to northern Vietnam (including the scene of French humiliation at Dien Bien Phu) ensured that it would once again be relentlessly in the front line. With the advent of American involvement the province was an integral part of the Ho Chi Minh Trail by which North Vietnamese forces supplied their compadre Viet Cong in the south. By the end of the '60s the Plain of Jars was part of one huge battlefield with American-sponsored Hmong militia battling North Vietnamese and Pathet Lao troops. Whole villages (including most of the state capital) were simply erased from the map by repeated saturation bombing. You see the rusting metal legacies taking the form of door jams, table legs, and many other practical household functions. Now 35 years since the horrors of the bombing, village life is returning to some semblance of normality and the area represents a vibrant mix of ethnicities.

PHONSAVAN

This town isn't winning any prizes for atmosphere or urban planning, but then one doesn't visit for the town itself. It is simply a base from which to explore the mysteries of the surrounding area.

GETTING THERE & GETTING AROUND

Lao Airlines flies from Vientiane to Phonsavan on Monday, Wednesday, Friday, and Sunday and from Luang Prabang on Wednesday, Friday, and Saturday. Their office is next to the post office. The **airport** is 4km (2½ miles) from town and a tuk-tuk costs around 50,000 kip to the town center. The **bus station** is in the center of town. Most of the departures are *songthaeaws* making short trips, but buses also depart for Vientiane, Luang Prabang, and Sam Neua near the Vietnamese border. Most long-distance buses leave early in the morning. It is 11 grueling hours to Vientiane and 10 no less grueling hours to Luang Prabang.

Tuk-tuks are the main form of transport here and they are not hard to find. You can also rent **bicycles** and **motorcycles,** but be aware that much of the surrounding country-side is littered with potentially explosive hazards.

⦅Fast Facts⦆ Phonsavan

Banks & Currency Exchange The Lao Development Bank (℡ 061/312-188) is on Rte. 7 and will change cash only. Most travel agents will also change cash.

Hospitals The Lao-Mongolian Friendship Hospital (℡ 061/312-166) can deal with very basic health problems only.

Internet Access There are a few Internet cafes around the center of town but the connections are painfully slow.

Post Office The post office (℡ 061/312-005) is on Rte. 7 and domestic calls only are available.

Tourism Information The Provincial Tourist Information Office (℡ 061/312-217) is a short way up the road to the airport and has limited information. Travel agencies are more helpful.

WHERE TO STAY & DINE

The **Auberge de la Plaine des Jarres** (℡ 061/312-044; $30 double) is a beautiful place overlooking town with open fireplaces and excellent food. The **Vansana Plain of Jars Hotel** (℡ 061/213-170; $30 single, $40 double, $50 suite) is also pretty grand for this part of the world, with TV, minibar, and bathtub. Its elevated situation means that many of the balconies have good views over the town. The **Puchan Resort** (℡ 061/312-264; $30 double) sits on top of a hill overlooking the town. Behind are rolling green hills and pine forests. Phuchan is made up of several large wooden bungalows. Each bungalow is divided into three separate areas with a bedroom and bathroom. Rooms are large, and simply but elegantly decorated. Bathrooms are very clean with a hot shower and Western toilet. Each bungalow has a large rear balcony, with good views of the rolling views. The **Maly Hotel** (℡ 061/312-031; $8–$50 double) has 30 rooms at a wide range of prices depending on size and facilities. It is efficiently run and the staff is helpful. The restaurant downstairs is one of the best in town (main courses 25,000 kip) serving both Western and Lao food. The **Poukham Guest House** (℡ 061/312-121; $3 double) is a simple affair directly across the main road from the bus station. It is popular with budget travelers. They are also highly regarded for their wealth of local knowledge and tours. The **Kong Keo Guesthouse** (℡ 061/211-354; www.kongkeojar.com; $3–$10 double) has seven clean rooms with private toilet and hot shower (solar cells) and six bungalows, also with private toilet and hot shower (solar cells). The lobby is in traditional Lao style. In the garden at the front is a wooden shack that serves as a bar, and stacked all around the

The Beauty of Vieng Xai ★★★

Vieng Xai, an incredibly beautiful area near the border with Vietnam, was the base of the Pathet Lao during the '60s and '70s. The rugged limestone karst formations that characterize the region are riddled with caves and it was from these that the Soviet-backed insurgents fashioned a series of subterranean complexes that enabled them to survive some of the most ferocious aerial attacks seen in the history of warfare. A series of more than 100 caves amounted to an impregnable fortress. After the Communist victory this remote area became home to thousands of those perceived to be loyal to the former regime and sentenced to "reeducation." This actually meant disease, hardship, starvation, and often death. It was these people who built the beautiful man-made lake in Vieng Xai. It is a beauty tinged with real hardship and tragedy. For years the closed attitude of the regime in Laos meant that this whole region, and its history both heroic and vicious, remained off-limits to visitors. The caves have been restored and are now opened to the public, though you must be accompanied by a government-accredited guide.

The caves sit in a natural and steeply walled limestone valley that affords them almost total protection from assault. The complex contained meeting rooms, hospitals, barracks, markets, and temples. A few of these caves are named for their celebrated former residents. Tours usually begin with **Tham Than Kaysone.** This was the headquarters of Kaysone Phomvihane, the effective leader of the Pathet Lao. From here he closely coordinated eventual victory with his north Vietnamese comrades shuttling every now and then over the border and on to Hanoi to receive direction. Inside the cave are a few relics of the Kaysone's time there including some appropriate Marxist reading. There is a reception room, kitchen, bedroom, library, and emergency headquarters

grounds are old bomb parts and other war relics. There are rooms in the main house and also newer bungalows at the rear, which are a better but more expensive option. It has a balcony restaurant. They run well-reputed tours to the Plain of Jars with the owner acting as guide.

When it comes to dining Phonsavan represents something of a black hole. Both the Maly Hotel and the Kong Keo Guesthouse represent acceptable if not exciting options. For Indian cuisine (which seems inevitable wherever tourists gather in Laos), head to **Nisha** (main courses 15,000 kip). The **Sa Nga Restaurant** (Rte. 7 near the post office; ✆ **061/211-013;** main courses 10,000 kip) serves reasonable Laos, Thai, and Chinese fare. If you want pizza or burgers, head to **Craters Bar and Restaurant** (Rte. 7; ✆ **020/ 780-5775;** main courses 25,000 kip).

ATTRACTIONS

Plain of Jars   Scattered over a large area in the middle of Xieng Khuang province, there are 160 individual jar sites on the Plain of Jars as a whole. The jars themselves are curious, huge limestone containers. In total there are about 4,000 of these mysterious objects. It is still unclear until what their purpose was, but the most likely accepted containing an oxygen generator in case of a gas attack. Kaysone's house sits at the front of the cave. **Tham Than Nouhak** is nearby and was the home of Kaysone's main sidekick and fellow Savannakhet native. **Tham Than Souphanouvong** is a cave fit for a prince, and indeed this figurehead of the Pathet Lao was half brother to his opposition leaders, Prince Phetsarath and Prince Souvannaphoumma. This war was a family affair at the highest echelons. The Red Prince lived here with his wife and 10 children from 1963 to 1973. The prince had a garage for his car and a patio on which to enjoy his breakfast. The cave is approached through a line of pomelo trees. **Tham Than Phoumi** was the home of the Phoumi Vongvichit, who became minister of information after Pathet Lao victory. It was enlarged using explosives. **Tham Than Khamtay** is named after Khamtay Siphandone, president of Laos from 1992 to 2006 and one of the Pathet Lao's most important military strategists. This is an artificial cave. Below it is a natural cave that was a barracks for hundreds of soldiers, but was also used for theatrical and sporting events as well as the occasional wedding.

Most people choose to stay in **Sam Neua** about an hour's drive away. This is best reached by **bus** via Nong Kiaow to Luang Prabang on Rte. 6 and then Rte. 1. This a 16-hour journey all the way (a stopover in Nong Kiaow is advisable). You can also reach it from Ponsavanh via Rte. 7 and then turn off left onto Rte. 6. **Lao Air** also flies to Sam Neua three times a week, although flights are often canceled due to fog or low passenger counts. Although there are plenty of accommodations in Sam Neua, the Bounhome Guest House (✆ **064/312-223;** 50,000 kip double) is regarded as the best, with a good second choice being the **Kheamxam Guest House** (✆ **064/312-111;** 50,000 kip double).

explanation is that they are funerary urns. This theory is supported by the more recent discovery of underground burial chambers. Some traces of human bodies have been found in the jars, while it is likely that the vessels themselves contained treasure. This has long ago been looted by the various rampaging invaders who have swept back and forth across these rolling hills. The jars appear in a number of different shapes, sizes, and positions; many lying prone on their side were most likely tipped over by avaricious looters.

Three of the biggest clusters of jars have been designated as officially recognized tourist sites, and an effort has been made to clear them of explosives. The whole area is still littered with the brutal confetti of war. Red markers around the sites tell you which areas have not been cleared. You should keep an eye on these and stay within the safely delineated areas.

Site One contains the most jars. This includes Hai Cheaum, or Cheaum Jar, the biggest jar of all. The scenery here is fairly uninspiring as opposed to the attractive locations in which you find other sites. It is the most popular site, and there are places set up selling snacks and drinks. Site Two is majestically situated on top of a small hill. There are some large and intriguing jars, with beautiful surrounding views. There are also quite a number of areas of remaining uncleared land mines, so keep a look out for those signs.

Site Three is the most impressive and atmospheric of all the sites, marked out by a backdrop of rolling hills dotted with bomb craters and wooded with pine trees. To reach it you walk across rice paddies and cross a small bamboo bridge. There are 130 jars here, some of which are in very bad condition.

To see the sites, there are a few options. Sensible restrictions (given all the things that can go boom!) mean that you cannot go alone without a proper guide. This means that quite a number of agencies catering to tourists have appeared in Phonsavan. They all offer day tours with a licensed guide. These cost around $10 per person, or you can rent a whole car or minivan for $50 to $100. Some guesthouses also run tours that are slightly cheaper. A van with a driver will cost you between $20 and $50 for the day, depending on where it is you want to go.

The Tourism Office offers five trips with a sliding scale of costs, depending on how many people are in the party. The Keo Kong Guesthouse, a popular option among the budget-minded, runs a tour daily for between $4 and $7.50, but will not go without a minimum of five people.

Avoid tuk-tuk drivers if they approach you offering trips to see the jars at a much better rate than that offered by official outlets. This is because they can't get permits to take passengers to all the sites, so it is a false economy since you will see very little.

The Xieng Khuang Tourism Office publishes a very useful pamphlet called "Do-it yourself activities around Phonsavan." It lists a number of interesting places to take in, as a complement to the more heavily visited sites. MAG (Mine Advisory Group) operates an office in Phonsavan and it is well worth a visit. Excellent information on the UXO (unexploded ordnance) problem in the area is on display and the office shows two award-winning documentaries on UXO clearance in Laos nightly. Donations go directly to UXO clearance.

Hot Springs   The natural hot springs at Muang Kham are government run. The actual pool where the hot water bubbles up from the rock up is fenced off, but you can get a view by taking a short path starting opposite the Hot Springs Resort. If you want to bathe then you have to go to the resort itself. It has a series of individual bathrooms in which you can soak in the warm spring water. It costs 5,000 kip.

Tham Piew   Tham Piew is a cave near Muang Kham, with a tragic and violent history. Some say it was used by locals as a shelter from aerial attack during the dark years of war. Others say it was a North Vietnamese Army field hospital. Whichever is true all those inside it were incinerated by an American rocket in the late '60s. The blackened walls bear testament to this tragic event. The journey there involves passing through both ethnic Hmong and Black Tai villages.

Muang Khoun

Muang Khoun was called Xieng Khuang and was once the provincial capital. Once capital of a royal kingdom, years of war and pillage compounded by obliteration from the sky meant that the town was all but destroyed. The temple, Wat Phia Wat, is worth a look. The enormous seated Buddha has a bullet hole through its forehead, and sits at the end of a row of towering brick pillars.

Central Laos

Central Laos is rarely at the top of anyone's list of most desired destinations and is often simply flown over or driven through on a night bus. That does not mean it is devoid of attractions. Both Savannakhet and Tha Khek are atmospheric towns strung out lazily along the Mekong facing, respectively, Mukdahan and Nakhon Phanom in Thailand. East of Tha Khek you'll find wild scenery featuring karst outcrops and some beautiful lakes. It is an area increasingly popular for trekking and ecothemed tours.

1 SAVANNAKHET

Savannakhet (or Savan) is one of the country's most important cities and shares with Luang Prabang an atmosphere of faded French colonial grandeur. Unlike Luang Prabang, however, Savannakhet is visibly crumbling, with little effort made to preserve its wonderful buildings. Savannakhet was very important to the French as an administrative center and transit point. It still fulfills many of those functions in Laos today. With the opening of the second Thai-Lao Friendship Bridge across the Mekong in 2006 and the complete renovation of Hwy. 9 from Thailand to Vietnam, Savannakhet is the gateway to one of the most important trading routes in Southeast Asia. The city is changing fast from the somnolent, crumbling echo of francophone times past to quite a vibrant (well, vibrant for Laos!) little place where there are still lights on after 10 o'clock.

SAVANNAKHET ESSENTIALS

GETTING THERE   Savannakhet is on the main north-south route from Pakse to Vietnam. The bus terminal is located near the main market, or Talat Nyai, in the north of the old town. There are three daily buses to the Lao Bao, Vietnam, border leaving at 6:30am, 9:30am, and noon. The journey takes 6 hours. You can also take a *songthaeaw,* but it's only advised if you are a masochist since it's a long journey and you will be cramped and unlikely to be able to see anything along the way. You can also cross the bridge from the very pleasant town of Mukdahan in Thailand. Take a tuk-tuk from

---

(Fun Facts   **Riding a Skylab**

In Savan, tuk-tuks are called "skylabs" for some unfathomable reason that probably has something to do with drug use by visitors in the 1960s and 1970s. These distinctly terrestrial vehicles charge between 50¢ and $1.50 around town depending on just how far you intend your orbit to stretch—or you could just ask them to beam you up direct.

Immigration to the old town for between $2 and $4, depending on your powers of persuasion.

Buses to Vientiane leave daily every half-hour throughout the day from 6am to 10pm and take about 10 hours to cover the 457km (283-mile) route. Going south to Pakse the first bus is at 7:30am and the last one is at 1:30am the following morning. The journey is 230km (143 miles) and takes 6 hours. You won't miss any great sights by traveling at night since it is a quite dreary road.

GETTING AROUND　Savannakhet's old town is small and perfectly walkable. Quite a number of guesthouses also rent out motorcycles for between $10 and $12 per day and bicycles for between $1 and $1.50. There are plenty tuk-tuks plying the streets. Just hop in and tell the man where you want to go.

(*Fast Facts*)　Savannakhet

Banks & Currency Exchange　The **BCEL** (Ratsavongseuk Rd.; ✆ **041/212-26;** open Mon–Fri 8:30am–3:30pm) changes cash and traveler's checks and gives advances on MasterCard and Visa. There is also an ATM issuing kip only. Around the corner the Lao Development Bank (Udomsin Rd.; ✆ **041/212-272**) also changes cash and traveler's checks and gives advances on MasterCard and Visa.

Embassies & Consulates　Given its location both **Thailand** (Thanon Kuravong; ✆ **041/212-373**) and **Vietnam** (Thanon Sisavangvong; ✆ **041/212-418**) have **consulates** in Savannakhet.

Post Office　You'll find the Post Office (Thanon Khanthabuli; ✆ **041/212-205**) is at the southern edge of town. There are many Internet cafes scattered throughout town. They generally close at 10pm.

Tourism Information　The **Provincial Tourism Office** (Thanon Ratsapanith; ✆ **041/214-203;** open daily 8–11:30am and 1:30–4:30pm), 2 blocks back from the river near the old immigration office, is well organized. When we went there the staff spoke English and some French. They had information not only on Central Laos but also other parts of the country. They can also provide tours and onward bookings.

WHERE TO STAY

Nong Soda Guesthouse　This hotel has one major advantage: It is by the river with two pleasant sitting areas, one downstairs and one upstairs. The outside rooms around the courtyard are large, clean, a little dark, and perfectly acceptable. It is possible to wander from your adequate bungalow onto the upstairs terrace and watch the sunset over Thailand on the opposite side of the Mekong. However, the service here is so bad it is comical. For the staff at Nongsoda, life is one TV-watching vacation. It was once a restaurant, but legend goes it failed on account of never actually bringing customers anything to eat. After 3 days of pushing we got them to boil a kettle (bring your own teabags, milk, and indeed teaspoon). This must have worn them out because after that the kettle was mysteriously "broken." Still, the staff is very friendly, despite their torpor.

Tha He Rd. ✆ **041/212-522.** 15 units. 100,000 kip inside; 120,000 kip courtyard. No credit cards. *In room:* A/C, TV, fridge.

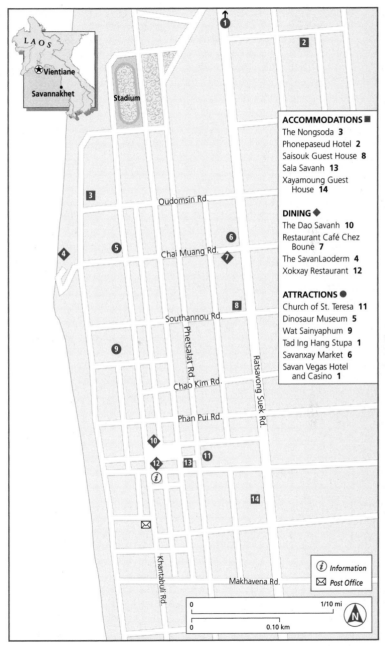

LAOS

★Vientiane

Savannakhet

Stadium

Oudomsin Rd.

3

4 **5**

Chai Muang Rd. **6**
  7

8

Southannou Rd.

Phetsalat Rd.

9

Ratsavong Suek Rd.

Chao Kim Rd.

Phan Pui Rd.

10

12 **13** **11**
i

✉

14

Khantabuli Rd.

Makhavena Rd.

ACCOMMODATIONS ■
The Nongsoda **3**
Phonepaseud Hotel **2**
Saisouk Guest House **8**
Sala Savanh **13**
Xayamoung Guest
  House **14**

DINING ◆
The Dao Savanh **10**
Restaurant Café Chez
  Boune **7**
The SavanLaoderm **4**
Xokxay Restaurant **12**

ATTRACTIONS ●
Church of St. Teresa **11**
Dinosaur Museum **5**
Wat Sainyaphum **9**
Tad Ing Hang Stupa **1**
Savanxay Market **6**
Savan Vegas Hotel
  and Casino **1**

i Information
✉ Post Office

0   1/10 mi
0   0.10 km

Ⓝ

CENTRAL LAOS

14

SAVANNAKHET

Phonepaseud Hotel ★   This is the best option in town for both midrange and top-range accommodations. It consists of a very pleasant series of semidetached bungalows in leafy grounds. You can park your vehicle right outside your bungalow, making packing and unpacking very easy if you are on a self-drive. The staff is friendly to the point of being playful, and they spend an awful lot of their time both looking at and talking about the giant whitefish in the tank in reception. Some of the rooms could be a little lighter but they are all large and comfortable. If you really want to splash out on the Super-VIP Suite for $100, you will be treated to a palatial space with a TV screen so large that it will cause you to feel positively Lilliputian. The one disadvantage of this hotel is that it is some distance from town. Getting a tuk-tuk seems to be no problem, however, and the staff will flag you down a ride and negotiate the standard price. There is an attached restaurant with a perfectly acceptable serving of local dishes and a Western breakfast (main courses 25,000 kip–35,000 kip).

Santisouk Rd. ✆ **041/212-158.** Fax 041/212-916. 69 units. $35–$45 VIP; $100 VIP suite. MC, V. **Amenities:** Restaurant; room service. *In room:* A/C, TV, fridge.

Saisouk Guest House   This is the backpacker option of choice and is very basic, but perfectly well maintained and well run. The English-speaking owners are friendly and understand their market well. There are 10 rooms, of which two are A/C doubles and the rest fan doubles (four with shared bathroom) in a fairly pleasant old wooden building. But don't expect to be encountering luxuries such as hot showers anytime soon.

Phetsalat Rd. ✆ **041/212-207.** 8 units. 30,000 kip fan and shared bathroom; 40,000 kip fan and bathroom; 60,000 kip A/C. No credit cards. In room: A/C (2 rooms).

Sala Savanh   In Lao this name means "Paradise Lodge." It is a renovated colonial building dating from 1926, located in the heart of the central district of the old city. It has charming grounds with a shaded sala in which to relax. The atmosphere is genuinely retro and cozy with a touch of faded grandeur. The rooms have a homey feel with dark-wood floors, slatted shutters, and rustic bedspreads.

129 Kouvoravong St. ✆ **041/212-445.** Fax 041/252-096. www.salalao.com. 5 units. $28 double. No credit cards. *In room:* A/C, TV, fridge.

Xayamoungkhoun Guest House   This is a clean but slightly run-down option in a very central part of town. The rooms are large and airy. The building itself is from the French colonial era and is airy with tiled walls (slightly flaky) and wooden floors. The nicest feature is the large second floor communal balcony. A major advantage of this place is that the management is very friendly and helpful. They also offer tours.

House 84, Ravongseuk Rd. ✆ **041/212-426.** 15 units. 50,000 kip fan double; 70,000 kip A/C double. No credit cards. In room: A/C (5 rooms), TV, fridge (5 rooms).

WHERE TO DINE

Where once Savannakhet was a bit of a trial on the food front, these days you have quite a number of attractive options both Lao and French. Apart from the many restaurants **the riverfront** near the old immigration building is a place to sit in low plastic chairs and chow down on steaming bowls of soup cooked at the table on earthenware pots full of hot coals. Around here during the day you will also find vendors selling *khao ji pâté* (warm baguette sandwiches with pâté and vegetables). All restaurants listed are cash only.

The Dao Savanh ★★★ Ⓕ FRENCH   This is an excellent authentic French restaurant in a beautifully renovated (in 2006) colonial-era town house. When you first

Dinosaurs in Laos

Quite strangely, the Savannakhet district has been the scene of some major dinosaur discoveries. The **Dinosaur Museum** (Thanon Khanthabuli; ℂ **041/ 212-597;** open 8am–noon and 1–4pm; admission 5,000 kip) displays some of the discoveries with captions in French and English. The biggest fossilized dinosaur is dubbed the "Big Lizard" and is an unfathomable 110 million years old.

There formerly was also a **Provincial Museum** at the southern edge of town containing artifacts of interest largely concerning more recent history. At the time of writing the museum is closed indefinitely, the mysterious explanation solemnly delivered being that "something is broken with it inside."

come across the property, it is a bit of a shock. Among the crumbling French architecture surrounding it gleams this perfect example of elegant restoration to old Indochina, displaying thoughtful design and good taste in furnishings and ambience. The food is authentically gourmet in quality with a fine range of wine. To compound its near perfection even further the prices may be higher than many restaurants around town, but for what you get it's an absolute steal. If you are tired of the road, wilting from the sun, or simply in need of pampering, the Dao Savanh is positively restorative. There is also a brand-new Internet cafe attached with well-maintained machines.

089/1, Unit 12, Simuang St. ℂ 041/260-888. Main courses 90,000 kip–150,000 kip; small plates and entrees 20,000 kip–26,000 kip; lunch menu 65,000 kip; tasting menu 165,000 kip. Daily 7am–10:30pm.

Restaurant Café Chez LAO/WESTERN   This is a very pleasant cafe/brasserie run by a Lao-French family native to both Savannakhet and Paris. There is a wide selection of French and Lao food, an excellent wine cellar, and above all a fantastic global selection of both tea and coffee. The Lao/Cambodian *luklak* (fried beef served with fries, salad, and a fried egg) is above average and the Western breakfast is very good indeed. The imported steaks are very expensive (120,000 kip), but the meat does come from France. A local steak is 56,000 kip in comparison. The place attracts an interesting NGO crowd.

Bane Xayaphoum, Chaimeunag Rd. ℂ 041/215-190. Main courses 56,000 kip. Daily 7am–11pm.

The SavanLaoderm ★ LAO   With the whole expanse of the Mekong spanning the town, it is amazing that there is only one riverside floating restaurant in Savannakhet. The SavanLaoderm is the place to come for the full celebratory communal family night out. It's on a large breezy platform on the Mekong with lots of wood and bamboo. The sunset views are superb and the atmosphere is not menaced by the tuneless wail of karaoke that can so often blight a situation such as this. The menu is encyclopedic and the steamboat-style delivery is popular among the large groups of both Lao and Thai visitors.

Thahae Rd. ℂ 041/252-124. Main courses 25,000 kip–60,000 kip. Daily 5–11pm.

Xokxay Restaurant ★ LAO   Just opposite the Dao Sanvanh this utterly unpretentious traditional Lao eatery offers a fine range of dishes, including many particular to Savanahkhet. The owner, Monsieur Nasirak, is justifiably proud of his Nam "Fer Nam," or Lao noodle soup. We would also recommend the *Mu Grob* (crispy pork) washed down with iced lemon tea.

107/16 Thanon Si Meuang. ℂ **041/213-112.** Main courses 12,000 kip. Daily 7am–9:30pm.

ATTRACTIONS

The main joy of Savannakhet is simply walking the streets and enjoying the atmosphere. The French left their legacy here in the city's now-decaying colonial structures. The central square of the old town, remains at the heart of the grid that made up the original town. Despite its appearance most of it is fairly modern, dating from the 1930s and 1940s. The pretty **Church of St. Theresa,** dating from 1930, is at the head of the square and is well maintained with a pale ocher facade and exterior. It is still very much a functioning church. The whole square would be impossibly pretty in a very Provençal way if it weren't actually falling down.

Wat Sainyaphum is the largest and oldest of all the wats in the area. It was first constructed in 1542, although most it is far more modern. Farther outside town is **Tad Ing Hang Stupa** (about 13km/8 miles heading northeast on Rte. 9; admission 5,000 kip). It dates from the 16th century and is second only in significance to Wat Phou among religious monuments south of Vientiane. There is a major festival here in February. Women will need to dress modestly and are also forbidden from entering the inner sanctum.

At the northern end of town is **Savanxay Market.** This reflects Savannakhet's status as a trade and transport hub for three nations. If you are sick of staring at the river, head east up Rte. 1 to Bungva Lake. It's a good place to relax by a different stretch of water.

A sign of Savannakhet's changing status is the area growing up around the bridge from Thailand including the brash and luxurious **Savan Vegas Hotel and Casino** (www.tycoonresort.com/main.shtml). This bizarre luxury complex will leave you feeling suitably starry-eyed if you have just come in from a remote area. It is glitzy, trashy, and utterly inappropriate. I love it. It is hard to guess what they will come up with next in this very un-Lao piece of Laos.

2 THA KHEK

The capital of Khammouane Province, the delightful riverside town of Tha Khek is undergoing something of a renaissance. Even only a short time ago, despite its obvious and compact charms, it definitely exuded an air of lost potential. It is a small French colonial town built around a central square right on the Mekong. Like so many of the major trading towns along the Mekong, the population is more Vietnamese than Lao, the French peopling their colonial administration with those considered more industrious from beyond the Annamite Mountains. Until recently Tha Khek was either muddy or dusty, the riverfront road nothing more than a rutted track. It has since undergone a face-lift with roads being paved, buildings being restored, and street lighting installed. The central square has been embellished with brand-new ornamental lampposts that local kids use as improvised basketball hoops. With the Mekong to its front and the maze of limestone karst mountains to its back, Tha Khek is in a dramatic setting. It is also a busy border crossing to Thailand, with small river ferries crossing the river constantly during daylight hours.

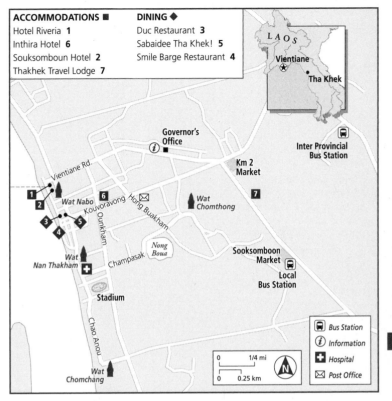

ACCOMMODATIONS ■
Hotel Riveria **1**
Inthira Hotel **6**
Souksomboun Hotel **2**
Thakhek Travel Lodge **7**

DINING ◆
Duc Restaurant **3**
Sabaidee Tha Khek! **5**
Smile Barge Restaurant **4**

Governor's Office

Inter Provincial Bus Station

Km 2 Market

Vientiane Rd.

Wat Nabo

Wat Chomthong

Nong Boua

Sooksomboon Market

Local Bus Station

Wat Nan Thakham

Stadium

Wat Chomchang

0   1/4 mi
0   0.25 km

🚌 Bus Station
ⓘ Information
✚ Hospital
✉ Post Office

CENTRAL LAOS

14

THA KHEK

GETTING THERE & GETTING AROUND

Tha Khek is on Rte. 13, the main north-south road, and buses go both ways on a constant basis (buses to Tha Khek depart every hour from Vientiane, Paksan, Savannakhet, and Pakse). The bus station is 3km (2 miles) away from the Mekong near the area of Souksomboun Market. There are plenty of tuk-tuks on hand to take you to the town center.

Although the town is quite sprawling the center is very compact. It is easy to walk anywhere you wish to go. If you do need to go farther afield **tuk-tuks** are everywhere. You can also hire **motorcycles** ($7 per day) and **bicycles** ($2.50 per day) from the Travel Lodge (p. 305).

VISITOR INFORMATION & TOURS

The **Travel Lodge** (p. 305) is affiliated with a local travel agent and they can organize tours locally. **Green Discovery** (p. 281; www.greendiscoverylao.com) is intending to open an office in Tha Khek soon and is the acknowledged expert in kayaking and trekking. Meanwhile, ask for information at the Inthira Hotel, which is owned by an affiliate company with the same management. You can also contact them at their offices in

Vientiane or Pakse before you arrive. **Remote Asia** (www.remoteasia.com) offers personalized tours in the area and they can be booked online via their website.

(Fast Facts   Tha Khek

Banks & Currency Exchange   **BCEL** (Vientiane Rd.; ℂ **051/212-686**) changes cash and traveler's checks and makes advances on MasterCard and Visa. The **Lao Development Bank** (Kuvoravong Rd.; ℂ **051/212-089**) will change cash only.

Internet Access   There are a number of Internet cafes on Kuvoravong Road leading straight up from the central square to Rte. 13. They are mainly devoted to kids playing computer games, so don't expect peace and quiet.

Post Office   Tha Khek's **Post Office** is on Kuvoravong Road.

Tourism Information   The **Tourist Information Office** (Thanon Vientiane; ℂ **051/212-512**) has plenty of information on local trekking options and tour operators, and can put you in touch with an English-speaking guide.

WHERE TO STAY

One drawback of the gentrification of Tha Khek is that there is a real dearth of decent midrange and budget accommodations. Until recently there were a couple of dilapidated but pleasant old French colonial hotels with black-and-white tiled floors and bad plumbing that more than made up for their logistical deficiencies through atmosphere and charm. They are now gone and what remains is fairly grim, with the notable exception of the Travel Lodge. The problem there, though, is that it is a long, long way from the river and the old town. If you are on a budget and want to stay near the river be prepared to grit your teeth slightly and put up with a fair amount of sleaze.

Hotel Riveria ★   From the outside, Tha Khek's only luxury hotel is a bit of an eyesore and evokes thoughts of just how bad totalitarian architecture can be. Once you're inside, this impression melts away. The hotel was totally renovated in 2008 and it was done very thoughtfully. On the upper floors you have splendid views of the river to the front and the limestone mountain ranges to the rear. The decor is "Lao lite," with silk furnishings and ornamental carvings. The rooms are not huge but are very respectable with plenty of light. The staff is very friendly and understated with a good command of English. This hotel is in no way spectacular, but it is perfectly pleasant.

Setthathirat Rd. ℂ **051/250-000.** Fax 051/252-188. www.hotelriveriathakhek.com. 56 units. $36 deluxe; $51 super deluxe; $56 executive suite; $66 VIP suite. MC, V. **Amenities:** Restaurant; room service; Internet; minibar. *In room:* A/C, TV, fridge, minibar.

Inthira Hotel   The sister operation of the hotel of the same name in Champasak tries to pull off the same trick of providing retro colonial luxury, but in this case fails. The problem is largely that the rooms are very dark and quite shabby. It is certainly not overpriced, however, being slightly only half the price of its more magnificent sister in the south. The staff is pleasant and friendly and speak good English. In all, though it fails to be what it wants to be, it is still not a bad option.

Anou Rd. ℂ/fax **051/251-237.** www.inthirahotel.com. 12 units. $18 double. MC, V. **Amenities:** Restaurant; bar; Internet; room service. *In room:* A/C, TV, fridge, minibar.

Souksomboun Hotel This hotel is simply bizarre. It is housed in a former French
police station and on first sight you might think you are entering one of those Indochina hangovers. You are not. It's more of a strange motel with some fairly suspicious "karaoke" activities taking place in an annex at the back. The building does have a quirky charm and a beautiful riverside location. It's a fun place to stay if you keep your sense of humor.

Setthathirat Rd. ℂ **051/212-225.** 23 units. $8. No credit cards. **Amenities:** Restaurant. *In room:* A/C, TV, minibar.

Thakhek Travel Lodge This is the best budget option, with large, clean rooms in a rambling house or around an adjacent courtyard. The staff is super friendly and helpful and they provide all kinds of information on things to see and do. They also rent out motorcycles and bicycles. What is there not to like? The drawback is its location. Tha Khek is about 3km (2 miles) away from the river and out of town on the bustling main road. If you factor in the $7-a-day motorcycle rental into your room cost, then it makes more sense, but since being in Tha Khek is largely about being by the river, it is a question of whether you would rather pay more or pay the same and put up with a grubbier riverside option. The Thakhek Travel Lodge also charges a $2 towel deposit, which is highly unusual.

BanVienviley Moung, Rte. 13. ℂ **030/530-0145.** 15 units. $2.50 dormitory; $5 double shared bathroom; $9 double with bathroom. MC, V. **Amenities:** Restaurant; motorcycle rental. *In room:* A/C.

WHERE TO DINE

Eating in Tha Khek is generally a fairly grim affair, especially when compared to Savannakhet. Lining the river are little shop-front outfits selling dubious barbecue. Most of the bigger hotels have restaurants serving a mixture of Lao and Western fare and, as ever in Laos, you can seek out the *khao ji pâté* vendors with their delicious warm baguettes. None of the restaurants below take credit cards.

Duc Restaurant LAO This is a place for no-nonsense Lao food, particularly noodles. It is in a very nice riverside location. There are other similar places along the riverfront, but this one is particularly popular.

Setthathirat Rd. No phone. Main courses $1.20–$2. Daily 6am–10pm.

Sabaidee Tha Khek! WESTERN/LAO This new restaurant is a very good option for Western food. They offer a range of dishes from fish and chips to noodle soup. It is very much in the standard backpacker tradition but it does do the job. The staff is very friendly if a little slow. A very bizarre but interesting dish on the menu is the "crabsticks with Japanese mustard very hot!" The warning was appreciated because the mustard is indeed hot enough to melt the paint from the body of a Toyota Corolla. If you have sinus problems, this culinary adventure may give you some relief. They also sell DVDs and they have a TV on generally showing the BBC, so it's a good place to catch up on with what is going on beyond the Mekong River.

Fountain Sq. ℂ **051/251-245.** Main courses $2–$3.50. Daily 8am–2pm and 5–10pm.

Smile Barge Restaurant LAO If you want to get even closer to the river than the vendors on the banks, head for one of the floating restaurants. The Smile Barge is the most popular. They also have a related nonfloating restaurant on the other side of the road facing the river. If you like the caterwaul of karaoke and think your skills will impress the locals, then you are entering heaven. If you don't, then you are most certainly entering hell. It's a typical Lao/Vietnamese affair and is very popular with the tone-deaf, and visiting groups of Thais from across the river in Nakhon Phanom. It is, in fact, all great fun if you don't mind crowds. It gets very busy and even a little raucous late in the evening.

Setthathirat Rd. © **051/212-150.** Main courses $3–$5. Daily noon–1am.

ATTRACTIONS

Tham Pha Pa   In 2004, a local man trying to trap bats discovered this long-hidden cavern 18km (11 miles) east of town containing 229 Buddha images. Ranging in size from 15 centimeters to as high as 1m (3¼ ft.), they had remained undiscovered for as long as 600 years. Tham Pha Pa has now become quite an important center of pilgrimage for both Lao and Thai people. The best way to get there is on a rented motorcycle. Alternatively you can hire a tuk-tuk for the day (around $15, depending on your haggling prowess).

Admission 3,000 kip. Daily 8am–noon and 1–4pm.

Wat Phra That Sikhotabong   This temple 6km (3¾ miles) south of town is Tha Khek's main attraction. The stupa is one of the most important pilgrimage sites in the region. Legend says that the present-day structure was constructed on the site of a much earlier chedi. This incarnation was built in the 19th century during the reign of the doomed King Chau Anou. It was restored a number of times through the 20th century. The golden stupa is in a typically Lao style and occupies scenic grounds right beside the Mekong. There is a major Buddhist festival here that usually takes place in February or thereabouts, depending on the phase of the moon.

Admission 3,000 kip. Daily 8am–6pm.

Mahaxai Caves and the Khammouane Protected Area ★★★   East of Tha Khek is a range of magnificent limestone karst formations and these natural glories are becoming a bigger and bigger draw for the town. The Mahaxai Caves that riddle the jagged mountains and ridges can be done as a day trip either by motorcycle or a tuk-tuk rented for the day. There are many caves, but the most visited is **Tham En,** named after the huge flocks of sparrows rumored to make this place home. On public holidays this is a popular picnic spot for locals and can get quite busy. **Tham Pha In** is often considered to be the most dramatic cave. There is a pool inside illuminated by an opening in the cave roof. The water glows emerald and in local folklore evokes the emerald green of the skin of the Hindu God Indra after which it is named. Don't touch the water. It is considered sacred. **Mahaxai** town is 50km (31 miles) east of the caves and is beautifully located nestled into the spectacular limestone scenery on the banks of the **Xe Bang Fai River.** It's a great place to simply sit and look at the view. To penetrate the **Khammouane Limestone formations** further it is best to go an organized tour since the area is remote (for operators, see p. 281). For many the **Tham Lot Kong Lo Cave** is the real highlight of a trip in this area. This is a naturally formed 7km (4⅓-mile) tunnel running right through a limestone mountain. The river flows through it until one emerges into a hidden valley. As kayaking adventures go this is a magical experience. Don't forget to bring a flashlight and some plastic sandals. In some places the water is shallow and you have to drag your vessel. Most tours will also organize a village stay giving you an insight into daily life in this remote area. There is also an **ecoresort** in the park, the **Sala Hinboun** (© **041/212-445;** fax 041/252-096; www.salalao.com/salalao/content/hinboun.htm). This all-timber offering is situated on the banks of the Hinboun River. Reached by bus and boat, it makes a convenient base from which to explore surrounding villages and caves.

Southern Laos

Southern Laos is often overlooked as eyes are drawn to the splendors of Luang Prabang and the dramatic scenery of the north. Southern Laos offers something different especially if you have a little more time or intend to travel from Laos across into Cambodia, a journey that is now very easy. Pakse is not as packed with old French colonial buildings and glittering temples as other cities but although it's a commercial hub it is a relaxed place to base yourself with a good location, good facilities, a compact and convenient center, and some good restaurants. Champasak is a riverine gem and the southern islands of Si Phan Don have become the favored chill-out zone of a whole new generation of budget travelers. The Bolaven Plateau provides a welcome relief from the heat. Above all the real gem of the south is the ancient Khmer temple complex of Wat Phou, one of a chain of several spectacular architectural relics running north of Angkor itself across Laos, Cambodia, and Thailand.

1 PAKSE

Pakse is the crossroads and administrative center of southern Laos. As crossroads go, it is a very relaxed and laid-back place. It is not packed with attractions but it is a pleasant city in which to pass a day or two. Being at the confluence of the Mekong and the Se Don rivers there are plenty of spots to enjoy a cool drink while taking in superb river views. Its geographical position as a center of commerce has been further boosted by the opening of the Lao-Japanese Bridge over the Mekong across which trundles an endless procession of trucks carrying goods from Thailand. This has increased trade and the modern part of town that adjoins it is a bustling area of markets, truck stops, and commerce. The old part of town (where the hotels and restaurants are) is far quieter. If you have limited time it makes sense to use Pakse as a base for day trips to Wat Phou, the Bolaven Plateau, and islands in the Mekong.

In terms of orientation pretty much everything you need is to be found on near Rd. 13 from the old French Bridge up to the roundabout next to the Champasak Palace Hotel.

GETTING THERE

BY PLANE **Pakse Airport** is situated 2km (1¼ miles) from town heading north up Rd. 13. **Lao Airlines** (Rd. 1.; ✆ 031/212-252; open 8am–11:30pm and 1:30–4:30pm Mon–Fri) has daily flights to **Vientiane** and twice weekly to **Luang Prabang.** A one-way flight to Vientiane costs $129. There are also international flights to **Siem Reap** and **Bangkok.** A jumbo from the center of town costs about $1. **Departure tax** on international flights is $10.

BY BUS   Hotels, restaurants, and travel agents lining Rd. 13 sell bus tickets with an inclusive shuttle to the terminal or pickup point. The **VIP bus** to Vientiane (you can't miss it—it's huge, luridly decorated, and costs 150,000 kip) picks up in town. The **Northern Bus Terminal** is located 8km (5 miles) to the north of the airport. Regular buses to Vientiane cost 100,000 kip. We recommend you take the VIP sleeper bus. It's a long way. This is the place to get transport to Vientiane and all towns along the route. It is also the terminal for buses to Vietnam via the Lao Bao and Lak Xao crossings. For excursions to the Bolaven Plateau, all destinations south, and to the remote east of the country head to the **Southern Bus terminal** 13km (8 miles) out of town heading south. Tickets to Champasak cost 10,000 kip and the bus to Don Kong (the drop-off point for Four Thousand Islands) costs 40,000 kip. The **VIP Bus Terminal** is along Rte. 11 heading near the BCEL Bank, although the buses pick up and drop off in town as well.

BY CAR   Pakse marks the junction between the main north-south Rd. 13 and Rte. 16 crossing west to east from Thailand to the Bolaven Plateau.

GETTING AROUND

Plenty of **tuk-tuks** ply the streets of Pakse, although you will need to haggle. On a shared ride reckon to pay about 50¢ to most places around town. You can rent step-through **motorcycles** at many hotels, restaurants, and travel agents around the central area along Rte. 13. The price is about $10 and some machines are certainly better than others. The Lankham hotel also has a few 250cc dirt bikes if you want something more serious. They cost $25 per day. If you want to travel engineless, bicycles are also available along the same drag for $1 a day (the ones at the Sang Aroun Hotel look good and they have gears). The Lao Chaleun hotel rents a **minivan** with a driver for $100 a day, which works if there are several of you.

VISITOR INFORMATION & TOURS

Pretty much all hotels and guesthouses have an affiliated travel agency on-site and they all run similar tours. Good travel agents dealing with tours in the south include:

GREEN DISCOVERY (Unit 47, 13 Rd. 13; ✆ **031/252-908;** www.greendiscoverylaos. com) runs a host of activity and sightseeing tours of all kinds around southern Laos. The staff is friendly and helpful and their English is good.

REMOTE ASIA (Rte. 13 Km 4, Vientiane; ✆ **020/202-2139;** www.remoteasia.com). Remote Asia is based in Vientiane but runs a whole variety of motorcycle and adventure tours around southern Laos, which you can book in advance online. They can offer you standard itineraries or you can be in touch with them by e-mail before your trip and they will assemble something individual for your needs.

XPLORE-ASIA (129 Rd. 13; ✆ **031/212-893;** wwwxplore-asia.com) can show you everything in the vicinity. For coffee aficionados they have a special coffee tour up on the Bolaven Plateau. You won't only drink it—you will see how it is created and meet the villagers who make their living producing it.

DIETHELM TRAVEL (Thaluang Rd. opposite the Thaluang Hotel on the road running parallel to Rd. 13 btw. Rd. 13 and the Se Don River; ✆ **031/212-596;** www.diethelm travel.com). This upmarket travel agency has a small Pakse branch.

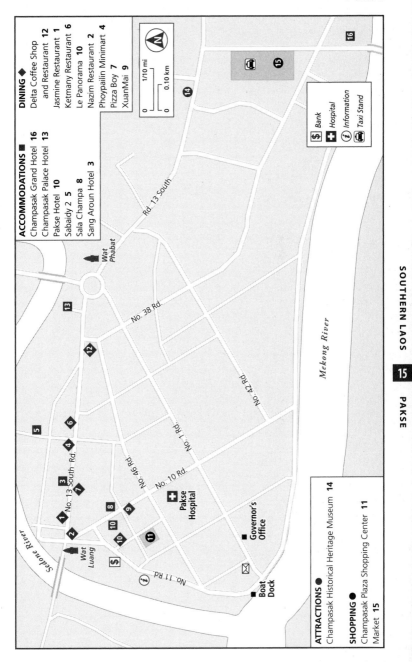

ACCOMMODATIONS ■
Champasak Grand Hotel **16**
Champasak Palace Hotel **13**
Pakse Hotel **10**
Sabaidy 2 **5**
Sala Champa **8**
Sang Aroun Hotel **3**

DINING ◆
Delta Coffee Shop
and Restaurant **12**
Jasmine Restaurant **1**
Ketmany Restaurant **6**
Le Panorama **10**
Nazim Restaurant **2**
Phoypailin Minimart **4**
Pizza Boy **7**
XuanMai **9**

ATTRACTIONS ●
Champasak Historical Heritage Museum **14**

SHOPPING ●
Champasak Plaza Shopping Center **11**
Market **15**

0   1/10 mi
0   0.10 km

$ Bank
✚ Hospital
ⓘ Information
Taxi Stand

Wat Phabat

Wat Luang

Sedone River

Mekong River

Rd. 13 South
No. 38 Rd.
No. 42 Rd.
No. 1 Rd.
No. 46 Rd.
No. 10 Rd.
No. 13 South Rd.
No. 11 Rd.

Pakse Hospital
Governor's Office
Boat Dock

(Fast Facts) Pakse

Banks & Currency Exchange **BCEL** (Rd. 11 along the river south of the old French Bridge; ✆ **031/212-770;** open Mon–Fri 8am–3:30pm) has a **currency exchange counter** outside at the entrance that changes cash and traveler's checks and can give advances on both Visa and MasterCard. There is also an ATM, which takes Visa and MasterCard. BCEL has three other ATMs scattered around town including one situated on Rd. 13 right in the center of the hotel and restaurant district. They only issue local currency up to a limit of 700,000 kip. They also apply hefty charges. You are better off using the exchange kiosk. The **Lao Development Bank** (Rd. 13; ✆ **031/212-168;** open Mon–Fri 8am–4pm) changes cash and traveler's checks and gives cash advances on Visa and MasterCard.

Hospitals The **Hospital** (✆ **031/212-018**) is situated on the corner of Rd. 10 and Rd. 46.

Internet Access There are many Internet cafes lining Rd. 13. Some of the machines are in serious need of technical support and a complete system reinstall.

Post Office The **Post Office** is south of the town center at the corner of Rd. 1 and Rd. 8.

Telephone The city code is **031.**

Tourism Information The Tourism Information Office (Rd. 11, 20m/66 ft. toward the river from the BCEL Bank; ✆ **031/212-021;** open 8am–noon and 1:30–4:30pm). This is a good place to find out about tours and onward transportation.

WHERE TO STAY

There are plenty of midrange options in Pakse. The true budget options are scarce, while in the luxury category there are two absolute gems of very different sorts: the Champasak Grand Hotel and the Champasak Palace Hotel.

Champasak Grand Hotel From the outside this brand-new international hotel looks like a bit of a skyline mistake. There are enough examples of new luxury hotels in Indochina being built with an eye to the surrounding French colonial architecture to make the exterior facade of the Champasak Grand an architect's folly. The building dominates the new town near the Lao-Japanese Bridge. Still, the location is superb, the rooms and facilities are well designed, and the service is good. All this comes with real newly minted luxury at a very cheap price. The views from the rooms, the pool area, and the restaurant are fantastic. You see the sweep of the Mekong both ways, and when the rains and thunderstorms come rumbling up the river during monsoon you have a ring-side seat for the show. Rooms have high ceilings, floor-to-ceiling windows, and tasteful decor. In low season (which is when the rains arrive) the rooms are discounted by up to 30%. For a couple of days of affordable luxury in a simply beautiful location this place is a winner.

Lao Nippon Bridge Mekong Riverside. ✆ **031/255-111.** Fax 031/255-119. www.champasakgrand.com. 115 units. $65 superior; $80 deluxe; $120 premier; $200 executive suite. AE, MC, V. **Amenities:** 2 restaurants; bar; Internet; outdoor pool; room service; spa and fitness room. *In room:* A/C, TV, fridge, minibar.

Champasak Palace Hotel ★ This hotel was described by one travel guide as an eyesore. Nothing could be further from the truth. It is gaudy, flamboyant, and absurd. All these things make it interesting and fun. It was originally constructed in the late '60s as a palace for Prince Chao Boun Oum, the last prince of Champasak and Lao premier between 1960 and 1962. He fled to France in 1974 as a Pathet Lao victory became imminent and he died soon after. It was renovated in the early '90s and now provides unique experience at a wonderfully cheap price. This vast rambling building is characterized by mosaic pillars, lots of gold-painted motifs, giant potted plants, and dark wooden floors. Some of the single rooms have small windows, which can make them seem quite dark although they are appointed in a suitably old-world colonial style. The VIP suites are huge, sitting on top of the building on a kind of plinth with a shaded veranda on all four sides. They have great views of the Se Don River (if you're there in May you will also be treated to the sight of the orange flowering frangipani). There is an elevator down to reception running down the outside of the building, but it is glass-sided so is a bit alarming if you have a problem with heights.

Rd. 13. ✆ **031/212-263.** Fax 031/212-781. www.champasak-palace-hotel.com. 115 units. $35 standard; $45 superior; $60 VIP suite; $100 queen suite; $200 king suite. MC, V. **Amenities:** Restaurant; bar; fitness room; room service; Wi-Fi (lobby and VIP rooms only). *In room:* A/C, TV, fridge, minibar.

Pakse Hotel ★★★ This is a superb midrange hotel. The building used to be a cinema. Recently renovated, the whole place has an understated class and style demonstrating perfectly judged taste. Some of the rooms have excellent views and all are well appointed. Service here is much better than average in Laos. It is a well-run operation. There is also a very nice (and refreshingly breezy) rooftop restaurant, which provides the perfect setting to contemplate a Mekong sunset.

Rd. 5. ✆ **031/212-131.** Fax 031/212-719. www.paksehotel.com. 63 units. $25 economy; $28 standard; $38 superior; $45 deluxe; $53 panorama; $71 minisuite; $96 VIP suite. AE, MC, V. **Amenities:** 4 restaurants; Internet room service. *In room:* A/C, TV, fridge, minibar.

Sabaidy 2 This very cheap and basic option is for the full-on backpacker niche market. If you are not into the international ethos of bongos, banana pancakes, and loosely fitting pajamas then you might want to steer clear. Sabaidy 2 receives excellent reviews from the market it serves and if you are on a supertight budget then it's definitely the one for you. This guesthouse is very popular and often full. There is a little restaurant-courtyard at the front where the initiated can swap yarns of the road.

Rd. 24. ✆ **031/212-992.** $2.95 dormitory; $4.70 single with shared bathroom; $6.90 double with shared bathroom; $10 triple with shared bathroom; $8 double with shower. No credit cards. **Amenities:** Restaurant.

Sala Champa This is a slightly rambling affair in one of Pakse's few old French colonial villas. Although the reception area has an incongruous air of decay the hotel itself is atmospheric, with polished wooden floors, old-world furniture, Lao silk furnishings, and pleasant leafy balconies. The rooms increase in price the higher up the house you go. There is one suite that is beautifully appointed, very much with an eye to the colonial Indochina aesthetic. Rooms in separate chalets lining the courtyard are considerably cheaper than those in the main house, because they are also considerably smaller. There is a pleasant sitting area between reception and the courtyard, and a restaurant and beer garden are attached.

Rd. 14. ✆ **031/212-273.** Fax 031/212-646. 17 units. $14–$26 double; $38 suite. No credit cards. **Amenities:** Restaurant; bar. *In room:* A/C, TV, fridge, minibar.

Sang Aroun Hotel   A very new, spotlessly clean, business hotel at a very good value. The foyer is positively gleaming with a slightly Orwellian air of efficiency. Indeed if you are on business with a small per diem this is the hotel for you. The rooms are large and well appointed. The service is good, but the hotel does lack character.

Rd. 13. ☎ **031/252-111.** Fax 031/252-555. 31 units. $23 standard; $30 deluxe. No credit cards. **Amenities:** Restaurant; bar; Internet. *In room:* A/C, TV, fridge, minibar.

WHERE TO DINE

As in most of Laos, Pakse is very much a cash economy, and all the establishments below take cash only.

Delta Coffee Shop and Restaurant ★ LAO/WESTERN   This is a good place for breakfast, but also a very viable option for every other meal of the day. With a bewildering display of carefully coded choices on the menu the indecisive could possibly starve simply as a result of pondering the wealth of options. Both the breakfasts and the coffee are superb. The terrace at the front is a pleasant place to watch the world go by.

Rd. 13. ☎ **020/543-0063.** Fax 031/213-634. Main courses 20,000 kip–45,000 kip. Daily 7am–11pm.

Jasmine Restaurant and the Nazim Restaurant INDIAN   These two very popular Indian restaurants are on opposite sides of the street on Rte. 13 in the heart of the hotel district. Their history represents something of a tortured soap opera. Travel guide folklore tells us that at one time they were one and that a heavenly schism tore them apart in a welter of rancor and bad feeling. Whatever the truth of it may be (and they both claim to be the "first"), it is certainly slightly odd that you have two groups of south Indians far from home who remain in such disharmony that they actually don't speak to each other. The Nizam used to be two doors up from the Jasmine under the now-defunct Ponsavanh Guest House. It has now moved across the road and is under the Royal Pakse Hotel. Both restaurants are hit-and-miss. In the Jasmine the quality of the masala dosa (south Indian pancake with potato filling) wildly varies. In the Nazim, a masala dosa was a sort of pea pancake, which was certainly original but not very Indian. When both restaurants are functioning, the food is good, but too often they count on the ignorance of their clientele and produce food that would have people laughing them out of town in Chennai. In both restaurants the Indian *chai* (tea) is the real deal.

The Jasmine Restaurant: Rd. 13; ☎ **031/251-002.** The Nazim Restaurant: Rd. 13; ☎ **031/252-912.** Main courses 15,000 kip. Daily 7am–10:30pm.

Ketmany Restaurant ASIAN/WESTERN   With a well-shaded leafy terrace, this is a pleasant place in the heat of the day. There is a good mix of Lao, Thai, Vietnamese, and Western food. The Asian food is better than the rather lackluster attempt at Western fare. Service is slow but friendly. The slowness might be because the restaurant appears to be woefully understaffed.

Rd. 13. ☎ **031/212-615.** Main courses 6,000 kip–12,000 kip. Daily 7am–10pm.

Le Panorama ★★★ Moments ASIAN/WESTERN   This restaurant on the roof of the Pakse hotel is one of the best in southern Laos. Whether you choose French, Lao, or Thai food, the chef produces great results. The surroundings are softly lit, and the restaurant has great views of the Mekong and the Se Dong rivers as well as the town of Pakse itself. The staff is super friendly and the service is good. The hotel Wi-Fi works here as well, so it's a good place to combine a bit of surfing with the closest that Pakse has to a

More Choice Eats in Pakse

There are plenty of food stalls and floating restaurants lining the Mekong on Rd. 11, just south of the main hotel and restaurant area on Rd. 13. It's hard to choose which is the best, although **Kamphong Sihavong** (✆ **031/213-240**), a floating restaurant specializing in seafood dishes, certainly draws a healthy crowd of locals. Best thing is just to wander slowly down the road, pick a spot where the view appeals to you, pull up a plastic chair, order an ice-cold beer Lao, and wait for the sun to sink in a satisfying ball of orange and red.

gourmet experience. Being French run, there is also a selection of wines from a well-stocked cellar. Come here to enjoy the sunset over the Mekong.

Rd. 5. ✆ **031/212-131.** Fax 031/212-719. www.paksehotel.com. Main courses 45,000 kip. Daily 5–11pm.

Phoypailin Minimart ★ ASIAN/WESTERN   This local favorite is right at the center of town, at a crossroads next to the main Honda dealer. There is a shaded sitting area in front of the shop. Good, basic Lao and Vietnamese fare is cooked up in a wok just near the cash till. The family that run this place is very friendly. It's also a good place to stock up on supplies. Many use it as a meeting spot, because of its obvious and central location. They open very early for breakfast, with strong coffee and fresh baguettes.

Main courses 6,000 kip–12,000 kip. Daily 6am–11pm.

Pizza Boy ★ LAO/WESTERN   Pizza Boy opened in 2006, serving delicious Italian food. They specialize in fruit shakes (about 8,000 kip) and pizza, both of which they do very well. The pizza is the best thing on the menu. They also serve pasta, as well as Lao and Thai dishes.

Next to the Lankham Hotel on Rd. 13. Main courses 20,000 kip–45,000 kip. Daily 8am–11pm.

XuanMai ASIAN   XuanMai is an intimate, traditional, and very unpretentious restaurant serving solid helpings of Lao and Vietnamese food. The staff is very friendly and the ambience is pleasantly Indochina-provincial. The fruit shakes and garlic bread are a treat.

Rd. 5 and Rd. 10. ✆ **031/213-245.** Main courses 13,000 kip–30,000 kip. Daily 7am–11pm.

SHOPPING

In the **Champasak Plaza Shopping Center** you will find many stalls selling souvenirs, silk, clothes, electrical goods, and pretty much everything else Pakse has to offer. Nonetheless, Pakse is not a great shopping town and if possible you are best served by hanging on to your kip until you reach Vientiane or Luang Prabang, where the choice is much wider. In the New Market (Talat Dao Hung, Rd. 38) in the new town near the Lao-Japanese Bridge you will find a variety of foodstuffs and motorcycle parts. This is a major commercial crossroads.

ATTRACTIONS

Pakse itself is not weighed down with things to see. The best sights are the river, the sunset, and the superbly kitsch Champasak Palace Hotel. The **Champasak Historical**

Heritage Museum (Rd. 13; open Mon–Fri 8:30–11:30am and 1:30–4pm; admission 5,000 kip) has a few interesting historical artifacts from ancient temples, interesting textiles, musical instruments, and a fair amount of dreary Communist propaganda. There are also quite a number of wats in the city, none of which are particularly distinguished.

2 CHAMPASAK

To describe this town as "sleepy" doesn't do justice to just what a quiet place it is. It is a really nice place to relax for a couple of days enjoying major events such as a dog barking or a chicken crossing the road. There are some very pleasant riverside guesthouses and hotels and you are only 8km (5 miles) from Wat Phou. Once accommodations were bare-bones, but that is changing with the recent inauguration of the Inthira Hotel. Astonishingly this scenic hamlet on the western side of the Mekong (you have to cross the river coming from Pakse) was once a seat of the empire with lands stretching from the Annamite Mountains right into what is now Thailand. Just as astonishing is that it was also a center of administration for the French, hence some of the distinctively beautiful French architecture you see up the main street.

GETTING THERE

Buses leave from Pakse's southern bus terminal and drop you off at the purely ornamental central roundabout. If you are coming on a rented motorcycle you will need to negotiate the ferry crossing. This is not hard. If you are nervous about loading the bike across the gangplank get one of the crew to do it for you. The ferry from Ban Muang on the eastern side of the river costs 10,000 kip. Make sure you bring a hat: There is no shade from the burning sun and the crossing takes 15 minutes. It is real heatstroke territory unless you are careful.

GETTING AROUND

Champasak is eminently walkable. Guesthouses also rent rattling bicycles.

Fast Facts **Champasak**

Banks & Currency Exchange The **Lao Development Bank** (open times Mon–Fri 8:30am–3:30pm) on the southern edge of town changes traveler's checks and cash. There is no ATM.

Internet Access There are a couple of Internet cafes up the main street. They tend to close very early; don't expect to be surfing past 7pm.

Post Office There is a **post office** where you can make international phone calls.

Tourism Information The **Chamapassak District Visitor Information Center** (© **020/220-6215;** open Mon–Fri 8am–4:30pm) can give you background on local sights and transportation options. They can also fix you up with a local guide.

In Champasak, most restaurants are also guesthouses and vice versa. Unless specified, credit cards are not accepted.

Anouxa Guest House   This is the best of a series of riverside guesthouses and restaurants. It is situated at the southern edge of town. Each room has its own river-facing veranda. You can enjoy with A/C or without. The staff is very friendly and the place is well maintained. The Lao and Western food is not adventurous but it is solid and satisfying (main courses 20,000 kip–40,000 kip).

1 mile north of the Fountain Circle. ✆ **031/213-272.** 17 units. 80,000 kip fan; 150,000 kip A/C. **Amenities:** Restaurant. *In room:* A/C.

Inthira Champanakone Hotel ★   This is a brand-new luxury boutique resort in an old French colonial house. It is beautifully adapted, the house being the restaurant and reception area. In the courtyard they have constructed a series of two-story minihouses, each one being a separate unit. The rooms are small but cute with polished wooden floors and a circular staircase leading to the sleeping area at the top. The restaurant serves a mixture of Lao, Thai, Italian, and French food (main courses 18,000 kip–55,000 kip). Inthira (Indira) is the name of the sun goddess in Indian mythology but more importantly is also the name of the owner's daughter.

Ban Vat Amard. ✆ **031/214-059.** www.inthirahotel.com. 8 units. $60 double. **Amenities:** Restaurant; room service. *In room:* A/C, TV, fridge, minibar.

Khamphouy Guest House   A basic but functional option with good views of the river and restaurant attached (main courses 20,000 kip–40,000 kip). They also have a well-maintained fleet of bicycles for hire.

Ban Watthong, 14 A Rd. (south of the circle). ✆ **031/252-700.** 8 units. 20,000 kip fan; 30,000 kip A/C. **Amenities:** Restaurant. *In room:* A/C.

La Folie Lodge   Located on Dong Daeng Island, across from Wat Phou, on the banks of the Mekong, this splendid operation allows you to bask in luxury, atmosphere, and history all at the same time. The cabins are super grand in a rustic and almost totally wooden fashion. If you wish to contemplate the mystic and eerie splendors of Wat Phou while also sipping cocktails by the pool, La Folie is the place for you.

Dong Daeng Island. ✆ **030/534-7603.** www.lafolie-laos.com. 24 units. $125 double. MC, V. **Amenities:** Restaurant; bar; outdoor pool; room service. *In room:* A/C.

ATTRACTIONS

Wat Phou (Wat Phu) ★★★   This spectacular temple on a hillside was designated a World Heritage Site in 2002. It is a dramatic complex of temples, steps, statues, and lakes stretching up a mountainside. It is one of the historical highlights of a visit to Laos.

   Wat Phou is one of a chain of spectacular Khmer ruins spanning Thailand, Cambodia, and Laos dating back from height of the Angkor empire when the Khmers ruled from the South China Sea to the Andaman sea and as far north as Burma. It has a more rundown feel than either Phimai or Phanom Rung in Thailand and certainly has yet to benefit from the energy of conservation that is taking place in Angkor Wat, although things are moving along. Wat Phou is situated at the base of Mount Phou Kao, 6km (3¾ miles) west of the Mekong. There was a temple on this site as early as the 5th century, but the ruins you see now are from the 11th century to the 13th century. The temple is unique in structure, all the parts leading to a shrine where a Shiva lingam (sacred Hindu phallus) was anointed with water from a mountaintop spring. The temple later became a center of Theravada Buddhist worship. It still is. In addition to interested tourists both local and foreign, many come here to make merit.

Initially Wat Phou was linked with the city of Shrestapura, which lay on the bank of the Mekong River due east of Mount Lingaparvata (which is now called Phou Kao). By the end of the 5th century the city was already the capital of a kingdom, which connected with the pre-Angkorian kingdoms of both Chenla and Champa. The first structure on the site was constructed at this time. The mountain was considered a home of Shiva and the river an echo of the holy Ganges.

Shrestapura was then superseded by a new city in the period of Angkorian dominance. The original buildings were replaced, recycling some of their stone blocks. The temple now seen was built primarily during the Koh Ker and Baphuon era of the 11th century. Some alterations were made during the following 2 centuries, before the temple, like most in the empire, was converted to Buddhism under Jayavarman VII. This carried on after the Lao superseded the Khmer. Like most Khmer temples Wat Phou faces east (although it's about 8 degrees off since it is aligned with the river). Including the barays (the lakes that are a feature of Angkorian temples) it stretches 1.4km (¾ mile) east from the source of the spring, past the base of the cliff and then 100m (320 ft.) up the hill. The accompanying city used to lie east of the temple, on the west bank of the Mekong, while a road south from the temple itself led past temples, its ultimate destination being Angkor itself. Approached from that lost city, the first part of the temple you reach are the barays. There is now one that still contains water. There used to be further reservoirs north and south of this and on each side of the approaching causeway.

Past the main baray, the two palaces flank a central terrace. They are known as the north and south palaces; it is thought they were the men's palace and the women's palace. The term "palace" is loosely used here. Their purpose actually remains unknown. The gender classification is also likely to be apocryphal. Each is made up of a courtyard with a corridor and entrance on the side and false doors at both the east end and the west end. The courtyards of both buildings were built of laterite although the walls of the southern palace were made of sandstone. Both buildings are fenced off and appear to be in a fairly derelict state although the northern palace is in a slightly better condition. The palaces are noted mainly for pediments and lintels.

The next terrace is home to a small shrine to Nandi the bull (Shiva's runaround vehicle in Hindu mythology). The road connecting Wat Phou and Angkor ran south from this temple. As you continue west, more staircases (with tough climbing!) lead up to yet more terraces.

In the penultimate temple a lintel portraying the god Vishnu on Garuda (Vishnu's runaround vehicle, a splendid bird) is found on the northeast wall.

After a hard, sweaty climb (bring both a hat and plenty of water) you reach the main sanctuary culminating in the seven sandstone tiers of the upper terrace and the final sanctuary representing heaven. There are great views of the plain below from here. The sanctuary is made up of two parts. The front section, of sandstone, contains Buddha images, while the rear part of the structure, which used to be home to the Shiva lingam, is empty. Water from the spring emerging from the cliff about 60m (37 ft.) to the southwest of the sanctuary was once channeled along stone aqueducts into this rear chamber, providing continuous bathing to the holy lingam. The sanctuary was built later than the north and south and belongs to the Baphuon period of the later part of the 11th century. The east side features three doorways from south to the north. The pediments show Krishna defeating the naga (snake) Kaliya, the god Indra riding Airavata, and Vishnu astride Garuda. The doorways to both north and south feature ornate inner and outer lintels with scenes from Hindu mythology, some of which are fairly violent in nature.

There is a Buddha footprint on the face of the cliff, and also boulders fashioned to resemble elephants and a crocodile. It is said that the crocodile stone may have been the scene of human sacrifice.

There is an interesting museum on-site, which is well worth a visit. A major festival is held at Wat Phou each March. During the festival, there are not only religious ceremonies but also exhibitions of traditional sports such as elephant racing, horse hockey, boat racing, and others.

Admission is 30,000 kip. Daily 8am–4:30pm.

3 SI PHAN DON (FOUR THOUSAND ISLANDS)

As the Mekong makes its way south to Cambodia it becomes peppered with islands, sandbars, and rocky outcrops. This area is known as Si Phan Don, which translates as "Four Thousand Islands." About 120km (74 miles) south of Pakse, this area is becoming increasingly popular as a getaway spot, particularly among budget travelers. The series of islands has major significance in terms of its natural beauty and the uniqueness of its wildlife, including the heavily threatened Irrawaddy dolphin. It is also where you will find the largest waterfalls in Southeast Asia, a feature that foiled plans by the French to use the Mekong as the major trade route they first intended when their empire was the major force in the area. **Khon Phapheng and Somphamit waterfalls** remain the major tourist attractions in the far south and given their dramatic nature one can only speculate on how disappointed the French colonizers were when they first came across them. The largest and most developed island is **Don Khong,** but both **Don Det** and **Don Khon** are very popular places to stay among hammock-swinging aficionados.

GETTING THERE & AWAY

Buses leave from the Southern Bus Terminal in Pakse. The turnoff for the islands is about 120km (74 miles) due south (about 3 hr.) and tickets cost 30,000 kip. From the main road it's a short tuk-tuk ride to the boat landing at Hat Xai Khun. Don Khong–bound *songthaeaws* also cross the river on the car ferry and can take you right into the main town of Muang Khong. It costs 10¢ per person and 50¢ for a motorbike. Departing *songthaeaws* leave from just in front of the main wat. A boat to Don Det or Don Khon costs $3 per person they leave when the boat is full.

GETTING AROUND

Bicycles cost $1 a day and are the most popular way to explore the islands. You can also rent small motorbikes for $12 a day.

DON KHONG

The major activity on Don Khong (apart from lying in a hammock) is cycling past rice fields and looking at the temples that dot the island. The sleepy town of Muang Khong is the major settlement on the island although there are small villages scattered along the edges. Some 8km (5 miles) west of Muang Sen at the southern end of the island are a marketplace and some floating restaurants from which you get good sunset views.

(Fast Facts **Don Khong**

Banks & Currency Exchange There is **money exchange** (open Mon–Fri 8:30am–3:30pm) at the **Agricultural Promotion Bank** near the Mekong Hotel. You can change Thai baht and U.S. dollars in traveler's checks or cash.

Internet Access There are a number of small Internet cafes around Muang Khong. They don't stay open very late.

Post Office The post office (open Mon–Fri 8am–noon and 1–4pm) is in Muang Khong to the south of the boat landing just after the first bridge.

Where to Stay & Dine

Auberge Sala Done Khong This is the best hotel in Don Khong and is made up of two wooden houses. It has a faded colonial kind of grandeur. The rooms are very well designed and some of the larger ones have their own verandas. On the ground floor is a restaurant open to guests only. This hotel is a very popular with tour groups.

100m (328 ft.) south of the ferry landing. (*) **031/212-077.** www.salalao.com. 12 units. $33 superior double; $25 standard double. No credit cards. **Amenities:** Restaurant. *In room:* A/C, TV, fridge, minibar.

Kangkhong Villa Guesthouse Although set back from the riverfront this hotel is in an old teak house with large clean rooms. A shaded communal balcony gives you good views of the river, and is a nice place to sit and chat with other guests. Rooms are large and well furnished in dark wood. The upstairs rooms are better because they are lighter. There are also A/C rooms available.

South of the ferry landing across the road from Wat Phuang Kaew. (*) **031/213-539.** 18 units. $10 double fan; $15 double A/C. No credit cards.

Pon's Guest House The owner of the Guest House of the same name is very helpful and is a useful source of information not only on Si Phan Don but also on transport options for the wider area including border crossings to Cambodia. The rooms here are very clean and big with either fan or A/C. An upstairs terrace has good river views, while the downstairs restaurant consistently gets very good reviews.

150m (492 ft.) north of the ferry landing. (*) **031/214-037.** 18 units. $15 double fan; $22 double A/C. No credit cards. **Amenities:** Restaurant; Internet. *In room:* A/C, TV, fridge.

DON DET & DON KHON

These two islands south of Don Khong are very popular locations with budget travelers and the atmosphere is one of endless relaxation. Facilities are very basic throughout both islands. The area is astonishingly picturesque with emerald green paddies and gently swaying palm trees. There is very little to see or do but that is exactly the attraction. Nor is it a place to come and enjoy Lao culture. It is very much a scene for meeting other travelers and for that reason is a major rallying point for budget travelers and backpackers.

Accommodations are basic but cheap on Don Det while on Don Khon there is a wider range of options in the mid range. Real luxury, however, has yet to make it down to Si Phan Don. There are no banks and no post office. There are a few places with Internet but painfully slow connections. For most things practical you will need to head to Don Khong. Don Det has no permanent electricity supply, generally only being lit up between 6 and 10pm.

Getting There

Boats leave **Ban Nakasang pier** (about 4km/2½ miles west of Rte. 13). A ride in a small boat to **Don Det** costs $3 and drops you at the most northern part of Don Det and the northern coast (facing Don Det) on Don Khon.

Where to Stay & Dine

Guesthouses renting out basic bungalows are clustered in both areas in large numbers. They mostly cost between $3 and $6 and are very similar to each other. They also serve food from basic kitchens, which are also similar. The **Auberge Sala Don Khone** (© **031/212-077**; www.salalao.com; $18–$30) on **Don Khon** is the most upmarket option. It was built in 1921 by Les Messageries Maritimes as its timber trading headquarters. This classic French colonial single-story bricked mansion has been used for various things, including a hospital. Each room is fairly large with separate bathroom and balcony. Lime-washed walls, bamboo paneled ceiling, hardwood flooring, and rattan armchairs all contribute to the ambience.

On **Don Det,** the **Monkey Bar** is foreign owned and stays open as late as 11pm if you are looking for a late night out. On Don Khon the **Bamboo Bar and Restaurant** (main courses $3–$5) is a floating restaurant that is often well spoken of.

Attractions

The most interesting and popular thing to see around Si Phan Don is the heavily endangered **Irrawaddy dolphins.** Often seen by local people as humans in another incarnation, they have a mystical significance. The south side of Don Khon is where you will find them. April to May when the weather is dry and the river is low is the best time of year to see these elegant creatures breaking the surface of the water often in pairs. Boats can be chartered for about $10 an hour in the village of Ban Hang Khon on the island's southern tip.

The Khon **Phapaheng Waterfalls** (admission $1) is the stretch of water that confounded French trade ambitions on the Mekong and when you see them you understand why. A huge volume of water surges powerfully downstream to Cambodia. When the rains are at their height and the river is high, it is a very impressive site. The Khon Phapheng falls are of local religious significance, being seen by Buddhists as a place that spirits become trapped. The same is true of the **Somphamit Falls** on the western side of Si Phan Don. Here you can also see local fishermen trapping fish from precarious wooden causeways using huge bamboo traps. The water is forced powerfully through the narrow walls of the rocky gorge through which it is flows.

The French may have had their trade ambitions stolen from them by the force of nature but in small way they tried to ameliorate the mighty force of the Mekong around Si Phan Don with a small **railway** across the islands designed to haul a modest amount of goods from Cambodia across the islands from pier to pier. There is still the remains of a **rusting locomotive.** You can follow the trail of the old track across the islands.

4 THE BOLAVEN PLATEAU

This is the coffee-growing gate to the remote southeast of the country where travel is hard and life is spartan. More and more adventure-enthused tourists take these roads and indeed the roads have been improved of late. The main attraction of the Bolaven is that its elevation provides a welcome reprieve from the hot season. After 45 minutes of driving east you will need to don a sweater even in May. The road climbs very gradually to **Paksong** (nothing more than a main road lined with a few municipal buildings, a covered market, and two very basic guesthouses in which you can stay). Paksong, however, is better done as a day trip from Pakse. Nearby Bolaven are some spectacular **waterfalls. Tat Fan, Tat Yuang,** and **Tat Meelok** are some of the ones more accessible from Paksong. Travel agents such as **Xplore-asia** and **Green Discovery** (p. 308) also run **coffee tours** showing you how the coffee is cultivated and manufactured as well as giving an insight into the lives of local people.

Fast Facts

1 FAST FACTS: CAMBODIA

AREA CODES The international dialing code for Cambodia is **855.** Area codes are listed in the "Fast Facts" sections of specific cities.

BUSINESS HOURS Business hours are generally between 7am and 7pm from Monday to Friday. Markets close earlier, generally by 5pm. Most banks are open from around 8am to 3 or 4pm from Monday to Friday. Some are also open on Saturday mornings until 11:30am.

DRINKING & DRUG LAWS In Cambodia, there are no regulations on drinking alcohol. Drugs are illegal (though marijuana is widely available), and if caught the police will likely attempt to extract large amounts of money from you.

ELECTRICITY The electrical system in Cambodia is 220 volts AC. Two-pin flat plugs are the norm. The electricity can often be cut without warning. It's a good idea to carry a flashlight, especially in more remote places.

EMBASSIES & CONSULATES The embassy of the **United States** is at the corner of St. 96/51 (📞 **023/728-000**). The embassy of **Canada** is represented by embassy of **Australia,** located at Australia Villa 11, St. 254 (📞 **023/213-470**). The embassy of **Ireland** is represented by embassy of the **United Kingdom,** at No. 27–29 St. 75 (📞 **023/427-124**). There is no New Zealand Embassy in Cambodia.

HOSPITALS In the event of a medical emergency, you should head to Thailand.

Healthcare in Cambodia is not good. Although the main hospital in Phnom Penh is the Calmette, it is not recommended. The **International SOS Medical and Dental Clinic,** at No. 161 St. 51 (📞 **023/216-911**), is the best place to handle minor emergencies. **Naga Clinic,** at No. 11 St. 254 (📞 **011/811-175**), is also recommended. For any major emergency or injury, however, you'll want to arrange medical evacuation.

In Siem Reap, the **Royal Angkor International Hospital** (No. 6 Airport Rd.; 📞 **063/761-888;** www.royalangkorhospital.com) provides 24-hour emergency care, ambulance, translation, and evacuation. Check on their website before departure to make sure your insurance covers you under their terms and conditions.

INSURANCE For information on traveler's insurance, trip-cancellation insurance, and medical insurance while traveling, visit www.frommers.com

LANGUAGE Khmer is the official language of Cambodia. English is increasingly widely spoken. Some older people speak French. See chapter 17 for a glossary of Khmer terms.

MAIL Mail services from Cambodia are unreliable and things go missing. DHL has an office in Phnom on No. 28 Monivong Rd. (📞 **023/427-726**), and FedEx is at No. 701D Monivong (📞 **023/216-712**). It costs 2000 riel to send a postcard to the U.S., and 300 riel to send a letter.

NEWSPAPERS & MAGAZINES Two English-language dailies are available. The *Cambodia Daily* carries plenty of local and national news and contains good analysis. The *Phnom Penh Post,* which for many years ran as a biweekly, has now been relaunched as a daily. The *Bangkok Post* is also widely available. Locally produced magazines come and go in Cambodia. The best of the bunch at present is the *Southeast Asia Globe.* Bookshops stock a range of foreign and international magazines.

PASSPORTS See www.frommers.com/planning for information on how to obtain a passport.

POLICE In Cambodia, the police are not your friends. They are generally corrupt, so stay out of their way if possible. The ones you are most likely to come in contact with are traffic police. The bribes will start high, but $5 is the maximum you should pay for an infraction either real or invented. If you have something stolen and need a police report for insurance purposes, you may find that the police will attempt to extract a "fee" for their services. If you can, bring a Khmer speaker with you to aid negotiation.

SMOKING Smoking is unregulated in Cambodia and remains very popular.

TAXES Taxes are levied in the form of VAT. A departure tax of $25 is payable on leaving the country by air.

TELEPHONES See p. 48 in chapter 3, "Planning Your Trip to Cambodia."

TIME Cambodia is 7 hours ahead of Greenwich Mean Time.

TIPPING Tipping is not generally a Cambodian custom but is appreciated in some tourist areas. Check that service is not already included. Tipping 10% of the bill is more than acceptable.

WATER Do not drink the water or brush your teeth with it. Bottled water is freely available. Make sure the bottle is properly sealed on purchase.

2 FAST FACTS: LAOS

AREA CODES The international dialing code for Laos is **856.** Area codes are listed in the "Fast Facts" sections of specific cities.

BUSINESS HOURS As with so many things in Laos, the definition of business hours is relaxed. Government offices open at 8am and close for lunch at noon, reopening at 1pm and closing at 5pm. Some offices also open on a Saturday morning. Banks tend to be open from 8:30am to 3pm from Monday to Friday, though this varies. Restaurants vary but tend to close by 11pm. Shops also vary but tend to open at 9am and close between 5 and 7pm. Even in Vientiane, everything (except a few nightclubs) is closed by midnight.

DRINKING & DRUG LAWS Regulations on drinking are not enforced and alcohol is widely available. Penalties for driving under the influence are severe. Drug laws are extremely harsh, especially trafficking narcotics, which is punishable by death.

ELECTRICITY The electrical system in Laos is 220 volts AC. Two-pin flat plugs are the usual. The electricity can often be cut without warning. It's a good idea to carry a flashlight, especially in more remote places.

EMBASSIES & CONSULATES The **United States** Embassy is located at 19 Thatdam Bartholonie Rd., Ban Thatdam, Vientiane (© **021/267-000**).

There is no **Canadian** Embassy in Laos. Use the Australian Embassy or contact the Canadian Embassy in Thailand (15th Floor, Abdulrahim Place, 990 Rama IV Rd., Bangrak, Bangkok, 10500, Thailand; ✆ +66 (0)2/636-0540; fax +66 (0)2/636-0566).

The embassy of **Australia** is at Nehru Street, Wat Phonsay area, Vientiane (✆ 021/413-6000; www.laos.embassy.gov.au).

There is no **Irish** Embassy in Laos. Use the Swedish Embassy (Sokpaluang Rd., Wat Nak, Vientiane; ✆ 021/315-003).

There is no **New Zealand** Embassy in Laos. Use the Australian Embassy or contact the New Zealand Embassy in Thailand (M Thai Tower, 14th Floor, All Seasons Place, 87 Wireless Rd., Lumpini, Bangkok 10330, Thailand; ✆ +66 [0]2/254-2530; emergency after-hours duty officer: +66 [0]81/837-7240).

There is no embassy of the **United Kingdom** in Laos. Use the Australian Embassy or contact the U.K. Embassy in Thailand (14 Wireless Road, Lumpini, Pathumwan, Bangkok 10330; ✆ +66 [0]2/305-8333; www.ukinthailand.fco.gov.uk).

HOSPITALS Medical facilities in Laos are very basic. Most foreigners living in Laos go to Thailand for treatment of all but the most trivial of ailments. The Friendship Bridge connecting Vientiane to Nong Khai in Thailand is open daily from 6am to 10pm. If there is a real medical emergency, then crossing out of hours is allowed. Many travelers go to **AEK International Hospital** (✆ +66-42/342-555) or the **North Eastern Wattana General Hospital** (✆ +66-1/833-4262), both of which are in Udon Thani about 55km (34 miles) from the border. Both hospitals have English-speaking staff. For less complex medical procedures, **Nong Khai Wattana Hospital** in Nong Khai, Thailand (✆ +66-1/833-4262) is also an option

Within Laos, the **International Medical Clinic** operated by Mahosot Hospital is situated on the banks of the Mekong on Fa Ngum Road (✆ 021/214-022; open 24 hr.). The Australian Embassy also operates a modern medical clinic. It is situated at Km 4 on Thadeua Road in Watnak Village (✆ 021/353-840; fax 021/353-841; open Mon–Fri 8:30am–12:30pm and 1:30–5pm). Most doctors and hospitals in Laos require payment in cash, regardless of whether you have health insurance. The Australian Embassy Clinic accepts both MasterCard and Visa.

INSURANCE For information on traveler's insurance, trip-cancellation insurance, and medical insurance while traveling, visit www.frommers.com/planning.

LANGUAGE Lao is the official language. Some English is spoken in towns, but you will help yourself if you learn a few words of the local language. A few older people speak French. See chapter 17 for a glossary of Lao terms.

MAIL The mail system is not very reliable in Laos. If you can, you are better off mailing from Thailand. Outgoing mail takes 10 to 15 days to reach Europe or America. When posting a parcel, you must leave it open for a Customs inspection. There is an Express Mail service to most Western countries, which is faster than standard mail and also automatically registers your letter. Both DHL and FedEx have offices in Vientiane. Post offices tend to be open 5 days a week between 8am and noon and 1 and 4pm. You can recognize them by their mustard-colored signs. It costs 30¢ to send a postcard to the U.S., and just under $1 to send a letter.

NEWSPAPERS & MAGAZINES The only English-language newspaper in Laos is the *Vientiane Times*. It is a little low on substantive news, since media is under tight government control. In Vientiane and Luang Prabang you can get the *Bangkok Post* in some bookshops and international magazines such as *Time* and *Newsweek*.

POLICE   In Laos, the police are not your friends. They are generally surly and corrupt. The most obvious way to avoid having contact with them is by not breaking the law. If you should find yourself having to deal with them for whatever reason, be polite but not fearful. If you have something stolen and need a police report for insurance purposes you may find that the police will attempt to extract a "fee" for their services. If you can, bring a Lao speaker with you to aid negotiation.

SMOKING   Smoking is banned in many public places, particularly in Luang Prabang, where it is forbidden near many of the famous sites. Smoking is voluntarily

banned in hospitals, educational facilities, and government buildings.

TAXES   Taxes are levied in the form of VAT. A departure tax of $10 is payable on leaving the country by air.

TELEPHONES   See p. 209 in chapter 10, "Planning Your Trip to Laos."

TIME ZONES   Laos is 7 hours ahead of Greenwich Mean Time.

TIPPING   Tipping is not generally a Lao custom but is appreciated in some tourist areas. Check that service is not already included. Tipping 10% of the bill is more than acceptable.

WATER   Do not drink the water or brush your teeth with it. Bottled water is freely available. Make sure the bottle is properly sealed on purchase.

Khmer & Lao Glossary

1 THE KHMER LANGUAGE

The language of Cambodia is called Khmer, a term that refers to the ethnic majority of the country but is also used to describe all things Cambodian: Khmer people (the Khmer), Khmer food, and Khmer culture. The Khmer language belongs to the Mon-Khmer family. Written Khmer script is based on Pallava script from south India. It is ancient and very complex. Unlike in neighboring Thailand and Laos, the Khmer language is not tonal and is thus more merciful to the casual learner. Basic pronunciation is still frustrating and difficult, however.

Khmer embraces many loaner words from French, Chinese, and now English, especially technical terms. Although many Cambodians used to speak French, that is no longer the case. The second language of choice is English these days and it is amazing how many people have learned to speak it, especially the young. In the major tourist centers, speaking slowly and clearly in basic English phrases will do the trick, but a few choice phrases in Khmer will get you far.

USEFUL KHMER PHRASES

English	Khmer
Hello	Sew sadday
Goodbye	Lia hoy
Thank you	Aw koon
Thank you very much	Aw koon chalan
How are you?	Sook sabai?
I am fine	Sook sabai
Yes (man)	Baat
Yes (woman)	Jaa
No	Ah tay
I'm sorry	Sum tow
Toilet?	Bangku oon?
Do you have . . . ?	Mien awt mien? (literally do you have or don't you?)
Water?	Took sawt?
How much?	Tlai bawn mahn?
Can you make it cheaper?	Sum joe tlai?
Do you speak English?	Nayuk jes pia-sah onglais tay?
I don't understand	Nayuk yuhl tay
Please speak slowly	Sohm niyay yeut yeut
Please repeat that	Sohm niyay muhdawng teeiht
What time is it?	Maung bohn mahn

TRANSPORTATION TERMS

English	Khmer
Airport	Jom nort yoo-un hohs
Motorbike taxi	Motodup
Bus	Lan tom

EMERGENCIES

English	Khmer
I need a doctor	K'nyom trauv ghar kru payet
Hospital	Montee payet
Help!	Chooee!
Call the police	Jooee howiemao powlih
I'm lost	K'nyom vung veing plaow

GETTING THERE

English	Khmer
Where is the . . .	Noe ai na . . .
bus station?	setanee laan kerong?
hotel?	suntakeea?
guesthouse?	tayah sumnat?
restaurant?	porjarneea tarn?

TOURING

English	Khmer
I want to go to . . .	K'nyom chong tow . . .
temple	wat
museum	sahrah montee
market	puhsaa
beach	chuhnay suhmoht
Please slow down	Som jin yeut yeut
Please stop here	Som chop new tee nih

RESTAURANT & SELF-CATERING

English	Khmer
I'd like the menu, please	Sohm menui
I would like . . .	K'nyom jang baan . . .
bread	num pang
egg	pong mowan
vegetables	buhn lai
beef/chicken/fish	sait gow/sait mowan/trei
stir-fried/grilled	cha/ang
The check, please	Sohm kuht lui

HOTEL

English	Khmer
Do you have any rooms?	**Nee'ak mien?**
single room	**bontop sumrab moi neeak**
double room	**bontop graiy pee**
with . . .	**mien . . .**
bathroom	**bontop tuek**
hot water	**tuek g'daow**
air-conditioning	**mahsin trocheyat**
a phone	**toorasahp**

NUMBERS

0	**Sohn**	12	**Dawp pee**
1	**Muy**	20	**Muh pay**
2	**Pee**	30	**Sam suhp**
3	**Bei**	40	**Si suhp**
4	**Boo-un**	50	**Haa suhp**
5	**Bruhm**	60	**Hohk suhp**
6	**Bruhm muy**	70	**Jet suhp**
7	**Bruhm pee**	80	**Pet suhp**
8	**Bruhm bei**	90	**Cow suhp**
9	**Bruhm boo-un**	100	**Muy roy**
10	**Dawp**	200	**Pee roy**
11	**Dawp muy**	1,000	**Muy poan**

2 THE LAO LANGUAGE

The Lao language resembles Thai, with familiar tones and sounds found in each. While some vocabulary words might cross over, the two tongues—spoken and written—are quite distinct. However, many Lao understand Thai (learned from school texts and TV), so if you've picked up some words and phrases in Thailand, they'll still be useful here; people will understand and correct you with the appropriate Lao phrase.

Thankfully, many people in Vientiane and Luang Prabang speak English, and older citizens will usually be able to speak French (often with a delightful accent). Russian is not uncommon, and Chinese is growing in accord with the rising Chinese population (mostly in the north).

Like Thai, Lao has no officially recognized method of Roman alphabet transliteration. As a result, even town and street names have copious spelling irregularities, so for the vocabulary below, only phonetic pronunciations are listed. Most Lao will understand you, even without proper tones, and will appreciate your efforts to speak their language.

When trying to figure out the correct pronunciation of certain names, it's helpful to remember that the original transliteration of Lao was done by francophones, so consider the French pronunciation when faced with a new word. For example, in Vientiane (pronounced wee-en-chan), the wide central avenue spelled Lane Xang is pronounced Lahn Sahng. Also in Vientiane, Mixay sounds like Mee-sigh. Phonexay is Pawn-sigh. It takes awhile, but it's easy to pick up.

English	Lao
Hello	**Sa bai dee**
Goodbye	**Laa gawn**
Thank you	**Khawp jai**
Thank you very much	**Khawp jai lai lai/khawp jai deuh**
You're welcome/it's nothing	**Baw pen nyahng**
No problem	**Baw mi banhaa**
How are you?	**Sa bai dee baw?**
I'm fine/I'm not fine	**Sabai dee/baw sabai**
Yes	**Chow**
No	**Baw/baw men**
Excuse me	**Khaw toht**
I don't understand	**Baw kao jai**
Do you speak English/French?	**Passah Angit/Falang dai baw?**
How do you say that in Lao?	**Ani passah Lao ee-yahng?**
Where is the toilet?	**Hawng nam yoo sai?**
May I wear shoes here?	**Sai gup pen nyahng baw?**
Do you have . . . ?	**Mii . . . baw?**
drinking water	**nam-deum**
a room	**hawng**
I would like . . .	**Kaaw . . .**
coffee (black)/with cream	**café dahm/café sai nom**
tea	**nam saa**
How much kip/baht/dollar?	**Tao dai keep/baht/dollah?**
Expensive/too expensive	**Paeng/paeng poht**
Can you make it cheaper?	**Loht dai baw?**

TRANSPORTATION TERMS

English	Lao
Airport	**Doen bin**
Motorbike	**Lot jahk**
Bus	**Lot**
Bicycle	**Lot teep**
Car	**Lot ohtoh**

EMERGENCIES

English	Lao
Help!	**Soi neh!**
Call the police!	**Toh-ha tam louat!**

English	Lao
Call a doctor	Toh-ha tam mor
I'm lost	Koy long tang

GETTING THERE

English	Lao
Where is the . . .	Yoo sai . . .
bus station?	sathanilot pajam thaang?
hotel?	hohng ham?
guesthouse?	heuan pak?
restaurant?	han ahan?

TOURING

English	Lao
I want to go to . . .	Khawy yak pai . . .
temple	wat
museum	pipitapan
palace	palatsawang
market	talat

RESTAURANT & SELF-CATERING

English	Lao
Do you have a menu?	Kaw kaikan ahan dae?
I would like . . .	Khoi ao. . .
bread	khao jii
egg	khai
vegetables	phaak
beef/chicken/fish	siin/kai/paa
grilled	piing
Not spicy	Baw phet
The check, please	Kaw sek dae

HOTEL

English	Lao
Do you have any rooms?	Mi hawng wang?
single room	horng norn teeang deeo
double room	horng norn teeang koo
with . . .	sai . . .
hot water	nam hawn
air-conditioning	ae yen
a bathroom	hawng nam

0	**Soon**	10	**Sip**
1	**Seung**	11	**Sipet**
2	**Sorng**	12	**Sip sorng**
3	**Sahm**	13	**Sip sahm**
4	**See**	20	**Sow**
5	**Hah**	30	**Sahm sip**
6	**Hok**	40	**See sip**
7	**Jet**	50	**Hah sip**
8	**Pat**	100	**Neung hoy**
9	**Gow**	1,000	**Neung pan**

INDEX

See also Accommodations and Restaurant indexes, below.

ACCOMMODATIONS— LAOS

Restaurants— Cambodia